credits and
collections:
management and
theory

credits and collections: management and theory

EIGHTH EDITION

THEODORE N. BECKMAN, Ph.D.
Professor Emeritus of Marketing, The Ohio State University

RONALD S. FOSTER, Ph.D.
Associate Professor of Finance, The Ohio State University

McGRAW-HILL BOOK COMPANY
New York   St. Louis   San Francisco   London
Sydney   Toronto   Mexico   Panama

credits and
collections:
management and
theory

Library of Congress Catalog Card Number 68-55262

ISBN 07-004142-3

13 14 15 16 17   KPKP   7 9 8 7 6

TO
SARAH LANGUE BECKMAN
ROSEANN L. FOSTER

PREFACE

This book has continually evolved through a series of periodic revisions since it was first published in 1924. The primary objective of all revisions, including the one for this eighth edition, has been to provide a basic textbook for a needed comprehensive and well-rounded course in credits and collections on the collegiate level—graduate or undergraduate. A secondary goal has been to provide a unified body of analytically practical and theoretical knowledge needed by businessmen in the management of the credit and collection phases of a business enterprise.

To present the fundamental background of the subject and the theory, principles, and practices of credit and collection management in teachable and meaningful form, it was necessary to treat all phases of the subject in the fields of consumer, business, and residential mortgage credit, with special attention to short- and intermediate-term credit and concomitant collection problems. Moreover, while the emphasis was on the managerial aspects, it was the deliberate judgment of the authors that the treatment should be founded in theory and that the subject must be set in its proper environmental perspective rather than confined to the narrowly conceived decision-making process of credit and collection management in a highly micro or atomistic sense. As a consequence, this present edition is characterized even more than were its predecessors by increased attention to the implications of changing social and economic conditions, individual attitudes toward credit, government actions and reactions, and technological progress on the varied aspects of credits and collections.

While the basic objectives, approach, depth and breadth of coverage, readability, and authoritativeness have proved acceptable to users of previous editions and have been effective pedagogically, a number of important changes in the form of improvements are reflected in this eighth edition, a few of which are the following:

1 All statistical materials are presented in an up-to-date and meaningful manner, always involving analysis and possible conclusions.

2 A completely new chapter on residential mortgage credit is introduced, in line with the increasing magnitude and relative importance of this type of credit in the economy.

3 Additional coverage is given to financial institutions dealing in short- and intermediate-term credit for business users and ultimate consumers.

4 A complete discussion of the concept of return on asset investment is added, and the basic objectives of credit and collection management are related to it.

5 Due attention is given to a most comprehensive discussion of bankruptcy in the contemporary setting.

6 A careful and selective treatment is directed to relevant court decisions throughout the book and to pertinent legislation, such as the Uniform Commercial Code, the "gold cover" act, and the Truth in Lending law, together with their impact upon certain aspects of credits and collections.

7 The nature of automation and data processing and their technological effects on the performance of credit and collection operations are discussed.

8 The latest developments in charge account banking systems and credit card plans are incorporated into the pertinent existing content.

9 A relevant discussion is devoted to the "checkless" and "cashless" society concept and its implementation, including an evaluation.

10 The new "common language" used in consumer credit reporting is introduced.

11 Material that has become obsolete or irrelevant is eliminated except where it has historical significance.

12 With the direct aid of the leading institutions in the field of credit, such as Dun & Bradstreet, Inc., all content has been revised and updated in order truly to reflect their operations and current usefulness.

13 While the basic overall and external structure of the book remains, the sequence of some of the chapters has been changed to make for even a better organization.

14 All material throughout the entire book has been reexamined, updated, and revised, thus the revision is thorough in every sense of the term.

Structurally, the book is organized to emphasize the management function in credits and collections but without disregarding the theoretical foundation, the social setting, and economic and other environmental effects. For this purpose, the 31 chapters of the book are divided into seven parts, each starting with a part divider which briefly explains the purpose of the part and how it is achieved by the contents of the chapters included in it.

Briefly, in Part I are presented some of the general aspects of credit—its nature, instruments, and role in the economic and social environment. Part II, entitled "Nature and Scope of Credit Management," deals with the basic objectives of credit management and the broad policies, practices, problems, and risk elements involved in the decision-making process for all forms and types of consumer and business credit. Part III deals with the consumer credit-granting function as it is or should be performed by sellers of goods and services or lenders of money to ultimate consumers from a profit-motivating as well as a social viewpoint. Similar treatment is given in Part IV to the management of the business credit-granting function. Part V is devoted to the *analysis* of risk in the different types of mercantile, financial institution, and foreign credit and to the effective use of credit information sources. Part VI covers the management of the collection function, including business methods and practices, the legal framework, and a comprehensive analysis of such subjects as adjustments and bankruptcy. Finally, Part VII is devoted to a discussion of overall management control of credit and collection operations from a strictly managerial point of view. Special attention is given here to credit insurance, credit limits, and measurement of credit and collection efficiency.

In the preparation of this edition much encouragement and assistance has come from sources too numerous to list. Specific references are made in the appropriate places in this volume to those who contributed

substantially to a given topic.   Help was received also from colleagues of
the authors, especially from Robert B. Miner, and from other university
professors who have used the older editions as a textbook.   Credit managers, credit bureau and agency officials, trade and credit association
executives, and recognized authorities on various phases of the subject
contributed much in time and materials essential to a sound work in the
field.   Substantial help has also come from certain leading business executives in providing special literature and important exhibits for reproduction
in this volume.   To all these the authors acknowledge their indebtedness
and express their sincere gratitude.

THEODORE N. BECKMAN

RONALD S. FOSTER

CONTENTS

nature
and role
of credit

Credit is so pervasive and so dominant a force that our economic system is often characterized as a credit economy. It is also a potent social force, touching the lives of everyone in several different and often intimate ways and giving rise to identifiable social and individual attitudes of consequence. As an institution, credit has significantly affected the business, political, and social environment and has reciprocally been affected by it, as will be revealed throughout this volume. Its instruments are varied, manifold, sometimes quite complex, and frequently misunderstood despite their common usage.

A comprehension of the nature, uses, and general functions of credit is, therefore, essential for businessmen, economists, social scientists, and consumers alike, as is a similar understanding of the credit instruments involved and the way in which credit affects economic and social conditions, systems, and institutions and is, in turn, affected by them. To provide the basis for such an understanding is the function of Part I.

CHAPTER ONE

nature, uses,
and functions
of credit

Credit has such a wide scope that treatment of the subject in its entirety is seldom undertaken in a single book or course. Generally it is taken up from the standpoint of the users of credit, the two broad categories being *public* and *private* credit. The former is concerned primarily with public finance and is but briefly referred to in this book. For careful study, private credit is usually divided into *consumer* credit and *business* credit, depending upon whether it is employed by personal consumers or business organizations.

The credit which is used by consumers for their personal needs is mainly of the four following types: *retail charge account* credit, *instalment sales* credit, *cash* credit, and *real estate* credit. The types of credit utilized by business firms include *mercantile,* or commercial, credit, *invest-*

ment credit, and real estate credit.   In addition most commercial and industrial concerns use credit in the form of short-term and intermediate-term financing provided by commercial banks and other financial institutions.

Sometimes additional classes of credit are presented from the standpoint of users, such as industrial credit or agricultural credit. These usually represent, however, combinations of the classifications identified in the preceding paragraph.   This is illustrated by the credit used by farmers: when it is in the form of long-term borrowing, it is in the nature of investment credit or real estate credit, as the case may be; in the form of short-term or intermediate-term borrowing, even through Federal farm lending agencies, it is like credit extended by commercial banks or other financial institutions; in the form of terms obtained on the purchase of equipment or supplies for the operation of the farm, it is essentially mercantile credit; and in the form of credit used to purchase goods or services for personal consumption by the farm family, it is consumer credit.

Definition of credit. In this volume the subject of credit is treated, *mainly,* in terms of mercantile and consumer credit; *substantially,* from the standpoint of credit obtained from financial institutions, including real estate credit; and *incidentally,* in terms of any other class of credit. Simply defined, *credit is the power or ability to obtain goods or services in exchange for a promise to pay for them later.*   Similarly, it is the power or ability to obtain money, by the borrowing process, in return for a promise to repay the obligation in the future.   *Futurity* is thus a basic characteristic of credit, and *risk,* which is necessarily connected with the time element, is an accompanying characteristic.   In every credit transaction the seller or lender assumes some risk, dependent upon the extent of the probability that the promise will be fulfilled.   When emphasis is placed on the high probability of repayment in the future, credit is sometimes defined as "man's confidence in man."

Properly defined, credit represents the actual or prospective debtor's power or ability to effect an exchange by offering his promise of future payment.   Popular usage, however, has turned the meaning of the word credit around, until it signifies something that the seller and not the buyer gives.   Strictly speaking, it is incorrect for a seller to state "we do not give credit," for it is the prospective buyer who gives or offers his credit in exchange for the merchandise purchased or services obtained.   The seller may accept or reject this intangible offering, depending upon whether, in his opinion, the buyer possesses the willingness and ability to redeem his promise at maturity.   Thus it is a solecism to refer to sellers on time as credit grantors.

Nevertheless, the popular and familiar application of the term is generally adopted, partly because it is difficult to inaugurate changes of this nature successfully. It is not, however, impossible to reconcile practical usage with the stated definition, for in a sense the seller is granting the buyer permission to use his purchasing power as represented by his ability and willingness to pay at a future time. John Stuart Mill's definition of credit as "the permission to use another's capital" is suggestive of this conception. Thus what the seller really grants is not credit itself but the credit privilege, a distinction that should be kept in mind whenever reference is made to credit granting or extending throughout the book.

From certain points of view the term "credit" may be more readily explained than defined. The explanation is varied, however, depending upon the standpoint from which it is viewed. Narrowly conceived, credit may be regarded as *a technical function of management,* dealing with such matters as the investigation of credit risks, authorization of credit transactions, and collection of accounts.

More broadly viewed, credit is *a type of business finance.* When actually used in connection with the purchase and sale of goods or in the borrowing of money, it is shown on the books of the seller or lender as an "accounts and notes receivable" asset, representing the value of goods exchanged for promises, and on the books of the buyer as an "accounts and notes payable" liability. When employed in long-term borrowings by a corporation, credit may be evidenced by bonds as a liability on the borrower's books but as an asset on the lender's. The management of funds going into and out of these accounts, and the choice of alternative methods of financing sales and purchases or loans and borrowings, is a function of credit management on an executive level. When thus viewed the finance aspect of credit is emphasized, and an explanation is found of why a course in credits and collections is often treated as part of a curriculum in finance.

More often, credit is regarded as *a phase of marketing* whose function it is to facilitate the movement of goods through the channels of trade and their ultimate consumption. Thus conceived, credit is used to sustain and to promote production, distribution, and consumption of goods and services. Without its use many businesses could not exist, many purchases would not be made, and consumption would be at a much lower level. Moreover, credit is a device by which payment for purchases can be adjusted to the circumstances of the market, be they personal, industrial, seasonal, cyclical, or secular.

Actually, credit is much more than all these phases combined. To be sure, the management of credit involves the application of management principles as in any other aspect of business management. It certainly deals with financial considerations, and in recent years credit has become a potent force in the marketing of goods and services.   In addition, however, the subject must be viewed from its impact upon our society and its overall economy.   This gives it the necessary breadth as the context within which operational policies and procedures must be discussed, analyzed, and interpreted.

Credit distinguished from debt. Properly to understand credit, one must distinguish it from debt, wealth, and purchasing power.   As pointed out above, credit is a *power, capacity,* or *ability. Debt,* by contrast, *represents the unpaid portion, or the outstanding balance, of past business done on credit.*   Credit may vary with different appraisals of debt-paying power; debt is definite and determinable.   Credit is a purchasing or borrowing capacity—used and unused; debt constitutes a legal claim of creditors for specific amounts resulting from actual past credit transactions.   The collective credit is inexpressible in quantitative terms, since much of it is potential, but the collective debt is always the sum of items *payable* as shown by debtors' books or as the sum of all *receivables* on the creditors' books.   To say that credit and debt are the same thing oversimplifies the matter and limits use of the term credit, first, to that part of it that has actually been used, and second, to that portion of the used credit that remains unpaid.   The statistics on so-called "consumer credit" in terms of amounts outstanding, as published by the Federal Reserve System, are thus actually statistics on consumer *debt,* not credit.

Even when credit is treated in the narrowest sense as the opposite of debt, measured as of a given date, differences are reflected in attitudes, ranging from William Shakespeare's well-known injunction "Neither a borrower nor a lender be" to a saying by Artemus Ward—an American humorist of the 1850's and 1860's—"Let us all be happy and live within our means, even if we have to borrow the money to do it."   Quite often the concept of "debt" evokes an emotionally derogatory or even antagonistic attitude at the same time that the concept of "credit," which is the source of debt and in the narrowest sense but the opposite side of it, may be highly regarded and creditworthiness even extolled.[1]

Credit distinguished from credit volume. Although total credit is immeasurable, the credit of any individual or firm is regarded as limited and fairly determinable at any given time.   While the limit of one's credit may restrict his power to purchase on credit at any given time, there may be no limit on the number of times he may use his credit.   In

---

[1] For an interesting discussion of this aspect of the subject, see *The Two Faces of Debt,* a monograph published by the Federal Reserve Bank of Chicago, 1963.

other words, assuming that his promise to pay is fulfilled each time he buys on credit, the total of successive transactions made on credit far exceeds *during a specific period* the credit which the buyer has *at any one time.* For example, a person with a $100 limit on a charge account in a given store may use it every month in the year, paying promptly by the tenth of the month. Thus he would never have *credit* in that store in excess of $100. Neither would his *debt* there ever exceed $100. But the store's annual *volume* of business done on credit with him would amount to $1,200.

Credit volume is the total amount of business done on credit, either with an individual customer or with all customers. It is the sum of all credit transactions that have actually taken place during a specified period of time, such as a year or month. In terms of annual credit sales, it is, except for instalment credit, usually several times the residual, or outstanding, debts resulting from this business. Even on instalment transactions, the volume of such credit exceeds the indebtedness. For example, for the year 1967 the extensions of consumer instalment credit were reported in the *Federal Reserve Bulletin* as $81.3 billion, or 8.1 per cent more than the $75.2 billion outstanding on the average during that year, and in the preceding two years they were 19.9 and 10.7 per cent more, respectively.

By dividing the amount of credit volume by debt outstanding, a turnover rate can be computed which is a measure of business efficiency similar to the merchandise inventory turnover rate. An objective of business management is to build credit *volume,* for profits usually have a direct relationship to sales volume.

Credit contrasted with wealth. Credit differs not only from debt and credit volume but also from wealth. *Wealth,* regarded from the viewpoint of society, *is any material or physical thing that satisfies a human want, provided that thing is limited in amount.* Wealth, in other words, consists of *tangible economic goods,* such as land, buildings, equipment, gold, or personal effects. Credit is a special means whereby one may acquire a right to use such wealth. At the same time, the legal forms or instruments used in credit transactions provide creditors with a right to receive payment for the goods which they have surrendered to a debtor in a credit transaction.

From the standpoint of society, credit transactions transfer but do not in themselves increase wealth. From the standpoint of the individual vendor or creditor, the credit *instrument* received represents a form of *intangible* wealth accepted in exchange for the *tangible* wealth surrendered. Thus each party in the transaction may claim personal wealth which in total exceeds the value of the physical goods reckoned as social wealth. It may be concluded, therefore, that whereas credit is not wealth, credit instruments are so regarded from the viewpoint of the individual creditor.

Nevertheless, while credit is not wealth, it is a factor contributing to the *increase* of wealth. Credit is an aid to production and distribution and consequently leads to more goods brought to the market than otherwise would be. Thus the wealth of society is increased not by credit but by the *use* of credit. Credit also adds value to goods brought to the market by facilitating their transfer to people who want to use them. Credit is also a service for which people are willing to pay money.

Is credit purchasing power? Because to the economist demand is generally deemed to consist of both willingness and ability to buy, a consumer sometimes thinks that whatever makes him an effectual demander in the market at the same time increases his purchasing *power*. If this were the case, the extension of credit to an impecunious customer would increase his purchasing power. Carried to its so-called "logical" conclusion, this concept would lead to a belief that the purchasing power of the entire population could be increased or decreased by manipulating the volume of credit. Such is not the case, however.

Credit is extended to a buyer only because of the vendor's confidence in his promise to pay later. Ability to fulfill that promise must be tied to some tangible capacity to pay, usually to the debtor's current income, although debt may also be paid out of savings (accumulated income) or out of wealth inherited or otherwise acquired. One's power to purchase, therefore, *on credit or for cash,* grows out of his tangible purchasing power. It is unrealistic to think that credit enhances one's purchasing power, except temporarily, when credit itself is based upon purchasing power. Consequently, it is illogical to think that by using credit one can, in the long run, buy *more* than he could with his cash income and supplementary purchasing power afforded by savings or other wealth. It is true that some vendors misjudge buyers' real purchasing and paying power and so *sell* them *more* goods than warranted, but this is a misuse, not a proper use, of credit.

Although credit does not *in the long run* increase purchasing power, it may have some definite effects upon the *use* of purchasing power. It may advance the use of purchasing power, enabling a buyer to obtain today what he might not be able for some time to buy for cash. Credit may also influence the types of things for which expenditures are made, as when a few durable goods are bought in preference to the many small purchases of nondurables which are usually made when cash is at hand to be spent.

To be sure, there is no complete agreement about the relationship of credit to purchasing power as discussed above.   While most careful students of credit hold to the view and theory herein developed, critics of our economic system, consumer-oriented writers, and persons who regard credit with a jaundiced eye obviously hold a belief to the contrary. Much of the confusion on this point, in so far as consumers are concerned, may arise out of failure (1) fully to comprehend the nature of credit conceptually, (2) to distinguish between purchasing and purchasing power, respectively, and (3) clearly to define the term "purchasing power."   For example, on the last point one would be hard put to find a definition of purchasing power in any discussion of the subject, except when it refers to such specific phenomena as the "purchasing power of the dollar" as measured by wholesale prices or by consumer prices, in which case it refers to the worth of money as determined by what it can buy in comparison with what it could buy at a specified previous time or period. To find such general definition of the term purchasing power one had to resort to *Webster's Third New International Dictionary* (unabridged), where it is defined as the "capacity of an individual, group of individuals, or the aggregate of prospective buyers as determined primarily by current income and savings—called also *buying power*." When these points are thoughtfully considered, it is evident, as one authority states it, that "What is sometimes called an increase in purchasing power due to instalment buying can better be described as an acceleration of purchasing"[2] and "as a device by which the consumer uses the income he has to get what he wants most into his possession as soon as possible."[3]

Credit involving business enterprises as users differs substantially in this respect.   Here it has a more direct relationship to purchasing power.   Available credit may actually create purchasing power for a business organization, for by its means the business obtains merchandise, equipment, and supplies with which it may operate and make a profit. Thus purchasing and paying power may grow directly out of the use of credit.

Extent of business transacted by means of credit. The extent to which credit is used is an indication of its importance in business. There are no data to show the *total volume* of credit business, but careful estimates based on United States census data and other sources indicate that about one-half of all retail store sales is on credit and that about 85 per cent of all sales by wholesalers and manufacturers' sales branches are on credit.   It is further estimated that about 95 per

[2] Reavis Cox, *The Economics of Instalment Buying*, The Ronald Press Company, New York, 1948, p. 398. For a comprehensive discussion of this entire aspect of the subject, see pp. 397–404.
[3] *Ibid.*, p. 404.

cent of all business transactions involve the use of some credit instrument, including checks and currency.

Evidence points to a gradual increase in the use of credit over the years. It was customarily extended by small retail stores in the grocery and drug trades even before its use was widened by the adoption of a credit policy by department stores during the latter part of the last century. Mercantile credit was so common in the early 1800's as to warrant the rise of credit-reporting or mercantile agencies, like the predecessors of Dun & Bradstreet, Inc., in the 1840's. Since 1900, some developments have reduced the use of credit—for example, the rise of nonservice retail establishments such as supermarkets, cash-and-carry wholesalers, and distributive cooperatives. On the other hand, this decrease has been more than offset by opposing factors to be pointed out later.

Instalment credit has experienced great popularity since World War I. Budget accounts have been added to charge accounts and instalment contracts, and various forms of instalment credit have come to be featured by even the most reputable stores. Credit can now be used in buying transportation, meals, hotel accommodations, and long-distance telephoning. Small vendors as well as large have resorted to the use of credit in the sale of their goods and services through new financial arrangements offered by banks. Continued efforts by banks and other organizations, for example, in the direction of the widely heralded checkless society should give added impetus to the use of credit.

Also contributing to the increased use of credit have been the Federal Reserve System and such Federal agencies as the Home Owners' Loan Corporation, the Federal Housing Administration, and the Veterans Administration. The role of government in sponsoring the greater use of credit has nowhere been more evident than in the agricultural segment of the economy. Throughout the years since the period of World War I, numerous legislative acts and executive orders have established credit facilities and loan funds on an ever-widening scale. Counted among the Congressional enactments of outstanding significance are the Federal Farm Loan Act of 1916, and amendments which created the Federal land banks, joint-stock land banks, and intermediate credit banks; the United States Warehouse Act, also of 1916, which facilitates the financing of products stored under the Act, especially through provisions for licensing of warehouses and the use of standard warehouse receipts; the Farm Credit Act of 1933, which established the production credit system and banks for cooperatives; and the Farmers' Home Administration Act of 1946, which set up a mortgage insurance system. Among the important administrative agencies created by specific legislation or executive order and specializing or dealing in part with agricultural credits are the

Farm Credit Administration, the Commodity Credit Corporation, the Federal Farm Mortgage Corporation, and the Rural Electrification Administration.

Obviously, credit wields a potent force in modern business activity. It penetrates every fiber of our economic structure and affects everybody, regardless of race, creed, or station in life. Credit, probably more than any other single factor, is responsible for the rapid development of American industry and for the continued progress of our country and its people.

Users of credit. Credit is used almost universally in America, not only by all types of people but in a variety of roles. First, people use it extensively as *consumers*. Data published by the Federal Home Loan Bank Board reveal that the consumer in his role as a home owner is one of the biggest users of credit in the American economy. At the end of the year 1967, for example, the amount of outstanding mortgage loans secured by one-to-four-family nonfarm homes was about $236 billion. Then, too, the most recent *Survey of Financial Characteristics of Consumers*[4] shows that approximately two-thirds of all consumer units owe some kind of debt. Debtors are in all income groups and in all ages for heads of spending units, but they are found most frequently in the middle or moderately high income levels and are most common among younger consumers who are heavy purchasers of durable goods for the building up and equipping the home plant. In addition to the consumer with *debt,* which is evidence that credit has been used, there are unnumbered others who use *credit* but who may have had no outstanding debt at the time of the survey. There are very few consumers, indeed, who do not use credit or who do not have access to it as members of a credit-using family.

Second, people use credit in the role of *businessmen.* Credit financing actually underlies American business, for it has been the means by which most entrepreneurs have been able to venture into the business field and to give expression to their ideas for making products, distributing them, and rendering service. The systems of finance and banking in this country have developed largely in conjunction with this desire and need of business for credit.

Third, people use credit in *governmental* roles. The Federal government is a familiar example of a public agency as debtor. When collecting income amounting to less than its expenditures, the government, in a manner unavailable to individuals privately, relies upon borrowing for the balance of its financial needs, thus increasing the national debt.

---

[4] Dorothy S. Projector and Gertrude S. Weiss, *Survey of Financial Characteristics of Consumers,* Board of Governors of the Federal Reserve System, August, 1966.

It always borrows on short terms to finance operations in the interim between dates of large receipts of income from taxations. National governments trade their credit for funds in the open money market and frequently borrow from governments of other nations. Similarly, state and local governments use credit temporarily to supplement deficit incomes and in meeting, on a long-time basis, extraordinary expenditures for such items as highways, school buildings, river control, and slum clearance. On the whole, the principles of public finance are very much like those of personal finance, except that, at least on the Federal level, the banking system *provides* the government with purchasing power when its income is inadequate, whereas no such provision is made for any other user of credit. Also, government, unlike a private debtor, possesses the power to tax as a means of raising funds for the payment of indebtedness.

Sources of funds. Because for every debtor there is a creditor, the picture of credit users in our economy must be matched by one of credit suppliers or sources of funds. Technically, creditors provide merchandise, service, or money in exchange for a promise of future payment. Actually, however, the essence of supplying credit lies in the *investment* in the *things* which are sold on credit, i.e., in the *money* which the things represent. Money must be supplied by someone in some way before credit can be used.

There are two general sources of funds which flow into credit transactions: (1) savings and (2) "created" funds. Savings consist of the money which an individual amasses and makes available to others. A person who saves from his income, or a business organization that has profit from its operations, is in a position to supply funds to others for personal or business use. Instead of providing it in the form of money, however, the owner may invest it in merchandise which he makes available on credit. Funds accumulated may be offered directly, through banks, or through finance and loan companies. The supplying of such funds transfers purchasing power from creditors to debtors; it does not, as has been explained above, automatically increase the amount of purchasing power. Such funds may not actually even advance purchasing *power;* they may only advance *purchasing* if they are made available to spenders by persons who would not have used it themselves. The limit of such credit obviously lies in the amount of funds saved.

In contrast to funds saved are those derived from the second source, namely, those which are *created* through the institutional provisions of our banking system. Funds for credit use are created through the Federal Reserve System, where loans may be made in some multiple of assets of member banks held as a reserve with a Federal Reserve

Bank.   Assume that member banks of the Federal Reserve System are, for example, required to hold 20 per cent of demand deposit liabilities in the form of vault cash and deposits with a Federal Reserve Bank.   Then a member bank, theoretically, may create deposits equal to a maximum of five times its reserves.   A bank holding qualified reserves of $100,000 could thus support $500,000 of demand deposits.   If the bank currently has $300,000 of demand deposits, the legal reserve requirement would be $60,000, and the bank could use the $40,000 of excess reserves for the purpose of supporting an additional $200,000 increase in loans and demand deposits.   Thus an appreciable expansion of credit can be financed in such a way as actually to *create* and to *increase* the purchasing power available in the market.   Most of the loans made in this manner are in the form of checking accounts, although they may take the form of Federal Reserve notes.   Loans by banks are made through accounts mainly to the government and to business, although a growing portion represents personal loans.

Functions of credit.   Credit performs functions which may be classified as economic, social, and managerial.

The first economic function of credit is to serve as *a medium of exchange* in the economy.   Money exchange is a cultural stage ahead of barter, but a credit economy is a step in advance of a mere money economy.   By the use of credit, transactions can be consummated quickly and easily on confidence without conveying coin.   Risk, as well as time and effort, is minimized.   Were credit arrangements to disappear, volume of business would drop precipitously for want of a suitable medium of exchange to support it.

A second economic function of credit is to *make capital available* for business purposes which would otherwise lie idle.   Induced by payment for use of their funds, individuals save to invest or to lend their money.   Not only they benefit from this, but borrowers do too, for, with funds made available through credit, profitable industry can be conducted where before only ideas may have existed.   The development of *large-scale* enterprise is also a result of the use of credit, for partially through such credit instruments as bonds and long-term notes small sums are amassed into the capital accumulations required for large-scale industry.   Society is the benefactor of the use of credit, for through large industries a greater variety of products is produced and distributed at lower costs and prices.

A social function of credit is to *make for independence* of thought and action.   Its use obviates the necessity for hoarding on the part of those who desire to save and leads them to place their funds in institutions where the principal is more secure than are cached hoardings.   This, in turn, provides uses for capital which people have no means of employing themselves.   Credit bridges the gap between capital and labor, enabling the latter to secure assistance in an attempt at independent enterprise.   It enables individuals, moreover, to secure an education on borrowed funds and to obtain all types of consumption goods, including homes, pending the receipt of income and before the entire purchase price is accumulated.

For the business manager credit performs several functions.   It is a *tool of business promotion,* with which he may expand his business by catering to customers who want to buy their merchandise on credit. With it he can attract a desired class of trade and offer an inducement to buy, which constitutes a competitive advantage.   Credit also affords him an opportunity to undertake his business with the funds of others and to *adjust his volume of capital to the varying needs of his business.* He may, by this means, enlarge the scope of his operation by borrowing additional capital during periods of extraordinary business activity and reduce it with the approach of dull periods.

Need for skill in credit management. Whatever role credit plays in our modern world, its success or failure depends largely upon the skill with which it is managed in individual transactions.   No credit is more sound than the promises which underlie it.   Yet no credit structure is vulnerable except through the weaknesses of its management, for the concept of credit is logical and it is practical when well administered. Not credit itself, but the abuse of credit and the incompetent administration of it cause credit ills, such as unwarranted credit extensions, excessive losses on credit accounts, business failures, and perhaps unsettling cyclical conditions.   Unwise credit management tends to harm both debtors and creditors and shakes confidence in business in general.

The remedy for the ills and abuses of credit and the best assurance of proper use of this vital institution in our society is a knowledge of credit principles and sound credit practices.   Through almost 65 years, credit has been methodically studied in our modern economy and much has been learned which has been proved sound in practice.   There exists a body of principles which is fairly common knowledge to trained and skilled credit managers and which may be learned and applied by any student of the subject.

A knowledge of credit principles is requisite today, however, not only for those who are in the business of administering credit.   Businessmen and citizens in general need to be acquainted with credit, for every phase of any business is related in some way to it.   Not merely *how* to extend credit but *whether* to extend it is a question deserving the attention of general management in business.   Moreover, because credit has become an economic institution greater than any organization's use of it, an understanding of it today is indispensable also to economists, sociologists, lawyers, legislators, and politicians.

QUESTIONS AND PROBLEMS

1 Explain why our economic system may be characterized as a credit economy. Indicate what effect you think the elimination of credit from our society would have upon the economy.

2 Is the use of credit and its management in a business enterprise a phase of marketing or of finance? Does it make any difference whether it is involved in connection with buying or with selling activities?

3 What different views regarding credit may be held by the following: consumers, businessmen, legislators, accountants, bankers, investment counsels, economists?

4 Why is it a solecism to say that sellers on time *give* credit?

5 It is sometimes claimed that credit is merely a technical function of management. Is this position justifiable?

6 What is measured by the most commonly used credit statistics of the Federal Reserve Board: credit or debt? Explain.

7 How can credit *volume* be increased without increasing credit or debt? What is the significance of credit volume?

8 Trace the logic which relates American economic prosperity with the use of credit.

9 Is purchasing power increased by the availability of credit? Is credit increased by the availability of purchasing power? Explain.

10 What difference is there between consumer purchasing power and business purchasing power, so far as the relation of each to credit is concerned?

11 Judging from past developments, should we expect the use and volume of credit in this country to increase, remain constant, or decrease? Why?

12 What is the significance of the terms "saved" and "created" in connection with credit?

13 In what ways are the credit privileges of the Federal government different from those of businesses or individuals?

14 List several basic ideas or concepts which you may have held, consciously or otherwise, that have been changed as a result of reading the contents of this chapter. Is that to the good?

15 There is considerable discussion in current literature concerning the movement toward a checkless society. Indicate what impact you think such a state would have upon the use of credit in our economy.

CHAPTER TWO

role of credit
in the economic
and social environment

When the study of credit as a business function was substantially begun in the first quarter of this century, interest in it arose mainly from a desire to understand and improve credit granting and allied operations. Attention centered around mercantile credit. Consumer credit other than that relating to real estate was not yet of any significance in the market, and finance and banking were subjects of interest more to economists and to some specially affected groups than to students of marketing or business generally. Gradually the study of credit came to include consumer credit, also some phases of finance proper. The object of study, however, continued to be primarily an understanding of the use of credit as a technique or a function of internal management. The *general* aspects of credit remained a consideration primarily of economic theorists. Since the beginning of the 1940's, however, credit has in-creasingly been recognized as having a place in our economic and social structure that far exceeds in importance the mere sum of the individual credit transactions.

Credit as a cause and as an effect of business conditions. In its economic setting, credit is viewed both as a cause and as an effect. Businessmen have long recognized that credit is a dynamic, causal factor in the business world. It produces business. It increases the volume of sales, opens markets of new buyers, facilitates selling, creates satisfied customers, and builds demand for some products beyond what it would be in the absence of credit. More broadly conceived, credit has been regarded as a stimulating, and therefore causal, factor also in the general economy. Economists have attributed in part to credit not only the grad-ual expansion of our economy, but also some of its cyclical character. Ours is a credit economy, as is evidenced by our banking and other finance institutions, our extensive use of credit instruments, and our almost universally favorable attitude toward credit. Consequently, the policies adopted to expand or to contract credit have had a direct bearing upon the scope and volume of business activity.

Credit, however, is not only a causal factor in the system, as though it were some independent device which could be arbitrarily insti-tuted or omitted for the creation of certain effects. It is also itself an effect—an effect of a variety of circumstances quite independent of credit management itself. For example, our use of credit is a result of a high level of moral and financial integrity among our people. It is an outgrowth of our systems of record keeping and communications, of institutions which are able to provide information upon which credit can be intelligently based. It is the result of cooperation among business-men, of our concepts of accounting, our philosophy concerning debt, our savings, and our financing organizations.

Its evolution as an institution has accompanied the rise of these conditions which underlie credit. In contrast to the early 1920's, when the market significance of consumer credit started to become more appar-ent, we are today dwellers in a nation and world made small by rapid transportation and communication. We are a highly productive people, extremely interdependent but imbued with a philosophy that there is no limit to the material prosperity which our research, production, and dis-tribution organizations can provide. We are capitalistic, appreciating the productivity of money and the opportunities which exist for the profitable employment of savings. Our wealth and our income are becoming more equally distributed. We accept without objection the standardization of products put out by our mass producers. We have imagination for devising schemes of financing and willingness to use the institutions which make credit available.   We do not fear or condemn debt.   This is the environment in which our use of credit is made.   Credit in our economy is the effect of all these conditions.

Types of credit in the economy. Being fundamentally a *concept,* credit is given many forms of expression throughout the economy.   Some of it is for short duration; some, for long; some of it is used for obtaining capital equipment; other is used for acquiring items quickly consumed; some of it is the credit of organizations; some is that of individuals.   The economic significance of credit in these various uses is obviously not the same.   In some roles credit has a more pronounced, and perhaps also a more direct, effect upon business and economic conditions than it has in other roles.

A number of the different types of credit have been referred to in the preceding chapter in order to illustrate the concept or character of credit.   For that purpose certain classifications of credit have been used that are in line with much of the later treatment in this book.   For purposes of general analysis of the behavior of credit in our economy, as well as for practical uses in later discussions, it is believed that the following classification has special value:

I Public credit (governmental)

　A Federal

　　Bonds, notes, certificates, bills, and currency

　B State

　　Bonds and notes

　C Municipal

　　Bonds, notes, and certificates

II Private credit

　A Business credit

　　1 Long-term (investment credit)

　　2 Intermediate-term

　　3 Short-term

　　　a Mercantile credit

　　　b Cash credit

　　　c Deposit credit

　B Real estate credit

　　1 Business firms

　　2 Consumers

　C Consumer credit

　　1 Sales of merchandise credit

　　　a Charge account

    b Instalment
  2 Service credit
    a Charge account
    b Instalment
  3 Cash credit
    a Single-payment loans
    b Instalment loans

The types of credit are thus identified not so much from the standpoint of mutually exclusive classifications as from the different viewpoints from which the entire general credit function may be regarded. In the first place, credit may be characterized by the type of user, whether it be employed by government, by personal consumers, or by business organizations. If by government, it is regarded as *public credit;* if by consumers, it is referred to as *consumer credit* or *real estate credit;* and if by business institutions, it is regarded as *investment credit, intermediate-term credit, mercantile credit, short-term cash credit, deposit credit,* or *real estate credit,* as the case may be. Second, depending upon whether merchandise, service, or cash is given in exchange for the debtor's promise to pay, credit is designated as *sales* or *merchandise credit,* as *service credit,* or as *cash* or *money credit,* and the creditors are distinguished as vendors or lenders.

A third useful classification of credit can be made on the basis of the manner in which the credit is repaid. From this standpoint, credit falls into two general classes: *instalment* and *single-payment credit.* The latter requires payment of the full amount due at the end of a given period of time, while instalment credit requires the credit user to pay his obligation in fixed portions or instalments at stated intervals. Fourth, depending upon the maturity or length of credit use, credit may be categorized as *long-term, intermediate-term,* or *short-term credit.* The latter is that credit for which the payment of principal is promised within 1 year, while long-term credit usually is defined to have a maturity in excess of 10 years. Obviously, intermediate-term credit is between short-term and long-term or, perhaps, as commonly defined, has a maturity from 1 to 10 years.

A fifth important distinction arises from the nature of the debtor's motive for the use of credit. From this standpoint, business concerns use credit to procure fixed assets and to carry on operations or to facilitate the movement of goods through the various stages of production and marketing. The primary motivation for the use of credit by consumers, on the other hand, is to obtain funds with which to acquire real estate or to obtain goods and services or money to facilitate the process of consumption.

Finally, credit may be characterized by the source of credit, whether it be from individuals, business concerns; financial institutions, or nonprofit organizations.   In some instances, that for which credit is exchanged exists in a limited supply, as is true of the credit exchanged for the limited quantities of cash or merchandise which a merchant or a lender possesses.   On the other hand, funds exchanged for credit are sometimes created and expanded as the needs for credit increase.   This is true particularly of the credit supplied the government through banks and other financing agencies.   The amount of this type of credit which may be used depends upon many factors other than a mere stock of goods or gold.   Such credit, therefore, may be regarded as *created*, rather than *loaned* from a finite supply.

GOVERNMENTAL
USE OF CREDIT

Credit in the business economy cannot be considered apart from its use in the political economy, since, for one thing, the government's use of credit and the institutions established by it for supplying it have an important bearing upon other forms of credit.

By the Constitution of the United States, Congress is vested with authority "to pay the debts . . . of the United States . . . : to borrow money on the credit of the United States . . . ; to coin money, regulate the value thereof. . . ."   Thus it is a basic and assumed principle that the Federal government shall use its credit in the discharge of its responsibilities.   This is done by borrowing through the issuance of bonds, Treasury bills, Treasury notes, and Treasury certificates.   All these are forms of promises to pay which are exchanged for the money, service, or materials needed by the government.   The exchange is usually made for checking accounts established for the government by banks, and an important role of the banking system which has been created lies in the extension of such credit.

Direct effect.   In the normal course of its activity, if the Federal government is maintaining its credit by sustaining confidence in its operations and promises, there is no question of the government's creditworthiness and virtually no limit, except the Congress-imposed limit to the national debt, to the amount of credit which the government can command.   Its monetary needs are regarded as paramount, and the Federal Reserve System is designed in part to meet these needs.

The credit which arises from governmental uses—and state and municipal governments also are privileged to issue bonds and notes to supplement their incomes—is, therefore, a direct *effect* of the undertakings initiated by the government.   In periods of an unbalanced budget, such as during wars and depressions, when for alleged common welfare the government is spending in excess of its income, its role as a debtor is accentuated by increased borrowing.   Because the credit thus obtained is in turn spent in the market place for commodities and services, a great increase in purchasing power is felt.   Rising demand from this source is inflationary, for it represents not only an increase in the quantity of money in circulation but also, because as the money gets into circulation it is spent over and over again, an increase in the velocity of money.

Indirect effect. Moreover, such credit extended to the government also *influences* the amount of credit that is *used by business.*   A commercial bank may usually lend up to about five times the amount of reserve maintained with the Federal Reserve Bank.   This reserve may be built up by the commercial bank at its Federal Reserve Bank by discounting with the latter loans backed by government securities or through rediscounting commercial paper accepted by it in its loans to business concerns.   A loan may, however, be made to a business concern as a direct result of credit extended the government.   Suppose, for example, that, upon authorization given the government by Congress to spend a sum which it must borrow from the banks, the government in turn contracts with a business organization for the items it needs.   On the basis of this contract, the concern obtains a loan from the bank; this it invests in the production of the things needed by the government.   The bank, in turn, may rediscount this commercial paper with the Federal Reserve Bank as legal reserve and then lend *additionally* up to five times the amount of the reserve so placed.   Thus by the nature of the banking system, credit is *created,* and it does not correspond in amount with any funds *saved* to be made available for loans.   The business loans made possible by this system of credit may also be extended to sales and personal finance companies and to retailers to assist in financing sales to ultimate customers.

Resulting control. The expansive influence of governmental credit, and that credit which is made possible as a consequence of it through the banking system, have made these forms of credit the objective of legislative and administrative control.   It has been the purpose of Congress and of the Federal Reserve Board to regulate bank credit in order either to stimulate depressed business conditions or to curb what would appear to be an overextension of business.   This is done mainly through the open market operations of the Federal Reserve System and by raising or lowering the reserves required to be maintained by member banks with their respective Federal Reserve Banks as a basis for loans.   It is accomplished also by varying the rediscount rates charged on advances made by the Federal Reserve Banks to their member banks.   Control of credit at this level is facilitated by the fact that authority is highly concentrated in the administrative agency and responsibility for complying with the control falls to banks operating throughout the country.   Thus control may be both widespread and effective.

BUSINESS CREDIT

A second major part of credit in our economy is that used by business. To the businessman, credit is a means to an end.   With credit he can engage in productive activity which promises to yield him profit.   Prospects of profitable activity create a demand for credit.   The very increase of our population affords opportunity for additional business enterprises or expansion of existing ones.   New technological developments and shifting competitive practices also invite business undertakings if sufficient capital can be obtained.   The flow of credit into the business economy is thus a reflection of business opportunity.

Business opportunity a basic factor. Whereas the most distinguishing characteristic of government credit is the fact that it can be *created* to meet the government's need, the truly unique aspect of business credit is that it is *productive,* or self-liquidating, credit.   Money, like materials, personnel, or other factors of production, is usually employed in business for the purpose of engaging in a profit-yielding activity. None is desired beyond what is necessary; on the other hand, some of it is indispensable for the performance of any activity.   Availability of assets on credit, therefore, makes possible business performance.   In other words, in a successful business venture the acquisition of assets on credit automatically provides the means for the payment of the debt contracted.   The credit used by an individual concern, or all concerns collectively, however, is limited by the opportunities for profitable use of the money, merchandise, or equipment obtainable by its means.

Theoretically, the volume of credit extended to business by financial institutions, mercantile establishments, and others is governed by business *opportunity*.   Actually, it depends upon creditors' *interpretation* of the business opportunity.   This means that actually the injection of credit into, or its withdrawal from, the business system is the result of many individual decisions and transactions, which may cause one segment of the economy to expand and another to contract.   The creditors' function is to estimate the various situations properly and to provide the credit which can be used.   As a precaution against the possibility of collective poor judgment as to when credit in general needs to be expanded or curtailed in the business realm, the government holds some power to influence it through the control of interest rates and reserve-loan ratios.

The influence which credit exerts to stimulate or to depress business stems largely from the credit extended *to* business rather than *by* business. The use of credit by which a business concern becomes a debtor is that which expands its activity. This form of credit, therefore, arises as a *result* of opportunity; it is, on the other hand, a *cause* of business activity.

Investment credit. Usually the first form of credit which is used by a business organization is investment credit. This is utilized for the purpose of obtaining funds with which to purchase fixed assets and to carry on minimum business operations. If an entrepreneur has his own capital, he may not need to borrow for financing the purchase of land, buildings, machinery, fixtures, delivery equipment, and certain intangible assets. When borrowing is resorted to for such acquisitions, the credit involved is known as "investment credit." In addition to fixed assets, however, a certain amount of working capital is also often provided in this manner, sufficient for the requirement of the concern in its normal, or at least minimum, business activity. Permanent working capital is that portion of the current assets of a business which is constantly needed from week to week and from month to month. It is the combined sum required to carry minimum amounts of accounts receivable, inventories of merchandise, supplies, and cash for paying wages and other current expenses. The original funds from which all these needs are first met are usually obtained through investment credit to the extent that they cannot be provided by the proprietors, partners, or stockholders.

Investment credit is obtained through the issuance of relatively long-term obligations in the form of promises to pay at a future time in exchange for the money which is borrowed now. These obligations take the form of bonds; promissory notes secured by chattel mortgages or equipment obligations; and long-term promissory notes without such security. All these are promises to pay definite sums of principal and, in most cases, also certain rates of interest. These loans are made purely for investment purposes, hence the term "investment credit."

The length of the credit period in any one case is determined primarily by the life of the asset which is to be acquired with the money secured through the utilization of investment credit. Thus, chattel mortgages issued on movable goods are usually of a much shorter duration than first mortgage bonds secured by real property. Sometimes, the permanency of the borrowing organization tends to determine the length of the credit period. Four principal sources are available from which long-term investment credit may be secured, namely, the ultimate individual investor; business concerns; financial institutions, such as trustees, life insurance companies, and mutual savings banks; and nonprofit organizations, including universities and foundations.

Intermediate-term credit. In addition to long-term investment credit, most commercial and industrial concerns frequently require funds for an intermediate period of from 1 to 10 years. Historically, long-term financing has been used to procure the necessary plant and equipment, to refinance existing long-term obligations, and to provide funds for permanent working capital requirements. In recent years, an increasing number of companies have, however, used intermediate-term credit for the purpose of financing the enlarged use of machinery and equipment in addition to other needs that may be considered cyclical in character. An example of the latter is the financing of assets required for government projects during emergencies. The common intention in intermediate-term financing is to refinance through the retained earnings that may be accumulated during the period of the intermediate-term credit. Sources of this type of credit include commercial banks, life insurance companies, finance companies, government agencies, and government-sponsored agencies such as Small Business Investment companies.

Mercantile credit. Mercantile or commercial credit is the credit one businessman extends to another when selling goods on time for resale or commercial use. Theoretically, it is the power to obtain merchandise for business purposes in return for a promise to pay an equivalent at a specified time in the future. It includes the credit granted by different sellers of goods in the process of production and distribution from the time the goods are in the state of raw materials until they reach the hands of the retailer or industrial consumer. The principal purpose of mercantile credit is to facilitate the movement of goods through the various stages of production and marketing. It does not include credit given by the retailer when selling on time, or that extended by manufacturers and functional middlemen when selling directly to the individual consumer.

Short-term cash credit. Businesses not only purchase merchandise on credit but also are heavy users of short-term cash credit for which they promise to repay the principal within 1 year. Such credit may be obtained through the sale of commercial paper or from short-term loans granted by commercial banks on an unsecured basis. Indeed, one of the primary functions of commercial banks since their inception has been to facilitate the exchange of goods through the channels of distribution by providing methods for settling obligations. Many business firms are, however, not in a position to sell commercial paper or to obtain unsecured short-term loans from banks. Instead, they must pledge or sell some of their assets in order to obtain the funds needed. Thus a large portion of short-term loans made by commercial banks is secured, as is an even larger portion of such loans made by certain other specialized financial institutions, including finance companies and factors.

Deposit credit. The primary source of funds for certain financial institutions consists of *deposits*. These include commercial bank time deposits and demand deposits, mutual savings bank deposits, and savings and loan association savings accounts. While there are significant legal and operational differences among these different types of deposits, each of the above financial institutions is able to secure funds on deposit only by selling its credit to depositors. *Deposit credit* may, therefore, be defined as the power which enables a financial institution to attract funds of depositors. Quite frequently, deposits are made in the form of checks rather than in so-called "money." In either event the deposit transaction is purely a dealing in credit.

REAL ESTATE CREDIT

Nature of real estate credit. Real estate credit is that credit in which the lender is given a real estate mortgage as the security for a loan. It is sometimes referred to as mortgage credit and frequently is divided into farm and nonfarm credit. The latter is also further classified into loans on one-to-four-family homes, used primarily by consumers for the purpose of obtaining funds to acquire real estate, and loans on multifamily and commercial properties used mainly by business firms and other institutions. The principal sources of real estate credit include savings and loan associations, commercial banks, mutual savings banks, life insurance companies, mortgage companies, individual lenders, and Federal land banks.

Importance of real estate credit. Since the end of World War II, the use of real estate credit has increased substantially. At the end of 1945, the amount of mortgage debt outstanding was under $36 billion. By year-end 1967, total mortgage debt had risen to approximately $369 billion, an increase of $334 billion over the 22-year period. In contrast, the outstanding national debt increased from $255.7 billion to $284 billion, an increase of $28.3 billion during the same period. Although not strictly comparable, these figures serve to show the relative importance of real estate credit in our economy.

CONSUMER CREDIT

Nature of consumer credit. *Consumer credit* may be defined as the *credit granted to consumers to facilitate the process of consumption.* From the consumer's standpoint, it is the power which an individual uses in obtaining goods and services, or in borrowing money, for consumption purposes, on the promise to repay an equivalent at a future time.

In a broad sense, consumer credit includes all credit extensions for personal use, whether granted by manufacturers and other producers who sell direct to consumers, by retailers, professional men, service organizations, or by the various types of financial institutions. Although fundamentally all these kinds of credit extensions are alike in principle, separate consideration is given in this book to mortgage loans on homes. Excluded from the discussions of consumer credit are pseudo-credit transactions, exemplified by loans against insurance policies, loans by banks against passbooks on savings accounts, and loans by saving and loan associations against borrowers' shares. Such loans are in reality forms of dissaving or withdrawals from previous accumulations which belong to the borrower but which he does not wish to disturb permanently. The treatment of consumer credit in this book is therefore confined to open book credit, to credit underlying instalment sales transactions, and to the credit arising out of cash borrowings by consumers.

Reasons for consumer credit. From the standpoint of the creditor there is but one principal reason for consumer credit, and that is profit. To the retailer it spells increased volume and remunerative business; to the lender of money, it means a worthwhile return on his investment and compensation for his efficient method of operation. From the point of view of the consumer, however, the matter is not quite so simple. In using credit, he is motivated by a complex of impulses and desires not so easy to unravel and comprehend. In general, however, the consumer may be said to be prompted by one or more of three sets of motives: *convenience,* the *desire to improve his lot,* and *necessity.*

Millions of consumers in the United States utilize credit because they find it convenient to obtain goods and services on that basis. Orders can be placed by telephone, better service is usually secured from stores when goods are bought on a charge account, and several members of the family can buy on a single account without the necessity of carrying cash. Periodic payments facilitate home budgeting, and the person who pays the bills at intervals can control expenses more readily.

Perhaps equally large numbers of consumers use credit, especially of the instalment type, to raise their standard of living, to better their condition, by purchasing costly commodities like radios, automobiles, refrigerators, washing machines, and the many other articles which make their home life more pleasant and their lot in general easier to bear.   Or they may borrow to finance a vacation, to make home repairs or improvements, or for educational purposes.   If they can ultimately pay for them, there is every justification for such purchases and borrowings.

Then there is the large and growing volume of consumer credit that has its *raison d'être* in necessity and in human want and misery. Millions of our industrial workers and others live from hand to mouth and have no ready cash until pay day.   Farmers must wait for the harvest and in the meantime need credit to tide them over.   Periods of temporary unemployment deplete the meager reserves, if any, and credit may be resorted to until work is resumed.   Consumer credit may be the only way to meet emergencies caused by sickness, death, and accident, or to meet infrequent or nonrecurring expenses, as in hospitalization, special dental care, and the like.   Another very important reason for consumer credit, especially for borrowing money, is to reorganize one's financial obligations by consolidating many relatively small but pressing debts into one amount owed to a single creditor who is more willing to wait.   Some of the old creditors may threaten garnishment of wages, repossession of furniture, or other drastic action that may prove detrimental to the consumer.   In addition, there is a miscellany of other reasons.   Funds may be needed to cover moving expenses, to purchase an automobile needed to secure or hold a job which requires the use of the vehicle, to help a relative in distress, to pay taxes, to care for insurance premiums, or to meet interest on a mortgage.

The credit which is used by consumers for their personal needs is mainly of the three following types: (1) retail charge account credit, (2) instalment sales credit, and (3) loans of cash.

Role of consumer credit in the economy. The role of consumer credit in our economy reflects the difference between the purpose of such credit and that of government and business credit.   Government credit is used for carrying on its activities for the protection, welfare, and in the interest of the *public;* business credit is used for conducting the activities of business in the service of its customers.   Consumers, on the other hand, use credit in the *satisfaction of their own wants.*   In other words, all forms of credit other than consumer credit only *indirectly* serve the consumer; consumer credit contributes *directly* in that final step for which much of the economic system is organized, namely, the satisfaction of consumers' needs and wants.

Consumer credit is further characterized by the fact that it rests squarely upon the creditworthiness of an individual *as consumer.*   Consumers cannot create credit or purchasing power for themselves, as the government can and does.   Neither do consumers expect, by the use of the credit obtained, to make themselves *directly* productive of an income out of which the credit may be paid, as business does, and thus making the credit self-liquidating.   The limit of the government's credit is its need for credit; the limit of a business concern's credit is its opportunity for turning that credit to profitable use; the limit of a consumer's credit is primarily his normal purchasing power.   It is evident, therefore, that both government and business credit may actually *increase* purchasing power; consumer credit, on the other hand, is an *effect of purchasing power*.

Consumer credit does stimulate the economy in ways, however, which cannot be overlooked, although they are often overestimated. While consumer credit may not directly increase *purchasing power*, it may increase, accelerate, and redirect consumer *spending*.   Thus it may *appear* in the short run even to increase purchasing power.   This illusion of purchasing power has been the cause of considerable controversy in the interpretation of consumer credit and has been the instigation of efforts to control purchasing power through the regulation of consumer credit.

The role of consumer credit in the economy, in other words, is to be discerned by determining, first, how the normal expenditure of purchasing power influences the use of credit and, second, to what extent and in what manner credit influences the economy.   The latter is admittedly the more difficult to demonstrate.   However, when a clear distinction is made among government, business, and consumer credit, and when the behavior of consumer credit which may be attributed to natural market conditions is isolated, the role of this form of credit is seen to be mainly an effect or resultant of both purchasing power and spending habits rather than a cause.   This appears in the evidence of the seasonal, cyclical, and secular behavior patterns of consumer credit.

Seasonal pattern of consumer credit. One of the simplest indications of how consumers use credit is found in their purchases on credit throughout the year.   The percentage of annual retail sales made on credit, charge account or instalment, varies from month to month.   Consumer borrowing also evidences a seasonal pattern.   More credit sales and more cash loans are made in November and December than in any other month.   Fewest credit sales are made during February and July. This pattern, however, is not peculiar to credit sales alone, for cash sales also have corresponding peaks and low points.[1]

---

[1] Such pattern can be readily discerned by an examination of the monthly data on department stores and on outstandings on all sales and service credit, as well as on cash loans, in the *Federal Reserve Bulletin* and other relevant data published monthly in the *Survey of Current Business*, U.S. Department of Commerce.

This pattern of consumer credit is mainly the result of consumer spending habits. We do not *live* evenly, economically speaking. The institutional influences of our culture prescribe heavy buying for Christmas. Commercialization of Easter, Mother's Day, and other such occasions also conditions our spending. Moreover, anticipation of summer and winter seasons stimulates purchasing. With the change of wardrobe for both seasons, clothing sales are peaked in spring and fall. The fall season is also one in which more back-to-school supplies are bought. Spring and summer, on the other hand, are the seasons in which the impulses to buy an automobile or a house, or to make real estate repairs, are most active. At the beginning of winter, one is more inclined to buy heating equipment, radios, and television sets. Thus *normal consumption habits assume a seasonal pattern;* it is natural, therefore, that consumers use more credit at certain times of the year than at others. Credit is sometimes used as a lever for stimulating sales out of season, but this is not effective to any great extent. It is thus unrealistic to assume that credit purchasing varies throughout the year because of the greater or lesser availability of credit.

Cyclical character of consumer credit. Business fluctuations and the turning of the economy from periods of boom or prosperity to periods of depression or recession are presumed to have a significant effect upon consumer behavior in the market. To an individual consumer, unfavorable economic conditions may result in loss of employment and/or a curtailment of income. He is then unable or unwilling to spend as much in total as formerly and he may alter his consumption pattern accordingly. The effect upon a family's consumption pattern exerted by changes in income was first given general recognition in a study in 1857 by Ernst Engel of Saxony (Germany) when he formulated what are known as Engel's laws of consumption. Similar studies of family expenditure patterns have been made on a more comprehensive basis by the U.S. Departments of Labor and Agriculture in our own society and for recent years, and one of them by *Life* magazine. As a matter of fact, it has been found that not only actual changes in the economy and in consumer incomes but *expectations* of such changes have a profound effect on how much consumers will spend and for what types or classes of goods and services. For that reason, expectational studies are designed to determine consumer buying intentions and thus possibly forecast consumption patterns.[2] Even more important in this regard is the *Index of Consumer Sentiment*

---

[2] For an elaboration of this point, see "Consumer Buying Intentions," and "Quarterly Survey of Consumer Buying Intentions," in *Federal Reserve Bulletin*, September, 1960, pp. 973–1003; December, 1960, 1332–1337; and March, 1962, pp. 283–288; survey conducted for the Board of Governors by the Bureau of the Census.

based on attitudinal data gathered by the Survey Research Center of the University of Michigan and published annually since 1960 in monograph form.

The increase in expenditures resulting from higher (actual or expected) incomes is not uniform across the board for all things bought. A smaller *percentage* of the augmented expenditures goes for food; a larger percentage goes in good times for clothing, housing, and household operation as well as for automobiles, other durable goods, and so called "luxuries." This is only normal behavior familiar to all of us: when we have more income, we buy the more expensive things and the goods and services which we might do without, while concentrating on the necessities of life in poorer times or when incomes are lower.

It would seem reasonable to expect that this cyclical pattern of behavior of the individual consumer in the market should be reflected in his use of credit. Such is actually the case to a certain extent. Credit sales, both charge account and instalment, increase with general prosperity, and so do personal savings, but they do not *in the aggregate* necessarily decline in poor times unless such times are extended over a considerable period. It is noteworthy, as shown by the data in Table 2-1, that disposable personal income since 1947—the first post-World War II year following reconversion to peacetime pursuits—did not deviate from the pattern as much as did Gross National Product during the recession years 1949, 1954, 1958, and 1960–1961. This may be explained in large part by the built-in income stabilizers from social security, unemployment compensation, etc., and in part by the limited duration of those recessions.

Destabilizing effect of consumer credit not demonstrated. It is the cyclical relationship of economic conditions to consumer credit that is most often regarded with misgivings. The theory that business cycles are induced, or at least accentuated, by expansion and contraction of consumer credit, has been widely held and taught. It is usually pointed out that instalment credit especially is an important cyclical influence. By using it, people supposedly commit their future incomes and in a period of growing economic strain are unable to sustain even their more necessary purchases because of the need to pay off old debts. The implications of this reasoning are serious, but it has not yet been established that the stimulation or withholding of credit *on the consumer level* caused the rise or fall of economic activity throughout the system. Business operates on the ground that credit is warranted when economic conditions justify it. Business does not extend consumer credit on the presumption that it will lift the economy by its own bootstraps. Nor does business withhold credit from consumers because the economy is

table 2-1 Use of Short- and Intermediate-term Consumer Credit (Total, Instalment, and Noninstalment), as Measured by Average Outstandings, in Relation to Disposable Personal Income, United States, 1947–1967*

(In millions of dollars)

| Year | Gross National Product[1] (col. 1) | Disposable personal income[1] (col. 2) | Consumer credit outstandings | | | | | |
| | | | Total | | Instalment | | Noninstalment | |
			Amount[2] (col. 3)	Per cent of col. 2 (col. 4)	Amount[2] (col. 5)	Per cent of col. 2 (col. 6)	Amount[2] (col. 7)	Per cent of col. 2 (col. 8)
1947	231,323	169,833	9,631	5.7	5,360	3.2	4,271	2.5
1948	257,562	189,138	12,800	6.8	7,937	4.2	4,863	2.6
1949	256,484	188,585	15,089	8.0	9,970	5.3	5,119	2.7
1950	284,769	206,940	19,063	9.2	13,216	6.4	5,847	2.8
1951	328,404	226,583	21,296	9.4	14,609	6.5	6,687	3.0
1952	345,498	236,312	23,970	10.1	16,764	7.1	7,206	3.1
1953	364,593	252,564	29,087	11.5	21,417	8.5	7,670	3.0
1954	364,841	257,445	30,512	11.9	22,648	8.8	7,864	3.1
1955	397,960	275,348	34,718	12.6	26,089	9.5	8,629	3.1
1956	419,238	293,179	39,579	13.5	30,050	10.3	9,529	3.3
1957	441,134	308,524	42,524	13.8	32,396	10.5	10,128	3.3
1958	447,334	318,826	43,241	13.6	32,824	10.3	10,417	3.3

1959†	483,650	337,315	47,128	14.0	35,885	10.6	11,243	3.3
1960	503,755	350,044	52,800	15.1	40,747	11.6	12,053	3.4
1961	520,109	364,424	54,688	15.0	41,995	11.5	12,693	3.5
1962	560,525	385,267	59,072	15.3	45,291	11.8	13,781	3.6
1963	590,503	404,604	65,163	16.1	50,440	12.5	14,723	3.6
1964	631,712	436,575	71,975	16.5	56,055	12.8	15,920	3.7
1965	681,207	469,092	80,003	17.1	62,955	13.4	17,048	3.6
1966	739,600	505,300	90,079	17.8	71,243	14.1	18,836	3.7
1967	785,000	544,700	94,929	17.4	75,209	13.8	19,719	3.6

* When the consumer credit statistics series were revised by the Board of Governors of the Federal Reserve System in 1956, the revision was carried back only through 1948 (see *Federal Reserve Bulletin*, October, 1956, pp. 1031–1045). A later revision carried the changes back to include 1947 at least for totals and for some components (see *Federal Reserve Bulletin*, November, 1959, p. 1416). Consequently, no comparable data are available for years prior to 1947.
† For the years beginning with 1959 includes data for Alaska and Hawaii, and to that extent the magnitude of consumer credit outstandings compared to previous years is exaggerated.

SOURCES: [1] *Survey of Current Business*, U.S. Department of Commerce, August, 1965, pp. 25 and 33, and April, 1967, pp. 6 and 8.
[2] For the years 1947–1954, annual averages were computed from the monthly data in *Federal Reserve Bulletin*, November, 1959, pp. 1416–1417; for the years 1955–1960, the annual averages were computed from the revised monthly data in *Federal Reserve Bulletin*, December, 1961, p. 1397; for the years 1961–1967, the annual averages were computed from the subsequent March issues of the *Federal Reserve Bulletin* for the respective years.

overexpanded. If it does so, it is because it has less confidence in consumers' ability to meet obligations.

It is extremely doubtful whether consumer credit as a whole, or even the instalment part of it, has ever been a destabilizing factor in the economy. The hypothesis to that effect has never been adequately verified; to the extent that it has been attempted, the verification rested on limited data of questionable validity, partly because they were in the nature of estimates many of them later changed substantially and partly because of the short periods covered by them.

As will be noted from a footnote to Table 2-1, comparable data on consumer credit outstandings are not available for years prior to 1947. During the period covered by the data there have been four generally recognized recessions, in 1949, 1954, 1958, and 1960–1961. In none of these recession periods did consumer credit decline or otherwise change substantially from the general pattern for the other years, either in absolute amounts or as a per cent of disposable personal income; thus consumer credit has been lacking in cyclical fluctuation of a magnitude that might conceivably be deemed disturbing to the economy. This is readily discernible from an examination of Fig. 2-1.

Secular trend of consumer credit. In modern times, beginning with 1947, as shown in Table 2-1 and Fig. 2-1, the secular, or long-term, trend of consumer credit as measured by outstandings has been steadily upward. Noninstalment credit outstandings have increased from 2.5 per cent of disposable personal income to 3.6 per cent in 1967, an increase of 44 per cent in a period of 21 years. The moderate increase has been slow and steady, despite the great efforts made through the use of universal credit cards and other devices to accelerate the growth in the use of such credit, for reasons suggested in a later chapter.

Instalment credit outstandings, on the other hand, increased substantially, from about 3.2 per cent of disposable personal income in 1947 (when durable goods were still scarce and only 35 per cent of new and used automobiles were sold on instalment credit as against about 60 per cent in more recent years) to 13.8 per cent in 1967. This is an increase of more than 331 per cent in 21 years and no doubt reflects our rising standard of living and the vigorous economic growth during that period. Nevertheless, it is this increase in instalment credit outstandings, especially when reckoned in absolute amounts or when improperly computed as a per cent of disposable personal income in a manner that would result in a much higher percentage than they actually are, that has given rise to a demand from politicians and selfish interests for legislation not only on a state basis but for the entire United States through some Federal law or laws.

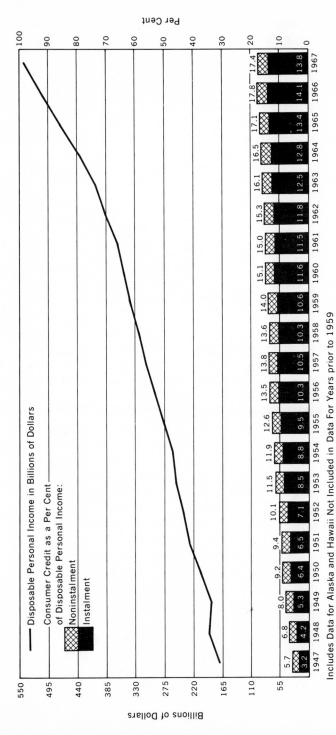

figure 2-1. *Consumer credit outstanding, total and instalment, respectively (average for the year), as a per cent of disposable personal income, United States 1947–1967. Source: Table 2-1.*

Includes Data for Alaska and Hawaii Not Included in Data For Years prior to 1959

Federal regulation of consumer credit. Because until the early 1940's consideration of the economic significance of consumer credit was mainly of theoretical interest, no attempts had been made to regulate it for social purposes. Theretofore regulation was confined to prohibition of usury and of deceptive practices in quoting credit terms. Popularity of the Keynesian doctrines relating to stimulation of the economy through spending and credit control, the occupation of Federal administrative positions by economic planners, and the need for bending every effort toward the achievement of military success combined in 1941 to evoke a new type of consumer credit regulation: regulation of the *amount*, or quantity, rather than the quality of such credit extended.

In 1941, controls of both a general and selective nature were placed upon credit. The general controls were effected through regulation of the discount rates and open market operations, presumably to affect the *total* amount of credit used in the economy. The selective controls were those imposed upon particular segments of the economy, one of which was consumer credit. Thus the restraints placed upon consumer credit through Regulation W were part of a broad program of credit control.

In general, Regulation W specified the down payments and contract periods allowed in instalment selling and froze charge accounts past due more than a specified length of time. The several purposes of this action were to reduce demand, particularly for durable goods, and to encourage savings which might be expected to be invested in War Bonds. By reducing demand, inflationary pressures should be relieved and strategic materials could be more easily diverted into war production. The administration of the Regulation was delegated to the Federal Reserve Board by Executive order of the President, who was vested with authority by the Trading with the Enemy Act of 1917. Following actual hostilities, the regulatory power of the Board was continued under Congressional legislation until the end of October, 1947, and then reimposed in 1948–1949 as an aid through the inflationary and deflationary transitional adjustments toward a peacetime economy. It was again imposed by Congressional action in 1950 as a result of the Korean conflict and remained in effect until May, 1952.

Being an unprecedented form of credit control and one based upon a regulatory philosophy unaccepted by some business groups, Regulation W produced uncertain results. To begin with, it represented a curb upon spending at a time when incomes were high but when civilian goods were unavailable. Consequently, sales of goods coming under the Regulation declined for reasons other than the Regulation. Prices, on the other hand, rose in spite of it and had to be regulated directly. Materials allocation, moreover, also had to be directly handled through priorities and quotas.   Upon the resumption of civilian production, the sales of durables increased before the terms of the Regulation were relaxed or removed.

Repeated attempts at permanent Federal regulation of consumer credit. From time to time attempts have been made to enact permanent consumer credit regulation of the W type just discussed on the ground that it is an effective means of stimulating depressed conditions and of tempering demand in an overactive market.   Opponents of such regulation, on the other hand, believe it to be an effort contrary to the normal habits of spending which underlie the use of consumer credit.   Moreover, there is little to support the alleged objectives of this and similar Federal legislation.

For example, a bill introduced in the Eighty-sixth Congress, Second Session, on which extensive hearings were held in 1960, stated in the Declaration of Purpose, in part, that "The Congress finds and declares that economic stabilization is threatened when credit is used excessively."   Since the entire matter centered around consumer credit, the declaration implied that such credit is a destabilizing factor in the economy, which is contrary to the facts shown in Table 2-1 and Fig. 2-1.   It also implied that consumer credit is used excessively, and that raises the question as to when such use may be considered excessive, not in any specific instance but for the economy as a whole.   From an overall or social viewpoint it would seem that consumer credit might be deemed excessive when its quality is so poor that the ratio of repayments to credit extended falls dangerously low or when losses from bad debts become too burdensome.[3]   That neither of these conditions has obtained since 1948—the first year for which data are available for a computation of the ratio of repayments to extensions for instalment credit—is evident from all known facts.   The repayments ratio, for example, has never gone below 85 per cent of the credit extended, and losses from bad debts have been extremely low.[4]

Consumer credit, being a unique *effect* of individual purchasing power, which is spent in accord with certain fundamental laws of human behavior, cannot be effectively changed by the type of Federal regulation contemplated, nor is there any basic or real need for such regulation

[3] Delinquency rates or ratios are obviously another index of consumer credit quality—a subject being studied by the Federal Reserve System (see "Consumer Instalment Credit" in *Federal Reserve Bulletin*, June, 1968, pp. 457–469.)

[4] For these and other facts bearing on the problem, see "Hearings before a Subcommittee of the Committee on Banking and Currency, United States Senate, 86th Congress, 2d Session, on S. 2755," especially the testimony of William McC. Martin, pp. 119–233, and of Theodore N. Beckman, pp. 279–324; also hearings on S. 1740, 1961, pp. 616–624 and 700–707. See also Table 8-1 and Fig. 8-1 in Chap. 8.

for the alleged purposes of preventing overall excessive use of consumer credit and of forestalling a destabilization of the economy.   When this became fairly apparent, political advocates of such legislation shifted their emphasis on the proposed solutions to the phantom phenomenon. Thus came into being a succession of so-called "Truth in Lending" bills, providing for disclosure of finance charges—usually referred to as interest—on a rate per annum basis.[5]   As will be seen from discussion of the subject in subsequent chapters, the type of regulation that is deemed necessary is already being provided with a high degree of effectiveness on a state basis.[6]   Nevertheless, political pressure behind such legislation, buttressed by popular voter appeal of "truth" and possible antagonism to "lenders," resulted in the enactment of Public Law 90-321, relabeled as the Consumer Credit Protection Act, effective May 29, 1968, with respect to the disclosure provisions.   As this law applies only to consumer *instalment* credit transactions, it is appropriately discussed in Chap. 8, except that the garnishment phase of the law is treated in Chap. 26.

QUESTIONS AND PROBLEMS

1 Point out the characteristics or distinguishing features of credit which may be used in classifying the various types of credit in our economy.

2 Appraise the contention generally emphasized that credit is a causal influence in our economy.

3 What interests in credit, and what viewpoints regarding it, would individuals in the following groups have: politicians, military leaders, welfare economists, Congress, labor groups, manufacturers, distributors, farmers, consumers?

4 What constitutes the "credit of the government"?   How does it differ from the credit of private interests?

5 How is credit "created" by the government?   Why do not consumers or businessmen have this power?   Has this power of the government any relation to everyday life?

6 In what way is business credit "productive"?   Why is this quality not found in government or consumer credit?   Of what significance is this aspect of credit in our society?

7 Name the types of business credit.   How and where may a businessman obtain each?

8 Contrast the motives of consumers with those of others in their respective uses of credit.

---

[5] For a brief but sound analysis of this type of legislation, see "The 'Annual Rate' Credit Bill," *The Credit World*, April, 1967, pp. 18–21.   Reprinted from *Here's the Issue*, Chamber of Commerce of the United States, Legislative Department, Feb. 24, 1967.

[6] Edgar Ray McAlister, *Retail Instalment Credit: Growth and Legislative*, The Ohio State University, Bureau of Business Research, Monograph 120, 1964.

9 Explain the interrelations of consumer credit, purchasing power, spending, and saving.

10 Are the seasonal variations in retail sales related to consumer credit?

11 Are seasonal variations in earnings the cause of seasonal variations in spending? In making purchases for cash or on credit?   Briefly explain.

12 Account for the increase in consumer debt between 1950 and 1967.

13 What prediction would you make as to the amount and character of consumer debt 10 years hence?

14 In what ways is consumer credit regulated?

15 Would you recommend the establishment of permanent regulation of consumer credit? If so, what type and why? On a Federal or state level? If not, how do you explain passage of the Consumer Credit Protection Act?

16 Indicate the measures or indexes that you would employ for the purpose of determining whether or not consumer credit was being used excessively on an aggregate or national basis that would likely affect the economy.

CHAPTER THREE

credit
instruments

Comprehensive knowledge of the various forms of credit instruments and their respective characteristics is essential to a full appreciation of some of the problems of credit management. In a sense, they constitute for the credit manager a kit of tools each of which is to be used appropriately, perceptively, and within the legal context. A credit instrument arises out of a credit transaction that has actually taken place and is, therefore, *evidence of an obligation to pay* at a future time in accordance with the terms agreed upon and often spelled out in the instrument itself. A credit instrument may be in writing, i.e., signed by the debtor, as in the case of promissory notes and checks, or it may take the form of an open book account or a bank deposit, neither of which bears the debtor's signature and hence is not regarded as being in writing. The promise to pay may even be implicit rather than explicit. The credit instruments commonly used may be classified as *promises to pay* and *orders to pay*.

Whatever their specific nature, all credit instruments have certain common essential characteristics: *futurity, risk,* and a *debtor-creditor relationship.* Credit instruments always involve *time* during which the creditor's confidence is placed in the debtor's promise. Until payment is received, there is *risk* that it will not be. Finally, the relationship between the parties is that of *debtor* and *creditor,* not of principal and agent nor of owner and trustee. By these features credit instruments are distinguishable from other commercial instruments that closely resemble them, including such facilitating documents as trust receipts, chattel mortgages, warehouse receipts, and bills of lading, all of which may be used as collateral for the credit instruments used.

PROMISES TO PAY

A promise to pay is a credit instrument, in writing or otherwise, which evidences a debt or obligation and expresses the intention to discharge it by payment. Such instruments include book accounts, deposits at financial institutions, promissory notes, and bonds.

Book accounts. The book account, sometimes called the "open book account," is probably the oldest form of credit instrument. It consists of *an entry on the vendor's books,* debiting or charging the customer with the amount involved. It is by far the simplest and most convenient form of credit instrument, and its extensive and pervasive use tends to stimulate business. Since, however, the seller's record alone is not the best type of legal evidence of either the debt or the amount thereof, *supporting* documents are commonly used in connection with it, such as signed sales slips or delivery receipts. Evidences of credit transactions represented by book accounts are carried on the vendor's records as accounts receivable and on those of business buyers as accounts payable.

Financial institution deposits. The written or implied *promise* of certain types of financial institutions *to return money deposited* with them constitutes another credit instrument of this group. These deposits may be made at commercial banks in the form of *demand deposits,* which are subject to withdrawal upon demand. Such deposits and currency (including coins) are the principal financial instruments that perform the essential functions of money in serving as a medium of exchange, as a standard of value, and as a readily available store of value. Demand deposits and currency outside banks together constitute the active private money supply.[1]   For some years bank demand deposits have amounted to almost four times the currency in circulation outside banks.

Deposits may also take the form of *savings accounts* at savings and loan associations, *deposits* at mutual savings banks, or *time and savings deposits* at commercial banks.   The latter include *negotiable time certificates of deposit* in which the depositor receives an instrument or receipt from a bank indicating the amount and date of deposit, the rate of interest to be paid by the bank, and the date on which funds may be withdrawn.   The fact that the bank promises to pay the amount of deposit plus interest to the bearer of the certificate allows it to be negotiable.   This has provided an impetus for negotiable time certificates of deposit to become important money market instruments.

Upon deposit of funds in any one of the several financial institutions, all the depositor receives as acknowledgment of the debt on the part of the institution is a certificate or a duplicate record of the account on the institution's books.   Thus the depositor exchanges his funds for the institution's promise to pay, on demand, upon advance notice, or at a future time.   Deposits are, therefore, fundamentally not unlike open book accounts arising out of commercial transactions.

Promissory notes. A promissory note is *a written promise of one person to pay another a definite sum of money, on demand or at a certain future time.*   It is essentially a very simple instrument; nevertheless, by common usage the promissory note has assumed a variety of forms which are noteworthy for their legal and practical significance.   Promissory notes may, therefore, be classified on the bases of negotiability, judgment action, and security.

Negotiability. Like some other credit instruments, promissory notes may be negotiable or nonnegotiable, depending upon their form. Both are equally meritorious, so far as the relations of maker and payee are concerned, but they are importantly different in their place in the market for credit instruments.   Those which are negotiable may, by endorsement, be discounted, sold, used as collateral, and otherwise disposed of in the finance markets.   Nonnegotiable notes, on the other hand, do not enjoy such flexibility; the holders thereof usually retain them in their own possession until maturity.

Certain features make for negotiability and should be scrupulously incorporated in notes when this quality is desired.   The following features

---

[1] *Federal Reserve Bulletin*, April, 1967, p. 609. For further information on the concepts, coverage, and measurement of the money supply, see "Revision of Money Supply Series," September, 1966, p. 1303; see also October, 1960, p. 1102, and August, 1962, p. 941.

$500.00   New Orleans, Louisiana, March 1, 19XX

Ninety days after date I promise to pay to the John Brown Company five hundred dollars, with interest at 7 per cent per annum, for value received.

(Signature of Maker)

figure 3-1. *Nonnegotiable promissory note.*

are essential to negotiability: the note must be in writing and signed by the maker; it must be an unconditional promise to pay a definite amount of money; it must be payable on demand or at a definite time in the future; and it must be payable to order or to bearer, and not only to a particular person or firm.[2] In addition, an instrument must ordinarily be delivered before it has legal effect. As such, promissory notes are among the most popular credit instruments and are given both by purchasers, in deferred payment for goods, and by borrowers, in exchange for funds or credit obtained from lenders.

The various forms of what are popularly known as "I.O.U.'s" are usually of the nonnegotiable type of promissory notes. Even when the promissory note is prepared in more formal fashion, as illustrated by Fig. 3-1, it may still be nonnegotiable, in this instance because payment is promised to a particular person instead of making the amount payable to the bearer or order. For the contrasting characteristics, see Fig. 3-2.

Judgment action. Promissory notes may also be characterized by features pertaining to the obtaining of judgments on them, those containing a clause in which judgment is confessed being known as "judgment" or "cognovit" notes. Upon default on an ordinary promissory note, judgment is obtained by bringing suit. The written promise is usually a sufficient basis for a judgment, but not until such judgment has been rendered after trial can collection efforts in the form of garnishment or otherwise be undertaken. To obviate the need for this time-consuming and tedious legal procedure, what is known as a cognovit clause is often inserted in promissory notes, as shown in Fig. 3-3. This means simply that the claim is ceded by the maker of the note and, judgment being obtainable without usual court proceedings, the holder of the note can begin at once to collect thereon. By the same token, abuses have developed in connection with the use of this credit instrument as when it is obtained by misrepresentation or false pretense and there is no way of bringing this out at a trial in court prior to the issuance

---

[2] For further elaboration, see the Uniform Commercial Code, which had been adopted by the middle of 1968 in all states (except Louisiana) and in the District of Columbia.

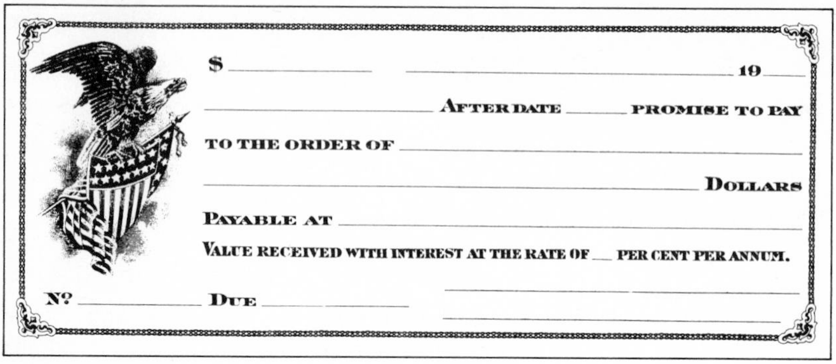

$ ______ ______ 19__

______ AFTER DATE ______ PROMISE TO PAY

TO THE ORDER OF ______

______ DOLLARS

PAYABLE AT ______

VALUE RECEIVED WITH INTEREST AT THE RATE OF __ PER CENT PER ANNUM.

No. ______ DUE ______

figure 3-2. *Ordinary negotiable promissory note.*

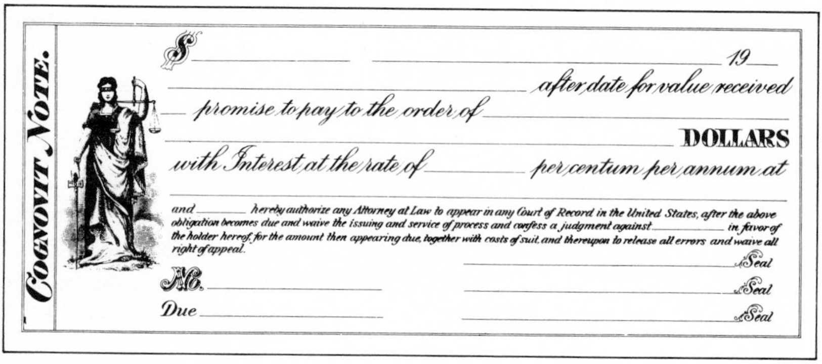

COGNOVIT NOTE.

$ ______ ______ 19__

______ after date for value received

__ promise to pay to the order of ______

______ DOLLARS

with Interest at the rate of ______ per centum per annum at

and ______ hereby authorize any Attorney at Law to appear in any Court of Record in the United States, after the above obligation becomes due and waive the issuing and service of process and confess a judgment against ______ in favor of the holder hereof, for the amount then appearing due, together with costs of suit, and thereupon to release all errors and waive all right of appeal.

______ Seal

No. ______ ______ Seal

Due ______ ______ Seal

figure 3-3. *Promissory note with judgment clause.*

of a judgment—a situation that does not arise when enforcing payment on a noncognovit promissory note. That is no doubt a basic reason why the cognovit note is not recognized in many states and is entirely prohibited in others, as shown in Fig. 3-4.

Security. On the basis of the security factor, promissory notes may be classified as *secured* and *unsecured.* Many promissory notes are accepted on the basis of a signature or signatures alone and hence are deemed to be unsecured. Others are secured by various types of collateral, such as mortgages on property or other negotiable credit instruments. Space is usually provided in the body of a secured note for a description of the security involved. In highly specialized notes, the specific use of this space may be indicated as in chattel mortgage note forms for the financing of automobiles, wherein space is provided for the motor number, serial number, and other identification of the vehicle.

Recognized or authorized	Not recognized or authorized		Forbidden	No statutory provision
Colorado	Alabama	Michigan	Indiana	Maine
Delaware	Alaska	Minnesota	Massachusetts	Nevada
Hawaii	Arizona	Montana	Mississippi	New Hampshire
Idaho	Arkansas	Nebraska	Missouri	New York
Maryland	California	New Jersey	New Mexico	Rhode Island
Ohio	Connecticut	North Carolina	Tennessee	Vermont
Pennsylvania	D.C.	North Dakota	Texas	
Utah	Florida	Oklahoma		
Virginia	Georgia	Oregon		
Wisconsin	Illinois	South Carolina		
	Iowa	South Dakota		
	Kansas	Washington		
	Kentucky	West Virginia		
	Louisiana	Wyoming		

figure 3-4. *Status of judgment notes.*

Factors determining use of promissory notes. Use of the promissory note offers definite advantages, particularly to the creditor. First, it serves as an excellent evidence of debt, practically eliminating disputes regarding the amount owed, due date, interest charged, etc. Second, notes are usually paid at maturity or renewed under favorable conditions. Third, because promissory notes are generally negotiable, they are readily transferable by endorsement and delivery. The fact that promissory notes may be transferred a great many times causes them to perform the function of a medium of exchange. Such function is greatly facilitated by the endorsement of the payee, which makes it a double-name paper, and by the fact that a third innocent party, namely, a bona fide purchaser, is ordinarily free from the defenses which may be advanced against the original payee. Lastly, promissory notes can readily be used as collateral for loans obtained from banks.

Notwithstanding the advantages of promissory notes, there are several limitations to their use. Consumers seldom give promissory notes in exchange for goods purchased from retailers, unless an instalment transaction is involved. This practice follows from the fact that retail credit is intended to make purchasing easy and thus to increase sales. The promissory note, however, is not so easily used as the charge account, nor is it conducive to the frequent repeat business which retailers attempt to develop. The same observation, though to a lesser degree, applies to dealings between retailers and wholesalers or between wholesalers and manufacturers.   It is still uncommon for a merchant to give a promissory note to the seller in the ordinary course of business, save when the account is past due and an extension is granted on that basis, or when the customer is regarded as an inferior credit risk.

The limited use of promissory notes in handling accounts between merchants is due primarily to two factors: namely, the use of "cash discounts," and the tendency on the part of merchants to buy frequently and in small quantities.   Many merchants are eager to pay cash within a specified period of time and to receive cash discounts.   If a note is to be given at the time of purchase, it is difficult to determine the exact amount when it is not known definitely whether or not the option of paying the bill in time to qualify for a cash discount will be exercised. Moreover, it is obviously inconvenient to handle by note numerous and frequent small purchases.   In addition to these reasons, it has also been found that adjustments are sometimes more easily secured before bills are paid when no written evidence of the debt is given; this fact, too, tends to lessen the use of notes.

In borrowing from banks or other financial institutions, however, the promissory note is the standard form of credit instrument.   The same applies to *commercial paper* sold directly to investors or through note brokers.   This term has been used traditionally to describe the various types of short-term credit instruments but, in recent years, has been employed more and more to mean specifically the short-term unsecured promissory notes issued by businesses to borrow funds in the money market.   These notes are negotiable and have a fixed maturity date, usually ranging from 4 to 6 months.   They bear a stipulated rate of interest but are sold at a discount.   The denominations of the notes vary but for the most part are made in multiples of $5,000.

Bonds. A bond also is a written promise by a corporation to pay a definite sum at a stated future time, but its characteristics distinguish it from the promissory note.   Bonds are issued for longer periods, usually for 5 years or more.   Short-term bonds as a rule mature within from 5 to 15 years from the date of issue; medium-term bonds have a life of from 15 to 40 years; and long-term bonds are for longer periods.   Even long-term notes usually mature in less than 5 years from the date of issue.   Bonds are issued for sums in round numbers or fixed denominations, such as $50, $100, $1,000, or more; notes are written for whatever amount is involved in the transaction.   Bonds are sometimes issued in series, many being offered at one time to raise large sums of money; notes are issued individually as the occasion for a specific need arises.

Depending upon the issuer, bonds are classified as government

(Federal, state, or municipal), railroad, public utility, mining, and industrial bonds. The rate of interest paid on bonds varies considerably, depending upon the nature of the security behind the instrument, credit standing of the issuer, current rate of interest at time of issue, anticipated long-run rate, and life of the security. On income bonds, interest payment is contingent upon earnings.

Bonds are transferable by endorsement and delivery. They can be utilized as collateral for loans and are especially valuable when listed on an important stock exchange, owing to the ready market in which they may be disposed of should need arise. This is not true of all bonds, however, since not all of them are negotiable, as for example, in the case of Series E bonds issued by the Federal government.

ORDERS TO PAY

The second main type of credit instruments consists of orders to pay, commonly called "drafts." Classified as to time of payment, they are either *sight* or *time* drafts. By character of the drawee, they are classified as *personal, commercial,* and *bank* drafts. On the basis of the residence of the drawee, drafts may be *domestic* or *foreign,* the latter usually known as "bills of exchange." Drafts are also classified as *ordinary* and *accepted,* and the accepted instruments may, in turn, be either *trade acceptances* or *bank acceptances.*

Checks. The common bank check is perhaps the simplest and most commonly recognized form of draft. The drawer in this instance is the depositor, who orders his bank (drawee) to make payment to a designated party (payee). The payee may actually be the drawer, as in the case where someone cashes his own check, but usually it is another person to whose order it is made out, payable on sight (see Fig. 3-5).

The popularity of the check may be accounted for by the convenience it affords. While promissory notes and other draft forms are used for long-term payments, checks are employed for cash and immediate settlements. It is the most popular of the mediums of exchange, and its use is still on the increase, owing, undoubtedly, to the existence of banking facilities and thrift on the part of the lower income groups of society. Final payment in the wholesale trade is almost invariably made by check, and the tendency on the part of customers to adopt a similar practice is continuously growing. Whether the "checkless" or "less check" society so widely advocated in banking circles will greatly diminish the importance of checks as credit instruments is still in the province of high conjecture.

Checks are negotiable instruments, are readily transferable, and

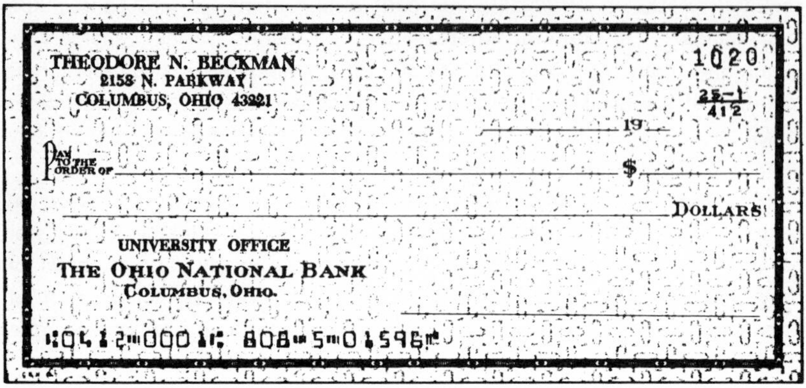
THEODORE N. BECKMAN
2158 N. PARKWAY
COLUMBUS, OHIO 43221
1020
25-1
412
19
PAY TO THE ORDER OF $
DOLLARS
UNIVERSITY OFFICE
THE OHIO NATIONAL BANK
COLUMBUS, OHIO

figure 3-5. *Common form of check.*

one check may, because of its free circulation, be used in the cancellation of many obligations. It facilitates payment not only locally, but also between debtors and creditors geographically far removed from one another.

Are checks credit instruments? Because checks are widely used in so-called "cash" transactions, the question is sometimes raised as to whether they are actually credit instruments. Receipt of a check virtually constitutes payment, and the risk involved in most check transactions is relatively small.

Notwithstanding the general soundness of checks, however, the check alone does not constitute payment. Payment is not really made until the check has been cleared and honored by the bank upon which it is drawn. The fact that merchants annually cash worthless checks amounting to many millions of dollars is testimony of the risk still present in their acceptance. As in all types of credit transactions, the risk is at times greater than at others. Bad check writers are still prevalent, and they present perhaps the greatest risk in the check as a credit instrument. Risk arises also from less intentional reasons: overdraft of accounts, unexpected delay in making deposits, and seizure of assets including bank accounts. In the past, bank failures constituted an additional risk, although now this risk is practically removed by modern banking practices and by the insurance of bank deposits by the Federal Deposit Insurance Corporation.

Bad check laws. Laws passed by all states concerning the prosecution of bad check makers furnish protection to creditors. The act of issuing a worthless check is regarded variously by the different states as a misdeameanor, felony, larceny, an extension of the false pretense law, or as simply unlawful. Punishments are prescribed accordingly by the respective jurisdictions.

Under most of the state laws the mere nonpayment of a check is taken as evidence of intent to defraud and of knowledge of insufficient funds at the bank. Usually, however, if the drawer makes actual payment within 5 or 10 days after receiving notice that his check was not honored, the presumption of fraud does not attach. Consequently few convictions are gained under these statutes, for either payment or direct denial of intent to defraud leaves the burden of proof to the state. Herein lies the chief weakness of the bad check laws.

As the statutes are not uniform or entirely clear, the procedure usually followed by a creditor upon receipt of a bad check is, first, to serve notice on the maker (preferably in person) and demand that the check be made good within 5 days or the number of days specified in the law. Failing to secure satisfaction, the creditor consults with the prosecutor or district attorney of the city or town in which the check was made and delivered (and hence where the crime was committed). This consultation may result in an arrest of the drawer, or it may lead first to an indictment by a grand jury, the latter precaution being taken in order to be immune to possible action by the drawer for false imprisonment.

Certified and cashier's checks. Precaution against acceptance of a bad check may be taken by insistence upon payment with a certified, cashier's, or a manager's check. Certification consists of having "Certified," "Good," or some equivalent word stamped across the face of a check by the cashier of the bank upon which it is drawn. This amounts virtually to a guarantee of payment by the bank, since the bank in effect deducts the amount from the drawer's account immediately, rather than after the check is presented for payment. An alternative method open to a depositor is to use a cashier's or branch manager's check, which is the bank's own order drawn upon itself and signed by the cashier or manager, payable to the payee designated by the depositor. Such checks are normally bought with cash.

Bank drafts. Another form of draft drawn by a bank, upon other banks, is known as a "bank draft." It is drawn upon out-of-town banks, as a rule, in which it maintains accounts. These drafts are used to facilitate making payments at a distant location. They are also convenient for persons traveling and reduce the risks incurred in transferring funds.

Money orders. Money orders are instruments which resemble checks and bank drafts. A *bank money order* is similar to a cashier's check in that it is drawn by a particular bank upon itself, but, unlike cashier's checks, bank money orders commonly are signed by the purchaser rather than a bank official. Bank money orders are, however, not available at all banks.

A *postal money order* is an order issued by one post office on another post office, requiring payment of the amount specified therein to the person designated in the instrument, or to his order. The maximum amount for which a single money order may be issued in the United States is $100. When larger sums are to be sent, additional orders may be obtained, since no limitation is placed on the number of orders which may be drawn on any office on any one day. Rates vary from 25 to 40 cents, depending upon the amount of the order.

An *express money order* is very similar to a postal money order except that the former is issued on the American Express Company and is sold at express offices and various retail establishments. Unlike postal money orders, express money orders may be transferred any number of times.

Travelers checks. Another credit instrument sold by the American Express Company, the Bank of America, and certain other banks consists of drafts known as "traveler's checks." These are drawn in four denominations ($10, $20, $50, and $100) on forms specially provided. These instruments are used extensively by travelers and have almost universal acceptability because of the reputation which these organizations have gained through draft redemption. All that is needed by the drawer to cash a traveler's check is his signature on the check matching the one that was placed there when the check was issued to him.

Commercial drafts. Drafts may be *drawn by sellers* ordering payment by buyers as well as by buyers ordering payment by banks. When drawn by one party to a business transaction upon another, the draft is commonly known as a "commercial" draft. Such drafts order payment to be made either upon presentation, in which case they are called "sight" drafts, or at a specified later time, in which case they are "time" drafts. Sight drafts are honored by immediate payment on presentation; time drafts are honored by payment when due or by acceptance, which consists of an endorsement by the drawee across the face of the draft with the word "accepted" followed by the signature. An accepted time draft is comparable to a promissory note in so far as its evidencing of a debt is concerned.

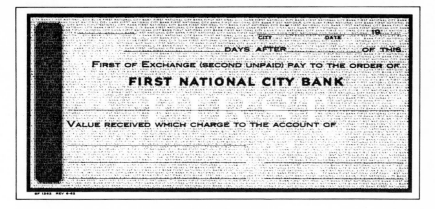

figure 3-6. *Common form of commercial draft.*

Commercial drafts, as credit instruments, are commonly used when open-account credit is not warranted and when the vendor desires payment or an accepted instrument before parting with his goods. Accordingly, such drafts may be accompanied by shipping documents. They are usually presented to the buyer through his bank. When the draft is honored, the documents are conveyed to the buyer, who may then obtain the goods. This instrument serves also to satisfy the buyer with delivery of the goods before payment is required. The simple form of a commercial draft is shown in Fig. 3-6.

Commercial drafts drawn between parties to foreign trade are commonly called *bills of exchange*. The usual procedure followed in making settlement by the use of this instrument when not prepared for acceptance by the drawee is for the seller of merchandise to draw upon the buyer, attach the draft to the various documents denoting shipment, and sell or discount the instrument at his local bank. This bank forwards the draft with attached documents to its correspondent bank in the country of the buyer. The draft is then presented by the correspondent bank to the drawee for collection or acceptance. If it is accepted as a time draft, it may then be sold by the drawer to others who will hold it until it matures.

Drafts or bills of exchange drawn by the seller of merchandise and accepted by the purchaser as payable at a definite future time are called "trade acceptances" (see Fig. 3-7). They are time drafts specifically arising out of merchandise transactions. Their use has been encouraged as a means of transferring the financing function in trade to finance specialists. This can be accomplished by the vendor-drawer's discounting his acceptances at his bank. Thus he liquidates receivables

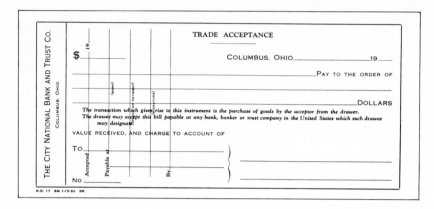

figure 3-7. *Trade acceptance in domestic commerce.*

he otherwise would carry, receiving upon acceptance of the draft the equivalent of money spent in production and distribution. The buyer, on the other hand, is not required to pay until he has had time to attempt to sell or use what he bought. The financing, in other words, is shifted to banks.

Efforts to popularize the trade acceptance have met with indifferent success. One of the major reasons is that the trade acceptance is not adapted to transactions involving short periods of time. It is not adapted to lines of trade in which purchases by customers are made in small amounts and at frequent intervals. For these reasons the acceptance has never been popular in the grocery trade and in other lines of business where the net credit period is 30 days or less and where customers have what may be termed "running accounts." Moreover, it involves difficulties where a cash discount is offered. The buyer may be reluctant to accept the draft for the net amount if he feels that he may be in a position to take the discount. In such cases he may be given the option of discounting the invoice within the discount period or signing the acceptance for the net amount. Furthermore, it is felt that use of the trade acceptance may convert some discounting customers into buyers by acceptance, thus lengthening the credit period. Finally, certain abuses have developed around the trade acceptance, such as using it to cover a past-due account, taking it from drawees who would not be given open-account credit, and extending credit to buyers merely because they are willing to sign an acceptance.

Bank acceptances. A bank acceptance is a time draft drawn by a seller upon, and accepted by, a bank with which a buyer has made an arrangement to accept such drafts as the seller may present. By this instrument, the bank's responsibility is substituted for that of the buyer, which obtains in the ordinary trade acceptance. Bank acceptances are commonly used in foreign transactions and generally carry a higher status than trade acceptances.

The bank acceptance has an additional and special usefulness in providing further credit for borrowers whose outstanding obligations to a bank may have reached the loan limitations of that bank. The National Banking Act specifically states that the total obligations owed by "any person, copartnership, or corporation, shall at no time exceed 10 per centum of the amount of the capital stock . . . and . . . unimpaired surplus fund" of a lending bank. This limitation applies regardless of the position of the obligor, whether he be drawer of a draft, maker of a note, endorser of discounted paper, or guarantor of an obligation. His aggregated obligations to the bank may not exceed the 10 per cent limitation. He may receive, however, additional financial assistance from the bank through the medium of *secured* bank acceptances. The Federal Reserve Act authorizes national banks and member state banks, where permitted by statute, to accept, even in excess of the 10 per cent limitation, such drafts, which may be used in connection with importation and exportation of goods, domestic shipment of goods, storage of readily marketable staples, and creation of dollar exchange.

Commercial letters of credit. Notice that a bank will accept drafts drawn upon it for shipments made to its client is often given to a vendor in the form of a commercial letter of credit. This is a statement issued by a bank, announcing the maximum amount of credit, the quantity and quality of goods to be purchased, the time within which shipment must be made, full instructions as to the shipment, the drawing of the draft, and the disposition that should be made of the documents, as a condition for the honoring of drafts presented by the seller. One copy is retained by the issuing bank, one is given to the buyer, and the original is sent to the foreign exporter or shipper. The shipper then presents the instrument, with the shipping documents and draft attached, to his local banker. The local banker negotiates the draft and thereupon forwards it, together with the documents, to the bank which issued the letter of credit, through his correspondent bank. If it is a time draft, the issuing bank accepts it, and if it is a sight draft payable on demand, the bank pays the amount involved. In each instance the shipping documents are surrendered to the issuing bank (see Fig. 3-8).

The importer finally secures the documents from his banker in exchange for a trust receipt executed by him whereby the banker is given a first lien on the merchandise until payment has been made on or before

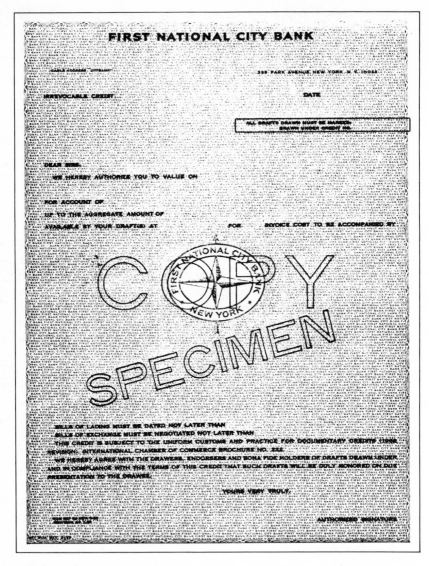

figure 3-8. *One form of a commercial letter of credit.*

maturity of the accepted draft.   If a sight draft, the importer is expected
to reimburse his banker before the shipping documents are surrendered,
unless arrangements are made with the bank for a loan of the amount
for an extended period.   Under the trust receipt the importer binds himself to hold the goods in trust, keep them insured in favor of the bank,

and to turn over all proceeds from the goods sold, to the banker until the full amount involved is repaid, when the trust receipt is surrendered.

It should be observed that the credit extended in the form of commercial letters of credit is secured solely by the merchandise imported. It is, therefore, essential that the goods be properly handled, well insured, and otherwise given good care. To avoid fraud on the part of the exporter and to guard against inability of the importer to meet his obligations at maturity, the issuing banker requires the purchaser of a letter of credit to sign an agreement to the effect that the terms of the contract will be closely observed and that, in case of depreciation in the value of the goods while in transit, he will furnish additional security as may be required of him, and that, in default thereof, the banker is given the right to dispose of the merchandise, irrespective of the maturity of the drafts drawn under the letter of credit.

Traveler's letters of credit. A traveler can also secure from his bank a letter of credit. A traveler's letter of credit may be defined as a request from a banker or firm to other banks or firms, with whom the former has credit relations or deposits, to advance money not exceeding the face value of the letter to the person named therein. It is the bank's agreement to accept the drafts of the traveler up to the face value of the letter, which is to be returned with the last draft. Its chief function is to facilitate the transfer of funds to foreign countries for the convenience of travelers. The purchaser of such an instrument has the right to draw at different times from different banks or firms up to the amount stated in the letter (see Fig. 3-9).

Each time a sum of money is drawn by the holder of the letter, the instrument is presented to the official making payment. He then notes on the reverse side of the letter the date when paid, by whom paid, and the amount drawn. The holder is also required to sign his name on a separate piece of paper so that his signature may be identified, by comparison, with that appearing on the letter of indication which is attached to the accompanying book of indication, in which are listed the names of all correspondents of the issuing bank.

Most traveler's letters of credit are made payable in London. If the traveler is, say, in Paris and finds himself in need of funds, he goes to a bank specified in the letter and identifies himself by means of a "Letter of Indication" issued to him by the bank that issued the letter of credit. The bank ascertains the price of pounds sterling at the time and draws a draft for enough pounds to equal the number of francs desired by the holder of the letter. This draft is then forwarded to London by the Paris bank, and proper notation is made on the reverse side of the letter of credit, which is then returned to the traveler, together

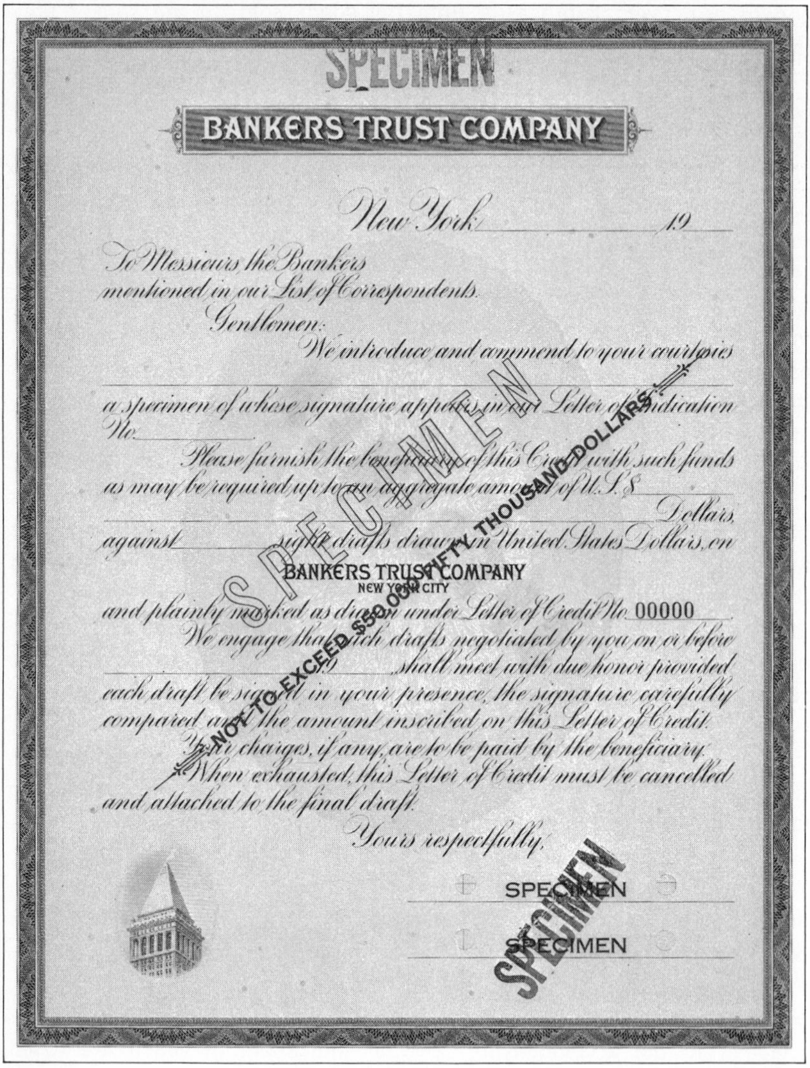

SPECIMEN

BANKERS TRUST COMPANY

New York ______ 19__

To Messieurs the Bankers
mentioned in our List of Correspondents.

Gentlemen:

We introduce and commend to your courtesies ______

a specimen of whose signature appears in our Letter of Indication No. ______

Please furnish the beneficiary of this Credit with such funds as may be required up to an aggregate amount of U.S.$ ______ Dollars, against ______ sight drafts drawn in United States Dollars, on

BANKERS TRUST COMPANY
NEW YORK CITY

and plainly marked as drawn under Letter of Credit No. 00000.

We engage that such drafts negotiated by you on or before ______ 19__ shall meet with due honor provided each draft be signed in your presence, the signature carefully compared and the amount inscribed on this Letter of Credit.

Your charges, if any, are to be paid by the beneficiary.

When exhausted, this Letter of Credit must be cancelled and attached to the final draft.

Yours respectfully,

SPECIMEN

SPECIMEN

SPECIMEN

NOT TO EXCEED $50,000 FIFTY THOUSAND DOLLARS

SPECIMEN

figure 3-9. *Traveler's letter of credit. The inside (shown on the opposite page) provides spaces for recording each date of payment, by whom paid, and the amount drawn.*

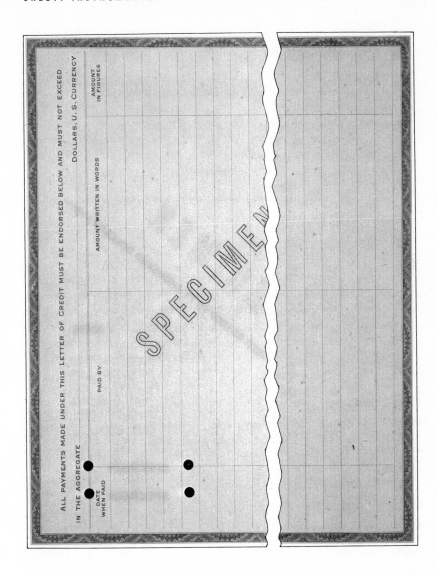

with the desired amount of money. The London bank then charges the issuing bank's account with the amount of the draft and forwards it to that bank. If the draft exhausts the letter of credit, the latter is retained by the Paris bank and returned through the proper channels to the issuing bank.

GOVERNMENTAL CREDIT INSTRUMENTS[3]

Credit instruments issued by the Federal government may take the form of money or of instruments that possess characteristics similar to those issued by commercial organizations. It is certainly true that since 1933 all the money in circulation in the United States has been credit money or in the form of credit instruments.

Long-term and short-term nonmonetary instruments. Probably the most familiar governmental credit instrument is the bond, through the sale of which purchasing power is obtained in exchange for a promise of repayment at some future date. Bonds are issued for different lengths of time, depending upon the purpose for which the funds obtained are to be used, extending to 10 years, 20 years, 30 years, or more. They carry interest rates reflecting current and prospective conditions in the money market and in the economy in general. Some are negotiable; others are nonnegotiable. Their buyers are commercial banks, other financial and business institutions, and the general public. Unlike some commercial bonds, those issued by the government can usually be readily disposed of, because of the government's disposition directly or through the banking system to support the market for its own securities.

In addition to the long-term credit instruments sold by the government, there are several types which are used to meet governmental needs for purchasing power for shorter periods—periods for which it would not be feasible to issue bonds. Such needs are met by the following credit instruments: Treasury bills, Treasury certificates, and Treasury notes. The bills are issued usually with a maturity of 3 to 6 months, the certificates up to 1 year, and the notes up to 5 years. Some banks hold such instruments as investment for their own funds; others dispose of them in the open market or sell them to the Federal Reserve Bank and thus increase their legal reserves.

Credit characteristics of currency. Throughout the financial history of the United States, the attributes of credit instruments have been

---

[3] While state, municipal, and other local governmental units often issue credit instruments, especially bonds, the discussion here is confined to the instruments used by the Federal government.

so closely associated with currency that monetary instruments themselves have been regarded as credit instruments. This association has existed to a greater or lesser degree depending upon the prevalent character of currency. Today, as already indicated, all currency is but credit money. With respect to paper currency, this is often referred to as paper money; after all, currency in the form of Federal Reserve notes as well as that in the form of United States notes is but in the nature of circulating promissory notes issued under conditions specified by law. Because of that, every form of currency, including token money, has the same essential characteristics as any credit instrument—time or futurity, confidence or risk, and a debtor-creditor relationship. The difference is not one of kind or specie but one of degree.

The same element of confidence which makes pieces of paper valuable as promissory notes or as checks, although for different reasons, gives value and acceptability to currency. In the case of commercial instruments, confidence rests in the debtor's willingness and ability to make due payment at a fixed time. In the case of currency, when it was issued under a system of gold redemption (in whole and later in part), confidence rested in the promise that the government would upon demand make payment in gold, in exchange for the currency previously issued in payment for goods and services. Under the circumstances of irredeemable currency prevailing since the early 1930's, confidence is placed in the hope that the conditions which give value and acceptability to the money will not so change as to destroy these two important attributes. Thus it may be seen that the confidence which is essential to credit instruments generally is fundamental to currency too, notwithstanding the fact that holders of currency are not often put to a test of their confidence and that currency circulates in a system quite apart from that of credit instruments as a whole.

The significance of this similarity of currency and other credit instruments lies not in a thought that they should be treated alike, but in a prospect that orderly business practice and economic welfare may be promoted by the support of an element common to both, namely, confidence in that which establishes their value and acceptability. Behind usual credit instruments stand the integrity of the maker or drawer, his ability to carry on his business profitably, his conformity to the standard usages of the instrument, his assets, and the like. The fact that these factors can be recognized, measured to some extent, and improved by various means lends security and efficiency to business practice. Similarly, warranted confidence in the character of currency also benefits the economy. While the government no longer holds itself obligated to redeem its monetary issues in gold, one may yet have confidence in the government's acting in other ways to support the meaning of its money.   One has confidence, in other words, in America's economic might, the solidity of its economy, the total overall soundness of governmental policies, and the continuing confidence in the dollar throughout the world. One has confidence that courts will continue to enforce contracts, that commercial banks will be run reasonably well, that the Federal Reserve Banks will not overexpand, that Congress will in the long run attempt to balance the budget, and that business will remain relatively sound. Moreover, there must be an institutionalized system whereby checks act as debits and credits on the individual banks, and there must be a clearing system.   If those conditions prevail, money will retain the value and merit the confidence which the public places in it.   If they are not maintained, loss of confidence and loss of value would strip creditability from money as the insolvency of a business firm would destroy the acceptability of its credit instruments.   Evidence of this can be seen in the countries of the world wherein economic conditions have deteriorated to such an extent that one scarcely knows what value money has as inflation progresses so rapidly, or that currency is arbitrarily devalued by the government in an attempt to balance affairs.

Notwithstanding the fact that at present all the effective money supply (currency plus demand deposits) may be considered as a form of credit, money and commercial credit instruments still differ mainly in their general acceptability.   Currency has what may be regarded as unlimited acceptability.   It circulates, is exchanged, and is retained for indefinite periods with practically no consideration of changes in value. This is not the case with respect to any ordinary credit instrument issued, although bonds of large corporations are regarded as "gilt-edged" and checks are passed as freely as cash.   The unlimited acceptability of currency is achieved partly as an institutional circumstance and partly by reason of the fact that the government defines it as legal tender.

Types of currency. In view of the close relationship between commercial credit, governmental credit, and money, it behooves the modern credit manager to familiarize himself with the conditions of each which may have a bearing upon his practice.   The effect of monetary conditions is produced both by the amount of money in circulation and by the types of it, through the variety of which our circulating medium assumes its character.   To credit managers, these conditions help to explain, in part, the general level of prices and thus aid in evaluating overall price-making forces and their influence upon different types of credit risks.   They also reflect the flexibility of the circulating medium and give some indication of the relationship that the money in circulation bears to the total amount of credit which the member banks' legal reserve would make possible.   The several kinds of currency currently outstanding and some of their more important characteristics are briefly discussed below.

Demonetization of silver and gold. Prior to any discussion of specific types of currency, two things should be borne in mind. One is that silver, to all intents and purposes, has been demonetized. Silver dollars have not been minted since 1936; hence the limited quantity of standard silver dollars, together with the monetized silver bullion and the silver certificates based thereon, is likely to be greatly diminished and may in time completely disappear. Subsidiary silver coins will tend to become silver*less*, as newly minted coins are made from nickel and copper alloys.

Two, gold coins have not been minted for more than a generation, and since 1933 it has been illegal for a private person even to hold a gold *certificate.* No such paper money could be turned into the Treasury for gold coins. Even the limited use of gold or its certificates as a backing of 25 per cent for currency in the form of Federal Reserve notes has been precarious in the face of mounting unfavorable international balances of payments. This finally led to the removal or lifting of the "gold cover" or backing for such currency, by an Act of Congress, effective March, 1968, thereby freeing this imprisoned gold for discretionary use as international monetary reserves and completely demonetizing gold as far as United States domestic affairs are concerned. The country is thus placed altogether on a managed currency basis, with chief reliance on extrinsic rather than intrinsic value of the currency phase of the money supply.

Federal Reserve notes. By far the most important and voluminous kind of currency in circulation is the Federal Reserve note, an obligation of the Federal government, authorized by the Federal Reserve Act. Its main purpose is to provide an elastic currency which can be readily expanded or contracted with the requirements of business. Through the Federal Reserve agents, the twelve Federal Reserve Banks can secure these notes by depositing, since March, 1968, 100 per cent of their value in government securities or in commercial paper and bills discounted by member banks. These notes have become the most useful and important kind of money issued, primarily because of their flexibility, so that at the end of 1967, approximately $42 billion were outstanding and in circulation. This represented about 88 per cent of all the circulating money (outside Treasury and Federal Reserve Banks).

Federal Reserve Bank notes came into existence under the provisions of the Federal Reserve Act of 1913, whereby national banks were given the privilege of retiring the national bank notes which they had previously issued. To maintain a market for the government bonds and at the same time to prevent a reduction in the volume of money in circulation, the Federal Reserve Banks were authorized to buy the bonds from the national banks and to issue Federal Reserve Bank notes against them.   Since then these notes have been regarded as emergency currency and have intermittently been issued and retired as the need arose.   In 1942 their issue was increased to assist in meeting the monetary requirements of the war period, but they have since been retired.

National bank notes were first issued in 1865, when the new national banks were given a monopoly of note issue against government bonds deposited in the United States Treasury.   In 1935 these notes were officially retired, and their withdrawal has been so rapid that virtually none of the money in circulation is in this form.

Treasury currency. The second kind of currency in circulation, called Treasury currency, is a composite of several different types. About 12 per cent of our circulating money is of this kind.[4]

Treasury currency includes silver dollars, silver certificates, fractional coins, and United States notes.   All these instruments are issued by the Secretary of the Treasury at his discretion within the power given to him by existing laws.   By reason of the restrictions imposed upon him, this currency does not entirely meet the requirements of flexibility expected of a monetary system.

United States notes, commonly called "greenbacks," came into existence during the War between the States.   They were issued as a forced loan, and the security behind them consisted merely of the general credit of the Federal government.   They were redeemable in gold from 1879 until the spring of 1933, when gold was nationalized, the redemptive feature withdrawn, and the President empowered to expand the issue to $3 billion.   However, a total of only $450 million was originally issued, of which some $323 million are still outstanding.

QUESTIONS AND PROBLEMS

1 What are the essential characteristics of credit instruments?

2 Define the term credit instrument.   How do credit instruments differ from credit itself?

3 As a recipient of a promissory note, what characteristics would you prefer it to have?

4 Is negotiability an essential characteristic of credit instruments?   Cite examples to support your position.

5 What credit instrument or instruments would you normally use in selling to each of the following:

a A fair credit risk in your vicinity

b A good risk across the country

---

[4] For the exact amount of any of the monetary instruments outstanding currently, see the latest *Federal Reserve Bulletin* (monthly publication of the Board of Governors of the Federal Reserve System).

    c A customer in England

    d A customer in Brazil

6 What instrument or instruments would a buyer normally use in purchasing from:

    a A regular source of supply

    b An unfamiliar domestic supplier

    c A long-known foreign supplier

    d A new foreign supplier

7 What kinds of drafts are drawn by sellers upon buyers? What kinds are drawn by buyers?

8 It is sometimes argued that checks are not credit instruments. Can you support this claim? Is there any more justification for regarding checking accounts in banks, rather than checks, as money, as is also done sometimes?

9 Why have practically all states enacted bad check laws? Does this fact help or hinder your argument that checks are credit instruments? How?

10 Distinguish between a certified and a cashier's check. Is there any difference in the procedure as far as the bank is concerned?

11 What steps should the holder of a bad check take upon learning that it has not been honored?

12 Explain the procedure involved when a commercial sight draft is used in connection with a bill of lading.

13 What is the difference between a trade acceptance and a promissory note from the standpoint of legality and trade practice?

14 Show, by diagram, the use of a commercial letter of credit by a New York importer in his purchase of woolens from England.

15 If you were to make a short tour through Europe, which of the following credit instruments would you use in providing yourself with the requisite financing: traveler's checks or traveler's letters of credit? Why?

16 What credit instruments are used by the Federal government? How do these compare with or differ from commercial credit instruments?

17 In what respects are there risk elements in currency similar to those in commercial credit instruments?

18 What kinds of currency are presently in circulation in our economy?

19 Explain the meaning and implications of the apparent demonetization of silver and the demonetization of gold. Briefly analyze the causes in each case.

nature and scope of credit management

The management of credit (and concomitant collections) is not unlike the management of any other major business function in so far as fundamental principles are concerned. It deals with the scientific planning, organizing, and controlling of the manifold activities that fall in its province. The same essential elements and reasoning are involved in each of the three components of credit management as in management generally. For that reason no elaborate general treatment of them is presented in this volume. Only those phases that are relevant to the management of credit are dealt with at appropriate places in connection with the subject matter to which they pertain.

Obviously, the management of credit must be in line with predetermined objectives of the enterprise as a whole and of the credit aspects in particular. The universal general objectives of credit management are discussed in one of the chapters in this part of the book. Again, credit work must be done in accordance with certain policies which may be formulated by top management or by the person in charge of the credit operation. These policies are discussed at various parts of the book deemed most appropriate from a theoretical or practical viewpoint. The same is true of discussions of the decision-making process, which continues from the time a prospective customer or borrower is given attention, through the entire period that the account remains on the books, and until the collection phase has been completed.

As already implied, credit management embraces the gamut of activities and responsibilities from the initial consideration of a prospective account until the completion of the collection aspect and a critical examination of the results achieved in the overall that might lead to alterations in policy and practice. In order to have a proper understanding of what is involved in all this, it is felt that at this juncture consideration should be given to the subject matter with which credit management deals and the type of management that is essential for effective performanc of the task. That is the purpose of the contents in Part II.

CHAPTER FOUR

the credit
manager

When a business organization sells on credit or otherwise deals in it, the administration of that credit becomes, on some level, a management responsibility. The nature and extent of management required is not the same in different types of institutions, nor is it always handled in the same way in comparable organizations. The level of management required for the administration of credit in a firm is determined to no small degree by the *concept* of the function prevailing there. In some instances credit is viewed narrowly as a simple function of approving credit transactions and making collections. Relatively little real management activity may be involved here. As the concept broadens, however, the credit phase of the business embraces sales and finance policy and other top management strategy and, consequently, becomes a management responsibility of a much higher order and of substantial magnitude.

Objectives of top management. Among the goals of top management of any business enterprise are two basic objectives. One is to see that the firm always has the means available to pay its bills on time or otherwise meet its current obligations. This is commonly referred to as the *liquidity objective*. Maintenance of adequate liquidity reduces risk to the firm and perpetuates its life. At the same time, top management must also seek the most profitable allocation of resources within the business. Thus another basic goal of top management consists in its *profitability objective*. Essentially, this means that top management must, without endangering the firm's liquidity, work toward meeting established company goals respecting net profit, return on owners' equity, and return on total asset investment.

Every dollar represented by an asset is a dollar invested by creditors or owners. Since the owners of a business want a satisfactory level of reward for themselves, its top management must strive for a reasonable rate of return on owners' investment normally shown on the company's balance sheet in terms of net worth or owners' equity. The return figure, all of which could theoretically be paid out to owners, is the amount of net profit after taxes, since all costs and expenses, including interest owed to creditors and Federal income taxes, must be paid first. Thus the *rate* of return earned by a particular firm on owner investment in the business can be determined by *dividing the amount of net profit after taxes by the amount of net worth*.

Achieving a high rate of return on owner investment is a two-step operation. First, management attempts to put money to work in assets in such a way that the rate of return to the business *as a whole* is as great as possible. Its responsibility is for the effective use of *all* assets through a proper allocation and efficient performance throughout the enterprise. Hence the dollar amount of net profit after taxes generated by the firm is an important measure of the amount of return earned by the organization as a complete entity. Thus the *rate* of return on total asset investment can be determined by *dividing the amount of net profit after taxes by the total amount of assets* held by the company. As evident from Fig. 4-1, maximizing (or optimizing) the rate of return on asset investment in any business requires planning and control of business volume, amount of assets, and the cost and expenses of operation.

The second step undertaken by top management toward achieving a high rate of return on owner investment is to arrange the firm's sources of financing in such a manner that the owners obtain as high a return as possible without incurring undue risks incident to excessive debt financing of a business. While debt financing makes it possible for owners to enjoy a greater return on their investment, the fixed obligations

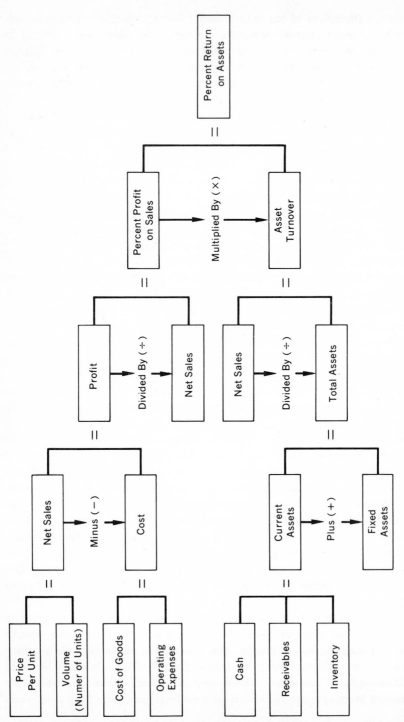

figure 4-1. *Computation of return on total asset investment illustrated.*

associated with debt financing also carry the risk that earnings may be partially or entirely insufficient to cover them.   At worst, this may mean loss of the business to creditors.   Top management of a company must, therefore, balance the chance of greater profits for owners through the use of debt financing against the possibility of fluctuating earnings and the risk of not being able to meet obligations of this type of financing.

PRINCIPAL OBJECTIVES
OF CREDIT MANAGEMENT

Not unlike top management, credit management too must keep the two basic goals of the enterprise in mind and, within its sphere of operation, contribute to their accomplishment.   Thus, in helping to achieve the company's liquidity objective, credit management must adopt policies, practices, and procedures regarding credit granting, credit limits, and collections that will enable the company to meet its obligations and will not jeopardize it through an excessive amount being tied up in receivables. Second, credit management must also help the business attain its profitability objective, particularly those elements that relate to net profits and return on asset investment.   Since the credit manager is usually not directly involved in the arranging of the firm's sources of financing, his contribution to the profitability objective must be limited to assistance in maximizing or optimizing, as the case may be, the company's rate of return on total asset investment rather than only on owner equity.

To meet the responsibilities related to liquidity and profitability, credit management must establish credit and collection policies and procedures that will enable the organization of which it is a part to (1) maximize or optimize sales or business volume, (2) control the amount of assets invested in receivables or other outstandings, and (3) control the costs of credit and collections.   In the accomplishment of these ends it is necessary for the credit department to cooperate with similar departments in other companies and with other departments in its own company.   This is so important that it may well be regarded as another objective of credit management proper.

Maximizing or optimizing sales or business volume. It is, of course, an objective of top management to attain that level of sales or business volume which maximizes or optimizes the firm's return on asset investment.   For practical purposes, among the tasks ordinarily assigned by top management to those functioning on a lower executive level, which usually includes the credit manager, is the obligation to *maximize* sales or business volume, since a policy of optimization involves considerations beyond the scope embraced by such executives.

To illustrate, the dollar amount of sales obtained by a business during any period of time such as a year is determined by two elements. The first is the *selling prices* charged on individual items of merchandise or service; these are multiplied by the second element, the *number of units* actually sold.   By the most progressive concepts, the cost of extending credit is regarded as an important consideration in establishing competitive pricing strategy in any firm.   Then, too, the volume of business done is usually related very closely to the policies and standards of credit and collection management.   No longer a passive function or a dead-weight expense, credit represents the assumption of a calculated risk, sometimes called a "marginal account,"[1] for the purpose of making sales.   By working in harmony with the sales department, suggesting sound business prospects, and assisting in the rehabilitation of poor ones, the credit manager administers a direct impulse to sales.   If he works wisely, he will not only win customers' business but also develop their ability as merchants.

In other ways, too, the credit manager may build the business of his concern.   He can revive dormant accounts by direct mail efforts. He can also solicit new credit customers and convert cash customers into profitable credit accounts.

Controlling the amount of receivables. Every dollar invested in an asset has alternative uses.   It could be in the form of cash as an aid to liquidity, or it might be in the form of some more profitable asset than receivables.   The longer such dollars are tied up in slow receivables, the less use the company is getting from those invested funds.   This may explain, in part at least, why some firms consider that the best use of available capital may be made by paying for the performance of the credit function by outside specialists, such as finance companies or factors, in which case little or no money of the vendor is invested in receivables.   In any event, a business must over time recover its money from receivables in order to meet its financial obligations and to reinvest, perhaps in other assets that would augment its profits. Whatever the reasoning, a company must control both the quality and the quantity of its receivables.

Once management has established the general role of credit in

---

[1] Some credit managers put so much emphasis on this aspect of their work that they measure the success of credit management by the number of marginal accounts handled and the effectiveness in doing so, all of which is rather shortsighted, especially when there is a tremendous difference of opinion as to what a marginal account is. Properly considered, it all boils down to the fact that a marginal account is one in which there is a substantial amount of risk—a matter which is really the sum and substance with which credit management is generally concerned. It must be remembered that risk is inherent in all credit transactions, the only difference being one of degree that is acceptable under given policies and conditions by astute credit managers.

its package of goods and services, several major factors determine the level of receivables. Some of these factors are essentially external, over which the company may have relatively little control, and other factors may be regarded as internal and hence subject to considerable control. The former include (1) customary credit terms of sale in the industry, (2) variations in the volume of credit sales due to fluctuations in the general level of business activity, and (3) changes in the volume of credit sales of a seasonal nature. Internal factors affecting the level of receivables include (1) credit policies and standards to be applied in the granting of credit, (2) policies and procedures to be used in establishing credit limits, i.e., the amount of credit to be extended, and (3) policies and procedures to be employed in collecting receivables.

In the protection of capital invested in receivables, it is the duty of credit management to adopt sound policies, procedures, and controls with respect to credit granting, credit limits, and collections. This is quite obvious. It is also the duty of credit management to adopt effective policies for such considerations as the charging of interest on past-due accounts, acceptance of collateral, and the taking of unearned cash discounts.

Controlling costs of credit and collection. A company incurs certain expenses in the extension of credit and in the collection of accounts receivable. These expenses include (1) bad debt losses, (2) wages and salaries of persons employed in credit and collection activities, (3) cost of funds tied up in receivables, (4) cost of fees and dues for credit information, (5) charges for outside assistance in making collections, (6) rent for space occupied by credit and collection personnel, and (7) depreciation of credit and collection equipment and fixtures. It is the responsibility of credit management to control these expenses as a means toward maximizing profits and return on asset investment.

Control of credit and collection expenses does not necessarily, however, mean minimizing expenses. A low percentage of losses from bad debts, for example, is not sufficient evidence of good credit management. Losses may be kept low by sacrificing sales which might yield profit in excess of the anticipated loss therefrom. This fact, however, even yet is often forgotten, especially in periods of doubtful conditions, and the fresh judgment which should characterize credit appraisal surrenders to the cautions of a too low level of credit management. What is desired is a minimum of bad debt loss commensurate with a maximum sales volume.

Minimization of account losses is gained not only by rejecting the determinably poor risks but also by sustaining and improving the risks which grow weak while being carried on the books. Some weaknesses develop internally, and it is the function of credit management to counsel and advise so that operating defects can be corrected and payment made.   Other problems are external to the risk and arise from the conditions of the community or trade in which he operates.   Good credit management may suggest actions to counteract the general conditions or plan for the least painful weathering of the storm.

In still another way, namely, by the maintenance of good collections, credit management may keep its losses low.   This entails the maintenance of adequate records and the prompt processing of delinquent accounts.   As will be shown in a later part of this book, this phase of the work requires an intimate knowledge of the legal remedies of creditors, adjustments, compositions, receiverships, bankruptcy, and the like.   Above all, it calls for an unusual degree of tact and diplomacy and strategy of a very high order, for, after all, the human equation is all-important in both credits and collections.

Cooperation with other credit departments. The successful performance of the above functions of credit management is dependent upon close cooperation with the credit departments of other business organizations, directly through interchange of credit information, indirectly through information furnished by credit bureaus and agencies, and through joint action in collection matters.   Probably no other form of business activity is so dependent upon collective action and cooperation as is credit work. The mutual benefits derived from the interchange of credit information and cooperation are so widely recognized that many credit managers are deterred from acting independently, even in cases of liquidation and bankruptcy, where preferences could be secured and an immediate gain obtained.

Furnishing aid to other departments of the business. As will be pointed out in a later chapter of this book, there is need for close cooperation with, and assistance to, the sales department of the credit manager's enterprise.   This is one way in which he may help to maximize sales volume and at the same time secure the assistance of the sales force as a source of credit information and possibly also in the collection process.   There is also need for close cooperation with the treasurer's office, since both are interested in financial aspects of the business. Similarly, close cooperation must be maintained with the accounting part of the business, because of the common interest in certain types of information maintained on accounting and credit records.

Need for cooperation with, or assistance to, the three types of business activity indicated above has generally been recognized.   Seldom, however, has the credit department been utilized, as it should be, in assisting the firm in its buying activity, through which aid can thus be furnished an analysis and unbiased appraisal of a supplier's responsibility, financial and moral, his ability to produce and furnish the quantity of goods agreed upon, and the possibility of enforcing the various parts of the contract should that become necessary.   Credit checking of prospective vendors may be just as fruitful as credit checking of prospective customers, and as the volume of business involved is much larger as a rule with any one supplier than with any one customer, it may be even more necessary.

The credit manager's training, experience, records, and knowledge of sources of information make him an invaluable aid to his firm in the formulation of financial plans and policies, in the analysis of statistical data of an internal or external nature, and in matters of public relations. Whether and to what extent this aid may be utilized depends upon the willingness and ability of the credit manager to place himself and his department at the disposal of his company on the one hand, and the discovery and realization of the great potentials in the use of such aid by management on the other.

EVOLUTION OF
THE CREDIT
PROFESSION

If credit management has today attained a degree of scientific proficiency, it is definitely the result of evolutionary development.   That is why viewing the current status of the credit manager and his work in historical perspective is so meaningful.   It explains in time-dimension terms present attainment, how it was achieved, and indicates the possible direction or prognosis.   There is also a space dimension to history.   What may have been true many years ago and no longer generally obtains today is still true of certain geographic areas and even of certain types of operation, as will be indicated briefly in the following paragraphs.   It is therefore erroneous to assume, for example, that since we are at present in the fourth stage of development of the credit profession, the preceding three stages have been completely superseded and are no longer in existence.   All that one needs to do to establish the falsity of such an assumption is to travel to the less developed countries or even to the less developed areas in the United States or delve into the operations of many of the smaller and growing individual enterprises even in the most progressive countries.   Thus the relevance of a discussion of all stages in the development of the credit profession becomes apparent.

Proprietor Stage. The *management* of credit is not so old as *credit* itself.   Lending has long been a business, but only relatively recently has the management of the lending business become something of a profession. Vendors have long sold on credit, but only with the development of mass distribution, based partly upon the widespread use of credit, has the management of mercantile and retail credit become a professional enterprise. From its earliest commercial use in this country to its present status, credit management has evolved through four stages.

During the first period, the "management" of credit, if such it can be called, devolved on the *proprietor* or head of the firm, who was personally in touch with his comparatively small number of customers and who was, consequently, familiar with the essential facts governing the determination of his credit policy and day-to-day credit activity. In the average small business establishment credit work is even yet performed by the proprietor or head of the firm, who may, in addition, have complete charge of other functions, such as buying, advertising, merchandising, financing, and general office management.

Diffused-responsibility stage. In the second stage, credit work was delegated to the *bookkeeper* and, in retail establishments, to the cashier-bookkeeper. This represented the passing from personal to impersonal supervision of accounts. The emergence of this stage can be identified with business recovery following the panic of 1873. With the opening of the Far West, the financial and commercial reconstruction following the War between the States and the business crisis that followed, the influx of large numbers of immigrants, and the rapid growth of individual business firms, the growing volume and scope of business made it impossible for the proprietor to perform all the work of credit management. It became imperative that some form of organization, although simple, be developed for the delegation of credit authority to individuals in responsible positions. Accordingly, the responsibility for dispensing credit, although primarily devolving upon the bookkeeper, was frequently shared by other individuals. Owners, managers, and salesmen, the latter because of their direct contact with the trade, all took part in the performance of this function.

Rise of the credit expert. A third stage was introduced by the formation of the National Association of Credit Management in 1896, marking the beginning of the evolution of the *credit expert* or *specialist* in the mercantile and banking fields. As trade grew and developed still further, the bookkeeper found it beyond his ability to handle both accounting records and credits successfully, for credit work alone required, in the majority of instances, the entire time of at least one person. Thus it came to pass that credit work was finally placed in the hands of a special man, who, though more or less of an expert, was at first in many instances given a rather inconspicuous place in the organization. This he still occupies in some of the smaller businesses which have not as yet expanded sufficiently or which fail to realize the importance of his services.

Emergence of the credit executive. The fourth stage in the development of credit management as a profession began during the depression of the early 1930's. This was the era in credit work distinguished by the transition of the credit man from the handling of mere technical matters to the formulation of credit policies in a somewhat *executive* or truly managerial capacity. The term "credit man" was replaced by designations such as "credit manager" and "credit executive." Behind this transition was the fact that during the depression the credit manager had been faced with difficulties of an almost insurmountable character.

POSITION OF CREDIT MANAGEMENT TODAY

The positions occupied by credit managers in companies today are identified by more than 150 different titles representing the gradations of authority and combinations of responsibility. On the officer level the credit position may be known as financial vice president; in lower echelons the positions are designated as credit manager and assistant treasurer, general credit manager, credit manager's assistant, branch credit manager, credit man, credit correspondent, chief bookkeeper, credit and adjustment clerk, and many other such titles.[2]

Irrespective of title, the performance of the credit work is the responsibility of positions of both line and staff character in an organization, positions which are specialized or not, depending upon the size and nature of the business. The functions falling to the different positions vary from credit-policy making at the top to the passing upon individual credit transactions at the bottom, and they are determined throughout by the combination of lines of merchandise handled, territories served, classes of customers served, and volume of business.

In companies where the management of credit occupies a top position, the credit manager or executive usually reports directly to the chief executive or chief corporate officer. The person in that position is responsible for the formulation of credit policies and the administration of credit operations that will maximize sales and profits, control costs of credit and collections, and control the company's investment in ac-

[2] *Analysis and Evaluation of Credit Management Functions*, Credit Research Foundation, Inc., New York, 1953, pp. 247–252. See also *Credit Department Organization and Operation*, American Management Association, Inc., New York, 1958, pp. 13–45.

counts receivable. This is accomplished through pertinent research into economic conditions and business practices; by establishing policies, procedures, and practices with respect to sales terms, financing arrangements, types of credit, and use of capital; by planning, developing, administering, and maintaining the necessary credit organization; by operating the credit department on sound principles and practices; and by maintaining with other departments and agencies, internal and external, relations essential to the achievement of the objectives. This level of management is not responsible for the detailed performance of credit work.

Where credit management does not occupy a top position but is still highly placed in the organization, the person in charge directs all credit and collection activities and is responsible for the interpretation of policy and its application. He staffs the credit organization and trains its personnel. He plans, executes, and coordinates programs for the operation of the credit department, approving major credit extensions, deciding borderline cases, and reactivating dormant accounts. He also directs the work of collecting. It is the task of employees on this level to maintain contacts with customers, credit and collection services used by the company, financial institutions, the trade, and professional organizations. In large companies the functions of this level are often applied to the administration of selected accounts grouped alphabetically, by product or brand, customer class, sales territory, or other geographical division.

In concerns where credit management is on the lowest administrative level, the person holding the position of credit manager or its equivalent is responsible for the actual extension of credit in accord with established policies. His chief duties relate to the extension of credit in analyzing requests, conducting investigations, evaluating risks, setting limits, and referring credits to higher authority. Making collections is another chief duty, which entails maintenance of controls, following up accounts, calling upon customers, representing the company at creditors' meetings, and supervision of collection correspondence.

QUALIFICATIONS
FOR CREDIT
MANAGEMENT[3]

For the proper and effective management of credits and collections, the person in charge, and in varying degrees those at lower levels in the

---

[3] Detailed descriptions of typical credit positions are presented in *Analysis and Evaluation of Credit Management Functions*, pp. 155–243. See also *Credit Management Handbook*, National Association of Credit Management, Richard D. Irwin, Inc., Homewood, Ill., 1958, pp. 88–97.

administration of the numerous activities that fall in its province, must possess certain personal, experience, and educational qualifications. With respect to the personal characteristics required, it would seem that, in Biblical terms, the ideal credit manager must have something of the patience of Job, the wisdom of Solomon, the courage of David, and the prophetic sense of John. In so far as all requirements which must be made by those who would engage in credit work are concerned, much depends upon the level of management on which the work is to be done. They are relatively few and unspecialized at the bottom, but as the management function of a given credit position broadens the requirements for education, experience, and personal competence of the person holding such a position increase.

Operational management. Most individuals enter the field of credit employment at the level of responsibility for actual credit extension, where applications are handled, discretion exercised, collections made, and the multitude of credit records kept. A high school education is essential for this position, and the employee should also have a knowledge of the rudiments of credits and collections, commercial law, and, in mercantile or bank credit departments, accounting and financial statement analysis.

If the position at this level includes the actual granting of credit and making of collections, familiarity with risks is beneficial. This may have been acquired through previous work in the field investigating risks or making collections, in handling the correspondence of the credit and collection department, in the preparation of reports or the analysis of statements and other credit information, or even in the work of selling.

The personal qualifications expected on this level begin with the ability to gather, organize, and retain the detailed information pertinent to accounts and to translate them into the operations of the credit routine. Such an employee should be capable of synthesizing facts and of communicating his ideas to his superior. In so far as he meets the public, he is expected to make a pleasing appearance and to speak and act in a manner that makes a favorable impression. Where judgment and discretion enter his work, he must be fair and just in his dealings.

Departmental management. Advancement in the credit profession usually represents the rising from one position to another, so that specifications for a departmental managership would generally include experience of 5 or 6 years in credit and collection work. Breadth of experience would also be necessary, and this should include exposure to the various aspects of credit activity. Management competence, however, arises not only out of thorough familiarity with operations but also from ability to organize people and to supervise them in their activities. Consequently, some experience along this line in either credit or other work is helpful.

Specifically, experience for this level of management should include risk research and appraisal, credit extension and collection supervision, office management, personnel selection and training, contact with other departments of the company, with customers, and with institutions related to the credit and collection functions.

Qualification for this position can be attained partly through experience, but it requires such mental development as can be acquired usually only through a college education or its equivalent. Many credit department managers, especially on the retail level, have no college degree, but those who expect to keep abreast of their work and the times enrich themselves by selective study. Knowledge in the same areas as in those required on the operational level, plus principles of business management and economics, although of deeper penetration, is desirable for departmental management.

On this level additional personal qualifications are required. It is essential to possess the maturity of outlook and stability of character which produce willingness to assume responsibility: for situations too difficult for others to handle, for risks which must be calculated as means to an end, for perseverance toward unformulated conclusions, and for the performance of those of limited capacity below him. Consideration for others both within and without the organization is important.

Executive management. In a few retail establishments, in many mercantile houses, and in most financing organizations, credit management reaches a level of executive capacity. It is attained by growth out of lower credit positions and by the encompassment of broader business activities. Education carried further in the principles and practice of credits and collections and in accounting and some practical experience with the credit aspects of finance, law, and business administration are desirable.

In addition to the usual operating and supervisor experience, close working with sales, accounting, order, shipping, and claims departments, as well as with higher executives in the line organization, contributes significantly to qualification for this position. Inasmuch, moreover, as work on this level is creative and initiatory, resourcefulness in the use of credit and in the use of finances is important. The executive manager must also be capable of eliciting confidential information.

Professional credit education. Through the National Association of Credit Management an effort has been made to professionalize credit and financial management, on the ground that a career in this work imposes responsibilities as important as those resting upon the lawyer, the doctor, the accountant, and the teacher.   The Association, accordingly, now under the direction of its affiliated Credit Research Foundation (chartered in 1949), has been promoting the National Institute of Credit (founded in 1918), the Graduate School of Credit and Financial Management, Credit Management Workshops, and some correspondence courses.

Through the activities of the Institute, carried on by many of its chapters, accreditation for work in the credit field is given in the form of Awards to those who fulfill stated academic and employment requirements.   The work may be carried on in colleges and universities, in local chapter classes, or by a program of correspondence study.   An Associate Award is granted for satisfactory completion of specified courses believed to be basic education for anyone entering the field of mercantile credit, provided the student has had 3 years of credit experience.   The Fellow Award is given to those who meet similar requirements with 6 years of experience.

The Graduate School of Credit and Financial Management, held for 2 weeks each summer at Stanford University and at Dartmouth University, provides for certification of those who satisfactorily complete the work of three yearly sessions.   Bringing together seasoned credit experts in diverse fields of business, this school makes a significant contribution to the development of credit managers of higher caliber.

In the financial institution field, much professional credit education is afforded under the auspices of the American Institute of Banking and of the American Savings and Loan Institute.   Dun & Bradstreet, Inc., is also offering a correspondence course in credit and financial analysis. In the retail field, courses in credit are offered under the auspices or through the encouragement of the International Consumer Credit Association and its numerous local associations.   In addition, courses for bureau personnel are provided in summer institutes by the Associated Credit Bureaus of America, Inc.

Business and social status of credit managers. To the individual contemplating a professional career in business, the role of credit manager holds forth promising opportunities, to men and to women alike.   In retail stores, a large percentage of the credit positions is held by women, the long tenure of whom bespeaks the stability of the work and its attractiveness from a career standpoint.   In the largest retail institutions, however, the manager of credits and collections is more often a man, under whom there are various assistants, the number depending upon the size of the organization and the credit task involved.   Mercantile and manufacturing establishments, likewise, employ credit experts or specialists, often on more remunerative terms than retailers, because of the greater breadth of training and experience which mercantile credit usually requires. Not least among the professional opportunities for credit management are those with the growing number of personal and sales finance agencies in the field of both consumer and mercantile credit. Banks, credit information agencies, and trade associations also employ many people in different phases of credit work. In addition to being reasonably remunerative, credit positions afford work of high value in social service and sufficiently varied to constitute a stimulating challenge to the progressive individual.

Through his cooperation with other members of his associations for the promotion of better standards of performance and higher standards of ethics in credit management, the credit manager makes a definite contribution to social welfare. Such cooperation has also resulted in a reduction in, or prevention of, commercial fraud on the part of credit users, and in better legislation with regard to checks, financial statements, bankruptcy, and other areas affecting members of society. The modern credit manager feels a strong responsibility to his profession, which, in turn, has a responsibility to the economy of this country as a whole. The credit profession may be likened to a gigantic valve which regulates the flow of credit through the economic system. When each credit manager, acting in his own self-interest in an enlightened way, i.e., with a social consciousness or responsibility, performs the credit and collection functions in a sound manner, the collective effect is to regulate the volume of credit and debt along sound lines from the standpoint of the entire economy.

QUESTIONS AND PROBLEMS

1 In what way or ways does credit management assist the firm in meeting its liquidity objective?

2 What are the major factors which determine the level of accounts receivable in a business organization?

3 In what way or ways does credit management differ from management generally?

4 What functions fall to credit management on different organizational levels?

5 What appraisal would you make of a credit manager who had no slow accounts and no bad debt losses?

6 How do credit managers contribute to an increase in sales volume?

7 When the credit manager has the title of assistant treasurer, what functions may he have other than those of maximizing sales and minimizing losses?

8 Is a college education indispensable, helpful, or irrelevant to the development of credit-management skill?

9 What contribution does credit practice make to manager development?

10 What on-the-job experiences help one progress from operational to managerial and then to executive work in credit administration?

11 What educational opportunities exist for learning about credit management?

12 What personal qualifications should a credit manager have? Which of them are uniquely significant for credit work?

13 In studying the historical development of the credit profession, is one dealing only with the past, or is the matter of consequence to the present and future as well? Explain.

14 Explain the difference between, and some of the implications of

   a Maximizing and optimizing sales or business volume

   b Minimizing and optimizing bad debt losses

CHAPTER FIVE

the credit
risk

In formulating policies and procedures for the credit-granting process, several basic steps must be taken by credit management. First, there must be determination of the grade or amount of risk that the firm is willing to accept. Second, each credit applicant must be investigated. Third, credit management must analyze the information obtained in its investigation in order to establish the applicant's creditworthiness. Finally, the credit manager or another person to whom such responsibility has been delegated must decide whether to accept or reject the applicant.

Risk is inherent in all credit transactions. It not only is pervasive through the various stages of credit granting but also persists through the entire collection process until collection or other final disposition is made, so that a user of credit is commonly referred to as a "credit risk"—a sort of personality. At each of these stages the credit manager

is confronted with problems incident to such risk.   In this chapter, however, attention is given primarily to the evaluation of a credit risk in
connection with the initial granting of credit, for the same factors and
decision-making problems are involved in all later treatment of credit
risks.

Tangible character of credit risks. The credit risk must be recognized, not as a vague, general condition to be appraised, but as a tangible
set of circumstances in the form of a person or a business entity such
as a firm or corporation.   In a sense, every individual or firm constitutes
a credit risk.   The myriad individualized circumstances of business are
the grist which the credit mill grinds into rejects and acceptances in
its processing of the flow of credit transactions.

Questions to be answered in judging a risk. Creditors generally
seek to avoid the "risky" transactions, for they would spare themselves
the losses and complications often resulting therefrom.   On the other
hand, it is not good business practice to reject *all* risk.   Were no risk
assumed and nothing ventured in the extension of credit, business would
not be what it is today.   It would revert to a cash basis or to the status
it held when credit was extended only to affluent and most reputable
buyers.   It has become good business practice to accept risk; the risky
transaction which is to be avoided is not the one which has *some* just
element of risk, but the one which has an *abnormal* and dangerous
amount of it.
    One of the chief functions of credit management is the analysis
of what constitutes the acceptable degree, or amount, of risk in an individual case.   When considering a new account, three decisions must
always be made in each case.   They take the form of three questions:
First, is the risk sufficiently good to be acceptable at all?   Second, if
the risk is satisfactory, to what extent should credit be granted, i.e.,
what shall be the credit limit?   Third, under what conditions or upon
what terms shall the credit and the extent thereof be granted?   These
are the three basic considerations in the mind of the credit grantor as
he appraises a risk.   Identical questions are posed when the account
wishes an upward revision of the limit or when a revision is necessitated
by changed conditions.   Again, the credit risk must be carefully examined
at certain stages in the delinquency in order to determine what additional
collection efforts, if any, are to be taken.

Measuring the credit risk. The measurement of credit risk is
made in terms of certain concepts and standards.   Because risk grows

out of debtors' unwillingness or inability to pay, every factor bearing upon these two sets of circumstances of *willingness* and *ability* to pay must be scrutinized in the investigation, and all available evidence bearing on them must be examined. This is an important part of the work of the credit grantor in accepting "calculated" risks. He develops acuteness in the perception of risk and skill in the measurement of it. Concluding that a credit applicant may be both unwilling and unable to pay a bill at maturity, for example, the vendor rejects him as a credit risk. Gaining assurance of payment, he may accept the risk but vary the amount of credit extended and the terms of sale, depending upon the circumstances. Thus he attempts to build business volume while keeping risk at a minimum.

Comparing risk to potential gain. After establishing to some extent the degree of risk involved in granting credit to the applicant, credit management should also consider the potential gain of the applicant's business before deciding whether to extend or reject the credit requested, and under what terms and conditions credit should be extended. Specifically, credit management should ask itself several key questions. First, what is the amount of annual sales that can be expected from the particular customer? Second, what is the dollar amount of net profit that can be anticipated from the applicant's business? Third, how much more will be invested in accounts receivable, inventory, and other assets if credit is extended to the customer? Fourth, what is the rate of return on asset investment? Finally, would the company use this amount of funds in another investment opportunity that offered this rate of return and had the same degree of risk of nonpayment? If the potential gain is acceptable in relation to the risk involved in granting the requested credit, the applicant should be accepted. But if the risk of nonpayment and the loss of investment is considered too high in relation to the potential return, credit management should establish other terms and conditions under which credit could be extended, sell the applicant on a noncredit basis, or not sell the applicant at all.

BASIC FACTORS
DETERMINING THE
CREDIT RISK

The principal factors to be taken into consideration in deciding whether or not to grant credit, in what amount, and on what terms and conditions, comprise what are commonly referred to in the credit profession as the "four C's" of credit—*Character, Capacity, Capital,* and *Conditions.*

Each of these terms has a meaning in connection with credit which may be different from their general usage.[1]

Character. Character comprises those qualities of a credit risk which make him *want* or *intend* to pay when a debt is due. Credit character and moral character or social reputation are not necessarily the same thing, although they are usually very closely related.

The character of an individual is the aggregate of mental and moral qualities which identify him. A person is thought to have character when he is governed by a high sense of what is morally right. Honesty is a foremost quality of character. Other qualities of character are integrity, fairness, responsibility, temperance, trustworthiness, industry, and the like. Character thus defined becomes credit character when these qualities combine to make one conscientious concerning his debts. It is conceivable that an individual of high rectitude, as for example a clergyman, may be indifferent toward his accounts and so lack credit character, while epitomizing all that is admirable in a moral sense. On the other hand, a gambler of low social esteem may enjoy a high credit character rating by virtue of a strong determination to pay his debts when due. In most cases, individuals are more consistent, so that a likely willingness to pay debts can be inferred from evidences of general character.

Judgment of character must be based upon evidence, and the seeking and appraising of evidence is one of the technical jobs of credit management. Perhaps one of the best evidences of willingness to pay is a long and consistent record of credit payment. The debtor who has an established credit record seldom, for reasons of character, deviates from his paying pattern. Others who have displayed their indifference to debt and their reluctance to meet just obligations may usually be expected to show such tendencies again in the future. Evidence of paying record is usually obtainable from other creditors, directly or through an intermediary organization.

Other evidences of credit character are found in positions of trust which an individual may hold in business or in social organizations; in the stability of his residence, employment, and business connections;

[1] Occasionally one adds another C to the four generally recognized C's of credit, as indicated by the title of an article "The Fifth 'C' of Credit: Coverage" (obviously referring to the coverage provision in credit insurance policies which some creditors carry), *Credit and Financial Mangement*, October, 1960, and at times one capitalizes on the popularity of the concept of C's of credit by carrying the matter to extremes as when adding C's for "Clairvoyance, Celerity, Candor" (*Credit and Financial Management*, August, 1960). Despite all such attempts at modification, whether taken seriously or with tongue in cheek, the four C's of credit herein discussed are of basic concern, of almost universal acceptance, and of applicability to all kinds of business dealing in credit.

in the extent and nature of his education and cultural development; and in the integrity which may be revealed in a personal interview.

When dealing with business customers, the willingness of the business organization to pay must be determined. In general, the character of small businesses, even when they are corporations, is the same as the character of the individuals who operate them. The corporate identity adds nothing to character if the management is deficient in honesty and trustworthiness. On the contrary, incorporation may indicate a willingness of incorporators to commit themselves for only a certain amount of debt in a particular venture. This should be recognized in appraising such a risk. The character of large business organizations, on the other hand, may be distinct from the personal character of its management, for their operations are usually based upon policy rather than upon persons. One would look therefore to evidences of policy in the management, their facilities for record keeping, the routinization of office functions, and their awareness of the competitive advantages inherent in the taking of cash discounts, in modernization, and other such practices. Here, too, the actual paying record is of paramount importance, for it is at least symptomatic or external evidence of the character (and capacity) that combined to build it.

Capacity. Capacity in credit signifies the *ability* to pay when a debt is due. However desirous a debtor is of paying, if he lacks money or the ability to obtain money with which to make payment, he is a poor risk.

Estimation of capacity, however, is not always simple; it involves several factors. It is primarily a question of earning power, for expenditures and payments almost always depend upon income rather than upon savings. Income alone, however, does not completely reveal capacity, for income may already be so committed to existing debt that a debtor would have no further capacity for credit. Moreover, the capacity of a consumer is affected by his expenditure pattern as well as by his debt. A family, for example, with a number of children would probably be a poorer credit risk for some luxury item than a childless couple with the same income. Time also affects capacity, for a credit obligation which one might be able to fulfill in a long period he may be unable to meet in a short time.

The most important evidence of capacity is income; this is so emphasized by some credit grantors that they neglect other evidences. Income, however, must be recognized as the product of other things, which also signify capacity, such as personal health, education in a profession or skill, age, personality, persistence and stability in employment, disposition to economize, resourcefulness, and progressiveness.

One's capacity in business, or the capacity of a business, likewise relates to factors affecting income, expenditure pattern, and existing debt. Business income is derived essentially from sales; whatever affects sales determines in some degree the credit capacity of the business. Advertising, salesmanship, store location, floor layout, fixtures and equipment, balance and age of inventory, services offered, competition, trade relations and sources, brands and agencies possessed—these are some of the factors of capacity in a business debtor. Capacity is determined by cost of operation as well as by sales, for the high cost operator is the less able to meet obligations on merchandise purchased on credit. Salaries, utilities, rent, and other items of expense are usually paid first out of income in order to keep the business going; merchandise creditors must take this into consideration in estimating the capacity of a firm to pay for its unpaid inventory. Capacity is influenced also by the existing debt structure of the organization. If debt is high in terms of equity investment, outsiders have claims which may impair capacity under some circumstances. Moreover, high debt of some kinds is accompanied by high interest costs.

Capital. Capital, for credit purposes, is the *financial strength* of a risk as measured by the equity or net worth of the business. It is the assurance that a debtor could be made to pay, in the long run, if character and capacity should fail. Capital is that which a creditor might seize as payment for the debt. Credit is not extended on the presumption that capital will serve as the means of payment, even when mortgages are taken, for a resort to capital usually means the termination of the business relationship. Credit is granted on the presumption that payments will continue and that subsequent sales will be possible.

Consumers usually have little capital. What they do possess is in the form of household furnishings and personal effects. Some may add to this some modest bank accounts; others may possess securities, real estate, and rights. The value of such capital for credit purposes is small and may be entirely intrinsic rather than market value. Moreover, part of one's personal capital may be exempt from seizure under the laws of exemption in the various states. Nevertheless, even the information on capital is of some value to the credit grantor, for it may at least cast light upon the character and the capacity of the individual.

The capital of business establishments is usually determinable from their financial statements. When assets are balanced against liabilities, however, a true estimate of capital must take market, rather than book, values of the assets into consideration, and attention must be given to a proper evaluation of all items contained therein for appropriateness of inclusion and for accuracy.

Special emphasis is sometimes given to collateral as a form of capital which is peculiarly favorable to risk evaluation. A bank making loans on security examines carefully the nature of the collateral offered for deposit, irrespective of the moral responsibility of the borrower. In selling automobiles to the ultimate consumer on credit, chattel mortgages are usually taken by the seller as security behind the promissory notes for the unpaid balances. In such instances the chattel or chattels offered as collateral must be thoroughly scrutinized, for it is the property thus conveyed upon which main reliance is placed in financing the transaction. Normally, however, this element of capital in the form of collateral is totally lacking in most mercantile and retail credit extensions.

Conditions. However creditworthy an individual may be judged from the standpoint of his character, capacity, and capital, it may not always be sound business to extend him credit. Creditworthiness is dependent not entirely upon factors that are inherent in the risk and over which he presumably has control; it is dependent in part upon the *economic environment* in which the risk exists. General business and economic conditions, over which individuals do not have control, may alter the ability of even the more capable risk to meet his obligations.

Both the long-run and short-run fluctuations of business must be taken into consideration in evaluating conditions. Some of these may be peculiar to an industry, to an industrial area, to a given geographic area, or to the nation as a whole. Some of the variations follow a more or less definable pattern of oscillation from prosperity to depression; others may be acute and of an emergency nature, unpredictable and conforming to no definite pattern. A credit executive must, therefore, constantly keep his finger on the pulse of conditions and sense the direction of changes. In a period of rising prices, men with little or no ability may succeed in business, whereas with an adverse change of conditions they could not exist. During a period of falling prices and general deflation, not only is capital often dissipated, but even character sometimes undergoes marked changes. Many an honest person is tempted by circumstances to resort to measures not sanctioned by credit managers.

Political as well as economic developments have a bearing upon credit risks in general and upon some of them in particular. Changing legislation and administrative attitudes, as well as judicial decisions, minimize or accentuate risk. Governmental subsidization of farmers tends to improve their credit status; the removal of import tariffs may lower the credit standing of domestic firms affected by this move. Disasters sometimes provoke the extension of credit to individuals not otherwise warranting it, mainly as a service in meeting extreme human need.

Exceptional business opportunities open to a credit applicant may also justify the extension of more credit to him than formerly.   Competitive conditions of a trade, too, have been known to influence the evaluation of credit risks, although from the standpoint of the creditor this is not always a salutary force.   Of not least importance is the condition of the money market in general, such as the availability of funds, the rate of interest charges, and the prevailing demand for credit.   All these conditions enter, consciously or unconsciously, into prudent credit judgment.

      Relative importance of the four C's. Appraising the credit risk requires the taking of all these factors into consideration.   Unfortunately, perhaps, they cannot be reduced to a prescription or a formula, for where such a large human element is involved, one strong factor may outweigh a number of other weaker ones.   Judgment is necessary, and judgment must rest upon a critical appraisal.   Moreover, the different factors may be present or lacking in varying degrees.   As the saying goes, there is a little bit of good in the worst of us and a little bit of bad in the best of us.   When it is said, for example, that a person or firm does not possess capacity, all that is meant by it is that it is deficient in that factor and not that capacity is *totally* lacking.   Again, this deficiency may vary in degree from relatively small to very high.   All these differences make an evaluation of a credit risk most difficult, though not impossible.

      Ranking the C's in importance is a matter of understanding what they represent and how the business of credit and collection is affected by them.   From what has been said above, it can be fairly concluded that credit is granted in a sale or loan in the expectation of receiving *money* payment to fulfill and redeem the credit promise.   The creditor does not wish, or may be unable, to repossess or replevin the item sold; neither does he wish to acquire other property upon which he may have taken a mortgage, except as an indirect means of obtaining his money.   It cannot be thought, therefore, that capital is a principal factor in credit granting.   It is a stopgap.   Credit would not be granted if replevin or attachment were expected to be the only or principal means of securing payment.   Credit is granted with the expectation that consecutive payments will be made against debt incurred or that if it is paid off in full, subsequent purchases and payments will be made.   Capacity is therefore generally more important than capital.

      As between character and capacity, there is sometimes disagreement concerning which is the more important.   The issue may be stated thus: Would the better risk be the individual who is honest but who lacks something in capacity to pay, or the one who is indifferent to his debts but who has the means to pay if he would?   It is sometimes maintained that the latter would be the better, for ultimately he could be made to pay through legal action if he has capacity, but that throws emphasis again upon capital and seizure.

The risk who has character, in the long run will usually find a way to pay.   This may demand patience of the debtor, but the honest debtor is usually scrupulous about working out his affairs.   In extreme cases, conscientious debtors who have gone through bankruptcy have sometimes later paid their obligations.   On the other hand, the risk who has either income or assets but who neglects, delays, or refuses to pay furnishes an entirely different picture.   He is a troublesome subject.   He must be watched and his account followed carefully.   He is a cause of collection expense and in many instances a reason for legally enforced collection.

The reasoning which assigns capital the first and capacity the second place of importance emphasizes that, especially in business credit, a credit seeker must display sufficient financial strength of his own to finance the volume of business he expects to do.   Next, the applicant must convince the credit grantor of his ability to conserve his financial resources through prudent management and to discount his bills or meet his obligations at maturity.   Finally, the applicant must show qualities of honesty and integrity, denoting willingness and intention to fulfill his obligations to creditors, irrespective of contingencies that might arise.

Although character is the least tangible of the factors in the determination of the credit risk, it is nevertheless *normally* the most important basis and is susceptible of definite ascertainment.   It is not extremely difficult, for example, to discover and separate the honest from the dishonest, the sane livers from the extravagant, the abstainers from the drinkers and gamblers, and the moral from the immoral.   Experience has shown that capacity and capital count for little when a clever crook deliberately determines to "beat" his creditors.   Where character is doubtful or distinctly inferior, no credit should be extended if the purchase of a lawsuit is to be avoided.

There is, on the other hand, something to be said in defense of the importance of capacity.   One survey concerning the relative importance of instalment credit standards disclosed that occupation and permanence of employment held first place.   This would reflect the emphasis placed upon the debtor's continued earning power, and it is suggestive of the fact that this is often the factor first to be regarded in consumer open-account credit, as well as in instalment credit.   A close second standard was the past payment record.   Thus it would seem that even under circumstances where capacity may be regarded as most important, character is held to be of almost equal significance.

The credit equation. Notwithstanding the fact that the ingredients of a credit decision must be judged mentally and pragmatically rather than mathematically, efforts are frequently made to reduce judgment to a formula.   These efforts usually consist of arraying factors regarded as important in the credit risk for the purposes of a particular credit grantor, of weighting these factors more or less arbitrarily or intuitively, and then reaching conclusions from the summary scores.   With the help of computers it is now feasible, by means of discrimination analysis, to examine the records of a company and from its experience to identify the significant factors that distinguish bad accounts from good ones, assign proper weights to each of such factors, determine more or less objectively the degree of risk involved, and by such credit-scoring system establish a minimum acceptable risk or cut-off point.   With experience of such a scoring system it may even be possible to develop a table showing the probability of an account with a given score going bad.

One Federal agency has used the following rating chart to estimate the risk on each borrower and found scoring effective and suitable to its needs.

Character	30%	Ratio value of property to	
Attitude toward obligations	15	annual income	7%
Ability to pay	15	Ratio monthly mortgage	
Prospects for future	12	obligations to income	6
Business history	10	Associates	5
		Total	100%

Regardless of what formula, if any, is used in the evaluation of a consumer credit risk, occupation has been found to be a very significant factor.   Studies on the subject have shown a high correlation or relationship between specific occupations or occupational classes and groups on the one hand and credit ratings or paying records on the other.   In general, consumers in the professional occupations rank the highest as credit risks, followed by skilled workers and clerical and office types of occupations, the lowest consisting of the unskilled labor groups.

While a number of reasons may be given for the high or low relative position on the credit risk scale of a given occupation, *stability* of income, rather than its size, is probably the most tangible characteristic of the better-rated occupations.   Thus the stable income of officers in the Armed Forces, school teachers, post-office employees, and office workers makes for much better risks than the equivalent total but irregular income of plasterers, coal miners, or musicians.   To be sure, occupation cannot be entirely divorced from character.   Certain occupations tend to attract persons of the highest moral integrity and credit character, while others offer less incentive in that direction.   Furthermore, some occupations, especially those of the professional and semiprofessional types, may be governed by codes of ethics that would preclude entry to persons of a questionable credit character.

It cannot be denied that the ultimate decision in a credit situation must be one of judgment and not of mere computation. Nevertheless, it may be of value to the credit manager who strives for some degree of exactness in his decisions to have a general guide as to the relative weights of the C's of credit without reference to the type or class of credit—mercantile, bank, or consumer—and without detailing the components of any of the C's. To this end it is suggested that the following weights may furnish a useful guide. If conditions are to be included in the weighting, character may be assigned a value of 35 per cent; capacity, 30 per cent; capital, 20 per cent; and conditions, 15 per cent. If conditions are to be excluded from the weighting on the ground that they apply generally to all risks in a given category and it is but desired to evaluate a specific risk within it, character may be assigned a weight of 40 per cent; capacity, 35 per cent; and capital, 25 per cent.

The weighting just suggested assumes, of course, that a given factor can be rated as totally present or totally absent. But, as already indicated, that is not usually the case. A given factor such as character may be rated as excellent and beyond the shadow of the slightest doubt or it may be good to all intents and purposes and yet fall short of the mark. Is the Character factor in such a case to be given full weight or only part of it? In such matters there is no substitute for judgment, tempered by experience.

Suggested practical uses of credit equations. Without attempting to reduce the credit equation to mathematical expression, it is still possible to state it in words that describe some of the degree of risk to be found in different combinations of the basic credit factors. Assuming normal transactions and the same conditions applying to all credit risks of a vendor, the credit equation may be stated for a specific risk as follows:

Character + Capacity + Capital = Good Credit Risk

If, however, any of the C's is impaired but not necessarily totally absent, the nature of the credit risk involved may be formulized as follows:

1 Character + Capacity + Insufficient Capital = Fair Credit Risk
2 Character + Capital + Insufficient Capacity = Fair Credit Risk
3 Capacity + Capital + Impaired Character = Doubtful Credit Risk
4 Character + Capacity − Capital = Limited Success
5 Capacity + Capital − Character = Dangerous Risk

6 Character + Capital — Capacity = Inferior Credit Risk
7 Capital — Character — Capacity = Distinctly Poor Risk
8 Character — Capacity — Capital = Inferior Credit Risk
9 Capacity — Character — Capital = Fraudulent Credit Risk

MODIFYING FACTORS
INFLUENCING
THE CREDIT EQUATION

It is natural that risks differ in quality, and part of the credit work is the determination of the amount and type of risk involved in a case. It is also true that credit managers may differ in their interpretation of the quality of a risk. Other factors modifying the credit equations, therefore, must be considered. Among them are the credit policy of the house, attitude of the credit manager, and the type of risk.

Policy of the house. In passing upon credit risks, the manager is governed by the policies of his house. He is influenced by the profitableness of the line he sells and by the operating conditions of his organization. With a high profit margin he can afford to take more risk in credit than could a firm with a low profit margin. Similarly, if his is an industry operating on a decreasing cost basis, he may find it advantageous to secure volume through liberal credit extension, thereby increasing the scale of operation and making for the economies resulting therefrom.

Policies in meeting competition also influence the credit equation. If competition is strong, liberal credit may be given as a matter of policy to attract trade. On the other hand, monopolistic or semimonopolistic enterprises are seldom, if ever, liberal in their credit policy. Even in the absence of competition, of course, maximum volume may be desirable, in which case credit is used as a promotional aid.

The type of its customers also affects policy and, in turn, credit granting. When customers are farmers or miners, more liberal terms may be required. Merchants dealing, on the other hand, with city trade are more likely to sell on shorter terms and to be more exacting in making collections.

Attitude of credit manager. Individuals in general and credit managers in particular differ in their subjective viewpoints. In their construction of the credit equation, some credit managers emphasize a customer's financial responsibility, others judge the risk primarily by character, and still others look to the management capacity of the risk. A few credit managers still regard the principal function of their work to be the minimization of bad debt losses; the majority views losses in relation to sales and bases its extensions upon this outlook.

Apart from their appraisal of the three C's, credit granting is influenced also by the managers' interpretation of general conditions. Some are more conservative than others; some are better informed; others are the better analysts. At all times they are influenced by their own personal experiences, the more recent ones occupying the more prominent position in their evaluation of credit risks. Thus the personal element enters credit work not only as the risk but also as the credit appraiser. It is this combination of factors which calls for skill and experience in the credit profession.

Types of risk. Banks and mercantile concerns have essentially the same credit problems, for they deal with the same type of clientele, both utilize the same sources of information, and both are interested in the business success of their customers. In these fields of operation, credit customers or applicants for such accommodations are frequently designated as "moral risks," "business risks," or "financial risks," depending largely upon which of the C's of credit predominates. Moral risks are those whose financial means are so limited that, from a credit standpoint, chief reliance is placed upon the character or determination to pay and secondly upon ability to run the business with reasonable efficiency. Many young men who possess these qualities when starting in business can obtain a limited amount of credit at least for short periods of time. The number of such risks is veritably legion. A customer is labeled a business risk if his chief asset is ability to run his business at a profit. If, on the other hand, the available capital of the subject is the main consideration in extending credit, the subject constitutes a financial or property risk which is best analyzed by an examination of the financial statement.

In the field of consumer credit, the number of so-called "moral risks" is much greater in absolute figures or in proportion to all credit customers than in banking or in the mercantile field. In these cases, moral risks are judged primarily by their integrity, paying habits, mode of living, and earning capacity. Thus, while all the C's of credit are universal in their application, capital has relatively little bearing in dealings with charge accounts used by consumers or when consumers borrow on their signatures. Consequently, more stress needs to be put on the moral character of the risk here than in other types of credit.

Changing nature of the credit risk. Any given credit risk may change in type, as from a moral hazard to a business risk, or vice versa.

This obviously suggests the possibility, or rather the probability, of a change in the quality of the risk resulting from changes in income, business progress, or composition of the enterprise. For such reasons it is essential that credit accounts placed on the books be reexamined periodically to ascertain whether substantial changes have taken place in the interim that might justify more favored or less favored treatment creditwise. Even under the most ordinary circumstances change of this kind is inevitable, especially so in a dynamic economy characteristic of this country in recent years.

QUESTIONS AND PROBLEMS

1 What are the basic steps in the credit-granting process? Is risk avoidable in this process?

2 At what point or points in credit dealings should a credit risk be analyzed? Why?

3 Is it possible to measure the credit risk quantitatively or must it be appraised and evaluated only qualitatively? In doing so, what factors must be considered and are these factors of limited or universal application, i.e., do they apply only to mercantile credit risks or are they of equal significance in judging risks for retail or commercial bank credit?

4 How would you, as a credit manager, proceed to judge an applicant's character? Give a specific Ilustration of the items of information you would wish to gather as a basis for your judgment.

5 What is the meaning of capacity? How does it differ in the case of a consumer, a retailer, a manufacturer?

6 Credit applicants and debtors are sometimes regarded as "moral risks." What is meant by this?

7 In judging a credit risk who applied for credit accommodation at a local department store, under which of the C's of credit would you classify each of the following items of information:

a Highest amount of credit extended by other stores

b Presence or absence of a checking or saving account at the bank

c Information secured from a neighbor

d Length of residence at the present location

e Assessed valuation of owned real estate

f Size of the family

g Social standing in the community

h Chattel mortgages given to creditors

i Size of the bank account

j Inheritance of property

k Mode of living

l Judgments held against the risk

m Position occupied and salary earned

8 Classify the items in the following credit report according to character, capacity, and capital:

J. B. Brown, aged 37, druggist. Net worth in business alone, $60,000. Married. Investment in real estate, $24,000. Business established 7 years ago. Prior to engaging in his own business was a salesman for a wholesale drug firm for 3 years. Business record apparently clear. One fire 4 years after started in business; cause unknown. Trade reports favorable. Good health. Secondary location. Recently installed modern fixtures. Carries satisfactory account at the bank. Spends most of his time in store. Employs two pharmacists and three clerks. Annual sales are about $230,000 and are increasing steadily. Growing emphasis on prescriptions. Encourages charge accounts. Inventory in store well arranged. Director of the local Retail Druggists' Association.

9 Why do some credit managers rely chiefly on a risk's character, while others base their decisions primarily on financial responsibility? Explain.

10 Once the type and quality of a credit risk has been carefully determined, is there any reason for reviewing it periodically? What is to be gained by such a review?

11 Why should the potential gain of a credit applicant's business be compared to the risk involved in granting credit to that applicant?

management of the consumer credit-granting function

Consumer credit plays an increasingly important role in the business of this nation and in the life of its people.   It takes several general forms, each intended to serve a special major purpose and each constantly evolving in new ways.   The secular or long-term trend has been definitely upward.   More consumers use credit and they use more of it.   It has thus become a growing business force and an ingrained characteristic of our society and its high and rising standard of living.

All of this raises questions as to possible excessive use of consumer credit, its probable effect on the economy, its costliness, need for and nature of control, and best ways of controlling it and/or curbing abuse.   On the matter of control, for example, not only does opinion or judgment differ widely but extremely strong positions are taken.   These range all the way from strict Federal control of both quantity and quality of consumer credit to complete *laissez faire*.   The former position is obviously based in the main on lack of trust in the integrity of private business enterprise in a competitive setting and in the belief of consumer general incompetence in credit matters.   The latter position, at the other extreme, is based on the ground that the consumer knows best his limitations on this score.

The reason for the extreme viewpoints and the numerous variations in-between is to be found mainly in lack of real knowledge and understanding of the essence of consumer credit in its various forms and its use and partly in the selfish motives of an economic, business, or political nature.   It is, therefore, the function of this part of the book to provide the basis for better knowledge and understanding of consumer credit.   Moreover, in the conviction that there are no built-in controls in the consumer himself despite his substantial sagacity in this regard, this part of the book also devotes considerable space to a discussion of the proper and effective management of the various forms of consumer credit by businesses engaged in it, the phase of credit management having to do with collections being reserved to a later part of the book where it can be treated on a common basis with other types of credit.   In the long run and in a competitive system, it is felt, control through effective management acquired by education, training, and experience on the part of credit grantors, coupled with more consumer education about credit, provides the summum bonum for all concerned including society at large.

CHAPTER SIX

consumer credit
information

Intelligent granting of consumer credit is based upon adequate relevant
information.   Both the assembly and the interpretation of this information
are important parts of the work of the credit department.   So highly
developed has the accumulating of it become, however, that it is far
beyond the province of each creditor to ferret the sources for himself.
While relying to some extent upon their own resourcefulness, creditors
have to a large extent turned to specialists supplying credit information.
These specialists, in turn, have become so respected for their work that
both the uses and the users of their services have substantially increased
in number.

Users of consumer credit information. Although retail stores are
still the most numerous users of consumer credit information, many other

organizations also need it and use it.   These others include manufacturers selling at retail; service establishments, such as garages, beauty
parlors, and undertakers; professional people like physicians, dentists,
and lawyers; insurance companies; building and loan associations; finance
companies; and commercial banks.   Governmental agencies, such as the
Home Owners Loan Corporation, the Federal Housing Administration,
and the Farm Credit Administration also seek information from credit
specialists in making their loans.   The Federal Bureau of Investigation
and the intelligence services of the Armed Forces, too, rely upon information assembled by credit agencies in evaluating credentials of individuals
to be entrusted with certain responsibilities, in ascertaining their loyalty,
and in judging security risks.   Moreover, lending organizations, brokerage
houses, real estate firms, individual mortgagors, hospitals, and hotels
are also interested in individual character credit reports.

Types of sources. Credit information concerning consumers may
be obtained from a variety of sources.   In general, the sources most
commonly used are the personal interview, references, credit bureaus,
credit-reporting agencies, and banks.

INTERVIEWS AND
APPLICATIONS

One source of information in the appraisal of a credit risk is the personal
interview, which has the advantage of providing firsthand information,
personal observation of the applicant, and an opportunity for instructing
him in the proper use of his account.   It is an occasion for a two-way
exchange of information which is usually not repeated in the life of most
accounts.

Who does the interviewing depends upon the organization of the
credit department.   In the larger stores, application clerks do this work;
in smaller ones, it may be done by the credit manager or by the proprietor
himself.   Whether a man or a woman be preferred for this function is
a matter of opinion in the profession, but each has certain peculiar qualifications.   Men may conduct themselves with what appears to be greater
impersonality and impartiality; women, on the other hand, are thought
to be more capable of meeting applicants on a common ground, inasmuch
as most applicants for credit, in retail stores at least, are women.

More important than who interviews is that it be done properly.
The interview is not a stern examination of the applicant.   It is an advantageous way of obtaining some pertinent information.   Some questions
may be asked directly; other information is brought out in conversational
discussion of the customer's need for credit.   The tone of the questioning

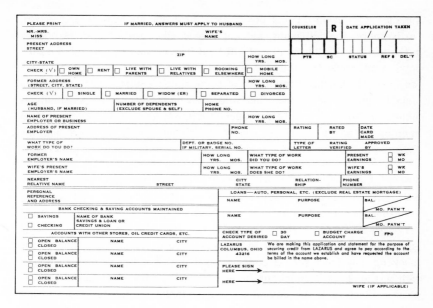

figure 6-1. *Application for charge account. Also serves as credit file card on the reverse side of which are provisions for data from the credit bureau, recheck, and comments.*

should put the interviewee at ease and dispel any feeling of having been singled out for this interrogation. Most applicants will be acceptable risks; the purpose of the interview, therefore, is to discover those who would not so qualify.

Application for credit. To guide the interview and to provide space for an orderly assembly of information, application forms are used by most stores. When no interview is held, these forms are filled out and submitted by the applicant. The forms used for this purpose are sometimes supplied to members by the local credit bureau. They take different shapes, sometimes being a card to be filed in the active credit files. Some stores make a duplicate of the application for submittal to the credit bureau. Whatever the individual nature, the application usually has space for entering the following information: name, residence, former address, employer, bank, property claimed, references, remarks, and signature (see Fig. 6-1).

Name in full. The first name as well as the middle name should be given in full to avoid confusion between some last names with similar initials.   Confusion on this point may cause embarrassment and losses. Furthermore, the full name will indicate whether the account is opened in the name of the husband *and* wife.   If it is in the name of the husband only, it becomes the duty of the store to ascertain the extent of his responsibility for the account, for in some states a husband is not responsible for debts incurred by his wife individually or his responsibility is limited in some way.   Under such circumstances, it is advisable that appropriate notice be served on the husband.   This will give him the opportunity to confirm or to decline the specified arrangement.

Residence and former address. The nature and location of an applicant's residence are often indicative of his means, rent expense, and social responsibilities.   In this item of information prudent credit managers often see certain danger signals that call for a careful investigation of the applicant prior to any favorable decision.   Any one of the following may flash such a danger signal: residence in a rooming house, with a friend, in a hotel, or in a furnished apartment; residence in a place or section of the city where questionable people are known to live or where slovenly or other bad conditions prevail; single persons living away from home; women who live under excellent conditions but refuse to furnish reliable references or sources of income.

The former address is usually needed for checking references and may be needed for tracing skips.   If the applicant is a newcomer, it is essential to determine whether he is but temporarily residing at the place given; in such case the full permanent address must be secured.

Occupation or business. An applicant's employment, its nature, place, and length of time thus engaged are a first consideration in evaluating the risk.   Some stores also require information concerning the salary or wage received from such employment.   As many persons resent disclosing such facts, diplomacy must be used in obtaining this kind of information.

The prudent credit manager is always on guard in treating applicants disclosing occupational danger signals and subjects the applications to careful investigation and scrutiny.   He is warned by any of the following illustrative situations: an unstable or hazardous occupation such as bartender, waiter, taxi driver, or laundry worker; employment in glamorous but relatively unstable jobs such as models and chorus girls; transient employees such as demonstrators and solicitors; employment with a relative, with a small and unknown firm, or with a business where either the employer is questionable or unreliable or the business is in a class regarded as unreliable or subject to rackteering; and "retired" persons for whom no evidence of income or wealth can be established.

Business address. In the event the applicant should later change residences, it will be a simple matter to locate him if his exact business address is known. Such knowledge is also required for the purpose of making an investigation, verifying the applicant's statements, and tracing him if he later moves to another town or city.

Bank. Possession of a deposit account by a customer usually indicates thrift and a desire to establish a credit balance. Knowledge of the bank with which the customer deals helps to verify facts stated in the interview and sometimes affords additional valuable information, depending upon the bank's willingness to cooperate in the exchange of credit experience with the depositor's actual or prospective creditors.

Property owned and encumbrances thereon. This can be readily verified through an attorney or a credit bureau. If the value of his equity is substantial, greater reliance can be placed on the customer's ability to meet his obligations ultimately.

Remarks. As already indicated, the credit manager in large establishments finds it impossible to interview all applicants personally. A statement given by the application clerk of his impression of the customer is, therefore, helpful in determining what decision should be rendered. These remarks are usually brief, and impressions are often expressed as "OK" "Unreasonable," "Bears watching," and the like.

Where application clerks are well trained, they will be on the alert throughout the interview for information that may put them on guard and furnish a basis for their remarks. For example, they would look with suspicion on any of the following situations that may be disclosed, sometimes inadvertently, during the interview: person suspected of being a minor, mentally unstable, or alcoholic; divorced or separated woman or widow who would not supply any references; person in extreme hurry to obtain credit before the application can be cleared; person attempting to impress one with his superior standing as a credit risk; applicant opened several new accounts on small or moderate income; large dependent family with modest income; and business applicant unable to furnish good bank or business references.

Signature. An applicant's signature is particularly important in stores where it is used for identification purposes when making purchases. If a store employs a coin, card, or Charga-Plate as a means of identifying charge purchasers, a customer's signature on the application is of less significance. A signed application is in reality a contract to which reference can be made, if need be, in the collection process.

Items bearing on instalment credit. Inasmuch as instalment purchases are very common, additional space is often provided on the application form for information relative to them. A credit manager is interested in the obligations already incurred by an applicant.

While the types of information indicated above are more or less standard, there are many stores which require more details: facts in regard to previous employers, exact occupation of the risk, his affiliations with lodges and churches. Many ask whether an account had previously been maintained at the store in question and call for the names of all persons authorized to buy on the account. Others provide space on the application for notation of the results of the credit investigation.

REFERENCES

Another valuable source of information consists of the references furnished by the applicant. Usually three names are required, including merchants with whom accounts have been maintained, other credit customers of the store, the present employer, and personal acquaintances who can speak about the applicant. Not all of them will be able to provide the technical information pertinent to the creditworthiness of the applicant, but the need for furnishing them has a salutary effect upon him when asking for credit, and such references also aid in tracing a debtor if he should skip.

Needless to say, all references should be consulted by telephone, wire, or letter without delay. Unfortunately, many investigators do not always do this, with the result that applicants learn that references have not been checked and therefore feel that they are unimportant.

RETAIL CREDIT BUREAUS[1]

The most important source of consumer credit information is the retail credit bureau, an institution developed mainly since the beginning of the twentieth century and primarily for the exchange of ledger information among associated creditors.

Rise and growth of retail credit bureaus. Prior to the turn of the present century, communities were smaller, consumers were better known, strangers rarely approached a merchant with a request for credit, and the bulk of retail business was conducted on a cash basis. The custom of trading in one place further aided in the effective maintenance

---

[1] In the preparation of the revised material for this part of the chapter, valuable assistance was given by some of the headquarters staff of the Associated Credit Bureaus of America and by William B. Price of the Credit Bureau of Columbus, Inc., which is gratefully acknowledged by the authors.

of direct and personal contact between merchants and patrons. Under these circumstances, the granting of credit on the basis of meager information then available might have been satisfactory. But conditions changed: towns and cities grew, population shifted, credit was asked for more freely, customers shopped around more, and the size of retail establishments increased.

Because of these changed conditions, it was impractical for merchants to rely upon personal knowledge for credit decisions. They then sought information about other charge accounts of the credit applicants, who did not always list all the stores from which they bought on credit. Moreover, applicants sometimes gave only the names of stores where their accounts were in good standing. Consequently, it became increasingly necessary for some comprehensive, impartial source of information to be established.

The remedy was found in the formation of credit bureau organizations, through which creditors exchanged information concerning their common customers. The first credit bureau was organized in Brooklyn in 1860. By 1906 there were 30 such bureaus, and in 1967, 2,200 of them. To facilitate interchange of information among bureaus as well as among members, in 1906 there was formed the Associated Credit Bureaus of America, Inc., an affiliate of the International Consumer Credit Association. Today, more than 100 million reports are written annually by the bureaus. Another affiliate organization is the Credit Bureau Reports, Inc., which was formed as an aid in providing a report service to national distributors who use the services of many credit bureaus. Mail order houses and gasoline companies, for example, may thus obtain one monthly bill for the hundreds of reports obtained from scores of widely scattered credit bureaus.

Organization. In general, credit bureaus specializing in consumer credit information are of two major types: those that are privately owned and operated and those that are mutually owned, controlled, and operated. The latter type may be in the form of a legal corporation, or a department of such an organization as a retail merchants association or a chamber of commerce. Most of these mutually owned bureaus are strictly cooperative, nonprofit, mutual benefit associations, operated solely for the convenience and protection of their members. Some of them set up specialized services for their membership, as illustrated by the Medical Credit Bureaus and by the Small Loan Exchanges or the Lenders' Exchange Bureaus.

The actual conduct of the business in all the bureaus is entrusted to a salaried official designated as "manager" or "executive secretary," who is elected annually by the board of directors. The relations of the members to each other and to the organization are governed by bylaws and by the contract entered into when a member joins the association. The contract usually outlines the means by which the member is expected to cooperate with the bureau and lists the services the association purports to render the member.

Practically all bureaus charge a regular annual fee, which entitles the member to all services of the organization and a stipulated number of inquiries for investigations of customers' records. All or a large part of the fee is credited to the member's account for services rendered at the scheduled rates per report. Reports are then charged at the stated rate, depending upon the type. Some bureaus base their charges on a sliding scale, the charge per report being reduced as the number of inquiries increases.

Contracts usually provide for one of three bases for charges: first, the "flat" charge for unlimited service on a monthly or annual basis; second, a flat charge for limited service to be rendered during a given period; third, the "metered" charge, according to which members pay for the service received at established rates per report. In smaller cities the tendency seems to be to retain the older method of charging flat fees, but in larger cities the trend has been toward the use of metered charges.

Method of operation. According to the terms of his contract, each member, upon joining the bureau, furnishes a complete list of his customers, giving for each the name, spouse, residence, former address, occupation, business address, and type of account. The new member also states his own experience with the customers in terms of date the account was opened, highest credit extended, and general remarks. Thereafter, similar facts are submitted for all new or reopened accounts. To the information thus obtained, the bureau adds facts gathered from publications, court records, and other sources carrying news about consumers.

The knowledge about customers thus acquired is then supplied to members upon request. Its transmission is effected by telephone, teletype, telautograph, mail, or messenger. Speed, accuracy, and completeness are the governing factors.

The heart of the bureau's records is what is technically known as the Master Card. On this is recorded the ledger experience normally gathered from members, particularly the length of time that the account has been outstanding and the amount due. Loose items such as clippings, reports, letters, arrests, public records, and the like also become part of an individual's credit record.

Services rendered by credit bureaus. The information assembled by the credit bureaus is disseminated in a variety of forms to meet the particular needs of members. It is presented in the form of reports, bulletins, ratings, and special services.

Reports. Reports constitute the principal service of the bureaus. They are made both orally and in writing, immediately or after necessary investigation, from strictly local sources or from out-of-town correspondents. The prices of the reports vary with their type and with the work involved in their preparation.

The basis of all reports is in the information on the Master Card. This alone is sufficient in many instances. The reading of ledger experience from this card and other data attached thereto over the telephone constitutes what is commonly termed an In-File oral report. It is the least expensive, costing as little as 60 or 75 cents to the volume user and $1 to other users, for it involves no particular investigation unless the trade experience is deemed to be too old, i.e., more than 6 months old.

Often a member desires to have a written copy of all the pertinent information on file with the credit bureau. This is known as a Full report. Credit bureaus throughout the country have adopted for this report, and most other written reports, the standardized credit-reporting form shown in Fig. 6-2. For a Full report the charge is usually $4.50; it is $5.00 if the information must be obtained from an out-of-town bureau.

In the "credit history" section of all written reports, credit bureaus now use an alphabetical-numerical code system, referred to as the "common language," to inform users about paying habits of their customers or applicants for credit service. This new system, adopted in 1966, consists of three symbols, two letter and one numerical, as shown in Fig. 6-3. The first letter is used to represent the "kind of business" which has reported ledger experience with the customer. The business classifications for which letter codes have been devised are those that most frequently report on ledger experience to the bureaus. The initial letter of each kind of business and the code letter are the same in most cases.

The second letter symbol pertains to the "terms of sale" or different types of consumer credit accounts. Open accounts are designated "O," "R" represents revolving accounts, and the designation "I" is used for instalment accounts. Any accounts which do not fit the classification O, R, or I are spelled out in detail. If the exact terms of sale are known, they are also summarized, showing length of the contract and amount of monthly payment. The third symbol is that of a

NAME AND ADDRESS OF CREDIT BUREAU MAKING REPORT

	SUMMARY REPORT	SINGLE REFERENCE	TRADE REPORT

CREDIT BUREAU OF COLUMBUS, INC.
170 East Town Street, Columbus, Ohio 43215
Telephone: 461-8400

	SHORT REPORT	[X] FULL REPORT	PREV. RES. REPORT

DATE RECEIVED	DATE MAILED	CBR REPORT NO.
8/15/67	8/16/67	--

DATE TRADE / CLEARED	DATE EMPLOY VERIFIED	INCOME VERIFIED
8/16/67	8/16/67	[X] YES [ ] NO

CONFIDENTIAL **Factbilt®** REPORT   FOR

IN FILE SINCE: 1957

This information is furnished in response to an inquiry for the purpose of evaluating credit risks. It has been obtained from sources deemed reliable, the accuracy of which this organization does not guarantee. The inquirer has agreed to indemnify the reporting bureau for any damage arising from misuse of this information, and this report is furnished in reliance upon that indemnity. It must be held in strict confidence, and must not be revealed to the subject reported on.

REPORT ON (SURNAME):	MR.,MRS.,MISS:	GIVEN NAME:		SOCIAL SECURITY NUMBER:	SPOUSE'S NAME:
DOE	Mr.	John Elwood		--	Lynn

ADDRESS:	CITY:	STATE:	ZIP CODE:	SPOUSE'S SOCIAL SECURITY NO.:
952 Plaza Place	Columbus	Ohio	43224	--

COMPLETE TO HERE FOR TRADE REPORT AND SKIP TO CREDIT HISTORY

PRESENT EMPLOYER AND KIND OF BUSINESS:	POSITION HELD:	SINCE:	MONTHLY INCOME:
Telephone Company-- Utility	foreman	1957	$ 667.

COMPLETE TO HERE FOR SHORT REPORT AND SUMMARY REPORT AND SKIP TO CREDIT HISTORY

DATE OF BIRTH:			
1926	NUMBER OF DEPENDENTS INCLUDING SPOUSE → 3	[X] OWNS OR BUYING HOME	[ ] RENTS HOME

FORMER ADDRESS:	CITY:	STATE:	FROM:	TO:
255 Forest Avenue	Dayton	Ohio	1926	1957

FORMER EMPLOYER AND KIND OF BUSINESS:	POSITION HELD:	FROM:	TO:	MONTHLY INCOME:
--	--	-	-	$ --

SPOUSE'S EMPLOYER AND KIND OF BUSINESS:	POSITION HELD:	SINCE:	MONTHLY INCOME:
Farm Bureau -- as stated	typist	1966	$ 290

CREDIT HISTORY *(Complete this section for all reports)*

KIND OF BUSINESS	DATE ACCOUNT OPENED	DATE OF LAST SALE	HIGHEST CREDIT	AMOUNT OWING	AMOUNT PAST DUE	TERMS OF SALE AND USUAL MANNER OF PAYMENT
D	5/59	7/67	450	129	00	R-1
F	6/66	6/66	1899	275	00	I$52-1
F	2/65	6/66	3890	3000	216	I$108-3
						prev I-1
F	2/66	4/66	1200	650	00	I$50-1
	also	2/66	2500	1035	00	I$69-1
D	10/65	--	49	00	00	O-2
O	records not local					
B	2/61	12/62	1200	00	00	I$32-2
						prev I-1

Real Estate Mortgage filed 4/1963 to Mortgage Company, amount $12,000.00 terms of $90.00 per month, balance of $9,950.00 property located at given address, open and prompt.
B   satisfactory checking and savings accounts.

PUBLIC RECORD AND/OR SUMMARY OF OTHER TRADE INFORMATION:
Collection 5/63, Oil Company for $39.00 Paid 6/63.
Collection 12/62, Department Store for $200.00 Paid 4/63.

Suit 9/1963 Central Finance Company vs subject; cognovit amount $329.22 paid 12/1963.

AFFILIATED WITH

Form 100   *Associated Credit Bureaus of America, Inc.*   *Credit Bureau Reports, Inc.*   Printed in U.S.A.

figure 6-2. *Full report prepared by a retail credit bureau. All identifying facts and other information are purely fictitious.*

pay rating, a number ranging from 0 to 9, indicating the customer's "usual manner of payment" on all the different types of accounts. Each classification is mutually exclusive, with enough classification numbers to cover completely the reporting needs of both bureaus and users. To illustrate the use of this common language, the first line under the "credit

A NEW LANGUAGE FOR CONSUMER CREDIT

We Agree

Credit granters and credit bureaus agree on the need for a common language—the same symbols should mean the same things throughout the consumer credit industry.

Through Research

These standardized abbreviations and terms have been developed through careful research. Representatives of major credit granting industries and credit bureau representatives consulted with each other to work out the best possible method of communicating precise information.

Let's Use Them

The new terms and abbreviations have been adopted. Now they must be put to use by everyone concerned.

It's So Simple

The new language is simple, and easy to learn. It is important that it be adopted as quickly and completely as possible.

KIND OF BUSINESS CLASSIFICATION

CODE	KIND OF BUSINESS
A	AUTOMOTIVE
B	BANKS
C	CLOTHING
D	DEPARTMENT AND VARIETY
F	FINANCE
G	GROCERIES
H	HOME FURNISHINGS
I	INSURANCE
J	JEWELRY AND CAMERAS
K	CONTRACTORS
L	LUMBER, BUILDING MATERIAL, HARDWARE
M	MEDICAL AND RELATED HEALTH
O	OIL AND NATIONAL CREDIT CARD COMPANIES
P	PERSONAL SERVICES OTHER THAN MEDICAL
R	REAL ESTATE AND PUBLIC ACCOMMODATIONS
S	SPORTING GOODS
T	FARM AND GARDEN SUPPLIES
U	UTILITIES AND FUEL
V	GOVERNMENT
W	WHOLESALE
X	ADVERTISING
Y	COLLECTION SERVICES
Z	MISCELLANEOUS

TERMS OF SALE AND USUAL MANNER OF PAYMENT

USUAL MANNER OF PAYMENT	SYMBOL
Open Account, 30 Day Account, 90 Day Account = 0	
Too new to rate; approved but not used	0-0
Pays (or paid) within 30 days of billing; pays 90 day accounts as agreed	0-1
Pays (or paid) in more than 30 days, but not more than 60 days	0-2
Pays (or paid) in more than 60 days, but not more than 90 days	0-3
Pays (or paid) in more than 90 days, but not more than 120 days	0-4
Pays (or paid) in 120 days or more	0-5
Bad debt; placed for collection; suit; judgment; bankrupt; skip	0-9
Revolving or Option Account = R or R$___*	
Too new to rate; approved but not used	R-0
Pays (or paid) according to the terms agreed upon	R-1
Not paying (or paid) as agreed, but not more than one payment past due	R-2
Not paying (or paid) as agreed, and two payments past due	R-3
Not paying (or paid) as agreed, and three or more payments past due	R-4
Bad debt; placed for collection; suit; judgment; bankrupt; skip	R-9
Instalment Account = I or I$___*	
Too new to rate; approved but not used	I-0
Pays (or paid) according to terms agreed upon	I-1
Not paying (or paid) as agreed, but not more than one payment past due	I-2
Not paying (or paid) as agreed, and two payments past due	I-3
Not paying (or paid) as agreed, and three or more payments past due	I-4
Repossession	I-8
Bad debt; placed for collection; suit; judgment; bankrupt; skip	I-9

*Where the monthly payment is known, it should be shown as in the following examples: R$20   I$78

figure 6-3. *Explanation of common language used by credit bureaus for consumer credit reporting.*

history" section of the report on John Elwood Doe shown in Fig. 6-2 has the following meaning: D, department and variety store; account opened, May, 1959; date of last sale, July, 1967; highest credit, $450; amount owing, $129; amount past due, $0; R-1, revolving account which is paid as agreed.

Except for credit bureaus in very small towns where the Master Card is normally revised every 6 months, such card is revised upon request of a member or subscriber. The ledger experience portion of the card alone may be revised, or the entire record, including verification of employment, marital status, and the like, may be refreshed. The former supplementation of the available data, when presented orally and usually within 2 hours, is known as an Up-to-Date oral report, for which the charge is the same as for an In-File oral report; the fuller investigation is called the Revised report and takes from 1 to 2 days unless a Rush Telephone or Rush Written report is requested by a member who thus assumes the extra communications charge.

Bureaus also prepare what are termed Indebtedness or Collection Aid reports, which contain evidence of a customer's buying activities and his approximate aggregate indebtedness as of a given time.   Upon receipt of a request for this information, the bureau makes inquiry of each of the member stores known to sell to the customer and asks for the amounts owing at that time.

Also upon request of a member, the bureau will trace missing debtors known as "skips" and issue Tracer reports, containing a summarized statement of the action taken and the results obtained.

Some bureaus furnish also Real Estate reports, compiled by special agents from real estate records in the county recorder's office.   They contain the name of the subject about whom inquiry has been made, street, original lot, sublot, foot frontage, ownership, tax value, mortgage and mortgage holder, amount, date, second mortgage and holder, amount, date, and additional comments of the reporter.   The purpose of such report is to check on the statement made in the application form concerning properties owned by the applicant.   When the merchandise is to be affixed to the home such information becomes indispensable. Another way in which this information is made available by the association is by keeping a plat of all the additions and subdivisions of the city, together with the names of the owners of property.   The record is kept up to date by rechecking daily with the real estate transfers as reported in the local legal journal.   All bureaus furnish what are called "property checks" at a cost of $1 per report, and these in a sense are modified Real Estate reports.

Credit guides. About 100 of the credit bureaus publish a credit guide, formerly known as rating books, giving in a highly condensed fashion a few main facts upon which a credit decision may tentatively be made.   Depending upon the size of the community and its retail trading area, such a book, often also called a "Blue Book" or a "Red Book," may contain listings for 10,000 to more than 300,000 names. Because of its limited circulation, which seldom exceeds 1,500 books in use at any given time, a retail credit bureau does not publish a credit guide more often than once a year.   To keep the information therein contained up to date, periodic supplements or revised sections are issued to all subscribers.

Credit guides usually contain for each listed name the following information: the full name and that of the wife, if married; occupation; residence of the individual rated; marital status such as widowed, etc.; and the rating. The rating itself may consist of a single symbol such as a number or letter. For example, in one type of rating book the rating 3 may be translated (according to its key) to mean that the individual thus rated is presumed to be good for $100 to $200 at several places on 30-day charge accounts, that he has a good income, and that he has always taken care of his personal accounts.

In most cases, however, the ratings are intended merely to show how the listed and rated persons have been meeting their obligations, without the bureau's passing judgment as to adequacy of income and overall manner of payment. In these cases ratings are expressed by symbols which indicate whether or not, and to what extent possibly, the person under consideration is entitled to credit accommodation, based upon the experiences of other creditors with the risk as contained in the rating symbols. Under such a system, for example, P may indicate prompt pay, S slow pay but good risk, and another type of symbol, say X, may indicate a poor risk or one that cannot be recommended for credit. It is also customary to indicate the number of merchants effectively consulted concerning any given name appearing in the book. For example, X4 would show that the individual cannot be recommended for credit by four or more merchants. P4 S3 means that the individual is reported as prompt pay by four or more merchants and three merchants report him as slow pay. The rule ordinarily followed is to extend credit rather freely when prompt pay predominates and to require cash or security when one or both of the other ratings predominate. It may be observed in this connection that, where names have carried several good reports and only one unfavorable, the latter is not generally published, but placed in the file record at the office and is published only in case an additional unfavorable report is received at a later date.

Credit guides usually contain the names of current buyers on credit only. They do not as a rule include names of transients, minors residing with parents, cash buyers, and persons concerning whom information is limited or conflicting. Neither do rating codes include the names of those individuals whose credit standing is so superior that no one has made any inquiries concerning them.

Special bulletins. Special bulletins are issued to all members, monthly, semimonthly, weekly, or at even more frequent intervals. All items of interest are contained therein, such as accounts of bad check passers operating in the city and other communities; information furnished by members regarding bad accounts on their books; notices of nonresponsibility for debts given out by husbands; new firms; changes of address; names and accounts of counterfeiters of currency, traveler's checks, etc. Some bureaus do not issue bulletins at stated intervals but put one out whenever there is something new or of special interest to the members at large. It is argued that, in the absence of regular intervals at which bulletins are to be issued, more interest is displayed by members, for they know that whenever the bulletin does come out there is something of special interest.

Derogatory information. The bureau keeps its members informed of happenings to an account in which they are interested. Thus, information concerning unusual activity in opening new accounts, buying unusually heavy on any one account, or when an imposter is buying on an account is automatically broadcast to all members interested. The bureau serves as a receiving station for all sorts of credit information. The organization usually has a working agreement with the post office department and sometimes with the express companies whereby the names of forgers, passers of "bad paper," and other suspicious individuals are reported to the association. Again, reports pour into the office daily, from members, of short and bad checks received. As rapidly as this information is received by the association, it is flashed by telephone to the stores likely to be interested in the names in question.

The bureau may furnish a service of supplying to the members daily, usually by telephone, of the names of individuals who were refused credit or whose accounts were closed by other members, and the reasons for such action. This is sometimes called "automatic notification service." Other information which is generally considered detrimental or derogatory, and, consequently, passed on to members whose codes appear on the Master Card, consists of suits for debts, assignments, collection accounts, mortgages, and the like. Finally, the members of the association are notified of the presence of short or bad check "artists" in the city, as soon as their presence becomes known to the bureau.

Periodic meetings. Monthly or weekly meetings of members of the credit bureau are held for the discussion of credit problems and the interchange of credit information. At these meetings demonstrations are given of methods of opening and closing accounts, and discussions are entered into relating to delinquent accounts, credit and collection policies, and similar matters.

Cooperation with detective agency. Whenever possible, the association supplies information to the detective agency employed by the retail merchants so as to facilitate in apprehending shoplifters who prey upon the big stores. In return, the detectives are frequently in a position to supply the association with useful information concerning such individuals likely to approach merchant members for credit.

Collection service. Most retail credit bureaus operate a collection department, as the information in its credit files helps considerably in the collection of accounts and, conversely, the collection phase of the work aids the credit-reporting task. In addition, most bureaus have letter systems, sometimes called Precollection Systems, that are sold to members. Each letter has a space at the top for inserting the delinquent's name and address, and space in the body for the name of the firm and amount due. These letters contain the bureau's letterheads and have an undoubted psychological advantage on the debtor's mind over letters sent directly by a single creditor. Because more elaborate treatment of this phase of credit work is reserved to another portion of the book, it will suffice to add here that the development of collection service by credit bureaus is largely an outgrowth of indebtedness reports which they are called upon to render. Credit grantors have found that they save time and money by referring the accounts to a collection service after other methods have failed.

Miscellaneous services. Retail credit bureaus render a number of other services which vary from bureau to bureau. They often furnish the member stores with special inserts to be used as direct mail pieces. Rubber stamps are sometimes supplied and other collection aids. Some bureaus prepare detailed personnel reports in order to unearth intimate but essential facts concerning people who are employed in a strictly fiduciary capacity or who may be required to handle large sums of money. Some bureaus make a special effort to assist debtors to reestablish their credit and to build better customer credit relations with member stores. A few bureaus publish monthly the collection percentages, classified by type of store. Others have a so-called "watch service," under which they issue warnings concerning an individual or send out notices that valuable information regarding a risk, in which the member is interested, has been received and suggest that a report on the subject be asked for. Still others conduct newspaper and billboard advertising campaigns designed to stimulate payment of bills on time, and keep members informed of favorable and unfavorable legislation pending and enacted.

Automation in credit bureaus. While credit bureaus have used electronic equipment for some years, many now contemplate the adoption of "on-line" computer systems to provide instantaneous reports to credit grantors. To aid credit bureaus in computerizing their credit reporting, the Associated Credit Bureaus of America, Inc., which is an international trade association of more than 4,300 credit bureaus and collection service offices, in cooperation with the Credit Bureau of Greater Houston, Credit Bureau Services of Dallas, and IBM Corporation, undertook a project study designed to develop an on-line computer credit-reporting system for use as a standard "package" by member credit bureaus.   In late 1967, the final testing phase of this pilot study began with the Dallas bureau operating both a complete manual service and, at the same time, a fully computerized credit bureau, thus enabling project officials to examine all aspects of the system.   When the computer package is completely operational, Credit Bureau Services of Dallas and the Credit Bureau of Greater Houston, scheduled to begin testing the same system in early 1968, will permit credit grantors to make direct inquiry into credit bureau files through the use of on-line terminals placed in the bureaus and in grantors' offices.

Acceptance of the standard computer system by most credit bureaus, which is the goal of the Associated Credit Bureaus of America, Inc., would result in reduced cost of obtaining information for both credit grantors and credit bureaus, increased efficiency in file maintenance, improved file security through information storage in computers, and greater accuracy and standardization in credit reporting.   It would also lead to a nationwide network of credit-reporting computers, giving credit grantors instant access to any consumer credit file in the nation from any other point in the nation.

Advantages of retail credit bureaus. The importance of these bureaus and their advantages to the members may be summed up in the following statement made by a writer on the subject:

> The . . . bureau is to the retail credit grantor what the clearing house is to the banks. It is a pivot around which retail credit business may circulate with reasonable safety; it is a clinic for the chronic credit abuser; it is the pulse of the retail charge business. It is a beacon light on an uncharted sea; a nucleus for a credit men's organization and for the promotion of a credit man's welfare. It is an educational center for disseminating among the public such propaganda as will aid a credit man's work.

Further proof of the advantages that accrue to members through the use of retail credit bureaus is afforded by various studies of the subject, which show that a larger percentage of the retailers is now using credit bureau service and that stores which use such service suffer fewer bad debt losses than those operating in the same field which have not taken advantage of it.   For these reasons it is considered good policy for a member to ask for a regular report on every applicant for credit and for an old customer when he becomes delinquent, when he suddenly increases his purchases, when information received from the bureau shows that he is opening many accounts at other stores, when unfavorable information is obtained from court records or the bureau, or when he starts buying again after the account has been dormant for some time.   Special reports should be called for as the occasion may require.

On the whole, there is a high degree of uniformity both in the method of operation and in the kind of service rendered, regardless of size of community, so long as the bureaus are affiliated with the same national organization.   In 1933 the National Retail Credit Association attempted to secure such uniformity when credit bureaus were part of that association by assigning exclusive territories to member bureaus and stipulating that reports were to be made available to members only. Against these latter practices the Attorney General of the United States issued a complaint which resulted in a consent decree by the association. Thus it is no longer possible for credit grantors to refuse to furnish information to any nonmember credit agency by virtue of a contract to that effect with the member bureau, although each store may of its free will refuse to give such information just as any merchant may on his own refuse to sell to a certain customer.

It is possible that as a result of this decree there may be somewhat less progress toward uniformity, which may be in some respects highly desirable.   It seems that retail credit bureaus act altogether too much like relay agencies and do too little independent work of a constructive nature.   There is no reason, for example, why some of the larger bureaus should not utilize the wealth of information on their master cards for studies that would lead to the establishment of credit limits on a more scientific basis than at present.   With the mathematical and statistical methods at their disposal such credit limits could be computed for each income group with gradient percentages for various influences such as size of the family, special expenditures, and the like.   Certainly, the national organization, through its members, would do well by means of bulletins or other publications to acquaint the public with the credit-granting system that has been developed in this country for effective service, as a basis for a better understanding between retailer and consumer.

SPECIALIZED CREDIT
BUREAUS AND
CREDIT-REPORTING
AGENCIES

Retail credit bureaus, whether privately or mutually owned and operated, are but one type, though the major one, of credit bureaus specializing in consumer credit information.   In addition there are credit bureaus of a specialized or particularized nature providing information and other service about customers or clients to a particular kind of business, line of trade, or profession.   There are also some credit-reporting agencies which operate in a substantially different manner from that described for the bureaus.

Medical credit bureaus. One of such specialized bureaus is the Medical Credit Bureau, whose dual purpose is to collect overdue accounts and to render a credit-reporting service which prevents delinquents from abusing the confidence of doctors and dentists.   For some time the medical profession has suffered from the unbusinesslike conduct of its practitioners, which resulted in tremendous losses from bad debts.   It is believed that the medical man's book accounts decrease in value faster than those of other types of accounts, partly because after he is cured the patient loses the desire to pay and partly because there is no material reminder of the debt in the form of goods that may be repossessed.   The physician himself, who is often more interested in the professional phase of the work than in its business aspect, is largely to blame for this condition.   Because of this, an attempt has been made to urge physicians and dentists to utilize the services of retail credit bureaus.   In some cities, however, they saw fit to establish their own bureaus whose offices are usually connected with the local academy of medicine and whose method of reporting and collecting can be dictated or controlled by the profession itself.   Among the earlier bureaus of this type is the Toledo Physicians and Dentists Credit Association.

Late in 1933 managers of a group of such bureaus operating in the Middle West organized what is now the Medical-Dental-Hospital Bureau of America, with main offices in Chicago, Ill.   The association acts as a clearinghouse of service and management ideas that tend to lead to the development and adoption of a uniform plan of operation for medical and dental bureaus.

Lenders' exchanges and other bureaus. In a number of cities companies making small cash loans to consumers have established what are commonly known as "lenders' exchanges" or "small-loan exchange bureaus," through which subscribing members obtain the necessary information for guidance in making both loans and collections.   It is the basic function of the exchange or bureau to keep track of all loans made by member companies, generally operating very much, though in much more abbreviated fashion, like retail credit bureaus and confining the information to loan experiences of members.

In some cases furniture stores and others dealing heavily in instalment sales have organized offices to provide them with credit information on their particular types of risks.   Coal dealers have at times followed a similar practice, as have home rental agencies and others who may be interested in a special kind of information about consumers.

Credit-reporting agencies. In addition to what are generally known as "retail" or "consumer credit bureaus," there are a number of privately owned and operated organizations or agencies specializing in consumer credit information. Most of them are small and are intended to serve primarily the smaller stores and miscellaneous types of creditors like insurance companies, real estate companies, lawyers, and others who may be interested in special kinds of information rather than in ledger experience alone.   Some of these agencies may be operating on a very large scale, as illustrated below.

Retail Credit Company. One of the largest of the independently owned credit-reporting agencies is the Retail Credit Company, of Atlanta, Georgia.[2]   Since 1899, this organization has gathered and disseminated credit information on an international basis, specializing in supplying information on individuals for insurance purposes.   The services of the company, however, are used not only by insurance companies but also by commercial concerns in connection with the consideration of claims, the extension of credit, and the selection of employees and representatives.   The home office of the organization is in Atlanta, but there are many branch offices and a much larger number of direct reporting stations maintained in cities other than those in which branches are located; in all of its activities more than 4,500 persons are employed on a full-time basis.   In the various branch offices, files on an estimated 22 million persons are maintained, containing both current-reports and older information of unusual value, as well as clippings from various sources and publications, and records from numerous governmental offices.

All the reports furnished by this company are intended to supply information necessary for making credit decisions, but because of the specialized needs in certain trades and for different kinds of risks, a variety of report forms have been developed.   Commonly used is the character credit report on an individual similar to that used by many retail credit bureaus and agencies.   Slight adaptations of this form are used for reporting similar information on farmers and small firms.   Other special report forms are used in connection with credit cards issued

[2] For an interesting account of the development of this company's function and its adaptation to changed conditions and emerging opportunities, see "History of Retail Credit Company," by William A. Flinn, an unpublished doctoral dissertation prepared under the general supervision of the senior author of this book, 1959.

by petroleum companies, small mail order credit accounts for wage earners, financing of automobile and truck purchases by consumers and dealers, delinquencies on instalment payments, disappearance of debtors, property checking, and employment of salesmen, office, factory, and executive personnel.   Unlike most credit-reporting agencies, the mainstay of this organization does not lie in rating books but in credit reports.

Credit Data Corporation. One of the newest consumer credit-reporting companies is Credit Data Corporation, an "electronic credit rating service," which in 1967 operated from two computer-center locations.   The one in Los Angeles began operations in 1965, with a San Francisco satellite added in 1967 by linking to the Los Angeles computer, servicing the state of California and contemplating an extension of the service area to cover the West Coast and some adjoining states.   A second center was opened in 1967 in New York to serve the metropolitan area of that city, with plans to extend the service through much of the Eastern Seaboard.   In addition, Credit Data Corporation plans to establish other regional centers, starting with Detroit, that would enable it ultimately to extend its operations throughout the nation.

From its computer centers, Credit Data provides subscribers (finance companies, retailers, banks, oil companies, and other types of consumer credit grantors) information that has been gathered and stored in its computerized central credit files, charging them about 50 cents an inquiry, on condition that they will contribute their records of historical and ongoing credit experience.   Subscribers use local, toll-free telephone service to obtain on-line credit reports.   Their calls are automatically routed by foreign exchange lines to the appropriate computer center. Credit Data operators retrieve the credit records from the computer and relay them to the subscriber, who has an oral report on an individual risk within 90 seconds.   On multiple inquiries, the average time for an oral report on each risk is reduced to 60 seconds.   When written reports, known as hard copy, are preferred, Credit Data provides them for an additional charge through its overnight delivery service.   Data in these reports include both positive information, i.e., an individual's current and past satisfactory credit transactions, and negative information, such as the fact that the individual has defaulted on a particular obligation.

Upon subscription for the service, a consumer credit grantor agrees to open his files to Credit Data Corporation, which uses portable microfilming equipment to obtain the credit information from ledger cards, file folders, and other records in the subscriber's office.   These data are later converted for entry into a computer.   Supplementary, up-to-date information to Credit Data is sent on magnetic tapes or punched cards by subscribers with computer operations and by others through the use of their own internal forms or special forms furnished by Credit Data. The central file is also augmented with information about bankruptcies, suits, judgments, liens, and other pertinent information gathered by Credit Data from public records.

As in all computerized credit service, files are safe through controlled access, data can be accepted from subscribers' EDP systems, responses are speedier than via manual systems, and costs of the service tend to be lower. Credit Data may also have an advantage of wide area coverage and of a wider variety of subscribers, especially banks, and thus make available a more complete record. It may suffer, however, from its more limited ability, compared to credit bureaus, to provide customized service, maintain intimate local contacts, and furnish such auxiliary services as involved in the collection of accounts. Finally, computerized credit service, unless strictly used only for credit purposes and in a most confidential manner, allegedly threatens an invasion of privacy generally deemed socially detrimental.

Other credit-reporting agencies. As consumer credit information became more and more important and the variety in both its users and the uses made of the information increased, a number of mercantile agencies have entered or expanded their activity in the field of consumer credit information. This is illustrated by the activity of Dun & Bradstreet, Inc., in the field of consumer credit reporting, even though it is known as "The Mercantile Agency" and specializes in information on mercantile and commercial bank credit. Since, however, this service constitutes but a small part of the company's reporting work, the organization cannot be regarded as a retail credit-reporting agency in the true sense of the term.

BANKS AS A
SOURCE OF RETAIL
CREDIT INFORMATION

Banks as a source of information. Although the banker's work lies in the province of financial transactions only, he is nevertheless, in a sense, classed as a retail credit grantor. He operates on the basis of the principles laid down for retail credit grantors every time he makes a loan on an unsecured note, with chief reliance on the borrower's financial and moral responsibility; hence the interest of the banker in the manner in which his borrowing accounts meet their obligations elsewhere. In order to obtain the required data from retailers, bankers find it necessary to reciprocate.

Methods of securing information from banks. Retailers acquire information from banks indirectly through the medium of retail credit bureaus. They also obtain data directly from banks, particularly those located in smaller communities. Such information from banks may be obtained by retail merchants by telephone or telegram, by messenger, or by mail.

Telephone inquiries are at best unsatisfactory, as judged by results obtained. This method usually involves a serious waste of time, due to the necessity for confirming the inquiry, unless the inquirer's voice is recognized by the person answering the telephone at the bank. In order to insure that the proper person obtains the information, both parties hang up the receiver and connections are reversed. Because of this, it is recommended that telephone inquiries be used sparingly and with a view of obtaining data which can be given with little delay. To secure data from out-of-town banks, inquiries are occasionally made by telegram.

It is customary for large stores in many cities to make inquiries through messengers or runners. These investigators make regularly scheduled trips to the banks from which data are sought. All special cases requiring immediate consideration are looked up at once. All other names on which information is desired are listed alphabetically and handed to the bank's reference clerk, whose function it is to furnish the data on names on file and have the replies ready when the messenger makes his next trip. Obviously, the better qualified the investigator, the higher the quality of information which he is likely to secure.

Inquiries by mail should be reserved for emergencies, or cases where more detailed information of a highly confidential nature is desired. The right sort of an inquiry personally directed to an officer of the bank and signed by the credit manager ordinarily brings the right sort of reply, showing the size of average bank balance, whether the prospective customer honors his notes when due, whether he overdraws his account, or makes unjust claims respecting his balances, and the like.

QUESTIONS AND PROBLEMS

1 List all the possible sources available to credit managers of retail stores in obtaining information about customers and prospects. Which are the most significant? Who is interested in this information besides retailers?

2 Point out the significance of the personal interview in retail credit granting. What kinds of information can thus be obtained?

3 Should an attempt be made to ascertain the applicant's salary during the personal interview? His instalment obligations? Give reasons for each of the answers.

4 How do you explain the existence of credit-reporting agencies or bureaus which operate for a profit while retail credit bureaus operate on a nonprofit basis? Why doesn't the latter supersede the former?

5 Prior to 1900, very few credit bureaus operated in the retail field, while today the number of such bureaus is over 2,200. How do you account for this tremendous development of credit bureaus within such a short time?

6 Mrs. Brown has applied for credit at the the X Department Store. What is likely to be the first source of information that will be used?

7 Assuming that a bureau report is wanted on Mrs. Brown, how may it be obtained and what kind of information does it usually contain?

8 Explain the meaning of "common language" as used in a retail credit bureau report.

9 Can you prove that the use of credit bureaus or similar sources of information redounds to the benefit of merchants using them? How?

10 Outline all other services, exclusive of furnishing credit information through various types of reports, which bureaus are prepared to render to the membership. What are the shortcomings of such bureaus?

11 The merchants of Littletown, Mo., have decided to establish a credit bureau. You were chosen to be the manager of the bureau. Indicate how you would proceed in the organization of such a bureau.

12 What use can the government make of retail credit bureau or agency information?

13 Explain the nature and purpose of each of the following organizations: International Consumer Credit Association, Associated Credit Bureaus of America, Credit Bureau Reports, Inc., Retail Credit Company.

14 How do you explain the development of specialized consumer credit bureaus, such as the Medical Credit Bureau?

15 Explain the nature of the operations of Credit Data Corporation. Do you anticipate an increasing need for the type of services provided by this firm?

16 Discuss the advantages to credit bureaus of a fully computerized credit bureau operation.

CHAPTER SEVEN

charge account
and service credit

From existing sources it is not possible to determine for recent years
either the number of retail and service establishments from which goods
and services can be bought by consumers on charge account credit or
the total amount of such business. To be sure, it is common knowledge
that such organizations as R. H. Macy's of New York and the J. C.
Penney Company have departed from their long-standing cash policy and
are now offering their customers charge account service as well as other
credit facilities. The same is true of oil companies and of numerous
service enterprises. At the same time, consonant with the ebb and flow
of economic and social change, some stores like those of the supermarket
or discount-house type have generally adhered strictly to a cash policy.
The tendency, however, has been unmistakably for the charge account
to be used in an increasing variety of merchandising and service establish-

ments, presumably encouraged by the wide use of multiplying so-called "all-purpose credit cards" of the Diners' Club, American Express, Hilton Carte Blanche, BankAmericard, and Eurocard variety.

Magnitude of charge account and service credit business. Direct data are not available for the measurement of the total magnitude of charge account and service *credit business volume* and changes therein. Indirectly, however, this can be determined through the data on *outstandings,* or amounts owed on such credit. Such data are presented in Table 7-1, separately for charge account credit and for service credit as well as in combined form. If it is assumed that the stated terms on such credit are 30 days but that the effective terms comprise on the average 45 days or one-eighth of a year, the total volume of such credit extended in a year can be computed by multiplying the outstandings by 8, assuming again that no charge in the receivables *ratio* has occurred from year to year.

At any rate, it is significant to note that while charge account outstandings in absolute amounts increased from 1947 to 1967 by 238 per cent, in relation to disposable personal income the increase was only 5.4 per cent. Moreover, the ratio of such outstandings to disposable personal income reached a peak in 1953 and since then has tended to decline. Service credit outstandings, on the other hand, increased during the period by 488 per cent in absolute amounts and by 85 per cent in relation to disposable personal income. For the two combined, the absolute amounts increased 319 per cent and the ratio to disposable personal income increased 31 per cent. Again, for the entire period covered by the data the combined outstandings in relation to disposable personal income increased at a rate of less than 1.4 per cent a year, and in the last 15 years the change in this ratio has been in the nature of a slight average decline.

All this relatively small change took place despite the aggressive merchandising of this type of credit by means of the all-purpose credit card to be discussed later and through various other devices. The simplest explanation is that charge account credit is used mainly for convenience, presumably by qualified credit risks who could pay cash if they had to do so; on such accounts a near-saturation point can be easily reached. Another explanation is, again as will be shown later, that there has been a tendency to convert many charge accounts into some form of instalment credit, especially through the device of the Option Charge Account plan and through the straight use of revolving credit. In terms of volume of business done, however, rather than outstandings, the charge account is by far the most important form of consumer short- and intermediate-term credit used.

From insignificant beginnings, the charge account has been ex-

table 7-1 Use of Charge Account and Service Credit, as Measured by Average Outstandings, in Relation to Disposable Personal Income, United States, 1947–1967*

(In millions of dollars)

Year	Disposable personal income (DPI)[1]	Charge account credit		Service credit		Charge account and service credit combined		
		Amount[2]	Per cent of DPI	Amount[2]	Per cent of DPI	Amount[2]	Per cent of DPI	Change in per cent of DPI
1947	169,833	1,882	1.11	905	0.53	2,787	1.64	11.0
1948	189,138	2,182	1.15	1,264	0.67	3,446	1.82	6.6
1949	188,585	2,299	1.22	1,363	0.72	3,662	1.94	6.6
1950	206,940	2,664	1.29	1,510	0.73	4,174	2.02	4.1
1951	226,583	3,042	1.34	1,726	0.76	4,768	2.10	4.0
1952	236,312	3,308	1.40	1,855	0.78	5,163	2.18	3.8
1953	252,564	3,553	1.41	1,921	0.76	5,474	2.17	(0.5)
1954	257,445	3,616	1.40	1,984	0.77	5,600	2.18	0.5
1955	275,348	3,861	1.40	2,094	0.76	5,955	2.16	(0.9)
1956	293,179	4,094	1.40	2,289	0.78	6,383	2.18	0.9
1957	308,524	4,297	1.39	2,506	0.81	6,803	2.21	1.4
1958	318,826	4,252	1.33	2,702	0.85	6,954	2.18	(1.4)

1959†	337,315	1.30	4,378	2,934	0.87	7,312	2.17	(0.5)
1960	350,044	1.28	4,480	3,229	0.92	7,709	2.20	1.4
1961	364,424	1.23	4,490	3,482	0.96	7,972	2.19	(0.5)
1962	385,267	1.19	4,590	3,855	1.00	8,445	2.19	0.0
1963	404,604	1.20	4,859	4,164	1.03	9,023	2.23	1.8
1964	438,096	1.19	5,224	4,493	1.03	9,717	2.22	(0.4)
1965	473,240	1.16	5,475	4,771	1.01	10,246	2.17	(2.3)
1966	511,568	1.17	5,979	5,042	0.99	11,021	2.15	(0.9)
1967	546,347	1.17	6,365	5,322	0.97	11,687	2.14	(0.5)

* When the consumer credit statistics series were revised by the Board of Governors of the Federal Reserve System in 1956, the revision was carried back only through 1948 (see *Federal Reserve Bulletin*, October, 1956, pp. 1031–1054. A later revision carried the changes back to include 1947 but not for service credit (see *Federal Reserve Bulletin*, November, 1959, p. 1416). Consequently, no comparable data are available for years prior to 1947.

† Beginning with 1959 the data include Alaska and Hawaii, and to that extent the magnitude of consumer credit outstandings as compared with previous years is exaggerated.

SOURCES: [1] *Survey of Current Business*, U.S. Department of Commerce, August, 1965, pp. 25 and 33; July, 1968, p. 28.

[2] For the years 1947–1954, annual averages were computed from the monthly data in *Federal Reserve Bulletin*, November, 1959, pp. 1416–1417; for the years 1955–1960, the annual averages were computed from the revised monthly data in *Federal Reserve Bulletin*, December, 1961, p. 1397; for the years 1961–1967, the annual averages were computed from the subsequent March issues of the *Federal Reserve Bulletin* for the respective years.

tended into practically every line of business and to all classes of customers. For some years department stores as a group, in terms of weighted averages, have done about 59 to 60 per cent of their total business on credit,[1] made up in recent years of about 37 per cent of total sales in regular charge account credit and the remaining 23 per cent in instalment and other term-account credit.[2]   The trend, however, has been for the regular charge account part of the credit business, relatively as a percentage of total sales, to decline and for the instalment account, including revolving credit, to increase.

In addition to many types and kinds of stores selling merchandise on charge account credit, such facility is now made available by service establishments such as dry cleaners, laundries, plumbers, electricians, and service garages; by physicians, dentists, lawyers, accountants, and other professional men; by mail order houses; by hotels, airlines, railroads, and restaurants.   It is not surprising, therefore, to find that the great majority of consumer buyers uses charge account credit and tends to use more of it.

On the other hand, it is equally significant that large numbers of our retail stores do *not* sell on credit and that the bulk of all retail store sales is *not* made on credit.   Throughout the evolution of the retailing structure, strong emphasis has been placed at times upon selling for cash only.   Chain stores, supermarkets, and discount houses are perhaps the best examples of stores consciously omitting the traditional charge account.   The same is true of novelty stores, of many specialty stores in the apparel trade, and of variety stores, some of which introduced credit in the late 1950's.

THE DECISION
TO SELL
ON CREDIT

The decision facing any retailer as to whether to sell on open account is a major policy question, for the basic character of an institution is usually determined by this factor.   Such a decision, however, is not always discretionary, for the practices of competitors may often determine whether or not credit in the form of charge accounts shall be made available.   Nevertheless, from an institutional standpoint and to the extent that choice may be exercised, there are a number of cogent arguments for and against the charge account policy.

---

[1] *Financial and Operating Results of Department and Specialty Stores in 1965,* National Retail Merchants Association, Controllers' Congress, July, 1966, p. 3.
[2] *Credit Management Yearbook,* 1964–1965, Vol. 31, pp. 152–162. Published annually by National Retail Merchants Association, Credit Management Division.

Arguments for retail charge accounts. The arguments which are generally made in favor of granting credit through regular charge accounts relate mainly to the amount and kind of business which such accounts stimulate.

Credit increases sales. Credit makes regular customers. Patrons with charge accounts usually give their entire trade in a given line to a limited number of stores. In this regard, one study revealed that charge customers of department and specialty stores also make a substantial number of cash purchases and, therefore, contribute significantly to the *cash* sales volume of the stores in which they have accounts.[3] Credit customers trade regularly in stores with which credit connections have been established, giving them preference and returning repeatedly to buy.[4] Cash customers, on the other hand, are everybody's customers.

Having a charge account is also often an inducement for patrons to buy more freely and perhaps more extravagantly than they otherwise would. The ability to charge purchases alters the sense of value of money, for it is more difficult to part with cash in hand than with funds dispensed at the month's end by check. This leads to credit customers' purchases exceeding on the average those of cash customers. Cash spenders are more inclined to be on the lookout for bargains and generally shop around. The credit customer is inclined to buy where he has an account, taking service as well as the merchandise into account and not quibbling over a small price differential. Some studies carefully conducted in order to ascertain the facts in this connection have revealed that the charge account customer on the average purchases about four times as much as the cash customer from a given store.[5]

Credit attracts better class of trade. Appealing to consumers who desire service, credit attracts not only those who respond to it as

[3] See "How Charge Accounts Affect Cash Sales," *The Credit World*, November, 1964, pp. 18–19.
[4] See Robert D. Breth, "The New Go-Go Era of Charge Account Promotion," *The Credit World*, November, 1965, pp. 13–15.
[5] See also the excellent article by Robert D. Breth, "How Much Is a Charge Account Worth?", *Credit World*, April, 1960, pp. 3-6. Belief in the importance of this type of credit business has given rise to the promotion by some stores of the so-called "Junior" or "Teen-age Charge Account"—a matter of considerable controversy. This type of account is usually of the revolving variety discussed later and is intended to offer young people a lesson in modern living in a credit age, where experience in managing a budget and self-discipline in meeting financial responsibilities are important to the proper use of credit. Opponents would prefer emphasis on thrift and call attention to the cost in using such accounts. It is quite possible that, with the aid of parents, all may stand to benefit from such an experience in the way of education as to the effective use of credit within limits allowed by the income and at a cost that can be justified. The risk involved from the standpoint of the stores is altogether moral, since payment cannot be enforced against minors. See *Credit World*, February, 1961, pp. 8–9.

a mere convenience but also those to whom it has a positive service value. The higher-grade stores featuring quality, style, and other aspects of a full merchandising program offer credit. Those which cut corners on cost, or which wish to appear to be doing so, either offer no credit at all or may substitute instalment credit for the open account.

The quality of a credit grantor's trade is determined in part by the confidence which credit instills. Based upon confidence, credit inspires good will. It facilitates selling because a credit customer knows that returns and adjustments are made more easily if purchases have yet to be paid for. Selling on credit makes for square dealing and honest representation. Buying on credit allays the fears of customers that they have been taken advantage of if merchandise should prove unsatisfactory.

Credit irons out business peaks. Credit makes for a better distribution of a store's business volume. Cash trade tends to peak on certain days, such as Saturdays and preholiday periods, or when wages or salaries are paid and cash is readily available. Credit customers, on the contrary, buy whenever goods are needed, irrespective of their lack of cash at the time. Credit not only evens out business throughout the week and month but, in farming and mining communities, it also provides a means of adjusting regular consumption to seasonal income. Credit also makes possible placement of orders by telephone and permits the delivery of goods in the absence of the purchaser.

Credit may reduce other operating costs. While reducing peaks in business, credit at the same time reduces the costs accompanying irregular business. Larger inventories and more selling personnel are required for a business with sales peaks. Moreover, cash sales, especially when they are in the form of C.O.D., entail special procedures and systems which are costly to maintain. Such business is usually segregated from other cash or credit business.

Arguments against retail charge accounts. Notwithstanding the aforementioned advantages, there are sound reasons why many successful retailers have avoided the adoption of a charge account credit policy. In any event, there are some disadvantages to those who sell on such credit, even though they may be more than offset by the advantages derived therefrom.

Credit increases cost of doing business. There is no question but that selling on credit increases the operating expenses of a store. To carry on a credit business, therefore, a store must be in a position to meet the additional expenses involved and to provide for the investment represented by accounts receivable.

The costs involved in credit are of two types: those which are budgeted directly to the credit department, such as payroll, bad debt loss, investigation services, and supplies; and those which, while they may not be budgeted to the credit department, are nevertheless a cost to the store, such as interest on invested funds, rent, and depreciation of equipment used. As is apparent from the data in Table 7-2, the total *budgeted* cost of operating the credit departments of department stores, expressed as a percentage of net credit sales, ranged from 2.25 to 2.52 per cent in 1963. Inasmuch as the credit sales of stores of this type approximate 60 per cent of their total sales, credit costs may also be stated as being approximately 1.3 to 1.5 per cent of *total net sales*. From other studies it is known that, depending mainly upon size of store and its ratio of credit sales to total sales, credit costs in stores range from less than 1 per cent to about 5 per cent of total sales. From such gross costs, of course, should be deducted the interest charges collected on past-due charge accounts and the service charges yielded by revolving credit and other instalment contracts including option accounts.

By and large, the biggest single item of credit operating cost is that of payroll. It *normally* amounts to about 50 to 60 per cent of total budgeted credit operating expenses. From the data in Table 7-2, however, it is evident that imputed interest on average receivables outstanding may take first place among credit operating costs, ranging from 40 to 46 per cent of total direct credit costs when figured on the basis of 6 per cent interest per annum. The reason for imputed interest taking first rank among operating costs in large department stores is the substantial proportion of the business done on instalment bases. This means that for stores dealing entirely or primarily in charge account credit payroll cost still occupies first position among operating expenses incurred by the credit business.

It is interesting to note that bad debt loss accounts for only about 7 to 15 per cent of credit operating costs, with the cost of postage sometimes being greater than the bad debt loss, particularly in the smaller department stores. The last point is to be explained by the fact that the larger stores have a greater proportion of their business on instalment terms.

Obviously, losses from bad debts vary considerably, depending upon the line of trade, type of customers served, nature of the credit facilities provided, and efficiency of the management. The same is true to some extent of payroll cost incident to credit operation, but this tends to become a larger percentage of total such costs for the smaller stores simply because there are certain irreducible payroll expenses like the salary of a credit manager that must be incurred even by the smaller stores. This is evident from the limited data in Table 7-2.

In appraising the cost of credit granting, the dollars spent in the performance of this function must be weighed against their effect upon the volume of business which the use of credit produces and the profits earned from the additional sales thus made. Merchants operating on a credit basis claim that the expense incident to credit granting is not unlike that incurred in advertising. It is argued that an expense is not an expense in the true sense of the term when the profit attributed to it exceeds the amount thus expended. Another way of stating the matter is that the cost of operating on credit is worthwhile, since it produces results that more than compensate for it.

table 7-2   *Cost of Operating Department Store Credit Departments, as a Percentage of Net Credit Sales, 1963*

	Annual credit sales volume			
Expense item	*$3–$5 million*	*$5–$10 million*	*$10–$20 million*	*Over $20 million*
Payroll cost	1.21	1.28	1.16	1.13
Stationery and supplies	0.13	0.14	0.12	0.10
Postage	0.32	0.39	0.29	0.27
Legal cost	0.11	0.09	0.12	0.11
Credit information	0.14	0.15	0.14	0.13
Net bad debt loss	0.25	0.33	0.48	0.69
Sundry and unclassified	0.09	0.12	0.04	0.09
Total budgeted cost	2.25	2.50	2.35	2.52
Imputed interest at 6%	1.51	1.64	1.97	2.18
Total expense*	3.76	4.14	4.32	4.70

* Reflects direct costs only and does not include such items are rent, light, heat, depreciation, telephone, telegraph, etc.

SOURCE: Adapted from *Credit Management Yearbook*, 1964–1965, Vol. 31, compiled by George P. Samit, National Retail Merchants Association, published annually by its Credit Management Division.

Cash customers pay for bad debts. It is frequently argued that cash customers as well as those who pay their bills promptly are penalized and that they are caused to pay for credit losses.   These classes of customers are charged the same prices as poor-pay customers, and since the prices in a store operating on both a cash and a credit basis are necessarily higher on account of losses from bad debts, the former are penalized and unduly taxed.

On the other hand, cash customers shop around considerably, buy less and in smaller quantities, and in many other ways raise the cost of operation, while credit trade rolls up volume—so essential to economical operation of a retail institution in the buying as well as on the selling end of the business.   Furthermore, the increase of total business which credit selling yields may so reduce the overhead allocable to cash sales that all prices may be lowered as a result.

Credit leads to extravagance and recklessness. Charge accounts undoubtedly induce some people to buy more and to live beyond their means.   Nevertheless, extravagance could be curtailed by proper education regarding the use of a credit system.   Besides, cases abound of wage earners who spend all their weekly income at one time, extravagantly and carelessly, and go without necessities until the following pay day.   Thus, extravagance is not practiced solely by persons purchasing on charge accounts.

Credit ties up capital. Charge accounts require a larger capital investment.   A merchant who wishes to engage in credit granting must possess more capital to secure a given volume of business than a merchant who operates on a cash basis only.   Capital turnover is decreased accordingly, but it is believed that the additional funds are well invested. More trade is secured, and economies from larger scale operation are gained which more than offset the interest cost of the additional investment.

Credit system invites complaints. Many credit customers feel their preferred position and take advantage of it.   More goods are returned, many complaints are registered as a result, and adjustments are asked for.   Some of them act occasionally as if they even owned the store.   In justification of this position, credit stores claim that credit customers, because of their concentration of purchases and savings effected thereby, are entitled to more attention and greater consideration. Besides, most complaints are not unreasonable, and an up-to-date merchant aiming at a maximum of service should welcome them, irrespective of their origin.

FACTORS DETERMINING
CASH OR
CREDIT POLICY

The arguments which may be made for or against the use of charge accounts are but one consideration in the decision a merchant must make regarding the adoption of a credit policy. The wisdom of selling on a charge account basis, as well as the benefits to be derived therefrom, arises from the nature and conditions of the business.

Class of trade. A basic determinant of whether a credit policy should be adopted is the class of trade to be cultivated. A retailer has the choice of emphasizing one or more of three types of appeal: price, quality, or style, in addition, of course, to stressing the reputation and superior service of the store. In choosing the price appeal, a merchant automatically eliminates some of that class of trade which is only secondarily interested in price. Obviously, a store emphasizing price attracts the trade of the lower economic stratum and of the habitual bargain hunters. When emphasis is shifted from price to quality or style, appeal is directed to a class of trade primarily concerned with the appearance or quality of the goods, and only secondarily interested in price. These customers desire services, of which credit extension is one, and are willing to pay for them, provided the additional cost is not unreasonable. Under these circumstances, it is advisable that a merchant meet the demand of the trade which he wishes to attract.

Line of goods. Another factor in determining credit policy is the line of merchandise handled. Goods within lower ranges of price lend themselves more readily to a cash system. While the credit card is occasionally used in connection with vending machines that dispense food and beverages, such use of credit is limited to employees of some large financial or similar institutions equipped with computer facilities whereby the charge to each employee may be readily made and deducted from his compensation at regular intervals. It is still customary to pay cash for relatively small purchases such as those made in supermarkets, although even small purchases may be charged when bought in a store in which a credit account is maintained. Ready cash to pay for substantial purchases is frequently not available, and it is customary to have such purchases charged.

Competitive conditions. A third factor consists of competition. To the extent that consumer goods become standardized and nationally advertised by manufacturers, price competition on the part of retailers is diminished in importance, save when articles are used as loss leaders in featuring bargain sales. The tendency then is for retail dealers to shift the basis of competition from price to service or quality, as in the case of private brands. Credit granting is one of the most important forms of service. Hence, retailers resort to it as a means of meeting competition, especially from chains and other stores granting the credit privilege. The keener the competition in a given community, the more likely are the stores to feature credit service as an attraction.

Community characteristics. Then, too, the character of the community incomes and the habits of the people must not be overlooked. In some parts of the country credit is more freely sought and used than in others as a result of such factors. The same applies to mining and farming communities, where ready cash is scarce between pay days and crops, respectively. In establishing a retail institution, local preferences should be duly considered, thereby avoiding the danger of adopting a policy that would necessitate running against the current.

Size of community. Again, the size of town in which the store is located must be given adequate consideration. In a large city there is always room for a limited number of cash stores even in lines of merchandise where credit is customary, for in them reside sufficient numbers of such people to support a few of these stores properly. In smaller communities cash policies should be adopted only after great hesitancy.

Capital commanded. The capital commanded by the store is a most significant factor in the determination of a cash or credit policy. Concerns with limited financial resources should either be satisfied with a limited volume of sales or else operate on a cash basis, for, to roll up a certain volume of business, more capital is required when trading is done on a credit basis. In addition to merchandise inventories, customers must be carried on the books, thereby tying up more capital in the enterprise.

TYPES OF
OPEN ACCOUNTS

In the extension of retail credit in connection with the sale of merchandise, numerous plans have been devised under the name of the open account. All of them have had the same objective of providing for continuous purchasing on the established credit. Each represents, however, some variation of the need or ability of the merchant to carry the accounts.

The regular charge account. The traditional retail open account is what is commonly known as the 30-day account on which the customer is free to make any number of purchases, provided that the total, when a limit is set on the account, does not exceed such limit. Purchases made during a month are billed monthly. Bills are due upon presentaion, although in practice they are outstanding on an average of from 45 to 60 days, depending upon business conditions. In other words, the terms *taken,* as judged by average of credit sales days outstanding, may be at substantial variance with the so-called "30-day stated terms." No specific charge is made for this form of credit, and the costs of its administration are absorbed in the overall operating expenses of the firm.

Scripbook and deposit accounts. A variation of the regular open, or charge, account is to be found in a plan for providing customers with scrip or coupons which can be exchanged for merchandise within the issuing store.   This plan may be used for the purpose of encouraging sales on the one hand and controlling the limit to which a customer may purchase on credit on the other.   The latter is accomplished by the requirement that the account covered by scrip purchases be paid before additional scrip will be issued.

Sometimes scrip is used in reverse as far as credit is concerned; i.e., it is given in exchange for a deposit of cash with the store, thereby allowing the customer the convenience of purchasing without having to pay cash at time of purchase.   Under such circumstances there is really no credit involved in the sale of merchandise by the store.   Instead of issuing scrip for the advance payment of cash, the store may carry what are known as "Deposit Accounts," which allow a customer to buy "on account" to the extent of the deposit credited to the customer on the store's books.   While no sales or merchandise credit is involved in such transactions, additional costs are involved as compared with strictly cash sales, in the form of much bookkeeping, billing, and probable payment of a rather high rate of interest on the deposits.

The option charge account. This type of account is a combination of the regular charge account and the revolving instalment credit account treated in the chapter that follows.   It is known by such designations as the Charge Account with Option Terms, Revolving Charge Account, All-purpose Account, but most often as the Option Charge Account.   It tends to eliminate the confusion caused by too many credit plans, and for that reason some stores have converted all their regular charge accounts and revolving accounts into this single form of credit.

Under this plan, the customer exercises the option at the end of the charge account period, usually some 10 days after the invoice or statement is received, of paying the full amount billed or only part of it (normally at least one-fourth of the amount owing, provided it is above a specified minimum in dollars) and deferring the balance until the end of the next month or billing when a similar option is again exercised by the customer.   In this way, the customer decides each month the manner of payment without the necessity of obtaining approval of the credit department, all purchases can be made by means of the same Charga-Plate or other identifying device, and buying is facilitated at peak periods because at such times the charge account can be automatically converted to an instalment form of credit without advance approval.

If the option is exercised and the charge account is converted to a revolving account in line with an initial agreement when the account is established, an interest and service charge is usually made at a rate of 1½ per cent per month for the amount outstanding at the end of the month—a practice much like that used for ordinary revolving credit. When such a plan is adopted by a store, the only other type of credit needed is the regular Instalment Account to take care of so-called "big ticket" items involving purchases of substantial amounts for which payments must be extended over a considerable period of time.

Charge account banking. A development[6] that has gained considerable momentum in the charge account area has brought into a common relationship stores, commercial banks, and consumers.   Under this arrangement a store that is unwilling or unable (because of limited capital, skill, and facilities) to sell on credit and thus carry receivables on its books and perform credit and collection operations may do so by having the bank assume all those responsibilities.   The bank investigates a consumer applicant for such credit.   If the risk is acceptable, the consumer is usually given a credit card entitling him to buy up to an assigned limit and such charge card is honored by all participating merchants.

When a credit sale is made by a participating store, the sales slip is forwarded to the sponsoring bank and the aggregate of such sale, less a merchant discount, or service fee, of 2 to 7 per cent,[7] is credited daily to the merchant's deposit account.   Each month the consumer receives a bill and the supporting sales slips from the bank covering all purchases made on credit in the participating stores, so that a single payment can be made for all of them to the bank.   For this service the consumer is charged nothing if remittance in full is made within a short period (usually 25 days) after billing for purchases made during

---

[6] It is said to have originated in 1951 at the Franklin National Bank, Rockville Center, N.Y.

[7] According to a recent study, the service fee charged by most banks is less than 4 per cent. For more details, see *Credit Card and Revolving Credit Survey*, American Bankers Association, Instalment Credit Committee, 1967.

the preceding month; otherwise the account is placed on an instalment basis and a carrying charge of 1 or 1½ per cent per month is added to the outstanding balance. The consumer is almost always required to repay at the monthly rate of $10 or one-tenth of the unpaid balance, whichever is greater.

The obvious advantages of charge account banking to the consumer are the convenience of charge accounts in a number of stores otherwise unavailable and of a single payment to the bank. On the other hand, while the consumer obtains the service free of charge so long as he pays his bills within the grace period, he is required to pay, not a rate of interest, but a service charge for additional time as if he had purchased the goods on the instalment plan. To that extent, he enjoys no special cost advantage over consumers buying from retailers on that basis in the first place.

The retailer no doubt secures some additional business from a charge account banking plan that he may not obtain without such accommodations to customers. The loss of potential income otherwise obtainable on its own instalment plans and the total of merchant discounts and other fees connected with bank credit card arrangements may, however, prove costly for a store that is in a position to handle its own credit and collection operations with equal or greater efficiency than the bank. It is, of course, realized that charge account banking operations involve much more than the mere making of a loan, for the bank is called upon to operate a credit department much like that of a department store, both on the credit-granting end and on the collection end of the business, and to engage in much record keeping and effective control devices. As shown in Table 7-2, it generally costs a department store about 4½ per cent of credit sales in direct expenses, and possibly less than 5 per cent if all costs were considered, to operate a credit department that deals not only in charge account credit but in the more costly forms of instalment credit as well. That may be why many banks have lowered the amount of service fees or have allowed refunds of the charged fee under certain conditions, as when the average charge exceeds a specified dollar amount. It may be the result of a realization that the basic charges provide too costly a service.

Commercial banks have found charge account banking a profitable source of business when sufficient volume is obtainable. Income to the bank is derived from two major sources, merchant discounts and instalment charges paid by the consumer for extended payments. Other sources of income received by the bank from merchants include membership fees on joining the plan, annual fees for the rental of sales-slip imprinters, and sundry charges made for certain operations such as for addressing customer envelopes and sending promotional literature to the merchant's customers. In addition to these direct sources of income, a bank credit card plan can also be used to attract new customers, both merchants and consumers, who in turn may make use of other bank services. On the other hand, a major disadvantage of this plan for the bank is the invariably high commitment of bank resources to the project, including outlays for advertising and promotional programs, enrollment of cardholders, and acquisition or use of processing equipment. Moreover, experience to date shows that larger retail merchants prefer their own credit arrangements and are reluctant to participate in bank credit card plans. As a result, the bank must attract a large number of small and medium-sized merchants if it is to achieve the volume necessary for profitable operations. In meeting this requirement, some banks appear to have indiscriminately mailed cards to anyone and everyone in their local area, without regard to creditworthiness.[8] As a result, these banks suffered high credit losses that might be expected from such unsound and unsafe credit practices.[9] While regrettable, this experience focused attention on the need for more effective selection of credit risks in charge account banking systems.[10]

The high credit losses and other operating costs associated with bank credit card plans may make this phase of the banking business unprofitable for a period of time until the break-even volume is obtained. The entire plan has, however, proved so inviting that in a number of communities, especially where charge account banking is not developed, some of the benefits are derived from a "Shoppers Charge Service" where a single card or credit plate is used for purchases in all participating stores identified by a specified emblem.

To reduce some of the problems associated with credit card plans, some banks have adopted two other alternative types of bank credit plans. One is "check credit," in which the consumer is given a book of checks, specially numbered or otherwise uniquely identified, rather than a credit card. Use of these checks, either to make a purchase or to obtain cash, constitutes a loan by the bank for which the consumer pays a service charge of ¾ to 2 per cent per month on the unpaid balance. In addition, the customer is often required to pay a fixed amount for each check. The second is the "overdraft" plan, which has been described

[8] See Richard F. Janssen, "Careless Issuance of Credit Cards by Banks Stirs Federal Reserve Worry over Risks," *The Wall Street Journal*, Aug. 21, 1967, p. 2.

[9] David D. Jordan, "Curbs on Credit Cards Issued by Banks Being Sought by Patman in House Bill," *The Wall Street Journal*, Aug. 29, 1967; see also "Chicago's Credit Card Crisis," *Business Week*, July 15, 1967, p. 35.

[10] Edward J. Brennan, "Credit Is the Key in Charge Account Banking," *The Credit World*, February, 1967, pp. 9–12.

as a "marriage between check credit and the regular checking account."[11]   Under this plan, the bank depositor obtains from the bank a line of credit in the form of an overdraft privilege on his personal checking account, and in addition he receives a supply of traveler's checks which are guaranteed by the issuing bank.   For these services, the consumer pays an annual fee of about $5 to $8, the regular checking account charges of the particular bank, and a service charge on the unpaid loan balance regardless of whether the overdraft results from the use of his personal checks or the special traveler's checks.

The advantages of check credit and overdraft plans to banks are that they are much simpler and less expensive to operate than a credit card plan.   There is no requirement for the bank to seek merchant membership in these plans and thus no pressure on the bank for a broad distribution of cards.   This enables the bank to eliminate much of the heavy startup cost and, perhaps, some of the high credit losses which have been associated with bank credit card programs.   Since check credit and overdraft transactions are normally for larger amounts than credit card purchases, the bank may also achieve greater profitability on a smaller number of transactions.   Neither of these plans, however, creates as many avenues for increasing the bank's total volume of business as does the credit card program.   Then, too, if either the check credit or the overdraft plan is to be successful, the participating bank must persuade consumers to use the checks liberally and retailers and other service organizations to accept the checks readily.

TYPES OF
CREDIT CARDS

The credit card was originally used almost altogether as an identifying device with no or very limited power to secure automatically authorization of purchases on a charge account basis.   In many retail and service establishments the credit card, which is usually made of plastic, is still used in that manner.   In recent years, however, the identifying function of the credit card, while still essential, has been subordinated to the authorizing function.   This means that the bona fide holder of a credit card is actually authorized to make purchases of goods and services by that means and uses the card accordingly.

Limited-purpose credit cards. Most credit cards may be used to purchase goods or services at only one or a limited number of types of retail or service establishments.   This is illustrated by Fig. 7-1A, which

---

[11] For an excellent discussion of charge account banking, see Robert W. Pullen, "Bank Credit Card and Related Plans," *New England Business Review*, December, 1966, pp. 2–6.

(A)

(B)

(C)

(D)

(E)

(F)

figure 7-1. *Credit cards used mainly for authorization of purchases under various credit card plans. (A) Limited-use credit card (Hilton Hotels); (B) limited-purpose credit card (Standard Oil Co.-SOHIO); (C) multipurpose American Express Credit Card; (D) multipurpose Carte Blanche; (E) multipurpose Eurocard; (F) multipurpose BankAmericard.*

entitles the holder to use it only in the hotels of the issuing organization. The same is true of the cards issued by most large department stores and the major car rental systems. Another example of a limited-purpose credit card is the one issued by the American Telephone and Telegraph Company and associated companies and used by the cardholder to charge long-distance telephone calls while away from the telephone to which the call is to be charged.

Fig. 7-1B is a card issued by one of the leading oil companies and is somewhat broader in its application. It entitles the holder to buy automotive, aviation, and marine merchandise and service from any station or dealer who wishes to honor it. The card being national in scope, arrangements have been made with other oil companies listed on the back and known as exchange companies to honor the card on the specified purchases until its expiration date unless it is canceled before that time.[12] Some oil companies have also established similar relationships with hotels, motels, and other types of retail organizations which permit the oil company cardholder to use his credit card to purchase a wide variety of mechandise items and services.[13]

Multipurpose or universal credit cards. While Diners' Club has been in existence for some years, the multipurpose or universal credit card plans did not develop until late in the 1950's when the American Express Company and Hilton, with its Carte Blanche, began to merchandise such plans aggressively. Among the newer organizations to issue a multipurpose card is Eurocard, established in 1965, with a credit card designed specifically for the traveler to Europe. The cards issued by such organizations as Diners' Club, American Express, Carte Blanche, and Eurocard are sometimes referred to as "travel and entertainment" cards. They are used primarily for dining and entertainment, for all sorts of travel, for accommodations at hotels, motels, and resorts, for personal transportation, and in other types of stores and service organizations as listed in a furnished directory. To obtain one of these multipurpose "travel and entertainment" cards, as shown in Figs. 7-1C, 7-1D, and 7-1E, an annual membership fee is required from the user, as contrasted with no such charge for any other type of credit card. All amounts charged by the use of these cards are billed monthly and are due and payable upon receipt of the statement; otherwise service charges may have to be paid on past-due accounts.

Another category of multipurpose credit cards includes those used in connection with charge account banking arrangements, such as the BankAmericard, as shown in Fig. 7-1F, Midwest Bank Card offered by a larger number of banks in Chicago and the Midwest, the Master

---

[12] Two interesting things may be noted from an examination of 7-1B. One is the absence of the cardholder's address, space being provided at the bottom of the card only for the name. This intentional omission is explained, first, by a desire to avoid the expense of issuance of replacement cards when customers change the address—a rather frequent occurrence—and, second, to make it more difficult for unscrupulous competitors to pirate accounts. The embossed dots and dashes (not reproduced on Fig. 7-1B) are symbol equivalents of the Scandex type numerals appearing above the dots and dashes and are designed for the use of different types of scanning equipment for electrically key punching the customer's account number.

[13] "Souping Up Gas Credit Cards," *Business Week*, Feb. 25, 1967, pp. 66–70.

Charge Card issued by a group of California banks, and the nationwide interchange system of Interbank Card, Inc. Most bank credit card plans are not presently truly national in scope, although the Bank of America, for example, has franchised several large regional banks to offer Bank-Americard and American Express Co. is using or franchising its Uni-Serv credit cards to banks across the nation. Such cards are, however, properly classified as multipurpose cards in the sense that they enable the cardholder to purchase a large number of goods and services for a variety of purposes from many different types of stores or organizations in his local or regional area.

There is no doubt that there are certain advantages to a multi-purpose credit card. It obviates the need for carrying cash, it provides a single billing for many purchases, it is convenient for keeping a record for tax purposes, and is regarded as a symbol of prestige. At the same time some weaknesses have been discovered. Such a plan must be carried out on a very large scale to justify the substantial investment in business machines for billing and accounting. To do so, it may become necessary to accept poorer risks, and that means greater possible losses from bad debts. Perhaps this can be accomplished by carefully selecting the risks and properly following up on the collections, just as any qualified credit manager would. Finally, there is a strong possibility of abuse.

In most states, legislation has been enacted making it a crime to use an expired, revoked, or stolen card or to use a card without authority of the party to whom issued. There have been reported, nevertheless, many instances of individuals and organized groups dealing in "black market" or "hot" cards and making extensive use of stolen cards to purchase goods and services.[14] One of the new techniques with the potential of reducing such fraudulent use of credit cards is Polaroid's "ID-2 Land Identification System." Under this system, a plastic identification card bearing a color photograph of the individual, as shown in Fig. 7-2, is issued to the cardholder. These cards are being distributed by Addressograph Multigraph Corporation, Cleveland, under the premise that the best way to verify the identity of a cardholder is by his photograph. Another, even more recent innovation, is the establishment of Telecredit, Inc. It is a computer system, centered at Columbus, Ohio, where, in a matter of seconds, by relaying inquiries through a touch-tone telephone into a data phone to the computers, use of a credit card fraudulently or excessively, anywhere in the United States, can be prevented by a credit card issuer subscribing to the service. Over one-half million inquiries a

---

[14] See "Credit Card Swindle Ring Uncovered, U.S. Agents Say," *The Wall Street Joural*, Nov. 13, 1967. See also "Credit Card Fraud Runs into Millions," *Columbus Citizen-Journal*, Aug. 7, 1967, and "Court Discloses Mafia Credit Card Thefts," *Columbus Citizen-Journal*, November 11, 1967, p. 2.

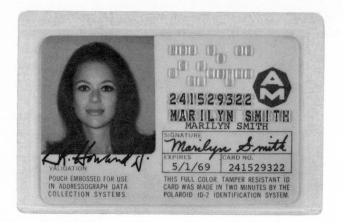

figure 7-2. *Credit card bearing color photograph of individual cardholder (color not reproduced) made by the Polaroid Identification System and distributed to retail establishments and banks by Addressograph Multigraph Corporation.*

month are already thus handled. Finally, some issuers of credit cards relieve holder of any liability if notified before any fraudulent use of it and otherwise limit the liability to a specified amount such as $100.[15]

To be sure, the cardholder himself can be of great assistance in the prevention of fraudulent use of credit cards by: not leaving credit cards lying around in the office, hotel room, in the glove compartment of the automobile, or even at home; not preserving out-of-date credit cards; not casually discarding unsolicited cards that are not expected to be used; destroying all cards not in use; and otherwise using caution as, for example, making sure that the card is returned after use. It has been suggested that the cardholder might well protect himself even by means of insurance.

COOPERATION AMONG RETAIL CREDITORS

The management of retail credit runs beyond the walls of each of the credit-granting institutions. Cooperation has developed among credit managers in many communities in what is known as a community credit policy. The extent to which they may agree to act in common fashion depends in part upon their willingness to do so, and in part upon the legal restrictions imposed upon collusive agreement among competitors.

[15] Al Bricker, "Columbus Computers Check Credit Cards," *Columbus Dispatch*, July 21, 1968, p. 23A.

One of the community policies is that of pooling ledger information in a credit bureau and of clearing all applications through the bureau before opening new accounts.   The policy may include also the uniform wording of application forms and the inclusion of certain essential items of information, the announcing in all statements of the terms on which merchandise is sold by the store, the adding of stipulated charges to an account for each month that it remains past due, and the establishment of common rules for collections.   Other rules may relate to terms to be used in the sale of certain articles on the instalment plan, the handling of "chronic returners," and the conditions under which accounts on the books should be suspended.   In a few instances the actual processes of investigation of applications and the billing of accounts have been turned over to a jointly supported office.

In some cities, merchants cooperate in suspending slow and undesirable accounts and in refusing to accept such accounts on a credit basis.   In others, periodic attempts are made cooperatively to educate consumers to pay their debts to merchants.   Special campaigns often feature such programs.

The major restraint upon community adoption of a credit policy was felt in connection with a desire to standardize instalment terms following the expiration of Regulation W.   Many retailers were satisfied with the terms of the Regulation, if not with the means by which the terms were enforced, and they hoped that some means would be found to prevent the collapse of credit granting to the level of the ridiculous terms which had prevailed before World War II.   Opinions were expressed by members of the U.S. Department of Justice, however, and by prominent attorneys well versed in credit matters, to the effect that agreements among competing merchants with regard to instalment terms would probably be regarded as in restraint of trade, and therefore in violation of the Sherman Antitrust Act.   No exception was made for the fact that the terms of such agreements would not be imposed upon unwilling competitors in the community or that no pressures would be brought to bear upon those who did not comply with the terms of the agreement to which they had subscribed.

**PRINCIPLES IN
THE SUCCCESSFUL
OPERATION OF CHARGE
ACCOUNT CREDIT**

Although qualifying conditions determine the exact nature of the charge account service, as well as whether such credit should be extended at all, underlying all phases of this business function are broad and fundamental principles obedience to which gives assurance of successful operation.

Principles of social significance. Some of the basic principles relating to charge account credit appertain to its role in society and in the economy. The following are illustrative of principles of this character:

1. Because of the convenience afforded most customers through the use of charge account credit and the consequent competitive attraction which such convenience constitutes, within the lines of trade in which it is commonly offered, the granting of this type of credit is, from the merchant's viewpoint, no longer a privilege but a competitive necessity.

2. Because charge account credit is primarily a service of convenience, it is inconsequential among the factors influencing total consumer purchasing power. For this reason, it cannot be regarded as an important cause, or even a concomitant, of cyclical business fluctuations. This is, in a sense, borne out by the data in Table 7-1.

Principles affecting individual customers or management. Another class of principles relates more to operational functions, and individually they approximate fundamental rules of action. The following illustrate such principles of charge account operation:

1. The probability of successful credit merchandising increases in the degree that the clientele of the institution is of moderately high income type, the merchandise handled is on the whole fairly costly, competition in the field is on a service basis, community preferences and size favor credit, and the merchant is adequately financed to carry the anticipated volume of accounts receivable without sacrificing variety of selection in his merchandise inventory.

2. Because the credit totality of the community or of the nation is no better qualitatively than the soundness of the individual credit transaction, both the individual and collective credit security of business rests upon intelligent credit analysis and application of results in each particular case.

3. To facilitate the use of charge accounts by customers and to expedite the consummation of credit transactions on the part of stores, such customers should be furnished a means of identification for credit purposes which is unmistakable, readily available, convenient to use, distinguishing, and revocable.

4. The amount of credit in a single transaction which an authorizer may pass upon without review should be proportional to the authority and responsibility of the individual in the organization. Small sums and routine risks may be handled uniformly by persons of little authority; larger sums and special risks should receive management approval.

5. Because of the routine and repetitive nature of credit investigation and appraisal, the management of this function should be an impersonal operation and, while allowing for the consideration of exceptional circumstances, should be based upon objective policies and standards.

6. The *collective* indebtedness and general credit character of an individual, being of more importance than *any one* of his debts or his attitude toward it, in the determination of his creditworthiness, it is to the mutual advantage of creditors to cooperate in the exchange or pooling of ledger experience.

7. The majority of consumers using charge account credit, and the great majority of credit customers being acceptable risks, the cost of credit extension may be increased disproportionately to the benefit derived by carrying investigation to the point where all bad debt losses resulting from errors in credit extension would be eliminated.

8. Collection efforts, being in part a function of credit practices, should conform in promptness and severity to the classes of credit risks involved.

QUESTIONS AND PROBLEMS

1 Arguments are often heard and specific examples are given to "prove" that charge account credit is growing or declining, as the case may be. To what extent and in what manner can the data in Table 7-1 be used to establish the true facts in this regard?

2 How can one explain the slow *relative* change in charge account credit outstandings and the consistent *relative* growth in service credit outstandings? Is the latter a good thing for society?

3 Department store A has a volume of credit sales equal to 60 per cent of its total annual business, while the credit sales of department store B are only 35 per cent of its total sales volume. From the standpoint of credit management, which of the two stores is probably the more successful? Why?

4 What is involved in the statement that "credit is a customary convenience"?

5 Does credit business tend to increase or decrease complaints from customers? What are the reasons for your answer?

6 In determining the costs of operating on a credit basis, what items should a store consider? Should such costs be expressed as a percentage of credit sales or total sales?

7 "Credit leads to extravagance and recklessness." What is the answer to this objection, if any? Does your answer apply equally to the use of the teen-age Charge Account?

8 J. Brown plans to open a store in the near future. One of his problems is to decide whether to operate on a cash basis or to adopt a policy of selling on credit. He seeks your advice. What would you recommend?

9 Show how J. Brown could, through the use of the charge account banking device, sell on credit without himself rendering a credit service to his customers. Is this desirable from the standpoint of sales volume and cost, respectively? Explain.

10 To what specific things may the carelessness of many retailers in credit granting be attributed? What remedies would you suggest?

11 "Cash customers pay for bad debts." If this is true, show that they are really benefited thereby.

12 How do you account for the fact that the loss from bad debts in a large store is usually a higher percentage of total sales than that of a small store in the line of business? Is this a crucial item in the costs of credit operations? Explain.

13 Retail stores selling for cash and open credit charge the same prices to credit and cash customers. Is this practice justified, or should such a retailer operate on a dual pricing system? Why?

14 What specific advantages does a retail merchant derive from the extension of credit to his customers? Would you recommend that most or all merchants operate on a credit basis in order to derive the same benefits? Explain.

15 In what ways may retailers in a community cooperate to the end of making retail credit business more sound? Does such cooperation relieve the merchant of individual responsibility? Explain.

16 Between the area covered by imposed regulations and that which is regarded as a violation of antitrust legislation, what opportunities are there for credit managers *collectively* to accomplish some of the ends hoped for in legislation and yet remain immune to action for engaging in allegedly restraining trade practices through agreement?

17 In what specific ways is the Option Charge Account a mark of progress in credit use and its operation? Can the same thing be said about charge account banking? Explain.

18 Is the development of the multipurpose charge account credit card to be welcomed or bemoaned? From whose point of view?

19 What are the advantages and disadvantages to the bank of the "check credit" and "overdraft" plans in comparison to bank credit card plans?

20 Is credit card abuse real? Show by citing evidence. Can it be prevented? Minimized? How?

CHAPTER 8

consumer
instalment credit

As will be shown later in a quantitative way, consumer instalment credit has grown over the years not only in absolute amounts but also relative to the economy as measured by disposable personal income. This is as might be expected from the increased production and consumption of expensive durable consumer goods, from the more extensive use of such credit by more classes of consumers, and from the constantly rising standard of living which necessitates its use on an expanding variety of goods and even services. Thus consumer instalment credit can no longer be regarded as a mere promotional sales device from a managerial point of view or of very limited application from the consumer angle. It has, indeed, become a permanent and fundamental part of our economy, affecting the entire productive process as well as consumption.

More directly, consumer instalment credit is of special concern to retailers and to financial institutions making loans for that purpose or dealing in the paper arising therefrom.   The first aspect of such direct influence is discussed in this chapter and the second is deferred to a later chapter in this part of the book.

Every retailer dealing in goods susceptible of instalment selling is confronted with certain administrative decisions concerning it.   He must decide whether or not he should use this type of credit and in what form or forms; what charge, if any, should be made for the credit service; and how the resulting outstandings should be financed.   Some of the basic decisions in this matter are often made for the retailer by the manufacturer whose goods are thus involved.   Similar management decisions must be made by those dealing in services equally susceptible of instalment selling.

Nature of instalment credit. Instalment credit is but one type of consumer credit.   When applied to the purchase of merchandise or service it differs from the ordinary type of retail credit primarily in one respect.   Instead of paying the full amount of the bill at the end of a given period of time, when instalment credit is used the purchaser is asked to pay his obligation in fixed portions or instalments at stated intervals as agreed upon at the time the sale is consummated.   In other words, an instalment sale is one in which part of the price of the goods is usually paid at once in cash or its equivalent, the balance owing being paid in fixed amounts at stated intervals.   The transaction is simply one of credit, and has no essential differences in its nature from other credit transactions.   In reality, though, it is broader than a mere type of *consumer* credit, for it is used to a considerable extent in the wholesale financing of automobiles and in the purchase of goods for industrial consumption.

The subject of instalment credit has often been approached from the standpoint of selling, buying, or financing.   It is this difference in point of view that is responsible for the many names given to it, some of which are confusing, misleading, or anything but descriptive of the actual process.   A few of the more familiar names which may be seen flashed before the public in newspapers and magazines are instalment selling, instalment buying, credit merchandising, time sales, deferred payments, partial payments, easy payments, revolving accounts, and various budget plans.   It is true enough that the process of selling on the instalment plan has its merchandising or selling and buying aspects, and that both buyers and sellers are vitally interested in it; the former regards it as a buying facility and the latter as a sales stimulant.   Nevertheless, it is the *credit* arrangement and nothing else that distinguishes this type of transaction from other types.   It is for this reason that the term "instalment credit" has been chosen as the most suitable designation of the economic process in which payments for goods or services are made in fractional amounts instead of in a lump sum.

Origin of instalment credit. There is nothing new about instalment credit as a business practice. In fact, it is a very old device, probably as old as credit itself. It is even older than Christianity, and was practiced on a limited scale in connection with marine insurance by the Babylonians and Phoenicians.[1] In Rome, according to Plutarch, Crassus, who was a contemporary of Julius Caesar, amassed a fortune by buying up houses during periods of great conflagrations, rebuilding them, and selling them on the instalment plan. The present type of instalment selling was introduced in England in 1828 by the Countess of Blessington, who, on her return from Paris, where it was apparently practiced by the store of Dufayel, suggested it to a firm of cabinet makers.

Evolution of instalment credit in the United States. In the United States, the instalment method of operation is also quite an old practice. It was introduced in New York as early as 1807 by the founder of the firm of Cowperthwait & Sons. It was first applied to furniture, which, incidentally, was a line not at first sold on charge accounts, and later spread to other articles. The building and loan associations which operate on this basis have been in existence for nearly a century. The Singer Sewing Machine Company adopted the plan about 1850 and has carried it to very large proportions. In the piano business, the instalment plan has been used since about 1875 and is now considered the prevailing practice in that field. The same is true of sets of books, which were thus sold for a long time by itinerant book agents. Many other lines of merchandise, including jewelry and reapers and binders, have been sold on the instalment plan for many years. Its adoption by the automobile industry gave great impetus to its growth and to its spread, since the middle 1920's, into many lines of trade and types of merchandise, including "soft" goods like women's wearing apparel and home furnishings, and into the homes of all income classes of the population. Instalment credit is now used by all income groups of consumers and by many of the "best" stores.

Importance of Instalment credit. It is not enough merely to say that instalment credit is important in our economy. Its importance is evident in a number of ways. It is shown, first, by the number of vendors using it. Complete statistics on the subject are unavailable, but the number is believed to be large, running into the hundreds of thousands of retail stores, service organizations, and direct-selling manufacturers.

[1] E. R. A. Seligman, *The Economics of Instalment Selling*, Vol. 1, p. 10, Harper & Brothers, New York, 1927.

Likewise, the number of consumers using instalment credit is also large, being in the millions.   The almost endless variety and types of merchandise sold on this plan of credit also attest its importance.   Consumer instalment credit is no longer limited to the financing of purchases of automobiles and other consumer durable goods of the common variety.   It has been extended to soft goods and to such goods and services as boats, airplanes, mobile homes, shell housing, air and steamship travel, and the financing of expensive vacations and of higher education.

More concrete evidence of its prominence is found in the volume of business done on instalment credit.   As shown by the data in Table 8-1, over a period of 20 years for which comparable information is available to date, extensions of consumer instalment credit have increased more than fivefold.   The increase has been somewhat greater for automobile paper, where the number of new passenger cars sold on instalment credit grew from 39 per cent in 1948 to from 60 to 62 per cent in more recent years.[2]   Moreover, the extensions increased each year except in the three recession periods 1954, 1958, and 1960–1961 (see Fig. 8-1), where the reductions are more than accounted for by the automobile part of the business.   This means that, as far as cyclical effects are concerned, the automobile phase is crucial, but even that consists of but about two-fifths of total consumer instalment credit extensions.   Parenthetically, it should be noted, as shown in Fig. 8-1, that repayments followed a more regular pattern and in times of recession approximated or exceeded the extensions.   The implications as to the overall soundness of instalment credit and the lack of cyclical influence on the economy are most significant.

Still another tangible evidence of the importance of consumer instalment credit is found in the volume of instalment debt outstanding, as shown in Table 2-1.   Here, too, the growth has been both absolute and relative to disposable personal income.   Furthermore, the increase in outstandings has proceeded at a faster pace than the increase in extensions, which is to be expected in a growing economy in which commitments are made in terms of a brighter future and in which such credit is extended on more and more "big ticket" items of merchandise and service and hence with longer maturities.   It is of importance to note in connection with the data in Table 2-1 that no cyclical effects in outstandings are to be discerned from the annual data and that the *relative* increase in the last few years covered by the data has not been disturbing.

Forms of instalment credit. Since the end of World War I, instalment credit has evolved from simple instalment-contract selling to a va-

---

[2] *Automobile Facts and Figures,* published annually by the Automobile Manufacturers Association.

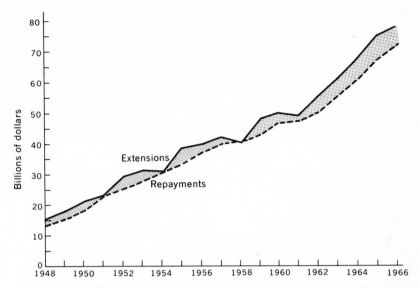

figure 8-1. *Consumer instalment credit repayments in relation to extensions, 1948–1966.*

riety of forms whose flexibility offers convenience to consumer-users and enhances the advantages of instalment selling for vendors.

Straight instalment contract. The oldest and most common form of instalment credit is that calling for a series of regular payments on an item following its purchase. Sale may be made on a security agreement or by means of a conditional sales contract or chattel mortgage. Each transaction involves a separate contract and its own terms of payment and is handled on the basis of the merits of the risk for that particular sale. A modification is the "add-on" account under which additional purchases may be made with a down payment and the balance is paid off without a substantial increase in the size of the instalment payment.

Deferred payment accounts. In order that successive instalment purchases may be facilitated, a plan known as the Deferred Payment Account, the Continuous Instalment Account, or the Budget Charge Account has been devised. This plan permits new purchases to be added to existing instalment indebtedness without changing the rate of charge or the rate of payment. In some cases the length of the entire payment contract is extended. The customer merely continues his payments at

table 8-1 *Consumer Instalment Credit Extended and Ratio of Repayments to Extensions, United States 1948–1967*
(In millions of dollars)

| | | Extensions | | Repayments Total | |
| | | | | | |
Year	Total[1]	Automobile paper[1]	All other[2]	Amount[1]	Per cent of extensions
1948	$15,585	$ 5,217	$10,368	$13,284	85.2
1949	18,108	6,967	11,141	15,514	85.7
1950	21,558	8,530	13,028	18,445	85.6
1951	23,576	8,956	14,620	22,985	97.5
1952	29,514	11,764	17,750	25,405	86.1
1953	31,558	12,981	18,577	27,956	88.6
1954	31,051	11,807	19,244	30,488	98.2
1955	38,944	16,706	22,238	33,629	86.4
1956	39,868	15,515	24,353	37,054	92.9
1957	42,016	16,465	25,551	39,868	94.9
1958	40,119	14,226	25,893	40,344	100.6
1959	48,052	17,779	30,273	42,603	88.7
1960	49,560	17,654	31,906	45,972	92.8
1961	48,396	16,007	32,389	47,700	98.6
1962	55,126	19,796	35,330	50,620	91.8
1963	61,295	22,292	39,003	55,171	90.0
1964	67,505	24,435	43,070	61,121	90.5
1965	75,508	27,914	47,594	67,495	89.4
1966	78,896	28,491	50,405	72,805	92.3
1967	81,263	27,221	54,042	77,973	96.0

SOURCES: [1] For the years 1948–1952, computed from monthly data in *Federal Reserve Bulletin*, October, 1956, p. .1110; for the year 1953, from February, 1960, issue, p. 200; for the years 1954 and 1955, from revised figures in December, 1961, issue, p. 1458; for the years 1956–1959, from the October, 1964, issue, p. 1318; and for the years 1960–1967, from the April, 1968, issue, p. A-50.
[2] Computed by deducting data for automobile extensions from data on total instalment credit extensions.

a fixed rate and at the stated intervals until the sum of his indebtedness is paid off.

Once a risk is investigated and his credit is established in connection with an initial instalment sale, a large part of the administration of this form of credit has been performed. Provision of opportunity for add-on purchases may require only reconsideration of the debtor's ability to meet his payments. This type of account is an inducement to buy and to make purchases at the store where credit is already established.

Budget accounts. A third form of instalment credit is the 90-day charge account on which one-third of the original balance is payable at the end of each of 3 months. This type of account is often used in the sale of clothing and household goods which cannot conveniently be paid for in 1 month on the regular charge account. No service or interest charge is usually made for this convenience. From the standpoint of the creditor, it serves as an attractive and orderly way of budgeting payment of an amount too large for regular open-account limits and authorization and too small to warrant the usual instalment contract.

Revolving credit account.[3] A fourth form of instalment credit provides for fixed monthly payments on whatever balance may be outstanding on this special form of open account. Charge privileges are extended for all types of merchandise up to a predetermined limit, which is established by multiplying the amount of the monthly payment by 6, 12, or 18. Assuming that the store operates on a 12-month plan, a customer agreeing to pay $10 monthly toward any outstanding balance may purchase up to $120 worth of merchandise at one time and make additional purchases to the extent that his balance is below that limit. If the monthly payment is increased to $20, the account ceiling is raised to $240. There is also the so-called "flexible revolving credit account" under which the customer just described would pay monthly not one-twelfth of the predetermined limit but a fraction of the outstanding balance which, when multiplied, say, by 12, would yield the new limit on the account. Thus the monthly payment changes up or down according to the amount of the unpaid balance. When such charges are made according to a chart furnished to the customer, it is known as the chart plan account. A charge usually amounting to 1½ per cent of the outstanding month-end balance is made on revolving credit accounts.

Both stores and customers look favorably upon this type of account, because of its fixed or flexible limit, its finance charge, and the

---

[3] See also the discussion of the Option Charge Account in the preceding chapter.

closer supervision given it, as a means by which charge account credit can be extended to more risky customers.   It is also a means by which a questionable risk may establish a good credit standing.   The flexible limit makes it possible for the customer to increase the limit without credit department approval, is convenient at peak buying times as in preholiday and preschool periods, and is a means of selling soft goods on a charge account plan with instalment account characteristics.

Factors affecting the decision to sell on instalment credit. The decision to offer instalment credit is a major policy decision for a vendor, for it affects not only his internal financial requirements but also the character of his clientele, the service he renders, and the attraction which he has to publicize.   Such a decision must be based, in part, upon a careful consideration of the factors discussed below.

Credit elasticity of demand.   The decision to sell on instalment credit is sometimes influenced by the likely effect of such credit upon the demand for the goods in question.   Demand expands and contracts in response to several factors.   Changes in price influence the demand for a product.   Changes in income, with price remaining stable, also affect demand.   Advertising, too, with price and income unchanged, may increase demand.   Similarly, the availability of credit in the sale of certain types of commodities offers a corresponding stimulus to demand.

The elasticity of demand attributable to instalment credit results mainly from the impetus such credit gives to *saving* and from the redirection it gives to *spending*.   Consumers are known to purchase proportionally more durable and so-called "luxury" goods as purchasing power increases.   With limited incomes, however, many people will not save voluntarily in order to make major purchases but dissipate their earnings in low-value items which are quickly consumed.   Credit introduced into this situation increases demand for the "instalment" goods, for it permits immediate acquisition and enforced subsequent saving.   It is thus that instalment credit has been instrumental in widening the market for automobiles, musical instruments, and innumerable electrical household appliances.   A vendor contemplating adoption of instalment selling, therefore, should consider the probable credit elasticity of the demand for his product.

Kinds of goods.   Originally, instalment credit was used mainly in connection with the sale of goods that were of a high unit value, durable, and of substantial repossession value.   All of this was obviously based on sound logic.   Relatively few consumers can buy an article of high unit value, such as an automobile or piano, for cash or on an ordinary charge account.   On the other hand, a consumer who cannot pay cash for an article selling for but a few dollars or buy it on a charge account is probably too poor a risk to be taken on any credit basis.   Similarly, it was felt that goods bought for immediate consumption or temporary use should not be paid for out of future income, as this would require payments for an article that is no longer in use or existence.   These two criteria are still deemed valid.   The third related to the repossession value, which under certain circumstances is still basic, as in the sale of a motor vehicle, where much reliance is placed on it.   In many cases, however, it was found through experience that it is of little validity, inasmuch as security and reliance are placed instead upon the moral aspects of the risk.   It must be remembered that even in the sale of so-called "soft" goods, the criteria of high unit value relative to the consumers' purchasing power and durability as measured by length of use of the article are still present and of importance.   The only abdication in the sale of such goods is from the criterion of repossession value.

Financial strength.   An instalment credit policy can be adopted only if the vendor possesses financial strength, or has access to financial resources, to enable him to carry the resulting receivables.   Instalment credit, involving large sums in individual transactions and extending for long periods, usually requires more working capital than do open accounts.

Working capital for instalment selling may be provided by owners of the business, but in recent years contract accounts have increasingly been financed through the aid of finance specialists.   Department stores and mail order houses often assign their instalment accounts to banks and to finance companies.   Automobile and appliance dealers usually work directly with sales finance companies in the initial financing of the transactions.   Vendors are thus enabled to concentrate their own resources on merchandising activities and leave the financing to others.   Ability to establish relations with satisfactory financial sources may be requisite for the adoption of an instalment credit policy.   There is also a tendency for some vendors to establish separate corporate enterprises as wholly owned subsidiaries for the financing of their sales on such credit terms.

ADVANTAGES OF
INSTALMENT CREDIT

Facilitates enjoyment of life. The phenomenal growth in the use of instalment credit represents but an attempt on the part of business concerns to respond to the wishes and demand of the public.   From the standpoint of the consumer instalment credit is desirable because it enables people to obtain, without delay, a great many commodities of high unit value and much usefulness, without the necessity of waiting or doing without them. The buyer is thus enabled to use the article while paying for it, and as a result can enjoy life more fully than would have been possible otherwise. Many individuals would never be able to own certain goods without this privilege, because of the difficulty or impossibility of accumulating a sufficient amount to pay for them in one lump sum. While it is theoretically possible to obtain desired articles by saving the purchase price in advance of purchase, in practice it is very difficult for most people to do so. They often save more effectively under the pressure of an obligation assumed.

From an economic standpoint, is there any reason why anybody should not have all of the comforts that he is able and willing to pro-duce? If a person desires to keep from going hungry and is able and willing to produce food, why should he not be allowed to do so and appease his hunger? If mankind wants to go on wheels and go fast, why not give it the opportunity to buy all the necessary automobiles, so long as it is willing to work and pay for them? The instalment plan is nothing more or less than a practical means of helping people to satisfy their desires, their wants, and their aspirations.

Encourages thrift. Instalment buying, statements to the contrary notwithstanding, tends to encourage thrift. It is an enforced form of saving. People will economize in order to be able to meet instalments when they become due but may refuse to economize for the mere sake of accumulating money. For example, a well-known automobile manufac-turer insisted some years ago that his prospective customers first save the money and buy the machine after they had accumulated a sufficient amount to pay for it, but the plan proved to be a complete failure. At the same time, other automobile manufacturers were exceedingly success-ful in selling their machines first and requiring that payments be made for them as they are put into use. "Pay as you ride," in the case of automobiles, and "pay while you play," in the case of pianos and other musical instruments, are very significant appeals, because they enable us to enjoy the use of the commodities while we can, and, besides, we can have the pride of possessing them, even though they have not been paid for in full. Few homes would be owned, indeed, if it were necessary to pay for them in full prior to obtaining possession. Yet few will deny the beneficial effect of home ownership, even on the time-payment basis.

The instalment plan is only another—and sometimes more effec-tive—method of saving so that higher-priced needs and comforts of life may be obtained. It provides the desired article first, and then encourages the buyer to put aside a certain amount weekly or monthly in payment for it.

Higher standard of living. The standard of one's living is judged today in large measure by the number and kinds of durable goods and costly articles in his possession, as well as by his consumption of items yielding cultural and aesthetic satisfaction. Instalment credit may be an aid to raising the level of one's living in terms of this standard.

In the first place, instalment buying tends to discourage the waste or dissipation of funds. If it were not for this method of operation, many persons would, no doubt, spend their money on articles of temporary gratification instead of buying goods that last, the satisfaction of which is being remembered and enjoyed. It is very likely that much of the income which is now used in buying substantial goods, such as automobiles and electric washing machines, would be expended for pleasure or goods that would give only immediate and temporary satisfaction. It is the consensus of opinion of authorities on the subject that frivolous purchases tend to be minimized as a result of instalment buying. Moreover, the instalment plan encourages culture, for it enables the poor as well as the rich to enjoy the better things in life. The better music and educational messages often heard over the radio or seen on television are but one illustration of what has been made available through instalment credit to the masses of our population who would otherwise be deprived of them altogether. The instalment plan has aided people in securing higher standards of living, education, comforts, conveniences, efficiency, recreation, and health. Not only that, but the added responsibility often causes them to do more and better work, for in order to meet these instalments, they must earn more. It has proved a strong incentive to work, to produce, and to secure those things which tend to make people happy. So long as we assume a dynamic social order and steady progress, instalment credit contributes to a higher standard of living not only over a short period of time, but in the long run as well.

Increases retailer's volume. That the instalment plan tends to increase the retailer's volume of business is no longer a matter of conjecture. Especially does it increase the demand for merchandise that is time- and labor-saving, health-preserving and pleasure-giving. It brings customers to the store at frequent intervals to make their payments. Each of these calls gives the retailer an opportunity to make additional sales, until it becomes an endless chain with the payments for one purchase leading to still another purchase. That is why some of the stores so urgently solicit instalment business and frequently offer leading articles even below cost just to enable them to bring customers into their stores and to open for them instalment accounts.

Lowers prices. Increasing consumer demand and retail volume as it does, instalment credit in turn furnishes a stimulus to manufacturers of commodities which are bought commonly on this plan, such as radios, automobiles, electric appliances, and furniture. Most of these industries operate on a decreasing cost basis, and consequently as their output is increased, the unit cost is materially reduced. This advantage of lower prices resulting from consumer credit inures to the benefit, therefore, of cash and credit customers alike.

Cash customers may enjoy still another price advantage from the general use of instalment credit. In the case of ordinary charge accounts, no discrimination whatever is made in price in favor of cash purchases. The person who buys for cash must pay the same price as the charge account customer. This is not generally true in instalment buying, however. Regardless of whether the basic price is a cash price or an instalment price, deviations are usually made in favor of the cash customer. Only the customer who buys on deferred payments is required to pay for the privilege, no other type of customer being required to pay the cost of instalment financing and of carrying the accounts on the books.

Other advantages. In addition to the distinctive advantages just outlined, instalment credit affords the same advantages as any other type of consumer credit. Furthermore, it helps to make for steady production, thereby furnishing regular employment. It is no longer necessary for a consumer to wait until he has accumulated a sufficient amount of cash to pay, in a lump sum, the full price of the article. A reasonable down payment will often be all that is necessary. Goods can thus be bought by a sufficiently large number of people to enable the plants to operate continuously and without serious interruption, avoiding sharp peaks and valleys in production. Finally, it is being used to liquidate slow pay accounts and to finance equipment purchased by hotels, restaurants, businessmen, and industrial users.

OBJECTIONS TO
INSTALMENT CREDIT

Notwithstanding the advantages of instalment selling in meeting consumer wants, building business volume for the vendor, and otherwise benefitting the economy, some potent arguments have been advanced against it from the standpoint of individual users and the economy as a whole. Those who use instalment credit generally favor it; critics and opponents often have not used it successfully or are ideologically allergic to it.

Promotes extravagance. Among the most common criticisms of instalment credit are: first, that it induces the purchase of luxuries by people who can afford only necessities; second, that it causes the mortgaging of future income; and third, that it leads to overspending, whether the purchases involve luxuries or necessities.

Even advocates of this argument cannot satisfactorily distinguish necessities from luxuries. The distinction lies not in the commodities themselves but in the importance of the goods to an individual's means or standard of living. Luxuries of one person are necessities of another; and luxuries of yesteryear are necessities of today. Bathrooms, hot water, telephones, electricity, central heating, and many articles commonly used today, such as pianos, radios, television sets, washing machines, ironers, toasters, and the like, are now *necessary* "luxuries." Their availability on instalment credit has encouraged not extravagance but the desire for a higher standard of living.

This wider use of comforts and conveniences does not always represent a freezing commitment of future income or overconsumption. Such a belief presumes a static future income. To the extent that increases are anticipated, adjustments can be made in the pattern of future expenditures, or other resources can be drawn upon, the increase of instalment sales can scarcely be viewed as an extravagance dangerous to our economic well-being.

Hampers thrift. The instalment plan is also criticized because it is supposed to exercise a detrimental effect on thrift and savings. That this is not the case will be revealed from an examination of statistics on savings, life insurance in force, deposits, and similar data reflecting thrift.

Apparently instalment credit has interfered very little with thrift in one form or another. Even if it had interfered to some extent, it might still have been justified, for there can be just as much wasteful saving as there can be wasteful spending. It is possible to save too much, just as it is possible to spend too much. What is needed is wise and intelligent saving, just as we need wise and intelligent spending.

Instalment credit is costly. Probably one of the most serious objections to instalment credit is its costliness. In addition to interest on outstandings and losses from bad debts, high costs of collecting accounts are generally incurred, except in the case of the more reputable stores.   Because of the chance of repeated default in payment, elaborate means must be provided for enforcing payment while at the same time keeping the customer satisfied with his purchase.   The repeated handling of collections alone involves an appreciable cost in this type of credit. For these and other reasons, payroll cost is the largest or second largest item of expense in instalment credit operations.

Alleged exorbitant charges and misrepresentation. Critics of instalment credit give the impression that, because administrative costs of this type of credit are necessarily high, charges for it are necessarily exorbitant.   It is true that both costs and charges are high and that some vendors abuse it by making exorbitant charges for the service.   It does not generally follow, however, that charges are exorbitant in the sense that they are illegal, unfair, or misleading.   Unfortunately, few consumers know, or even care, what instalment charges they pay and therefore are sometimes surprised to learn how high they are.   But consumer education, state provision for maximum sales financing rates and other charges, and Federal Trade Commission policing of advertised rate statements have measurably reduced abuse and deception with respect to charges.[4]

Not only rates charged but other instalment sales practices have shared criticism.   These include concealment of charges; rebates and bonuses given by finance companies to dealers; extra charges or "packs" added by the dealer to the amounts required by the finance companies; special fees for delinquency, recording of the credit instrument, and refinancing pastdue amounts; hasty repossessions and "fixed" auction sales; taking extra security such as wage assignments and endorsements of other parties; overcharging for insurance and failure to place insurance paid for by purchaser, as well as requiring extra coverage; inadequate or no refunds for payment of unpaid balances before they are due; and one-sided legal protection provided for in the sales agreement.

Methods of computing true, actual, or effective rates of charge. It is often argued that the best assurance against certain undesirable instalment practices is a knowledge of what rates are actually charged on instalment transactions, if any such charges are specified separately in dollar amounts.   This belief has formed the basis for the so-called "Truth in Lending" bill which has been proposed in several sessions of Congress and was finally enacted into the Consumer Credit Protection Act, effective May 29, 1968.   Among other things, it requires that finance charges on all instalment purchases be stated in terms of a "simple annual rate." It is alleged that a consumer would be in a position to decide whether the finance charge is reasonable, whether to take or reject an offer, or to find

---

[4] See also possible effects of new Federal legislation discussed below.

alternative means of financing his purchases, assuming, of course, that such alternative means are available to him.

First, it is important that rates of charge on instalment transactions should not be confused with *interest* rates charged for the mere use of money,[5] since the part of the total charge for the use of money is much smaller than the remainder of the charge which is made largely for service connected with credit granting, record keeping, and collections. Stated in another way, the cost of money to the instalment credit grantor, both explicit and imputed, even in the broad terms explained in footnote 5, is seldom over one-third of his total cost of such an operation.

In setting the total charge for instalment credit, interest and service, the grantor must consider the fact that every transaction is unique with respect to the creditworthiness of consumers, the amount of credit granted, and the nature of collateral. It is, therefore, not surprising that, in meeting the diverse needs for credit by consumers, grantors have developed several different methods of stating the finance charge. Generally speaking, this charge is expressed or ascertained in one of three ways. First, the charge may be quoted as a percentage rate expressed in relation either to the original indebtedness or to the unpaid balance outstanding. The second method is that in which the finance charge is stated as a flat dollar-and-cent amount rather than a percentage. Finally, some grantors state only the amount and number of payments, so that the consumer must calculate the amount he is to repay and compare that sum with the cash price of the goods to determine the amount of finance charge. The difference is referred to as the "time-price differential." The first and the third methods are perhaps the most common, although the instalment charge may be a combination of two of these forms.

Comparison of instalment credit charges is facilitated by the consumer and others involved when the instalment credit charge, interest and service, is expressed not only in amounts but also as a rate per annum under the so-called "time-price" principle or doctrine. To be of greatest usefulness, such a rate must be determined when the transaction is consummated. To do that may be utterly impossible, extremely difficult, or at best only approximate.

In some types of credit transactions, as in revolving credit where the charge is based on the month-end balance, an actual rate on average

---

[5] Even what is normally regarded as interest for the mere use of money actually consists of three parts. One is what the economist treats as *pure interest* in terms of rent paid for the use of capital in which no risk or expense is involved. Another is payment for the risk assumed through possible loss of principal. A third part is in the nature of a reimbursement for management expenses incurred in making and servicing an ordinary loan that is repayable in a lump sum and a net profit on the transaction.

outstandings *during* the month can never be determined accurately either in advance or even after the fact in the absence of prohibitively costly records of daily average outstandings for each such account.   In most other instances vendors would not know how to determine an actual rate of finance charge on a per annum basis for the quoted rates, the difference being that the former is based on the amount of debt outstanding at any given time while the latter is based on the original unpaid balance of the principal when the arrangement was effected.

Even among authorities on the subject there are substantial differences of opinion on the proper or best method of converting a so-called "nominal" rate of charge, such as is often quoted, or the amount of charge in dollars, into a so-called "effective" or actual rate per annum. Although the traditional amount of time used in financial matters for the computation of rates is the year, there are differences in both opinion and practice as to whether the calendar year of 365 days shall be used or a year of only 360 days in terms of 30-day months.   Which year length is to be used may become crucial in figuring the time elapsed between 2 dates within a year on large sums of money.

Much more important is the choice of method for converting finance or credit service charges into annual rates.   To this end there are several possibilities.   Obviously, the *actuarial method* is by far the most accurate but also the most complicated.   Hence, resort must be made to some other method.   One in common use is what is known as the *constant ratio method,* whereby a constant fraction of each payment is allocated to the finance charge and the remainder to the repayment of the principal or unpaid balance.   Another is the *direct ratio method,* based on the month-dollars in actual use by the consumer and is often referred to as the "78ths method" or the "sum of the digits method" according to which the finance charge is allocated among the months in direct ratio to the total month-dollars in use by paying 12/78 of the finance charge in the first month, 11/78 in the second month, etc.   Then there are the *minimum yield* and *maximum yield methods,* depending upon whether the finance charge is deducted from the earliest or the latest payments.

After an appropriate method for making the computation has been chosen, there still remains choice of the procedure or process of actually making the computation.   For this purpose a number of varying procedures have been developed including different formulas or other short cuts.   As to which is best even for a given method, authorities differ widely.   This, in turn, has led to the preparation of charts and "gimmicks" which, in the opinion of some students of the subject, facilitate the task and in the opinion of others are deemed to be absurd, at best only approximate, or not fitting varying conditions and differing credit arrangements.

Because of all these difficulties, it would be too much to expect the average businessman to know how to make the computation, and certainly it would be preposterous to expect consumers to know much about it. What is, therefore, intended in the following discussion is to present a method of computation for *students* of the subject as prospective managers of credit and for those already engaged in that type of management activity in order that they may be more sophisticated about it. Even this is intended to apply mainly to large individual sales of the regular instalment type.

For the sake of a logical approach to this problem, as well as in the interest of simplicity, a method for computing the actual rate of charge per annum, no matter how the charge is quoted, is suggested below and the computation is to be made in five simple mathematical steps as indicated:

1. Determine the cost of credit required. As noted earlier, the cost of instalment credit is usually expressed or ascertained in one of three ways, or as a combination thereof: as a percentage carrying charge, as a dollar-and-cent carrying charge, or as a differential between credit and cash prices. Consequently, the first thing to determine in figuring the actual rate is the sum of the costs incurred.

Suppose, for example, that merchandise such as a refrigerator, priced at $400, is sold on the instalment plan and that a charge of 6 per cent is made for the financing service. The charge remains the same although it may be stated that $4 must be paid for investigation, $3.50 for opening the account, $8 for the interest on the outstandings, 50 cents for filing the security agreement, and $8 for other services. On the other hand, the merchandise may have been priced as follows: "Instalment price—$424; Cash price—$400." Thus the same charge is shown to be expressed in different ways. The charge actually involved, however, is complicated by the combination of these methods of expression and by the fact that the consumer is not adept at figuring the *rate* when a cash discount is offered from the instalment price of the goods. Nevertheless, it is imperative to state *in terms of dollars and cents the total cost incurred* by reason of the use of instalment credit.

2. Determine the amount of credit required. The amount of credit needed in any transaction is simply the *amount of money which* the purchaser would have needed to make the purchase on a cash basis. It is the amount of cash he would have to borrow if he wanted to pay the vendor in full. It is the portion of the purchase price which the seller must wait for.   In practice, the credit needed may be assumed to be the difference between the cash price of the product and the amount of the down payment required when it is sold on the instalment plan, for it may be assumed that the buyer already *has* the amount of the down payment.

The credit required is easily confused with the original unpaid balance when the credit *charge* is added to the purchase price in the original entry on the creditor's books.   By no stretch of the imagination, however, can it be reasoned that the charge is part of the credit *extended*. While it may be part of the sum due from the debtor, the debtor was not financed for the charge in the purchase of the *commodity*.   The credit needed relates to the financing of the commodity; the charge for the credit relates to the cost of that *service* given in addition to the commodity.

In the case illustrated above, if the customer has no money at all, he obviously lacks $400, regardless of the manner in which the charge is expressed.   If a down payment of $50 is required, perhaps in the nature of an allowance on an old refrigerator, the buyer lacks only $350.   This is true even in the third instance, for one could not say that he lacks $424 less $50, or $374, because the price of $424 is arbitrarily determined by the charge made, and had he had $350 more than the $50 for the down payment, he would have made a cash purchase for $400.   It is theoretically unsound to reason that the vendor extended credit for $374, for that would imply that a service charge was being made on the cost of the credit.

3. Ascertain the nominal rate of the credit charge. The object of this step in the computation is to determine a *rate* of charge, unless the nominal rate is already stated in the terms of the agreement.   The nominal rate is found by dividing the cost of the credit by the amount of credit used.   Thus, if the $400 item were bought entirely on credit, without any down payment or allowance on a traded-in product, and the service charge amounted to $24, the nominal rate would be 6 per cent. On the other hand, if a down payment or allowance of $50 were made, the $24 charge would be collected for extending $350 of credit; the rate would then be 6.86 per cent ($24 divided by $350).

4. Compute the nominal rate per annum. For comparative purposes rates must be related to a time period, and the most common rate period in matters of money is the year.   Nominal rates, however, are not always quoted on an annual basis.   It is therefore necessary to convert them to an annual rate.   The general relationship may be expressed by the following equation:

Nominal rate: time involved = nominal annual rate: one year

Another way of achieving the same result is to divide the nominal rate by the time involved (months or weeks) and multiply the quotient by the number of such units in a year (12 or 52).

In the illustration, assuming that the contract extends for 6 months, 6.68 per cent: 6 months $= r{:}12$ months. This means that $6r$ equals 82.32 (6.86 times 12), and the nominal annual rate, represented by r, is 13.72 per cent (82.32 divided by 6).

Strictly speaking, r should be computed on the basis of the time required to repay the *credit used*, and not the sum of the credit used *plus* the charge for the credit. To make the error of including the latter gives the effect of using the credit for a longer period than was actually the case; it understates the rate charged.

5. *Convert the nominal annual rate into an actual or true annual rate.* In view of the fact that the credit in use is reduced as each payment is made on the principal owing, the simple nominal rate per annum does not present a true picture of the relationship between the actual or true rate of charge and the average amount of credit in use. This conversion of the nominal annual rate to an actual rate per annum may be accomplished by the following formula.[6]

$$R = \frac{r(2n)}{(n+1)}$$

In this formula, R is taken as the actual annual rate charged, r stands for the nominal rate of charge per annum, and n represents the number of instalments required to repay the principal. A contract to pay one-twelfth of a given sum at the end of each month for 12 months is equivalent to a contract to pay the entire amount at the expiration of $6\frac{1}{2}$ months (one-half of the number of instalments and one-half of another instalment). Thus, the service charge of 13.72 per cent in the above illustration becomes 23.52 per cent, determined as follows:

$$R = \frac{13.72\%(2 \times 6)}{6+1} = \frac{13.72\% \times 12}{7} = \frac{164.64}{7} = 23.52\%$$

A number of other methods and formulas have been developed in more recent years as short cuts in ascertaining the actual annual cost rate on instalment transactions.[7] One of the best of these formulas is the following:

---

[6] This formula was first developed by the senior author in 1924, and was incorporated in the second edition of this book, published in 1930.

[7] For a detailed presentation of various formulas of a similar character, see Milan V. Ayres, *Instalment Mathematics Handbook*, The Ronald Press Company, New York, 1946; and especially M. R. Neifeld, *Neifeld's Guide to Instalment Computations*, Mack Publishing Company, Easton, Pa., 1953. See also Robert W. Johnson, *Methods of Stating Consumer Finance Charges*, Columbia University, Graduate School of Business, 1964.

$$R = \frac{2\,(\text{payment periods in year})}{(\text{original unpaid balance}) \times (\text{number of payments} + 1)} \times (\text{total amount of finance charge})$$

usually expressed as

$$r = \frac{2pC}{A(n+1)}$$

The only disadvantage to this formula is that it fails to reveal the logic involved. Furthermore, if the terms express the charge as a per cent, such charge must first be converted into an amount, in dollars and cents, before applying this formula.

POLICIES AND
PRINCIPLES IN
INSTALMENT CREDIT

Successful selling on instalment credit is not merely a question of finding this form of credit adaptable to one's business and of making a conventional charge for it. Numerous other aspects of the credit relationship must be considered and policies formulated concerning the sales contract to be used; the size of sales to be financed; the amount of down payment required; the size, frequency, and number of instalment payments to be made; the fees to be charged; and the collection practices to be followed.

Instalment contract required. Because in instalment selling risks are relatively large and financing is required for a considerable period of time, the creditor should use a written contract, along with a promissory note, as a means of minimizing his risk. The contracts used in connection with instalment sales include conditional sales contracts, chattel mortgages, and bailment leases. In the states which have adopted the Uniform Commercial Code (49 states and the District of Columbia by 1968), these contracts are still used, but another document, the security agreement, is becoming more common.[8] Under the Code, each of these forms conveys to the creditor a *security interest* in the goods, and this interest is, in most instances, identical in effect regardless of the contract form used.

The Uniform Commercial Code provides that a security interest is not enforceable against the debtor unless the latter has signed a security agreement which contains a description of the collateral. It further

---

[8] For further information on this subject, see Uniform Commercial Code. See also the *Credit Manual of Commercial Laws*, issued annually by the National Association of Credit Management.

stipulates that a security interest in most kinds of personal property is protected when the creditor or his agent takes possession of the collateral. In the event of the buyer's default, the creditor usually has the right to declare all remaining payments due by virtue of an acceleration clause in the contract. If complete payment is not then made, the creditor has the right to repossess the goods.

Upon default and nonpayment of the total debt by the debtor, the secured creditor may, therefore, elect to take possession of the pledged property, which he may repossess in any peaceable manner. Under the Code, after repossession has taken place, the creditor may proceed to resell the collateral or keep it in full satisfaction of the debt. If the creditor elects to keep the goods, he must notify the debtor in writing of his intent and, if he does not receive objection from the debtor within 30 days, he may retain the property as his own. If the debtor objects, the collateral must be sold.

There is another situation where the creditor *must* sell the goods. If collateral consists of consumer goods, if the debtor has paid 60 per cent or more of the debt prior to default, and if the debtor after default has not signed a statement renouncing his rights in the property, then the creditor is required to sell the goods within 90 days after repossession. At any time prior to resale or retention after notice, the debtor may redeem the property by tendering the amount necessary to pay the debt and the expenses incurred up to that point. The money received at a sale is applied first to expenses, second to the debt, and third to a junior lien if one exists. Any resulting surplus belongs to the debtor. The latter is liable for any deficiencies resulting from the sale of the goods.

Minimum sale. Another principle is that each instalment sale should bear at least in part the credit costs incurred in the transaction. Inasmuch as the direct costs on instalment business are relatively high, there is a problem of determining the minimum sale that can be made on that basis. This problem did not exist when only goods of high unit value were sold in that manner. With the adoption of various budget plans and "storewide" systems whereby all kinds of goods can be bought on deferred payments, a minimum must be set or else the purchases may be so small as to make the business definitely unprofitable. It is not suggested that every sale share its proportionate cost, any more than it would be suggested that every article in a store be sold at a profit. But it would be sound practice to have every instalment sale bear the direct costs and contribute as much as possible to the general overhead.

Reasonable down payment. It is important in planning instalment terms that the buyer have an appreciable initial investment in the goods he buys. This can be accomplished only by requiring a down payment large enough to create a feeling of actual ownership. How large this must be will vary for different commodities and the total amount of the transaction.

From the seller's standpoint, a reasonable down payment is one that covers at least initial depreciation of the goods. This is often measured by the amount of gross margin on which the vendor operates. On automobiles, it varies from 25 per cent to one-third of the purchase price of new cars, and 40 per cent on used cars, which not only covers initial depreciation but provides an added margin of safety. On most other goods it is not practical to be governed by this criterion, hence the requirement that the down payment should be at least as large as any subsequent instalment payment, which thus reflects the buyer's ability to comply with the terms of the transaction. The usual down payments on certain goods are as indicated: 10 per cent on furniture, home furnishings, housewares, refrigerators, oil burners, leather goods, silverware, and radios; 10 to 25 per cent on furs; 20 per cent on women's apparel, stoves, and certain items of furniture; and 25 per cent on men's apparel and automobile tires.

Goods to outlast time of payment. Similarly, the goods sold on the instalment plan should outlast the time of payment or the length of the contract. When the number of instalments is strung out too far, the owner's equity is impaired and the article is worth less than what is owed on it. It is but natural for the customer under such circumstances to let the store repossess the product and thereby relieve him from further responsibility. A definite relationship seems to exist between the average loss on each article repossessed and the number of instalments required to complete payment for the purchase.

It would seem advisable to make buyers pay faster than the goods depreciate, so that their value may at any time exceed the liability of the purchaser. Above all, payments must end before the satisfaction from the goods disappears. The reluctance to pay for an object that has been consumed is too great an obstacle for the average instalment purchaser to overcome. The life of the contract must also be related to the customer's anticipated continuing ability to pay.

In general, long contracts are undesirable. They add to the uncertainty that the goods will at all times exceed in value the amount of the obligation and to the uncertainty of the customer's ability to pay. More capital is required to carry such contracts, the consumer pays more in carrying charges, and the losses from bad debts and repossessions are higher. They may also retard further purchases, even of perishable goods, until the contract has been liquidated.

A principle suggested by one authority in determining the length of the contract *for nondurable or soft goods* is that the down payment, the length of the contract, and the frequency of the instalment payments should be so arranged as to result in a collection percentage on this type of business equal to that obtained by the vendor on his regular charge accounts. Thus if a store has a collection percentage on its regular accounts of 50, the same percentage can be obtained on its deferred-payment business through a down payment of 20 per cent and four monthly payments of the balance or through a down payment of one-third with five monthly payments of the balance. The reason for this suggestion is that such goods are of the charge account type and should not be sold on longer terms, lest the store suffer in its accounts receivable turnover and jeopardize its seasonal business. In the case of durable goods, the nature of the merchandise is a primary determinant of the size of the down payment and whether the period within which payments are to be completed should be long or short. Goods which are of a seasonal nature, even though they may last more than one season, should generally be paid for during the first season.

Frequency of instalments or schedule of payments. The dates of payment of the instalments should coincide with the receipt of income by the customer. If the purchaser receives his wages weekly, his instalments should be arranged on a weekly basis. If most of the customers buying a certain type of goods such as automobiles receive their income monthly, in the form of salaries, they should be required to pay their instalments monthly. Furthermore, the size of the payment must bear a close relationship to the amount of income which the buyer normally receives and to the frequency of the payments. The shorter the period between instalments, other things being equal, the smaller the amount of each instalment.

Some houses encourage payment by the week. It brings customers to the store more frequently, thus giving the store an opportunity to make additional sales. It is also less burdensome for some people to pay in smaller amounts by the week than in larger sums once a month. Other people look favorably upon the idea because small payments weekly do not seem to disturb their budgets or normal mode of living and financing. Against these advantages must be weighed the tremendous amount of bookkeeping and additional collection effort incident to the weekly payment plan.

Reasonable but adequate carrying charges. Another principle is to levy a reasonable but adequate carrying charge. This means that each customer should pay most of the costs involved in selling to him on credit and in carrying his account.   It is believed that many vendors charge too *little* for the instalment privilege on the ground that it is a sales builder.   While a so-called "6 per cent" charge, which actually amounts to about 11 per cent per annum, may be adequate for very large transactions, it is altogether inadequate for small purchases.   Failure to make a reasonable carrying charge may in the short run attract additional business, but in the long run it may gain the dissatisfaction of regular charge and cash customers and the resentment of competitors.

Once ascertained, the carrying charge should be expressed truthfully, as suggested in a previous discussion, in amounts and in percentages where possible, so that a customer may make comparisons of charges by different vendors.   Furthermore, if the balance is paid before maturity, an equitable proportion of the carrying charge should be refunded.   To encourage collections, a schedule of refunds can be established and made known to all customers.

Prompt collections essential. Finally, it is essential that the vendor insist on compliance with the contract that has been executed at time of sale.   When a customer becomes delinquent for a considerable period of time, then he fails to have an equity in the product, since the depreciation of the commodity reduces its value to a point where all equity is wiped out.   Under such conditions he will not resent any attempt at repossession.   An efficient and effective collection system will keep the percentage of repossessions and, hence, losses due to bad debts down to a minimum.   It would prevent a customer, except under certain conditions as when he meets with some unforeseen misfortune, from becoming delinquent or from remaining delinquent over a considerable period of time.   It is the practice of some firms and finance companies, even now, never to allow delinquency to extend over a period longer than two monthly instalments.   Whether such a rigid practice is advisable will depend largely upon the rate of depreciation or length of life and usefulness of the product and the extenuating circumstances responsible for the delinquency.   According to one study of thousands of accounts, 90 per cent of all instalment customers violating their agreements had not made second payments.   This suggests the need for vigorous action if the first or second instalment is missed.

Many difficulties in the collection of instalments will be avoided if due care is exercised in the selection of credit risks and in the construction of the terms of sale.   Good collections always begin with good credit extensions.   The principles underlying instalment collections in no way differ from those that govern the collection of other past-due accounts, a more detailed discussion of which will be presented in subsequent chapters.

FINANCING
PURCHASES
OF CONSUMERS

Not all instalment sales credit is financed directly by the vendor. A large part of it is carried by commercial banks, sales finance companies, credit unions, and other organizations, which finance instalment transactions directly or by purchasing the notes or accounts of the vendor. Approximately 80 to 82 per cent of the outstanding consumer instalment debt is held by financial institutions and only about 18 to 20 per cent by the retail outlets that sold the goods. According to data shown in Table 8-2, commercial banks hold about 40 to 45 per cent of the paper, a large portion of which is purchased from department stores, furniture stores, automobile dealers, and sales finance companies. That held by sales finance companies represents mainly sales on instalment of automobiles, major household appliances, and materials for home repair and modernization. Retail outlets, in other words, although they may *sell* on the instalment plan, directly *finance* only one-sixth to one-fifth of the sales so made. Special consideration is warranted, therefore, of the commercial bank and the sales finance company, both of which play such an important role in this method of distribution.

By commercial banks. The instalment purchases of consumers are financed by banks in three different ways. First, commercial banks make instalment loans directly to consumers for the purpose of financing the acquisition of automobiles, appliances, or other durable goods. The second form is through the purchase of instalment paper generated by time-payment sales of automobile dealers or other merchants of consumer durable goods. Third is the even more indirect process of granting loans to sales finance companies and other financial institutions which then, in turn, either purchase instalment paper or make direct instalment loans.[9]

In the past, commercial banks hesitated to make direct instalment loans, but they were willing to lend indirectly on instalment paper by lending to finance companies which held the paper. In recent years, banks have engaged most actively in direct instalment lending and the purchase of instalment paper. Many banks, however, enforce higher standards for loans directly made than are applied to purchased paper. Part of the explanation for this practice is that when loans are directly made, credit protection, such as that supplied by the reserve for the

---

[9] Purchasing instalment paper and lending to organizations partake more of the character of business credit granting, a subject discussed in some detail in a later chapter.

table 8-2 Instalment Debt Outstanding from the Sale of Merchandise, by Holder, United States, 1948–1967*

(In millions of dollars)

End of year	Grand total	Financial institutions Total	Commercial banks Total	Per cent of grand total	Sales finance companies Total	Per cent of grand total	All others	Retail outlets Total	Per cent of grand total
1948	5,919	4,043	2,122	35.9	1,620	27.4	301	1,876	31.7
1949	8,261	5,928	2,811	34.0	2,712	32.8	405	2,333	28.2
1950	10,873	7,975	3,927	36.1	3,488	32.1	560	2,898	26.7
1951	10,852	7,682	3,761	34.7	3,315	30.5	606	3,170	29.2
1952	13,907	10,085	5,013	36.0	4,310	31.0	762	3,822	27.5
1953	16,614	12,572	6,160	37.1	5,504	33.1	908	4,042	24.3
1954	16,560	12,442	5,817	35.1	5,711	34.5	914	4,118	24.9
1955	21,078	16,570	7,347	34.9	7,930	37.6	1,293	4,508	21.4
1956	22,954	18,211	8,190	35.7	8,443	36.8	1,578	4,743	20.6
1957	24,062	19,394	8,912	37.0	8,780	36.5	1,702	4,668	19.3
1958	23,035	18,052	8,453	36.7	7,882	34.2	1,717	4,983	21.5
1959	26,839	21,163	9,992	37.2	9,090	33.9	2,081	5,676	21.0
1960	29,213	23,598	10,895	37.3	10,267	35.2	2,436	5,615	19.2

1961	29,080	23,485	37.9	11,012	9,911	34.1	2,562	5,595	19.2
1962	32,145	25,893	38.8	12,459	10,572	32.9	2,862	6,252	19.4
1963	36,289	29,536	40.5	14,696	11,611	32.0	3,229	6,753	18.6
1964	40,788	33,381	41.9	17,095	12,590	30.9	3,696	7,407	18.2
1965	46,536	38,244	43.6	20,297	13,670	29.4	4,277	8,292	17.8
1966	50,795	41,704	44.6	22,636	14,220	28.0	4,848	9,091	17.9
1967	52,525	42,852	45.3	23,777	13,976	26.6	5,099	9,673	18.4

* Exclusive of repair and modernization loans held by financial institutions which are for the most part in the nature of improvements of real estate occupied as houses, a large part of which is represented by labor cost rather than merchandise.

SOURCE: Computed from data published in the *Federal Reserve Bulletin*, as follows: for the years 1948–1952, from October, 1956, issue, pp. 1035–1038 and 1040–1042; for the years 1953 and 1954, from the October, 1960, issue, pp. 1164–1165; for the years 1955–1959, from revised data in the December, 1961, issue, pp. 1397–1400; and for the years 1960–1967, from the February, 1968, issue, pp. A–48 and A–49.

absorption of credit losses used when instalment paper is purchased from a dealer, does not exist.   Second, the rates charged by commercial banks on direct loans generally tend to be somewhat lower than those charged by sales finance companies.   This is natural and consistent with the higher quality of customers sought after and generally secured by banks.   Then, too, some banks try to limit the number of small loans by using a lending minimum, such as $300, in order to eliminate some of the fixed charges associated with very small loans.

By sales finance companies. The sales finance company is a private corporate venture in the financing of distribution through the purchase of vendors' instalment sales contracts.   Although its most familiar activity is in the financing of automobile purchases by consumers, much of its business volume is in financing the purchase of automobiles by dealers from the manufacturers.   Sales finance companies, of course, do not confine themselves to the transportation industry but furnish capital to vendors of all types of goods sold on instalment.   In more recent years they have also somewhat diversified their business by making consumer cash loans.

The operations of sales finance companies run into billions of dollars annually, and the capital funds of the three largest of these companies—Commercial Credit Company, C.I.T. Financial Corporation, and General Motors Acceptance Corporation—are about two-fifths of the combined capital of the nation's three largest banks.[10]   This status they have attained since the beginning of this century, when the first sales finance companies were conceived and organized.   Evolving from the practice of factoring accounts, they began to buy open accounts on the nonnotification plan and to purchase the drafts and notes receivable of manufacturers, wholesalers, jobbers, and other types of distributors.   They did not originally buy retail accounts.   As the production of automobiles increased, the necessity of financing their sale on a periodic plan of payment became increasingly apparent.   Sales finance companies gradually assumed responsibility for this function after 1913 and grew in number to almost 1,700 by 1925.   Because of the declining need for their services during the depression and World War II periods, in addition to increased competition from banks and other lenders for passenger-car loans in recent years, the number of sales finance companies decreased to approximately 1,200 in mid-1965.[11]

---

[10] C. W. Phelps, *The Role of the Sales Finance Companies in the American Economy*, Commercial Credit Company, 1962, p. 11. See also C. W. Phelps, *Financing the Instalment Purchases of the American Family*, Commercial Credit Company, 1963, pp. 35–39.

[11] "Survey of Finance Companies, Mid-1965," *Federal Reserve Bulletin*, April, 1967, p. 536.

A typical sales finance office. Naturally, the organization of the offices operated by the different finance companies varies in some respects. On the whole, however, there is a high degree of uniformity and the differences are usually slight. A typical office is headed by a manager who supervises the work of the branch or office, including passing on purchaser and dealer credits above certain brackets, routine office operations, bookkeeping, correspondence, collections, and adjustments. In some cases, a credit and collection manager is employed whose duty it is to pass on consumer and dealer credits up to a certain stipulated sum and to handle all collections. An outside sales manager or solicitor, usually coordinate with the credit and collection manager, to secure dealers' accounts is another member of the office staff. If a given make of automobile is financed through a single company, the solicitor or outside sales manager's services can be dispensed with.

One or more adjusters or outside representatives are generally employed in a sales finance company office to investigate delinquent accounts, make reports on them, and attempt to effect adjustments. To him the company looks for a future credit and collection manager, new business solicitor, or branch manager. Furthermore, he is the one who meets the customer under rather adverse circumstances. He must therefore be a man of considerable tact, friendly disposition, and supported by a good education.

A clerk, stenographer, and accountant, who perform the office work and care for the files, complete the organization. Among the files maintained may be one for dealers' work sheets, one for mortgage or other contract duplicates, one for insurance policies, and one or more collection follow-up files.

Granting the loans. The usual procedure in the financing of an automobile purchase by a consumer is for the buyer to fill out an application, giving in complete detail information concerning his status, source of income, and use to which the car is to be put. The application is signed and witnessed by the salesman or dealer. At the same time, the dealer fills out a work sheet that contains a full statement of the transaction and terms of the sale, showing also the amount which the finance company is to deliver to the dealer if the deal is approved. The usual contract is prepared, which may be a security agreement, chattel mortgage on the vehicle, or conditional sales agreement, and a negotiable promissory note is executed by the purchaser which specifies the number of instalments and the amount of each payment. All these documents are then turned over to the finance company. The risk is then investigated, either by the dealer or by the finance company. If it is done by the dealer, a summary of the results is made on the dealer's work sheet and the decision is recorded thereon.   If the transaction is approved, the account is opened and a record for the customer is established.   The security agreement, chattel mortgage, or conditional sales contract, as the case may be, is placed in the credit folder where all papers bearing the customer's signature are kept.   A copy of the contract is filed with the proper court, one copy is retained in the files of the dealer, one in the files of the finance company, and one is given to the purchaser.   At the same time the finance company notifies the consumer that his note has been purchased, advises him of the insurance coverage, and supplies him with a book of coupons, if the coupon book plan is used, indicating payment dates and the amount and date of each payment.

Collecting the instalments. Consumers usually make payments at the office of the finance company, and their accounts are credited accordingly.   When the final payment is made, the original of the security agreement, chattel mortgage, or sales agreement is returned to the purchaser and the one filed at the court is canceled.   If the customer defaults on a payment, his record is tabbed, and a form letter is usually sent inquiring whether a coupon book has been given to the customer, reason for default, etc.

If notices fail to produce results, the account is classed as delinquent and placed in the follow-up file.   At regular intervals, usually every 3 or 4 days, depending upon the policy of the company, the credit and collection manager refers to it and takes the necessary collection steps by correspondence, making one appeal after another.   If no reaction is obtained as a result of these communications, a field representative or adjuster may be directed to make a personal call on the delinquent and report on the case.   If a satisfactory adjustment is not effected during this call, the credit manager may, on the basis of the report, attempt to straighten out the account through further correspondence or a personal interview.   If no satisfactory results can be obtained, the car is repossessed.   In practically all cases the dealer is kept informed of delinquencies through a list furnished him at stated intervals.

Handling repossessions. The customer's promissory notes, which are handed over to the finance company by the dealer, may be indorsed with or without recourse.   If the former obtains, the dealer himself may repossess the car on order from the finance company, or else the repossessed car is turned over to him by the company and the dealer is required to pay the balance due, less rebates allowed for finance and insurance charges for the unexpired period.   He then reconditions and sells the car, retaining all proceeds for himself. Under the nonrecourse plan, most common today, the repossessed car remains in the hands of the finance company, which must assume full responsibility for the uncollected amount and the reconditioning and resale of the vehicle. A third plan, known as the repurchase system, has developed, whereby the finance company has no recourse to the dealer but enters into an agreement with him to repurchase from the finance company the repossessed product. This relieves the finance company from handling used cars in competition with the dealers whose car sales it finances and obviates the necessity for maintaining garages, repair and sales personnel, and equipment.

In connection with the recourse plan of financing, finance companies are attempting to offer the dealer protection against losses by special dealer reserves. In the first place, the company usually agrees to recover the car for the dealer free and clear of encumbrances, and the car must be delivered to the dealer's place of business. The dealer reserve is accumulated from amounts set aside out of the finance charges collected from customers. It ordinarily amounts to about $1\frac{1}{2}$ to 2 per cent on the amounts advanced on new cars and approximately 2 or 3 per cent on amounts advanced on used cars. The reserve is set up on the books of the finance company and, when it is declared earned, is paid to dealers in good standing. Payments are made periodically so that the dealer may be reimbursed on repossession from two regular sources, the resale of the car and the accumulated dealer reserve.

Financing charges. Instalment sale contract rates are not governed by moneylending laws, but are determined by competition within ceilings increasingly being established by specific state statutes. By 1967 there were 41 states with regulatory legislation in effect having some bearing on instalment selling. Among these, 40 states had legislation covering the sale of motor vehicles, 26 covered the sale of other goods and/or services, and several states specifically included revolving credit in the coverage. Many states set maximum finance charges on instalment sales. Sales of motor vehicles are more extensively covered in this respect (34 states) than are other instalment transactions (17 states).[12] Methods used to express these maximums differ considerably among the various states but most frequently are stated in terms of dollars per $100 per year.

An Ohio law, for example, which became effective in 1949, fixes the maximum base finance charge at the rate of $8 per $100 per year,

---

[12] For more details, see Edgar R. McAlister, *Retail Instalment: Growth and Legislation*, The Ohio State University, Bureau of Business Research, Columbus, Ohio, 1964. See also *Credit Manual of Commercial Laws, 1967*, National Association of Credit Management, pp. 184–193.

computed on the *original* balance of the retail instalment contract. This effectually provides at the outset for an actual rate of approximately 15 per cent on a 1-year contract. In addition, it permits a maximum service charge of 50 cents per month on the first $50 unit or fraction thereof and 25 cents per month on each of the next five $50 units or fraction thereof of the original principal balance for each month of the term of contract. On a contract of $300 and payable in 12 monthly instalments, the base charge in this case would be $24 and the service charge $21. The actual rate involved, therefore, is about 28 per cent. The charge on a 12-month contract for $500 by the same computation is about 23 per cent. On payments delinquent more than 10 days, an additional charge may be made of 5 cents for each dollar of delinquent payment but not in excess of $3 on any one instalment. Fees actually paid by seller, even when collected from buyer, for filing, recording, or releasing an instrument are not considered part of the financing charge, nor is the cost of insurance, where that is agreed upon, so considered.

Scope of operations of sales finance companies. From the foregoing discussion it must not be inferred that sales finance companies are concerned solely with the financing of automobile dealers and consumers in their purchase of motor vehicles. For many years they have been extending their service to the financing of music merchants and the purchase by consumers of such musical instruments as pianos. In more recent years their usefulness has increased through the financing of sales of electrical merchandise. In this latter area the field has been constantly broadening as new types of commodities have been added. Thus, instead of confining financing operations to the sale to or purchase by consumers of such standard items as radios, refrigerators, vacuum cleaners, ironers, ranges, washing machines, food mixers, and storage water heaters, these operations have extended to include dishwashers, disposers, clothes dryers, oil burners, home freezers, mobile homes, boats, and airplanes. Finally, there has been a tendency for sales finance companies and others engaged in similar types of operations to extend the service to the financing of other durable goods such as furniture, either by the purchase from the store of individually selected accounts or by making funds available to the store on the basis of a number of its accounts pledged as security in bulk without revealing the names of the individual accounts thus included in the pledge. This type of financing and accounts receivable financing, however, partake more of the character of factoring, a subject to be discussed in some detail in a later chapter.

The consumer credit protection act. For some eight years Federal legislation has been sponsored consistently and vigorously under the popular and politically attractive but utterly misleading label "Truth in Lending," as if there had been no truth in the statement of finance charges on credit transactions by the hundreds of thousands of business firms selling to consumers on credit or making loans to them, as if there were only one way of telling the truth about such charges, as if no attempt had been made at the truth in the numerous state laws relating to the subject, and as if the contemplated law pertained only to *lending* which has already been substantially covered by state legislation instead of applying to all types of consumer instalment credit transactions.   With the passage of the Consumer Credit Protection Act, the "Truth in Lending" misnomer, apparently deemed to have served its purpose, has been properly relegated to a minor position as a possible substitute of Title I.

Principal disclosure requirement. Of primary importance for this brief discussion is Title I, effective on July 1, 1969, which indicates that the basic requirement of the Act is *disclosure* of credit terms and finance charges made on consumer instalment credit transactions *before* credit is extended, not only as the total cost in dollars and cents but especially in terms of an approximate annual percentage rate.   For this purpose the finance charge, as spelled out, includes not only interest, but also service or carrying charges; loan fees, finder's fees, or similar charges; time-price differentials; investigators' fees; costs of any guarantee or insurance protecting a creditor against default or credit loss if they are a factor in the extension of credit; and any amount payable under a point, discount, or other system of added charges.   Thus, even though the finance charge may be several times the true interest cost or charge involved, it must be expressed as a percentage per annum just as is done in simple annual rates of *interest,* as if all of the finance charge were in the nature of interest to which the annual rate expression is indigenous.   Exempt from the requirement of expressing the finance charge as an annual percentage rate is a charge not over $5 on a transaction involving less than $75 or a finance charge of not over $7.50 applicable to an amount of credit over $75.   Civil liability for failure to comply is for twice the amount of the finance charge, with a minimum penalty of $100 and a maximum of $1,000 plus debtor's costs of the action with reasonable attorney's fees as determined by the court.   There are also other credit transaction exemptions from the Act, but they are not deemed of direct interest to this treatment.

Administrative enforcement of the Act. This is one of the most intricate phases of the law.   On the one hand, the Board of Governors of the Federal Reserve System is charged with the responsibility of prescribing regulations for carrying out the purposes of the Act, preventing circumvention or evasion, and facilitating compliance.   At the same time, the enforcement is placed under 10 different Federal agencies, depending upon the status of the creditors involved, of which each may have its own regulations in addition to those of the Board.   For example, enforcement of the law for national banks is lodged in the Comptroller of the Currency, any common carrier affected is subject to enforcement by the Interstate Commerce Commission, etc.   All those not specifically committed to some other Federal agency, which includes all sellers of goods on credit as well as many lenders like small-loan companies, are subject to enforcement by the Federal Trade Commission which normally has jurisdiction only over those engaged in interstate commerce—a point that may prove most troublesome despite the statement contained in the law that the Commission shall enforce compliance "irrespective of whether that person is engaged in commerce or meets any other jurisdictional tests in the Federal Trade Commission Act."   Criminal liability for a willful and knowing violation involves a fine of not more than $5,000, imprisonment of not more than one year, or both.

Determination of annual percentage rate.   While the Federal Reserve Board is given authority to prescribe various methods that will simplify the computation of the annual percentage rate, including the development of formulas and rate charts, two methods are specifically suggested in the law.   One is the complicated *actuarial* method for computing the simple annual rate on the declining balance, previously referred to in this chapter.   This assumes a uniform periodic rate applied to a schedule of instalment payments, multiplied by the number of periods in a year.   The other suggested method is the *constant ratio* formula, already discussed here, which assumes that all scheduled instalments are equal, payable at equal intervals, fall on due dates which are the same day of each month or other payment period, and that the debtor makes all payments as scheduled both as to time and amount.   These are the suggested methods of converting a possible *nominal* rate that is based on the original unpaid balance into an approximately *effective* rate that is based on a declining balance.   The Act is decidedly confusing when it refers to the approximate effective rate as a nominal annual rate.

Finally, in the case of open-end credit transactions, such as are involved in revolving credit where finance charges are computed on the unpaid balances from time to time, in addition to multiplying the monthly rate by 12 in arriving at the required annual percentage rate, the creditor may also disclose the average effective annual percentage rate of return received from accounts under the plan for a representative period, which would typically be lower.   Alternatively, under certain circumstances, he may disclose a projected rate of return to be received from accounts under the plan.   In any event, the disclosure for such transactions must indicate the basic conditions of the plan and the billing system or method of determining the balance upon which the finance charge is to be imposed.

Summary. The Act requires disclosure of terms and finance charges in credit *advertising* effective July 1, 1969, similar to what has already been discussed.   In Title II it deals with extortionate credit transactions, which are obviously illegal under various existing laws, but declaring a Federal offense the wrongful use of actual or threatened force, fear, or violence, subject to severe criminal penalties (a fine of up to $10,000 or imprisonment of up to 20 years, or both).   Title III deals with wage garnishment, discussed in Chap. 26 of this volume, and Title IV provides for the formation of a National Commission on Consumer Finance, which should result in considerably enhanced knowledge in the field of coverage.   There is no doubt that, on the whole, the law is complex and most difficult of enforcement.   In the face of a questionable need for it when all factors are duly considered, the wisdom of its enactment, effectiveness of its operation, and most of all its real contribution to sound credit management and general consumer welfare only time and experience will provide the necessary proof and justification.

QUESTIONS AND PROBLEMS

1 In what way does consumer instalment credit differ from the ordinary type of retail credit?

2 If the importance of instalment credit in our economy should be questioned, what evidence would you present to meet the challenge?

3 In what ways has the original concept of instalment selling been modified to increase its usefulness to both consumers and retailers?

4 Exactly what can be learned from the ratio of repayments to extensions of consumer instalment credit shown in the last column of Table 8-1?

5 In the January, 1961, issue of *Reader's Digest* there is an article entitled "We Went Bankrupt—On the Instalment Plan" in which instalment credit is blamed for all the bad judgment of both debtors and creditors.   From such a situation the inevitable conclusion to be drawn is that instalment credit is a curse or a plague to be avoided.   Assuming that the facts are correctly stated and that there are other similar cases of hardship attributed to the unwise use of instalment credit, would you be justified in applying the so-called "inch-mile" principle and generalize from such cases that instalment credit per se is detrimental to our society and its economy and should perhaps be forbidden? On the basis of data and other information presented in this chapter for the economy as a whole, explain and elaborate your answer.

6 A customer of too low credit standing to quality for an open account arranged for a revolving credit account with a store that provided them on a 12-month basis.   It was understood that the customer could afford to pay $20 a month to this store, and the account was opened. What limit was set? Assuming that the customer used his credit immediately to the extent of the limit, how much would his service charge be at the end of the first month at $1\frac{1}{2}$ per cent? At the end of the second month? How much would he be "open to buy" at the end of the third month?

7 How would you proceed to advise each of four merchants as to whether they should undertake to sell on instalment credit? One operated a gift shop; the second, a furniture store; the third, a used-car lot; and the fourth, a ready-to-wear store.

8 Is there any alternative to having adequate financial strength if all other factors are favorable to instalment credit operation? Briefly explain.

9 What beneficial effects has instalment selling had upon Americans individually? Collectively?

10 What in your opinion is the most valid criticism of instalment credit? Is this a criticism of instalment credit or of the use made of it?

11 A mail order house advertised in its catalogue that purchases could be made on the instalment plan. From the explanatory material included in the catalogue and the "payment table" therein presented, it was clear, for example, that if a customer purchased $150 worth of the merchandise on that plan, he would have to pay down 20 per cent at time of purchase, $15 would be added as a service charge, and the unpaid balance would have to be repaid in monthly instalments of $11 each. What would be the cost of such credit service in terms of simple rate per annum? Another illustration taken from the same source referred to the purchase of an article for $67, on which the down payment would be 20 per cent, the service charge $7, and the monthly payments $7 each. What would be the cost of such credit service in terms of simple rate per annum? How does this compare with the cost on the $150 transaction, and how do you explain the difference? Is there any justification for computing such cost in terms of simple rates per annum? Explain.

12 The total delivered cash price for an automobile which you have just purchased is $3,850, including all accessories and taxes. In purchasing the car, you were given a trade-in allowance on your old car of $1,750. The balance is to be paid in 24 monthly instalments of $100 each. What is the actual rate of charge per annum involved in this transaction? Show all steps taken in making this computation.

13 You are considering buying a TV set from a local dealer. You have chosen one priced at $350, but you do not feel that you can pay for it in cash at this time. The dealer suggests that you buy it on the instalment plan and offers you the choice of two payment plans. Under Plan A there is a 10 per cent down payment and a financing charge of $\frac{1}{2}$ of 1 per cent per month on the original unpaid balance. Under Plan B there is no down payment and a financing charge of 8 per cent on the original unpaid balance. While under either plan the number of months to pay for the set is flexible, it was decided to pay for it

in 15 months. Which of these two plans offers you the better deal as measured by the value of R? What is the dollar-and-cents cost of each plan to the purchaser?

14 Mr. Brown purchased an automobile on the following terms:

   a Cash purchase price, $2,795

   b Down payment, $900

   c Seller advanced insurance cost for 2 years amounting to $215

   d Buyer had to sign a promissory note in the sum of $2,380, repayable in 20 months at the rate of $119 per month

   What was the cost of financing the transaction as a per cent (true rate) per annum? (Show all the steps taken in making this computation.)

15 The X store advertised a sale of electrical appliances on the instalment plan. An illustration of monthly payments reveals the following terms: An appliance is offered for sale at $295. A down payment of $30 is required, $31 is charged for the easy payments, and the unpaid balance is to be cared for by monthly instalments of $25 each. What was the cost of financing this transaction as a per cent (true rate) per annum?

16 A good used car was purchased for $1,750. As a down payment the purchaser's used car was offered and accepted at a value of $650. The vendor agreed to advance $90 to cover the insurance premium for a period of $1\frac{1}{2}$ years. A finance or service charge of 12 per cent of $1,190 was added to the unpaid balance. The purchaser was required to sign a note for $1,332.80, payable in 17 monthly instalments of $74 each and the eighteenth instalment of $74.80. Compute the actual cost of this transaction in terms of a true rate per annum.

17 What bearing does the Uniform Commercial Code have upon the choice of contract by a vendor of goods on the instalment plan? Explain.

18 A common fallacy is to confuse finance charges on instalment transactions with charges for the mere use of money, in so far as expressing rates is concerned. Why it it a fallacy to do so? Explain in some detail. Assuming this to be desirable, can it be done on all forms and types of instalment sales credit? Why or why not?

19 Propose a program for instalment policies which might be adopted by a vendor contemplating selling on instalment credit.

20 Explain the role which the sales finance company plays in the distribution of consumer goods.

21 Explain the ways in which the instalment purchases of consumers are financed by commercial banks.

22 What are the requirements for determining the annual percentage rates of finance charges on instalment transactions under the Consumer Credit Protection Act (the so-called "Truth-in-Lending" law) and how do they affect the method or methods discussed in this chapter?

23 Evaluate the Consumer Credit Protection Act from the standpoint of need for it, its possible effectiveness, and special problems to be encountered in its inforcement.

CHAPTER NINE

management of
retail credit

Retail credit management usually requires organization for the work, since the activities to be performed are too varied and voluminous for a single person and many of them are too specialized and technical to be combined with the duties of personnel doing other work. The extent to which organization for credit work has developed in any given enterprise, and its relation to other parts of the business, depend upon a number of factors. Whatever the size, however, and whatever the particular variants of the task, the management of credit and collections involves essentially the same problems under all circumstances, and the same principles govern the successful administration of the task.

Place of the credit department in the store. Retail organizations vary considerably in size. This, in turn, affects the place of the credit

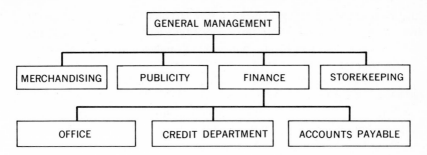

figure 9-1. *Location of credit department in organizational structure of a retail store.*

function in the enterprise and the organization for the task. In most of the grocery stores and drugstores selling on credit, as in many other types of small retail stores, there are no separate departments for the handling of credits and collections. In fact, departmentization of functions, or even of merchandise, may be totally lacking. Even specialization in personnel may be out of the question; all office work may have to be done by the proprietor himself in addition to managing the buying and selling phases of the business.

Where a separate credit department is maintained, it is often merged with other management functions. Some of these other functions are closely related to that of credits and collections and may be actually but parts of the latter. Among these are the supervision and management of the accounts receivable, credit sales promotion, and adjustments. Others, like office management, accounting, statistical control, and detective work, may also sometimes come under the jurisdiction of the person in charge of the credit function. Such person may also be an officer of the company, functioning in the capacity of treasurer, assistant treasurer, vice-president, secretary, or assistant secretary. The usual position of the credit department in a retail store is in the finance division, as shown on Fig. 9-1.

Types of retail credit department organization. The personnel of the retail credit department and the distribution of its functions obviously vary again with the size of the store. For example, a typical specialty store for women's ready-to-wear with approximately 5,000 charge accounts has seven employees including a credit manager, an assistant, a charge-approve clerk, an authorizer, a bookkeeper, and a stenographer. On the other hand, a fairly large department store in the Middle West employs 17 people in credit work, comprising a credit manager, three divisional credit managers (one of whom is handling deferred accounts), two interviewers, three authorizers and refer clerks, three agers of past-due accounts, one name and address clerk, one follow-up clerk, and one outside collector.

In general, retail credit departments are organized on either divisional or functional bases. If the *divisional plan of organization* is used, the charge accounts are divided alphabetically into two or more units of approximately 20,000 accounts in each unit or division, while the Deferred Payment Accounts are usually set up in a separate division. An assistant manager placed in charge of each division is responsible for the whole gamut of credit and collection activities pertaining to the accounts in his division as if he were in charge of a small credit office. Under this arrangement each division is further segmented into sections, with a credit clerk in charge of his block of accounts, subject to the immediate supervision and direction of the divisional credit manager.

The divisional method of organization has several advantages. The broader range of credit activities under this plan provides good training and wide experience. Through diversification of activity, the work is more attractive and less fatiguing. It enables a person to become familiar with many of the accounts under his jurisdiction and thus render more prompt and better service to customers, at the same time safeguarding the interests of the store. As direct responsibility can be placed upon those in charge of sections and divisions and the work in each area is fairly comparable, there is greater opportunity for comparison and control. The chief handicap in this plan of organization is that it does not permit of any high degree of specialization or uniformity of treatment or emphasis on a specific function.

Under the *functional arrangement,* collection functions are separated from those dealing with credit granting, and the latter are subdivided into the charge accounts section, which handles applications, identifications, and credit limits; an authorization section, in charge of a manager who supervises authorizers, refer clerks, tube-room clerks, and others; a credit sales promotion section, with its supervisor, clerks, and typists; an instalment accounts section, with its manager, interviewers, credit clerks, collection clerks, typists, and analyzers; and an accounts receivable section, with its manager, bookkeepers, control clerks, bill adjusters, etc.

The functional plan is on the whole the better of the two and is by far the more widely used. As indicated above, under this plan there is room for considerable specialization. One group of persons may be primarily engaged in taking applications for credit, another may assume responsibility for investigating the applications and the establishment of the account files, a third may go over the accounts for special attention, a fourth may handle the stenographic work, and so on. Such

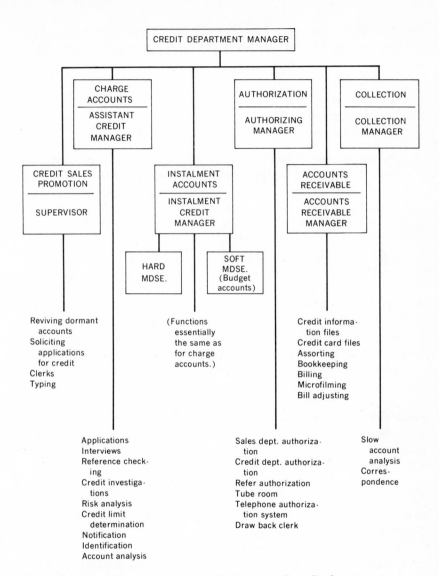

figure 9-2. *Functional organization of a large retail credit department.*

specialization usually spells greater efficiency, but is subject to the weaknesses gleaned from an examination of the advantages of the alternative plan of organization.

An illustration of the functional organization of a credit department in a department store of substantial size is shown in Fig. 9-2. Inasmuch as the functions are essentially the same in all stores similarly operating, regardless of size, the type of organization shown in this figure can be readily adapted to the needs and circumstances of much smaller stores.

FUNCTIONS OF
THE CREDIT
DEPARTMENT

The purpose of organization is that the various major functions and subdivisions thereof might be performed with greater efficiency and less cost.   In credit work, therefore, organization is an administrative aid in the opening of accounts, authorization of credit sales, billing, collection, and the maintenance of credit records.

The opening of new accounts. A main function of credit management is the opening of new accounts.   This is a continuing work, and it represents an effort made to gain additional sales volume by increasing the number of customers buying on credit.

New accounts come from a variety of sources.   Some may be opened by encouraging the store's own employees to establish their credit.   Others are obtained by personal or mail solicitation of current cash patrons, by opening accounts for prospective customers newly come to the community or recently attaining a status which indicates creditworthiness, or merely by accepting credit applications voluntarily submitted.   There is no limit to the ways of enlarging the list of charge or instalment credit customers and of developing them into profitable accounts.   The activities involved in opening new accounts are discussed in the following paragraphs.

Handling the application. Applications may be received at any time in the course of business, but they are often submitted when a customer is in the store to buy something.   The credit department must be prepared to handle applications promptly, for a sure way of creating a favorable impression upon customers is by displaying efficiency in credit operation.

If the customer presents his application personally, an interview may be had and sufficient information gained to authorize an immediate purchase which he may wish to make.   This would be followed by the usual investigation of the risk.   Applications received by mail are handled in the routine of investigation.

Investigation. Increasing numbers of retail credit departments are using numerical point-scoring systems for evaluating credit applications. As discussed in Chap. 5, these systems involve assigning weighted values to each of the various items obtained on the application. The points, or scores, from a number of such predetermined factors are then added together to derive an individual applicant's total score which, when compared to a standard established by the store, serves as a guide in distinguishing between acceptable and undesirable accounts, establishing account limits, and determining the type of account suited to the applicant's ability to pay. These systems establish merely a *frame of reference* for the credit staff. They do not substitute for good judgment and they do not necessarily reduce the need for investigating other sources of information on many applicants. The following are the sources from which relevant information may be obtained:

1 Credit bureau reports and rating books
2 Other creditors who have extended credit to the applicant
3 The applicant himself, his landlord, employer, or neighbors
4 Banks, attorneys, and others given as references
5 Court records
6 Published registers, directories, etc.

The number of these sources which will be used in any one case depends upon how creditworthy the applicant appears to be, the quality of the information obtained, and the amount of credit involved. It also depends upon the resources and facilities of the credit department. The need for speed, size of the order in question, apparent quality of the risk, the budget for investigation, all of these factors additionally determine the nature and extent of the investigation.

Assigning a credit limit. When the investigation is completed and the risk found creditworthy, the account is established and a limit set for it. The limit, however, is seldom announced to the consumer, except in the case of revolving or instalment accounts where limits are an integral part of those forms of credit. Limits, nevertheless, are usually determined and are used for the benefit of the store in authorization and in collection work. The function of such limits and the methods of determining them are discussed in a later chapter.

Notification of credit applicants. When the credit application is approved, the customer is notified so that he may proceed to use his credit. Forms of notification vary, ranging from formal, dignified announcements to effusive letters of welcome and highly promotional sales pieces. Whatever the tone of the communication, the notification affords an incomparable opportunity for instructing the customer in the proper use of the account and in the terms of payment upon which the account is based. Simultaneous notification of the opening of an account should also be given the accounting department, and proper records should be prepared for credit authorizers.

If opening of the account is delayed or if the application is rejected, notification should be so couched as to benefit the applicant with whatever advice or recommendation may reasonably be given him, to avoid imputation of lack of character or competence, and to preserve future business relations on a cash, if not on a credit, basis.

Identification of charge customers. Once an account is established, it becomes the duty of the credit department to devise a system for the handling of charge purchases on such an account that will enable the department to exercise as complete a control over such transactions as is practical. If the system used in authorizing charge purchases is poor or inadequate and errors creep in at frequent intervals, the success of the credit department, together with the reputation of its manager, is seriously jeopardized.

Proper treatment of authorization routine and responsibility calls for a distinction between "charge taken" and "charge sent" purchases. These are frequently designated as "charge take with" and "charge send" transactions, or merely "takes" and "sends." The principal reason for this distinction lies in the problem of identifying customers, inasmuch as this arises chiefly in connection with "take with" purchases, when the customer must be properly identified before leaving the store with the merchandise. In case of "sends," however, the address to which the goods are delivered and the signature of the recipient on the delivery slip serve as adequate means of identification.

In a store of any size, the problem of identifying charge customers in order to make sure that the purchasers on credit are entitled to buy on the specified accounts is complicated by the large number of transactions on a single account and by the fact that more than one person may be authorized to buy on such account. It is extremely important that the identification means used by the store should possess certain characteristics: it should be distinctive, economical, durable, revocable, flexible, convenient, and retainable. While several devices have been employed to this end, as discussed below, the problem of properly identifying those who may be entitled to buy on credit on certain accounts still remains largely unsolved.

Identification by signature. Identification by signature is still the most widely used form of identification. At times the signature given in connection with a purchase is checked against other signed credentials which the individual may be carrying and which he may be asked to display "for identification." Drivers' licenses, organization membership cards, Social Security cards, and the like furnish such a basis for comparing signatures. At other times the signature written on the sales slip is compared with the customer's signature on his credit application in the credit department. This latter method is especially effective when used in conjunction with the pneumatic tube system of authorization, by which the signed sales slip is sent directly to the credit department. In some stores, signature verification is also being made through the use of closed-circuit television which transmits a picture of the signed sales slip to the credit department.

Whatever method of comparison is used, the signature identification has several advantages. It has a unique psychological effect upon people with fraudulent intentions. It also makes easier the tracing of fraudulent purchasers when the attempt is repeated and the securing of a conviction once they are apprehended. The signature method is also helpful in carrying out instructions of patrons. Because of domestic difficulties, for example, a husband may wish to stop all purchases by his wife made on his account. He may then instruct the credit department not to approve any purchases unless the sales checks bear a certain signature, which may be his own name signed in a certain way or may consist merely of the telephone number or street address instead of the signature. On the other hand, unless some comparison of the signature is made at the time of purchase—and this is not always done—positive identification is somewhat sacrificed in consideration of the time saved by a simple method, and in recognition of the fact that relatively few people identify themselves falsely in connection with charge accounts.

Credit cards. A widely used method of identifying charge customers is by means of credit cards, such as those depicted in Fig. 7-1, and other tokens that might be furnished by vendors to their charge account customers especially in the form of Charga-Plates. This type of device serves to identify credit customers as those to whom the store has given a symbol of its confidence in them. The tangible evidence of their charge account constitutes also a reminder of the store and thus may increase the buyer's patronage. The identifying device facilitates credit authorization in the sales department, for it furnishes sales clerks with a recognizable and uniform basis for making charge sales. This is especially true of the Polaroid card, which is being distributed by Addressograph Multigraph Corporation (see Fig. 7-2). The color photograph encompassed in this card drastically simplifies the positive identification of credit customers. Still another feature of some credit cards is that they are marked as valid until a stated date. The need for periodic renewal is also an opportunity for the store to reconsider its accounts, to restrict their credit, or even to close an account if that step should be warranted.   This type of identification thus has several advantages over the signature alone, for it may aid in credit control as well as in its authorization.   Many retailers have, however, eliminated the expiration date on credit cards primarily because of the costs of maintaining such a system and issuing replacement cards.

Credit cards, however, pose problems which are not found in the use of signature identification.   One is the frequent neglect of the customer to carry his identification card when shopping.   To accommodate the account under such circumstances, it is usually necessary that the signature be accepted even though cards have been furnished.   Another difficulty grows out of the loss or theft of credit cards and their subsequent use by unrecognized finders, as discussed in Chap. 7.   Of less importance is the soiled appearance which cards acquire from much use and the consequent necessity to replace them, now overcome by the use of plastic cards.   The effort to remedy such weaknesses as these has led to the development of still other means of identification.

Identification by floormen. Because of the objections to coins and cards, customers are identified in many stores by the floor managers. Where this system is used, the floorman is generally required to identify customers whose purchases exceed a certain amount, say, $25, before the charge is referred to the authorizer in the credit office.   Otherwise, the sales slip or the information thereon is transmitted directly to the authorizer, depending upon the mechanical equipment in use, where the charge is authorized or rejected.

Obviously, it is impossible for a floorman to know all customers possessing accounts at the store.   He is therefore required to exercise some judgment in the matter, for he is generally more responsible than the average sales clerk in the store.   He may ask the customer to present some means of identification, such as a letter addressed to him or her, a driver's license, a bank passbook, a store's monthly statement addressed to the customer, a Social Security registration card, or something of like nature.   At best, the plan is haphazard and represents a weak link in the credit system.

Charga-Plate identification. About the middle 1930's the Charga-Plate token came into vogue.   It is now used by many of the large department stores throughout the country.   It usually is a small plastic plate and has on it the name of the customer, the account number, a space for the customer's signature, and sometimes the credit limit and address of the customer.   When a charge purchase is made, the customer hands the Charga-Plate to the salesperson, who inserts it in an addresser that prints the name and address on the sales check.

The chief virtues of this method of identification are that (1) it saves time since it is faster than handwriting the address; (2) it prints the name and address clearly and accurately, thereby minimizing errors in billing and delays in delivery; (3) it obviates the necessity of spelling out one's name and address within the hearing of others. Additional plates for persons authorized to buy on a given account can be secured upon application of the charge customer.

This device, however, is subject to several disadvantages. As with cards, many people do not remember to carry the Charga-Plate with them and sometimes postpone shopping until this convenient form of identification is brought along. Other customers dislike the idea of carrying small objects in their purse or pocket. There is also a possibility of its being lost or stolen. If found by unscrupulous individuals, the plate may be used to make purchases, to the detriment of the store. It is possible, moreover, that certain abuses will be made of this identification, for in case an account is stopped by the credit department, there is no way of recalling the plate from the customer. Consequently, there is a possibility that purchases will be made by its aid, at least occasionally, even though clerks are informed of such possible abuse. Finally, there is the cost of operating the system. Stamping the plates involves some cost, as does the purchase or rental of the Charga-Plate imprinters by which the impression of the plate is transferred to the sales slip.

To increase the usefulness of Charga-Plates, several stores in some cities have joined together in the use of common plates. The plate is thus prepared with a notch representing each of the cooperating stores in which the customer has an account. This notch then fits the plate for insertion in the presses of that store. The value of the plate is thus enhanced in the eyes of the customer, who may use it in the several institutions. It is also likely that, surmising that if the credit is good in one store it probably would be in another of the cooperating stores, customers may be encouraged by this plan to open additional accounts and so to lessen their loyalty to the store of their original account.

AUTHORIZATION
OF CHARGE
PURCHASES

Authorization is the function of credit administration that involves approval of specific purchases by customers after they have been duly identified. It is aimed principally at keeping the amounts of credit extended within reasonable bounds, in relation to the limits that are deemed warranted for the respective accounts, and partly as a protection against possible dishonest practices of salespeople. Inasmuch as this function is usually performed against the pressure of time, authorization practices represent the measure of accuracy and security which is sacrificed for speed and economy. As a rule, authorization occurs on three distinct levels of credit operation: on the sales floor, from the credit department records, and from the credit manager. In an ascending order of authority, these three forms of authorization are, first, the simpler charge transactions, second, the ordinary charges, and third, the exceptional charge sales, respectively.

Sales floor authorization. Authority to accept identification presented by customers and to release merchandise on a charge sale is delegated in part to the sales personnel. Usually they may authorize sales up to $10 upon signature alone and up to $25 upon presentation of tokens such as Charga-Plates. In thus expediting the approval of these small transactions, the store eliminates the tedious, time-consuming, and costly reference of every charge sale to the record files. Time is saved for both store and customer. Although some losses of necessity occur as a result of this casual method of operation, the saving is supposed to exceed the loss.

Credit department authorization. Credit sales involving sums greater than are wisely trusted to the discretion of sales personnel are authorized by the credit department after reference to its account files. By brief examination of the authorization file or the ledger record of the buyer in question, the authorizer in the credit department can find whether any reason exists why credit should not be given in the particular instance to the person presenting his identification. Accounts are sometimes temporarily stopped for a number of reasons: they may have reached or exceeded their limit, the debtor may be far behind in his payments, he may have failed to communicate with the store upon request, the customer responsible for payment may have restricted the account, etc. This condition of the account may be shown by a tab or signal attached to the authorization file, by the statements filed with the ledger record, by the fact that the record has been moved to a separate file of "stopped" accounts, or by other similar devices intended to designate the account as one requiring individual consideration at the time a sale is made to it. Depending upon the condition of the particular account, authorization is either given or refused; if the latter is the case, the party seeking the use of the account is usually requested to go to the credit department, where the cause of the refusal can be discussed and possibly removed.

Unless an efficient system of record keeping is maintained, such credit department authorization would obviously consume time and personal effort.   In order to combine maximum speed with sufficient security, two general methods of authorization have been developed: negative authorization and authorization directly from the credit files.   By the *negative authorization* method, each sales inquiry referred to the credit department is checked against a list of *accounts on which credit has been stopped.*   If the name in question is found there, the immediate transaction is not authorized.   If it is not found there, it is assumed that the account remains among those whose credit is good, and no direct reference is made to those cards before authorization is given. With this method it is possible, therefore, that a customer with ill-gotten identification and no account might obtain authorization for a purchase because the name did not appear on the list of *bad* accounts.   While this abuse infrequently occurs, it is felt that the time saved in checking only the doubtful accounts may exceed in value the losses resulting from this imperfect check.

In direct, or positive authorization, a check is made against the credit record in the main files of the department.   There, the present status of the account—up to the time of the last posting of sales slips and payments—can be seen, and ample evidence observed for the authorization of the present transaction.   This is the more careful method, but it does involve more physical effort and time, or at least more elaborate facilities, for in large credit departments the thousands of cards may require several rows or aisles of tables.   The task of locating the record for every account called for from the sales floor is no small undertaking.

A number of the larger stores place two credit limits on the authorization file, one to be used primarily by the regular authorizer and the other for main use by the "refer" authorizer.   The first symbol for so-called "preliminary" authorization usually consists of a numeral representing a certain money value.   For example, numeral 1 may equal $25, 2 may be equal to $50, and so on.   The second symbol representing the account limit ordinarily consists of letters, so that letter A may equal a credit limit of $50, B may represent a limit of $75, etc.   Thus a credit limit of 1B would mean that the authorizer could allow a charge up to $25, although the refer authorizer may allow purchases up to $75, including the balance owed.   Special symbol designations are used for the unusually poor and for the unlimited accounts, respectively.   With many stores the procedure is much simpler, only one credit limit being assigned to each customer, which is expressed either in numbers or in letters.   One such store, for example, uses the following arrangement: 1 represents a credit limit of $10, 2½ equals a limit of $25, 5 equals

$50, etc.   A certain department store with around 80,000 accounts uses the following code for credit limits: G = $25; H, $50; K, $100, L, $150, N, $250; O, $500; and T, unlimited.

Authorization by credit manager. Ordinarily the credit manager does not concern himself with authorizations on accounts once they are opened and maintained in good order.   His approval is usually required only on the initial transaction when the account is opened, or at the time of subsequent sales involving extraordinary amounts of credit, as might be the case in purchases of furniture, major electrical appliances, tailored apparel, etc.   The manager in these instances may possess no more information than is available to other authorizers in the credit department, but the requirement of his approval forestalls the possibility of major credit transactions escaping his attention and he no doubt is more capable of using sound judgment in the matter.

Authorizing "charge sent" purchases. When retail charge purchases are to be delivered, the problem of handling them is greatly simplified.   It not only obviates the necessity of providing means for identification, but it also makes possible authorization at a central point.   If the purchases are within certain limits, they are likely to be authorized in the charge authorization section located in the delivery department.   If a large amount is involved, or if alterations are to be made, the sales check is sent to the refer authorizer in the credit department or the charge phone may be used for the purpose.

AUTHORIZATION
FACILITIES

All retail credit authorizations made off the sales floor require that the sales slip, or the information contained thereon, be referred to the credit department in order that the customer's name and amount of purchase may be checked with the status of his account by the authorization file or by his ledger record.   To handle this transfer, several types of communicating equipment have been developed, consisting of authorization telephones, pneumatic carrier tubes, telautograph systems, and mechanical carriers.

Authorization by telephone. One of the methods in use throughout the country involves authorizing by means of especially designed telephone systems, such telephones being also known as "charge phones," "OK telephones," "electric charge phones," or "Touch Tone" and "Touch Calling" telephones.   The telephone equipment of many of these systems consists of telephone units located in the selling departments throughout the store and a master switchboard in the credit office where the necessary credit files are maintained.   Connection is made by the sales clerk with the authorizer by a number of methods, including push buttons, dials, or simply picking up the headset of the phone.   Whatever the method, connection is established, and the salesperson conveys to the authorizer the necessary information from the completed sales check regarding the transaction, including the customer's account number, name, address, and the amount of the sale.   The authorizer refers immediately to the authorization file or ledger records and if the charge is in order, transmits an O.K. to the sales clerk.   If authorization cannot be made, the salesperson is advised as to what steps to take.   If it is difficult for the authorizer to identify the customer because of wrong address, wrong initials, wrong spelling, or if the authorizer finds that restrictions have been placed on the account, the charge is transferred to a refer authorizer for consideration.

Telephones are also used in computerized authorization systems, such as illustrated by the "Touch-Tone Card Dialer" shown in Fig. 9-3. Under this system, the clerk inserts the customer's credit card into the automatic dialer to establish connections with the computer and identify the account.   By the use of the push buttons to record the amount of sale, the computer can be queried as to whether the purchase may be authorized.

The pneumatic tube system. Under this system a number of tube dispatch stations are placed throughout the store at certain strategic points.   In case the tube system is used in conjunction with a central cashiering station, the carriers must be distinguished by some color. Thus, in many stores using this system, cash sales checks together with the cash payments are carried in gray-capped purses or carriers.   These are opened and handled by the cashier and the change, if any, together with the sales-check copy for the customer, returned by way of the cash carrier belt conveyor, moving along the desk of the cashier to the carrier return dispatcher and thence back to the department making the sale. Charge sales checks are carried in red-capped or in green-capped purses, which are relayed in the tube room to the credit office, unless a charge authorization section is located in the tube room, which is very often the case.   To distinguish further between "charge taken" and "charge sent" purchases, the entire carrier of one or the other may be painted red or any other color.   In this manner, it is possible to give preference to those transactions which require immediate attention.

Just before entering the authorization room, charge and cash transactions may also be separated by a projection on the side of the

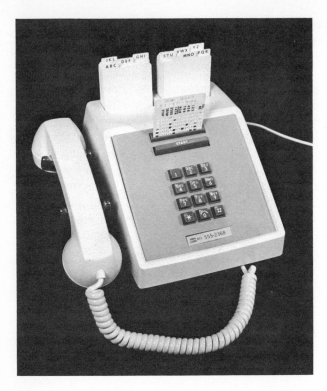

figure 9-3. *Touch-Tone Card Dialer used for access to computer for immediate credit checking of inserted credit card account and possible authorization of the amount indicated by caller's pressing of buttons. The cards at top contain numbers called frequently, which, when inserted, are dialed automatically. (American Telephone and Telegraph Company.)*

carrier. Charge slips may then be placed in a carrier having a smooth surface on both sides while cash sales slips are placed in the other type of carrier. When the rough edge comes in contact with a certain point in the tube, the carrier is switched over to another tube which leads to the cashier. The smooth-edge carrier continues on its way to the authorizer. The carriers from the various stations are numbered and are thus returned to their respective points of origin.

When personal checks are offered in payment, they may be approved by floormen or department managers, if within certain limits, and handled as cash transactions. Should these limits be exceeded, the bank checks are forwarded, together with the sales checks, to the charge authorization desk and, if approved, a rubber band is placed around the

carrier. The rubber band signals the cashier located in the tube room
to open the carrier and handle the transaction as a cash sale.

The original sales checks are placed in bins as soon as approved.
From these they are collected at frequent intervals by messengers from
the bookkeeping or auditing department. In this manner practically all
the charge sales are posted in the ledger and otherwise handled by the
auditing department during the day the sales are made.

The telautograph. Another system for authorization is an electrical mechanical writing device known as the "telautograph." Combined
receiving and sending stations are placed in the credit department and
on the different floors, and all communication is carried on by means
of writing which is electrically transmitted to the desired station. All
sorts of confidential inquiries can be thus made and replies received
without the customer overhearing anything. No telephones are tied up
while waiting for a reply, and signatures or initials of the persons communicating may appear on the slip as a means of fixing responsibility.

The carrier system. The so-called "cash carrier system" offers
another method of authorization, particularly for the smaller stores. The
carriers are fastened to a belt which is propelled by an electric motor.
This belt transfers the carriers from station to authorization room and
return much the same as in the case of the tube system. The belt
is constantly moving, and the carriers come in contact with it only when
forced, a rough edge of the carrier forming the contact. This system
is much slower than any of the systems described in these pages and
frequently fails to work. It permits, however, centralized control of credit
transactions which stores of any size could not secure unless they could
afford to install one of the other systems of authorization.

Principles governing choice of authorization system. In view of
the fact that mechanical conveyor systems are generally too slow for
large organizations and telautographic devices are not yet widely in use,
for practical purposes choice of system lies between telephones and
tubes. The merit of either for a particular installation must be judged
from the capacity of either to meet the requirements of such a system,
as judged by the following factors:

Speed. Speed in consumer credit authorization is of primary importance so long as it is consonant with accuracy. It is claimed that
by using telephones, transactions can be completed in from 10 to 30
seconds. Tubes are reputed to require a somewhat longer time; however,
the producer of tube systems claims that only 40 seconds is necessary

for cash sales and less than 1 minute for charge authorizations. Inasmuch as carriers move through the tubes at a rate of 30 to 40 feet a second, contact may be established with department authorizers almost as quickly by one method as by another. The length of time required to complete the transaction then depends in part upon the record facilities maintained at the authorization center and in part on the necessity of withdrawing the sales slip from the carrier and inserting it back for its return to the appropriate sales station.

Flexibility. To accommodate the constant ebb and flow of sales volume among different departments and on different days, it is imperative that any authorization system be adaptable to a wide variety of conditions. Provision is usually made in systems of both tubes and telephones for the addition of other outlets. Additional telephone units are sometimes connected in different locations to supplement the permanently installed junctions.

Tube systems may be regarded as flexible in that additional ones may be installed with outlets in areas subject to business peaks. This, of course, involves installation costs and an investment for equipment unused during periods of normal business. The operation of tube systems is more flexible than their installation, inasmuch as compressor systems are so developed as to permit the operations either of individual tubes or of the entire system. In so far as the addition of cash registers and telephones entails mainly a wiring job, it is easier in many instances to increase this facility than to increase or redirect the tube capacity, notwithstanding the fact that in modern store construction wall and floor ducts are often provided for enlarging pipe, wire, or tube installations.

Cost of installation and upkeep. Neither type of system is inexpensive, and the cost of each depends upon whether a new or old building is being equipped and the elaborateness of the facilities desired. While extensions of tube systems are often difficult and costly, the equipment is not so expensive to install initially. Sales-department tube outlets are comparatively simple, and the bulk of the complicated and costly apparatus is behind the scenes, but in the case of telephones, the authorization facilities must be supplemented by cash registers. These vary in cost, but in larger institutions they frequently become very expensive. Thus not only are tube installations somewhat less costly than telephone authorization, when cash register provisions must also be furnished, but their maintenance cost is also reported to be low and the depreciation of the installation is slight.

Miscellaneous considerations. A further requirement of the authorization system is that it safeguard accuracy and privacy, at the same time aiding in all possible ways in the keeping of records. The telephone eliminates the handling and rehandling of the sales check, which results in its becoming folded and crumpled and in its sometimes being returned to wrong sales departments by the tube system. It obviates any possibility of mixing one transaction with another.

On the other hand, only by seeing the sales slip with its signature can an authorizer give his best judgment on the authenticity of the buyer's identification. Telephone usage requires that the authorizer rely upon the salesperson to scrutinize the credentials of the buyer. Moreover, another objection to telephone authorization of "charge takes" is the possibility of impostors buying on the accounts of bona fide patrons as a result of their having heard the patron's name mentioned over the telephone. It is then not difficult for the person with fraudulent intentions to go to another department and purchase on the account which he has found in good standing. Yet the proper use of the telephone may be a good remedy for fraudulent buying, for by it quick communication may be made with the store's protection department, which can act at once to apprehend the impostor.

BILLING

Charge account administration has for many decades followed a conventional plan of posting and billing, which in recent years has in the larger stores undergone some radical changes in the interest of increased efficiency. The standard procedure has been to post each day's credit sales slips to the ledger card of the account, showing both the description of the purchase and the amount. At the end of the month the customer's ledger statement is summarized and a bill prepared for mailing to him.

Under the new plan, posting and billing are both simplified and staggered. Sales slips are filed each day with the customers' cards in the active ledger file. No posting to the ledger is done, however, until the time for billing the account, when all sales are posted and the sales slips, after being microfilmed, are attached directly to the bill and sent to the customer. Instead of all bills being prepared at the month's end, certain alphabetical sections of the files are billed each day, the complete billing being performed once each month. This is called *cycle billing*.

This plan of billing has the obvious advantage of spreading the work, thereby eliminating month-end peak loads and the need for additional equipment and personnel. Incoming payments, moreover, are received throughout the month, and collections are facilitated by accounts coming due continuously rather than at monthly intervals. The advantages are sufficient to have induced most large stores to adopt the new billing plan, and its use is becoming increasingly widespread.

WATCHING, REVIVING, COLLECTING ACCOUNTS

Because credit is perishable and consumers' habits changeable, continual review of accounts is necessary. One purpose of this review is to learn if account holders are continuing to buy on credit. Another is to see that they are using their accounts in accord with the terms agreed upon.

Watching the accounts. Once an account is accepted, to guard against running up charge purchases beyond the limit warranted and in order to obtain and file all relevant facts pertaining to the account, it is essential that a good credit office system be established. Such a system should provide means for securing and filing all credit information in a manner which will make the data available for quick reference. It should facilitate the handling of changes of condition and address in order always to keep the files corrected. It should provide an automatic check on a customer when the limit is approached too closely with a possibility of exceeding it. Finally, a good credit department system should have a definite means of keeping the proper department informed concerning changes in residence, deaths, divorces, changes of names by marriage or otherwise, and any other changes which would affect the mailing lists or which offer possibilities for soliciting patronage effectively. Most of these ends are provided through the proper adaptation and use of the types of files and facilities discussed later in this chapter.

Reviving dormant accounts. Although attention is directed primarily toward opening new accounts in the credit department, revival of inactive ones is a no less important activity. Dormant accounts represent an investment of money spent originally to get the accounts opened, a sum estimated at between $10 and $20 each. For reasons of dissatisfaction with indifferent or discourteous treatment and poor service, unadjusted grievances, too high prices, the influence of friends shopping elsewhere, removals, and deaths, credit customers discontinue use of their accounts. Thus business amounting to the product of the number of inactive accounts times the average store sales per customer is lost. Through proper credit management, directed through conversational but sincere letters serialized in from 3 to 12 mailings, a large percentage of this lost business can be regained in reactivation of the account.

Stimulating active accounts. It must not be assumed that all technically active or nondormant accounts are as active as they should be when judged by the business volume obtained on the average from customers in the same income class or in terms of potential. Moreover, based on our propensity to consume, even reasonably active customers could no doubt make more use of the store's facilities and thus spend more on its merchandise and services.   Much can therefore be done through effective credit sales promotion to secure more business from active customers to the benefit of all concerned.

Collecting accounts. The tasks of extending credit and making collections are allied not only in the fact that the one is a functional outgrowth of the other, but in their use of common records.   For these reasons, the credit manager is also directly or indirectly responsible for collections.   The extent to which collections are a specialized, functional activity, however, depends partly upon the size of the institution and the volume of its credit business.

In some instances, the need for collection activities is the result of improper credit granting, for when the character, capacity, or capital of an applicant are misinterpreted or the conditions surrounding the risk are disregarded, credit may be granted to unworthy persons.   Collecting then becomes the effort to obtain from the buyer a payment for which his normal mode of living makes no provision, and the success of the endeavor depends upon the persuasiveness, diligence, and perseverance of the collector.   On the other hand, in many other instances the delinquency of debtors does not really represent an error in credit granting, but only a temporary default of a fundamentally good risk.   By disposition, individuals are often negligent and forgetful, with the result that it is a common condition of retail credit that accounts are outstanding longer than the terms provided and yet without serious disturbance or concern of the business.   In both these instances, however, the duty of the person in charge of collections is to initiate proceedings which will gain payment, whatever the cause of the delay may be.

To collect overdue accounts with a minimum of bad debt loss on the one hand and good will of customers on the other is a task that calls for a scientific approach to, and handling of, the problem.   Routines must be established, letters are carefully prepared, arrangements are made for telephoning debtors, and policies are formulated for enlisting the aid of collection agencies and attorneys or for enforcement of payment by legal means.   Adaquate and competent personnel must be charged with the reponsibility of this work.   The various important aspects of the subject of collections are covered in detail in a number of chapters later in this volume.

CREDIT FILES
AND RECORDS

The records of the credit department constitute one of the most valuable and voluminous sets of records in the retail store.   They are also one of the most-used sets of records. Consequently, they must be set up with an interest not only in their permanence and preservation but also in their accessibility and usefulness.

Although many variations in the types of equipment are found, there are basically a few types of files which are used in most credit departments: the tickler file, with dated compartments for automatically bringing items to attention at predetermined times; the credit history card, or ledger record file; the authorization file; the credit folder; the card index; the inactive file; the microfilm file; and the collection file. How many of these will be in actual use depends upon the size of the organization, the prominence of credit in the business, and the attention given to order and routine therein.

The credit history card file. The records in most frequent use are those contained in what is commonly known as the *credit history card file.* For each account opened a card is made out bearing the name, address, credit rating, and credit limit of the individual. Other information on it may include some of the facts learned in the interview or in the credit investigation made in connection with the opening of the account. In fact, the credit card may be the same card as the interview form.

The credit history card is usually designed to fit the facilities of the department. A 3- by 5-inch index card placed in one or more drawers may be used for this purpose and filed vertically in accordance with a decimal system of numbers and split letters. This system is not adapted to large establishments, however, for it is too slow and inaccurate. There is always the possibility of cards being misfiled, particularly when handled in large numbers. Furthermore, it does not show at a glance all the information desired. For these reasons more elaborate tray files and visible indexes have been substituted, which show at a glance all the essential data an authorizer wants to know. Cards so filed furnish authorization instructions, and they serve also as a repository for credit sales slips which are accumulated until the time of billing.

For such records, commonly used for authorization of credit purchases, two types are in general use by progressive stores. One is the flat-drawer type of visible index and record. Although it requires frequent opening of the drawers and the use of one drawer may interfere with the use of another, its chief merit is that it obviates the necessity of thumbing cards. It also shows all the essential data for authorization purposes at a glance. It thus increases productivity of personnel in a vital work station area.

The other is the rotary-type file, as shown in Fig. 9-4, which has been developed over the years into a highly efficient unit. By pushing

figure 9-4. *Rotary-type file used for credit authorization and other purposes.* (*Diebold, Incorporated.*)

a button the desired tray containing the record sought is automatically brought to the front of the clerk and held there by a latch-type button as long as needed. The file can be stopped in motion by pressing a "stop" button, the lightweight short trays make all records accessible, and a single file unit may contain numerous records.

It is generally considered good practice for authorizers to keep records of their work to make possible intelligent planning for improvements. These records show the number of charges passed on daily and the number reserved until the day following. In addition, the refer authorizer should have records showing purchase and payment habits of the account; ratings; restrictions, if any; extra or special instructions; reference number of folder file; and the signature of the customer.

System for small stores. It stands to reason that for small stores with but a few hundred credit accounts no elaborate filing and authorizing or record-keeping procedures are needed. In fact, simple trays next to the cash register where such transactions are handled may be sufficient. This accommodates the ledger cards and statements in one index; it provides instant balances on accounts that are mechanically computed; furnishes the customer an itemized record of each item purchased, the total, previous balance, and the new balance; and provides the store a daily control of total outstandings. On the other hand, the system is too expensive for stores with, say, fewer than 300 charge accounts and too cumbersome for stores with more than 1,000 accounts. Furthermore, it is not well suited to stores that are highly departmentized. Too many slips would accumulate in such cases within a very short time and clutter up the register.

Credit folder file. In this file is kept detailed and miscellaneous information concerning the account, such as reports on the customer collected from agencies, bureaus, references, bankers, attorneys; and clippings from newspapers and trade publications which have a bearing on the subject in question. These folders may also contain copies of the monthly statements sent the customer as well as copies of all unpaid invoices. In smaller concerns no separate file may be kept for credit, collection, or adjustment correspondence, but all letters would be kept in the credit folder. If the number of accounts is small, even credit history, or ledger record, information may be placed on the outside of the folder so as to obviate the necessity for a separate record. To accommodate all this information, some type of vertical folder or envelope large enough to hold 8½- by 11-inch forms is used and filed alphabetically.

Card index. Two other files are generally found in many credit departments. One suitable especially for the company selling over a wide area is the card index consisting of two sets of cards bearing the name and address of customers and their file number. One set is arranged alphabetically; the other is arranged according to geographical location and serves as a cross index for the alphabetical list and for all credit records and folders alphabetically arranged. A third set of cards is sometimes prepared for selected groups of accounts, such as those which have been placed in the hands of attorneys or collection agencies, or those which are in financial difficulties and need special watching.

Inactive file. The records kept in the inactive file are those of accounts which have at one time or another been active but which for a continuing period have been in disuse. Policies for the segregation of such accounts vary, but after a certain length of time the separation is made in order to facilitate operations. For accounts which have been inactive 6 months, the ledger card alone may be placed in the inactive section; after 1 year of inactivity both the ledger and application credit record cards may be put in that section.   Cards are kept in the inactive file indefinitely, so that they may furnish a convenient basis for reactivating an account when further use of it is sought by the customer.   This file is also the repository for closed correspondence concerning an account.

Microfilming equipment. Developments in microfilming have been adapted to the needs of the credit department as a means of preserving some of its records.   All charge sales slips, monthly statements, and checks in payment of accounts are filmed, and the rolls of film are filed conveniently in a cabinet in the credit department, where it is accessible to a supervisor who may need to discuss an item with a customer by means of a projection machine.

Filming conserves space and has been particularly useful in conjunction with the cycle billing procedures, whereby the charge sales slips are filed daily with the customer's ledger record and accumulated until the time of the month when that alphabetical portion of the tray files is billed.   By this plan these sales slips are not only totaled on the statement but attached to it as evidence and explanation of the items billed.   Except for the filming of these records, no copy of the sales slips would be retained by the store for any extended period.   Consequently, the microfilm has provided a simple means of permanently preserving these records in a small amount of space.   When they need to be reviewed, the film is inserted in a projection machine, and at the touch of a button it is quickly spun to the evidence sought.

Clipping service. Every credit department of a store of some size should have a clipping clerk to record all relevant data pertaining to accounts carried on the books, especially concerning business difficulties involving lawsuits, judgments, foreclosures, and bankruptcies; bad checks; marriages, divorces, separations, and deaths; and records of real estate transactions and registering of deeds.   These points are at times very illuminating and invariably shed some light on the affairs of a customer.   Some of them may indicate substantial changes in a customer's financial responsibility, of a favorable or derogatory nature, which no creditor can afford to overlook.

Every credit department should also be provided with a form for passing instructions to the authorizers.   As has been previously pointed out, accounts may be restricted for various reasons, requiring changes in the indexes of the authorizers' records.   Authorizers should be informed of these changes with the least possible delay.   This may be accomplished by the use of a form which has sufficient space in which are printed in abbreviated fashion all possible changes and instructions, thereby necessitating merely the insertion of the name and address of the account and several check marks opposite the appropriate spaces in the form.

Records for collections. The records of the credit department are generally the basic ones for making collections. In the first place, the evidence of the nature of the risk furnished by the credit history card or ledger record and the credit folder is suggestive of the manner in which collection should be undertaken. Accounts are designated as of different quality, expressed sometimes in the limits set and sometimes by other identifying symbols. Different types of accounts merit different treatment in collection, the best accounts, in general, being given the greatest consideration and handled most leniently. Reference may be made to the accumulated information in the credit folder to find a possible explanation for the nonpayment. Moreover, it is only by an examination of the monthly statements, together with the credit history card, or ledger record, that it is discovered that the account has not been paid. This discovery is usually first made at the time a second monthly billing is prepared, and the account may be flagged to bring it to the attention of the collection supervisor before it is time for a third statement preparation or for some other effort provided by the collection system. In the case of accounts which are designated for caution when opened, routine examination during the month following the first billing may be the basis for commencing collection effort. In all these respects, therefore, performance of the credit and the collection functions may require the use of the same records.

When the collection function is sufficiently large to warrant specialized personnel for handling, certain separate records may also be kept for this work. It is often desirable to maintain a separate file of accounts which are past due. This obviates the necessity for repeated reference to the credit history card files and other records, which are in constant use for other purposes. This collection file, too, may be organized alphabetically or in tickler fashion, depending upon the need and choice of its manager.

The function of the collection manager pertains in part to the keeping of records on the nature and progress of delinquent accounts, but this is only as a means to the efficient performance of his other duties. Letter writing is another important activity, both in the preparation of form letters for similar cases and in the composition of individual messages for unique cases. Telephoning and interviewing are also part of the work of this position, as are other matters incident to enforcement of payment, all of which are discussed in some detail in subsequent chapters devoted to collection.

ELECTRONIC DATA PROCESSING AND THE CREDIT DEPARTMENT

When a retailer turns to computerized electronic data processing, one of the first functions ordinarily converted to the computer is the handling of accounts receivable. Use of the computer does not change the approaches to credit management discussed previously in this chapter, but it does enhance the speed, accuracy, and consistency of credit operations.

Large store operations. A very large store usually purchases or leases its own computer. When this occurs, the store ordinarily establishes a data processing department and sets up a staff to administer and program the operation. Managers of the various departments expecting to use the processing services become deeply involved in the development of the programs affecting their operations, because every procedure to be automated must be defined in minute detail. In this respect, the credit manager is no exception.

When a new computerized processing system is installed, the credit department usually must establish a new numbering system for the accounts. Most often, an alpha-numeric system is used, under which a clerk can find an account easily, without cross reference, whether by number or name, because the accounts are in sequence both alphabetically and numerically. Gaps must be left between assigned numbers, however, to allow for addition of new accounts without destroying the alphabetical sequence. Furthermore, each assigned number must carry a check digit for use in a special mathematical test designed to detect common entry errors, such as transpositions. It is applied by the computer every time it reads an account number in order to prevent the application of charges or payments to the wrong account. Before the data processing system starts to process accounts receivable, new credit cards in the form of Charga-Plates bearing the recently assigned numbers are issued to charge customers.

Most stores with computerized accounts receivable systems have adopted the *negative* method of authorization. Each time the accounts receivable files are undated, the computer generates a printout of *bad* accounts. If a name is not on this list, charge purchases are authorized. If the *positive* method of authorization is employed, the current balance of all accounts is recorded on a massive random access file. Information on stolen or lost cards is applied immediately to the file. For a routine request, the authorizer enters the account number and amount of the purchase into the computer, which is programmed to calculate a current "open to authorize" amount for the customer, based on assigned credit limits minus outstanding account balance and pending authorization memos.   If the "open to authorize" amount exceeds the amount of the purchase, the computer registers approval automatically.   If an authorization request exceeds the "open to authorize" amount calculated by the computer, the transaction is referred to a supervisor who makes a judgment according to a more detailed study of the particular case.   When lost or stolen Charga-Plates are presented, the computer detects such cases and signals the authorizer immediately.

Charga-Plates may be used to complete a charge transaction in the conventional manner, by imprinting the name, address, and account number of the customer on the sales slip, or the plate may be inserted into the register and read directly.   A register-readable plate is shaped like the end of a punched card and has small rectangular holes punched in it to represent the account number.   Special registers, of course, must be used for this purpose.

The advantage of using the register to read the number from the plate is that the opportunity for clerical error is practically eliminated. Even though the computer is programmed to test the account numbers, the test cannot be perfect.   Errors which result in the application of charges to the wrong account may at best offend a good customer.

The registers usually capture information for processing by printing the entries in special, stylized type font on the journal tape.   Periodically, the printed tape is removed from the register and sent to the data processing department, where it is read into the computer at electronic speed by an optical scanner.

The information printed on the journal tape includes not only the customer's account number and the amount of the purchase but also code numbers identifying the items purchased, or their general classifications, and the itemized amounts.   This additional information is usually captured as the basis for merchandising reports, but it also enables the store to switch to "descriptive" billing.

Most noncomputerized large stores now use "country club" billing, a method in which sales slips are photographed on microfilm, sorted by customer, used in the development of the monthly statement, and then mailed with the statement to the customer.   If the store has a large credit department, this procedure entails many hours of clerical labor.

When the store adopts "descriptive" billing, the sales slips are merely filed for reference, perhaps on film, by register and by day.   The data processing system reads the charges from the register tapes, sorts the information electronically, prints the statements on the appropriate day with a brief description of each item purchased. The hours of clerical labor which are thus eliminated help to support the system.

An important advantage of computerized billing is that it narrows the time gap between closing the books and mailing the statements. The controller of one large department store maintains that each day eliminated reduces the store's investment in accounts receivable 0.8 per cent, a considerable amount of money for major stores.

Another advantage of the computer is that it makes possible a fully consistent approach to dunning and collections. Without a computer, decisions in these areas are made by employees who vary among themselves and each from day to day. With a computer, formulas for decisions can be established precisely and incorporated into the programs. The computer automatically prints a code for the dunning level on the statement to initiate the established routine. Of course, the computer can also be programmed to recognize an exception, so that the well-to-do customer who prefers to pay annually does not receive a dunning letter.

Small store operations. The smaller store offering credit to its customers has special problems. Such a store ordinarily endeavors to keep its office staff at a minimum size to reduce expenses. This condition is further complicated by a tendency to use office people on the sales floor during busy periods. As a result, record keeping falls behind during periods when charge sales are at a maximum. Statements are not mailed out as regularly as they should be. The investment in accounts receivable grows larger than it should, and the office staff falls behind in following up delinquent accounts.

A small store, however, does not have to have a proprietary interest in a computer in order to adopt data processing methods and thus alleviate some of the conditions mentioned above. Instead, many smaller stores are now using the services of data processing centers, which offer accounts receivable processing service to retailers. Under the National Cash Register system, for example, the store captures information at the register in the same way the larger stores do, and the register tapes are periodically forwarded to the processing center, where the computer prints a credit-management report as well as statements for the customers soon after the end of the month. The monthly statements may be mailed to the customers by the processing center or returned to the retailer for mailing.

The computer applies carrying charges, if the retailer wishes, to all credit amounts over a month old. This is a service the smaller retailer usually cannot perform for himself because the computations require more man-hours than he has available. When the computer does it for him, he usually finds that the charges speed payments, reduce his accounts receivable investment, and help to support the processing service.

The credit-management report reveals the activity under each account during the month, and provides an age analysis of all overdue accounts. The computer flags the overdue accounts by printing the address and telephone number under the name of the customer. As a result, it is a simple matter for a retailer to find a delinquent account, review its current status, decide what action to take, and telephone or write the customer or turn the account over to a collection agency.

QUESTIONS AND PROBLEMS

1 Diagram the organization of a credit department in the overall organization of (1) a department store, (2) a medium-sized specialty shop, (3) a small single-line store.

2 Contrast the divisional and functional plans of organization.

3 Should credit applications be submitted in writing? Should they be taken during an interview? Should they be signed? Explain.

4 Contrast the sources which would be used for obtaining information for (1) a poor risk, (2) a good risk.

5 What role is played by the credit limit in retail credit?

6 Should a customer be told of the reasons for rejecting his credit application?

7 Compare the various methods of identification with respect to security, cost, availability, authorization, and revocation.

8 What is the difference between "granting credit" and "credit authorization"? Who should be responsible for credit authorization?

9 Under what circumstances would authorization telephones be preferable to pneumatic tubes, and vice versa? Obtain sales literature from manufacturers of this equipment for sake of comparison.

10 Is "negative" authorization *ever* advisable?

11 What improvements has cycle billing made upon regular billing?

12 Where in a well-organized department would you expect to find records of dormant amounts? What actions would you recommend for reviving them?

13 What functions are served by the credit history card file and the credit folder file?

14 When should an account be regarded as inactive? Should credit sales promotion be confined to this type of account or should it also be extended to so-called "active" accounts? Why or why not? Would society benefit from it?

15 The credit card has become an increasingly popular device, medium, or instrument. Does it serve the same purpose for which it was originally intended? Explain.

16 Explain how the use of electronic data processing equipment by credit management in large stores differs from that in smaller stores.

CHAPTER TEN

consumer cash
credit and its
management

Consumer credit in the form of charge accounts, instalment sales contracts, and other accounts facilitates selling and makes buying of goods
and services both convenient and possible.   These are not the only forms
in which consumers use credit, however.   Cash, as well as merchandise
and services, is obtained by them on time for various uses and reasons,
as indicated in this chapter.

Basic nature of consumer borrowing. As explained in the first
chapter, borrowing of money for personal use has occurred in all ages
of recorded history.   The need to borrow is today greater than ever before, partly because of the dependence of people upon a complex money
and credit economy that is subject to many uncertainties and partly as

table 10-1 *Consumer Debt Outstanding from Personal Loans, by Holder, United States, 1948–1967**
(In millions of dollars)

End of year	Total	Instalment loans					Single-payment loans		
		Total	Com-mercial banks	Sales finance com-panies	Con-sumer finance com-panies	Credit unions	Total	Com-mercial banks	Others
1948	3,669	2,224	839	166	853	334	1,445	1,261	184
1949	3,963	2,431	913	142	973	438	1,532	1,334	198
1950	4,635	2,814	1.037	162	1,286	590	1,821	1,576	245
1951	5,291	3,357	1,122	276	1,555	635	1,934	1,684	250
1952	6,231	4,111	1,374	341	1,866	837	2,120	1,844	276
1953	6,968	4,781	1,521	377	2,137	1,124	2,187	1,899	288
1954	7,800	5,392	1,676	402	2,257	1,342	2,408	2,096	312
1955	9,114	6,112	1,916	466	2,623	1,678	3,002	2,635	367
1956	10,042	6,789	2,118	570	2,940	2,014	3,253	2,843	410
1957	10,946	7,582	2,351	676	3,124	2,429	3,364	2,937	427
1958	11,743	8,116	2,612	781	3,085	2,668	3,627	3,156	490
1959	13,515	9,386	3,196	946	3,337	3,280	4,129	3,582	547
1960	14,987	10,480	3,577	1,066	3,670	3,923	4,507	3,884	623
1961	16,392	11,256	3,798	1,201	3,799	4,330	5,136	4,413	723

Year								
1962	18,099	12,643	4,285	1,452	4,131	4,902	5,456	4,690	967
1963	20,581	14,464	4,950	1,754	4,590	5,622	6,117	5,205	912
1964	23,182	16,228	5,542	2,030	5,078	6,458	6,954	5,950	1,004
1965	26,036	18,354	6,333	2,345	5,606	7,512	7,682	6,587	1,095
1966	27,954	20,110	6,952	2,606	6,014	8,549	7,844	6,714	1,130
1967	29,957	21,690	7,692	2,772	6,294	9,169	8,267	7,064	1,203

*The data given in this table are as reported in the sources indicated below, except for the first 2 years for consumer finance companies, the figures for which were obtained directly from the Division of Research and Statistics, Board of Governors of the Federal Reserve System, for a previous edition of the book. It will be noted that the sum of the data on instalment loans shown for the several types of holders exceeds the *total* reported, probably because the data for personal finance companies and perhaps also for credit unions include other than strictly personal loans.

SOURCES: Computed from or taken as given in data published in the *Federal Reserve Bulletin*, as follows: for the years 1948–1952, from the October, 1956, issue, pp. 1035–1038 and 1040–1042; for the years 1953 and 1954, from the October, 1960, issue, pp. 1164–1165; for 1955–1959, from revised figures in the December, 1961, issue, pp. 1399–1400; and for 1960–1967, from the February, 1968, issue, pp. A–48 and A–49.

a result of desire for a constantly rising standard of living that could be financed in some measure the same way as are the requirements of a business enterprise—mainly out of future income. Consequently, as can be seen from the data in Table 10-1, year-end consumer debt outstanding from personal loans *increased* in the 20-year span covered by the available data more than 8 times. Even when related to disposable personal income, the *increase* in proportion is more than 50 per cent.

Types of consumer-lending institutions. To provide for consumers an adequate supply of lendable cash in correspondence with their need of or desire for it, two important problems had to be resolved. One had to do with a change in thinking about the concepts of interest and usury and the anachronistic attitude toward borrowing and lending for consumption purposes. The moral and legal restrictions upon so-called "interest taking" that resulted from this often hampered the process so that such loans had to be made secretly and illicitly. Growing social sanction following some enlightenment on the subject has taken form in new institutions and practices for meeting consumer needs for cash. Thus, the system of lending institutions which has evolved during this century and mainly since the 1920's now provides consumers with various types of cash loans, much as they are supplied in businesslike fashion with other forms of credit connected with the acquisition and purchase of merchandise and services. In fact, much of the borrowing of money discussed in this chapter is directly or indirectly related to the acquisition and purchase of goods and services.

The second thing that had to be recognized, even though ever so feebly, is that borrowing by consumers or lending to them is vastly more than a matter of merely providing money without risk, cost, service, and numerous special considerations. As in the sale of merchandise on credit, so in the lending of cash to consumers, there are many different markets, services, and prices. People sometimes need large sums, sometimes small; at times they can offer security for a loan, at other times they cannot. Some loans are made for purchasing new goods; others are for paying off old debt. Some borrowers know how to handle and use money intelligently; others do not and hence require budgeting counsel from the lender. Lending, therefore, to consumers is not merely the dispensing of a uniform commodity, money, but rather *the serving of a diversity of needs for money.* The variety of consumer-lending institutions in a sense expresses the effort in a competitive society to meet the diverse needs. Furthermore, this calls for a treatment of the prices charged not as interest or per annum rates—ideas that have developed through the ages in connection with the use of money in large sums for business purposes—but as service charges involved in the lending of money to consumers.

Among the leading consumer finance institutions are the following: consumer finance companies, personal loan departments of commercial banks, industrial banks and loan companies, pawnbrokers, and credit unions.   The relative position of each of several of the leading types in the industry and changes therein are shown in Table 10-1 by the amount of outstanding consumer debt held.

CONSUMER FINANCE COMPANIES

Consumer finance companies, often referred to as small-loan companies, and sometimes as personal finance companies,[1] are one of the principal sources of small loans made to consumers on the instalment plan.   As revealed by the data in Table 10-1, they generally account for about 30 per cent of all instalment loan debt held by all consumer-lending institutions.

These companies are typically private corporate enterprises whose stock in trade is their capital, which they use for lending purposes.   Their funds are obtained mainly from stock subscription, although they themselves borrow heavily from other sources.   They operate under the provisions of state laws, under which they are licensed and regulated with respect to certain lending practices.   Such companies frequently function on a sectional or national scale, with branch offices in cities of all sizes, each office constituting a separate licensee.

The position which the consumer finance companies hold among lenders today is largely the result of the small-loan laws enacted by the states.   Following the turn of the present century, the attention of many socially minded persons and of certain institutions was attracted to the plight of wage earners and other consumers of small means who were forced to rely upon the then available sources of loans.   Foremost among the institutions concerned with the loan situation, as a phase of general social conditions, was the Russell Sage Foundation, an organization philanthropically endowed in 1907 to work "for the improvement of social and living conditions in the United States of America."   This

---

[1] Pertinent official definitions are as follows: *"Personal finance companies* are engaged principally in making personal cash loans.   Consumer loan companies licensed under State small loan laws and industrial loan companies specializing in personal cash loans are included here."   *"Sales finance companies* are engaged principally in purchasing instalment paper which arises from retail sales of passenger automobiles or other consumer goods or from outlays for residential repair and modernization."   *"Business finance companies* include commercial finance companies and factors engaged principally in financing or factoring business accounts receivable" and in financing sales of business equipment. *Federal Reserve Bulletin*, April, 1967, p. 541.

organization undertook a comprehensive investigation of the small-loan field and uncovered many bad conditions, including the inadequacy of facilities for small loans and numerous abuses on the part of existing commercial lending agencies.   After a 9-year study of the consumer credit situation and after some legislative experiments in several states in attempts to solve the small-loan problem,[2] this Foundation in 1916 drafted a model bill for submission to the state legislative bodies for enactment into law.   This model bill has since become known as the Uniform Small Loan Law; it has been revised several times to keep abreast of the times and to incorporate into it the results of experience and accumulated wisdom.

The Foundation has continuously urged this law for adoption by the states and it has been this type of legislation which has given birth to the modern consumer finance or small-loan company.   In 1945 the Foundation withdrew from the field, and its then seventh draft was superseded by a new model prepared by the National Consumer Finance Association.   While the new model differed in many details, the basic principles of the Foundation's model were left intact.

Provisions of the uniform small-loan law. Small-loan laws are now in existence in 49 states (not enacted in Arkansas and the District of Columbia), but are deemed to be in effective form only in 44 states that applied the following principal provisions of the uniform code:

1 *Amount of Loan.*   Loans at the specially authorized rates may be made up to $300.   Many states have deviated from this antiquated limit.

2 *Interest and Charges.*   An interest rate or charge of $3\frac{1}{2}$ per cent per month on unpaid balances of $100 or less than $2\frac{1}{2}$ per cent per month on the remainder up to $300 limit is recommended. It has been proposed that in further revisions these rates or charges be lowered to 3 per cent and 2 per cent, respectively.   Interest or the charge is to be made only on the unpaid balance and cannot be deducted in advance.

3 *Security.*   The signed promissory note may be secured by a chattel mortgage, by securities, or by the signature of a co-signer to the note.

4 *Fees.*   No special fees may be collected on the loans, except recording fees, nor may any charges be made other than the rates applying to the unpaid balance.

5 *Supervision.*   Companies operating under the law are licensed, the licenses being renewed annually, and bonded and are required to submit to state inspection and examination.

[2] The first state small-loan law was enacted by pioneering Massachusetts in 1911, followed by Pennsylvania in 1913 (declared unconstitutional and reenacted in 1915), New Jersey in 1914, and New York and Ohio in 1915.

6 Capital Requirements. At least $25,000 capital must be provided by the licensee. Some states place this minimum at $10,000.

7 Penalties. Specific penalties are provided for violation of the principal provisions of the law.

Numerous variations of the so-called "uniform law" are to be found in the legislation enacted by the states. For example, in a number of states the maximum loans permitted are $1,000 or more and as high as $5,000 in California. In most cases the rates of charge are graduated, decreasing with the increased size of loans, and the higher than legal contract rates allowed usually being limited to loans up to $300, $500, or $600. As a safeguard against evasion or violation of the small-loan law, quite a few states prohibit the operation of another business in the office of the small-loan company. In some states the licensee is permitted to require that insurance be carried on the security for the loan, and in a few instances he is authorized to assist in the sale of such insurance or to collect a fee for it. In a majority of the states small-loan licensees may also make loans under provisions of industrial loan laws or consumer discount acts, and in some states they are allowed to purchase instalment paper and do some business financing.

There is a definite tendency for the small-loan laws to become more realistic and adjust to modern times and conditions. This is well illustrated by the revision of the Ohio law in 1961. First, the limit was raised from $1,000 to $2,000, thus obviating the necessity for a consumer to borrow from more than one source and to resort to possible subterfuges in doing so. Partly because of the reduced purchasing power of the dollar and partly because of phenomenal increases in the standard of living even in the so-called "lower income groups," the original limit of $300 is indeed an anachronism.

Second, the maturities were adjusted to the sum borrowed by the consumer. Thus, in the new Ohio law the maximum length of time for the repayment of the loan is 25 months for amounts under $1,000, but for loans in excess of $1,000 and up to the new maximum of $2,000 it is 37 months. An extra 15 days is allowed so that the first payment need not be made until 45 days from the date of the contract. For the country as a whole the average length of a loan contract is about 24 months.

Third, and very important, the law has been changed to provide for an expression of the loan or finance charge as an add-on in dollars and cents rather than in percentages. Under the new law, the maximum charges that can be made on a loan are $16 per $100 per year for that part of the original unpaid principal not exceeding $500, $9 per $100 per year for amounts in excess of $500 but not exceeding $1,000, and $7 per $100 per year on amounts in excess of $1,000 up to the maximum limit of $2,000.   This is now modified by the Consumer Credit Protection Act as discussed in Chap. 8.

Scope of operations. Partly because of the great need for this service and largely as a result of the businesslike mien brought to the small-loan business, growth in the number of licensees, though not in companies, and the number of consumer-borrowers has indeed been phenomenal over the long run, especially when viewed in absolute terms. It is generally claimed by the industry that one family out of every six or seven borrows from small-loan companies, with an average loan of $558 in 1965 compared to $238 in 1950.[3]   The increased size of the average loan may be explained by at least three factors.   One is the maximum loan or ceiling permitted by law, which has been raised in many states in recent revisions or amendments.   Another is the need for larger amounts due to increases in the cost of living.   For example, from 1950 through 1965 such cost increased 31 per cent, which means that the $238 average size of loan in 1950 would have had to be no less than $312 in 1965 for the same purchasing power.   Third, probably incident to rising standards of living and more generous use of credit accompanied by increased indebtedness, a greater demand would naturally be expected for larger loans within the permissible legal limits.

The industry's growth can be measured in more than one way. According to the data in Table 10-1, the amount of consumer debt outstanding held by consumer finance companies increased 53 per cent by the end of 1965 over 1960.   In terms of cash loans made by personal finance companies as reported in the 1967 *Finance Facts Yearbook* the increase in a similar period was 96 per cent—a rise from $3.6 billion to $7 billion.

Major characteristics of market served. In 1965, about one-half of consumers borrowing from consumer finance companies had an annual income under $6,000, and over 70 per cent had monthly incomes from $300 to $750.   Skilled and semiskilled workers make up the bulk of the borrowers, followed by service workers (including government personnel).   Nearly one-half of the loans are made for the purpose of enabling borrowers to consolidate existing indebtedness, and while certain others are listed under other categories, they are of similar essence.   Some of these are presumably contracted under conditions of emergency and

---

[3] Except when otherwise specified, figures used in this portion of the discussion of consumer finance companies are taken from or based upon data in the 1967 *Finance Facts Yearbook*, largely based on a survey of such companies, which operated 3,584 offices in 1965. National Consumer Finance Association, Washington, D.C.

represent a disruption of the family budget, as might be suggested by medical, dental, and hospital bills.   Many of the other loans are made for paying regular recurring bills, such as taxes, insurance, and rent for which individuals have not accumulated the necessary funds in advance.   Still other loans are made, not for indebtedness previously incurred, but for taking advantage of opportunities for which no means of purchase on credit are offered; travel, vacation, and educational requirements are typical examples.

Advantages to consumer borrowers. Consumers derive many advantages in borrowing from personal finance companies.   First, no cosigners are needed.   The signature of the borrower, with perhaps that of his wife, is sufficient.   Consequently, secrecy is maintained.   Second, no security may be required.   Loans to the extent of a borrower's monthly salary, known as salary loans, are often made on signature alone.   Chattels on automobiles or on furniture, or wage assignments where lawful, may be taken, but furniture loans are seldom enforced and are purely in the nature of psychological security or collateral.   Some companies no longer take wage assignments, even when permitted by law.   Third, borrowing can be accomplished quickly and easily.   The routine of operations and the pressure of competition combine to cause loans to be made promptly.   Fourth, assistance in budgeting can be obtained from loan companies which will help borrowers extricate themselves from debt.   In many instances this has developed into full-fledged consumer credit-counseling service of much broader scope, which has enlisted the cooperation of many civic-minded leaders throughout the United States.

PERSONAL LOANS BY COMMERCIAL BANKS

The lending of small sums directly to consumers[4] is a practice which commercial banks were slow to adopt.   As far as loans are concerned, their business was with commercial enterprises, and when consumer financing began to develop during the 1920's commercial banks would have none of it.   Gradually, and at a faster pace during the depression years of the 1930's, commercial banks began to appreciate the market for money which lay among consumer-borrowers, and they proceeded to equip themselves for handling this business.   Today over 80 per cent of the nearly 14,000 commercial banks and their numerous branches regularly make instalment loans to consumers, and, as shown by the data

[4] Indirectly, consumer loans are made by commercial banks through the purchases of consumers' notes, conditional sales contracts, and leases from dealers who have sold goods on such bases.

in Table 10-1, they account for about 35 per cent of all instalment loan debt held by all consumer-lending institutions.   They cater more largely to a higher class of risk than do personal finance companies, and a smaller proportion of the loans is made for the purpose of paying off existing indebtedness.   Furthermore, the average size of loan by commercial banks is over twice that of consumer finance companies.

Banking laws and consumer loans. The role which the commercial bank plays in direct consumer lending can be appreciated only as it is seen against the background on which the bank operates.   It must be remembered that the commercial bank has been an institution established and equipped for lending primarily to businesses, for *commercial* purposes.   Fairly large sums are usually involved in such loans.   Moreover, the attitude of the bank by nature and tradition has been notably conservative.   Furthermore, the bank has its earning power on loans fixed by the legal and contract rates permitted by law in the states.   For example, while the legal rate chargeable may be 6 per cent, 8 per cent may be charged where the specific rate is agreed upon by the parties involved.[5]   Consequently, in the light of these particular features, the commercial bank has not been in the most advantageous position for making and encouraging small loans to consumers.   Such loans were regarded as too small to be of interest to the bank, too risky for the responsibility the bank felt for its purpose, and too costly to be permissible within the limits of the rates authorized by law.   Today, however, many states have laws specifically permitting banks to make instalment loans at effective rates which are higher than the usual legal and contract rates.   Charge account banking, on which $1\frac{1}{2}$ per cent per month is normally charged on consumer past-due accounts, to the extent that it proves a successful enterprise should tend to promote the amount of consumer credit extended by commercial banks.

Character of consumer loans by commercial banks. All in all, commercial banks have found the consumer loan business an increasingly profitable field of operation, as indicated by the data in Table 10-1.   Their consumer loans are made more largely to clerical workers, salespersons, employers, managers, and officials than are those of small-loan companies or industrial banks, and relatively less to the laboring classes.   In most

---

[5] Legal and contract rates differ widely among the states.   In the great majority of instances the legal rate is 6 per cent, although in one state (North Dakota) it is as low as 4 per cent, and in four states (California, Georgia, Nevada, and Wyoming) it is as high as 7 per cent.   Contract rates have an even wider dispersion, with 8 to 10 per cent being the most common rates.   On the low side there are nine states with a 6 per cent rate, and on the high side there is Rhode Island with 21 per cent. Three states (Maine, Massachusetts, and New Hampshire) permit any rate agreed upon in a contract.

instances these borrowers constitute the better risk with which the commercial bank feels it must protect itself. The loans also are on the average somewhat larger than those of the other small-loan agencies. The rates charged vary with the type of borrower, the purpose of the loan, and the length of time for which it is desired. Nominal charges of from 5 to 8 per cent per annum are usual, which amount to an effective rate of approximately 10 to 15 per cent. Additional charges are often made in the form of investigation fees or penalties for delinquencies. Consequently, the true rate usually amounts to about 17 or 18 per cent per annum. Repayment is usually made on a monthly plan, although for short-term loans of from 30 to 90 days a one-payment arrangement may be made. For small loans of short duration it is also sometimes customary for the bank to make a flat charge, perhaps of no more than $1, to defray costs when interest collected will be small at best. Considerable care is exercised by the bank in making its loans, and an effort is made to avoid the risks which may result in loss of the loan or in costly collection activities. In this wise expenses are kept to a minimum, and for this reason, too, commercial banks often require some form of collateral for its loans, such as securities and chattel mortgages of automobiles or other durable goods.

Commercial banks engage most actively in the sales finance function, providing money for the purchase of automobiles, refrigerators, and other durables and taking a chattel mortgage on such goods as security. Moreover, they cooperate with distributors in arranging sales finance service, and also render financial assistance to merchants in the carrying of their inventories and in cashing their accounts receivable. Thus the aid given to the financing of consumer goods may be indirect and in the form of a loan for business purposes; thus it is, too, that some of the statistics on the volume of consumer loans come to include business loans which are not properly so classified. This, it might be added, is a difficulty encountered in appraising the volume of consumer loans made by all types of lending agencies, namely, that they include some loans for business purposes which are made on the instalment plan. Again, many single-payment loans reported by banks as consumer loans are in reality business loans.

INDUSTRIAL BANKS AND
LOAN COMPANIES

Industrial banks and loan companies are institutions chartered and supervised by the states, mainly for the purpose of making nonbusiness loans to be repaid by borrowers out of income. Some states have industrial bank laws and permit institutions chartered thereunder to accept deposits, in which case they are called industrial *banks;* in other states in which there are no such laws and hence deposits are not permitted, the institutions are known as industrial *loan companies.* In their modern form, both these types of institutions are an outgrowth of the organizations started by Arthur J. Morris about 1910 which became known as Morris Plan banks or companies. They differ from personal loan companies in that they offer a greater variety of services of a banking nature, and they differ from commercial banks in that they deal mainly in consumer, rather than commercial, loans.

By 1934 this new kind of banking became so well established that the American Industrial Bankers Association was formed, and by 1937 no fewer than 33 states had passed legislation permitting the "Morris Plan" type of operation. Industrial banking was then at its peak, with about 1,000 such institutions in business. During World War II their number decreased considerably, since many of the original "Morris Plan" banks and industrial loan companies have been transformed into regular commercial banks in order to offer checking account services and enjoy other advantages. As late as 1952 data were reported separately in the *Federal Reserve Bulletin* for industrial banks and industrial loan companies, but since 1953 they have been included under "Other" lenders.

Nature of operation. Perhaps the most distinguishing characteristic of the industrial bank is its acceptance of deposits. This service, however, was not one of its original features. Because legislators of state banking laws did not give consideration to the repayment of loans in instalments, authorized interest rates were predicated upon the assumption that loans would be outstanding in their entirety throughout the whole period for which they were made. Gradual repayment of the principal, however, yields an effective rate in excess of the legal rate. To avoid accusations of usury, industrial bankers conceived a plan whereby payments would be credited to a "deposit account" rather than be deducted from the loan principal. When the deposit equalled the loan, the loan was "paid off" in a so-called "one payment." Existing laws in 10 states relating to industrial banks would permit such banks to accept deposits under conditions that would qualify them for membership in the Federal Deposit Insurance Corporation. In 22 other states, however, industrial banking or loan companies operate under laws which allow them to issue *certificates* of one kind or another for savings but which apparently do not qualify them for membership in the FDIC.

Several features of their service distinguished the method of operation of industrial banks, one of which is the fact that a great percentage of their loans is made on promissory notes bearing the signatures of one or two co-makers.   Thus the borrower must seek from among his friends, relatives, business associates, or fellow employees someone who will share his responsibility in the loan.   This often proves to be a real stumbling block, both because of the reluctance of people to sign another's obligation and because of the unwillingness of would-be borrowers to ask such a favor and thus to reveal their financial situation to others. This requirement of co-signers is a competitive disadvantage of industrial banks; consequently, many such banks now make character loans and loans secured by other considerations.   Nevertheless, no other consumer loan agency places such emphasis on co-signatures as does the industrial bank.

Character of loans and interest rates. Another feature of the loans of these banks is the amount which they will lend.   In general, up to $5,000 may be borrowed by any one person, although a few industrial banks lend less than that and some slightly more.   In actual practice, however, such loans average around $1,500, or about three times the average loan made by personal loan companies.   Repayments are made monthly, semi-monthly, or weekly, and may extend for as long as 2 years, although they are normally limited to 1 year.

The rates charged by industrial banks have a wide variation, but perhaps the most common charge is a discount of 6 per cent plus an investigation charge of another 2 per cent, both charges being *based on the full amount borrowed*. Thus in view of the fact that the principal due is reduced with each payment, the rate of charge is greater than appears, being nearer 15 or 16 per cent, depending upon the time involved.   In some cases, the rates have been as high as 34 per cent per annum, but the usual true or effective rate charged by industrial banks figures around 16 per cent.

Competitive status of industrial banks. The competitive position of industrial banks is determined, on the one hand, by the nature of its services and its charges and, on the other, by the restrictions imposed upon it by state law.   Its bank services, where permitted by law for industrial banks or where such banks have converted their charters to those of commercial bank status and hence really ceased to be industrial banks, include checking, personal, and savings accounts, as well as financial advice and insurance for co-maker loans.   Its loan services are equally diversified, including co-maker, collateral, and single-signature types of loans.   According to purpose, they may be classified as personal, business, rental lease, sales finance, and real estate loans.   So common have these various loan services become, in fact, that it is not unusual to find industrial banks actively competing with both personal and sales finance companies, financing instalment sales by direct loans to consumers, through merchants, or by loans to merchants on their own responsibility. Segregated departments are sometimes established in the industrial banks for handling this business as distinct from the co-maker type of loan. On the other hand, the chief advantage which the industrial bank holds over the commercial bank in consumer loans is its reputation for being primarily a *consumer* loan agency. Specializing in this type of loans, and being comparatively less conservative in its policies, the industrial bank has served a broader market than have commercial banks.

Notwithstanding the competitive advantages of the industrial bank, it suffers some significant disadvantages in its effectual competition for small-loan business. Perhaps foremost is that of the requirement of co-maker signatures. Unwillingness or inability to obtain the cooperation of a co-maker may cause some borrowers to resort to personal finance companies and to pay the higher rate required. Such recourse is made also for the reason that the industrial bank is unwilling to lend sums as small as can be obtained from other lenders. Business may be lost to commercial banks also when the borrower possesses security or reputation which qualifies him in such banks for a loan under their terms.

While the industrial bank is defined as a distinct type of institution under its creative legislation, like all types of modern small-loan makers, it has assimilated many of the characteristics of other institutions as well. Consequently, as the proportion of its business done with different classes of borrowers waxes or wanes, the industrial bank tends to change some of its inherent character. For this reason, many industrial banks have chosen to transform themselves into regular commercial banks; others have changed to the category of industrial loan companies, which are essentially the same as industrial banks except that they cannot accept deposits and do not have the advantage of Federal deposit insurance; and still others have tended to become more of the sales and personal finance type of lender.

PAWNBROKERS

The pawnbroker is one of the most familiar institutions engaged in consumer cash lending, not so much by reason of the volume of loans but because of the long and traditional role which this agency has filled in the lending business. The unclear line of distinction which long existed between pawnbrokers and so-called "illegal lenders" has in latter years been better defined. Although in the minds of many people the pawnshops still charge exorbitant sums, they are today a licensed and inspected lending agency. They must, therefore, be recognized as a bona fide lending institution.

Distinguishing characteristics. A distinguishing characteristic of the business of a pawnbroker is that in order to obtain a cash loan the borrower must leave something of value as "security" for the loan. Jewelry, musical instruments, radios, luggage, and sometimes clothing are items commonly left as pawns. In consideration of this, the pawnbroker may lend up to approximately one-third the value of the item pledged. Loans, however, are usually for very small sums and, except in shops specializing in jewelry, seldom average more than $10. Loans are made for short periods, usually a month, at the end of which they may be repaid along with attendant charges, extended by the payment of accrued charges, or neglected and thus implying willingness to surrender the article pledged. The law requires that "precious" items be retained for a specified length of time, sometimes 6 months, before being offered for sale. Other articles are held for shorter periods if no word is heard from the borrower. Eventually, the pawnbroker notifies the borrower by registered mail of his obligation and, if in a reasonable time no reply is received, the article may be sold.

Interest and service charges. Charges made by pawnbrokers are stipulated in the laws under which they are licensed. A rate of 5 per cent per month is allowed by some laws, with 3 per cent the maximum rate applying to the portion of the loan which exceeds $25. In addition to this, however, there is often a "storage" charge of 25 cents per month. Thus a loan of $10 may cost 75 cents for one month; one of $20 may cost $1.25. The rate charged for such small loans, therefore, is something in excess of 60 per cent per year, depending upon the amount borrowed. In return for the legal privilege to charge such relatively high rates, pawnbrokers must be registered with the appropriate state agency, licensed, and inspected periodically.

Although such rates may seem unjustifiably high, it must be remembered that they are much less than those charged by "loan sharks," who have extracted sums representing rates of from 120 to 1,200 per cent per annum from unsuspecting or defenseless borrowers. On the other hand, the pawnshop method of borrowing is not without its advantages under certain conditions. No promise is made to pay the amount borrowed, for the pledge is virtually sold with an option to repurchase it. In case of nonpayment, no risk is assumed other than loss of the pledge. The borrower is not pursued by collectors, nor is he in danger of having his wages attached. These are no inconsequential considerations to some people. Besides, *rates* become meaningless when dealing with small sums like $2 or $5, just as percentage changes are meaningless on figures of 2 or 5.

ILLEGAL LENDERS

Unlicensed lenders, commonly referred to as "loan sharks," operate in all states, but abound and do a thriving business in those states which have failed to enact small-loan legislation or which have enacted defective laws and set the maximum rates too low to attract regular small-loan companies.   In such states, illegal lenders are the only source available for a large majority of wage earners in need of financial assistance.   While they accept all kinds of security, illegal lenders favor a wage assignment, especially in states where garnishment laws fail to limit drastically the amount that a creditor may attach.

Some of the unlicensed lenders may attempt to supply a need at a reasonable rate, but most of them have been found to be unethical and outside the law.   The rates charged are exorbitant, ranging from 10 per cent a month and up, with 20 per cent per month being rather usual.   On an annual basis, the rates vary from 120 to 1,200 per cent, with a usual rate of about 240 per cent.   Interest payments are collected indefinitely, so long as the principal remains unpaid.   But, worst of all, it is the aim of loan sharks not only to get a person in debt but to keep him there.   This is accomplished by urging the borrower to renew the loan, by using various so-called "legal devices" to collect more than can be paid, and by having the loan, when it cannot be paid, refinanced by a fictitious company owned by the same lender so that a heavy re-finance charge may be collected in addition to the usual rate.

CREDIT UNIONS

A credit union is a cooperative organization formed for the purpose of (1) encouraging thrift among its members and (2) making loans to them at relatively low rates of interest.   Systematic savings are promoted through the regular purchase of shares in the credit union, and loans may be made to members for any "provident and productive" purpose.   A credit union is thus a type of cooperative savings and lending association, formed under a special law, for the benefit of members only.   At the end of 1965, according to the 1966 *International Credit Union Yearbook,* there were in the United States and its territories 22,182 active credit unions with 16.7 million members, over $10.6 billion in total assets, and about $8.3 billion in loans outstanding.   Even more important, by the end of 1967 credit unions held 42.3 per cent of all consumer debt outstanding from personal instalment loans.

Peculiar characteristics of a credit union. To operate as a credit union the organization must be chartered under a state law, where such exists and is deemed suitable and preferable, or under The Federal Credit Union Act passed in 1934 as amended to date. Under the charter a credit union can be organized to serve a *particular* group having a common bond of interest and association by reason of employment; membership in a church, fraternal order, or labor union; or residence within a well-defined area or closely knit community of limited size. Being essentially a cooperative, it must open its membership to all in the particular group, and it must be operated on a strictly democratic basis.

Its capital is obtained from membership savings invested in the credit union's shares, supplemented by borrowings which are within the limits allowed by law and which are in relation to unimpaired assets. For example, a Federal credit union can normally borrow an aggregate amount not exceeding 50 per cent of its paid-in and unimpaired capital (savings represented by shares purchased by members) and surplus. Under most of the laws the dividend that may be declared on members' shares is limited to a maximum of 6 per cent, but the average more nearly approximates 4 or 5 per cent.

A Federal credit union may make loans to its members, with maturities not exceeding 5 years, in any amount, except that a loan to a director, officer, or member of a committee is limited to the amount of his holdings as represented by the shares he owns in the organization; nor can such a person endorse notes for borrowers. Under some of the state laws there is provision for a maximum amount of loan to a member on his own signature and another limit on a loan that is secured. For the latter it is the general practice to make use of co-makers or co-signers, who are usually members of the same credit union. It is common to lend up to $300 or $400 and as high as $1,000 on the borrower's signature alone and more with security, which could consist of pledged shares in the union. As of the end of 1965, loans outstanding to members averaged $496 per member.

Under the Federal law the maximum rate of interest that may be charged by a credit union is 1 per cent per month on the unpaid balance, while under most of the state laws the maximum rate is either 1 per cent per month on the unpaid balance or 6 per cent per annum on the entire amount deducted in advance, which amounts to about 11 per cent a year.

Advantages and limitations of credit unions. Several advantages may be claimed for the credit union plan of saving and lending. First, it encourages thrift by making possible and convenient, at place of employment and in small amounts, the regular purchase of shares of small denominations.   Such savings were largest during the most prosperous post-World War II years, probably because those were the years in which many members had substantial amounts to save.   Second, there is the low cost of operation.   Except for some of the very large unions, office space is often donated by the employer or other sponsor of the credit union, management services other than those of the treasurer are given by members free of charge, and the union is exempt from all taxes other than on real estate.   Only as the union grows and becomes of some size is full-time clerical and other assistance employed.   It is interesting to note that in the United States and its territories there were in 1965 but 10,709 credit unions, or less than one-half of the total number, with payroll deductions and that the total number of full-time employees was only 20,582, or less than one per credit union.

Third, losses from bad debts are very small, partly because the employer may make payroll deductions to stimulate loan repayments as well as regular savings.   Fourth, the return on capital to shareholders is limited to not more than 6 per cent but averages but 4 or 5 per cent, thus providing a source of funds at low rates and at the same time making the savings relatively profitable.   Fifth, the rates charged by credit unions are much lower than those charged on similar loans from the standpoint of size and type by other commercial lenders, being limited to a maximum effective rate of 12 per cent per annum.   Sixth, each loan is protected at the union's expense by loan protection insurance, known as "credit life insurance," through the Cuna Mutual Insurance Society.   Seventh, the credit union's funds are protected by law, by the supervisory committee, through bonding of all employees handling money, and via reserves set aside to cover uncollectible loans.   Eighth, and so important that it is listed among the three objectives or purposes of a credit union by the Ohio Credit Union League, credit unions "provide members an opportunity for learning how to improve the management of their financial affairs through a cooperative and democratic organization."

In view of these advantages it is easy to see why credit unions have come to occupy the first position among the several financial institutions holding consumer debt outstanding from personal loans.   Moreover, this leadership was attained by a growth of 118 per cent during the 1960's as compared with a growth in total such outstandings of but 92 per cent.   It must not be concluded, however, that the future of credit unions is so bright that they will in time supplant other loan agencies.   First, credit unions can operate only for groups with a common bond and those that are closely knit.   To insure success, participants must all be members of the same church, lodge, club, labor union, teacher association or group, residents of the same neighborhood, employees of the same governmental bureau or department, or employees of a single business firm or industrial plant. Second, a credit union must have a substantial number of members in order to operate with a reasonable degree of efficiency and to provide sufficient funds for lending. Most employers in this country have fewer than 50 workers each. This at once limits the organization of unions among employees of industrial and commercial enterprises. Third, with some exceptions, they do not seem to operate in harmony when the membership is very large. Fourth, credit unions have not as yet learned to extend credit safely without sacrificing the secrecy which small borrowers ordinarily seek. Finally, it remains to be seen what effect adverse economic conditions such as a serious depression may have upon the operations of credit unions. So far, all real growth of credit unions has been experienced since the depression of the 1930's. It is important to bear in mind that even in the years of greatest net growth a number of credit unions were being liquidated because would-be member borrowers would take their business to commercial banks and private finance companies. Also potentially threatening to the success of credit unions is the opposition of private consumer-financing institutions to the preferential advantage enjoyed by credit unions through tax exemption privileges. If this advantage were to be removed from all types of consumer cooperatives, credit unions would be adversely affected to some extent. It is certain, however, that credit unions have become and will no doubt remain an integral and substantial part of the consumer finance structure in our economy.

PHILANTHROPIC AGENCIES

Advances by relatives and friends. There is always a certain amount of lending taking place between members of the same family and between friends. In times of economic stress and unemployment, it may assume large proportions and prove unusually burdensome on the lender and far from satisfying to the borrower. Sometimes such loans are placed on a business basis, a promissory note may be given and even some security offered, but this basis is frequently more apparent than real. Few relatives and friends enforce payment of the principal, let alone payment of interest charges.

Special loan funds. Employers sometimes set aside special funds out of the company's treasury for the benefit of employees who are in need of temporary assistance. Funds are maintained by many colleges and universities to help deserving students in emergencies. A number of philanthropic organizations, fraternities, and church societies have also provided funds for such purposes. Very often, however, the students themselves contribute to funds for loans to be repaid after the borrower has graduated and established himself. On such loans no interest is charged, and quite frequently no principal is collected. Consequently, many of them take the form of outright contributions. Then there is a host of free loan societies of one kind or another making small loans which are usually repaid; hence the funds are said to have a great velocity. Then there are special funds, such as the Benjamin Franklin Fund and the Provident Loan Society of New York, provided by philanthropists. All of these will be greatly overshadowed by loan funds made available by the Federal government for large numbers of students under special conditions.

Remedial loan societies. These organizations, which operate in some of the larger cities, make loans on indorsed notes, pledges, or chattel mortgages. The average loan is around $100, and the rates charged range from 12 to 36 per cent per year, depending partly upon the society's policy but largely on the nature of the security offered and type of loan. Usually, the rates are lower than those charged on similar loans by commercial lenders. The number of such societies is so small, however, and their funds are so limited that little assistance can be expected from such a source by the majority of consumers in need of financial aid.

COMPARATIVE RATES
CHARGED BY
CONSUMER-LENDING
INSTITUTIONS

If the rates charged by either sales or personal finance companies on consumer loans are compared with those charged by commercial banks on commercial accounts, the former appear to be exceedingly high. If, however, the comparison is made with the rates charged by commercial banks on instalment consumer loans or with those charged by industrial banks, it is much more favorable. When the comparison is made with the rates charged by pawnbrokers, the charges of finance companies appear low indeed. It should be stated parenthetically that in such a comparison only legally authorized rates are considered and no attention is given to the outrageously high rates often charged by illegal lenders known as "loan sharks." The differences in the rates of charge made by the several types of consumer-lending institutions legally operating are explained in large measure by the several factors discussed in the paragraphs that follow.

Cost of capital. The money which lending institutions make available to borrowers is not equally costly to all of them. Commercial banks obtain much of their capital from deposits, most of which are demand deposits on which little or no interest is paid depositors. Even on the so-called "time deposits" little interest is paid. Usually, a bank has eight times as much in deposits as in its own capital and surplus, which means that it has practically no cost or very little cost on eight-ninths of the funds which it can lend. Industrial banks are also favorably situated in this respect. They, too, attract deposits, often to the extent of two to four times their own capital. Again, credit unions obtain much of their capital for lending purposes from savings of members invested in shares on which a relatively low dividend is paid. Finance companies, on the other hand, cannot accept deposits, but must supply their own funds or borrow from banks and other financial institutions. While the amounts borrowed may approximate three or four times their own capital, higher rates must be paid than those paid by banks on deposits. Higher rates must also be paid to investors in finance companies because of the greater risk nature of the business.

Cost of investigation. Relatively little expense is incurred by a commercial bank in investigating the risk. On commercial accounts an audited financial statement is usually demanded and secured and other information is obtained from the borrower, all at the latter's expense. To a large degree this is also true of consumer borrowers, especially when the loan is secured. Practically no such expense is incurred by credit unions. Finance companies and industrial loan companies, on the other hand, especially on signature loans, must conduct a complete investigation at the lender's expense which is included in the charge.

Size of the loan. The average size of a business loan made by commercial banks is several times the average size of a consumer loan made by the same institutions, and the average size of a consumer instalment loan made by such institutions is over twice the average size of a loan made by a personal finance company. Furthermore, loans made by sales finance companies and others in connection with the purchase by consumers of automobiles average around $900 on used cars and about $2,000 on new cars, while loans made on signature alone by the same institutions and those made by small-loan companies are substantially smaller on the average.

This means that, because of the difference in size of loan alone, no comparison can be made between rates charged on consumer loans with those charged on business loans. Even on consumer loans the rates may vary considerably, largely because of the difference in the type and size of loans.   Assume, for example, a monthly cost per account of $4.   On an average account loan of $2,000 this cost amounts to 2.3 per cent per annum, on an average account loan of $500 it is 9 per cent, and on an average account loan of $250 it is 18 per cent.

Risk incurred.   Generally the losses from bad debts suffered by well-managed commercial banks are very small and those of credit unions are almost negligible.   Because of the differences in the nature of the risks, losses are much heavier for sales finance companies and still greater for personal finance companies.   In computing the rate to be charged, bad debt loss experience must be taken into consideration.

Service rendered. Obviously the service rendered on an instalment account is vastly different from that required on a single-payment

table 10-2 *Major Components of Net Finance Charges on Consumer Credit, by Type of Lender, 1959*

Item	Nine consumer finance companies	Ten sales finance companies	Nine commercial banks	All federal credit unions
Net finance charge,* per cent of average outstandings per annum	23.87	13.69	9.42	9.13
Major components, per cent of net finance charge:				
Operating expenses	59.7	56.7	44.3	36.1
Cost of funds:				
Borrowed	16.6	29.5	15.9	1.4
Equity	12.2	5.9	25.7	62.5
Total	28.8	35.4	41.6	63.9
Income taxes	11.4	7.8	14.1	0.0

* Gross finance charges, less dealers' share when purchasing paper from them, and exclusive of insurance charges or costs.

SOURCE: Computed from basic data in Table 1 of Paul Smith, *Cost of Providing Consumer Credit,* National Bureau of Economic Research, Inc., Occasional Paper 83, New York, 1962.

loan. The privilege of the borrower to repay the loan in instalments rather than in a lump sum calls for much additional work of a clerical nature. Each payment must be recorded and handled. The borrower must be reminded of delinquencies, for he has many opportunities to become slow in meeting his obligations. An elaborate system must be devised to handle this kind of business. Moreover, even on the same general type of loans some institutions render more service to borrowers than others. For example, in the personal finance field some companies have gone to considerable length in educating or counseling consumers to the need for budgeting their expenses and improving their buying of various goods, in order that they may get their money's worth and extricate themselves from the financial embarrassment which usually brings them to seek aid from these companies. In this connection the various state associations of personal finance companies are rendering a notable service. Their educational activities have been emulated by individual companies, and their incessant efforts are constantly raising the level of service in the business.

Net profit. This may be regarded as the compensation for managerial ability and entrepreneurial capacity. An adequate net profit must be provided to attract the efficient management needed to run the business and to secure the capital required. The newer the type of enterprise, the greater the risks assumed, and the less prestige a business enjoys in the public mind, the higher the net profit required to attract both capital and management.

A few of the important reasons for differences in the rate of finance charge are revealed by the limited data shown in Table 10-2. To be sure, the types of lenders are not strictly comparable in terms of operations. For example, the consumer finance companies deal largely if not entirely in cash loans to consumers, while the sales finance companies and commercial banks finance largely the purchases of durable goods by consumers. Nevertheless, the data throw light on certain basic matters. For one thing, they show that, except for credit unions, the cost of money even in the most inclusive fashion that embraces both borrowed and equity capital is but one-third to two-fifths of the net finance charge. Second, operating expenses, which include salaries, occupancy costs, advertising, bad debt losses, travel, office supplies, legal fees, credit information expense, etc., range from over a third to about 60 per cent of the net finance charge. Third, except for credit unions which are exempt, income taxes absorb about one-tenth or more of the net finance charge. Fourth, there is an extremely wide variation in the cost of equity funds as measured by dividends plus retained earnings, ranging from about 6 per cent of the net finance charge for sales finance companies to 62.5 per cent for credit unions.

Conclusion. From the above discussion it should not be inferred that all the rates now charged by finance companies or others are justified and that no possible reduction can be effected. As a matter of fact, some companies may charge rates that are as low as conditions permit, while others may charge rates that are too high, although within the brackets permitted by law. Rather is this discussion offered as an explanation of differences in rates now existing as between different types of lenders. There is no doubt that these rates may in some instances be reduced through a greater volume of business per office, through a better selection of risks, through improved collection techniques, as a result of better business conditions and more regular employment, and through a more sympathetic attitude on the part of the community and the government toward the kind of business that provides essential financial help to consumers on a sound basis.

QUESTIONS AND PROBLEMS

1 Trace the influence of changing economic conditions upon the development of consumer-lending institutions since 1900.

2 Interpret the competitive relations of lending institutions, as shown in Table 10-1. Explain the relative and absolute increases in loans by each type of institution.

3 Are personal finance companies licensed in your state? If so, under what terms could a new licensee office be established? May anyone with the required capital open a new loan office, or any existing company establish a new branch? If there is no small-loan law in your state, what market is there for lending institutions?

4 Does the Uniform Small Loan Law now meet the need of borrowers as well as it did in 1916, when it was first put on a statute book? Explain.

5 Compare personal finance companies, industrial banks, commercial bank personal loan departments, and credit unions with respect to the following: aggregate volume of loans outstanding: number, volume, and size of loans outstanding per loan establishment: source of loanable funds; loan rates; legal lending restrictions; cost of operations.

6 What was the reason for the disinterest of commercial banks in consumer loans prior to 1930 and their change of attitude thereafter? Indicate the possible effect of charge account banking.

7 Contrast the operations of industrial banks and commercial banks.

8 In view of the fact that most consumer-lending institutions make a wide variety of types of loans, are there points at which one may not encroach upon business legally reserved for another?

9 If credit unions lend at lower rates than some other types of consumer loan agencies, why does not everyone borrow there?

10 Distinguish between the advantage enjoyed by credit unions because of their superior efficiency and those which exist for other reasons. Compare credit unions with other lenders from the standpoint of both explicit and implicit operating costs.

11 Contrast the nature and operation of personal finance companies and sales finance companies.

12 Why should the charge for money loaned to a consumer, even when expressed as a per cent per annum, be regarded as a rate of finance *charge* rather than as a rate of *interest?* Explain. Ilustrate with data used in the discussion of personal finance companies in this chapter.

CHAPTER ELEVEN

residential
mortgage credit

The United States has often been described as a nation of home owners. By the end of 1967 approximately 64 per cent of all families in this country lived in owner-occupied dwellings. As will be shown later in a quantitative way, one of the contributing factors to this high rate of home ownership has been the significant increase in the use of residential mortgage credit. Although it is fundamentally similar in principle to other kinds of consumer credit extended for personal use, the distinctive characteristics of residential mortgage credit are of special interest to home mortgage grantors, borrowers, legislators, and others concerned with the terms, availability, and magnitude of home mortgage loans.

Nature of residential mortgage credit. Mortgage credit is that credit in which the lender is given a real estate mortgage as the security for a loan. It is also referred to as real estate credit, commonly divided into farm and nonfarm. The latter is further classified into loans on multifamily and commercial properties, used mainly by business firms and other institutions, and loans on one-to-four-family residences, called residential mortgage credit or residential real estate credit.

While consumers generally use residential mortgage credit to purchase existing homes or construct new dwellings, this type of credit also embraces loans made to refinance existing loans held by other lenders, to acquire building lots, and, mainly through later additions to the original loan, to modernize and repair existing facilities or provide funds for any other purpose, such as a college education or vacation, in which case a mortgage on real estate is given as security for the loan. From the viewpoint of the various lenders engaged in extending such loans, some of the basic decisions involved are similar to those confronted by retailers and other institutions making other kinds of consumer credit extensions. There are, however, certain special features of residential mortgage credit which have brought about the development of numerous distinctive practices and policies in its administration.[1]

First, as noted earlier, it is usually advanced against the security of real property, which is immobile. This requires that the lender pay special attention to all factors that are likely to affect the value of the specific parcel of real estate during the period of the loan, including the property's economic life, structural soundness, location, design, and marketability. Second, mortgages or similar instruments are used to pledge the property as security for the obligation. The laws and procedures of mortgaging real estate are generally much more complex and technical than those involved in many other types of consumer credit transactions. The lender must, for example, determine whether the borrower actually is capable of mortgaging the property, whether he owns it or such interest in it as he claims to possess, and the extent of all preceding claims outstanding, if any, against the property.

A third consideration is that most residential mortgage credit is long term in character. As a result, the lender not only must analyze the risks that may arise from any anticipated future changes in general business conditions, local economic conditions, consumer preferences, and the property itself during the life of the loan; in addition, he must consider those factors which may affect the borrower's desire and ability to repay the loan over a long period of time. Finally, relatively large sums of money are usually involved in the extension of residential mort-

---

[1] For a detailed treatment of the characteristics and risks of mortgage lending along the lines herein mentioned, see Arthur M. Weimer and Homer Hoyt, *Real Estate*, 5th ed., The Ronald Press Company, New York, 1966, pp. 425–426 and Chap. 20.

gage credit, so that parties to the transaction take precautions not typically found in consumer credit.

Importance of residential mortgage credit. It is not sufficient merely to say that the consumer in his role as a home purchaser is one of the biggest users of credit in our economy. The importance of residential mortgage credit is, however, evidenced in several ways. While direct data are not available for the measurement of the total number or dollar volume of home mortgage loans made in any given period,[2] it has been estimated that long-term credit is used in the purchase of more than 75 per cent of all single-family homes.[3]   In the case of new, one-family homes built for sale, it has been estimated that 95 per cent of all such dwellings sold in 1965 used mortgage credit to some degree.[4] More concrete evidence of the relative importance or residential mortgage credit is found in a comparison of residential mortgage debt outstanding relative to other major types of debt in our economy. As shown by the data presented in Table 11-1, at the end of 1956, the amount of outstanding loans on one-to-four-family residences was $99 billion, and by year-end 1967 it had risen to $235.6 billion, an increase of $136.6 billion, or 138.0 per cent over the 11-year period.   Not only does residential mortgage credit constitute one of the largest credit sectors in our economy but, in absolute terms, the increase in home mortgage debt over a period of 11 years has been greater than that of most other major types of debt.

Still another significant evidence of the importance of residential mortgage credit is found in the balance sheet of consumers, as shown in Table 11-2.   Home ownership represents one of the most important single types of assets held by consumers.   Since most families are not able to accumulate sufficient amounts to pay cash for such large expenditures as their homes, it is not surprising that home mortgage debt constitutes the largest component of consumer liabilities.   Just as business firms frequently use long-term credit to finance the purchase of capital goods, so have consumers financed the acquisition of homes through the use of home mortgage loans.

Most of these loans in recent years have been of the *direct-reduction* type.   Under this plan the borrower pays a fixed amount at regular intervals, usually monthly, to the lending institution.   Part of this pay-

---

[2] For many years the Federal Home Loan Bank Board published a monthly statistical series, *Nonfarm Mortgage Recordings*, which reported the number and dollar volume of mortgage recordings of $20,000 or less made by six types of lenders. The Board, however, suspended publication of the series in February, 1965.

[3] See Loring C. Farwell (ed.), *Financial Institutions*, 4th ed., Richard D. Irwin, Inc., Homewood, Ill., 1966, p. 610.

[4] "Monetary Policy and the Residential Mortgage Market," *Federal Reserve Bulletin*, May, 1967, p. 729.

ment is for interest due, and the balance is immediately used to pay off part of the principal amount of the loan. The outstanding loan balance is thus reduced with every payment, and the amount which the borrower has to pay in interest each month is correspondingly less. In this manner, the borrower's equity in the home is increased with each payment.

The liberal use of residential mortgage credit has, no doubt, been largely responsible for the substantial increase in the home ownership segment of the total assets of consumers. Moreover, repayment of home mortgage debt through the direct-reduction method has contributed to an expanded consumer net worth, which, as shown by the data in Table 11-2, has increased by nearly $710 billion during the period from 1956 to 1967, or by 61.8 per cent over an 11-year period.

From an economic point of view, the rising volume of residential mortgage debt has, however, caused some consternation over its soundness and led to the development of numerous statistical methods for determining its quality. Some economists, for example, have been somewhat concerned that the ratio of home mortgage debt to disposable personal income has risen rather steadily from about 22 per cent in 1950 to approximately 43 per cent in 1967, which might be explained, among other things, by the cumulative effect on the debt structure of longer

table 11-1 *Selected Types of Debt Outstanding, End of Specified Years, United States, 1956–1967*

(In billions of dollars)

Type of Debt	1956	1961	1964	1965	1966	1967
Mortgage debt on one-to-four-family dwellings	99.0	153.1	197.7	213.2	223.7	235.6
Mortgage debt on multifamily and commercial properties	30.5	49.1	76.2	85.7	95.3	105.0
Short- and intermediate-term consumer debt	42.5	57.7	78.4	87.9	94.8	99.1
Federal debt	225.4	249.2	267.5	270.3	273.0	284.0
State and local government debt	42.7	65.0	85.2	95.1	100.9	110.1
Long-term corporate debt	100.1	149.3	192.9	211.3	232.4	261.4
Farm debt	19.5	27.5	36.0	39.3	42.1	45.4

SOURCES: *Federal Reserve Bulletin,* August, 1968, p. A-40, and other issues; *Savings and Loan Fact Book,* 1968, p. 32.

terms of mortgage contracts. Other indexes which have been employed to evaluate the quality of home mortgage credit are vacancy, foreclosure, and delinquency rates.

It is true that in some localities, vacancies have created some alarm, but examination of available data indicates that, on a nationwide basis, the supply of vacant units has remained relatively constant in relation to the total number of residential units during the period from 1963 through 1967.[5] In regard to foreclosures, estimates by the Federal Home Loan Bank Board reveal that there has been a persistent rise in the *number* of nonfarm mortgage foreclosures but that the foreclosure *rate* is less than 0.5 per cent of all mortgaged structures, and this rate

[5] *Savings and Loan Fact Book*, 1968, p. 49; annual publication of the United States Savings and Loan League, Chicago.

table 11-2 *Consumer Balance Sheet, End of Specified Years, United States 1956–1966*

(In billions of dollars)

Item	1956	1961	1964	1965	1966
Currency and bank deposits	163.2	189.7	245.4	268.9	276.5
Savings shares	36.8	75.7	108.6	118.0	122.3
Insurance and pension reserves	171.4	201.3	250.5	271.0	280.7
Government securities	90.1	103.9	114.5	119.1	130.1
Corporate and other securities	305.8	489.3	572.3	618.6	540.5
Total current assets	767.3	1,060.0	1,291.4	1,395.5	1,350.1
Nonfarm family home ownership	352.2	420.0	501.0	517.0	530.0
Value of durable goods	170.3	216.5	255.5	275.5	296.3
Total assets	1,289.8	1,696.5	2,047.9	2.188.0	2,176.4
Residential mortgage debt on 1-to-4-family houses	99.0	153.1	197.7	213.2	223.7
Short- and intermediate-term debt	42.5	57.7	78.4	87.9	94.8
Total liabilities	141.5	210.8	276.1	301.1	318.5
Consumer net worth	1,148.3	1,485.7	1,771.8	1,886.9	1,857.9

Note: Parts may not add to totals due to rounding.

SOURCES: *Finance Facts Yearbook*, 1967, p. 36, published annually by the National Consumer Finance Association, Washington D.C.; also appropriate issues of the *Federal Reserve Bulletin*.

has changed very little in recent years.[6]   Another recent study, conducted by the Mortgage Bankers Association of America and reported in the *Federal Reserve Bulletin,* also showed that, over a 7-year period, only from 3.04 to 3.47 per cent of home mortgage loans became delinquent and, further, that only about one-fourth to one-third of these delinquent loans were delinquent for a period of longer than 30 days.[7]   In final assessment, it should be noted that as yet there is no consensus of what size the home mortgage debt should be or what rate of vacancies, foreclosures, or delinquencies will produce sufficient problems to have a deleterious effect upon the quality of residential mortgage credit.   All of these remain for determination by future research and in terms of experience.

TYPES OF HOME
MORTGAGE LOANS

When acquiring a home on a mortgage, the borrower may use one of three different types of mortgage loan plans.   These include conventional loans, loans insured by the Federal Housing Administration, and loans guaranteed by the Veterans Administration.

Conventional loans. In conventional mortgage loans, the lending institution advances funds to a borrower at its own risk without any Federal government backing.   Any loss resulting from the borrower's failure to repay the loan must be absorbed by the mortgage lender.   In recent years, however, some lenders have insured certain conventional mortgage loans against loss through private insurance companies.

There is considerable variation in the features of conventional loans, depending upon the credit standing of the borrower, location and value of the property being mortgaged, laws and regulations under which the various lending institutions must operate, and managerial policies and practices of the different lenders.   Conventional loans are normally extended for a period of 20 or 25 years even though some institutions are legally permitted to make 30-year conventional loans.   The maximum loan is usually limited to 80 or 90 per cent of the appraised value of the property, but $66\frac{2}{3}$ to 75 per cent is more common.   The rate of interest charged on conventional loans naturally is influenced by the stage

---

[6] *Federal Reserve Bulletin,* August, 1968, p. A-51.   Confusion in this area is often caused by expressing the rate per *thousand,* which on a percentage basis (always per *hundred*) should be reduced by 10; also by frequent use of the rate per thousand of mortgaged *units* instead of *structures,* on the basis of which mortgage loans are actually made, thus tending to enhance the rate of foreclosures when, for example, a structure with three units for which a single mortgage loan is made is counted in the rate as three instead of one.

[7] *Ibid.*

of the business cycle and the condition of the money market. Then, too, some lending institutions charge a lower rate for borrowers who have a high credit rating or who make a large down payment. During the period from 1963 to 1967, the rates charged on conventional loans by all institutions in the United States have averaged from about 5.75 to 7.59 per cent.[8] In addition to interest, the borrower must pay certain fees which are commonly referred to as *closing costs*. These may include such items as property appraisal fees, mortgage-recording fees, legal fees, title insurance cost, documentary stamps, and initial service charges. The total closing costs vary widely among institutions, usually averaging under 1 per cent of the mortgage loan.

Most conventional loans contain a *prepayment provision* which permits the borrower to make a rapid repayment of the principal, without penalty. Another feature found in some conventional loan contracts is the *open-end advance clause,* under which the original mortgage may be used as security for future borrowings so that the borrower can increase the amount of his mortgage loan after the original amount has been paid down over a period of time. If the original loan, for example, was $15,000 and had been reduced by payments to $12,000, the borrower could then secure an open-end advance in an amount up to $3,000.

While open-end mortgage borrowing can be used to obtain additional funds for any number of reasons without a completely new mortgage loan, a borrower who does not have an open-end clause in his mortgage but who wants additional money for the purpose of making improvements to his home may obtain a *conventional property improvement loan.* Such loans are made by many lending institutions to finance such property improvements as plumbing repairs, grading and landscaping, built-in appliances, lawn-sprinkling systems, and even home furnishings, such as carpeting. Property improvement loans differ from mortgage loans in that the former are not secured by real estate or any other assets of the borrower and thus are very similar to unsecured cash loans made to consumers.

FHA-insured loans. FHA-insured home loans are granted by private lending agencies, and the agencies are insured by the Federal Housing Administration against loss if a borrower fails to meet the payments on the loan. In addition to the interest rate, the borrower must pay the lending institution, which in turn pays the FHA, an annual insurance premium of $\frac{1}{2}$ per cent, computed monthly, on the outstanding balance for the full term of the loan.

---

[8] For detailed information on interest rates and other features of conventional home loans, see the periodic releases by the Federal Home Loan Bank Board on "Conventional Mortgage Rates and Terms."

To qualify for insurance under the FHA home mortgage program, the loan must meet the requirements of the statutes and FHA regulations, which have been changed several times in recent years. During the summer of 1968, the maximum interest rate that a lending institution could charge on FHA loans was $6\frac{3}{4}$ per cent. This is in addition to the $\frac{1}{2}$ per cent insurance premium, for a total charge of $7\frac{1}{4}$ per cent. Such loans may be made for a maximum period of 30 years on existing properties and 35 years on proposed construction, but in no case may the loan extend for a period in excess of three-fourths of the remaining economic life of the house. The minimum down payment on FHA home loans is 3 per cent for the first $15,000 of appraised value, 10 per cent for the next $5,000, and 20 per cent for the balance over $20,000. The maximum loan limit is $30,000 on a single-family home.

FHA loans are direct-reduction loans, with the borrower paying the same amount per month. These loans may be paid off faster than provided in the original contract. In fact, the borrower may repay up to 15 per cent of the original principal amount, in addition to his regular payments, during any 1 year without any penalty. If the entire loan is repaid in a lump sum at any time during the first 10 years, the borrower is, however, charged a penalty of 1 per cent of the original amount of the loan.

The FHA carries on several other activities under different titles of the National Housing Act. One of these insures lending institutions against loss on loans made for the repair, improvement, or modernization of single-family property, such as building a garage, painting the house, or repairing the roof. These FHA improvement loans are unsecured loans and may be made up to a maximum of $3,500 and 5 years and 32 days to repay. They are discount loans and carry an effective interest rate up to nearly 10 per cent. The lender now has insurance coverage of 90 per cent of any loss incurred on each individual loan, which, in effect, makes him a co-insurer of up to 10 per cent with the FHA on each FHA property improvement loan it makes.

VA-guaranteed loans. The original loan guarantee program of the Veterans Administration was part of the Servicemen's Readjustment Act of 1944. The guarantee section of this Act has been amended several times, primarily to extend eligibility under the program for a longer period. As a result, loan benefits for World War II veterans were extended up to the cut-off date of July 25, 1970, while the eligibility termination date for veterans of the Korean conflict is Jan. 31, 1975. A new loan guarantee program was incorporated in the Veterans Readjustment Act of 1966 to provide benefits for members of the Armed Forces who have served 181 days or more since Jan. 31, 1955.

GI loans, as they are popularly known, are made to eligible veterans by private lending institutions, or they can be made by individuals. On properly granted loans, the VA will guarantee the lender against losses up to a maximum of $7,500 or 60 per cent of the loan, whichever is less.   The loans can be made up to 100 per cent of the purchase price, at the discretion of the lender, provided that this amount does not exceed the valuation placed on the dwelling by an appraiser approved by the Veterans Administration.   Amounts above $12,500 are, however, not subject to the guarantee and are handled on whatever loan-to-value ratio is agreed to by the lender and the borrower.   The maximum rate of interest which can now be charged to a veteran on a VA home loan is $6\frac{3}{4}$ per cent.   GI home loans can be made with a maturity up to 30 years, but the loan may not be made for a period longer than the remaining economic life of the property.   The lender is allowed to assess reasonable closing costs, including a service charge, but no prepayment penalties can be charged on VA loans.

SOURCES OF FINANCING
HOME OWNERSHIP

The principal lending institutions that provide funds to meet the needs of home owners for residential mortgage credit are savings and loan associations, commercial banks, mutual savings banks, and life insurance companies.   Individual investors also provide funds for this purpose, as do certain governmental agencies, mortgage companies, pension funds, educational institutions, and other organizations making occasional investments in real estate.

The relative importance of the various suppliers of residential mortgage credit is revealed in the data presented in Table 11-3.   The total mortgage indebtedness outstanding on one-to-four-family nonfarm homes was $235.6 billion at the end of 1967.   Approximately $103.2 billion of this amount, or nearly 44 per cent, was in the portfolio of savings and loan associations.   The remaining 56 per cent was divided almost equally among commercial banks, mutual savings banks, life insurance companies, and other lenders, including individuals and government agencies.   The lending practices of individuals vary so widely that it is difficult to generalize about their mortgage-lending practices.   Special consideration is warranted, however, of the more important sources of residential mortgage credit.

Savings and loan associations. Savings and loan associations are referred to in various parts of the country as building and loan associations, savings associations, homestead associations, or cooperative banks.   Laws, regulations, and tradition limit the investments of these institutions primarily to loans secured by residential real estate.   Historically, savings and loan associations also have been direct lenders, originating loans which were held in their own portfolios, and generally have limited themselves to financing properties within a rigidly defined geographical area. More liberal regulations in recent years have, however, permitted them to acquire or sell a participating interest in conventional mortgage loans beyond their usual lending area.

In addition to concentrating their lending on local homes, savings and loan associations specialize in conventional loans as distinguished from VA or FHA loans. On conventional home loans, they may lend up to 90 per cent of the appraised value of single-family properties on terms up to 30 years. Most associations, however, do not grant such liberal terms. According to one study, the *average maturity* and *average loan-to-price ratio* on conventional loans made by all savings and loan associations for the purchase of previously occupied houses during August, 1968, were 23.1 years and 74.8 per cent, respectively. The corresponding averages on loans for the purchase of new homes were 25.8 years and 76.1 per cent.[9] Average interest rates during August, 1968, on conventional loans were 7.12 per cent on previously occupied houses and 7.06 per cent on new dwellings. The rate of interest, closing costs, maturity, loan-to-price ratio, and other characteristics of conventional loans naturally vary with different associations, time periods, customers, geographical regions, and other considerations.

Commercial banks. During the period from 1961 to 1967, commercial banks increased their relative importance as a source of residential mortgage credit. While they make FHA and VA loans, banks generally have concentrated their lending on conventional mortgage loans on one-to-four-family homes. National banks and most state banks legally may lend for terms up to 25 years and advance amounts up to 80 per cent of the appraised value if the entire loan is amortized by the end of 25 years. If the mortgages are, however, guaranteed by the VA or insured by the FHA, these provisions do not apply.

The importance of commercial banks as suppliers of residential mortgage credit is greater than is indicated merely by examination of published data on the dollar amount or proportion of outstanding home mortgage debt they hold.[10] First, the trust departments of many commercial banks acquire residential mortgage loans in the exercise of trust functions, but these loans do not appear on the banks' record of assets and typically are not shown in published data as part of commercial banks' share of outstanding mortgage debt. Second, banks occupy a significant position in the short-term financing of building operations,

[9] *Ibid.*
[10] For discussion along the lines herein mentioned, see Weimer and Hoyt, *op. cit.,* pp. 449–450.

table 11-3 *Mortgage Loans Outstanding on One-to-Four-Family Nonfarm Homes, by Holder, United States, 1947–1967*
(In billions of dollars)

End of year	Total	Savings and loan associations	Commercial banks	Mutual savings banks	Life insurance companies	Federal gov't. agencies*	Individuals and others†
1947	28.2	8.5	6.3	2.3	3.5	0.6	7.0
1948	33.3	9.8	7.4	2.8	4.9	0.7	7.6
1949	37.6	11.1	8.0	3.4	6.1	1.2	7.9
1950	45.2	13.1	9.5	4.3	8.5	1.5	8.3
1951	51.7	14.8	10.3	5.3	10.6	2.1	8.6
1952	58.5	17.6	11.3	6.2	11.8	2.5	9.1
1953	66.1	21.0	12.0	7.4	13.2	2.8	9.7
1954	75.7	25.0	13.3	9.0	15.2	2.8	10.4
1955	88.3	30.0	15.1	11.1	17.7	3.0	11.4
1956	99.0	34.0	16.2	13.0	20.1	3.5	12.1
1957	107.6	38.0	16.4	14.1	21.4	4.7	13.0
1958	117.7	42.9	17.6	15.6	22.4	4.7	14.5
1959	130.9	49.5	19.2	16.9	23.6	6.3	15.4
1960	141.3	55.4	19.2	18.4	24.9	7.1	16.3
1961	153.1	62.4	20.0	20.0	25.8	7.3	17.5
1962	166.5	69.8	22.1	22.1	26.4	7.4	18.7
1963	182.2	79.1	24.9	24.7	27.3	6.2	20.0
1964	197.7	87.2	27.2	27.4	28.7	6.0	21.2
1965	213.2	94.2	30.4	30.1	29.9	6.4	22.2
1966ᵖ	223.7	97.4	32.8	31.7	31.4	8.8	22.6
1967	235.6	103.2	34.5	33.6	30.0	10.7	23.6

* U.S. agencies are FNMA, FHA, VA, and Farmers Home Administration.

† Includes mortgages held by trust departments of commercial banks, pension funds, philanthropic and educational institutions, fraternal and beneficial organizations, casualty and fire insurance companies, real estate and mortgage companies, other organizations, and individuals.

SOURCE: Federal Home Loan Bank Board, *Savings and Home Financing Source Book*, 1967, p. 38.

much of which is permanently financed by some other type of mortgage-lending institution upon final completion of construction. Finally, commercial banks extend substantial amounts of short-term credit to other financial institutions, particularly to mortgage companies. The mortgage company is an organization whose principal activities are to grant residential mortgage loans, hold an inventory of such loans only for a short interim until this inventory is sold to institutional investors, and service the loans for these ultimate investors.[11] Mortgage companies rely heavily on commercial bank credit to finance their mortgage inventory until it is delivered to other financial institutions such as life insurance companies, mutual savings banks, or pension funds.

Mutual savings banks. At the end of 1967, there were only 503 mutual savings banks in the country, and these were found in only 18 states, mainly in the New England and Middle Atlantic regions. Of the total number of savings banks, 456 were concentrated in six states. The extent of their orientation toward residential mortgage investments is indicated, however, by the fact that 14.3 per cent of all nonfarm home mortgage debt in the entire country was held by mutual savings banks.

In sharp contrast to other major suppliers of residential mortgage credit, the mortgage portfolio of these banks consists largely of FHA and VA loans rather than conventional loans, to the point that they rank first among all types of financial institutions in holdings of FHA and VA mortgages. The importance of mutual savings in the FHA and VA mortgage markets since 1950 is due, in part at least, to the passage of legislation permitting them to invest in federally underwritten mortgage loans secured by properties located beyond their state boundaries. According to latest estimates, these institutions hold approximately $13.6 billion in mortgage loans on out-of-state properties in non-savings bank states. Mutual savings banks also have maintained their relative importance in the mortgage markets within most of the states in which they are located. Part of the explanation for this is that these banks have charged lower interest rates on conventional home loans than many other institutions[12] and, in addition, have specialized in FHA and VA loans, which offer attractive terms to borrowers.[13]

Life insurance companies. Mortgages constitute the largest single category of life insurance company assets. As shown by the data pre-

---

[11] Saul B. Klaman, *The Postwar Rise of Mortgage Companies*, The National Bureau of Economic Research, Inc., New York, 1959, p. 1.

[12] See Federal Home Loan Bank Board, "Conventional Mortgage Rates and Terms," August, 1968, p. 3.

[13] For more detailed information, see *Mutual Savings Banking*, annual report published by the National Association of Mutual Savings Banks, New York.

sented in Table 11-3, life insurance companies have increased substantially the dollar amount of their investment in home mortgage loans. The relative share of total home mortgage debt held by these firms has, however, declined constantly each year, from 20.3 per cent in 1956 to 12.7 per cent in 1967.

Life insurance companies grant conventional, FHA, and VA home loans. They generally have shown a definite preference for larger loans and have tended to extend longer terms than other institutions. They are limited by law as to the loan-to-value ratio but may lend from $66\frac{2}{3}$ to 80 per cent of the value of the property, depending upon the loan maturity and the percentage of life insurance company assets invested in mortgages. A number of these firms are active in residential mortgage lending over a wide geographical area and commonly acquire out-of-state mortgages through the use of mortgage companies.

PRINCIPLES IN THE
SUCCESSFUL OPERATION
OF RESIDENTIAL
MORTGAGE CREDIT

As noted earlier, the principles underlying the extension of residential mortgage credit are basically the same as those governing other types of consumer credit service. Successful administration of home mortgage credit requires the application of these fundamental rules of action in conjunction with other principles which emphasize more specifically the operational functions of residential mortgage lending. The following illustrate such principles:

1 Because most home mortgage loans are granted for long periods, during which time a multitude of unforeseen and undesirable events can affect the borrower's liability to meet his loan commitment, such loans must be satisfactorily backed by good real estate security, pledged to protect the lender agains financial loss in case the basic contract cannot be carried out for any reason.

2 Since it is the aim of mortgage lenders to avoid, if at all possible, foreclosure losses and disagreeable experiences that may result from the forced sale of mortgaged property, the borrower must possess the willingness and capacity to meet the terms of the loan agreement.

3 Because the possession of real estate, each parcel of which is unique and immobile, does not indicate ownership, the instruments of residential mortgage credit must be carefully detailed and the laws regarding the mortgaging of real estate must be properly followed.

4 Since relatively large amounts of money are involved in residential mortgage credit, parties to a transaction must analyze cautiously each feature of the loan contract.

5 Because mortgage lenders must not only protect their suppliers of funds but also seek a reasonable return for these suppliers, a mortgage loan must provide sufficient gross income to cover all costs connected with granting and administering the loan, share its burden of the costs of providing the variety of services desired by the lender's customers, and thus enable the lender to build up its reserve position against possible future losses and earn a reasonable rate of return.

QUESTIONS AND PROBLEMS

1 Explain why mortgage credit might properly be classified either as a type of consumer credit or as business credit.

2 What are the distinctive characteristics of residential mortgage credit which have contributed to the development of special practices and policies in its administration?

3 What evidence would you present to indicate the importance of residential mortgage credit in our economy?

4 Explain what is meant by a direct-reduction loan. How has the use of this type of loan contributed to the increase in the net worth of consumers in our economy?

5 What statistical data would you examine for the purpose of determining whether or not consumers have overextended themselves in the use of residential mortgage credit?

6 As a potential borrower seeking a home mortgage loan, why would you prefer a loan agreement that contained an open-end advance clause?

7 Explain the differences between FHA-insured home mortgage loans and VA-guaranteed loans.

8 What is a property improvement loan? How does it differ from a mortgage loan?

9 What changes have taken place since 1947 in the relative importance of each of the principal home mortgage-lending institutions?

10 Explain why a mortgage company might properly be considered as a middleman in the field of mortgage credit.

11 Do you think that the Federal government will play a larger or smaller role in the area of residential mortgage credit in future years? Why or why not?

management
of the business
credit-granting
function

Short-term business credit, whether used in connection with the purchase and sale of merchandise and services or through the facilities of financial institutions, antedates by many centuries the modern form of consumer credit and is of vastly greater magnitude and pervasiveness. Not only is such credit used throughout the mercantile field on the buying or selling end of business operations or both, but it is used in the everyday conduct of business dealings and in substantial amounts.

Because of the tremendous scope of short-term business credit and its complexity, the credit-granting function in this area is given special consideration in two parts of the book. In this part the treatment includes an introduction of mercantile credit and the variety of terms of sale in common use, followed by a chapter on the management of mercantile credit and one on the management of financial institution credit. In all three chapters comprising this part the discussion is confined to the phase dealing with credit granting, the collection part, which is an essential concomitant, being deferred for treatment later in the book. Moreover, much of the substance underlying effective management of the credit-granting function of mercantile concerns and financial institutions, because of its technical yet important nature, is reserved for treatment in a separate part of the book that follows.

CHAPTER TWELVE

terms of
sale in
mercantile credit

Mercantile credit is the credit used in connection with the purchase or sale of goods and services for resale in the same or altered form or for use in the conduct of the business enterprise. Its users may be profit-motivated business concerns, nonprofit and cooperative organizations, or governmental institutions. In essence mercantile credit is confined to wholesale transactions and represents the power of a business or institutional enterprise to obtain goods and services in exchange for a promise of future payment.

A principal function of mercantile credit is to finance goods through the channels of trade, largely as a matter of necessity governed by custom and by the need of customers for such financial assistance. Another major function is of a purely marketing character and has to do with the facilitating of the movement of goods from production to consumption; more specifically its aim is to open and widen outlets for the goods in order that they may flow more freely from points of production through the channels of trade until they reach the retail outlets or end up in the industrial or commercial consumption destination.

Productive character of mercantile credit. Mercantile credit involved in the transfer of goods is presumed to be "productive," while consumer credit involved in such a transaction is not generally so regarded. By this is frequently meant that the very occasion giving rise to mercantile credit provides for or yields the funds by which the credit obligation is later discharged, thus making the debt so incurred, in the normal course of business activity, self-liquidating. For example, when a retailer buys goods from a wholesaler or manufacturer for resale to consumers, he resells them in the normal course of business at a price that covers his purchase price and yields him an amount sufficient to compensate him for his contribution to the marketing process. This quality of being "productive," in the narrow sense in which it is thus used, pervades mercantile credit and so makes it in one way less risky than consumer credit. Nevertheless, it calls for constant vigilance in credit administration in order to be fully aware of all the pertinent factors that affect the continued profitable conduct of the customer's enterprise.

To say, however, that mercantile credit is "productive" and consumer credit is not, is, in a broader sense, an economic fallacy and sheer nonsense. Nothing that is creative of utility can truly be said to be unproductive. There is certainly no question but that the ability to obtain goods and services on credit serves a usefulness and satisfies a need of ultimate consumers even as of industrial and commercial consumers, the former being on the consumer credit level and the latter on the mercantile credit level. It is, therefore, both sound logic and good economic theory to regard both types of credit as productive. An understanding of this fact would silence many arguments that consumers are "required" to pay credit charges but get "nothing" in return, that the costs incurred in granting credit are a competitive waste and a social loss, or that consumer credit is an "evil" while mercantile credit is an unquestioned benefit. False notions regarding this point are evidence of a failure to recognize that services, as well as commodities, have value and that, after all, the aim and end of most economic effort is consumption.

History and development of mercantile credit. Traces of mercantile credit may be found in antiquity. It is doubtful, however, whether it had come into extensive use before the money economy system had

been definitely established.   As late as A.D. 847 the trade carried on by
the wandering Jewish merchants—the Radanites, from the Persian words
"rah dan" (knowing the way)—who carried on the commerce between the
East and Europe, was conducted mainly on a cash basis or on barter,
although mercantile credit was already in use.[1]   This type of credit was
used to some extent in the days of Roman domination, but its most
rapid development awaited the establishment of fairs and other periodical
markets in Europe and Asia.   At the fairs which thrived during the latter
part of the Middle Ages, obligations incurred at previous fairs or on other
occasions were settled, usually by offsets or a kind of clearinghouse
method.   Since the fairs were held at intervals of from 3 to 12 months,
the bills of exchange arising out of the commercial transactions ran for
a relatively long time.   Gradually mercantile credit grew in importance
until in some lines of business it became a dominant feature, giving rise
to special institutions dealing in such credit, as exemplified by factors in
the woolen industry in England, which already occupied an important
position in the seventeenth century.

As the factory system of production assumed its place in our
economy, the wholesaler came to the front as the outstanding middleman
serving both manufacturers and retailers.   One of his major functions
was to finance the manufacturers who operated on a small scale and
were weak financially and to extend credit to retailers for several months
at a time.   As manufacturers grew in size, large-scale retailing came
into being, and banking made important strides, the dependence upon
the wholesaler for financial assistance diminished, but it resulted in no
diminution in the use or volume of such credit; it merely shifted part
of the burden to manufacturers and others or shortened the period of
time for which such credit was extended.

Terms of sale—nature and components. In the transfer of goods
on time at the wholesale level, a credit relationship is established upon
a certain basis.   This basis is expressed in what are known as "terms
of sale," which has customarily come to have a special and restricted
meaning that may, perhaps, be more aptly expressed by the phrase "terms
of payment," rather than referring to *all* the conditions surrounding the
transaction.   Popular usage throughout business and industry, however,
dictates use of "terms of sale" in the more restricted sense as relating
solely to terms of payment.   In the mercantile credit field such terms
usually comprise two distinct elements: the length of time for which credit
is given, known as the "free," or "net," credit period, and the cash
discount that is commonly coupled with it.

---

[1] J. Jacobs, *Jewish Contributions to Civilization*, The Conat Press, 1920, Chap. 6.

THE CREDIT PERIOD

The length of time for which credit is extended is called the credit period, which varies from 30 days to 120 days in most lines of trade. A number of factors determine the length of the credit period in a given line of business or for a given creditor, the more important of which are briefly discussed in the paragraphs that follow.

Rate of stock turnover. In general, the free credit period tends to vary in length with the time required by the buyer, in his normal course of operations, to sell the goods purchased on credit and convert them into cash or into receivables. It is the same as saying that the length of the credit period varies inversely with the rate of stock turnover on the general type of merchandise involved—that the higher the rate of turnover, the shorter the credit period, and the lower the rate of turnover, the longer the credit period.

Location of customers and transportation facilities. The rate of turnover is, in turn, affected by such considerations as the geographical location of the customer and the transportation facilities available for shipment of goods to him and the time consumed in the process. The longer the goods are in transit, the slower the rate of turnover, since larger quantity purchases are necessitated and more merchandise must be kept on hand; therefore, the longer the credit period that is required of sellers.

Terms of sale granted by preceding sellers. Both the length of the credit period and the cash discount offered by a seller to his customers are determined in large measure by the terms of sale granted by such seller's sources of supply or the preceding sellers. He may thus merely pass on the same terms or may modify one or the other of the two component elements.

Competitive conditions. Deviations from so-called "regular" terms of sale are often the result of extremely active competition in a given line of business. Under such circumstances customers tend to take advantage of the situation and run their accounts even beyond the extended net period, thus tending to lengthen the credit period.

Character of commodity. Distinction in terms of sale is frequently made on the basis of the character of the commodities in the transaction, even though such goods are sold by the same concern. For example, some of the products on the same invoice may carry no cash discount, probably because they yield but a narrow margin to the seller, while on others the cash discount may be quite substantial. Again, on some of the products the net credit period may be as short as a week, despite the normal length of 30 days on the other items; in fact, some items may be sold only for cash. Ordinarily the credit period is short when the product is perishable, highly standardized, bought for current and immediate use or enjoys a brief marketing period, and when the margin of profit is relatively narrow. By the same token a longer credit period is granted on new goods, on seasonal merchandise, and on articles that yield a relatively wide margin of profit.

Quantity involved in transaction. Very often terms are stricter on large shipments than on smaller ones, probably because the larger quantities are sold at less advantageous prices to the seller. Thus, carload lots of meats are usually shipped by packers on S.D.-B.L. terms, which involve neither cash discounts nor a free credit period, while smaller shipments of the same merchandise are normally made on net weekly terms.

Classes of customers. Terms of sale often differ with the classes or types of customers served, usually as a matter of industry or trade practice. For example, manufacturers of cigars allow 30 days for net payment by wholesalers and 60 days to retailers. Even on the same level of distribution customers may be classified for such purpose, so that department stores, for example, may receive different terms of sale from other types of retailers.

Nature of credit risk. When the credit risk is inferior, the net credit period, if any is allowed, is usually much shorter than when the risk is of a high order. That is, no doubt, why bakers sell to small restaurants on C.O.D. terms, to the larger and more responsible restaurants on a 7-day basis, and to the larger chain restaurants on 30-day terms.

Sectional differences. The distribution of income throughout the year in different parts of the country, even in a single type of business or occupation, may vary sufficiently to affect the length of the net credit period required. Farming, for example, is more seasonal in single-crop areas than it is in dairy sections or in other diversified areas. Obviously, the terms of sale, in so far as the length of the credit period is concerned, are adjusted in conformity with such sectional differences in order that the bills due may more closely coincide with the time income is received by purchasers of the goods.

Attitude of the credit manager and policy of the seller. Unfortunately, there are still some credit managers in important mercantile enterprises who are of the firm conviction that their principal, if not the only, task is to eliminate all losses from bad debts or at least bring them down to, and keep them at, an irreducible minimum. Such a narrow conception of credit management has sometimes influenced a seller unduly to shorten the credit period, to make the credit period coextensive with the cash discount period, to bolster the cash discount by including in it a quantity discount ingredient available only to those who pay within the stated period and probably in violation of the Robinson-Patman Act, and to take strict measures with respect to those who fail to pay within the so-called "credit period." Despite the rationalization of such an attitude or policy, it is in conflict with the fundamental objectives of credit management and under normal competitive conditions cannot long survive as a constructive force in the seller's business.

THE CASH DISCOUNT

The discount used in connection with terms of sale is commonly referred to as a "cash discount," and is thus distinguished from a trade discount, a functional discount, or a quantity discount. As such it is granted to induce a purchaser to pay in a shorter time than called for by the free credit, or net, period stated or implied in the terms of sale. In essence, then, a cash discount is a premium for payment of a bill *before* due date, and not for so-called "prompt payment" as it is sometimes construed. It necessarily follows that, to be a bona fide cash discount, there must necessarily be in the terms of sale a free, or net, credit period beyond the date on which the cash discount period expires. Failing that, the cash discount is such in name only, not in substance or in indicated purpose.

Advantages of cash discounts. From the standpoint of vendors, there are several advantages to be derived from the cash discounts they offer customers. First, quick possession of the money induced by the discount enables vendors to reemploy it in their business and so make it productive of further activity, and so to increase their working capital turnover as to permit the conduct of business with fewer invested funds. Second, early collection of accounts receivable induced by the cash discount reduces credit and moral risks, as well as losses from bad debts. Third, operating costs incident to collections are reduced when many of the bills are discounted. Finally, the taking of a cash discount by buyers tends to promote and to maintain a spirit of good will between seller and customer, there being less occasion for friction.

From the standpoint of the buyer, the cash discount offers two worthwhile advantages. In the first place, considerable savings can thus be effected, since the discounts normally offered by sellers are much higher than current rates of interest. In the second place, a buyer who takes the cash discounts offered to him becomes a preferred customer. Consequently he is given superior treatment and is much sought after by vendors.

Significance of the cash discount. The significance of the cash discount can be fully appreciated only upon the determination of the equivalent rate of interest per annum. To determine that, the intervening period—in days—between the optional dates of payment should be divided into 360 days—the number of days contained in a year as reckoned by banks—and the quotient multiplied by the rate of discount under consideration. To illustrate, assume that a bill of goods is invoiced on April 1, and that the terms are 2/10, net 30 days. Under these terms the bill may be paid by April 10 and the 2 per cent discount taken by the buyer, or remittance may be made on April 30, the date the account is due net. If the first option is exercised, the seller pays 2 per cent for receiving his money 20 days ahead of time. If the second option is exercised, the purchaser indirectly pays (by losing) 2 per cent for the use of the amount of the bill for 20 days—the intervening period between the two optional dates of payment. Since there are 18 times 20 days in a year, the equivalent rate of interest per year, whether viewed from the seller's or purchaser's angle, is 2 times 18, or 36 per cent.

The above computation, while accurate enough for all practical purposes, calls for adjustment if *complete* accuracy, rather than a practical method of computation, is desired. This is so because the computation was based on the total amount of the invoice instead of the amount after deduction of the cash discount. For example, if the invoice covers a sale of $1,000 worth of merchandise and the terms are 2/10, net 30, as stated above, the amount payable when the discount is taken is $1,000 less $20, or $980. Since payment of $980 in cash earns $20 for the unexpired part of the net credit period, or $20 for a period of 20 days, the earnings for a full year at this rate would be 18 times $20, or $360, making the actual rate $360/$980, or 36.73 per cent, instead of 36 per cent as previously figured.

Attention must also be called to the fact that the computed rate, by whatever method, does not necessarily reflect the net earnings to a buyer who takes the discount either as a *net rate* or as a *net amount* for a year. In the first place, in order to take the discount it may be necessary to borrow the money at a bank. Whatever rate is paid to the bank for the loan must be deducted from the computed equivalent per annum rate yielded by the cash discount.   Thus, if the bank loan should call for a payment of, say, 5 per cent, the *net rate* earned would be only 31 per cent under the first method of computation and 31.73 per cent under the second method.   Second, in the various computations presented the concern is only with the *rate* per annum, not with the *amount* per annum.   The amount for a whole year as indicated by the rate would be earned by a discounting customer only if he would discount bills successively throughout the year.

Misuse of cash discount. The term "cash discount" is misused or misapplied at least under two sets of conditions.   The first is when the terms of sale involve a cash discount that is unreasonably high.   A case in point is a discount of 5 per cent in terms of 5/10, net 30 days, the equivalent rate per annum being 90 per cent.   If the business is so lucrative that a seller can offer such a rate of return for advance payment, its credit standing would necessarily be good enough to enable it to borrow from financial institutions at relatively low rates of interest. If, on the other hand, the business is so poor and unprofitable as to require payment of 90 per cent for money, its span of life would be considerably shortened by such payments.   It seems that when cash discounts exceed the equivalent of 30 or 40 per cent per annum they are, *in fact,* a combination of "cash" and "trade," or "quantity," discounts.   It seems, further, that some of these inordinately high cash discounts continue today from sheer custom that prevailed many decades ago when credit periods were approximately 6 months in length and hence the large cash discounts were justified.

Second, there are many terms of sale which do not have a net credit period, so that the cash discount loses all significance as such and becomes instead a form of trade discount.   That is true of such terms as 2/30; 1/10; or 8/10, E.O.M.   In none of these is there a net credit period, hence the cash discount cannot be regarded as a premium for payment *before* the debt actually becomes due or as an inducement to pay before the purchaser has to pay.   The so-called "cash discount" allowed under such terms is given to all who pay within the credit period by the end of which payment can be legally enforced, and so approximates the nature of a trade discount.

Abuse of the cash discount. A very serious matter which credit managers have to cope with constantly is that relating to the practice on the part of many buyers of taking unearned discounts.   Although allowed only as a premium for cash payment within a specified time definitely stated on the invoice, or otherwise agreed upon, nevertheless many purchasers deduct discounts even when remittance is made long after the expiration of the discount period.   This abuse has originated principally as a result of the practice which leaves the matter of taking cash premiums to the honor and good faith of the buyer.   It is generally believed that no such difficulties would be experienced if provision were made at the outset for the buyer to remit the full amount of the invoice and for the seller either to credit his account or return a check covering the amount of the discount in case remittance is received within a specified time.   As it is, the buyer has the power to deduct the premium.   The cash discount is attractive.   Not wishing to lose it, he therefore makes every effort to exact it, even though it necessitates the use of threats.

So long as the buyer enjoys the privilege of determining whether the cash discount is to be taken when making remittance, this abuse is likely to continue.   The vendor is then faced with several alternatives. In a desire to be obligingly lenient, he may simply disregard such infractions upon the terms of the sales contract in the hope that few buyers will take this unfair advantage.   Second, the seller may accept payment but inform the customer of the irregularity with the expectation that the abuse will not be repeated.   Third, the creditor may either bill separately for the amount of the cash discount which was unjustly deducted from the invoice or may add the amount to the next invoice, in each case notifying the customer of the action taken and reasons for it.   Finally, if a very strict policy is to be pursued, which is seldom justified, the check for the inadequate sum may be returned and one for the full amount required.   Under all circumstances it is essential that sellers insist upon the closest observance of cash discount terms, pointing out to buyers that cash discounts are contract terms, not unlike those relating to price, quality of merchandise, and delivery.

Loading. Another abuse that has crept into the cash discount system is that buyers of large business organizations frequently insist upon receiving extra large discounts for cash.   These unusual terms are demanded in full knowledge of their superior position as buyers on the one hand and the fear of sellers of losing trade on the other.   Thus, some store buyers make it a practice to shop for cash discounts rather than merchandise.   The condition of affairs is due partly to the method employed by some stores of penalizing departments whose buyers fail to secure a specified minimum discount.   If the buyer fails to receive the required discount, his department is charged with the difference between the discount obtained and the discount required.   Similarly, the department is credited with any discounts which are secured in excess of the required figures.   This practice is known as "loading," and is regarded by the enterprises which use it as a means of making sure that buyers secure the largest possible discounts.   Another argument in its favor is that it enables executives to judge the abilities of various buyers on a uniform basis.   Furthermore, the advantages gained by securing a large cash discount are equivalent to a price reduction when considering the net profit of the department.   Finally, terms once established are usually granted on future transactions.   Because of this loading practice, hard and unusual terms are demanded of sellers, with the result that the cash discount system is greatly harmed and sentiments are thereby created for its abolishment.

Attempts to eliminate cash discounts. For some years a strong feeling was developing in favor of eliminating cash discounts from terms of sale.   Several arguments are generally advanced for such a step, which admittedly can be taken effectively only by all competitors simultaneously.   First, it is argued, cash discounts scarcely represent a true reduction in price, inasmuch as prices are set initially in anticipation that the discounts will be largely taken.   Second, cash discounts are obsolete and outmoded; they originated when banking facilities and the money supply were exceedingly limited, profit margins were high, and the credit periods were very long, and hence they are an anachronism.   Third, they are discriminatory, being unfair to customers who do not take them and giving an advantage to those who discount their bills.   This, by the way, is the same as saying that cash discounts are effective and accomplish the purposes intended.   Fourth, cash discounts have at times been used as a competitive weapon, despite the probable illegality under the Robinson-Patman Act and constant urging by credit leaders against such a practice.   Fifth, cash discounts are an economic cost for customers who do not take them and thus penalize the financially weak concerns.   Sixth, abuses of cash discounts on the part of customers make their administration difficult.

The conviction in favor of eliminating cash discounts was strengthened during World War II by the fact that such an incentive was unnecessary to encourage payments by the Federal government or by private organizations that during the war were eagerly seeking scarce goods and all of which had in those prosperous years adequate funds to meet all such obligations.   The continuous rise of prices during that period also stimulated vendors to find ways of increasing their prices without discouraging patronage.   All these factors combined to cause a number of manufacturing concerns to announce the discontinuance of their cash discounts.   In some instances list prices were lowered by the amount of the discount; in others no changes were made in list prices.

Strong opposition to attempts to eliminate cash discounts from terms of sale, some of it in an organized manner, slowed, stopped, or reversed the action with respect to the elimination of cash discounts. Those objecting to the change argued that the elimination of cash discounts would remove a customary source of income, that it would eliminate incentive to pay early, that outstanding accounts would become slower and larger in amount and thus require more working capital on the part of the vendor for the same volume of business, customer relations would deteriorate, and the cost of operating on a credit basis, including the making of collections, would rise substantially.

There is no doubt but that much of the argument in favor of the complete abolition of the cash discount, rather than modernizing it where needed, arises out of a failure fully to understand the function of such a discount, which can probably be appreciated better from an analysis of its advantages to both buyer and seller than from a review of economic and business conditions which motivated it. Whatever may be said of the alleged obsolescence of the cash discount, it still remains an incentive for prompt payment and is a screen by which *preferred* credit customers are distinguished from the merely *good* ones. Being generally taken by buyers when it is offered, it constitutes more of a penalty to those *unable* to take it than a discount to those who take advantage of it. It appears, therefore, that purely from the credit administration standpoint of the vendor there is merit in its retention, while from the standpoint of pricing and sales promotion there may be some valid arguments for its elimination. The customary status of the discount will probably be the strongest factor tending to perpetuate its use.

Anticipation. Expressly or by custom most sellers allow customers an anticipation rate, equivalent to a more or less satisfactory rate of interest per annum varying from 6 to 8 per cent, on the amount paid after the discount date has expired but before payment is due net. The purpose is to encourage customers to anticipate payment even after they have lost the privilege of the cash discount, by allowing them a reasonable rate of interest for the period of advance payment. Sellers opposed to such a policy usually state on their invoices "No Anticipation Allowed."

An anticipation rate may be allowed when the terms do not include any cash discount; under these conditions there can be no ambiguity about such a rate as to extent and the time for which it may be taken. When, however, the terms include a cash discount that is to be taken within a relatively short time after date of invoice or of receipt of goods, as the case may be, such as the usual 10 days of grace, it must not be construed that the anticipation rate is allowed *in addition* to the cash discount, for it is really *in lieu thereof* for payment *after* the cash discount date but before due date.

The only exceptions to this are to be found in connection with "dating" terms and "extra" terms discussed later. Under these circumstances the true or so-called cash discount may be taken a long time after date of invoice, so that the anticipation rate is used to encourage payment even before the cash discount period expires. To illustrate, under terms of 3/10, 60 extra, as will be shown later in detail, a so-called cash discount of 3 per cent of the amount of the invoice can be taken if payment is made by the end of 70 days (10 days and 60 days extra) and the net amount is due the next day. Should an anticipation rate of 7 per cent per annum be allowed in connection with these terms and should payment of an invoice amounting to, say, $500 be paid 40 days after date of invoice or 30 days in advance, the amount that may be deducted from the invoice would be 3 per cent of the invoice value for the so-called "cash discount," or $15, and $2.83 as anticipation for 1 month at the rate of 7 per cent per annum on $485 ($500 — $15). Unfortunately, there is a tendency for big buyers to take both the true cash discount and an anticipation rate—an abuse that should not be countenanced under a proper interpretation of the terms of sale.

TERMS OF
SALE CLASSIFIED
AND EXPLAINED[2]

Terms in any given trade are often referred to as "usual," "common," or "regular," meaning thereby that such terms are considered well established and general in the trade under consideration, fixed by custom or contract, and sometimes by resolution of an associated group in the trade. By accepted usage, the period of credit extension dates from the time of shipment or invoice of the order, and not from date of receipt of the goods by the buyer, unless R.O.G. (receipt of goods) or other terms are agreed upon by the contracting parties or adopted by a vendor.
     The customary terms of sale in mercantile transactions consist of C.B.D., C.O.D., Cash, "Ordinary," E.O.M. and M.O.M., Proximo, R.O.G., "Extra" or Dating Ahead, and Season Dating terms.

     C.B.D. and C.O.D. terms. C.B.D. (cash before delivery), C.W.O. (cash with order), or C.I.A (cash in advance) terms are applied to bad risks when the seller is unwilling to extend any credit whatever. Under these terms no credit is extended and no risks are assumed by the seller. The terms are rather uncommon, since C.O.D. (cash on delivery) terms are usually employed instead.

---

[2] For a fairly comprehensive list of customary terms of sale, see Appendix.

If the purchaser on C.O.D. terms refuses to accept the goods unless credit is extended, the seller, of course, must have the goods returned, and thus lose the freight both ways, and perhaps suffer on account of deterioration of the products while in transit, or else resell the goods to another customer in the locality of the original consignee or thereabouts.   C.O.D. terms are, therefore, a poor substitute for C.B.D. terms and must not be used unless some confidence is had in the purchaser, or unless a deposit is made by the buyer sufficient to cover the freight charges.

Occasionally, or regularly in certain lines of trade, terms are quoted "S.D.-B.L.," meaning thereby that a sight draft to which an order bill of lading is attached must be honored before delivery.   This arrangement closely resembles C.O.D. terms, and may be said to constitute one way of enforcing them.   Here, as under C.O.D. terms, the seller need not deliver the goods (the receipt for them given by the carrier) until after the buyer has made payment in cash.

So-called "cash" terms. The terms discussed in the preceding paragraphs are what may be called true types of *cash* terms.   There are, however, other so-called "cash" terms that are in reality nothing but short credit terms.   Not infrequently sellers state their terms as "cash" when they really contemplate a short period of credit, varying from a week to as much as 14 days or longer.   Sometimes concerns deem transactions to have been consummated on a "cash" basis if payment is made when the salesmen next call on the customers or within a certain number of days that may be specified or implied.   As there is no option to be exercised by the buyer as to time of payment, there is no cash discount in these credit terms.

Ordinary or typical terms. Terms involving no special features, such as datings and extras, are, for lack of a better name, termed as "ordinary" or "typical."   They consist of nothing more than specific reference to one or both of the component parts of terms of sale—the free credit period and the cash discount—simply and definitely stated.   If no cash discount is involved, the terms will be stated as *net;* if neither free credit nor cash discount is allowed, the terms are likely to be stated as *net, net.*   In all other cases, under these terms, the references to the cash discount and the free credit period are taken literally and without any inferences or special interpretations.   For example, when sales are made on 3/10, net 60 terms (3 per cent, 10 days, net 60 days), it means that if the bill is paid within 10 days from the date of invoice, a deduction or discount of 3 per cent from the face of the bill is allowed, and that the bill becomes due at the end of 60 days from the date of the invoice or shipment.   It is optional with the buyer, who may either pay in 10 days or else make remittance in 60 days and void the discount privilege.

E.O.M. and M.O.M. terms. Both E.O.M. (end of month) and M.O.M. (middle of month) terms are special forms of datings. All shipments under E.O.M. terms made during any one month are subject to the stated credit terms, both the cash discount and the free credit period, as if they were all made at the end of the month. For some lines of trade, mostly in dry goods and apparel, the end of the month is considered to be the twenty-fifth day of the month in which the invoice is dated. M.O.M. terms are an amended form of E.O.M. terms, in that the reckoning of the discount or net credit period begins from the fifteenth of the month for all goods shipped between the first and fifteenth of such month and from the end of the month (or the first of the following month) for all goods shipped between the fifteenth and end of the month, the terms beginning to apply on the fifteenth of the current month and the first of the next (proximo) month, respectively.

The primary purpose of these terms of sale is to accommodate "running" or active accounts, especially where the transactions are numerous and involve relatively small amounts. Under such circumstances it is convenient for the buyer to settle once or twice a month for all his purchases from any one supplier, instead of making the frequent settlements which would otherwise be necessitated. It is equally convenient to the seller from the standpoint of record keeping. E.O.M. terms are also in common use in the dry goods and apparel trades even when the transactions are substantial in amount, because they are advantageous to buyers, afford convenience, and facilitate financial control over departmental operations.

The terms are subject to serious abuses, however. There is danger that sales will slump toward the end of the month unless the seller is persuaded to date the shipments as of the following month, thus extending the credit period by 30 days. Some customers may insist for various reasons that their purchases be billed as of the first of the month following when goods are bought toward the end of the month, thereby forcing the seller to discriminate among customers. In any event, these terms are longer than the ordinary stated-period terms such as 30 days or 90 days, because the counting of the number of days, both for purpose of the cash discount and for the net credit period, is suspended until the middle of the current month or the beginning of the month following.

Proximo terms. In reality there is little difference between proximo, or prox., terms and E.O.M. terms, the former merely specifying a date in the month following in which the cash discount must be taken if it is to be taken at all, such as the tenth, fifteenth, or twentieth. Usually, these terms include both elements—the cash discount and the net credit period—and are stated in the following manner: 2%, 15th proximo, net 60 days, or 2%, 15 days proximo, net 60 days.

If the terms are stated as "3% 10th prox." and there is no net credit period stated or implied, then the so-called "cash discount" is in truth a form of trade discount, just as it is in the terms often used in connection with manufacturers' sales of women's wearing apparel of 8%, 10 days, E.O.M.

R.O.G. terms. R.O.G. (receipt of goods) or A.O.G. (arrival of goods) terms are not very common and are used for the purpose of accommodating distantly located customers who wish to make payment before the expiration of the cash discount period but yet desire to inspect the goods before such payment is made. For that reason, the terms are applicable only to the cash discount period. Assuming that the terms are 2%, 10 days R.O.G., net 30 days and the shipment is made on Mar. 5 but arrives at destination on Mar. 17, for purposes of the cash discount the reckoning begins with Mar. 17 (otherwise payment would have had to be made before the goods reached the buyer), but for purposes of the net credit period the reckoning begins with Mar. 5. Such terms also facilitate competition with sellers who are located in closer proximity to the buyers, at least for cash discount purposes.

"Extra" terms. Under these terms the discount does not begin to operate until the expiration of the "extra" period, and the net amount becomes due at the same time. Thus the terms of 2 per cent, 10 days, 60 days extra, often expressed as "2/10-60," granted by cotton cloth mills on finished goods mean that, when payment is made 10 days after expiration of the extra period or at the end of 70 days from date of invoice or shipment, 2 per cent may be deducted from the invoice as a so-called "cash discount." Since, however, payment must be made by that time if the bill is not to become past due, the 2 per cent in reality is not a cash discount but more in the nature of a trade discount, and hence no equivalent rate per annum for such a discount can be computed. Undisguised, and assuming no implied additional discount for advance payment, these terms really amount to 2 per cent, net 70 days.

Season dating terms. Season or long datings, which may run from 60 days to 3 or more months, constitute merely an extension of the credit period, similar to the nature of any other sort of dating ahead. Season dating may issue, for example, from the unwillingness of manufacturers to carry the entire burden incident to advance planning of production and to possible unfavorable market changes. Wholesalers are thus frequently required to place their orders with manufacturers or importers considerably ahead of production or importation. To induce them to do so, season datings are allowed which extend the time for payment to coincide with the seasonal sales of the products. Similarly, season dating is a device to induce retailers to share the risk and carry part of the burden incident to advance ordering of a stock of goods. While the buyer under these conditions may have to carry the goods for a longer than normal period, unless he buys them subject to later shipping instructions, he has the advantage of earlier possession of the goods, if desired, and a known price which he is to pay at a much later date. Most important, by such arrangements responsibility is at least partially shifted by manufacturer or importer to wholesaler and by the latter to the retailer. They also enable the wholesaler and the manufacturer or importer to plan ahead and provide the goods that will be later needed by the retailer.

Criticism of terms of sale currently in use. The terms of sale now in use in the mercantile field are subject to criticism on several scores. The more important of these are pointed out briefly in the paragraphs that follow.

Unscientific construction. Many of the terms of sale now in use are too complicated for a clear understanding of what is involved. Not infrequently, the cash discounts are confused with trade discounts, as has already been pointed out earlier in the chapter. Sometimes, the terms are so constructed as to invite delays in taking the cash discount. Occasionally, the terms of sale are so absurd that they cannot stand any analysis whatsoever.

Lack of uniformity. Throughout the entire mercantile field, lack of uniformity in terms of sale is characteristic. Even in a single industry or trade different sellers quote different terms of sale to customers of like standing. The effect of such a lack in uniformity of terms of sale within a single industry is anything but wholesome. The tendency, under such conditions, is to compete for business on credit terms. This invariably leads to laxity in the observance and enforcement of whatever terms are granted. While terms should and must vary as between different industries and lines of merchandise because, among other things, of differences in margins of profit and rates of stock turn, it is of supreme importance that they be uniform within each industry and when goods are sold under similar conditions. Only in this way will proper standards be developed that will place credit dispensation on a plane even higher than that occupied at present.

Lack of enforcement. It is a matter of common knowledge that little effort is directed toward the enforcement of terms of sale. This is probably one of the greatest weaknesses in the system. Extenuating circumstances, which are in reality nothing more than a desire to meet competition, are usually offered as an excuse for deviation from a policy which is supposedly in existence but seldom exercised.

Terms of sale under the Robinson-Patman Act. In the late 1930's terms of sale gained official scrutiny in the administration of the Robinson-Patman Act, the principal purpose of which was to prohibit economically unjustified *price* discrimination. It remained the evident intent of Congress, nevertheless, that price discrimination effected by means of prohibited discriminatory credit terms should also be considered illegal.

In the light of a reasonable interpretation of the law and the action so far taken under it by the Federal Trade Commission, it would seem that giving a larger cash discount to some buyers than to others in the same general class is definitely a prohibited discrimination in price. It would also seem congruous with the decisions of the Federal Trade Commission in other aspects of the law to believe that variations in the cash discount periods offered customers buying and paying under similar circumstances would be regarded as unlawful. It is not clear, however, whether allowing a favored customer a longer time in which to take the cash discount or in which to pay the net amount of the bill would be considered a prohibited discrimination. This reasoning seems to be borne out by the few specific cases adjudged by the Federal Trade Commission. For example, in one case the Commission definitely prohibited the granting of cash discounts of 1 to 2 per cent to certain purchasers of baker's yeast and not to others who paid in the same manner and within the same time.[3] In another case a dairy company and two of its subsidiaries were prohibited from discriminating in the price of fluid milk by giving favored dealers cash purchase discounts of 2 per cent.[4] In a third and more recent instance, the Commission prohibited a grocery firm and its subsidiary through which it made and sold bakery and fountain supplies, among others, from giving a favored customer 2 per cent on cash purchases while nonfavored customers received only 1 per cent.[5]

All in all, the general effect of the Robinson-Patman Act upon terms of sale should be to bring greater uniformity into their usage. For

[3] Federal Trade Commission Dockets 3903 and 3926, 1941.
[4] Docket 6737.
[5] Hudson House, Inc., et al. Consent to cease and desist, 1959. Docket 7215.

many years a trend toward simplification of terms of sale structures has been in evidence. The incentive offered by legal restraints, especially of the type contemplated by the Robinson-Patman Act, should accentuate this tendency.

QUESTIONS AND PROBLEMS

1 Explain what is meant by the statement that mercantile credit is limited to wholesale transactions.

2 Why is mercantile credit often regarded as productive, while consumer credit is not so regarded?

3 Is the use of mercantile credit more largely a matter of convenience or of necessity in business? How does the history of this type of credit bear out your answer?

4 What is meant by "terms of sale"? Is this meaning used in a broad or a narrow sense? Explain.

5 List the factors that affect the length of the free, or net, credit period. Do these factors affect the size of the cash discount? If yes, is the effect direct or indirect and why?

6 What is the purpose of cash discounts? In what respect does a cash discount differ from a trade discount?

7 Show good reasons why cash discounts should be taken by purchasers. Suppose you had no ready cash available; would it be worth your while to borrow at your bank in order to take the discount? Why or why not?

8 Garfield purchased a bill of goods amounting to $1,000. The terms designated payment at the end of 30 days, with a 2 per cent discount for payment within 10 days from date of shipment. Assuming that Garfield could borrow money from his bank for any length of time that he desired, how much will he save by taking advantage of the cash discount, through payment of the bill with funds secured from the bank at the rate of 7 per cent per annum?

9 A buyer for a department store received a 3 per cent cash discount on goods billed at $3,000. The standard discount required by the store is 4 per cent.
  a At what price were the goods charged to the department?
  b To what abuses might such practice lead?

10 A creditor has sold a bill of goods to a customer on terms of 10/10 proximo, the 10 per cent being understood as a cash discount. The debtor failed to remit by the tenth proximo.
  a What is the real significance and meaning of the 10 per cent?
  b Can the debtor legally deduct part of the 10 per cent on the theory that it is to that extent a trade discount?

11 A dealer in builders' supplies bought a shipment of goods, billed at the regular terms, at $3,500, on Apr. 12. What is the amount of cash discount and when must the bill be paid in order to take advantage of it?

12 What is meant by an "anticipation rate" and how is the practice justified?

13 Suppose that an invoice for highly seasonal goods is actually made out on Mar. 1 but is dated ahead to Apr. 15, the terms are 3/10 days, net 60 days, and an anticipation rate of 6 per cent per annum is allowed by the seller.

   a Is the buyer permitted to deduct from the invoiced amount of $1,000 both the cash discount and the anticipation rate if payment is made on Apr. 1?

   b If the answer is in the affirmative, what would be the amount of the total deduction from the invoice and how would it be computed?

14 In what respects are E.O.M. and R.O.G. terms similar? How do they differ? What is the chief purpose of each?

15 The usual terms of sale in the following lines of business are assumed to be:

   a Confectionary: 2/15, net 30

   b Cotton cloth mills, on finished goods: 2/10, 60 days extra

   c Hardware, wholesale: 2/10th prox., net 30 days

   d Children's clothing, manufacturers: 8%, 10 days, E.O.M.

   Briefly explain the meaning of each of these terms of sale and compute the equivalent rate of interest involved in the respective discounts given to purchasers of such goods.

16 If you were (1) a manufacturer, (2) a department store operator, (3) a small retailer, what attitude would you probably have in each case toward attempts to eliminate cash discounts? Why?

17 Under what circumstances might the offering of different cash discounts or free credit periods be justifiable under the Robinson-Patman Act? What differences would not be justifiable: (a) on the basis of specific decisions on the subject to date? (b) on the basis of theory and perhaps probable decisions in the future? Explain.

CHAPTER THIRTEEN

management of mercantile credit

The importance of the credit function in the mercantile field cannot be overemphasized, whether it be reckoned in terms of sales and profits potentialities or only on the basis of actual accomplishments. The latter involves somewhat of a quantitative evaluation, which is made possible only in part, on the basis of some data for certain segments of the mercantile field made available for some census years by the United States Bureau of the Census.

Magnitude of mercantile credit and its management task. In Table 13-1 are shown data concerning mercantile credit only for wholesalers—a segment covering over two-fifths of wholesale trade as conceived for census purposes on an establishment basis. The most recent year for which the limited data shown in the table are available is 1963. Dur-

table 13-1 *Importance of Receivables in the Operations of Wholesalers in Specified Kinds of Business, United States*

Kind of business	Reported as selling for cash only, per cent of total sales	Reported as selling on credit		For establishments selling on credit		
		Per cent of total sales	Sales per establishment, in relation to sales per establishment selling for cash only, per cent	Year-end receivables as per cent of sales	Bad debt loss as per cent of sales	Year-end inventory* as per cent of sales
All wholesalers	4.0†	80.0†	253	9.5	0.19	9.5
Air conditioning, refrigeration equipment, supplies	0.7	81.2	471	14.7	0.37	11.5
Apparel and accessories	1.7	76.3	185	12.4	0.22	9.5
Beer	36.6‡	54.7	191	4.6	0.11	4.7
Automobiles and other motor vehicles	3.6	70.2	340	5.3	0.12	8.0
Automotive equipment	1.2	82.9	363	10.6	0.25	18.3
Drugs:						
General line	0.7	96.5	140	11.3	0.14	14.4
Specialty line	3.3	82.2	273	9.6	0.15	10.7
Dry goods, piece goods, notions	1.1	77.2	213	12.0	0.15	12.2
Electrical supplies, apparatus	1.1	89.1	222	13.6	0.24	11.2

Kind of business						
Electric appliances, TV, radio sets	0.7	88.9	630	12.6	0.25	10.8
Electronic parts, equipment	1.5	81.9	358	12.9	0.34	16.7
Furniture, household	2.2	71.4	329	11.2	0.31	9.4
Groceries, general line	3.3	90.7	213	3.9	0.09	6.5
Hardware:						
General line	0.0	97.2	344	12.1	0.20	17.2
Specialty line	0.7	80.9	452	12.1	0.32	15.8
Heating equipment and supplies	0.3	89.9	643	14.1	0.42	15.1
Home furnishings and floor coverings	0.6	81.9	331	13.4	0.33	13.1
Industrial machinery and equipment	1.3	76.2	345	13.3	0.21	11.0
Industrial supplies	0.7	88.4	291	10.4	0.19	12.5
Jewelry	1.9	83.8	648	20.4	0.29	17.0
Lumber and millwork	0.4	77.2	368	11.0	0.26	7.0§
Optical goods	1.7	77.6	625	13.0	0.20	13.6
Paper, coarse, printing, fine	0.3	91.1	526	10.3	0.19	8.3
Plumbing fixtures and supplies	0.5	89.4	774	13.2	0.42	15.5
Sporting goods	0.8	76.1	221	14.5	0.31	15.0
Stationery and office supplies	1.4	69.3	234	12.4	0.25	11.7
Toys, games, fireworks	3.8	82.3	411	16.8	0.36	10.5
Wallpaper	1.4	76.5	278	14.9	0.39	14.8
Wines and distilled spirits	8.0	88.4		10.9	0.10	11.5

* While year-end inventories are given at cost and receivables are in terms of selling prices, the dollars invested in each of the two assets are strictly comparable.
† This means that wholesalers' establishments accounting for 16 per cent of total sales for wholesalers did not report to the census on this item. Similar percentages can be computed from the data given here for each kind of business.
‡ Some states prohibit wholesale sales of beer on credit.
§ Lumber wholesalers without yards, commonly known as drop shippers, carry an inventory of but around 1 per cent of sales, compared to about 15 per cent for lumber wholesalers with yards, yet they account for about 27 per cent of all sales in this category, hence the low inventory shown here.

SOURCE: Computed from most recent data published by the Census of Business in terms of establishments operated by wholesalers.

ing that year wholesalers (designated by the census as merchant whole-salers) operated 208,997 wholesale establishments with total sales amounting to over $157 billion.

Even from these limited data the importance of credit in the mercantile field can be appreciated.   For one thing, the sales per establish-ment for wholesalers reporting as selling on credit were about $2\frac{1}{2}$ times those made by establishments reporting as selling only for cash, and these ranged for different kinds of business from almost $1\frac{1}{2}$ times for general-line drugs to as high as nearly 8 times for sporting goods.   Sec-ond, selling on credit involves a tremendous investment in receivables. According to the data, 9.5 per cent of all sales made by wholesalers selling on credit were carried on their books as year-end receivables, and this figure ranged as high as 20 per cent for jewelry wholesalers.

To appreciate the significance of a wholesaler's investment in receivables when selling on credit, comparison should be made with the investment in merchandise inventories, which for all wholesalers as a group was the same percentage as the amount invested in receivables.   In 13 of the 29 kinds of business covered by the data in Table 13-1, the investment in receivables was in excess of the investment in inventories. Yet normally little attention is given to the management and control of receivables relative to the attention devoted to planning merchandise re-quirements, buying, and stock control.   From the facts just presented it is clearly evident that a wholesaler's investment resulting from credit operations in the form of receivables is, on the whole, as substantial as is his investment in year-end stocks of merchandise—presumed to be the largest single asset of a wholesale enterprise.   In many lines of trade the former investment is even more substantial.   Knowledge of these facts should behoove management of wholesale concerns to han-dle and safeguard receivables, on the credit-granting side as well as on the collections aspect, by every means available through sound and scientific policies and procedures.

Finally, while the losses from bad debts for all wholesalers in the aggregate were only 0.15 per cent of total sales and 0.19 per cent of *credit* sales, they amounted to $239 million, which is a substantial sum worthy of careful treatment.   This should not be construed, however, as implying that such losses are high or too high.   In fact, they may be too low if they resulted from the acceptance of too few calculated credit risks and the consequent unreasonable reduction in sales and profits potentials.

From the fragmentary data available on the items analyzed above for wholesalers there is every reason to believe that substantially the same conclusions apply to the sales of manufacturers and of certain other segments of the mercantile area.   Consequently, the several figures computed for wholesalers can be derived for the others by the application of similar percentages to the known sales volume. When this is done, the magnitude of the mercantile credit task—measured by credit sales volume, year-end receivables, and losses from bad debts—as computed for wholesalers, can no doubt be trebled or quadrupled. The implication of this is crystal clear. It means that the management of the mercantile credit function deserves the careful attention of top management fully as much as the management of the investment in inventories or in fixed capital assets and that the direct management of the credit and collection task must be placed in most reliable hands.

Varying importance of mercantile credit by lines of trade. The data briefly analyzed above are in the form of aggregates for all wholesalers—a macro approach to the subject. The matter takes on greater significance, however, from a management point of view when they are analyzed by lines of trade so that each concern in a given line can compare its experience with the totality for its trade. That is why data are presented in Table 13-1 for 29 selected kinds of business operated by wholesalers. From an examination of these data it will be noted not only that for 13 of the 29 lines of trade for which data are given in the table the investment in year-end receivables exceeded the investment in year-end inventory but also that in another four lines of trade the investments in the two types of assets were approximately equal. Finally, while bad debt losses for all wholesalers selling on credit were only 0.19 per cent of sales, for some lines of trade this percentage was more than double. For microanalysis as when a given firm compares its accomplishments with others operating in like manner, such information is much more significant than are the aggregate data for an entire segment of the mercantile field such as wholesalers. When thus viewed, the importance of mercantile credit and its proper management take on special significance.

THE MERCANTILE CREDIT DEPARTMENT— PLACE AND ORGANIZATION

To perform the manifold major tasks and the numerous routine operations necessary for the proper and effective management of the credit function in a mercantile establishment, an adequate organization must be developed, usually in the form of a mercantile credit department. In the organization of such a department, the principal objectives are (1) to establish lines of authority and relationships between it and related parts of the enterprise; (2) to provide the facilities necessary for procuring, appraising, handling, and preserving the information which is essential to credit granting; and (3) to provide the framework upon which to hang the operational elements that make for effective functioning.

Place of the credit department. A matter of prime importance is that of placing the credit department in the structural organization of the enterprise. Obviously, the work of a mercantile credit department is closely related to the activities of several other parts of the business, including order filling, shipping, and billing. The relationship is especially close to the organizational parts that deal with sales, financing, and accounting. That is, no doubt, why the credit department is in some wholesale and manufacturing concerns placed in the sales division, in others it is joined with the financial aspects of the business, and in still others it is in the auditor's or accounting division.

At least two seemingly important arguments are advanced in favor of placing the credit department in the sales division under the general supervision of the sales manager. First, both sales and credit tasks are intended to accomplish the same end, i.e., to maximize or optimize sales volume. The credit manager, for example, can maximize sales by increasing customer good will through prompt credit decisions. He can cooperate with the sales organization by persistently following up collections on all due accounts, on the theory that since credit is extended in limited amounts, less business can be expected from customers who are delinquent in their obligations and have therefore used up part of or all their credit with the seller. He may also have other opportunities for cooperation with sales personnel. Second, it affords an opportunity for securing the greatest degree of cooperation from the sales force in gathering reliable credit information, in following up accounts, and in making collections. It must be remembered, however, that the kind of cooperation contemplated under such an arrangement is likely also to maximize losses from bad debts and prevent the credit manager from performing his functions objectively and in a manner that will maximize sales on the one hand and minimize losses on the other.

Advocates of the plan calling for united effort on the part of the credit manager and treasurer argue that both are directly and vitally concerned with the financial aspects of the business. It is the duty of the credit manager so to dispense credits as to keep his compnay's funds intact, to venture into the future and prophesy what conditions in collections will obtain several months hence, to provide the financial officer with the data, and to speed up collections when business require-

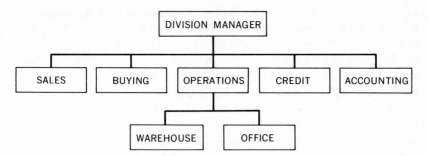

figure 13-1. *Place of the credit department in the organization of a typical division of the company performing all the functions of a wholesaler in its own community.*

ments call for additional cash. Both he and the treasurer are financial officers of their concern. Besides, credit policy has a profound effect upon the determination of the company's financial plan, and particularly on the amount of current financing that must be provided by the treasurer. Such an organizational arrangement is likely, however, to prove detrimental to the goal of maximizing sales, as pressure for funds may be translated into a strict credit-granting or collection policy which will, in turn, reduce sales volume.

In view of the foregoing, there is much to be said in favor of placing the credit and accounting departments under a single administrative division head. Both departments use many of the same records, so that much duplication can be eliminated by merging the two functional activities. At the same time, the credit department, when thus combined with accounting, suffers from none of the disabilities incident to any other combination.

Where the credit function is of strategic importance, as in the sale of such appliances as cash registers or business scales, or where the top management deems it of great consequence, the credit department may occupy a position coordinate in rank with that of sales, buying, operations, accounting, or any other major division. Such an organization is illustrated by Fig. 13-1.

Reasons for an independent credit department. Regardless of the division of the business in which the credit department is placed, it is of utmost importance that the department, while administratively under the jurisdiction of a division manager (sales manager, treasurer, or controller), always maintain a position of complete independence in its everyday work. Several important reasons may be advanced in support of this view. To begin with, credit work is complex and intricate, requiring the full time of an experienced and properly trained executive. A credit manager is a specialist; the technique of credits and collections involves all the intricacies of the business world. It therefore requires a man of broad knowledge and experience. Because of the technical nature of this work, other department heads will frequently fail to appreciate the credit man's position and proceed to issue orders in ignorance of probable consequences.

A second argument in favor of this independent position is that it facilitates unbiased opinions and decisions, based upon actual evidence at hand, without fear of displeasing a superior officer under whose direct supervision the credit manager works. Furthermore, the sales and credit departments represent two different viewpoints. Salesmen are by nature optimistic and are likely to overestimate a debtor's ability to meet his obligations, whereas credit managers must of necessity remain conservative and grant credit with great care and caution if bad debt losses and other costs are to be kept at a minimum. As a result, clashes will often ensue, unless a credit manager's authority is clearly defined.

Finally, the plan of establishing an autonomous credit department substitutes voluntary cooperation for cooperation through compulsion. If anything, it tends to develop an *esprit de corps*. No one realizes the benefits of cooperation, the cornerstone of the present-day credit system, to so great an extent as the credit manager. He knows, as all other department heads should know, that the various departments must constantly work in closest harmony with one another. Should there exist the slightest friction between the sales and credit managers, for example, their company would be carrying an expensive load. A willing and competent credit manager cannot properly manage the credit for his concern if he is compelled to work with an incompetent and disgruntled sales manager, and vice versa. The fact remains that the ultimate object of both is to increase profitability for their company. As soon as the credit manager assumes an antagonistic attitude toward the sales force or salesmen refuse to cooperate with the credit department, they are defeating the very purpose for which they are employed and developing a condition which militates against the interest of both and which inevitably proves detrimental to the entire organization. Hence, unity between them is essential; each must have full confidence in the other. The absolute necessity for teamwork, perfect harmony, and cooperation in its truest sense needs no argument. But it can be best accomplished not through dictatorship but through a volition born out of a complete and sympathetic understanding of the position of others, and the ultimate aim which all the departments are striving to attain, namely, greater net profit for the concern as a whole.

Credit department organization. Much of the success of any credit manager depends on the organization of his department and upon the system or lack of system with which the work is handled. If he is to occupy a position of a true executive, as he should, and have time for constructive thinking and careful judgment, he must not permit himself to become overburdened with a mass of detailed and routine work. Hence the importance of a system that will permit much of the detailed work to be handled efficiently by an assistant or clerks. Whatever the system employed, it must provide for accuracy of the records, efficiency in handling them, and accessibility so that the credit department force can locate them with promptness and certainty.

Obviously, credit department systems vary in different concerns with the size of the house, number of accounts handled, line of trade, and the degree to which this department is separate and distinct from other departments in the business enterprise. It is not intended, therefore, to submit a description or analysis of every system in existence. Rather an attempt is made to describe briefly a typical plan, which is subject to almost infinite adaptations of handling orders from both new and old customers, and to indicate ways in which credit work may be efficiently controlled.

**MERCANTILE CREDIT
DEPARTMENT OPERATION**[1]

Form of organization is to the credit department what the skeleton is to a body. It provides the framework for the various operational elements consisting of facilities, methods, policies, and personnel. Together these elements comprise the credit system, the efficient and coordinated functioning of which determines in large measure the success of the credit department. While the credit system embraces collections as well as the credit-granting phase of the work of the department, this chapter is confined to the treatment of the credit-granting function. Furthermore, even in this limited way the requirements of the system differ sufficiently in the handling of credit orders from new customers as against those

---

[1] As the operation of a mercantile credit department is extremely dynamic and subject to the influences of technological developments and the introduction of new or improved mechanical and other devices, it is not intended in this section to deal with details pertaining thereto. To keep abreast of such matters, much can be learned from the various issues of *Credit and Financial Management*, published monthly by the National Association of Credit Management, and from many other periodicals.

from customers whose accounts are already established to justify separate treatment of each.

Handling orders from new customers. When orders reach the credit department, they are stamped with a receiving stamp and submitted to the proper person for credit checking. Each order is then examined to determine whether it is from a new or from an old customer.

Follow-up credit file. Should it be discovered that a given order is from a new customer, a folder is prepared and an investigation of the applicant's credit and financial responsibility instituted. In the meantime the folder containing the order is placed in what may be termed a "follow-up credit file" several days ahead. This file is a sort of a tickler, which makes for accuracy and efficiency. It is almost indispensable where many new accounts are constantly being investigated and old accounts are undergoing revision. This file consists merely of 31 divisions, one for each day of the month, each containing folders of accounts that are being investigated.

Scope of investigation. Obviously, the amount of the information needed before making shipment depends upon the line of business in which seller and buyer are engaged, whether the order is for immediate or future shipment, and whether it is small or large from the standpoint of the seller as well as the buyer, considering the customer's location and general condition of his business as set forth in the salesman's report. When an order is small and ratings are favorable and agree with and substantiate the salesman's report, a first order may, under such circumstances, be shipped on that basis alone, but additional data should be sought for as soon as possible in order to establish a credit limit. On the other hand, if the order is substantial or ratings indifferent or in conflict with the contents of the report submitted by the salesman, additional facts must be obtained before accepting it. Just how much additional data are required would depend on the eagerness of the seller to roll up volume, the amount of apparent reliability of the facts made available by the several sources of information, and the extent to which they agree or differ among themselves.

Another point to be emphasized in this connection is that pertaining to the type of data most desired. In some instances it may be advisable to investigate thoroughly a customer's willingness to pay, or character; on other occasions financial data may be deemed most significant; while in still other cases general local conditions and ability to succeed may be stressed considerably. For this reason it may be advisable for a credit manager to classify the various sources of information according to the type of facts which they are best able to supply.

There follows a list of all possible sources of credit information that may be resorted to by credit managers in the process of securing adequate credit data. These sources are arranged in what is considered the order in which they are chronologically called into service. Thus, for example, salesmen's reports are listed first, because in many concerns salesmen are required to submit a report with every first order. Again, mercantile agency ratings and commercial agency reports appear in the two following places, respectively, since most mercantile establishments subscribe for the services of one or more of these agencies. Reference to subsequent chapters on sources of information will at once reveal a substantial duplication in the type of data which some of them ordinarily furnish. A credit manager should, therefore, exercise judgment in the selection of those sources from which the most needed and reliable facts may be obtained with the least outlay. These sources of information are as follows:

1 Salesmen's reports
2 Mercantile agency rating or reference books
3 Mercantile agency reports
4 Credit interchange reports
5 Special agency reports
6 Trade bureau reports
7 Credit application and financial statements secured directly from applicants
8 Direct inquiries to trade
9 Bankers' reports
10 Attorneys' reports
11 Direct investigation
12 Court records
13 Corporation cards and services
14 Corporation manuals
15 Registers and directories
16 Trade and financial papers
17 Other customers in same line or location
18 Other sources of a miscellaneous character

Credit application. When a first order is solicited by a salesman without his filing a standard credit report on the new customer, or when an unsolicited first order has been received, it is customary to request a more or less formal credit application from the risk. In some instances, this consists of a letter by the applicant explaining his requirements and furnishing essential qualifying information regarding himself and his

APPLICATION FOR CREDIT

DATE ____________

BUSINESS NAME ____________ PHONE NUMBER ____________

FULL NAME OF PRINICIPALS ____________

BUSINESS ADDRESS ____________ CONTRACTOR'S LICENSE NO. ____________

RESIDENCE ADDRESS ____________ KIND OF CONTRACTOR ____________

FORMER ADDRESS ____________ HOW LONG AT PRESENT ADDRESS ____________

NAMES OF FOUR FIRMS WITH WHOM YOU HAVE ESTABLISHED CREDIT

	NAME	ADDRESS
1.		
2.		
3.		
4.		

BANK WITH ____________ BRANCH ____________ KIND OF ACCT. { CHECKING ☐ SAVINGS ☐ LOAN ☐ }

DO YOU OWN REAL ESTATE? ____ VALUE ____ ENCUMBRANCES ____________

HOW LONG IN BUSINESS FOR YOURSELF ____________

ESTIMATED MONTHLY CREDIT REQUIREMENTS ____________

DO YOU CARRY WORKMEN'S COMPENSATION AND PUBLIC LIABILITY INSURANCE? ____________ ____________

SIGNATURE

(THIS APPLICATION MUST BE COMPLETELY FILLED OUT IN INK)

figure 13-2. *Example 1 of a credit application form used by mercantile creditors.*

business. Although many buying firms realize that such information is wanted and needed for opening an account in their name, it remains necessary frequently, nevertheless, for credit managers to request the information. For this reason, many of them have prepared application forms which may be sent with or without the accompaniment of a standard financial statement form. Two examples of such application forms are shown in Figs. 13-2 and 13-3.

Through mercantile credit applications information is sought on points covered also in retail credit applications, but in addition facts are solicited which show by contrast some of the differences between mercantile and retail credit applicants. For instance, specific statements are expected concerning the credit limits which the customer himself thinks he will need. Capital conditions, including encumbrances, are relatively more important to the mercantile creditor. Moreover, the importance of public liability and the insurance coverage thereof is emphasized. Such applications in general call less for character factors directly and more for references and other information from which not only character, but capacity and capital as well, can be discerned.

The credit history card record. When an adequate amount of information has been collected, the folder from the tickler file and the reports that have accumulated in the meantime in the "pending" file are referred to the credit manager for his decision. If the order is re-

NEW CUSTOMER REPORT

Date_____

Name _____

Address _____

PARTNERS OR OFFICERS

_____   _____

_____   _____

Kind of Business?_____How long in business?_____

Previous business or experience?_____

Estimated value of stock?_____Appearance of store_____

Is location in a business or outlying district?_____ What insurance carried?_____

Any nearby competition?_____

What help is employed?_____

Does stock appear well-kept and balanced?_____

What proportion of sales are made on credit?_____Are they good collectors?_____

What Real Estate is owned?_____

In whose name held?_____Value?_____Amount of mortgage?_____

Any outside investments or interests?_____

Reputation for meeting obligations_____

PRINCIPAL SOURCES OF SUPPLY

NAME	ADDRESS
_____	_____
_____	_____
_____	_____
_____	_____
_____	_____

Does banking with_____

figure 13-3. *Example 2 of a credit application form used by mercantile creditors.*

fused, the information should be organized in such shape that it may be presented to the sales department, if need be, to convince it of the wisdom of the credit manager's decision. Only by adopting an attitude which expresses willingness and readiness to show reasons for refusing an order will all possible friction between the two departments be eliminated and unquestioned confidence and cooperation gained. Thus, it is the practice of many houses first to pass all information obtained to the assistant credit manager to be written up according to some pre-determined plan of procedure.   Another reason for transcribing much of the data is that the original information becomes so voluminous in a few years as to require too much space for filing and imposes an extra burden on the clerical force.   Accordingly, it becomes necessary to boil it down in a compact and efficient way by summarizing only the important and relevant facts.   A method which has found much favor in some concerns is that of classifying the data according to character, capacity, and capital.

If the order is approved, terms and a credit limit are assigned, and a credit history card record is made out, which is filed in a credit history card record cabinet in strict alphabetical order or alphabetically under the proper geographic unit, whereby the cards are coordinated with mercantile agency books, thus facilitating revision when new books are issued.   This card contains a synopsis or summary of all credit information from the various sources, including the name and address of the customer, type of organization, bank, terms, ratings of the general mercantile agency, summary of credit interchange reports, credit limit assigned, and remarks (see Fig. 13-4).   As soon as the proper data are recorded on this card, the order is sent either to the order department for registration and for pricing or direct to the shipping department for filling.   In some cases the credit history card is combined with the ledger card and through a flagging system by means of colored tabs also includes information as to the method of collecting the account and the dates on which collections should be expected.   Going through such records weekly or at other frequent intervals, the credit manager notes the purchases, payments, and whether the balances are kept within the limits set.

The credit folder. This folder contains all credit reports on customers which have been collected from agencies, bankers, attorneys, and bureaus; financial statements secured from the customer himself; and clippings from newspapers and trade publications which have a direct bearing on the name in question.   These folders also contain copies of monthly statements forwarded to the customer as well as copies of all unpaid invoices.   They probably constitute the single most important file in the credit department.   Folders are usually filed alphabetically.   In the smaller concerns no separate files are maintained for credit, collection, or adjustment correspondence.   Under such circumstances all current correspondence is kept in the credit folder.   If the number of accounts is relatively small, even credit history card information may be placed on the outside of the folder and made a part of it so as to obviate the necessity for a separate record (see Fig. 13-5).

	CARD NO.
NAME	
POST OFFICE	DUN & BRADSTREET
STORE LOCATED	BANK
SHIP FREIGHT EXPRESS TO	ATTORNEY
ROUTE VIA	INTERCHANGE
BUSINESS	CREDIT LIMIT
BANKING CONNECTION	SALESMAN

REFERENCE	SOLD	H.C.	OWE	P.O.	RISK

CREDIT CARD NO.

NAME OF FIRM _____
BUSINESS ADDRESS _____
PRINCIPALS _____

DATE _____
SALESMAN _____
PHONE NO. _____
LICENSE NO. _____
KIND OF CONTRACTOR _____

REPORT OF REFERENCES	B M D C A		RECORD OF PURCHASES		
	YEAR	CODE	1940	AMOUNT	PAID
TRADE REFERENCE			NOV.		
			DEC.		
TRADE REFERENCE			1941		
			JAN.		
			FEB.		
TRADE REFERENCE			MAR.		
			APR.		
TRADE REFERENCE			MAY		
			JUN		
			JUL.		
BANK REFERENCE			AUG.		
			SEP.		
			OCT.		
			NOV.		
CREDIT APPROVED _____			DEC.		

figure 13-4. *Credit history card records used by manufacturers and wholesalers.*

Card index and inactive files. Two other files are generally found in many credit departments. One is a card index containing the name and address of customers and their file numbers. The card index may be divided into two or more sections. One of these sections consists merely of an alphabetical list of all accounts. Another contains a geographical list of all customers and serves as a cross index for the alphabetical list and for all credit history cards and folders if alphabetically arranged. A third section may contain an alphabetical list of accounts

NO.	NAME		

NAME	TOWN	NO.		
ST. ADDRESS	STATE	LED. NO.		
SALESMAN	BUSINESS			
ACCT. OPENED		METHOD OF PAYMENT CHECK		
TERMS	DISCOUNTS	PROMPT AT MATURITY	C.O.D.	
CREDIT LIMIT	10 DAYS	30 DAYS	SLOW	VERY SLOW

DATE OF REPORTS	RATING			
	DUN & BRAD.	SPECIAL AGENCY		

REMARKS		

figure 13-5. *Credit folder which is used also as a source of information for checking credits.*

that have been placed in the hands of attorneys or agencies for collection, or those which are in financial difficulties and need watching.

In the inactive file are placed all finished correspondence and other unnecessary and old material in order to prevent an undue accumulation of antiquated data in the credit folder. Similarly, when payment is received on an account, all paid items are checked on the proper statements which, together with paid invoices, are removed to the inactive file, which may sometimes be kept in the general offices for a stated period of time.

Together, all these indexes and files are kept in facilities such as those shown in Fig. 13-6, which are so located in the department as to be most readily accessible to the various individuals who will use them for checking orders, filing, billing, correspondence, etc.

Handling orders from old customers. To handle expeditiously orders from old customers as soon as they are received by the credit department, they should be checked at least twice by the credit manager himself or by his assistant. No matter what kind of checking system may be in use, it is advisable that the credit manager himself make it a point to examine all orders which represent fairly substantial

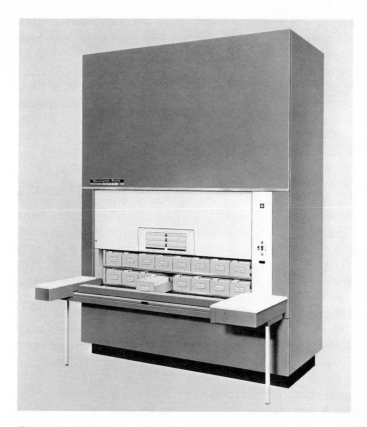

figure 13-6. *Ledger card and credit files such as are used in mercantile credit departments.*

amounts. In this way little irregularities which might not attract the attention of assistants may be caught by the trained eye of the credit manager.

In the first checking, all orders should be checked against the credit history card as to name, address, credit limit established by the credit manager, and instructions under "Remarks." In some houses celluloid cards or tabs of various colors accompany all credit cards, each color bearing a certain significance: thus, yellow may signal caution; red may indicate poor credit standing; clear, good credit standing; and so on. Orders easily cleared are let through quickly in this first checking and dispatched to the shipping department for immediate filling. In some houses, the credit history card file or a duplicate thereof is maintained in the Order Register department where the first checking takes place and only orders from delinquents or from customers who have exceeded their limits or who are otherwise restricted are submitted to the credit department for action.

In the second checking special attention is given to the information in the credit folders. By means of a "Please Get" rubber stamp, clerks make the necessary folders available within a short space of time for the second checking. As a result of this process many more orders are either refused or accepted and sent on to the shipping department.

The remaining orders are probably retained on account of inadequate information of a recent character. They are, therefore, placed in the follow-up credit file and an investigation is instituted as in the case of orders from new customers. To be sure, in a majority of cases the revision investigation will be far from exhaustive, consisting, in all probability, of a request for a recent mercantile agency report or a Credit Interchange Bureau clearance. As the new information is collected, proper notation is made on the credit history card and the new reports are filed in the credit folder. From this point on, orders from both new and old accounts are handled in a similar manner. If an order is held pending receipt of payment by the customer, the bookkeeping department is notified so that the credit manager will be informed when payment is received and the order will be released for shipment.

Changing nature of mercantile credit department systems. Earlier in this chapter it was pointed out that it is not intended to present a description or analysis of every mercantile credit department system in existence. Nevertheless it should be noted at this juncture that in the performance of the credit function, as in the field of office management generally, many innovations are being adopted and credit systems are being constantly modified as more efficient devices become available (see footnote 1). For example, one objection to the usual credit history card file is that the cards tend to stick together and are easily misfiled. To overcome this objection there is now available a visible filing system where at the touch of a finger a whole section of magnetized cards fans out, and the individual cards stay in position until the needed information is spotted.

The innovations have run the gamut from some simple device to meet a specific need like that indicated above to the development of a completely ledgerless accounts receivable system which eliminates posting operations altogether. Instead, all invoices, credit memos, and other such items are placed in a pocket for each customer, on the front of which there is inserted in slits a credit history card containing the usual information including the dollar credit limit, thereby making all information pertinent to a credit decision available in one place and in an accessible location. This is presumed to make for speed, accuracy, and economy of operation and for relative simplicity in performing both the credit and the collection functions.

Credit operation costs. As in the operation of a retail business on credit, in the mercantile field, too, manpower as reflected by payroll is one of the largest single items of cost when selling on credit. Also important is the interest cost, actual or implicit, on the receivables normally carried on the books. At the beginning of this chapter it was shown that 9.5 per cent of all sales made by wholesalers selling on credit were carried on their books as year-end receivables. At the end of 1963, this amounted to about $12 billion. At an average rate of interest of 6 per cent per annum, this item of cost approximates $720 million. Another significant credit operating cost is that of losses from bad debts, which for wholesalers selling on credit were $239 million, or about 33 per cent of the interest cost. Other items of expense include the cost of credit information, collection agency fees, rent for the space occupied by credit personnel, depreciation of credit and collection equipment and fixtures, utilities, and supplies.

In the absence of studies to this end, no authoritative statements are now possible with respect to the total cost of operating the credit phase of a mercantile business. Available data on the magnitude of some credit operating costs do, however, strongly suggest the need for management of mercantile credit departments to know the amount of such costs and to consider the potential impact on the various cost items resulting from contemplated changes in credit and collection policies and procedures. This means that credit managers should encourage the application of sound and scientific cost studies to credit and collection activities as a means toward more effective management.

QUESTIONS AND PROBLEMS

1 From the facts presented in the early part of this chapter, explain the importance of the credit function in a wholesale house. Does this afford a complete explanation? Why, or why not?

2 What objectives is the organization of a mercantile credit department designed to accomplish?

3 Identify the functions and activities which relate the credit department to other areas in a wholesale establishment, and indicate the significance of these relationships to the place which the credit department should be given in the organization.

4 What is the difference between organization and systems as those terms pertain to the mercantile credit department? Is either fundamental to the other? Explain.

5 A writer in one of the leading business publications advocated the abolition of the credit department. His contention was that more sales could be made as a result of a lenient policy in credit extension and that the profit obtained from the additional sales would more than offset the added losses from bad debts. It follows, therefore, that the absence of a credit department would result in a maximum of sales and, while the losses from bad debts would naturally increase, they would be far exceeded by the added profits. He further proceeded to state that most people are honest and that the abandonment of the credit department would be a good thing from the creditor's standpoint. Do you agree? Explain.

6 In a wholesale firm with a volume of business of approximately $1,800,000 a year, what position should the credit department occupy on the organization chart?

7 Would your answer be the same if the volume of business were $10,000,000?

8 The ABC manufacturing company was just organized for the production of a variety of drug items to be sold to wholesalers and to a certain extent also direct to retailers. You were placed in charge of credits and collections. What records and files would you deem absolutely necessary for your operations? What other records and files would you consider advisable to have?

9 How would such records and files come into use:

a In the checking and handling of first orders?

b In the checking of orders from old customers?

10 In the event that information must be secured as a basis for judgment whether a first order should be accepted or rejected, what factors would determine just how much and what kind of information should be gathered?

11 Outline the procedure for handling orders:

a From new customers

b From old accounts in good standing

c From old accounts that are delinquent

12 What are the major items of cost incurred in performing the credit function of a mercantile business? Which of these items are the most important? What bearing does this have upon the layman's thinking that bad debt losses represent the cost of operating on a credit basis?

CHAPTER FOURTEEN

credit
management of
financial institutions

While business firms rely upon mercantile credit to acquire much of the goods and services required for the normal conduct of operations, they also use substantial amounts of short-term funds made available by financial institutions. These funds are employed for a variety of purposes and are obtained from different types of institutions. In this chapter are considered the major types of financial institutions that supply short-term credit to business enterprises, as well as the need of businesses for such credit.

Need for short-term credit from financial institutions. Almost every business makes use of current debt financing for which payment of principal is promised within 1 year, for several reasons. A most important one is that certain types of current financing are often available when long-term sources of funds are not. Second, under normal circumstances, the interest rate or rate of return paid for short-term funds is less than for long-term sources of funds. A third explanation is that it is normally possible for the borrowing business to repay the suppliers of current financing at will without substantial penalty. Fourth, unlike some forms of long-term funds, the use of short-term financing does not disrupt the voting control of the firm. The major disadvantage in current financing is that the borrowing firm commits itself to repayment within a short period of time and, in comparison to long-term sources, has relatively little time to plan new sources of funds to meet such obligations. If payments are not paid when due, the borrower runs the risk of financial embarrassment or even forced liquidation.

As a general rule, it is desirable, therefore, to finance permanent needs with long-term sources of funds and temporary requirements with short-term funds. This is based on the assumption that permanent financing of temporary needs leads to higher financing cost for the firm, more frequent and higher idle cash balances, and a lower level of profitability, while temporary financing of permanent needs is a very high-risk operation. In order to apply this general rule of business finance, management must decide which requirements are temporary and which are permanent. In most businesses, fixed assets such as land, buildings, delivery equipment, furniture, and fixtures are thought of as permanent needs throughout the life of the business. A large portion of current assets must also be considered as permanent requirements. This amount commonly is termed *permanent working capital* or *fixed working capital;* it is the minimum dollar sum needed in the business to carry normal or at least minimum inventories and supplies, to provide for the carrying of normal or minimum investment in receivables, and to insure that there will be adequate funds on hand to meet operating expenses and other cash disbursement requirements.

Every business enterprise also requires temporary additions to its long-term financing. Seasonal peak sales, for example, require advance expansion of inventory followed by proportionately heavy increases in accounts receivable. Anticipated price increases in inventory, unfavorable court decisions, or uninsured property losses are among the many other situations that may require varying amounts of temporary capital, sometimes referred to as *variable working capital.*

As suggested above, these temporary asset needs should be financed with flexible short-term debt that may be expanded or contracted with corresponding fluctuations in the assets. It also would be *ideal* for a firm to obtain all of its permanent capital requirements from equity sources or long-term borrowing. This is an extremely difficult task for many companies, particularly small businesses, which do not have as many long-term sources of supply available to them. It is rather common, therefore, to provide for a substantial proportion of temporary asset requirements, in addition to significant amounts of permanent working capital needed for inventories, receivables, and other assets, through the use of trade credit and short-term credit extended by certain types of financial institutions.

General nature of short-term credit from financial institutions. The major types of financial institutions that supply short-term credit to business firms include commercial banks, commercial-paper houses, sales finance companies, and business finance companies. As shown later, such credit extended by some of these institutions is made on the basis of unsecured loans. In other instances, short-term funds are supplied through loans that are secured by a specific pledge of collateral or property, intended to reduce the risk incurred by the lending institution. It may also be used to enable the borrower to obtain a more liberal loan in the form of a larger amount, longer maturity, or lower interest rate than otherwise would be possible. In some loans, security is necessary to conform with what has become the customary arrangement offered by the particular financial institution. The collateral offered may consist of marketable securities, accounts receivable, notes receivable, merchandise inventory, real estate, equipment, or other property, both tangible and intangible.

COMMERCIAL BANKS

In some respects, credit in the economy comes to a focus in the commercial bank, an institution chartered under a state or Federal banking act[1] that enables it to accept demand deposits and time and savings deposits, create money, and make loans and investments within the legal provisions of the charter. It is an institution in which personal and business funds are deposited and used as a basis for investments and loans to others. Such a bank acts in part as a free, competitive enterprise and in part as a publicly supervised organ of society catering to the diverse financial needs of the community.

The main function of the commercial bank is to provide for the

---

[1] Of the 13,767 commercial banks in operation at the end of 1966, slightly less than 35 per cent were national banks and about 65 per cent were state banks, but the national banks accounted for approximately 58 per cent of the deposits in commerical banks. Of all the commercial banks, only about 45 per cent were members of the Federal Reserve System, but because they were the larger institutions, they accounted for about 83 per cent of the deposits in all commercial banks.

varying credit needs growing out of commercial and other business under-takings.[2]   The financial needs of business calling for short-term commercial bank credit are rather specialized ones.   First, they are needs for cash, not for the tangible assets which are usually available on open-account or other forms of credit.   These assets, however, are sometimes bought with the cash obtained through a bank loan.   Second, they are needs of a relatively temporary nature, often for fewer than 90 days and sometimes for as long as a year.   Indeed, the chief purpose of short-term commercial bank credit is to assist businessmen in meeting their *current* needs for funds that would facilitate the processes of production and distribution.   That is why commercial banks ordinarily grant such credit only for short periods.   When a business establishment borrows money from a bank for periods longer than 1 year, it is presumed to be using the bank as a source of intermediate or permanent working capital.   Consistent lending for periods longer than 1 year is contrary to the original intent of such banking institutions.   As further proof of this intent, attention should be called to the fact that all banks expect their borrowers to *clean up* their accounts by being out of debt to the bank for at least 1 month each year.

Nature of short-term business loans. Although in borrowing from a commercial bank actual cash may be obtained, the loans are usually made in the form of a drawing account in the name of the borrower. Checks may be drawn by the borrower up to a certain amount in return for his promise to repay an equivalent amount at a specified date in the future or on demand, as the case may be.

A bank may lend on any one of a number of credit instruments, as has already been pointed out in Chap. 3.   A secured loan is one made by the bank on a note or draft secured by some form of collateral. Security offered may consist of real estate, bonds, stocks, warehouse receipts, bills of lading, merchandise, notes receivable, or other property. Thus "commodity paper" is secured by a warehouse receipt attached to the note, "collateral notes" are secured by a deposit of bonds and stock, etc., and "mortgage notes" are secured by mortgages on property. Collateral deposited in numerous cases consists of bonds and stocks. Securities listed on an important stock exchange are the most desirable for such purposes, owing to the relative ease with which they are convertible into cash.

Unsecured loans are based upon the financial and credit responsi-

---

[2] While the traditional function of commercial banks in the field of lending is to make short-term business loans, there has been a tendency since 1933 to make also intermediate-term business loans of 1 to 5 or 10 years in maturity and to engage in the mortgage loan business, as shown in Chap. 11, and in consumer credit, as revealed in Chaps. 7, 8, and 10.

bility of the maker or makers, acceptors, or endorsers. These loans involve no specific pledge of property as security. Firms enjoying a long-standing relationship with a bank may borrow on an unsecured, line-of-credit arrangement. A *credit line* is customarily established on an annual basis and reflects an understanding between borrower and bank as to the maximum limit that can be borrowed during a year without a credit recheck by the bank. Although a line-of-credit agreement does not constitute a binding contract on the part of the bank, banks usually honor the terms of such agreements unless radical changes occur. The borrower can use any portion of his line whenever he needs funds and can reduce his loan when the need is passed. When the borrower wishes funds, he signs unsecured notes which ordinarily are in multiples of $1,000 or $5,000 and have maturities that allow for repayment as desired. When a line of credit is not used, the bank will treat each unsecured loan as a separate agreement and the borrower signs unsecured notes for the specific amount involved.

The interest on some bank loans is collected at maturity. It is, however, common practice for banks to *discount* loans, especially in the case of unsecured loans. This means that the bank will deduct the interest in advance from the principal amount of the loan and credit the account of the borrower with the balance. These practices give rise to what are designated as loans and discounts. In both instances, the interest rate is quoted as a per cent of the total amount of the loan; hence, when the loan is discounted, the effective rate of charge on the money that the borrower actually gets to use is somewhat higher than the stated percentage. On a $10,000 loan that matures in 6 months, for example, a stated rate of 6 per cent (annual rate) discounted is the equivalent to approximately 6.19 per cent, since the borrower is paying $300 for the use of $9,700 for 6 months.

A substantial number of commercial banks also require borrowers, particularly those with a line of credit, to maintain balances in their demand deposit accounts of from 10 to 20 per cent of the principal amounts borrowed. These are often referred to as *compensating balances*. Such a requirement also increases the *effective* rate of interest in excess of the *stated* rate under those circumstances wherein the minimum compensating balance is greater than the borrower would normally keep in his bank checking account. If a 20 per cent balance were required on a 6-month, 6 per cent $10,000 loan, the borrower would be paying $300 interest but would have the use of only $7,700. This would be an effective rate of about 7.79 per cent.

Bank credit policy. Formulating and implementing a sound commercial loan credit policy is among the most important responsibilities of bank directors and management.[3]   With approximately 13,740 commercial banks in this country serving diverse credit needs in different localities, it is impossible to suggest a uniform credit policy that is equally applicable to all banks.   In the granting of credit, it should be noted, however, that significant differences exist between the standards of banking institutions and those of commercial concerns.   Banks are, for the most part, far more conservative than mercantile concerns in the extension of credit, for at least three major reasons.

In the first place, they deal with other people's money in a fiduciary capacity.   When a bank acts in the capacity of custodian for the funds of depositors, whose deposits furnish the basis for the bulk of the loans made, a high degree of certainty and confidence is required concerning the bank's ability to meet its obligations at all times, particularly at maturity, lest it experience a "run."   Unlike a mercantile house, a bank cannot ask for extensions of its obligations without jeopardizing its reputation and good will.   Such a request may result in the cessation of its business activity and consequent failure.   This delicate situation in which a commercial bank finds itself requires a high degree of liquidity, which the various bank examiners, representing the Comptroller of the Currency, the Federal Reserve System, the Federal Deposit Insurance Corporation, or the state bank department, make it their business to enforce.

A second reason for the bank's conservative attitude, as compared with mercantile creditors, is to be accounted for by the difference in margins of profit as a per cent of loans made compared to margins as a per cent of merchandise sales.   Banks normally operate on comparatively narrow margins; consequently they cannot afford to assume undue risks.   A third element in the situation is the relative size of the loan. Most businessmen deal with a single bank but buy merchandise from many sources of supply.   Thus, comparatively large sums are borrowed from banks.

To reduce risks to a minimum, a bank credit department is forced to investigate its risks more thoroughly, scrutinize its information with greater care, and base its loans wherever possible on collateral capable of quick realization.   An attempt is also made to diversify loans in regard to lines of business, location, and maturities.   Businesses dealing in staples selling on short-credit terms are usually given preference over

[3] For a discussion of the considerations involved in the formulation of a bank's credit policy, see Julian J. Clark and John B. Pipkin, II, "Establishing a Bank's Policy," *The Banker's Handbook*, Dow Jones–Irwin, Inc., Homewood, Ill., 1966, Chap. 19. See also Howard D. Crosse, *Management Policies for Commercial Banks*, Prentice-Hall, Inc., Englewood Cliffs, N.J., 1962, Chap. 10.

those dealing in luxuries or lines which sell on long-credit terms. Finally, well-established concerns, the managements of which are known to be conservative, are sought in preference to new and unseasoned organizations.

If local banks are unwilling or unable to finance some of the mercantile transactions, particularly when large amounts are involved, the necessary funds may be secured from other financial institutions, which in turn frequently borrow from their respective banks. In recent years, some commercial banks have become reluctant to finance small business in its seasonal operations. Hence, a greater burden has fallen upon the large manufacturer or wholesaler who, in addition to extending credit on the merchandise sold, must assume responsibility for financing the smaller customers.

Departmentization of credit work in banks. As is true of all functional organizations, the need for departmentization of credit work in commercial banks depends primarily upon two factors. One is the nature of the work to be done, and the second is the size of the bank and its volume of business.

Functions performed. Regardless of the size of the institution, bank credit management generally involves three principal functions. The credit standing of applicants must be investigated; bank credit records must be constantly revised so as to keep the bank officers informed of the status of their accounts; and credit information must be furnished correspondent banks and other creditors who seek it. Some institutions go so far as to investigate prospects before soliciting their business; these are still in the minority, for most banks undertake no investigation until an application for credit is made. Information concerning risks is constantly pouring into the credit department from many sources. These facts must be sorted and related to the accounts so that limits may be altered or assistance given a customer who is getting into difficulties.

The problem of gathering the necessary credit facts and properly keeping them is none too simple. To be sure, no elaborate systems or special records need be kept in the small banks. Here the cashier may know personally all his customers and may, in addition, possess a substantial degree of knowledge of local conditions affecting their credit standing. With the growth of cities, size of deposits, and number of borrowers, personal contact can no longer be relied upon. The work then requires careful and sometimes minute subdivision, memory alone becoming inadequate. An up-to-date credit department, which collects all the necessary credit information and properly files it, thus becomes a necessity.

Size of the bank. The type of organization of a bank's credit department must necessarily vary with the size and character of the institution and the nature of the community it serves.   There are banks in which two or three officers, together with a loan committee, perform all the necessary functions.   At the other extreme, there are some of the largest banking houses with as many as a hundred employees and in which the work is highly departmentized.   In such institutions the credit department is in charge of a credit manager, who may rank as vice president or assistant cashier.   Between these two extremes there are a large number of medium-sized banks located in growing communities in which the executive officers sooner or later reach a point where they find it impossible to maintain a personal and immediate contact with all customers whose names are carried on the books.

In order to overcome these difficulties and to assist them to keep in touch with borrowing customers, such banks generally conclude that the installation of a credit department, which gathers and files all valuable information and makes it readily available as occasions arise, will solve their problems.   The bank credit department came into being toward the end of the last century, was generally established in the large banks in the second decade of this century, and since 1920 gained wide acceptance among medium-sized institutions.   The *raison d'être* of every bank credit department is invariably found in the need of the loaning officers for assistance in assembling and interpreting facts and opinions that will help them to determine intelligently whether credit should be extended and in what amounts.

Bank credit department organization. Unlike credit management in a commercial or industrial enterprise, credit management in a bank is not usually the responsibility only of the credit manager.   Even the term credit manager is a misnomer in connection with bank credit, for no one person in a bank bears the entire responsibility for credit authorization and management, and the so-called "credit manager" is in reality the manager of the bank's credit department.

It is not intended to make the exposition of the organization and operation of a bank credit department so broad as to cover all sorts of banks.   An attempt is made rather to explain the operations of credit departments of medium-sized banks, for it is believed that a comprehension of this typical organization will enable every resourceful student of the subject so to modify the structure and credit systems to be described as to conform with the needs of the particular bank under advisement.

Bank directors and officers. In common practice, the actual preparation of overall credit-policy statements is usually carried out by the president or senior loan and credit officer, but the final policy must be established by the board of directors.[4] A statement of credit policy usually includes references to the types of loans made by the bank as well as the credit basis upon which the various loan applications are considered acceptable. Only important applications or matters of credit policy are referred to the directors at their periodic meetings. By considering all loan applications over established amounts, the full board, loan review committee of the board, or some other designated subdivision of the board regularly reviews and interprets credit policy by actions it takes on the various applications. If the majority of directors disapproves the loan in question, that decision is final, the opinion of the president and of other officers to the contrary notwithstanding.

Since in the majority of banks all directors do not meet each week, it is customary to delegate much of the loan-making power to a loan committee, which is usually composed of three or more designated officers. To this committee must be submitted all applications for loans exceeding the stipulated amounts of the individual officers' loan authorities. Besides approving or recommending action on specified credit applications, this committee makes a complete report of all applications handled each week or month, as the case may be, and the decisions rendered to the directors under whose supervision it operates.

Next to the loan committee, the president exercises the greatest amount of control over bank credits. All important loans are referred to him by the credit manager or senior loan officers for approval or disapproval. Ordinarily, the president does not go into the matter in great detail and acts largely on the recommendations of his subordinate officers, who analyze the situation with great care. Then follow the vice presidents, one or more of whom may be placed in charge of certain classes of accounts and who pass upon most credit matters. Where the number of accounts handled is large and the lines of business served are numerous, assistant vice presidents and assistant cashiers may be engaged in credit work. These officers interview customers and review the financial condition of borrowers with a view to establishing lines of credit, the same as their senior officers, except that they are likely to handle smaller and, consequently, less important accounts. Finally, the

4 See Clark and Pipkin, *op. cit.*, p. 249.

manager of the credit department may have authority to make small loans on good security or those which are otherwise reasonably safe.

Credit department manager. The manager of the bank credit department exercises general supervision of the entire operation of his department. Among his numerous duties, one is daily to look over the new-account cards which are filled out when a customer opens an account. The information requested on the form may be useful in appraising the risk or in determining whether any investigation should be then initiated.

The department manager also interviews customers and prospects for the purpose of obtaining information needed by the loaning officers in making loan decisions. He acts as an intermediary between the loan committee and his department. Often serving as secretary of the committee, he knows not only the voted decisions but also the opinions of the individual members of the committee, and thus is well informed in carrying out the policies and wishes of his executive officers.

Still another function is to communicate with other banks and commercial houses requesting credit information and to receive and classify information from credit applicants and others. He must regularly examine incoming financial statements and mark for copying those portions which are to be transferred to the "comparison of statements" form. Finally, he inspects all new and revised folders prepared during the day by his assistant.

Assistant manager of the credit department. The assistant is generally charged with the task of running the department smoothly under the manager's supervision and solving problems of minor importance. It is he who allocates work to other employees, initiates where necessary the assembly of information about a new account or for an account revision, supervises transcription of pertinent portions of replies to inquiries and of financial statements marked for copying by the manager, and consolidates into the credit folder file all data secured from other departments of the institution.

Credit department systems. Many systems and mechanical appliances have been devised and new ideas are being evolved constantly by manufacturers of electronic equipment, indexes, card systems, and cabinets. In choosing one of these systems, each credit department manager should bear in mind the results to be attained rather than the mere means. In the broadest sense, the credit system to be used in connection with business loans involves providing bank management with the basic information essential for processing, reviewing, and collecting the loan. The filing system and facilities for record keeping are, therefore, an integral part of the overall credit system and the backbone of the credit department. With more extensive use of computers, particularly by the large banks, no doubt much credit information and record keeping will be put on computers in the future.

The credit folder. Although there is considerable lack of uniformity among bank credit departments in regard to their filing systems, because of differences in requirements and comparative age of the institutions, each bank credit department nevertheless uses some sort of a system for filing credit information folders. These folders differ in makeup and content according to the policy of each particular bank. Many banks use folders made of letter-sized expansion pressboard type, while others use the lighter manila style. In some instances, the former are used for the more important and active accounts on which much information is likely to be collected, while the latter are reserved for accounts of a less popular character, concerning which comparatively few data are to be assembled.

To facilitate the use of credit folder information, especially when its contents become voluminous, many institutions arrange the folder on the order of a book, separating its several divisions by index sheets. At least five divisions are ordinarily made. The first contains all financial statement information concerning the risk, including the "comparison of statements." The second contains notes and memoranda obtained from interviews and investigations as well as direct correspondence with the customer. For example, if the subject is a borrower in the open money market, a notation of the date on which his note was purchased, the amount involved, due date, rate, and name of the broker may be preserved. The "opening sheet," or form filled out by the new-account clerk, is also sometimes placed in this section. The third contains mercantile agency reports as well as reports from credit interchange bureaus. In the fourth is placed all correspondence with banks, brokers, and trading houses, as well as carbon copies of letters requesting information from these sources. In the fifth section are kept miscellaneous items gathered from newspapers, magazines, court records, and the like.

Some credit departments prefer to classify information contained in the credit folder into only two divisions: one for that obtained from direct sources and the other for information from indirect sources. The direct source information division begins with the "opening sheet." Following this is the borrowing sheet, showing the date, amount borrowed, due date, rate, and remarks; financial statements; and interviews with brokers, officers, or partners of the borrowing concern. The indirect information division contains the descriptive material concerning the risk, trade and bank references, memoranda of inquiries, clippings, results of interviews with references, and reports of mercantile agencies and credit interchange bureaus.

The index card file. Every credit department should have some type of central information file system or index card system for every account, giving the name and address of the account and the folder and file numbers or other symbols by which they are designated. Index cards are always filed alphabetically, and are indispensable when files are divided into several separate sections or when folders are filed geographically. Through the index card file one can immediately learn in what division a given folder is located. Another advantage derived is that the index file acts as a check on the folder files, thereby preventing losses through misplacements and inaccurate filing. Folders are sometimes removed by one of the loaning officers without knowledge of the filing clerk. Reference to the index will at once reveal the fact that a folder has been made out for the account in question but that it has either been misfiled or deliberately removed by one of the bank officers or employees. Further to obviate such annoyance arising from inability to locate folders rapidly, some banks require that a person removing a folder from the files place a slip bearing his name in place of the folder. When strictly adhered to, good results may be obtained from this method. An official, when careless or in great haste, however, may take the privilege of not conforming strictly to the rule, thereby giving rise to the difficulty just described. A third advantage closely connected with the one preceding is that the index file furnishes definite knowledge whether or not there is a folder on the name under consideration.

Some banks have, in addition to an alphabetical index, a trade index. Such an index facilitates the work if a revision of all names in a given line of business is necessitated by certain conditions. Index cards filed by lines of business or industry also lend themselves to uses for solicitation purposes, an item of considerable importance to some institutions.

The pending file. Many matters come up in the daily routine of the department which cannot be settled for some time. The installation of a pending or tickler file obviates the possibility of delaying or forgetting important matters. Such a file may be divided into 12 monthly divisions with 30 or 31 subdivisions under each. A simpler plan is merely to have 31 divisions, one for each day of the month. Papers filed under each daily division are to be arranged alphabetically. For example, a folder of a new customer would be placed in one of the divisions under the date when the receipt of information is expected and the matter is to come up again. Unless matters are postponed more than 30 days, it is quite evident that one monthly division containing 31 subdivisions would suffice.

Filing credit information. There are differences of opinion regarding the best methods of filing. Some credit department managers prefer to file all information in strict alphabetical order; others prefer a geographic division of the files, with alphabetical subdivisions by names of accounts under each geographic unit; still others find it advantageous to divide the files in accordance with the types of names handled. While it is difficult to describe all systems of filing in use at the present time, an attempt will be made nevertheless to indicate some possibilities for arrangement of files on the basis of logic and convenience. A filing system must be fitted to the bank and no attempt should, therefore, be made to adapt the bank to the system. For example, in some banks, files and folders covering bank accounts are not regarded as belonging to the credit department; accordingly, they are kept in another department. In other banks, these names are handled together with commercial accounts.

Two separate divisions may be had for deposit and loan accounts and for commercial paper names. In both of these divisions folders are usually arranged alphabetically. Where these two classes of names are filed together, it is advisable to distinguish them by means of colored index tabs placed on the folder. Similarly, one or more files may be had for bank names, one for correspondents, one for bank nonaccounts, etc. These folders are ordinarily filed geographically. Where more than one class of bank names is included in one file, distinction should be made by use of colored celluloid tabs.

Information on commercial nonaccounts and on miscellaneous names arising from inquiries is frequently kept in a separate file division. These folders are filed alphabetically and may also be classified and distinguished by colored index tabs. Bank nonaccounts may be kept separately or filed together with commercial nonaccounts and the miscellaneous file. If kept separately, they are filed on a geographical basis.

The loaning process. The amount and nature of the information secured concerning a borrower vary with the nature of the loan (whether it is open or secured), the amount requested, the purpose for which the loan is to be used, and the status of the borrower. Few sources are used for old reliable customers, just to verify their condition, but on a large loan application from a new borrower, all available sources of credit information may be checked.

CITY NATIONAL BANK
BRANCH COMMERCIAL LOAN APPLICATION

NAME OF APPLICANT AND ADDRESS		OFFICE
BUSINESS		DATE
MANAGEMENT OR PRINCIPALS		

CREDIT APPLIED FOR	AMOUNT	RATE	TOTAL BANK DEBT IF APPROVED

COLLATERAL, ENDORSERS, GUARANTORS	
PURPOSE	
MATURITY & SOURCE OF FUNDS FOR REPAYMENT	

PRESENT LOANS OUTSTANDING (To include loans to endorsers, guarantors, affiliates, etc.)		TYPE OF LOAN — COLLATERAL & VALUATION	MATURITY	RATE	BALANCE
	COMMERCIAL				
	OTHER				

PRIOR LOANING EXPERIENCE	
AVERAGE BALANCES (To include related accts.)	

FINANCIAL STATEMENT	DATE:	TYPE:
		FISCAL ☐ INTERIM ☐ AUDIT ☐ UNAUDITED SIGNED ☐ UNAUDITED UNSIGNED ☐

COMMENTS (For additional space use other side)	
RECOMMENDATION OF BRANCH	

APPROVALS	APPROVED BY:	DATE:	RECOMMENDED BY:	DATE:

figure 14-1. *Application for a loan at a commercial bank branch, made by a business borrower.*

Application for a loan. In each case, the "Application for Loan" provides a basis for the analysis of the risk (see Fig. 14-1). The executive officer who takes the application fills in the necessary information, determines the market value of any property offered as collateral, secures a new financial statement if necessary, may have the real estate checked from the public records to verify the items listed in the financial statement, and obtains all available data from the bank's own records. In connection with this, he checks all affiliated accounts which might include a church or club account over which the applicant has control, his wife's account, or any other account in which he has an interest or for which he assumes responsibility. The borrower's previous record with the lending institution is filled in under "Remarks." Additional facts may be obtained from Dun & Bradstreet, Inc., from the Credit Interchange Bureau, or from one or more of the other sources already cited.

All commercial accounts whose initial deposits are substantial are ordinarily marked for investigation. Requests are thereupon forwarded to mercantile agencies for reports, and letters are sent to bank and trade references requesting information on the subject under consideration. If the bank is a member of a credit interchange bureau, an inquiry ticket is sent to that organization. In the majority of cases, a form letter is sent simultaneously to the new account expressing appreciation of his business and requesting him to fill out an enclosed financial statement blank and return it in the stamped enclosed envelope. It is usually explained in the letter that it is to the borrower's advantage to furnish the bank with a statement of his financial responsibility, so that the bank's replies to legitimate inquiries regarding his credit standing may be made advisedly and intelligently.

Information sources within the bank. In addition to the credit department itself, there are a number of sources within the bank from which information may be obtained for original approval or subsequent revision of accounts. One of these is the loan committee. In his capacity of secretary for the loan committee, the credit manager acquires knowledge concerning reasons for specific action taken by the committee. Second, from the loan department he also learns of loans actually made and sometimes of approaching maturities. Lists of names involved should be furnished daily by the loan department, containing the amount of the note, whether secured or unsecured, total indebtedness, rate of discount, and remarks. It should also be shown whether an extension was asked, whether such extension was granted or refused, and whether payment was made early, on due date, or after.

A third source of information is the new-account desk, which at the end of each day sends to the credit department a card for each account opened that day. This card, known as the signature card, gives the name, address, character of the account opened, amount of initial deposit, and other information. Fourth, the correspondence files provide other data invaluable to the credit department. All finished correspondence dealing with the establishment of an account or the extension of credit is stored in these files and is available to the credit department. From such files the credit department ascertains who the borrowers are, the negotiations developed, and specific agreements and provisos relative to the establishment of the various accounts. This information forms the basis of the credit files maintained by the credit department.

A fifth source of information is that obtainable from the analysis or auditing department which, among other tasks, deals with the average net and ledger balances, the proportion of these balances to credit extensions, and the profitability of the account since it became active. In some banks the records of this department are sent monthly to the credit department; from these are copied the facts stated, on a card provided for that purpose.

Sixth, the demand deposit and time certificate ledgers provide other useful data. From them can be obtained information on the checking habits of the borrower. They show whether there is a margin of safety at all times and whether there are frequent overdrafts. Time deposit ledgers tell something of the financial wisdom of the customer. If a time deposit is being maintained, it is favorable, for it shows that accumulations are made for emergencies. Finally, something about the investment habits of the customer may be learned from the bond department. Bond men usually know who among the risks are speculators and who are seasoned investors.

The analysis. If the application is for a small amount, the matter may be passed on immediately by the loan officer and routinely reviewed by the credit manager and the loan committee, even without waiting for a new financial statement, especially if the applicant is a regular customer of the bank. In all other instances, the loan officer makes a careful and complete analysis, normally with the assistance of a member of the credit department, of all the information collected, particularly of those items that bear directly on the risk's financial responsibility. For this purpose, many banks use the ratios developed by the Robert Morris Associates, showing relationships that exist between certain financial statement items for a given line of business. With these so-called "standard," "normal," or "average" ratios are compared those computed for the applicant's business, and in the light of the results as well as in consonance with the other information, the analysis is completed and a recommendation made to the responsible loan officer or the loan committee as the case may be.

Making and watching the loan. The power to make loans for the bank is one which is delegated by the board of directors. The cashier, vice presidents, and president are allowed to make loans up to amounts specified by the board of directors. The loan committee accepts or rejects those loans which are beyond the purview of the individual loan officers' authorities. Later, at its regular meeting, the board formally accepts all loans made by the loan committee. Each loan application is read in full to the loan committee, showing the needs of the applicant, his plans for repayment, and his past record at the bank. The accompanying financial statement is studied. Current assets are carefully examined and current liabilities are noted. To approve a loan some banks require the unanimous consent of all members of the committee. The credit department manager's report and recommendations are gone over with care. If the loan is approved, the application for the loan is so marked and signed by the secretary to the committee. Under certain conditions, the applicant may be asked to come in for a conference in order to discuss some of the weaknesses that have been discovered during the investigation, and unless he is willing to take advice and make the necessary changes, the loan may not be granted or else only part of it may be approved, and that under certain stipulations. Generally, it is a bank's policy not to lend more than five times the borrower's average balance for the year, but this rule or policy is very elastic in actual practice.

From the time the loan is made until it is repaid, the credit department must keep a watchful eye on the progress of the customer, all newspaper clippings being filed in the proper folder and other information being properly recorded and appropriate action taken when justified. About 10 days before maturity a date slip appears in the tickler file, at which time the borrower is informed of the approaching maturity. In the meantime, a summary containing up-to-date information and the bank's experience with the risk is prepared and presented to the loan committee to determine whether the loan would be renewed if requested. The results of the decision are then sent to the loan cage or department, where they remain until the debtor asks for a renewal of the loan, in whole or in part, or makes full payment.

Making loans through branch banks. When an application for a loan is made at a branch bank, of which there is a large and growing number, the manager of the branch secures all the necessary information, including the application form properly filled out, the financial statement, and the information which he personally has of the applicant concerning his method of doing business, habits, and general reputation in the vicinity. This information is sent to the credit department of the main office of the bank, where a real estate check may be made and various reports obtained to complete the investigation. The results are then submitted in the usual way to the loan or other committee for action. If the branch manager is fully informed of the prospective borrower's financial condition, he may be authorized to grant the loan at once after obtaining permission by telephone from the credit manager at the main office. The branch manager may be even given power to make loans up to a certain amount without referring them to the main office, especially if they are secured by highly marketable collateral. A duplicate application form is retained by the branch office, where the note is filed. The latter is often a cognovit note which eliminates the necessity for proving the validity of the debt by acknowledging on its face that the signer is duly indebted to the holder and confesses judgment when presented before the proper legal authorities. The branch attempts to collect the loan, but when unable to do so in the usual course, the matter is turned over to the main office.

LOANS THROUGH SALE OF COMMERCIAL PAPER

Some well-established business firms borrow on a short-term basis through the issuance of *commercial paper*. This form of obligation consists of unsecured promissory notes which are negotiable and carry a fixed maturity date. The notes are ordinarily in denominations of $5,000 and have maturities ranging from 30 to 270 days. They do not bear a stated rate of interest, but are sold at a discount from their face value.

Commercial paper may be sold directly by the issuer to institutional investors, which include such diverse groups as commercial banks, nonfinancial corporations, pension and trust funds, insurance companies, and university endowment funds. This direct channel of distribution has been utilized primarily by finance companies, while industrial, wholesale, and retail firms normally sell their commercial paper through dealers. These dealers, commonly referred to as *commercial-paper houses,* are middlemen who buy the notes from the issuer and resell them to investors at a slightly higher price than they paid for the paper. In addition, the commercial-paper house typically receives a commission of $1/4$ per cent of the face value of the notes for its marketing services.

Advantages of selling commercial paper. For borrowers who are in a position to use this type of financing, commercial paper offers several advantages in comparison to other methods of obtaining short-term funds. To begin with, the borrower can issue these notes usually at rates of interest lower than those that can be negotiated directly on short-term loans from commercial banks in the locality in which he is located. A large borrower also may find that the statutory limitations on a loan to a single borrower by his local bank necessitate obtaining funds from additional banks, particularly during peak seasons. Through the sale of commercial paper, the borrower not only acquires needed funds but may establish additional banking connections. Furthermore, a borrower who issues this paper, rather than secure an ordinary bank loan, need not be concerned with a compensating balance requirement and thus gets the use of the full amount of money borrowed. Then, too, when borrowing in the open market through commercial paper, the business borrower's name becomes known to many institutional investors and his credit standing may improve substantially when the obligations are promptly discharged. This may enhance the firm's ability to borrow in the long-term capital markets. Finally, the extended investigation with reference to open market paper indirectly benefits the borrower by keeping the firm "on its toes."

Disadvantages of selling commercial paper. From the standpoint of the vast majority of business enterprises, the major argument against the sale of commercial paper is simply that this method of financing is not available to them. The nature of the commercial-paper market is such that only very large companies with exceptionally high credit ratings and well known to investors can issue these notes. These rigid requirements explain in large part why the total volume of commercial paper outstanding is small relative to short-term bank credit used by business firms. While the commercial and industrial loans of commercial banks amounted to nearly $88.4 billion at the end of 1967, the total volume of commercial and finance company paper outstanding was about $17.1 billion.[5] This relationship should not, however, obscure the fact that the use of commercial paper has expanded significantly and, indeed, nearly quadrupled in the 7-year period from December, 1960, to December, 1967.

A second disadvantage of commercial paper stems from the impersonal relationship that exists between borrower and lender. Investors who purchase this paper are not hesitant about switching to more attractive short-term investments that may become available. Consequently, the supply of funds to the commercial-paper market is volatile and unreliable from the borrower's viewpoint. Moreover, the notes must be paid when due and no extension of maturity is possible, as may be the case in a short-term bank loan. Finally, some borrowers object to the frequent inquiry to which a borrower using this method is subjected. He is asked for a great mass of more or less detailed information over and over again. This in itself has two objectionable features: first, it may arouse

---

[5] *Federal Reserve Bulletin*, August, 1968, pp. A-24 and A-35.

suspicion among borrowers' commercial creditors; second, it necessitates a complete removal of the secrecy which many houses regard as essential to success.

Advantages of buying commercial paper. From the standpoint of the investor, paper purchased in the market is usually regarded as a particularly attractive investment. This kind of commercial paper is highly marketable and readily convertible into cash. Maturity dates can be chosen to provide for liquid funds to meet current needs. Comparatively high rates on commercial paper are often available. A minor advantage is that these notes can be had in practically all denominations. Moreover, few of these notes are renewed. There is no obligation on the part of the investor to renew them even when requested to do so. Last but not least, the security is of a prime character. Although legally commercial-paper houses are merely guaranteeing the genuineness of the signature, in practice their responsibility is greater than is apparent. They frequently have their own funds invested to a certain extent in the paper they handle, but, most important, they have a reputation at stake, which constitutes a substantial part of their stock in trade. In addition, they give investors, as a rule, a 10-day option within which to investigate the credit standing of the borrower, and, if results of the investigation do not warrant the purchase, the notes can be returned, without any further obligation to the investor.

SALES FINANCE
COMPANIES

The general term *finance company* is used broadly to refer to three different types of financial institutions. These include *consumer* finance companies, which are engaged primarily in making cash loans directly to consumers and were discussed in Chap. 10, *sales* finance companies, and *business* finance companies.

Major functions of sales finance companies.[6] Sales finance companies are engaged in the performance of two main functions. The one for which they are most well known is that of financing the instalment purchases of automobiles and other durable goods by ultimate consumers. The operations of sales finance companies in the performance of this function were discussed previously in considerable detail in Chap.

---

[6] For more details, see C. W. Phelps, *The Role of the Sales Finance Companies in the American Economy*, Commercial Credit Company, 1962. See also C. W. Phelps, *Instalment Sales Financing: Its Services to the Dealer*, Commercial Credit Company, 1962.

8. The second important function of these institutions is *business* financing, a principal type of which is generally known as "floor planning."

Nature of floor planning. This is a method of financing the purchases by dealers and distributors of inventories of automobiles and other types of high-unit-value durable goods, especially major household appliances. This is normally regarded as wholesale financing and may best be illustrated from the automobile field. The manufacturer of automobiles usually insists upon cash payment on delivery of his products to the dealer. This is done through a sight draft drawn on the dealer and payable by him on receipt of the goods.

Under the ordinary wholesale or "floor" plan of financing, the dealer acquires the new cars, stores them in a warehouse or displays them in his showrooms, and executes a trust receipt for the benefit of the finance company. In this way, the dealer remains in possession of the merchandise, which he can display and attempt to sell, but does not have legal title to it. Such title vests in the finance company, the dealer merely holding the goods in trust. The promissory note or trade acceptance given by the dealer may be secured by a security agreement, warehouse receipt, or some other type of wholesale lien instrument instead of the trust receipt.

When a sale is made, the proceeds must be immediately turned over to the finance company before the car can be moved off the floor. The amount loaned seldom exceeds 90 per cent of the invoiced cost of the article. Interest charged on such loans approximates 0.5 per cent per month, since risk is relatively small and the turnover of such loans fairly rapid.

BUSINESS FINANCE
COMPANIES

According to the "Survey of Finance Companies" published in the *Federal Reserve Bulletin,* business finance companies include those financial institutions which are engaged principally in providing funds to business firms through factoring, accounts receivable financing, or time-sales financing of commercial, industrial, and farm equipment.[7] Instalment financing of equipment purchases is more properly included in a discussion of intermediate business financing. Special consideration is warranted, however, of factoring and the assignment of accounts receivable.

Factoring accounts receivable. Contrary to common notion, factoring is much more than a mere method of financing accounts receivable.

[7] "Survey of Finance Companies, Mid-1965," *Federal Reserve Bulletin,* April, 1967, pp. 534–559.

In fact, the financing aspect may be subordinated to the credit and collection management phase of the factor's operations and to the protection or insurance against bad debt losses which factoring affords.

What factoring involves. As normally practiced, a factor purchases accounts receivable from a client, without recourse, and assumes all credit risks thereon. This means that for such a client the factor performs three sets of functions. First, he substitutes cash for the accounts receivable, placing the client's extension of credit on a self-liquidating basis as though he were selling for cash. Second, he assumes the credit risk for all accepted accounts and takes full responsibility for the solvency of such customers to the extent of the accepted or approved amounts. Third, he checks the credits and collects the accounts. To enable him to assume all credit risk on accepted accounts, the sales orders must necessarily be approved by the factor. For the same reason, he must have full responsibility for collections, and that is why the client's customers are notified by a printed statement on each invoice that the bill is assigned and payable only to the factor named and at the address indicated. In doing this work, the factor acts as an expert credit manager for his client.

There are, of course, some deviations from the usual functioning of the factor as indicated above. There is such a thing, for example, as non-notification factoring, used occasionally for a client who wishes to withhold such information from his competitors. Under this plan the client collects the accounts, and as payments are received by him from customers they are immediately remitted to the factor. The so-called "Factoring Maturity Plan" is another deviation from normal operation. This plan is designed for a client who is not concerned with the financing of accounts receivable during the free credit period but who wishes to be relieved of the credit risks and of the credit and collection management tasks. In such a case the factor pays for all accepted invoices remaining unpaid at maturity dates, assumes all credit risks on them, and collects the accounts. Obviously, emphasis is placed here on the risk and credit and collection management aspects of the factor's operations rather than on the financing of receivables. It is even possible for a client to utilize the factor only for the credit service without involving any advancing of funds on the receivables.

Extent of factoring. Factoring is still largely concentrated in the textile industry and its various branches and allied lines, where they also advance funds against merchandise inventories. Its services have also been extended, however, to such varied lines as rubber goods, shoes, paper, petroleum products, glass, coal, lumber, metal products, and other types of products and lines of trade.   Furthermore, not only bona fide factoring companies but to some extent also the organizations known as finance companies, discount corporations, or acceptance companies are engaged in this work, and in recent years a few commercial banks have entered this field.

General method of operation. As the functions performed and the specific tasks undertaken by a factor for a given client may differ substantially from those required by another client, the exact relationship is usually spelled out in a contract between the two parties.   As of the effective date of the agreement and after the accounts receivable already on the client's books have been assigned initially, the operations that usually take place may be summarized as follows:

1. Each day the client submits to the factor, in duplicate, a list containing the names and locations of the customers, amounts of the orders for each, terms of sale, and delivery dates, for approval.

2. The factor's credit department checks each account for its creditworthiness.   If approved in its entirety or within a certain limit, the order is properly initialed; if not, the word "rejected" or "declined" is written, and a copy of such list with the proper notations is returned to the client.

3. As orders are filled and shipments made, the amounts are tabulated on a Sales Assignment Sheet, which is sent in duplicate, together with the invoices and duplicates as well as shipping documents, to the factor for acceptance.   This is indicated by proper signature and one copy is returned to the client.   If the sales sheet includes amounts that have not been previously approved and hence cannot be accepted, such amounts must be guaranteed by the client, who is duly informed of that fact.

4. Usually the client mails the original invoice directly to the customer and sends two copies of it to the factor.   One copy goes to the bookkeeping department for posting to the account of the client's customer.   The other copy is for the accounting department, but is reviewed by the credit department of the factor for the purpose of determining whether the shipment was made with prior credit approval by the factor and thus made acceptance of the invoice obligatory.   If not, the shipment would be considered the client's responsibility and, in the event of failure to collect from the customer, the loss would be assumed by the client.

5. Each day the factor credits the account of the client with the face amount of the invoices accepted and guaranteed, less an agreed percentage retained as a reserve to take care of claims, returns, and

allowances. Usually, 90 per cent is thus credited, the balance of the 10 per cent being credited when the accounts become due regardless of whether they are then paid. The funds so credited each day are available for daily remittance to the client, but it is the exception rather than the rule when the client requests funds in this manner. Remittance schedules are generally set up on a predetermined basis such as every 10 days or twice monthly, as desired by the client.

6. At the end of each month the factor bills the client for all charges, which are composed of two elements. One is interest on the money advanced, normally computed at 6 per cent per annum on the basis of actual daily net debit balances. The other is a factoring service commission, which can be as low as $\frac{1}{2}$ per cent of the accounts financed but is usually around $1\frac{1}{2}$ or 2 per cent when all normal factoring services are rendered.

Advantages of factoring. In lines of trade where factoring is recognized as a sound business practice, there are several advantages to be derived by a seller from such service. First, it obviates the necessity for any investment in accounts receivable. The client sells on credit but secures cash immediately. Second, it eliminates all work and expense connected with credit and collection management. This, however, is not a complete savings, since there is some work and expense incident to the maintenance of proper relations with the factor in the daily and other operations. Third, factoring eliminates all risk from credit selling, by shifting it to the factor. This in a sense provides complete credit insurance so long as the credit sales are limited to the accepted accounts and amounts. Fourth, factoring provides the seller with constantly available funds with which to pay bills in time to take advantage of purchase cash discounts. Finally, factoring improves the seller's current ratio over what it would have been in its absence, assuming that the cash received from factoring is used to pay off some of the current obligations. This is the same as saying that, under the conditions indicated, factoring increases the client's net working capital though not the total working capital.

Possible disadvantages. When factoring is not normally used in a given line of business, resort to it by a member of that industry or trade may be interpreted as a sign of financial weakness and thus impair its credit standing. A more important alleged disadvantage is that a seller's credit business may be restricted, since it is limited to accounts and amounts acceptable by the factor who tends to be conservative in order to reduce his credit risks to a minimum.

To say that a seller's business might be restricted by factoring would, however, appear to be unrealistic for several reasons.   First, a seller, by reason of limited funds, may be precluded from taking a risk which the factor, because of his far greater financial strength as compared with that of a client and because of the nature of his operation, can and will take.   Second, the seller does not have the vast store of information which is available to the factor's credit department and which enables the latter to calculate a risk in a more thorough and expert manner. Third, it may be added that customers may pay the factor more promptly than they would pay the client because of fear of offending the factor who represents many sources of supply.

Lastly, it is sometimes argued that the service is too costly.   To be sure, the factoring commission may range from $\frac{1}{2}$ per cent to $1\frac{1}{2}$ per cent or sometimes a little more, depending on the client being factored, and there is an interest charge, usually at the rate of 6 per cent in simple interest per annum on whatever funds are obtained from the factor before maturity date of the invoices sold to him.   But these two percentages cannot properly be converted into a single annual rate and then compared with the rate of interest a firm may pay a lending institution for the mere loan of money.

The factoring commission which is deducted daily from gross receivables sold to the factor can under no circumstances be considered as a charge for the use of money, but must be properly regarded as a charge for credit granting, bookkeeping, and collection services (including the absorption of bad-debt losses) rendered.   The seller should evaluate the cost of factoring to him in terms of what the cost would be to him if he performed the services rendered by the factor.   He would have to compare the aggregate amount of commissions paid to the factor during the year with what it would cost his own firm to maintain a fully staffed credit and collection department and accounts receivable personnel, to pay for supplies and services required, and to assume credit losses.   Of course, he would have no assurance that actual credit losses would not exceed the amounts estimated.   In short, the seller might well look upon the factoring commission part of the total charge as merely a monthly or annual expense of doing a credit business; it is definitely not an expense for mere borrowing of money.

Assignment of accounts receivable. When accounts receivable are financed by other means than factoring, they are either pledged as collateral for a loan or are assigned and sold to a finance, discount, acceptance, or credit company.   In the latter instance the accounts are sold with recourse, at least to the extent of the margin covered by additional accounts, the lender does not assume any credit risks, customers are usually not notified that their accounts were assigned, and collections are usually made by the assignor as agent for and on behalf of the assignee. The amounts advanced by the lender usually range from 80 to 90 per cent of the face value of the receivables assigned, the remainder being held as a reserve for possible deductions and shrinkages, including bad debts.

Reasons for assignment. This may be approached in two ways. One is the use of assignment rather than factoring. The explanation for this may be found in the fact that the assignor is not interested in credit protection, he is not seeking relief from credit and collection management work, his needs for such financing may be seasonal rather than continuous, or the use of factoring and consequent notification may be misinterpreted in the given line of business. The other is to inquire into the reasons for assignment at all.[8] These necessarily include all the various reasons for borrowing money for short-term purposes on a continuous basis instead of obtaining it on a long-term basis through debt or a greater dilution of equity, assuming that those avenues are available. It certainly enables business firms to secure cash on a flexible and elastic basis as required by expanded sales volume or by the opportunities for profitable purchases. Not unimportant is the fact that firms that make use of receivables financing may also obtain from the finance companies other types of financing such as loans on inventory or for the purchase of machinery and equipment. Finally, the assignment of accounts receivable is used to raise cash for seasonal needs or for emergencies.

Advantages in assigning accounts receivable. From the wide and growing use of the practice of hypothecating as collateral for a loan at a bank or of direct sale of accounts receivable to a finance company, it must be inferred that there are not only reasons for it but also advantages to its users. Some of them are revealed from the very statement of reasons for assigning accounts receivable. A special advantage is the improvement in the showing made by the assignor's financial statement, since it substitutes cash for about 80 to 90 per cent of the accounts receivable, leaving the remainder as they were except for the prior claim of the assignee to which they are subject if the amount advanced cannot be collected.

The charges made by the leading finance companies range from around 10 to about 15 per cent per annum, and are in the form of a single figure which can be readily converted into a true annual rate. It

---

[8] For a more comprehensive discussion of the subject, see C. W. Phelps, *Accounts Receivable Financing as a Method of Securing Business Loans,* Commercial Credit Company, 1963.

is, however, difficult to compare accurately the charges for accounts receivable financing by leading banks and leading finance companies because, in addition to interest, some banks make an additional so-called "service charge," may also require borrowers to carry compensating balances, and may carry the proceeds of assigned accounts in a cash collateral account instead of immediately reducing the loan.   All such practices cause the total true annual rate to be substantially in excess of the rate apparently charged by the bank for accounts receivable financing.

Objections to assignment of accounts receivable. The objections have come principally from some unsecured merchandise creditors and from those of the commercial banks that have not as yet engaged in accounts receivable lending.   It is unfair, they claim, to expect credit accommodations on single-name paper or merchandise on a mere verbal promise to pay at the same time that the finance company or bank is secured by the borrower's accounts receivable, one of the most liquid assets.   As a result of such security, the finance company or bank is a preferred creditor in case of bankruptcy, while the others are simply general creditors.

Second, it is claimed that strong concerns do not have to resort to this method of financing, while weak ones cannot afford it.   While this may have been true to some extent in earlier years of the practice, that is certainly not generally the case today, partly because of the reasonableness of the charges and partly because the use of receivables as collateral may arise when the concern is successful and is suffering from growing pains.   Third, the ease with which additional funds can be procured in this manner, it is further claimed by opponents, may tempt the small and unsophisticated merchant to overtrade and expand his business on an unsound basis.   Actually, such temptation is believed negligible.

Fourth, in the past, one of the most frequently voiced contentions of the opponents of accounts receivable financing was the fear that it might afford unscrupulous and dishonest merchants an additional method for misleading their creditors as to the real status of their financial responsibility until it would be too late for the general creditors to take protective measures.   It was argued that, if such measures were not required by law to be recorded, too often the first notice creditors would receive concerning an assignment would come when failure would be precipitated and discovery made that the debtor's accounts could not be relied upon.   As a matter of fact, funds received by accounts receivable financing have seldom been used to commit frauds against unsecured creditors.   Moreover, the Uniform Commercial Code requires the filing of public notice of assignment of accounts in those instances in which such an assignment, alone or in conjunction with other assignments to the same assignee, transfers a significant part of the outstanding accounts of the assignor.

In the fifth place, it has sometimes been argued that raising funds by assigning accounts might be unfavorable to the assignor on the theory that the business reputation might suffer should his customers learn of the assignment and interpret it as a sign of financial weakness. However, the number of firms making use of the practice, as well as the volume of funds provided by this method of business finance, has steadily increased, particularly since the late 1940's.

Sixth, the cost of borrowing funds in this manner, whether from a bank or other financing institution, is necessarily higher than the rates charged good customers on ordinary unsecured loans. It has, therefore, been argued that merchants cannot afford to pay the higher costs without experiencing adverse effects. The cost of a method of financing must, however, be compared with the profits it makes possible and business firms, the vast majority of which are small businesses, usually can obtain more funds by pledging or assigning accounts receivable than by resorting to unsecured loans or other methods.

Seventh, it is claimed that although the sale of accounts receivable immediately places the assignor in a stronger financial position, by substituting cash for open book accounts, ultimately he is worse off. For one thing, the cash is not likely to remain long in the hands of the borrower and, if it is used to speculate in merchandise or for investment in fixed assets, the borrowing concern is placed in a position of having as a result a smaller portion (since the assignor receives but from 80 to 90 per cent of the amounts pledged or assigned) of a slower asset in place of accounts receivable. But such an exceptional case (speculation or unwise use of funds or credit) is just as possible when the firm obtains the cash by any other method or when it secures merchandise from trade creditors.

In fact, financing companies operate with a definite understanding that their special function is to extricate concerns from their financial difficulties when no other usual institutions are willing and able to help them, to serve customers whose needs exceed bank lines, and to enable their more successful clients to grow to the point where they can qualify for bank and open market lines of credit fully adequate to their needs. In performing this function they render a valuable service.

Factoring versus other financing of accounts receivable. From the foregoing discussion it is clear that the factoring of accounts receivable is essentially different from the financing of such receivables by assignment to a finance company of one type of another. There is a difference in the purpose, reasons for the action, functions required of the financing organization, method of operation of such an organization, relationship between the two parties to the arrangement and of the customers whose accounts are involved, and in charges for the services. For these reasons, the two types of financing accounts receivable cannot and must not be treated together as if they were interchangeable. Much of the confusion on the subject has resulted from such a procedure. There is no doubt but that each method has its place and can be fully justified when used appropriately and handled in an economical and sound manner.

QUESTIONS AND PROBLEMS

1 Explain the reasons why business firms use such large amounts of short-term debt financing.

2 What is the difference between "permanent capital" and "temporary capital" requirements? Why is this distinction important in the selection of a firm's financing?

3 The Old Commercial Bank has agreed to grant the XYZ Company a 6.5 per cent, $20,000 loan that matures in 4 months. If the bank "discounts" the loan and requires a 20 per cent "compensating balance," what is the effective rate of charge to the XYZ Company?

4 Commercial bankers have long had a reputation for conservatism. What are the reasons for this?

5 Contrast the functions of a commercial bank's credit department with those of a mercantile establishment's credit department.

6 Explain the functions of the directors, loan committee, and credit manager in regard to commercial loans by a commercial bank.

7 What is the purpose served by the "credit folder?"

8 Trace the steps through which an application for a bank loan goes. What sources of information are used?

9 Explain the advantages of selling commercial paper. Why are small companies not actively engaged in the sale of commercial paper?

10 Explain the role played by the sales finance company in the "floor" plan of financing dealer acquisition of new cars.

11 How does the factoring of accounts receivable differ from their assignment to a finance company? Be specific as to all points of material difference.

12 If you found it necessary or advisable to assign some of your accounts receivable, would you notify your customers of that fact? Your creditors?

13 Is it good practice to assign accounts receivable? Give reasons for your answer.

14 The X company incorporated for the purpose of manufacturing a certain staple product in the drug field. It is planning to purchase a site and erect a structure at a cost of approximately $800,000. The company will require machinery valued at about $150,000; an inventory of raw materials, goods in process, and finished products involves a minimum investment of $200,000 and a maximum of $300,000; and some $30,000 is required for the purchase of delivery and drayage equipment. In addition the company will have to finance its sales, which are to be made on 30-day terms. This will require a minimum of $250,000 to carry the receivables during the slow seasons and as much as $400,000 to care for them during seasons of peak activity. A few thousand dollars will also be needed to care for the first payroll and for other immediate expenses. Show how and to what extent these financial needs can be provided through the use of the different classes of credit.

investigation and analysis of mercantile and financial institution credit risks

In analyzing the credit risk for a mercantile concern or financial institution, whether it represents an active or prospective account, it is necessary to secure essential information bearing on its character, capacity, and capital, as well as on the general and peculiar business and economic conditions affecting it. Such information is available from a variety of sources. Although these sources are similar in some respects for all users, they are much more varied for creditors dealing with business organizations than for those dealing with ultimate consumers, and the information supplied greatly differs. In this chapter and in the several chapters that follow is presented a discussion of the sources of such information at the disposal of mercantile and financial institution creditors.

Sources of credit information in the mercantile and financial institution fields. For the sake of clearness and brevity the various sources of credit information available to mercantile and financial institution creditors may be classified as follows, based partly on the order in which they are commonly brought into play but largely on their relative importance:

I Mercantile agencies:
   1 General.
   2 Special.

II Other creditors, through direct interchange:
   1 Orally, by means of personal contact and through trade-group meetings.
   2 By correspondence.

III Credit bureaus for the interchange of ledger experience:
   1 Credilt interchange bureaus maintained by associations of credit managers.
   2 Trade credit bureaus operated under the auspices of trade associations.

IV Special representatives who are familiar with the risk's locale:
   1 Salesmen of the creditor.
   2 Attorneys.
   3 Banks.
   4 Insurance companies.

V The credit risk itself, through:
   1 Personal interviews.
   2 Financial statements furnished directly upon request of the creditor.

VI The creditor's own records of past dealings with the risk in question. This applies only to old accounts.

VII Current business and professional publications.

VIII Miscellaneous sources, such as:
   1 Corporation manuals.
   2 Corporation financial services.
   3 Trade and financial publications.
   4 Credit character reports.
   5 *Credit Manual of Commercial Laws,* published annually by the National Association of Credit Management.

It is imperative that every credit manager be thoroughly familiar with all these classes of sources supplying credit information. He must know what they are, the kind of data they are prepared to supply, the value of each source as to the completeness of its service and freshness of the information, how quickly the intelligence may be secured, what the cost of the service is, and how to use the various sources under different circumstances. Only through such an intimate acquaintance will the credit manager be able to tap them at the proper time, properly and correctly interpret the information thus secured, and keep the costs of credit management within budgeted limits.

CHAPTER FIFTEEN

Dun & Bradstreet, Inc.—
the general
mercantile agency

A mercantile agency is, as far as is known, a uniquely American institution in origin, and its task is to collect and disseminate credit information to subscribers or members. As will be shown in this chapter and the one following, there are many such organizations, all operating as *agencies* for legal reasons and competing for the business of subscribers or members, but for some time there has been only one such agency that may be termed general—hence the designation *the* General Mercantile Agency. As the welfare of our economy has been in no small measure tied up with the effectiveness of the work of such an agency, it may be well to discuss briefly the history of the organization and the impelling motives that gave it birth and accounted for its development to date.

Origin of the general mercantile agency. The mercantile agency system was an immediate outgrowth of the crisis which occurred in 1837. Prior to that date, Western and Southern merchants visited their sources of supply in the Eastern market once or twice a year. Credit relations were then established through personal contact and through recommendations of old customers in good standing.

In those earlier days there was but little definite information accessible to the seller concerning his customers' character, capacity, and financial strength; confidence was, therefore, not infrequently badly misplaced. The means of travel were slow, uncertain, and difficult, and the traveling salesman had not yet made his appearance. Communication facilities were equally inferior and inadequate, so that but meager data, of an uncertain nature, could be obtained through mail inquiries. As a result, credit was injudiciously dispensed and during times of stress the losses incident thereto were appalling. To be sure, a few of the larger houses employed agents whose duty it was primarily to collect accounts and incidentally to gather all sorts of data pertaining to the customers' credit standing. The vast group of smaller houses, however, found this method prohibitive from the standpoint of cost and were forced to base their credit decisions upon the inadequate and uncertain information obtained principally through the personal interview.

The avalanche-like movement which finally swept the country as a result of the crisis of 1837 carried with it destruction and ruin to numerous banking institutions and business houses, the effect of which was felt the more keenly and painfully in the market of the East where most of the sellers and hence creditors were located. With the passing of the clouds, merchants throughout the country began to realize that one of the chief contributory causes of the crash and the depression that followed was inherent in the conditions which governed credit granting in this country. No other factor was responsible to any greater extent for the extensive speculation and overtrading which prevailed in the West prior to the panic than the assumption of unnecessary hazards involved in the unsystematic and unscientific credit extensions by Eastern vendors. Thus the crisis of 1837 brought creditors face to face with the necessity of closer and more thorough scrutiny of credit risks. The eagerness with which information was sought for by sellers of goods on time finally resulted in the establishment of the mercantile agency.

Salient facts in the history of Dun & Bradstreet, Inc. The only *general* mercantile agency in existence today is a product of developments which started soon after 1837. Among the business firms which failed in that year was A. Tappan & Co., a New York silk jobbing house, whose credit manager, Lewis Tappan, had so carefully recorded all information he could gather in selecting his firm's customers that subsequent collection of his accounts ultimately enabled the company to meet its own liabilities. Recognizing the value of his information files, Lewis Tappan began in 1841 operating as the first general mercantile agency and invited businessmen to cooperate in pooling their credit information and experiences with him. Initial reluctance on their part soon gave way to the logic of, and need for, the service he undertook to provide.

In 1849, a similar organization under the name of the Bradstreet Company was formed in Cincinnati by John M. Bradstreet, an attorney to whom a large insolvent estate was assigned for handling on behalf of creditors. While performing his duties, he acquired a great deal of information concerning debtors and creditors of the estate, residing in and near Cincinnati, the most important city then on the American frontier and where credit risks were the greatest and concerning which information was most difficult to secure by the Eastern manufacturers and wholesalers. Thus, the second general mercantile agency had its origin near the so-called "source of raw material," from the standpoint of credit information, while the first was located in the center which "consumed" this information. After a coexistence of more than 80 years, the two merged in 1933 under the trade style of Dun & Bradstreet, Inc.

ORGANIZATION AND OPERATION OF THE GENERAL MERCANTILE AGENCY[1]

Organization of Dun & Bradstreet, Inc. The executive or central offices of Dun & Bradstreet, Inc., from which general control is exercised over the entire system, are located in New York City.

The United States is divided into 43 districts. Each of the districts may also operate one or more suboffices and reporting stations, as dictated by the size of territory included in the district and the amount of business transacted. Both suboffices and reporting stations are located at the focal points in the district and are used as headquarters for field reporters as well as a means of facilitating service to the respective sections of the district. District offices are usually self-supporting and constitute central points at which credit information is conveniently assembled and transmitted to subscribers and other interested offices of the company. Sometimes offices are maintained at great expense

[1] In the preparation of the revised material for this chapter, much valuable assistance was rendered by the headquarters personnel of Dun & Bradstreet, Inc., especially by Glenn L. Johnson, Public Relations Manager, all of which is deeply appreciated and gratefully acknowledged by the authors. Also acknowledged with gratitude is the helpfulness of R. J. Price, District Manager, Columbus, Ohio.

for the same reasons that unprofitable items are knowingly carried in stock by merchants. There are 140 district offices, suboffices, and reporting stations in the United States. A private wire network connects 86 of the offices, and most regular inquiries for reports are transmitted over the network.

In the United States all communities are covered by the general mercantile agency through headquarters, district offices and suboffices, many reporting stations, and thousands of representatives and correspondents, who are busily engaged everywhere, investigating local business concerns and new enterprises. By the establishment of branch offices in practically every area of mercantile or industrial importance, a corps of investigators is assured whose acquaintance with businessmen in the territory they cover and whose knowledge of local affairs place them in a position where they can secure information otherwise not obtainable.

To assist in foreign trade, Dun & Bradstreet, Inc., has extended its activities to cover all areas of the Free World. Through Dun & Bradstreet of Canada, Ltd., it operates branches in that country, and additional offices are maintained in other countries under the ownership of separate subsidiary corporations of Dun & Bradstreet. In some parts of the world information is obtained by Dun & Bradstreet, Inc., through special arrangements with foreign mercantile agencies.

Services of Dun & Bradstreet, Inc. The principal services of Dun & Bradstreet, Inc., obviously pertain to the supplying of credit information. It has, however, with the passing years added other services and publications as basic aids to top and middle management in the areas of credit, sales, general marketing, finance, education, and economics.

Basic service. This consists of the publishing for the exclusive use of subscribers credit reports on commercial enterprises and reference books, revised bimonthly, that contain listings with credit ratings of businesses in the United States and Canada. It is supplemented with a special service in the apparel trade, through its Credit Clearing House Division, including the *Apparel Trades Book*—a reference book listing apparel wholesalers and retailers. Finally, through its Commercial Claims Division, it collects commercial accounts.

Other publications and services. Through its Municipal Service Division, the company publishes investment reports on states, counties, municipalities, school districts, and other authorities that issue bonds to the public through underwriters. The company also publishes the *Million Dollar Directory*, listing businesses in the United States worth $1 million or more; the *Middle Market Directory*, listing businesses in the United States worth $500,000 to $1 million; the *Metalworking Directory*, listing metalworking plants in the United States having 20 or more employees; and International Market Guides for (1) Mexico and Central America, (2) the Caribbean area, (3) South America, and (4) Continental Europe.   It also publishes, through the Dun & Bradstreet Publications Corp., *Dun's Review*, a monthly business management magazine; *Business Abroad*, a monthly magazine for those selling or operating overseas; the *Exporters' Encyclopaedia*; and *Service*, a credit newsletter. In addition, the company publishes pamphlets and handbooks on subjects or studies, as well as a series of economic trend data of interest to business management and the business professions.

The company, through its Marketing Services Company Division, makes market research studies.   Finally, through its Business Education Division, it conducts correspondence courses in (1) credit and financial analysis, (2) personal investment, (3) profitable management for small business, (4) salesmanship, (5) business English, and (6) accounting. This division also publishes a series of paperback handbooks on business subjects.

International services. Through subsidiaries, the company provides similar credit and related services in South America, Great Britain, Continental Europe, South Africa, and Australia, and from correspondents obtains information from all areas of the Free World.

Collecting credit information. The basis of the principal services rendered by the general mercantile agency is the credit information it assembles from all parts of the business field it covers.   Its principal objective is to possess up-to-date and complete information on the credit status of every business concern in which its subscribers may be interested.   To fulfill this ambition, it is necessary that the collection of information be pursued both extensively and intensively; use is therefore made of a number of methods including correspondence, personal investigation, and published materials.

Mail inquiries. Credit information concerning all commercial and industrial business enterprises in the United States is sought by mail from both the enterprises themselves and from their creditors.   All business houses are thus contacted every January by means of a mailed financial statement form, as shown in Figs. 15-1*A* and 15-1*B*.   Through this effort the timely cooperation is solicited of all concerns about which credit information may be needed, and an attempt is made to obtain the latest evidence of the subject's condition as revealed in his year-end financial and profit and loss statements.   As these financial and profit

INFORMATION FURNISHED TO

STATEMENT FORM C

Credit -
MAN'S CONFIDENCE
IN MAN . . . .

Dun & Bradstreet, Inc.

As a Basis for Credit, Insurance, Marketing and other business decisions by its customers

NOTE: Transmittal of financial statements on this particular form is optional. Financial statements on your own stationery or on that of your accountant will be equally useful. The full report of your accountant is preferred.

Business Name
Used for Buying _____

Other Name or
Style Used, if any _____

Street Address _____

Business _____

City _____ State _____ ZIP _____ County _____

FINANCIAL CONDITION AS OF _____ 19 ____

IS THIS
FISCAL ☐
OR INTERIM? ☐

ASSETS		LIABILITIES	
CASH _____ $		DUE BANKS $	
GOVERNMENT SECURITIES _____		Unsecured _____ $	
MARKETABLE SECURITIES _____		Secured _____	
NOTES RECEIVABLE (Customers) _____		NOTES PAYABLE-TRADE ACCEPTANCES	
ACCOUNTS RECEIVABLE (Customers)		Merchandise _____ $	
Not Due _____ $		Machinery & Equipment _____	
Past Due _____			
Less Reserves _____		ACCOUNTS PAYABLE	
INVENTORY		Not Due _____ $	
Finished Goods _____ $		Past Due _____	
In Process _____		ACCRUALS	
Raw Materials _____		Salaries & Wages _____ $	
OTHER CURRENT ASSETS			
_____ $		TAXES (Except Federal Income) _____	
		FEDERAL INCOME TAXES _____	
TOTAL CURRENT		DUE RELATED CONCERNS	
FIXED ASSETS		Loans & Advances _____ $	
Land _____ $		Merchandise _____	
Buildings _____		LOANS & ADVANCES	
Machinery and Equipment _____		From Officers _____ $	
Furniture and Fixtures _____			
Less Depreciation _____		LONG TERM DEBTS.—DUE WITHIN 1 YEAR	
INVESTMENTS—RELATED CONCERNS		Real Estate Mortgages _____ $	
Stocks & Bonds _____ $			
Loans & Advances _____			
Accounts Receivable _____			
INVESTMENTS—OTHER		TOTAL CURRENT _____	
_____ $			
		LONG TERM DEBTS.—DUE AFTER 1 YEAR	
PREPAID—DEFERRED _____		Real Estate Mortgages _____ $	
MISCELLANEOUS RECEIVABLES			
Officers & Employees _____ $			
DEPOSITS _____		PREFERRED STOCK _____	
SUPPLIES _____		COMMON STOCK _____	
_____		CAPITAL—PAID IN SURPLUS _____	
_____		EARNED SURPLUS—RETAINED EARNINGS _____	
		NET WORTH (Proprietor or Partners) _____	
TOTAL ASSETS _____ $		TOTAL LIABILITIES AND CAPITAL _____ $	

BASIS OF INVENTORY VALUATION _____

RECEIVABLES PLEDGED OR DISCOUNTED _____ YES ☐ _____ NO ☐

CONTINGENT LIABILITIES $ _____ (SEE OVER)

SUMMARY STATEMENT OF INCOME

NET SALES $ _____ FROM _____ TO _____

FINAL NET INCOME (LOSS) $ _____

DIVIDENDS OR WITHDRAWALS $ _____

5G-10 (82561)

(Use the reverse side of this form for submitting important supplementary details)

ABOVE FIGURES
PREPARED BY _____

Name _____ Independent Accountant Yes ☐ No ☐

BUSINESS NAME _____

SIGNED BY _____

TITLE _____ DATE _____

figure 15-1A. *Statement form mailed each January to known business concerns with capital of $20,000 or more. A shorter form is used for smaller businesses.*

and loss statements are returned, they are incorporated into credit reports and promptly distributed to all interested subscribers. In addition, creditors are also solicited for their ledger experience with accounts in question. This information is sought, on the form shown in Fig. 15-2 when the report on a risk is being revised or when information is first collected

STATEMENT OF INCOME	SURPLUS OR NET WORTH RECONCILIATION

From_____, 19____TO_____, 19____

STATEMENT OF INCOME

NET SALES............................$

COST OF GOODS SOLD.....................

GROSS PROFIT (LOSS) ON SALES..................

EXPENSES

  Selling ....$

  General ....

  Administrative ....

NET INCOME (LOSS) ON SALES..................

OTHER INCOME

..................$

OTHER EXPENSES

..................$

NET INCOME (LOSS) BEFORE TAXES

  Federal Income Tax..........$

  Other Taxes on Income........

FINAL NET INCOME (LOSS)..................$

SURPLUS OR NET WORTH RECONCILIATION

SURPLUS OR NET WORTH AT START..................$

ADDITIONS

  Final Net Income..........$

DEDUCTIONS

  Final Net Loss..........$

  Dividends ....

  Withdrawals ....

SURPLUS OR NET WORTH AT END..................$

When financial statements prepared or certified to by independent accountants are transcribed to this form, indicate whether the statements transcribed are identical with the accountant's statement(s) Yes ☐ No ☐. If No, please describe adjustments. Attach copy of accountant's certificate.

THE FOREGOING STATEMENTS, IF CONSOLIDATED, INCLUDE THE FIGURES OF WHAT OTHER CONCERNS?..................

ANNUAL RENT $................ LEASE EXPIRES................ 19...... FIRE INSURANCE ON: Merchandise $................ Machinery & Equipment $................ Furniture & Fixtures $................ Bldgs. $................ ARE OFFICERS AND EMPLOYEES BONDED?................

IS BUSINESS INTERRUPTION INSURANCE CARRIED?................ IS BODILY INJURY AND/OR PROPERTY DAMAGE INSURANCE CARRIED?................

BASIS OF VALUATION OF: Fixed Assets................Marketable Securities—Investments................

ARE LIABILITIES SECURED IN ANY MANNER? Yes ☐ No ☐ If Yes, describe the security and the manner of payment................

STATE AMOUNT OF EACH CONTINGENT LIABILITY: (Describe)................

REAL ESTATE—LOCATION	Title—In Name Of	Value Mkt. ☐ Cost ☐	Mortgage	Due Date	Net Income—R. E.
		$ $			$

BRANCH LOCATIONS:................

NOTE: Comments will be appreciated on any phase of your operations, including developments since the statement date.

Full Names of all Officers, Directors, Partners or Proprietor. If Partners, state if General, Special or Limited

FULL NAMES AND TITLES	% of Ownership	Year of Birth	Marital Status	Life Insurance Carried for the Benefit of the Business
A.				
B.				
C.				
D.				
E.				

figure 15-1*B. Reverse side of Fig. 15–1A.*

about the risk as the basis for a rating or for a credit report requested by a subscriber. This ledger experience is always used to supplement the information obtained directly from the subject of the inquiry.

Personal investigation. Personal investigators gather much of the information which goes into the credit reports (see Figs. 15-3*A* and

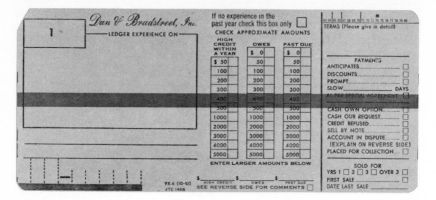

figure 15-2. *Form used to obtain ledger information from creditors of a risk.*

15-3*B*).   For this work a staff of about 1,800 full-time reporters is maintained.   In addition, the company uses the services of thousands of independent correspondents in locations removed from the cities and towns where company offices are maintained or resident reporters are situated. The object of the system of personal investigators is to provide a group of interviewers that can cover the field of business regularly and methodically and at the same time be prepared to make special investigations as needed.

In the city areas where company offices are maintained, including smaller localities where resident reporters are available, credit reports are revised on a scheduled basis, or as inquiry may determine, through direct calls made by the reporters.   Interim and special investigations are also handled by these reporters.   City reporters are assigned to certain districts of the city or to groups of business concerns in the same line of trade or in allied lines of business.

In the areas away from these city locations, traveling reporters call on each concern annually according to a prepared schedule.   These reporters revise and bring up to date the credit information on each name on their schedule and gather initial information on new commercial enterprises not yet investigated.   Interim investigations in these areas between the scheduled visits of the traveling reporters, as well as spot investigations of new enterprises, are handled by the correspondents. This group consists principally of attorneys, bankers, established merchants, and others who are informed on local situations.

Public and published records. A third source of credit information consists of legal recordings and of current news items.   In order to learn of the former, including all recorded items such as deeds, mort-

Dun & Bradstreet, Inc. **BUSINESS INFORMATION FORM**

Information furnished to Dun & Bradstreet, Inc., as a basis for Credit, Insurance, Marketing and other business decisions by its customers

SIC DUNS

NAME & STYLE ☐ OR ☐ CD DATE ______ LINE ☐ A ☐ N STARTED RATING

Address ______ (NO.) (STREET) (P.O. BOX)

(TOWN) (STATE) (ZIP) (COUNTY)

TEL. (AREA CODE) (TELEPHONE NUMBER)

H ☐

N ☐

Principals (Name & Title) ☐ Copy from previous as corrected

☐ List only Pres. (or Chief Exec.) here if 4 or more officers shown. List only Senior Partner here if 7 or more partners shown

SUMMARY

PAYMENTS	☐ GEN	☐ ANTIC	☐ DISC	☐ PPT
	☐ SLOW ___ (days)	☐ CASH	☐ UNDETERMINED	
SALES	$ ______ (ANNUAL ONLY)			
WORTH	$ ______ (MUST BE IN CAPITAL RANGE OF RATING)			
EMPLOYS	______ (TOTAL) (______ here)			
RECORD	☐ CLEAR		☐ INCOMPLETE	
	☐ BUSINESS		☐ INDIVIDUAL	
CONDITION	☐ STRONG		☐ GOOD	
	☐ FAIR		☐ UNBALANCED	
TREND	☐ UP	☐ DOWN	☐ STEADY	

Directors: ☐ The officers ______

PAYMENTS ☐ Copy 6X's attached ☐ Copy ______ ☐ Management declined reason for slowness

☐ Management stated slowness caused by ______

FINANCE (☒ See Reverse Side)

HISTORY ☐ Copy previous as corrected ☐ Copy all officers (if 4 or more) as first paragraph of History. Copy all partners (if 7 or more) as first paragraph of History

☐ Incorporated ______ (STATE) on ______ (DATE) ☐ Auth. Capital $ ______ Paid in capital $ ______

☐ Style registered on ______ by ______ ☐ Style unregistered

☐ Business started ______ ☐ Partnership formed ______

☐ Ownership acknowledged ☐ in signed statement ☐ verbally by ______ on ______ ☐ ______

IF BUSINESS UNDER 3 YEARS OLD COMPLETE THE FOLLOWING:

☐ Starting capital $ ______ derived from ☐ savings $ ______ ☐ loan $ ______ ☐ ______ $ ______

______ born ______ ☐ married ☐ ______

______ born ______ ☐ married ☐ ______

______ born ______ ☐ married ☐ ______

☐ FIRE RECORD ______

☐ PERFORMANCE RECORD (IF A CONTRACTOR) ______

☐ Antecedents under investigation ☐ Continued (copy attached)

OPERATION ☐ Copy previous as corrected ☐ Retails ☐ Manufactures ☐ Wholesales ☐ ______

(Product or line) ______

☐ General Contractor engaged in ______

☐ ______ Contractor Does work for ______

☐ Financing obtained from ☐ Local bank ☐ Savings & Loan Assoc. ☐ ______

Accounts ______ Terms ______

☐ Non-Seasonal Employs ______

Seasons ______

Employs (range) ______

☐ Branches are located at:

☐ Copy from previous as corrected

☐ Copy branches from PBR-Col 5

☐ Copy branches from PBR-Col 6 } OR's ONLY

☐ Copy branches from PBR-Col 7

LOCATION ☐ Owns ☐ Rents ☐ ______ sq. feet on ______ floor of ______ story ______ building

In ☐ good ☐ normal ☐ poor condition. Housekeeping ☐ good ☐ normal ☐ crowded ☐ poor

(Special Fire Hazard) ☐ ______

5G-7(670210)

figure 15-3*A*. *Investigation form used by Dun & Bradstreet reporter for the Regular reports.*

gages, suits, judgments, and other instruments, representatives are maintained in most county seats.[2] Finally, clippings are made daily of mate-

[2] Much of this type of information can also be obtained from a *Daily Reporter*, which is a daily publication in various cities containing legal news and items pertaining to real estate, finance, and allied matters.

FINANCE Information furnished to Dun & Bradstreet, Inc., as a basis for Credit, Insurance, Marketing and other business decisions by its customers.
☐ Copy comparatives from ☐ attached ☐ previous CD   ☐ Copy statement from ☐ attached ☐ previous
On _____ 19 _____
                                    NAME   TITLE
☐ Submitted statement dated _____ . ☐ Submitted estimates (below) ☐ Declined statement but submitted partial figures (below)
☐ Declined financial information. ☐ Was absent. ☐ Investigation indicates the following condition:
☐ Declined statement but gave partial figures, indicated *, which, when supplemented by other investigation indicates the following condition:

ASSETS			LIABILITIES				
Cash	$		Accts Pay	$		☐ Annual ☐ Mo. ☐	
Accts Rec			Owe Bank			Sales	$
Mdse ☐ Cost {EXPLAIN OTHER			Owing			Gross Profit	
						☐ Sal (and) ☐ Draw	
						Net Profit	
Current			Current			Dividends	
Fixt & Equip			Mortgages			Monthly Rent	
Real Estate						Lease Expires	
						Fire Ins Mdse	
			Capital Stock			Fixt	
			Surplus			Bldg	
			Net Worth				
Total	$		Total	$			

REAL ESTATE	TITLE	VALUE ☐ MKT ☐ COST	MORTGAGE	MORTGAGE DUE DATE	☐ ANN PAY ☐ MO PAY	☐ ANN INC ☐ MO INC

Accountant _____

Date _____ Name of Business _____
Signed _____ Title _____

(Comments:) ☐ _____ said _____
            (PERSON INTERVIEWED)

_____
_____
_____
_____
_____
_____
_____

(Supplementary information: Suits, Judgments, Liens & Code Filings) _____
_____

(If a Contractor) Work in Progress _____
_____
_____ ☐ Continued (copy attached)

BANKING ☐ Cash confirmed ☐ by Bank ☐ by _____ ☐ Non-borrowing account
☐ Principal stated ☐ Balances average _____ ☐ Does not borrow ☐ Borrows on   on an ☐ unsecured basis
                                                                        ☐ _____ basis
☐ Loans granted to _____ ☐ Unsecured ☐ Secured by _____ ☐ Now owing _____
☐ Terms of repayment _____ ☐ Relations satisfactory (Bank Identification) _____

REPORTER *				☐ DIRECT CALL ☐ LIMITED INTEREST	MINIMUM STANDARD FOR THIS REPORT – CONSULT 2 AUTHORITIES ☐ Management Interview ☐ 1 AUTHORITY (for Travelers ONLY)	
STATEMENT	P & L	SALES	# REFS		(INDIVIDUAL)	(CO.)
FIN EST	BK EST					
☐ ☐	☐ ☐	☐			(INDIVIDUAL)	(CO.)

figure 15-3B. *Reverse side of Fig. 15–3A.*

rial published in newspapers, financial journals, and trade periodicals, so that no pertinent items will be missed.

Compiling the report. When all pertinent data have been assembled, including the reporter's observations, financial statements, ledger experience, legal evidences, and comments of references, the credit report must be compiled. This is usually the work of the reporter. He writes the pertinent facts in standard terminology of the company and in a form used for all subjects. After accurately stating the condition of the subject of inquiry, the reporter gives the firm a rating. If there is any doubt about what rating best reflects the credit status of the subject, the case is reviewed by a committee which makes the decision.

Once written, the report is duplicated in numbers thought to be sufficient for meeting the demand for it during the ensuing period. Few calls come for reports on some subjects; many come for those on others. Copies of a new report are sent automatically to subscribers who have inquired about the subject during the year, and the remainder are filed for answering subsequent inquiries.

CREDIT REPORTS
AND THEIR USES

Notwithstanding the fact that a subscriber to the Dun & Bradstreet service may begin his credit analysis by making reference to the rating book and then possibly requesting a report on the subject, an understanding of the reports is of primary importance, for upon the reports are based the ratings and many other services of the agency. Credit reports, in other words, are the backbone of the agency's operations.

When reports are used by subscribers. Credit report needs vary with the type of business, kind of accounts sold, amounts of the orders, and selling terms. Generally speaking, subscribers draw reports whenever they feel the need for more or more recent detailed information than they have in file or is indicated in the Reference Book listing. Types of situations where reports are used are:

1 First orders and new accounts, especially unsolicited orders.

2 Marginal accounts, especially those that can be built into profitable customers.

3 Accounts where credit exposure requires all the facts obtainable.

4 Accounts where management has changed.

5 Problem accounts of any kind.

6 Prospects to provide salesmen with background data for credit judgment.

General reliability of the reports. It should be stated in this connection that the agency has no possible motive to injure or misrepresent any businessman, for its only and true interest, for obvious reasons, is to convey as nearly as possible the whole truth in every report. The prosperity of the agency is directly proportional to the extent to which the reports prove beneficial to subscribers. Accordingly, should a report exaggerate the financial and moral responsibility of a trader, subscribers would be apt to trust him in like measure and the agency would be blamed for the losses suffered because of the reliance upon such report. Should a trader be reported too unfavorably, subscribers, by denying credit, would be losing a good paying customer, and the institution would be equally blamed. It must be conceded, therefore, that the entire success of a mercantile agency system depends upon the general truthfulness and complete impartiality of its reports and records.

In the interests of truth and satisfactory service to subscribers, it sometimes becomes necessary to report unfavorable information that may prove damaging to the character or credit position of the subject of the inquiry or that may even indicate evidence of fraud or other illegal acts. In such cases extreme caution must be exercised. Agency reporters are asked to "talk out the unfavorable," so long as there is no violation of a source of confidential information, with the subject of the report himself, so that possibility of error may be minimized and the subject may have an opportunity to explain the matter from his standpoint. In general, a credit report is considered a "privileged communication" so long as it is prepared and given without malice aforethought to a subscriber upon request. Under these conditions the maker of the report is absolved from liability under libel action.

Principal types of reports issued by Dun & Bradstreet, Inc. When a subscriber requests a credit report from Dun & Bradstreet, Inc., he receives the report which is already available in the files or which the agency then prepared. This may be an Analytical report, which the agency prepares on large, complex concerns, or a Regular report, which it prepares on all others. Both cover essentially the same subject matter. The determination of the type of report to write is solely the agency's decision. It depends upon a number of factors such as the size of the subject organization, its method of operation, the complexity of its financial structure, the number of inquiries received concerning it, and probably also the nature of the competition from special mercantile agencies.

Regular reports. The "Regular" report of the agency is illustrated in Fig. 15-4. In addition to the heading, which contains the identifying features of the subject and the latest available rating, the report is divided into five parts designated as Summary, Trade, Finance, Operation, and History. The content of each section of the report is as follows:

Heading. The heading of the report has several elements. The very top line contains the report designation such as OR meaning Original, or First, Report, CD meaning Condensed Report, AD meaning Additional

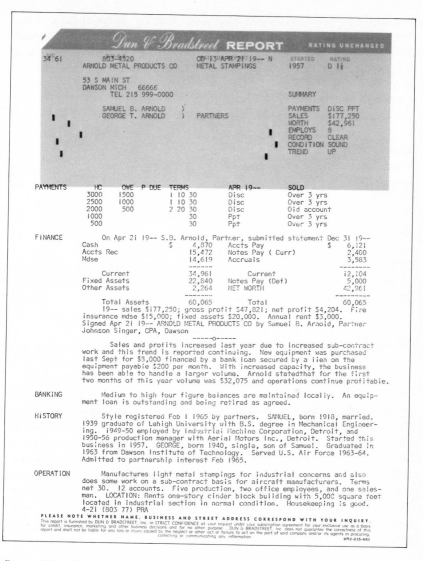

figure 15-4. *Specimen of a typical, though fictitious, Regular report prepared by Dun & Bradstreet, Inc.*

Report, etc.; office of the company that prepared the report (by numerical designation); date of the report; and a designation for internal use of A for Apparel or N for Nonapparel line.

Next below the date line appear the identifying data which coincide with the elements of the listing in the Reference Book, namely, the Standard Industrial Classification Code Number, name of the concern, line of business, year the business was started or came under present control or management, and the rating. All other data appearing in the heading are self-explanatory except that in the case of individual proprietorships the name of the owner is given below the trade style if the style is listed in the Reference Book.

Summary. This is a brief statement summarizing the important aspects of the report. In conjunction with the captioned credit data appearing just above this statement, it gives a quick "flash" of the salient information in the body of the report.

Trade. In this part of the report are presented, in tabular form, the ledger experiences of a number of suppliers with the subject. It shows for each reporting creditor the highest amount of credit extended within a year to the account, amount owing, amount past due, terms of sale, and the manner of meeting obligations—whether prompt, slow, discounts, anticipates, and the like.

Finance. This section of the report contains information about the financial position of the business and its operating trend. In most instances it consists of a detailed statement of assets, liabilities, and net worth, together with sales and earnings figures. If available, comparative statement summaries are given for 3 years. In addition to footnotes describing the source of the figures and other supplementary details often given, this section also includes comments by the reporter explaining significant financial items and updating the information as when some time may have elapsed since the date of the statement. The objective of the reporter is to obtain as complete financial information as possible and when detailed financial statements are not available directly from the owners he endeavors to obtain reliable outside estimates. This may involve many sources, and often does. Likewise, estimates furnished by the owners can thus to some extent be verified in outside quarters.

Operation. Here is provided the opportunity for a deeper insight into the physical characteristics of the business, for this part of the report indicates what kind of business it actually is, what products it handles or produces or what services are rendered, how it is operated, number of people employed, character of the place of business, selling terms, selling seasons, trading area covered, etc. If there are subsidiaries, they are usually described briefly at this juncture. Under the subcaption Location is given a brief description of the premises, size, location, and, in some instances where pertinent, the nature of the adjoining properties, especially if they represent an unusual fire hazard.

History. This section includes the antecedents of the principals as well as the background of the business. If it is a corporation, the data relate to the incorporation; filing information on trade styles; relevant details on successions, if any; mergers; and the like. Antecedents of the principals cover age and marital status, educational background, previous business experience, and identity of other concerns with which they may also be connected.

Analytical reports. These reports are prepared for the larger firms for which more detailed information is not only available but also needed for credit purposes. Whether a credit risk be a large or small enterprise, essentially the same sets of facts must be taken into consideration in appraising its creditworthiness. The amount and detail of such information for the smaller concerns, however, is usually limited and as the credit involved is generally modest there is no urgent need for much detailed information concerning the risk. For the larger concerns, where the amounts of credit involved are substantial, the need for considerable credit information exists and the possibility of securing it is greatly enhanced. Small firms frequently possess little financial and statistical data concerning their activities; their managers sometimes have meager technical qualifications and business records; and the nature of their business operations is so simple as to be readily evident from a superficial investigation. On the other hand, as organizations increase in size and complexity, they afford opportunity for more penetrating analysis of their financial and credit condition. In fact, the only meaningful way in which complicated business structures can be studied is through an analysis of their internal and external relationships as revealed by records. It is natural, therefore, that as larger credit users lend themselves to more detailed study they also make possible the preparation of more detailed reports about their activities and status.

As shown in the report reproduced in Figs. 15-5*A* to 15-5*E*, a detailed analysis is presented in this type of report of the nature and composition of the organization, its method of operation, and its financial structure. Among the items upon which it enlarges beyond what is encompassed by the other types of reports are matters pertaining to personnel, capital structure, comparative financial statements for 3 years, ratio analysis of such statements, and banking relations. Because of the extensive credit required by such large enterprises and by reason of which even general creditors have virtually an equity interest in those firms,

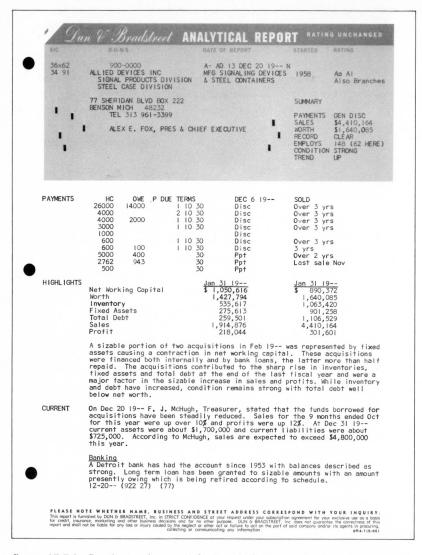

figure 15-5A. *Specimen of a typical, though fictitious, Analytical report prepared by Dun & Bradstreet, Inc.*

the Analytical report gives emphasis to capital conditions and long-run prospects of success.

Special reports. Occasionally credit managers need more information than is provided in the standard credit reports.   This need is supplied

ALLIED DEVICES INC
BENSON MICH

A CO PAGE 2
12-20---

Figures of Jan 31 19-- were prepared from a balance sheet signed by Frank J. McHugh,
Treasurer. Mitchell and Mitchell, CPA's, accountants.

FINANCIAL STATEMENTS

	Jan 31 19--	Jan 31 19--	Jan 31 19--
Cash	$ 396,666	$ 393,818	$ 301,802
Marketable Securities	189,128	201,340	
Accounts Receivable	154,011	179,342	356,116
Inventory	452,616	535,617	1,063,420
TOTAL CURRENT ASSETS	1,192,421	1,310,117	1,721,338
Fixed Assets	202,171	275,613	901,258
Investments	92,000		
Prepaid-Deferred	4,916	8,622	38,407
Other Assets	9,725	92,942	85,611
TOTAL	1,501,233	1,687,294	2,746,614
Accounts Payable	44,456	66,587	117,913
Accruals		38,301	136,040
Taxes (Exc Fed Inc)		12,572	18,601
Federal Income Taxes	161,644	126,542	383,412
Long Terms Liabs (curr)			175,000
Other Curr Liabs	43,210	15,499	
TOTAL CURRENT LIABILITIES	249,310	259,501	830,966
Long Term Liabs			275,563
Common Stock	190,000	190,000	210,100
Capital Surplus	11,313	11,313	11,313
Earned Surplus	1,050,610	1,226,480	1,418,672
TOTAL	1,501,233	1,687,294	2,746,614
NET WORKING CAPITAL	943,111	1,050,616	890,372
CURRENT RATIO	4.78	5.02	2.07
TANGIBLE NET WORTH	1,251,923	1,427,794	1,640,085

At Jan 31 19-- accounts receivable shown net less undisclosed reserves. Inventory
valued at cost on first in-first out basis. Fixed assets shown net less reserve for
depreciation $235,612.

(CONTINUED)

figure 15-5B. *Page 2 of Fig. 15–5A.*

in Key Account and Special Purpose reports, which are designed to furnish
comprehensive data based on investigations made specially for the subscriber. The Key Account reports provide facts on credit problems with
large concerns or "big risks" that may continue over a period of time;
the Special Purpose reports are designed to assist management in the
formulation of policy decisions.

ALLIED DEVICES INC
BENSON MICH

A CO Page 3
12-20---

INCOME STATEMENTS AND SURPLUS RECONCILIATION

	JAN 31 19--	Jan 31 19--	Jan 31 19--
Net Sales	$ 1,825,171	$ 1,914,876	$ 4,410,164
Cost of Goods Sold	922,930	1,129,964	2,932,205
Gross Profit	902,241	784,912	1,477,959
Expenses	485,933	401,399	768,112
Net Income on Sales	416,308	383,513	709,847
Other Income	6,427	46,100	19,255
Other Expenses	37,010		42,501
Federal Income Taxes	210,014	119,369	385,000
Final Net Income	201,666	218,044	301,601
	===========	===========	===========
SURPLUS START	888,925	1,050,610	1,226,480
Add: Net Income	201,666	218,044	301,601
Deduct: Dividends	39,981	42,172	109,409
SURPLUS-END	1,050,610	1,226,480	1,418,672
	===========	===========	===========

SUPPLEMENTAL DATA Footnotes appended to the Jan 31 19-- statement showed no contingent
debt. Annual rent shown at $62,000, lease expiring 1985.

According to management, the item other assets represents (1) $50,000 cash held in
escrow by the landlord who pays interest on that sum. (2) Balance consists mostly
of a mortgage receivable on property in Edison Township, Mich. which was sold in 1964.
Management states that more than $2,000,000 in fire insurance is carried on inventories
and fixed assets.

Feb 19-- the company acquired for an undisclosed cash consideration the outstanding
capital stock of Signal Products Corporation and Steel Case and Tube Co. both of which
were established and profitable. A bank loan of $1,000,000 was obtained at that time.
A portion of the loan was voluntarily prepaid and was reduced to $450,563 at Jan 31
19--. $175,000 of that amount is due this year, payable quarterly and the balance is
due over the next two years.

Records show a financing statement entered Feb 15 19-- naming Allied Devices Inc. as
debtor and Saginaw Machine Tool Co. as secured party. Collateral: Specified Machinery.
File #108761. According to F. J. McHugh, Treasurer, the company purchased 2 high speed
Turret lathes at a cost of $28,500 payable over 36 months.

(CONTINUED)

figure 15-5C. *Page 3 of Fig. 15–5A.*

In ordering such reports, the subscriber indicates on a special
request form the nature of the information desired. The report is then
written individually to meet the particular need. Because of the greater
amount of work that goes into the preparation of such a report, the
cost of it is usually relatively high.

ALLIED DEVICES INC
BENSON MICH

A CO Page 4
12-20---

HISTORY   Incorporated Michigan laws June 30 1920 as Railroad Devices Corp. Name changed to present style Feb 1 1960.

Authorized Capital Stock: 1,000 shares no par value common stock, increased to 4,000 shares latter part of 1958.
Outstanding Capital Stock: $210,000 at Jan 31 19--.

Control: The General Holding Corp., New York City owns 35% of the outstanding capital stock which is held in voting trust by the Detroit National Bank, Detroit, Mich. 40% acquired by A. E. Fox in 1958. Balance owned by Sanborn, Caputo and McHugh.

In early 19-- the company purchased the outstanding capital stock of Signal Products Corporation, Fairdome, Ky. and Steel Case & Tube Co., Minneapolis, Minn. for an undisclosed cash consideration. Late in that year these corporations were merged into Allied Devices Inc. and their activities are now conducted as divisions.

General Holding Corp., New York City, is an investment and holding company. It was formed under New York laws 1900. At Dec 31 19--, that company had a net worth of $20,816,112, and a strong financial condition. According to McHugh there are no intercompany loans, guarantees, endorsements or merchandise transactions between the two companies.

OPERATION   Products: Manufacturers electric signaling devices including crossing gates 60% and steel containers 40%.

Distribution: Sales made to railroads throughout the United States to approximately 100 active accounts.
Terms: 1 10 Net 30 days.
Seasons: Fairly steady throughout the year
Salesmen: Six on commission basis. A. E. Fox and J. S. Caputo are active in sales.
Employees: 148

At headquarters Benson Mich., leases 20,000 square feet in a 3 story brick building where signal devices are manufactured. 62 employed.

Branches are located at FAIRDOME, KY., MINNEAPOLIS, MINN. and branch sales offices at New York, N.Y. and Los Angeles, Calif.

Signal Products Division, Fairdome, Ky., leases 12,000 square feet in a 1 story frame building where railroad crossing signal gates are manufactured. 39 employed.

Steel Case Division, Minneapolis, Minn., leases 15,000 square feet in a 2 story brick building where steel enclosed containers are manufactured. 47 employed.

(CONTINUED)

figure 15-5D. *Page 4 of Fig. 15-5A.*

Continuous service. When an inquiry has been made by a subscriber concerning a business firm, his interest in the subject usually continues, especially if credit is extended to the customer on the basis of the initial inquiry. To accommodate this continuing interest, continuous service has been developed, by which the inquirer is provided, throughout a year following his inquiry, all information pertinent to the

ALLIED DEVICES INC   A CD Page 5
BENSON MICH   12-20---

ALEX E. FOX, PRES   JOHN S. CAPUTO, V PRES (SALES)
FRED W. SANBORN, V PRES (PROD)   FRANK J. MC HUGH, TREAS
HARRY K. LITTLE, SEC   MARY (MRS. GERALD) LOY, ASST TREAS

DIRECTORS: A.E. Fox, F.J. McHugh, Edward Raines and P.J. Walsh.

MANAGEMENT BACKGROUND

FOX born 1908, married. Employed by the Pennsylvania Railroad latterly as Freight
Operations Manager from 1925 to 1958. Since 1958 has been with this company as Chief
Executive Officer. Life is insured for $200,000 with this corporation as beneficiary.

SANBORN born 1913, married. Princeton graduate 1934 BA Degree. 1935 to 1943 employed
by Ford Motor Company in production control. Joined this company in 1944, became
General Manager 1951 and elected Vice President in 1958. Life is insured for $100,000
with corporation as beneficiary.

CAPUTO born 1916, married. 1940 to 1955 employed by Steel Case and Tube, latterly was
General Sales Manager. Joined this company as a divisional sales manager and elected
a Vice President in 1958.

MC HUGH born 1909, married. Employed by this company since 1939 as an inside accountant. Elected Assistant Treasurer in 1948 and Treasurer in 1958.

LITTLE born 1932, single. Served U.S. Army 1951 to 1953. Employed by this company and
elected Secretary in 1960.

MRS. LOY employed here since 1959 and elected Assistant Treasurer in 1963. Her husband
is an Associate Professor of Mathematics, University of Detroit.

RAINES is a practicing attorney in Detroit and general counsel. WALSH is Executive
Vice President of Detroit National Bank, Detroit, Mich.
12-20--- (922 68)

figure 15-5E. *Page 5 of Fig. 15–5A.*

subject that is subsequently obtained by Dun & Bradstreet, Inc.   This
is supplied at no charge over and above the cost of the original report.
Additional information concerning the subject may be obtained during
the ensuing year from the traveling reporter's investigation, in conjunction
with a later special investigation, or as a result of general news reports
on the individual.   Upon receipt of an inquiry from a subscriber, his
number is placed opposite the name inquired about, and when new infor-

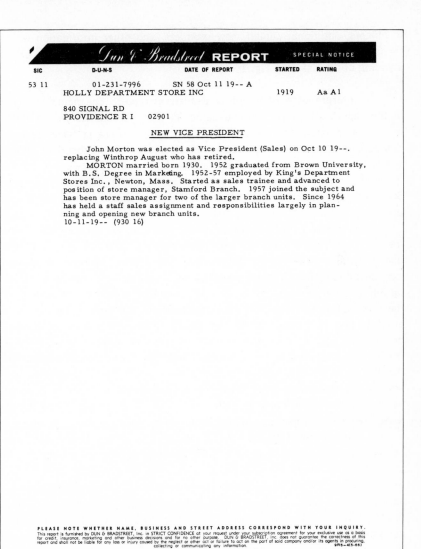

figure 15-6. *Special Notice informing subscribers of a change in management and a refinancing of the business that was under way. Names and addresses are fictitious.*

mation about the subject is reported, copies are sent to all who have made inquiry about that account.

Part of this system of continuous service consists of Special Notices to all interested subscribers reporting newsworthy matters such as lawsuits, assignments, foreclosures, bankruptcies, mortgages, changes in officers, additional capital, new products, and other information which tends to detract from, enhance, or in any other way affect the credit standing of the risk (see Fig. 15-6).

Interpretation of a Dun & Bradstreet report. The name as given in the report, which is also the name as given in the Reference Book, is the name which the concern uses in buying.   Care is taken to have this name appear exactly as used by the business.   The subscriber should compare the name as it is given on the purchase order with the name in the Reference Book or the report to be sure that they are identical. Some names are similar to others so that this careful examination may prevent confusion or even in extreme cases prevent loss from fraud.

From the kind of business many things can be learned concerning the risk.   If the business is of a highly seasonal character, the information at hand may not be recent enough, the amount of credit requested may be unduly large if in off season, and slow payment may be expected during certain periods.   The kind of business indicates the extent of the risk, nature of price and other competition, the type of persons who are attached to it, attitude of the public toward it, how it is affected by business depressions and periods of recovery, degree of stability in production and distribution channels, and the credit requirements.   In the light of this intelligence, a credit man can determine whether the amount of credit asked for is in line or excessive, whether it is to be used for other operations or side lines, and, other things being equal, what chance the subject has of succeeding in it.

Closely allied to the kind of business is its location, since local conditions of an adverse nature, such as crop failures or shutdowns of factories in a single-industry town, may have a profound effect upon it.   Its location in relation to sources of supply is an important factor, as well as the specific site on which the business is conducted.   Some locations require too high rentals, or heavy investments in fixtures and equipment which have relatively little value in case of liquidation, or they are out of the beaten paths of customers.

The names of the principals and their history are of great significance in appraising a credit risk.   Their record may point to the necessity for injecting new blood, either because of incompetence, advanced age, or undue attention to other interests.   Some of the principals may be mere figureheads, and the outside interests may prove even detrimental to the business in question.   For the same reason, changes in the directorate or officers should be watched for a clue as to underlying reasons. Obviously, the history of the enterprise is closely tied up with the personnel.   No business can run itself; it must be managed.   How successful has the management been?   Has there been any financial embarrassment in the past?   Has any attempt been made to avoid lawful obligations? What changes have been made in the legal form of the organization?   All these can be obtained from the History section of the report.   Similarly, in this section of the report light is thrown on changes in the capital structure of the concern, changes in ownership, acquisitions, and relationships to other concerns.   Frequent changes in ownership or management may signify instability.   A history of frequent mergers may reveal a tendency toward overexpansion.   If the concern is a subsidiary, what is its legal liability as well as that of the parent concern?

From the section of the report on method of operation, one can determine whether the business is conducted soundly, to what extent it is subject to weather or other natural hazards, what the marked potentialities are, and how much it depends upon factors beyond its immediate control, as when it operates on an agency basis the contract for which is subject to cancellation by the principal.   The fire record is scrutinized in order to evaluate the moral hazard of the subject, while the facts on insurance will indicate the adequacy of coverage.

If no financial statement is presented in the report, the risk is regarded in an unfavorable light, unless the other information is exceptionally good.   If a statement is given, its value is enhanced if it is signed, audited by a certified public accountant, and of recent date.   A comparison with previous statements shows the general trend.   If the items on the statement are in round figures they have probably been estimated and should be greatly discounted.   When the risk is that of an individual or partnership, it is important to know whether the statement contains merely the business assets or includes those outside the business.   A few of the items can be checked, such as the amount owed to the bank or the total amount owed to merchandise creditors, the former through the bank and the latter through a credit interchange report.   The existence of chattel mortgages, judgments, or liens should be watched. Liens may signify financial stress unless incurred in the ordinary conduct of the business.   Judgments may have been the result of claims which the risk had a right to contest or may have been caused by unwillingness of the subject to meet his just obligations.   Chattel mortgages may also represent a danger signal, unless they arise out of the purchase of new equipment.   The latest statement presented in the report should be carefully analyzed according to the ratio method even though a fairly complete analysis has been made by the agency, provided, of course, that the credit man is capable of doing it.   Unless the credit man is skilled in statement analysis, it is probable that the agency can do a better job of it.

In judging the trade investigation part of the report, one should first ascertain whether the number of creditors reporting is sufficiently representative and whether the amounts extended by these creditors are typical for the business. Paying habits shown here may be used as a check upon the accuracy of the financial statement. If a few large creditors are being paid promptly but not the others, it may show a necessity for doing this or losing principal sources of supply; small creditors would then be handicapped. On the other hand, if only the very small creditors are being paid promptly, it may mean that the concern is unable to pay the larger amounts but wishes to maintain a good standing with a few small creditors for reference purposes.

It is best for the credit manager to reach his own conclusion and then to compare it with that reached by the agency. Any change in rating shown calls for a more careful analysis of the report itself to ascertain which factors have been responsible for the change and whether such factors are of great significance for the specific purpose under consideration.

RATINGS AND THEIR USE

Although the preparation and use of credit reports are the backbone of the agency's business, the ratings are no less important. It is with the ratings in the reference book, in fact, that most credit managers would begin to appraise a risk. In this highly concentrated summarization of certain aspects of the subject's business condition, sufficient evidence of his creditworthiness may often be found.

Nature and significance of ratings. Dun & Bradstreet ratings consist of two symbols representing (1) the financial strength and (2) the composite credit appraisal of the subject. As shown in the Key to Ratings, Fig. 15-7, except for A-rated subjects, letters signify estimated pecuniary strength, or net worth position of risk; numerals and fractions are used to express the general credit grade of the subject. The letter denotes capital resources and reflects the estimated tangible, going-concern, yet conservative, value of the net worth after appropriate deductions and allowances for intangible items, assets of questionable value, and assets exempt under state laws. In this capital range are included concerns from the smallest to the largest, showing a net worth from less than $3,000 to over a million dollars and involving 14 classifications.

The second symbol denotes the grade of credit and is based upon an investigation as to the manner of payment, length of time in business, financial condition, business ability, personal habits, and similar factors which affect the success of a business. To express this position of the risk, four classifications are used, representing "high," "good,"

Key to Ratings

Estimated Financial Strength Composite Credit Appraisal

			HIGH	GOOD	FAIR	LIMITED
AA	Over	$1,000,000	A1	1	1½	2
A+	Over	750,000	A1	1	1½	2
A	$500,000 to	750,000	A1	1	1½	2
B+	300,000 to	500,000	1	1½	2	2½
B	200,000 to	300,000	1	1½	2	2½
C+	125,000 to	200,000	1	1½	2	2½
C	75,000 to	125,000	1½	2	2½	3
D+	50,000 to	75,000	1½	2	2½	3
D	35,000 to	50,000	1½	2	2½	3
E	20,000 to	35,000	2	2½	3	3½
F	10,000 to	20,000	2½	3	3½	4
G	5,000 to	10,000	3	3½	4	4½
H	3,000 to	5,000	3	3½	4	4½
J ⎫			J 3	3½	4	4½
K ⎬	Up to	3,000	K 3	3½	4	4½
L ⎭			L 3½	4	4½	5

K & L are being phased out

Classification for both Estimated Financial Strength and Credit Appraisal

Financial Strength Bracket ⎰ Explanation

1 **$125,000 and Over**

2 **20,000 to 125,000**

3 ⎱
4 ⎰ **Up to 20,000**

4 is being phased out

When only the numeral (1, 2, 3, or 4) appears, it is an indication that the estimated financial strength, while not definitely classified, is presumed to be within the range of the ($) figures in the corresponding bracket and that a condition is believed to exist which warrants credit in keeping with that assumption.

"INV." shown in place of a rating indicates that the report was under investigation at the time of going to press. It has no other significance.

Not Classified or Absence of Rating

The absence of a rating, expressed by two hyphens (--), is not to be construed as unfavorable but signifies circumstances difficult to classify within condensed rating symbols. It suggests the advisability of obtaining a report for additional information.

Absence of a Listing

The absence of a listing is not to be construed as meaning a concern is non-existent, has discontinued business, nor does it have any other meaning. The letters "NQ" on any written report mean "not listed in the Reference Book."

Year Business Started

The numeral shown is the last digit of the year date when the business was established or came under present control or management. Thus, 8 means 1958; 9 means 1959. No dates go past ten years. Thus the absence of a numeral indicates ten years or more. This feature is not used in connection with branch listings.

Key to Ratings

figure 15-7. *Key to Ratings used by Dun & Bradstreet, Inc.*

"fair," or "limited" credit, or first, second, third, and fourth credit grades. An assumption underlying the ratings is that a close relationship exists between the capital strength of a business, as evidenced by its estimated net worth, and its general credit standing, as reflected by willingness and ability to meet obligations promptly.

A *high* credit rating is reserved for concerns which have been established in business for some time, have a good record, discount their bills or anticipate payment, and are otherwise well regarded. If the subject fails to qualify for this rating by some small margin, he may be assigned the *good* rating. Only essentially sound concerns which pay their bills promptly are rated as good. A *fair* rating is assigned to firms which may be slow in paying but are in fairly sound financial condition and for whom prospects are conservatively favorable. Finally, the *limited* grade indicates a relatively poor risk from whom payments may be forthcoming rather slowly. A concern thus rated may operate for a long time without actually becoming financially involved, but there is considerable hazard in selling to it on time. If a subject is actually in financial difficulty or on the verge of such embarrassment, it is not likely to be assigned any rating at all. Likewise, if there is inadequate information on which to base a rating or if other circumstances preclude it, no rating may be assigned. Absence of a rating, whether indicated by the dash (–) or by two hyphens (--), is not to be construed as unfavorable but signifies circumstances difficult to classify within condensed rating symbols and suggests the wisdom of making a further investigation of the risk.

In certain circumstances it is difficult to assign a "capital" rating by the usual letters, yet the concern is in good credit standing. For example, where financial data are inadequate or in a situation where the ownership of the business rests with an estate and it is not easy to determine what assets of the estate actually pertain to the business, no meaningful capital rating is possible. A numeral rating, ranging from 1 to 4 is used in such cases. The meaning of 2, for instance, is that the assets are presumed to be in the broad range of $20,000 to $125,000 and that a condition is believed to exist which warrants credit in keeping with that assumption. This is known as a "one-legged" or numeral rating.

Reference books. The reference books published by the general mercantile agency are often regarded by the credit profession as credit encyclopedias. They are intended to give a general idea of the credit standing of concerns whose ratings are included, and are issued six times a year (bimonthly), tne date of each book being the month of its publication. The Reference Book set, in four volumes divided alphabetically by states, etc., covers businesses located in the United States and Canada. Several other books are published for various sections of the United States. The division of the field in this manner prevents waste, since a subscriber who does business exclusively in the Southwest, for example, has little use for ratings of concerns located elsewhere, except possibly in the selection of his sources of supply. Such a subscriber may be satisfied with a sectional book covering his area of operations, which he can obtain at lower cost than the amount charged for the use of books for the entire country. The number of names included in the reference book volumes covering the United States and Canada is close to 3 million. The books are loaned and not sold to subscribers, with the provision that no one outside the subscriber and his employees is entitled to use them.

Briefcase editions of any of the states included in the volumes loaned to subscribers can be obtained from the agency for the convenience of the subscriber's representatives, especially salesmen. These editions are exact replicas of the information contained in the larger volumes, are conveniently bound in flexible covers, are printed on lightweight paper, and may be secured only by regular subscribers for an extra charge as per schedule published in the company's reference books. The price per copy of these editions of the reference books varies according to the size of the state.

Contents of reference books. Reference books contain the ratings of merchants, manufacturers, and traders generally. They are arranged alphabetically by states and the different communities within each state, with the names of the business concerns in each locality similarly presented. The plan of arrangement calls for the listing of the community, whether it is a city, town, village, or hamlet, in which a place of business is to be found; the county in which the community is located; its population; post office facilities; and bank facilities. If the community has no bank or banker, the nearest town or city having such accommodations is indicated. This information is followed by the listing of business firms in strict alphabetical order. Each name is preceded by a Standard Industrial Classification code number, designating the specific kind of business in which the subject is engaged. Following the name of the enterprise, the line of business is indicated in abbreviated form. Then follows a numeral indicating the year the business was established if started within 10 years. To the extreme right of this information is the rating proper. If the name listed is new, an A, meaning additional name, is shown at the left of the business classification code number; if the rating has been changed in the current issue, the letter C is printed in the same position.

Utility of reference books to credit managers. Credit managers generally hold reference books in high regard. In fact, many of them rely too heavily upon ratings contained therein. Most credit men, however, use ratings with caution, realizing their general weaknesses: that they may have been based upon insufficient information; that they merely express opinions of the editors of the reference book and those in the various offices who prepared the reports upon which the ratings are based; that through sheer error wrong ratings may have been assigned; and, further, that ratings are subject to change. Sometimes reporters fail to secure pertinent data. Whatever facts are gathered may be misinterpreted in the office of the agency. It is conceivable that the opinions of the agency officials may be divergent from the views of the credit managers using the ratings and that the latter might have reached different conclusions had they had the same facts before them. Containing so many names, it is possible that errors have crept in and that wrong ratings appear opposite certain names. To avoid all errors in a monumental task of this sort is humanly impossible, although in justice to the agency it should be said that such errors are relatively few.

Business conditions are constantly changing and ratings are, consequently, subject to considerable revision. It is estimated that changes in names and ratings average about 5,500 each business day so that notwithstanding the correctness of a rating at date of publication, it soon may become less useful. The nature of these changes affecting ratings, favorably or unfavorably, and the proportion of each type of change to all changes are shown by the following table, covering changes in 1966 of more than 1.2 million names:

	Number	Per cent
Names added	342,462	28.1
Names deleted	331,447	27.2
Rating changes	545,682	44.7
Total	1,219,591	100.0

The above figures concerning changes in the reference books do not include the many thousands of revisions that do not affect capital or credit ratings but are merely of an editorial nature. In view of the foregoing, ratings must not be relied upon as the sole basis for reaching credit decisions. They are, as stated in the reference book itself, immediate guides, and should be used chiefly for *orientation* purposes. Thus, if the rating is extremely good and the amount of the order is relatively small, it may serve as the sole guide to credit authorization and to quick approval of the order. Similarly, if the rating is quite limited, credit may be restricted regardless of the amount involved. In most cases, however, ratings are useful guides in determining whether the order should be given consideration and what additional credit information would be deemed desirable to obtain prior to reaching a decision.

Another profitable use of the ratings is in making periodic revisions of the credit files. A downward change in a rating as shown by latest reference book or special report may necessitate a new investigation of the customer thus affected, whereas an improvement in the rating may point to the advisability of revising the credit limit upward.

Third, ratings should be used as a check upon other sources of information, particularly the credit reports that are normally submitted by salesmen, at least with first orders.

A fourth use made of reference books by credit managers is in cooperating with the sales department. By this means, lists of prospective customers with desirable ratings may be compiled for promotional purposes, thereby preventing the solicitation of inferior accounts and thus effecting a worthwhile saving of time on the part of the salesmen who might otherwise attempt to secure undesirable trade. An alternative to the preparation of specific lists for solicitation is for the credit manager to instruct the salesmen of his firm not to call upon prospects whose ratings are below a certain minimum. When this is done, it is essential that salesmen be furnished briefcase editions of reference books for their respective territories. Salesmen may also be equipped with letters of introduction, which can be obtained on request, that entitle the bearers to consult the reference book or ask for credit information at any of the agency's offices.

A fifth use of ratings by credit managers is to determine or set credit lines. Some credit managers set arbitrary lines for all accounts having a certain rating, and thus develop a whole table for that purpose, similar to the practice of credit insurance companies in determining the amount of coverage to be allowed on each account under the policy in question. These matters will be more adequately discussed in subsequent chapters.

Finally, the reference books are utilized by credit men as an aid in securing additional data for credit and for collection purposes as well, since from them one can ascertain whether or not there is a bank in a given community wherein a given risk is located, as well as the name of the bank and some of its officers. Such a bank can then be used both as a source of credit information and as an agency for the collection of accounts by means of drafts.

Use of reference books outside the credit department. Sales departments that are alert to their opportunities make effective use of reference books in their sales research in all or part of the territory covered, in the selection of the most desirable outlets from a credit standpoint, in compiling mailing lists for sales promotional purposes, in measuring the purchasing power of the customers or prospects, in routing salesmen, in judging results of salesmen by territories, in determining the number of outlets for their goods, and in estimating the number and approximate size of competitors.   In making purchases, the buyer or the subscriber may find it useful to ascertain from the reference book the status of the source of supply, financially and functionally, to verify statements regarding manufacturing facilities and the like, and in other ways to check upon the reliability of his resources.   Retailers frequently use these books for similar purposes.   Banks, naturally, make constant use of the reference books for the same purposes as mercantile creditors.   In addition, they use the books to check on unknown names appearing on paper presented to them by clients for discount.   Finally, market planning staffs sometimes make use of reference books in determining the scope and characteristics of a market.

OTHER PUBLICATIONS
AND SERVICES OF
DUN & BRADSTREET, INC.

Although the reports and reference books constitute the principal credit services to the business community, Dun & Bradstreet also performs a number of other significant services.

Credit advisory service. Through its Credit Clearing House Division, the agency serves the apparel trades and their affiliated lines of business with specific advice and recommendations as to whether to accept an order on credit.   This is known as credit checking and is discussed in some detail in Chap. 16.

Collection of overdue accounts. The Commercial Claims Division, upon request, will undertake to collect past-due accounts for clients, both by means of personal call and through the mail.   Because of the great prestige of Dun & Bradstreet in the business world, this method often brings results.   Forms of a reminder are supplied to subscribers free of charge, but if they fail to produce payment, the account may be turned over to the agency for collection.   Personal presentation of the subscriber's claim against a debtor is made only in the important trade centers. If litigation is found necessary, the account is turned over to an attorney for action.

Dun's Review. This much-quoted periodical contains an analysis of current business conditions, features special articles on trends and developments affecting industry, trade, and finance, and regularly reports on marketing, executive methods, production, product development, employee relations, and government policy.

Business Abroad. This is a bimonthly magazine edited for those who ship, sell, or operate abroad. It includes articles of timely interest as well as such matters as tables of currencies, shipping regulations, and the like.

The business economics department. This department publishes basic statistical data including records of commercial failures, bank clearings, building permits, and commodity price indexes. Most of this material is republished in the various newspapers and financial magazines, for a great deal of such data is compiled firsthand by the agency. Dun & Bradstreet's weighted price index of 30 basic commodities is an illustration of such information.

Business education division. As an outgrowth of its principal function of collecting and supplying credit information, a great many facts are obtained concerning business enterprises in the various fields of business activity. Many of the facts are made available to businessmen through free publications, such as the *Failure Record, Key Business Ratios, Growth in Importance of the Credit Function,* and many others. The company has also developed several correspondence courses in previously specified subjects. A 1967 color motion picture, *Credit,* is also available.

The directory division. As already indicated in an early part of this chapter, this division publishes the *Million Dollar Directory,* the *Middle Market Directory,* the *Metalworking Directory,* the *Reference Book of Manufacturers,* and *Dun's Reference Book of Corporate Management.* In addition, it publishes Trinc's *Blue Book of the Trucking Industry* and *Trinc's 5 Year Red Book,* two directories that provide comprehensive statistics on the trucking industry and individual truckers in the Class I and Class II groups of United States motor carriers of property, and *Dun's Reference Book of Transportation.*

Marketing services company division. This is a specialized research organization. It concentrates on solving business and marketing problems for clients on an individualized basis and provides computer-stored data for sales and marketing usage.

Municipal service division. It provides reports analyzing the creditworthiness of bonds issued by states, counties, cities, school districts, toll roads, and municipal electric and water systems. This information is for primary use by banks, insurance companies, bond dealers, estates, and individuals who invest in municipal and revenue bonds.

Cost of agency service. The cost of securing information from the general mercantile agency varies directly with the extent of service required. Some concerns spend as little as $100 a year for directory service; others spend as much as $50,000 for comprehensive service covering nationwide and international sales efforts.

The variation in costs depends in part upon the type and number of reference books and mainly upon the number of reports obtained. If only sectional books are required, the contract price is less than when it provides for the one covering the entire United States or the United States and Canada. Similarly, although as many as six editions of any of the books, published bimonthly, may be obtained, as few as two, renewed each 6 months, may be subscribed to at a lower figure. Likewise, while as few as 25 reports may be contracted for with whatever type and number of reference books, a larger number of reports can be contracted for or bought singly at an increased price. In each case the needs of the subscriber are determined and service is recommended accordingly.

Criticisms of the general mercantile agency service and their validity. Notwithstanding the generally excellent job done in its unique position and in rendering a comprehensive service, the general mercantile agency is continually striving to improve its performance and to correct misconceptions of its service.

It is sometimes claimed that inaccuracies in the reports reduce their trustworthiness. It must be recognized, of course, that where such errors exist they are sometimes the result of changes in conditions since the report was written. Some are no doubt attributable to uncooperativeness on the part of respondents from whom information must be obtained. To the extent that they stem from the human frailties of Dun & Bradstreet's own personnel and management, it can at least be said that they are not in accord with the standards for reporting set by the company.

Another criticism is made of the length of time required for obtaining a credit report. This can be made of but a small portion of the service, for it is claimed that 75 per cent of all inquiries are answered directly from the files. Also, the installation of the private wire network in 1958 speeded up the transmission of inquiries between offices. The computerization of this network and extension of it in 1966 further speeded service.

In other instances, reports are delayed for the laudable purpose of supplementing or refreshing the information they should contain. Most of the substantial delays occur when a first report must be written on a new business located in a place not easily accessible to a reporter. Under such circumstances, however, probably no speedier service is obtainable by a subscriber anywhere else. When specified by the subscriber, he may obtain the benefit of one-way or two-way "Priority Service" whereby, for an additional fee, the inquiry is given preferred handling over routine requests for information.

A third criticism relates to the infrequency with which reports are revised. It is claimed that the standard of semiannual revision of reports is not always maintained and that the organization is unable to keep pace with the continual changes in names and creditworthiness. On the other hand, too frequent investigation of risks is bothersome to businessmen, and it unreasonably increases the agency's cost of doing business.

Complaint is also current to the effect that many of the reports received by subscribers do not contain financial statements. The fact is, however, that the agency is constantly exerting effort to secure statements. This is done through its annual requests mailed to every business in the United States, through personal contacts of reporters, and through mail followups. As a result, statements are obtained for about 75 per cent of all reports written, though not necessarily for as large a percentage of the reports received by a subscriber who draws reports only on the poorer and off-rated accounts.

Much of the responsibility for the refusal of merchants to submit statements to the agency and to sign them must be placed upon creditors rather than the agency. If credit managers would require and insist upon financial statements from their debtors, the latter would in time become educated to the fact that rendering statements is good business and justifiable from many viewpoints. The agency is, nevertheless, gradually overcoming this difficulty and is thus diminishing the validity of the criticism.

Finally, it is claimed that the trade opinions furnished in credit reports are insufficient to give a complete picture of the subject's paying habits. The agency maintains, however, that not all ledger experiences received are published in the reports; those which are included are re-garded as typical and representative of those received.   In many cases a long list of creditors' experiences is given.   Nevertheless, it may be desirable and advantageous to the subscriber to have in the report as complete a list of trade opinions as is available or as can be obtained in the course of the agency's normal operations.

QUESTIONS AND PROBLEMS

1 Name and classify the sources of credit information available to credit managers of banks, wholesale establishments of all kinds, and manufacturing enterprises.

2 Why should a credit manager familiarize himself with all the sources of credit information when, as a matter of fact, he may use but few of them?

3 Is it essential that a creditor know how the various credit agencies function in the gathering of data for their reports to members and subscribers? Give reasons for your answer.

4 What is the connection, if any, between the panic of 1837 and the establish-ment of mercantile agencies?

5 What significance may be attached to the fact that one of the two general mercantile agencies began its operation in New York and the other in Cincinnati?

6 How is it possible for mercantile agencies to supply derogatory information without subjecting themselves to prosecution for libel or slander?   Explain.

7 List the various services performed by Dun & Bradstreet, Inc., for its subscribers and for the business community, respectively.   What information is basic to this service of Dun & Bradstreet, Inc.?

8 As a credit manager, what services of Dun & Bradstreet, Inc., might you find useful?   Which of its services would be of value to businessmen engaged in other than credit management?

9 Which might be regarded as the "backbone" of the agency's business, the reference books or the reports?   Explain your standpoint and show the relationship of the two.

10 List the different types of reports prepared for subscribers by Dun & Bradstreet, Inc., and indicate their specific purposes and uses.

11 Analyze the report reproduced in Fig. 15-4 and indicate what decision you would reach as to the desirability of the risk and the amount of credit that might be extended to the subject.   Compare your decision with that given in the summary of the report.

12 Why are Dun & Bradstreet reference books rented instead of being sold?   What other precautions are taken in its services for the same reason?

13 Explain just what a Dun & Bradstreet rating is and show what uses may be made by the credit department of the ratings contained in the reference books. Are any other departments of the subscriber's business interested in ratings, and for what specific purposes?

14 What evidence is there that a Dun & Bradstreet rating heavily weights the capital factor of the credit C's?

15 What qualifications are especially lacking when a subject is assigned an inferior rating? Does a "limited" credit rating necessarily reflect a bad financial condition or an undesirable credit risk? Explain.

16 In the light of the reasons for the continuous changes being made in names and ratings, to what extent would you be hesitant to rely upon a Dun & Bradstreet rating on the ground that it lacked freshness or up-to-dateness?

17 Under what circumstances might a rating alone be relied upon for purposes of credit granting? Under what circumstances would it be necessary or advisable to request a report?

18 Examine a copy of *Dun's Review* and report what value it would have for a credit manager in his work.

19 Indicate the alleged deficiencies in the services of the general mercantile agency and show in what ways attempts have been made to overcome them.

20 In what specific ways has the private wire network installed in 1958 to connect 79 of the Dun & Bradstreet offices been of help to subscribers and to the company? How has this been improved since 1966?

CHAPTER SIXTEEN

special mercantile
agencies

In addition to Dun & Bradstreet, Inc., the general mercantile agency, there is a large number of special mercantile agencies of varying size and importance, sometimes referred to as "trade agencies." These are distinguished from the general agency in several respects. The scope of their coverage is often limited to a single trade or to a limited number of allied trades, instead of covering all lines of business. Their operations are sometimes restricted to particular localities or trading areas, rather than extended to cover the markets of the entire Free World, as in the case of the general agency. Moreover, their services are at times more varied and complete than those of the general agency; in other instances they are more limited, consisting mainly of ledger experience. These special agencies hold an important position in the administration of mercantile credit, but it is one which is measured more by the value of their services to users than by the number of subscribers thereto or by the scope of their operations.

Types of special agencies. Special agencies may be classified on the bases of scope of operation and functions performed. From the standpoint of *scope of operation,* they may be placed in three categories. The first comprises those serving a single trade or line of business, as illustrated by the Packer Produce Mercantile Agency. A second group includes some of the larger mercantile agencies covering several allied or special trades, an outstanding example of which is the National Credit Office, which serves several fields of activity. Finally, there are agencies which are territorially restricted and which report on local names without respect to trade lines.

According to the *functions which they perform,* special mercantile agencies may be further divided into four classes. One class is engaged primarily in supplying types of ledger experience such as certain lists of past-due accounts or only names of other creditors who have had dealings with a subject. Other special agencies collect and disseminate complete ledger information, including terms of sale, highest credit extended, amounts owing and past due, and manner of payment. Most of the mutual agencies are of this character. Still other special agencies interpret the facts assembled and make recommendations to the trade on the basis of such information.

In the second functional class are agencies which offer services similar to those of the general agency, although they are usually heavily spiced with trade flavor. The services performed by them may include rating books, special reports, trade bulletins, derogatory news, and collections. The agencies of this type are, as a group, larger, older, and more powerful than those belonging in the other categories. In this group belong the Lyon Furniture Mercantile Agency, the Produce Reporter Company, the Packer Produce Mercantile Agency, the Jewelers Board of Trade, the Graphic Arts Board of Trade, the Lumberman's Credit Association, Inc., the National Credit Office, and the Alfred M. Best Company, which reports on insurance companies other than life.

The third functional class consists of but few agencies that offer a service known as "credit checking," a plan under which the agency makes definite recommendations on whether a specific order shall be accepted. The leading exponent of this service was the Credit Clearing House, which for several years offered this service only, later added other functions until credit checking became "just another service," and in 1942 was absorbed by Dun & Bradstreet, Inc. The Credit Exchange, Inc., is another well-known agency rendering a credit-checking service covering the textile trade.

In the fourth and final functional category belongs a group of special mercantile agencies which make personal and special investigations for their members or subscribers, principally to establish the existence or absence of moral responsibility of the risk. Proudfoot Reports, Inc., may be given as an example. Bishop's Service, Inc., O'Hanlon Reports, and the Hooper-Holmes Bureau are also of this type.

MAJOR FUNCTIONS OF
SPECIAL AGENCIES

Special agencies disseminate credit information through reports, periodic supplement sheets, and rating books. They also engage in collecting delinquent accounts for their members.

Reports. Special reports similar to those of the general mercantile agency are issued upon the request of subscribers by most of the special agencies. Such reports cover antecedents, financial resources, trade experiences secured largely from other creditors who are subscribers for the agency's service, general comments by the special reporter or correspondent who made the investigation, and the most recent rating assigned. In the place of such reports, some of the cooperative bureaus merely furnish unfavorable information which they have gathered from the members. Thus, one organization requires that each member list with it at certain intervals the names of all his customers who have become delinquent, are being sued, have been found disagreeable to do business with, make unjust claims, or those concerning whom he is in possession of information that would tend to detract from their credit standing. Such agencies obviously aim to protect their members or subscribers by making available to them only unfavorable experience. This abbreviated service, while meritorious in some respects, tends to have a negative effect in that it prevents losses from bad debts, but does not serve as a business builder, which only a complete picture of the credit risk, dealing with both favorable and unfavorable experiences, would make possible.

Periodic supplement sheets. Supplement sheets bearing changes in ratings are issued periodically, usually weekly, under the designation "service sheets," "credit report sheets," or bulletins.

In addition, these service sheets supply derogatory information obtained through court records and other sources. They aim to warn subscribers of the financial weakening of their customers and of impending business disaster, citing transactions involving suspicious transfers of property, assignments, bankruptcies, dissolutions, records of fire, and the like. They report protested checks, judgments entered, executions issued, claims placed with attorneys and collection agencies for collection, loss by swindle, appointment of receivers, and all other changes in the credit standing of customers which would naturally be of interest to creditors. Sometimes it may also be suggested by means of these sheets that subscribers make inquiry and request special reports on certain names listed therein, especially when important new reports are available for distribution.

Reference books. Practically all special mercantile agencies that are privately owned, and a few of the mutual type, publish rating books, often designated by their color and known as "Blue Books" or "Red Books." They are published annually, semiannually, or quarterly and contain the credit ratings of all names which the respective organizations cover.

In general, the ratings of special agencies follow the plan of those of the general mercantile agency. They often consist, however, of *three symbols* instead of two, thus designating not only credit standing and capital resources but also paying habits and, sometimes, special credit conditions. Manner of payment is shown usually by the third symbol, which indicates whether the merchant discounts his bills, pays promptly at maturity, or is slow in making settlement. Such ratings are based on majority reports received concerning the subject rated. Conditions of special interest to creditors are indicated in either the first or third symbol, wherein may be shown such practices as the following: habitual registering of complaints without cause, disregard of terms of sale, deduction of unearned discounts, and the like. A key interpreting the conditions reflected by the various signs is furnished each subscriber and is an integral part of the rating book.

Collection departments. Special agencies ordinarily provide a collection service for the trades they serve. The collection department thus maintained is not only an important source of revenue but also serves as an excellent source of information for the credit files of the agency.

**ADVANTAGES AND
WEAKNESSES OF
SPECIAL MERCANTILE
AGENCIES**

Being essentially a variation of the general mercantile agency, except for those offering a credit-checking service, special mercantile agencies must be appraised on the basis of their peculiar characteristics.

Specialization. One definite advantage of this agency type lies in its specialization. By a concentration of its interest, it may come to know its subjects more intimately. Solicitors enjoy a confidence based upon their constant circulation among the same traders and credit managers. They become familiar with the merchants and the trade. They learn the problems of subscribers' customers, their methods of doing business, typical operating expenses incurred, seasonal fluctuations in demand, and normal rates of stock turnover. It then becomes relatively easy to discover poor management or to detect impending financial embarrassment.

Promptness in reporting. Lacking the elaborate organization and wide scope of the general agency, special agencies may institute immediate investigations, and being local in character in some cases, they are in a position to interview at once all those who possess information regarding the subject of investigation. A report can thus be rendered on the same day on which the request is received, or shortly thereafter, even when a clearance must first be made. Furthermore, they aim to anticipate inquiries by maintaining complete records on file.

Superiority of reports. Special agencies are said to be particularly strong in the number and quality of trade opinions which they furnish. These ledger facts are secured directly from the creditors of the risk and are generally complete, as to both contents and number. Another conspicuous feature of these reports is a record of collection items handled by the agency and of complaints registered against the subject. The reports contain a good bit of trade flavor, are frequently revised, usually every 3 months, and are as a rule complete, detailed, analytical, and sometimes even interpretive, in the sense of making recommendations and suggesting decisions.

Complete ratings. As a rule, a third symbol, denoting paying habits, is added to the other two symbols, which express capital resources and general credit standing, respectively. The object is to overcome an objection voiced against the inadequacy and shortcomings of general agency ratings and to avoid generalizations wherever possible. Some agencies have an additional symbol denoting special conditions as per a code shown in the key to the ratings.

Limited facilities. On the other hand, because the special agency's facilities for gathering information are sometimes limited, it must rely upon the cooperation of its subscribers. Such dependence may constitute one of its weaker characteristics. No small agency can maintain the extensive and elaborate equipment which is usually required in order to assemble all the essential facts reflecting the true status of a customer. Few branches are maintained by special agencies; information must be gathered largely through local attorneys, who act as correspondents, and from trade sources, and much of it may go unchecked. Fortunately, however, subscribers and other creditors in the trade covered generally cooperate with the agency, which is regarded more or less as part of the trade itself.

Limited references. Chief among the weaknesses of these organizations is the inadequacy of ledger information from the standpoint of variety of references interviewed or otherwise consulted. Operating within a restricted line or territory, special agencies will likely consult only those creditors who are confined to the special line of trade under consideration or who sell within a limited geographic area. In this way many merchants from whom large purchases may have been made by the subject of the inquiry are automatically excluded, merely because such sellers deal in a different line of goods or operate chiefly in a different district.

NATIONAL
CREDIT OFFICE

In the following pages are described and critically analyzed the services of several of the more prominent special mercantile agencies, one of the largest of which is the National Credit Office, New York City.[1]

History and development. Founded in 1900 to serve as a specialized agency in the textile field, reporting on manufacturers (cutters), converters, wholesalers of dry goods, and large retailers, this agency has steadily expanded in both coverage and service. In 1931, the company was acquired by Dun & Bradstreet, Inc., by which it has since been operated. In 1933 it became a subsidiary, and in 1962 a division of Dun & Bradstreet, but it still retains its identity and autonomy of operation. Today, in addition to its headquarters office in New York, branches are maintained in Atlanta, Boston, Chicago, Cleveland, Detroit, Los Angeles, and Philadelphia. The types of business which its specialized service covers include metals (aeronautical, appliances, automotive,

[1] In the preparation of the revised material for specific mercantile agencies included in the earlier editions of this book, as well as for inclusion herein for the first time, much valuable assistance was rendered by top personnel of the respective organizations, and new forms were supplied with permission to use them, all of which is most gratefully acknowledged by the authors.

machinery, metal products, radio-television); mobile homes; paint, ink, and rubber; shoes and leather goods; commercial paper; menswear; dress and blouse; coat, suit, and intimate apparel; textile mills; converting and household goods (including furniture); and wholesale and retail (including department stores, chain stores, discounters, and other large retailers handling piece goods, dry goods, knit goods, and floor coverings).

Services. Unlike some of the other special mercantile agencies, National Credit Office publishes no *general* rating book as such, although it publishes credit-rating books or marketing directories on a number of the industries in which it specializes. These credit and marketing directories include the:

> NCO Survey (Metals & Electronics)
> Distributors of Electronic Parts
> NCO Credit Guide of High Fidelity and Sound Specialists
> High Fidelity and Sound Specialists (geographical list)
> NCO Credit and Marketing Guide of Leather Goods Manufacturers
> Electronic Marketing Directory
> ACS Mobile Home and Travel Trailer Credit Guide
> Mobile Home and Travel Trailer Dealers of the United States and Canada (geographical list)
> Mobile Home and Travel Trailer Manufacturers (geographical list)
> NCO Credit and Marketing Guide of the Chemical Coatings Industry
> NCO Credit and Marketing Guide to the Wholesale and Retail Textile Markets
> Electronic Sales Representative Service

These marketing or credit directories list concerns, usually showing name and address as well as certain data about each. They are arranged either alphabetically or geographically, depending on the purpose of the directory. The data listed about each concern may include rating, credit line, net worth, volume of business, number of employees, name of purchasing agent, payments record, trade comments, year established, telephone number, product and distribution breakdown, divisions, and branches. Services are, however, given mainly through credit reports and a number of extra forms of assistance. The reports are in three parts: Current Information, Management and Products, and Financial Statement (see Figs. 16-1*A*, 16-1*B*, and 16-1*C*). In the first part is presented all available information of late date, such as recent financial condition and trends, business trends, ledger reports of other creditors, and new information about the firm. In addition to these facts, which are more or less common in credit reports, there is another less common feature. It is a "credit suggestion," or a recommendation as to the

nco. **specialized credit report**

FEMINA FOOTWEAR CO., INC.   MFR. SLIPPERS & PLAYSHOES
123 West Kerry Ave.   Dept. 964
Buffalo, N.Y. 14020   Analyst: Jeffrey Jones
Phone: 716-477-3602

JUNE 5, 196-

CREDIT SUGGESTION - (A) - BECAUSE OF FURTHER PROGRESS AND VERY LIQUID
CONDITION, REQUIREMENTS ARE NOW SUGGESTED.

NEW INFORMATION - Management recently advised that sales so far this year
have shown an increase of about 9% over the corresponding period
of last year with profits also ahead of a year ago.

ANTECEDENT COMMENT - Records clear. Originally formed 1935. Present
management in control since 1938. Manufacture general line of
slippers and playshoes. Management experienced and well regarded.

FINANCIAL -	12/31/6-	12/31/6-	12/31/6-
Cash	$ 5,000	$ 12,000	$ 20,000
Receivables	126,000	114,000	134,000
Merchandise	181,000	239,000	184,000
Current Assets	312,000	365,000	338,000
Current Debts	68,000	107,000	65,000
Working Capital	244,000	258,000	273,000
Fixed Assets	44,000	34,000	32,000
Net Worth	353,000	369,000	388,000
Sales	1,234,000	1,336,000	1,423,000
Profit	28,000	32,000	38,000
Dividends	14,000	16,000	19,000

Auditor: Paul D. Hartman & Co., CPA., Buffalo, N.Y.

TRADE - EXCELLENT

HIGH CREDIT	OWING	PAST DUE	TERMS		PAYMENTS
$ 25,000	10,000	0	2/30		ant
15,000	7,000	0	2/15	prox	dis
11,000	5,000	0	2/30		ant
10,000	6,000	0	2/15	prox	dis
6,000	5,000	0	2/15	prox	dis
5,000	0	0	2/15	prox	dis
2,000	2,000	0	2/15	prox	dis
1,000	0	0	2/30		dis

Union Tanning Co., Boston, Mass.   Smith Leather Co., N.Y.C.
Chelsea Heel Corp., Chelsea, Mass.   Fancy Leather Corp., Boston, Mass.

ANALYSIS - This is a well established business which has shown a consistently progressive trend over the years. Steady increases have
been shown in both volume and profits in recent years. Financial
condition has been good for a number of years and was quite liquid on
the last statement which featured all indebtedness covered more than
twice by the total of cash and receivables. Financing is assisted
by unsecured loans from two banks and a small amount was owing to one
bank at recent investigation date.

cd

figure 16-1A. *Specimen of a specialized credit report such as is typically
issued by the National Credit Office. While typical, this is a
sample and fictitious report.*

NCO® *specialized credit report*

MANAGEMENT & PRODUCTS

FEMINA FOOTWEAR CO., INC.
123 West Kerry Ave.
Buffalo, N.Y. 14020
Phone: 716-477-3602

MFR. SLIPPERS & PLAYSHOES
Dept. 964
Analyst: Jeffrey Jones

JUNE 5, 196-

John W. Sussler, Chairman of Bd.
Peter G. Field, Vice-Pres.
F. J. Richman, Secy.

Edwin W. Delray, Pres.-Treas.
Rosanne S. Dooley, Vice-Pres.

DIRECTORS: John W. Sussler, Edwin W. Delray, George H. Lee, and
Ronald Lockhart.

HISTORY - Established as partnership 1935 as Adorable Shoe Co. Succeeded
1936 by Femina Footwear Co., N.Y. Corp. 1938 change in control
occurred and certain of former interests retired. Charter surrendered
and business re-incorporated under N.Y. laws under present style.
Plant formerly operated at Manchester, Vt., was discontinued 1949.
Moved to caption address 1955.

PERSONNEL - Sussler, born 1900, principal financially, maintains general
supervision over production and purchasing. Long associated with
line and officer with subject since 1938. Previously Vice-President
and General Manager of Adorable Shoe Co. Originally employed by
others as an auditor. $50,000 insurance carried on his life with
company as beneficiary. Elected Chairman of the Board 1962.

Delray, born 1911, associated with subject since 1938, is active in
production. Elected Director 1950. Shortly thereafter elected
Secretary and assumed the additional office of Vice-President 1959.
Elected President and Treasurer 1962.

Richman, born 1930. Employed by subject since 1950. Elected
Assistant Secretary 1955 and Secretary 1962.

Field, born 1928. Associated since 1954. Elected Vice-President 1963.

Dooley, born 1924. Employed as stylist and designer since 1956.
Elected Vice-President 1959.

Lee, is a local attorney. Lockhart, is also President of Lockhart
Gear Works, Buffalo, N.Y. and has been associated with that company
throughout his business career.

METHOD OF OPERATION - LINE - Manufacture women's and children's turn
process padded sole and cement process hard sole house slippers and
playshoes. Retail price range from $3.95 to $10.95 a pair. Approximately 50% of production is for in-stock and 50% against orders.
DISTRIBUTION - Direct, nationally, about 75% to department stores and
25% to individual retailers. Terms of sale 3/10EOM. Use trade styles,
"Femina", "Kittens", and "Play-Cats".
EQUIPMENT - Lease quarters on first floor of three-story building.
Rents 30,000 sq. ft. Output 2,000 pairs daily. Employs about 125.

BANKS - First Marine Bank, Buffalo, N.Y.
Manufacturers Bank of Buffalo, Buffalo, N.Y.

cd

figure 16-1B. *Page 2 of Fig. 16–1A.*

amount of a general line of credit of which the subject is worthy. The
second main part contains background information, including the names
of officers and directors, history of the company, personnel, and method
of operation. The third section is a photograph of the company's complete financial statement.

One of the "extras" making for a complete credit service is

FINANCIAL STATEMENT SUBMITTED TO **NATIONAL CREDIT OFFICE**

Name **FEMINA FOOTWEAR CO. INC.** Business **Mfr. Slippers & Playshoes**
Street and No. **123 West Kerry Avenue** City **Buffalo** State **N.Y.** Zip **14020**

STATEMENT OF (DATE) **DECEMBER 31 196—**

PLEASE LIST SUPPLIERS AND BANKS ON REVERSE SIDE

ASSETS		LIABILITIES	
CASH IN BANK $		ACCOUNTS PAYABLE $	19,989.81
ON HAND $ 19,902.51		DUE CONTRACTORS (without other)	2,222.42
U S GOVERNMENT SECURITIES.		UNSECURED LOANS PAYABLE	
RECEIVABLES for Mdse Sold to Customers		To Banks.	
("Age at Foot of page)		To Partners or Officers.	
ACCOUNTS $ 680.10		Total $	
Less Res. for Discounts $		SECURED LOANS PAYABLE	
Less Res. for Bad Debt $	133,883.89	Owing to	16,190.91
NOTES & TRADE ACCEPTANCES (Less $ discounted)		ACCRUED WAGES & EXPENSES	
DUE from FACTOR or FINANCE CO		TAXES—Accrued and Payable	
		a. Withholding & Payroll	13,368.18
		b. Federal & State Income.	10,897.02
PHYSICAL INVENTORY OF MDSE (Valued at Cost or Market)		c. All Other.	2,213.00
Raw Materials $		RESERVE for Income Taxes since last closing	
In Process $		MORTGAGE—DEFERRED DEBT— Due within 12 mos.	
Finished Mdse $ 183,974.92		CURRENT LIABILITIES	65,233.22
CURRENT ASSETS	337,761.32	MORTGAGE—DEFERRED DEBT— Due after 12 mos.	
Due from Partners, Officers, or Employees		LOANS Subordinated on (date)	
Due from Affiliated or Assoc. Companies		**TOTAL LIABILITIES**	65,233.22
LAND & BUILDINGS $		IF CORPORATION	
Less Depreciation $		Capital Stock Pfd. $ 20,000.00	
MCHY., EQUIP., FURN. & FIXT. $ 79,231.58 Less Depreciation $ 46,804.91	32,426.67	Com. $ Capital Surplus	388,345.74
INVESTMENTS (Describe on opp. page)		Earned Surplus $ 208,345.74	
PREPAID & DEFERRED CSVLI $ 77,389.97	6,000.00	Undist. Earnings Sub-Chapter S	
Goodwill $	1.00	Deficit (red). $	
		CORPORATE, PARTNERSHIP or INDIVIDUAL......NET WORTH	
TOTAL ASSETS $	453,578.96	**TOTAL LIABILITIES & CAPITAL**	453,578.96

ACCOUNTANT—Was above statement prepared by an outside accountant? Yes ☐ No ☐ Is he C.P.A.? ☐ Registered? ☐ Licensed? ☐
Accountant's Name **Paul D. Hartman & Co.**
Address **Buffalo, N.Y. 12/31**
How often are books audited? **Annually**
MERCHANDISE—If not valued at Lower of Cost or Market, state basis used.
Is original inventory record retained by you? No
Is merchandise pledged as security for any debt? **No**
If so, state amount so pledged $
INSURANCE—Fire: Mdse $ ____ Bldgs & Fixt. $ **Full**
Use & Occup. Surplus $ ____ Business $ **20,000** on **George Sussler**

RECEIVABLES
For goods shipped during months of:
a. Dec. $ 185,561.45
b. Nov. $ 45,212.21
c. Oct. $ 3,110.23
d Prior Months.
Do these include any consigned goods, uncredited returns, or unshipped merchandise? Yes ☐ No ☐
Have all bad accounts been written off? Yes ☐ No ☐
During the past year, have you paid, traded, sold or collaterized accounts or notes receivable? Yes ☐ No ☐

PROFIT AND LOSS STATEMENT

FOR PERIOD FROM **Jan. 1 '6—** TO **Dec. 31 '6—**

GROSS SALES	$	1,471,188
Less RETURNS $ 25,347		
Less DISCOUNTS $ 22,734		1,423,107
NET INCOME FROM SALES	$	
Inventory—begin'g $ 239,479		
Purchases—Net $ 603,105		
Labor $ 360,522		
Factory Overhead $ 119,370		
Total $ 1,322,476		
Inventory at end $ 183,975		
Cost of Goods Sold		1,138,501
GROSS PROFIT ON SALES		284,606
Selling & Shpg. Exp. $ 90,226		
Salaries—Officers or Principals $ 65,200		
Adm. & Gen. Exp. $ 51,740		
Bad Debts $ 1,705		
Depreciation $ 5,103		
INCOME or (LOSS) ON SALES		71,232
Other Income (exclude discount earned) $	Total $	71,232
Deductions from Income		
NET PROFIT or (LOSS) before Income Taxes		71,232
Provision for Fed & State Income Taxes.		33,179
NET PROFIT or (LOSS)		38,053

RECONCILIATION OF SURPLUS OR NET WORTH

Beginning (date)	$	369,293
ADD: Profit for Period	38,053	
Other Credits to Surplus $		
	Total $	407,346
DEDUCT: Loss $		
Div. & Wdrwls $ 19,000		
Other Charges. $		
NET WORTH or SURPLUS at end.	$	388,346

INVESTMENTS—Describe (if subsidiary or affiliate state % owned)

LIABILITIES—Merchandise received or charged to you but not received. $
Amount of Contingent Liabilities.
Are any liabilities secured in any way? $ ____ If so, state amount, creditor and nature of security.
Annual Rent $ ____ Lease Expires.
NET WORTH—Has this been decreased since statement date by withdrawal, retirement of capital, payment of dividends, bonuses, or personal income Taxes? $
If so, by what amount? $
TAXES—Have all Federal, State, and Local tax assessments been paid or shown accrued on statement? **Yes**
Tax Closing date? **Dec. 31** Date of latest return examined by Internal Revenue Service?

OWNER — PARTNERS — OFFICERS AND DIRECTORS

Name	Title	% Ownership	In charge of
John Sussler,	Ch. of the Bd.	60%	
Edwin Delray	Pres.-Treas.	30%	
F. J. Richman	Secy.	10%	

TO **NATIONAL CREDIT OFFICE**, a division of Dun & Bradstreet, Inc. The undersigned warrants that the foregoing figures and answers are true and accurate in every respect and orders this statement marked to you with the intention that it shall be relied upon as the expression of credit or insurance by such concerns...

Dated at **Buffalo** this **20** day of **April 196—**
Signed by **Femina Footwear Co., Inc.** (Name of Corporation, Partnership or Proprietorship)
By **Edwin Delray**

INDEPENDENT ACCOUNTANT'S OPINION (Please use your own letterhead if additional space is necessary)
We have examined the above balance sheet and profit and loss statement. Our examination was made in accordance with generally accepted auditing standards and included such tests and procedures as we considered necessary. In our opinion the statements present fairly the position of the company in conformity with generally accepted accounting principles applied on a basis consistent with that of the preceding year.

Signature: **Paul D. Hartman, C.P.A.**
Address: **Femina Footwear Co., Inc., Buffalo, N.Y.**
Date **4/19/6—**

figure 16-1C. Page 3 of Fig. 16-1A.

an Industry Current Comment report, an annual roundup by department heads or senior partners, presenting the trends, problems, and prospects for the various trades plus annual composite financial and operating statements. Borderline accounts are listed on the Marginal Account Registration, providing an opportunity for easier and more frequent revision of files. A monthly listing of concerns, by industry, is also published under the title of *NCO News*, showing major changes in principals, financial conditions, and credit lines, development of financial difficulties, and names of new concerns.

Other specialized services. In addition there are other specialized services which are offered clients for a separate fee. These include:

Correspondence and lecture courses in credit and financial analysis

Special line service designed for lines of credit which are abnormally large or where the risk is a marginal one

Specialized claims service—provides a complete collection service for National Credit Office members only

Management services—assist clients in finding solutions for a wide assortment of management problems

Market planning service—helps establish sales potentials, sales quotas, sales territories; evaluates sales performances; makes special market studies.

Principal features of the National Credit Office service. The National Credit Office claims to be operating on three basic principles, as indicated below:

1 *Specialization.* Within each industry, the reporters and investigators specialize on a limited group of concerns. This gives them an opportunity to become familiar with the fundamental conditions as they exist in the unit on which they are reporting. It also allows them to become personally acquainted with the important individuals in the group comprising the unit and to obtain a fairly thorough knowledge of the operations of the unit as a whole.

2 *Centralization.* Each department aims to serve a large percentage of the concerns selling to the trades on which the department reports. Inquiries, therefore, reflect the activities of those concerns and are frequently a first indication of a situation which may not otherwise be detected until a much later date.

3 *Interpretation.* The company feels that financial statements, ledger experiences, and information from banks and other factors which enter the complete investigation of an account have a practical significance which may be lost, unless there is a definite understanding on the part of the investigator that what he is doing leads to a definite conclusion regarding the account.

LYON FURNITURE
MERCANTILE AGENCY

The oldest and largest of the special mercantile agencies is the Lyon Furniture Mercantile Agency, established by Robert P. Lyon in 1876. It specializes in reporting on credit risks in the furniture, carpet, home furnishing, interior decorating, and electric-appliance trades, as well as department stores and general stores that carry furniture. The organizations rated are those customarily buying from manufacturers, jobbers, and wholesalers of furniture, carpeting, floor covering, upholstery materials and supplies, mirrors, lamps, appliances, veneer, plywood and hardwood lumber, and related items, as well as the manufacturers, jobbers, and wholesalers of such products themselves. Offices are maintained in New York, where the headquarters of the company are located, and in Boston, Chicago, Cincinnati, High Point, N.C., Los Angeles, and Philadelphia. Its services consist of a rating book issued semiannually, weekly supplements and interchanges, confidential credit reports, and collection assistance.

The Lyon Red Book and supplements. The reference or rating book issued by this agency is known as the "Lyon Red Book," a volume of some 1,500 pages, in which a three-symbol rating is given for the subjects listed. The content of the reference book is organized alphabetically by states and by cities within the respective states, with county and population given for each city. Rated risks are listed by corporate name, trade style, or personal name of the proprietor, cross reference being used to facilitate identification. The address, business classification, and symbols indicating whether the subject sells on the instalment plan, from a residence, office, or catalogue are given, in addition to a two- or three-symbol indication of the credit conditions, capital, and paying habits of the risk.

The credit ratings, as shown by the key in Fig. 16-2, consist of three symbols, two numerical and one letter. The first numeral, ranging from 12 to 31, represents special credit conditions or some details of the risk's business or trade practices. The letter symbol pertains to capital ratings, specifically the financial worth of the company. The degree of financial responsibility of the risk may also be expressed by a letter symbol, when no data are available for a real capital rating. The third symbol is that of pay rating, a number ranging from 1 to 9, indicating whether the risk claims to buy always for cash, or the manner of his payment on credit transactions. Thus a rating of "13 S 6" has the following meaning: 13, Inquire for report (and comment covering the subject would appear in the "Trade Investigation" portion of the report); S, $2,000 to $3,000 capital; 6, Very slow. Although three such symbols

NAME_____ Sub. No._____

THIS CREDIT REFERENCE BOOK IS THE PROPERTY OF LYON
FURNITURE MERCANTILE AGENCY and is LOANED on Annual Subscription Agreement only: NOT SOLD. THIS BOOK MUST BE RETURNED
upon termination of Subscription Agreement or upon delivery of a new
book. (See Page "D" for further conditions).

LYON RED BOOK — CREDIT KEY

CAPITAL RATINGS Estimated Financial Worth	PAY RATINGS Based on suppliers' reports
A ....$1,000,000 or over B .... 500,000 to $1,000,000 C .... 300,000 to 500,000 D .... 200,000 to 300,000 E .... 100,000 to 200,000 G .... 75,000 to 100,000 H .... 50,000 to 75,000 J .... 40,000 to 50,000 K .... 30,000 to 40,000 L .... 20,000 to 30,000 M .... 15,000 to 20,000 N .... 10,000 to 15,000 O .... 7,000 to 10,000 Q .... 5,000 to 7,000 R .... 3,000 to 5,000 S .... 2,000 to 3,000 T .... 1,000 to 2,000 U .... 500 to 1,000 V .... 100 to 500 Z-No financial basis for credit reported.	1—Discount. 2—Prompt. 3—Medium. 4—Variable, prompt to slow. 5—Slow. 6—Very Slow. 7—C. O. D. or C. B. D. 8—Pay rating not established, but in- formation favorable. 9—Claims to buy always for cash.

INDEFINITE RATINGS	SPECIAL CONDITIONS
F—Estimated financial responsibility not definitely determined, pre- sumed high. P—Estimated financial responsibility not definitely determined, pre- sumed moderate. W—Estimated financial responsibility not definitely determined, pre- sumed small. Y—Estimated financial responsibility not definitely determined, pre- sumed very limited.	12—Business recently commenced. 13—Inquire for report. 21—Buys small, usually pays cash. 24—Name listed for convenience only. 29—Rating undetermined. 31—Financial statement declined, or repeatedly requested and not received.

| The omission of a rating is not un-
favorable, but indicates that sufficient
information is not at hand on which
to base rating. | SYMBOL INTERPRETATION
● or 12 — Business recently
commencced.
✦ or 116 — New Statement recently
received.
▲—Indicates information of unusual
importance.
⊙—Sells on installment plan.
(?)—Sells from residence, office or
catalogue. |

CREDIT GRANTORS—NOTE

No system of ratings can ALWAYS convey an accurate summarization of
existing conditions. Book ratings reflect conditions believed to exist when
assigned, and are based upon information obtained from financial statements,
from the trade, special reporters, correspondents, financial institutions and
other sources deemed reliable, but the correctness therof is in no way
guaranteed.

Conditions are constantly changing, and changes as made are shown in the
"LYON Weekly Supplement and Report", and in Lyon Credit Reports.

Should any error, or inaccuracy in rating be noted, it should be reported
immediately to the Agency, in order that correction may be made.

Inquire for Detailed Credit Report on all NEW ACCOUNTS, and make
inquiry at least once a year on old accounts or when change in rating is
indicated in the "LYON Weekly Supplement and Report."

A

figure 16-2. *Illustration of ratings used in reference books of Lyon Furniture
Mercantile Agency.*

may be used, in the great majority of cases only two are provided: capital and pay rating. Only occasionally is the third symbol employed for additional information. Subscribers under contract may also obtain, for use by their salesmen, state editions of the pages of the Red Book bound separately for each individual state or combination of states.

A semiannual supplement to the Red Book is issued in January and July, containing changes in capital and pay ratings, names of new business concerns with their classification and ratings, and business successions which have occurred while the Red Book was in press, thereby giving practically a current up-to-date book at the time of its release. More current information on such changes is made available in the *Lyon Weekly Supplement and Report,* a leaflet which also carries statistics on business failures of the past month, dissolutions, assignments, receiverships, trusteeships, bankruptcy petitions, current rating changes, and accounts placed for collection with the Lyon Furniture Mercantile Agency.

Trade experience reports. In addition to issuing the reference book and its supplements, the agency also conducts and makes available to subscribers a weekly interchange of trade experience. Risks about which further information is desired are listed on the *Tracer* sheet, which is circulated throughout the trade for the purpose of soliciting recent experience on the manner in which the risk is making payment, the amount owing, and the amount past due. When trade comment has been accumulated, all contributors are entitled to receive a summary thereof, issued in a *Result of Tracer* report.

Credit reports. Supplementing the rating information and the results of the tracer investigation, the Lyon agency furnishes credit reports which contain detailed facts concerning the subject risk and serve as a basis for thorough credit analysis, as indicated by the following headings and items covered:

Heading	Names and ages of principal personnel; address
Antecedents	Origin of business; business history of owners and officers; fire record
General Information	Nature of business; plant and equipment; progress
Financial Information	Financial statement; comparative summarized statements
Analysis	Items and ratio analysis of important statement items
Bank Information	Report of bank comment on risk
Trade Investigation	Report of trade experience
Summary	Condensed statement of outstanding facts contained in the report; current rating

Collection. A feature of the agency's collection service is the prestige it enjoys as an authoritative source of credit information.   Recognizing that delinquent customers in the trade know that with a poor credit rating they cannot expect favorable terms, the agency, on its own letterhead, solicits payments for creditors who request this assistance. As is often the case, the strength of its appeal to the preservation of a credit standing may bring an immediate response.   If payment is made by the delinquent debtor within 10 days of notification, no charge is made for the service.   If, however, further collection effort is required, it is understood that the creditor subscriber will pay the usual collection fee.   Such service is based upon the assumption that the credit task is not finished until collection is made.   Collection effort, therefore, is regarded as an integral part of the service of this credit agency.

THE JEWELERS
BOARD OF TRADE

The Jewelers Board of Trade is illustrative of special mercantile agencies that are mutual, nonprofit membership associations.   While organized for the promotion of *all* interests of the jewelry trade, its main purpose is to provide information and other assistance on *credit* matters.   In 1933 it emerged as a consolidation of two separate organizations previously existing—The National Jewelers Board of Trade and The Manufacturing Jewelers Board of Trade.   Accordingly, its present membership includes manufacturers, wholesalers, and importers of jewelry, watches, silverware, and stones—precious, semiprecious, and imitation.

General method of operation. Essentially, the backbone of the operation of The Jewelers Board of Trade is its Reporting Department, which maintains a vast file of credit information pertaining to makers and sellers of what it calls "jewelry store merchandise."   It considers this a "living record" because the information is kept alive or up to date by a corps of trained investigators supplemented by carefully selected correspondents throughout the United States and through mail communication.   Its reports, supplied to members upon request as privileged communications, are not unlike in content and make up to those issued by Dun & Bradstreet, Inc., or by other similarly operating special mercantile agencies.   At the same time, the organization claims to provide "a highly specialized service to its members" and, "because of its nonprofit and cooperative nature, is rendered at the lowest possible cost."

Reference books. The Jewelers Board of Trade publishes a reference or rating book semiannually, commonly known as the "Red Book."

It is published in three styles—large desk size, complete pocket size, and in sectional form—a copy of each being supplied to every member. This book covers all engaged in manufacturing, importing, distributing, and retailing jewelry, diamonds, stones (precious, semiprecious, and imitation), silverware, watches, and kindred items of merchandise. Symbols are used to designate the business classification of the subject rated, such as manufacturer, wholesaler, department store, etc. The rating proper consists of but two symbols, a letter (from AA for the highest to S for the lowest) designating the estimated capital, i.e., the tangible financial resources subject to execution or available to creditors, and a numeral in one of the four grades designating the credit standing of the subject. Thus, according to its "Rating Key," a rating of K 53 would mean that the subject has an estimated capital (in the sense used for such purposes) of $35,000 to $50,000 and a credit standing in the third grade or column.

Other services. This organization, with headquarters in Providence, R.I., and branches in New York City, Chicago, and San Francisco, provides additional credit services to its members. One of them is in the form of a *Service Bulletin,* published weekly, which contains news of changed ratings, removals, deaths, establishment of new outlets, financial embarrassments, and other information of interest and of immediate importance. The *New Name Bulletin,* published weekly, contains new names that will appear in the next issue of the reference book and on which credit reports have become available. This bulletin is obtainable "at a low subscription rate," as well as the Continuous Service provided for 12 months following a completed report to a member for an extra annual charge. Supplementary services of a research character or that would facilitate collections complete the list.

CREDIT–CHECKING SERVICES

There are at least two major organizations that specialize in what may be termed as credit-checking service, one of them being operated by Dun & Bradstreet, Inc., and the other as an independent specialized mercantile agency.

Credit Clearing House, division of Dun & Bradstreet, Inc. Notwithstanding that Dun & Bradstreet, Inc., is a general and not a special mercantile agency, its Credit Clearing House operates for all practical purposes like a specialized mercantile agency. It features a service of credit checking, sometimes also called a credit advisory service.

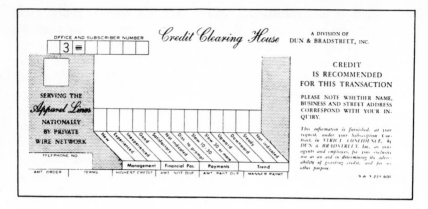

figure 16-3A. *Credit Clearing House form recommending credit for a transaction.*

Nature of credit checking and method of operation. The essence of the credit-clearing service is not merely the supplying of credit information but the offering of a recommendation on the advisability of accepting a *specific order* on credit, taking into account the actual dollar amount of the order. It is a service furnished only for the men's, women's, and children's apparel and accessories lines, made necessary because of the need for speed and accuracy in answering credit inquiries in this industry that is characterized by keen competition, style hazards, and a rapid turnover of retail outlets. Sellers in this industry, moreover, especially on the manufacturing level, are seldom large enough to employ a full-time credit manager, so that management of the credit function is delegated to someone occupied primarily with other duties.

In response to their inquiries, subscribers receive a recommendation slip. It may contain the specific advice "Credit Is Recommended for This Transaction" (see Fig. 16-3A). In addition, there are certain situations which require a qualified recommendation. A special recommendation form is used to indicate that "Credit Is Recommended for This Transaction Provided:" (see Fig. 16-3B). The subscriber is then given provisions, as checked or otherwise indicated on the slip, which apply to the specific credit situation. A third form is employed to show that "Credit Is Not Recommended for This Transaction for Reasons Indicated" (see Fig. 16-3C). Finally, when a new recommendation is available, all interested subscribers are informed to that effect (see Fig. 16-3D).

Credit Clearing House recommendations are based on the judgment of a staff of trained analysts, familiar with the purchasing habits,

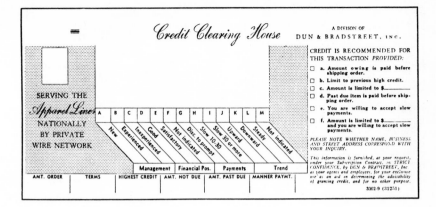

figure 16-3*B.* Credit Clearing House form making a qualified recommendation.

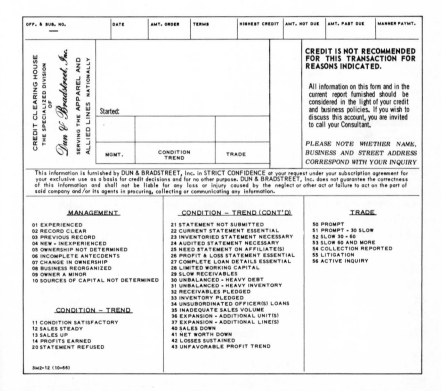

figure 16-3*C.* Credit Clearing House form indicating that credit is not recommended.

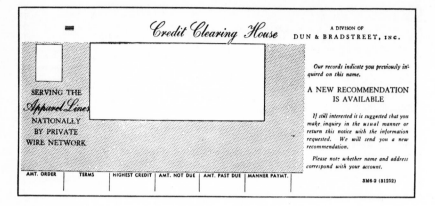

figure 16-3D. *Credit Clearing House form indicating that a new recommendation is available.*

trade customs, buying seasons, and credit problems in the apparel industry.   The analysts arrive at their opinions through the review of the Dun & Bradstreet credit reports on accounts under their jurisdiction, and through a constant watch of the Master Card on which are recorded for each account the daily purchases, payment experiences, and other pertinent information furnished by subscribers when they place their inquiries.   By means of the Master Card the analysts are kept informed of the day-to-day buying and paying pattern of accounts as inquiries come in daily from subscribers all over the country; it is an aid, too, in highlighting any abnormalities such as overactive buying, out of season purchases, and increasing slow payments.

Headquarters of Credit Clearing House are located in New York City; there, credit opinions on apparel outlets located throughout the country are set up and maintained.   Credit advisory service is available, however, to subscribers outside the metropolitan area, for in the Dun & Bradstreet branch offices which actively serve Credit Clearing House subscribers, an equivalent of the New York answering index is maintained. Information assembled in New York City is microfilmed and then printed on microcards, which are provided for the respective branches.   Thus the branches can furnish immediate credit information on apparel outlets located anywhere in the United States.

Apparel trades book. A distinctive feature of Credit Clearing House is the publication of a specialized reference book listing retailers and wholesalers located in the United States that handle apparel merchandise exclusively or in connection with other lines.   The book is re-

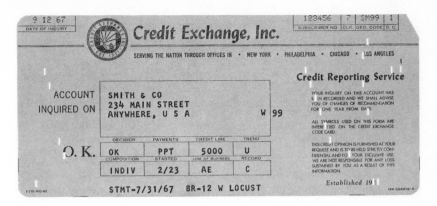

figure 16-4A. *Credit Exchange, Inc., O.K. report to a subscriber on a given subject or transaction.*

vised four times annually, to coincide with the retail sales seasons of men's, women's, and children's wear.

The ratings in the reference book are comprised of three symbols designating estimated financial strength, payments appraisal, and composite appraisal. An example is H 2 C, wherein H stands for a financial strength between $50,000 and $100,000, 2 denotes the second of four scales of payment-habit ratings, and C is the third of four scales of overall credit appraisals. Special features of the Apparel Trades Book include the trade style listings of the rated names; symbols to indicate the lines of merchandise handled by each concern; and symbols to distinguish wholesalers, wholesalers and retailers, and operators of more than one store.

Credit Exchange, Inc. This is another organization, established in 1921, that provides a credit-checking service in the wearing apparel, gift, and sporting-goods industries. With headquarters in New York City, it maintains branch offices in Chicago, Los Angeles, and Philadelphia. In addition to the credit-checking service, the company operates a collection division through Credit Exchange Service Corp. and Allyn M. Schiffer, Inc., and an adjustment division through Credit Agency of America, Inc.

Recommendations of Credit Exchange, Inc. The recommendations in electronic card form include an O.K. report (see Fig. 16-4A), a Not Recommending report (see Fig. 16-4B), which is in contrast with the policy of Credit Clearing House previously discussed, a so-called "automatic reference" on which current ledger experience is reported by the

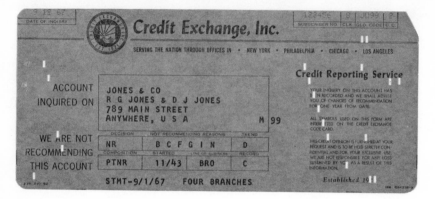

figure 16-4B. *Credit Exchange, Inc., Not Recommending report on a given account.*

subscriber, a notice of revision being conducted, a change of recommendation report if such change is made, a special notice card, and a notice of investigation card, the results of which will be reported as soon as the investigation is completed.

When an O.K. recommendation is made, the company considers it practically as a report, even though detailed credit reports are also made available if desired by the subscriber.   The reason is that, in addition to the decision, payment record, and high credit suggestion which have been given for many years, the recommendation card now includes in symbols or otherwise also the composition of the business, date started, lines of merchandise carried, trend over the past few seasons, previous insolvency record if any, and significant remarks about the account. Similarly, when an account is not recommended, reasons for such action are stated in symbols.

This agency differs from Credit Clearing House in another respect.   It does not publish a rating book, but prefers the method wherein a subscriber contacts it by mail or telephone on each order on which it supplies him with a recommendation or report as desired.

Advantages and disadvantages of credit-checking service. This service obviously has its advantages and limitations.   Perhaps foremost among those advantaged by it are the firms whose volume of business does not warrant the employment of a credit manager.   Other firms not wishing to establish a credit department are similarly benefited.   Moreover, there are at times individuals engaged in business who are unfit, by ability or experience, to handle complicated situations, or who are utterly unfamiliar with the methods of credit management.   For such organizations and such individuals credit checking supplies a real need, saving both time and worry, especially when an immediate ruling on a doubtful risk is urgently demanded.

Even large concerns with trained credit executives may consider this service an important credit tool because of the value of comparing their own opinion with that of a source which, through a pooling of its inquiry from subscribers in cities all over the country (or at least in the important markets), records at a central point on master cards the buying activity of customers in the apparel and allied fields. As there are thousands of potential sellers to any single retailer or other customer in these lines, no individual seller can possibly know where or how much his customers are buying or how they are paying their bills from season to season or day to day, but an agency of the type rendering a credit-checking service can supply this information. To be sure, as will be shown in the next chapter, many credit bureaus have been developed to provide some such information, but their scope is more limited in the lines of trade in question.

Probably the greatest objection to a system of credit checking supplied from without is the effect of such service upon the sales volume of the subscriber. In making an affirmative recommendation the service is bound to be ultraconservative. Its success will be proportionate to the amount of loss incurred and is not so much tied up with the volume of business done or lost by the subscriber. Keeping losses to a minimum is, however, only one of the functions in credit management. The other major function, that of maintaining as high a sales volume as possible, is fully as important and must not be neglected.

Another objection to credit checking is the difference in standards of various creditors. Inasmuch as the margin of profit varies with different houses and, since the experience of different firms in connection with credit risks also varies considerably, credit standards used for the measurement of risks are bound to differ with different concerns, but, so long as orders are checked by an outside organization, they are likely to be based on a single standard for all creditors who are subscribers for the service, obviating the use of independent, intelligent judgment by subscribers.

In the third place, credit managers ordinarily desire to have all the facts on which judgments are based. Their individual interpretation of such facts might vary considerably from the interpretation given by an outside credit-checking service. To overcome this, detailed Dun & Bradstreet reports are made available at the request of subscribers by Credit Clearing House and similarly by Credit Exchange, Inc. Moreover, the recommendation cards supply fairly detailed information in symbol form of considerable value when properly interpreted by the subscriber.

OTHER TYPES
OF SPECIAL
MERCANTILE AGENCIES

As may be inferred from the foregoing, there are many special agencies in different lines of business. Some are more widely known and used than others, but even less well-known agencies are significant in their particular operating areas. The following are several of such specialized agencies.

Produce Reporter Company. With headquarters in Wheaton, Ill., and offices in New York City and Los Angeles, this company has served the produce industry since 1901. Its *Fruit and Produce Credit Book*, commonly known as the "Blue Book," reports on shippers and dealers in fruits, vegetables, and other food products in the United States and Canada and is intended to serve as a credit and marketing guide "adapted to the daily needs of wholesale handlers and users of perishable fresh fruits and vegetables." The book is published twice a year, and the listings and ratings in it are kept up to date through Weekly Credit Sheets, which, in turn, are summarized in a Monthly Supplement. Each week's Credit Sheet is accompanied by the *Exchange Bulletin* whereby merchandise and buyers can be located easily and quickly.

The industry served by the Produce Reporter Company is characterized by certain unusual features. First, many changes are constantly taking place. Two, the goods are for the most part extremely perishable. Three, shippers and receivers are usually far removed from one another in distance. Four, there are many unusual credit risks in this fast-moving business.

What this means, for one thing, is that terms of sale are as nearly on a cash basis as possible. That is why so much attention is given to pay descriptions as revealed by reported pay practice in terms of days after arrival of the goods. Preferred customers, from this standpoint, are those who pay at least 35 per cent of the time within 2 days and all within 5 days, rated as AA. Next best, with an A rating, are those who pay 58 per cent of the time within 5 days, and the poorest, with an E rating, are those whose payment practices are reported to be uncertain. Most commission merchants generally follow the policy of making remittance immediately after the sale has been completed, while the brokers generally remit immediately following collection.

It also means that the ratings in the Blue Book must be highly specialized, detailed, and specific. This involves a detailed classification of the business that is rated (whether retail grocer, receiver from distant shippers, jobber, buying broker, or a combination of all of these and others), symbols for the goods in which it specializes, and the ratings themselves.   These generally consist of three sets of symbols: the credit worth as expressed in thousands of dollars available to creditor upon liquidation; the moral responsibility or the integrity-ability-pay rating, ex-pressed in X's and therefore referred to as the X rating; and the pay description, expressed in symbols from AA to E.   A rather common simple type of rating might be expressed as follows:

JR 200 FV   30M XXX B

in which a jobber and receiver of 200 carlots of a general line of fruits and vegetables during the year is rated with a financial-responsibility of $30,000 and a good moral responsibility and pays his bills at least 70 per cent of the time within 10 days after arrival of the merchandise. A much more detailed rating, assuming that the information is available, is illustrated by the following actual rating and shows to what length this information goes:

RCJ 850 CitAPrDecLetCtCabCantsStSpFV 75M XXX 148

Translated, this means that the business is classified as Receiver (from distant shippers), Commission Merchant, and Jobber; handles about 850 carlots; deals in the following specialties: citrus, apples, pears, deciduous fruit, lettuce, carrots, cabbage, cantaloups, strawberries, sweet potatoes, fruit (general line), and vegetables; estimated financial worth is $75,000; reported general credit standing is Good (XXXX being Excellent, XX Fair, X Doubtful, and X — Poor); and 148 stands for the comment "Have conflicting reports—rating indicates reported general experience."   In addition, the subject's telephone number is given in the Blue Book as well as the bank to which drafts may be sent to cover shipments.

A third thing growing out of the peculiar characteristics of the in-dustry mentioned above is that the writing of comprehensive confidential reports has become a rarity.   Instead, in about 90 per cent of the cases, the firm needing the information calls on long distance for the information, which is given from the files if available or is otherwise obtained by telephone and similarly transmitted.

The Packer Produce Mercantile Agency. This company, established in 1924, covers the wholesale fresh fruit and vegetable industry.   Its service is used by firms engaged in that trade and by allied concerns manufacturing or distributing machinery, materials, and supplies used by the industry in the production and marketing of perishables.   Its headquarters are located in Kansas City, with principal branch offices in New York, Chicago, and Los Angeles.   Field offices are located at numerous other points throughout the country.

The reference book of the company, first published in 1925 and titled "The Packer Red Book," lists and rates all kinds of wholesale fresh fruit and vegetable dealers.   It is published semiannually, with weekly bulletins and bimonthly consolidated supplements serving the purpose of keeping ratings and listings in the reference book revised and up to date between publication dates.   Detailed credit reports are available, as are other services incidental to a credit reporting and rating agency.

The principal section of the reference book contains the listings and ratings arranged alphabetically by state, town, and name.   Another section, called the Index, lists the same firms by name and town, alphabetically by name, for cross-reference purposes.   A third section, called the "Red Book's Special Chain Store Directory," lists important chains, voluntary groups, and cooperatives in the food field, alphabetically by name.   Each listing attempts to provide the information needed by shippers and sellers of fresh produce to reach the proper person or division buying such items.   In effect, this section is but a convenient and useful cross reference of concerns in this type of operation which are also listed in the principal section of the book with the appropriate ratings.   A fourth section lists and rates by state, town, and name truck transportation brokers who serve shippers by arranging for transportation of fruits and vegetables from shipping point to market destination; although such "truck brokers" are not classified as dealers, they are considered part of the industry as a whole.   Basic listing in the principal geographical (state-town-name) section consists of firm name, address, telephone number or numbers, personnel handling buying or selling, type of operation such as shipper, grower, packer, broker, jobber, etc., specific commodities handled, estimated annual volume of business in truckloads or carlots, and rating.

Ratings are composed of three parts, as follows: (1) an estimate of net worth as indicated by code letters, (2) general business methods and practices as indicated by number of stars, and (3) paying practices as indicated by Roman numerals I, II, III, and IV.   Illustrative of such a rating is the following actually taken from the book:

RecJobBan C **** I

Translated via the Rating Key, this means that the concern is a Receiver and Jobber specializing in bananas, with a financial or net worth estimate of over $250,000, an Excellent rating for business methods and trading practices (*** = Good, ** + = Fair to Good, ** = Fair, and * = —), and paying habits Mostly Prompt (II = Generally Satisfactory, III = Slow, and IV = —).

Proudfoot Reports, Inc. This enterprise was formed in 1900 by Louis A. Proudfoot, a New York attorney. Proudfoot knew so much about people of prominence and notoriety that other lawyers sought his opinion about more or less well-known characters. In 1900 he supplemented his personal knowledge by starting a card index of all judgments and bankruptcies in New York County and of clippings from New York newspapers regarding the questionable antecedents and activities of individuals who found their way into print. This service was initially developed in behalf of other lawyers.

Special comprehensive and confidential reports are now prepared on individuals, partnerships, corporations, or associations in almost every line of business or service in the United States for the purpose of aiding clients in forming an opinion as to the desirability of the extension of credit, among other things. The subject to be investigated might be a business enterprise. The inquirer might ask about the responsibility of an individual who is seeking employment or admission as a member to a stock exchange or to a country club. It might be regarding the history and reputation of an accountant in behalf of a corporation that is changing its auditors or in behalf of a banker who has been offered the accountant's audit by one of his borrowing accounts. It might be for his election to the board of directors or to an official position in the company. It might be on a Wall Street investment dealer in behalf of a concern the securities of which are traded in the market. While the scope of Proudfoot's service is extremely wide, it is flexible and lends itself to confidential inquiries with discretion.

Reports on individuals, no matter why the inquiry is made, cover age, place of birth, home life, extent of education, business activity, and dates of former business connections and club memberships. Suits, judgments, bankruptcies, and criminal records, if any, are reported. Then follow comments on past record, financial responsibility, method of paying bills, bank and other credit information, integrity, moral standing, and business reputation. Similar comprehensive information is obtained on partnerships, corporations, associations, and professional firms.

The index of suits, judgments, and bankruptcies now consists of millions of 3- by 5-inch cards. Reports are rendered to concerns in all lines of business and service activities and to many commercial banks, trust companies, investment bankers, security dealers, and stock brokers, as an agent under an agreement that the information requested is for use of the client, shall be strictly confidential, and is not to be communicated to others. These reports are made for the client's specific need, and in placing such an order it is essential that a full reason for the investigation be disclosed to the agency so that the report may be pointed in the right direction and supply the answers to the problem.

Bishop's Service, Inc. Also specializing in custom-made reports for cases of exceptional importance is Bishop's Service, Inc., a New York firm serving since 1895 such clients as banks, security houses, industries, attorneys, public relations consultants, government agencies, research consultants, and educational and public institutions. As described by Bishop's, their reports "begin where ordinary 'credit' reports leave off and supply comprehensive information which no financial statement by itself can disclose." Their reports are designed to give background from the start; the capital setup and the financial position, including the bank account; personalities of officers or partners; present activities and future prospects; and the record of litigation. Unusual information or that which is difficult to obtain they take pride in supplying. Each investigation is conducted separately; however, when the file copy of a recent report meets a client's need and where clearances of confidential material can be effected, arrangements are often made for inspection of a copy of the report for a modest fee.

QUESTIONS AND PROBLEMS

1 In what ways do special mercantile agencies differ from the general mercantile agency? To what extent are these differences advantages or limitations, from the viewpoint of the user of their services?

2 Distinguish the bases upon which special mercantile agencies may be classified and cite an example for each type.

3 What characteristics of a special mercantile agency's rating symbols are distinctive? How are they to be read and interpreted?

4 What are the purposes of supplement sheets? What kinds of information do they generally contain?

5 Compare and contrast the reports issued by special and general mercantile agencies.

6 What factors might a credit manager in the furniture or apparel trades take into consideration in deciding whether to subscribe to services of the special mercantile agency in his field or to those of Dun & Bradstreet? Might he need the services of both? Why?

7 Point out some of the unique features of the National Credit Office and appraise them from the creditor's point of view.

8 Some special mercantile agencies furnish only unfavorable experiences. How valuable is such service? What are the chief weaknesses of the plan?

9 What services other than ratings and reports are supplied by special mercantile agencies? How valuable are these other services? Explain.

10 Under what circumstances might you engage the services of Proudfoot Reports, Inc.?

11 How would you account for the fact that many of the special mercantile agencies began their operations early in the twentieth century? Contrast their origins with that of Dun & Bradstreet, Inc. What relationship had these events to the beginning of formal study of the subject of credit?

12 Describe the nature of the credit-checking service of Dun & Bradstreet and indicate how it differs from that rendered by Credit Exchange, Inc.

13 As a credit manager for a flour mill selling its products to wholesalers, large bakeries, and to chain stores, what would be your attitude toward a credit-checking service for your company? Explain. Would your attitude differ if you were the credit manager of a manufacturing concern producing women's apparel? What would it be if you were the *owner* of the latter enterprise? In what single important respect do the credit-checking services discussed in the book differ, and how can such difference be explained?

14 Explain the difference in the estimated capital rating used by Dun & Bradstreet, Inc., and The Jewelers Board of Trade, respectively, even though in both instances a letter is served to designate it. Which of the two is the more significant from a creditor's point of view and why?

15 It has become fashionable in certain modern academic circles to place emphasis on the general and look askance at the teaching and learning of the detailed and specific. Assuming such a position to be valid as a rule, how can you, as a prospective credit manager, justify the detail and the specific material contained in this chapter, even when presented in a somewhat analytical fashion?

interchange of ledger experience among mercantile and bank creditors

In the conduct of a comprehensive credit investigation of a risk, information relevant to all the four C's of credit must be sought, secured, and weighed. Such information may be obtained from various sources and may be of varying quality or significance to a given situation. One type of information, however, that is of universal value and of high quality in judging a credit risk is that which reflects creditors' experience with it over a period of time. It is commonly known as "ledger experience," "ledger facts," "trade information," or "trade opinion." It consists of information made available by creditors who have had experience with the risk as reflected on their respective ledgers or other books of account.

A composite of such experiences is deemed to afford the best immediate answers to the questions, "Does he pay?" and "Will he pay?" It is based upon the assumption that the way in which a risk discharges, or has been discharging, its obligations to creditors, individually and collectively, will establish the manner in which it will tend to react to still another creditor. Moreover, much of this type of information is self-explanatory and does not call for any special or unusual skill for analysis and interpretation.

While it is dangerous, or at best unwise, to rely solely on ledger experience as a basis for judging a credit risk, certainly for long-run purposes or where comprehensive and basic knowledge of the risk is required that would *explain* the payment pattern behavior, it is undeniably a valuable kind of information. That is why it is included as an integral part of a mercantile agency report, is sought by direct reference to those creditors who have the information, and why certain intermediary organizations have been formed to supply it indirectly

DIRECT INTERCHANGE
AMONG CREDITORS

Obviously, ledger experience must be supplied by those creditors who have had it with the risk in question. This experience may be shared with others interested in the account by direct reference or indirectly through mercantile agencies or credit interchange bureaus specializing in this type of information.

Securing references. In order to obtain ledger experience directly from creditors, it is necessary for the interested mercantile concern to ascertain who those creditors are. To secure such references, several methods are available which can be used simultaneously to advantage.

The simplest way is to ask the risk for references, keeping in mind that only the most favored ones are likely to be given and hence should be used mostly for the leads it may suggest. Second, from the nature of the risk's business it is often possible to locate selling concerns to which it is probably known. For example, when a dry goods name is being investigated, it is safe to assume that some of the well-known houses in the same area handling knit goods, notions, gloves, hosiery, and underwear would have dealings with the risk. Third, supplementary lists of references can be secured through the company's traveling salesmen. Fourth, a bank may quite readily discover the names of concerns selling the subject in question by glancing over canceled checks, provided that the subject is one of the bank's accounts.

Methods used for direct interchange. The direct interchange of ledger experience among creditors may be effected orally—by personal contact and through trade group meetings—or by correspondence.

Personal contact. The simplest yet perhaps the least satisfactory means of credit interchange among creditors is through personal contact of the inquiring party with the credit managers who are known to have had experience with the subject of the inquiry. This method often results in a multiplicity of investigations, especially when the credit risk is undergoing changes the probable effect of which is to weaken his financial condition. Besides, too much valuable time of the occupied credit manager would have to be devoted to the process of calling for, over the telephone or in person, or furnishing credit information were this method to be widely adopted.

Practically all banks of substantial size and many of the large commercial houses effect this personal contact through a credit investigator whose principal duty is to assist the credit manager in obtaining ledger experiences and trade opinions by going after the information instead of waiting for it to come to his house.

Trade groups. A highly convenient way for creditors selling in the same market to exchange ledger and other valuable facts is afforded by the meetings to be described presently. These gatherings are usually restricted to members of the respective local credit men's associations, each of which conducts one or more meetings at frequent intervals, usually weekly or semimonthly. Thus, all creditors selling to grocers, bakers, general stores, and allied lines of trade form a provisions division, consisting of wholesale grocers, meat packers, produce dealers, etc. In the larger cities the Credit Men's Association may have organized as many as a dozen or more trade groups, such as women's wear, dry goods, furniture and hardware, printers and stationers.

The purpose of group meetings is to offer a ready means of exchanging information respecting applicants for credit, slow-pay customers, and all accounts which show abnormal and hitherto unexpected developments. Each of the participants turns in to the group chairman the names of the accounts on which further information is sought, stating the reason for his action. As the name of the inquiry is called off, all those who previously have had experience with the subject voluntarily relate their experiences. Where the trade divisions are large, a limit is placed on the number of delinquent accounts or first orders that may be brought up by any one member. It should be noted that not only ledger data enter into the discussion, for an extremely important phase of the work is the exchanging of confidential facts gained through personal contact by some of the participants with the risk in question, involving at times a most intimate knowledge of strictly personal affairs that may be favorable or derogatory.

Among credit trade groups in the very large cities, this work is more formalized and direct interchange practices are highly developed and adapted to the relatively large number of participating members. Before each meeting any member is permitted to send to the secretary of the group three names on which he desires a report. These names are consolidated into one list, a copy of which is sent to each member requesting him to furnish his ledger information. These facts are then returned to the secretary, who prepares the complete reports, which are distributed to all members attending the meeting. Reporting firms are identified by code numbers for the sake of security, but because members possess keys to the codes they can know who is reporting what experience. Knowing this enables them to appraise the information accordingly, and to seek by telephone additional data for which the regular report was no proper reporting medium. In addition to this exchange of information, a weekly news bulletin is sent out by the secretary, carrying urgent and timely news which members believe would be of interest to other members. These weekly sheets are sometimes exchanged with groups in other cities, thus providing both information and contacts which may later be followed up by telephone.

While the interchange of ledger experience is the basic service of trade groups, these gatherings also serve other useful purposes. Thus, it is not uncommon there jointly to arrive at a decision to place an account in the hands of the adjustment bureau, or to throw a debtor into bankruptcy, or to take other measures which require concerted action. They are also used as a medium for bringing about much needed standardization in credit practices; for the regulation of trade abuses; the concentration of claims for collection, investigation, prosecution, and adjustment; for the promotion of educational and research work; and for such other matters as may be deemed desirable to discuss. They truly afford an excellent means of elevating the work of the credit manager even to a higher plane from the standpoint of both efficiency and ethics.

Credit group meetings operating in a manner somewhat similar to that described above are also used by trade associations which, in furthering the main purposes for which they have been formed, have found it essential to render a credit service to their members or to the members of their respective industries. As the coverage of such a trade association is likely to be national in scope, however, these groups may have to be organized on a sectional geographic basis, and even then they may be unable to meet more often than monthly or quarterly.

Interchange by correspondence. Expediency often demands direct interchange of ledger experience among creditors by correspondence. To facilitate and encourage the system which makes for safe clearance of credit risks, the National Association of Credit Management has approved and adopted a special form, and in addition has drawn up a number of rules for the strict observance on the part of both receiver and giver of credit information. Most of these rules are printed on the back of the forms.

Advantages of direct interchange. Speed in obtaining the desired facts is no doubt the principal advantage of direct interchange, whether accomplished orally or by correspondence. Second, the information obtained is fresh and up to the minute. Third, if obtained orally, the information may be of superior quality and may include items which discretion would forbid imparting on paper. Fourth, there is no specific charge or direct cost for this information. Finally, the direct contact among credit men, especially when personal and at trade group meetings, is of great value, as it fosters and encourages cooperation in preventing customers from getting into difficulty, in rehabilitating those who have become financially embarrassed, and in constantly improving credit standards and ethics.

Objections to direct interchange. Foremost among the objections is the multiplicity of investigations which inevitably results from this direct method. Widespread adoption of this means of securing ledger experience and other credit information would necessarily place a heavy burden on the valuable time of credit managers and cause unnecessary duplication. Second, when many inquiries are made concerning a given credit risk, especially when such risk is not in a particularly strong financial position, suspicion of creditors is likely to be aroused, thereby unduly embarrassing the subject of the inquiries. Third, the system lends itself to abuse. Since there is no direct cost involved, unscrupulous credit managers may make investigations, not because of an existing interest in the account, but with a view of determining whether or not the subject's trade should be solicited.

Indirect interchange of ledger experience. To overcome the objections incident to the direct exchange of ledger experience among credit grantors, a number of intermediaries have developed. While trade opinions or ledger experiences were always obtainable to some extent from the mercantile agencies, few organizations existed prior to 1900 with the sole object of collecting quickly and with a minimum of effort comprehensive ledger figures and making them conveniently available to their respective members or subscribers. The greatest development of such intermediaries, specializing in the handling of ledger information, has taken place since about 1915.

Today, at least two modes of securing ledger experience through some sort of a specialized bureau maintained cooperatively are at the disposal of the alert credit manager:

1 The credit interchange bureaus maintained by local associations of credit managers

2 Trade credit bureaus, reporting on a single line of trade or on a limited number of allied trades and maintained by trade associations

CREDIT INTERCHANGE BUREAUS OF THE NATIONAL ASSOCIATION OF CREDIT MANAGEMENT[1]

Early history. The early organizations of this type were known as "reference bureaus," probably because they rendered no reports on creditors' experiences. When a member wanted information he called the bureau, secured the names of other creditors, and by direct communication obtained the necessary ledger facts. The first bona fide credit interchange bureau to have assumed the responsibility of soliciting information from creditors and issuing it to interested members in the form of reports is said to have been established in 1901.[2] Since that time such bureaus were being organized by different groups of businessmen or by trade associations to meet the growing need for such information on the part of creditors. For some years these bureaus operated on a local-market basis, but it was discovered that information confined to a single market or territory was not sufficient. Accordingly, in 1912 a central bureau was organized in St. Louis to enable the various bureaus, although independently operated, to exchange their reports and experiences and to make the clearances more valuable because of the wider area covered in the investigation. In 1919 this central bureau was taken over by the National Association of Credit Men (later changed to National Association of Credit Management), and in 1921 it began to function as a unit of the Associated system under the management of the Credit Interchange Bureau Department. At first only 15 bureaus participated in the national system, but now there are 61 such bureaus covering most of the major and minor markets of the country, and the tendency is to develop a single medium for the cooperative exchange of ledger

---

[1] Much of the information for the revision of this chapter was obtained through the courtesy of present and past managers of the Central Credit Interchange Bureau of the National Association of Credit Management.

[2] R. Young, *Industrial Credits*, Harper & Brothers, New York, 1927, p. 25.

information through some of the trade credit bureaus joining in the system of the National Association of Credit Management.

Organization and purpose. The purpose of the Credit Interchange Service of the National Association of Credit Management, as stated in its published literature, is to provide executives with "impartial, complete, up-to-date facts in answer to that single question paramount in credit work: Can and does he pay?" This is accomplished by providing an impartial medium between debtors and creditors and between creditors themselves, whereby those who are interested in any account may freely and unreservedly interchange the facts contained in their ledgers, (1) without the necessity of direct reference, each to the other; (2) without divulging the information under their own name; and (3) receiving, in exchange for data contributed by them, a summary of experiences of all others interested in the account.

This National Credit Interchange System is now comprised of 61 bureaus, plus a coordinating unit—the Central Credit Interchange Bureau, located in St. Louis. Each of the 61 bureaus is an independent corporation owned and operated under the supervision of a local association or associations of credit men, or in some few instances, under the supervision of the National Association of Credit Management. The principles of (1) member direction and control and (2) service on a cost-of-operation basis prevail in all instances. Each bureau is inspected annually by the Director of the Credit Interchange and Industry Service Department of the national organization and, in the event of emergencies or complaints on the part of one or more of its members, a special inspection may be conducted. The national office also retains the power to recommend to the local board of directors the dismissal of its bureau manager, under penalty of expulsion from membership in the National Association of Credit Management in case its recommendation remains unheeded, unless satisfactory cause for ignoring it is duly given. Membership of this bureau system is strictly limited to manufacturers, wholesalers, jobbers, and financial institutions that are members of the National Association of Credit Management, and the accounts dealt in are those of *business* firms and not of individuals as consumers.

Method of operation. Credit interchange operates on the basis of information accumulated in the local bureaus by their requiring each member participant in the service to supply current ledger experience on his accounts. Each local bureau operates on a "zone of operation" basis, the zone of operation being the normal trade territory of the market served by it. Each bureau is responsible for controlling and writing

MEMBER INQUIRY		F-1	IMPORTANT List other sources of supply below. The bureau will endeavor to obtain their information.	PRO. NO.

CREDIT INTERCHANGE   BUREAUS
7th Floor, 21 Ottawa Ave. N. W.,   GL 9-3371
Grand Rapids, Mich 49502

SEND US A REPORT ON   DATE

NAME

TRADE STYLE

STREET ADDRESS

TOWN		STATE		ZIP CODE
TYPE BUSINESS				
MEMBER	CHECK FOR AUTOMATIC REVISION	☐ SEND PRELIMI- NARY REPORT	REVISING FILE ☐	
	☐ 4 MONTHS	☐ SEND ONLY COM- PLETED REPORT	1st ORDER ☐	
	☐ ___MONTHS			

LIST ADDITIONAL REFERENCES ON REVERSE SIDE

NAME   ADDRESS

BANKS WITH
SUBJECT HAS
BRANCHES AT:

figure 17-1. *Member's inquiry ticket.*

all reports on members' customers located *within* its zone of operation, as assigned to it by the National Association of Credit Management, and, in addition, must cooperate in sending individual creditors' ledger experience on subject accounts *outside* its zone of operation to the bureau in whose zone such customers are located. Thus, when a clearance is made, members of all bureaus having dealings with the subject under investigation are canvassed for information without regard to industry or location.

Each member is furnished with "member inquiry tickets," as shown in Fig. 17-1. These tickets are sent to the local bureau when the member wants information on prospective customers or current accounts, but in most cases the member makes his request for a report from the bureau by telephone. Upon receipt of an inquiry ticket or phone request, the local bureau checks its files to determine whether or not a report had already been written on the subject customer. Prepared reports are taken from the files to be sent immediately. Should the latest report be more than 120 days old, however, or in the event that no report is available concerning the subject of the inquiry, the current ledger experience of all known creditors is sought and an up-to-date report is prepared therefrom.

A bureau obtains current information from members in its immediate trade area by means of an "Inquiry Sheet" (see Fig. 17-2), which lists all accounts within such trade area for which the bureau has received an inquiry or desires current creditor experience. These Inquiry Sheets are mailed to each member of the bureau. The member fills in the information on the sheet where it is available and applicable and reports it to the bureau by telephone, sometimes at an agreed time of the day

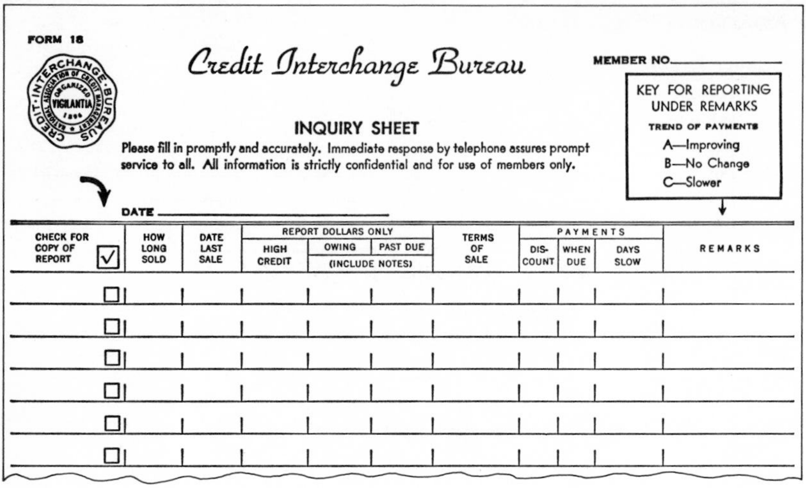
FORM 18

Credit Interchange Bureau

MEMBER NO.______

INQUIRY SHEET

Please fill in promptly and accurately. Immediate response by telephone assures prompt service to all. All information is strictly confidential and for use of members only.

KEY FOR REPORTING UNDER REMARKS
TREND OF PAYMENTS
A—Improving
B—No Change
C—Slower

DATE ______

CHECK FOR COPY OF REPORT ☑	HOW LONG SOLD	DATE LAST SALE	REPORT DOLLARS ONLY			TERMS OF SALE	PAYMENTS			REMARKS
			HIGH CREDIT	OWING	PAST DUE		DIS-COUNT	WHEN DUE	DAYS SLOW	
				(INCLUDE NOTES)						
☐										
☐										
☐										
☐										
☐										
☐										

figure 17-2. *Inquiry Sheet sent daily by the bureau to all members, containing spaces for 33 accounts on a sheet.*

and at a prearranged call from the bureau. If research for sources uncovers nonmember creditors known to have had dealings with the risk under investigation, possibly because such nonsubscribers have been given as references, a postcard request for information is sent to those creditors if a telephone charge is considered too expensive.

As noted previously, each bureau must write all reports on subject customers located within its zone of operation. Thus, if all known creditors were located in the local zone, a report could be prepared upon receipt of the ledger information from all the members in that zone. Since, however, creditors of the subject are no doubt also located in other zones, a request is sent to the bureaus of those zones, which, in turn, accumulate information from interested creditors and forward it to the inquiring zone, where the complete report is written (see Fig. 17-3*A*). On the other hand, should an inquiry be made on a subject located outside the zone of the inquirer (see Fig. 17-3*B*), the bureau of inquiry first canvasses creditors within its area, sends a copy of this preliminary report to the inquirer if so requested, and forwards the information gathered to the bureau of the zone in which the subject is located, where a national clearance is instituted. Finally, all the assembled information is incorporated in a report written by the bureau making the national clearance and in whose zone the subject is located. It is then duplicated and sent to each of the contributing bureaus, which forwards it, in turn, to all interested or inquiring members.

(A) SUBJECT OF INQUIRY LOCATED WITHIN THE ZONE OF THE INQUIRER. BUREAU OF INQUIRY PREPARES FINAL REPORT

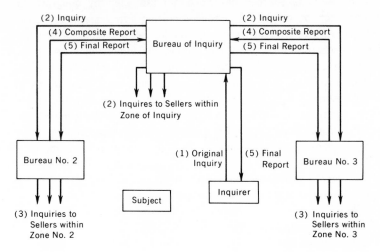

(B) SUBJECT OF INQUIRY LOCATED OUTSIDE THE ZONE OF THE INQUIRER. BUREAU NO. 2 PREPARES FINAL REPORT

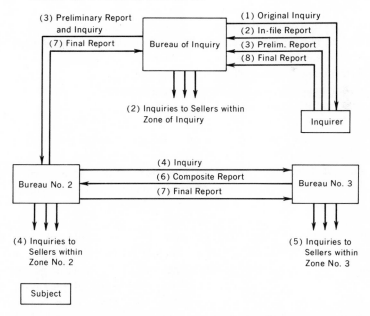

figure 17-3. *Procedure for assembling and reporting information embodied in a Credit Interchange Bureau report. (The numbers indicate the order in which the steps of the procedure are carried out by the various parties involved.)*

Contents of a Credit Interchange report. The ledger facts gathered from the various sources described are tabulated by geographical units, under each of which the proper reporting firms are listed more or less indiscriminately. The report shows in the first column the line of business of each contributor. Then follow the individual experiences, showing length of time sold to the account, date of last sale, highest recent credit extended, amount now owing, amount past due, terms of sale, paying record, and comments. Under "paying record" three classifications are to be found, into which all customers may be conveniently divided. These purport to show whether the subject discounts his bills, pays promptly at maturity, or permits his accounts to lapse into slowness. If slow, the extent to which that is true is indicated, usually in days.

Changes in payment and similar data of material significance, either favorable or derogatory, are generally included in "comments." This item, consequently, discloses whether claims against the subject have been placed in the hands of an attorney or a collection agency, whether the subject returns merchandise unjustly, whether further credit has been refused, and the like (see Fig. 17-4).

Interpretation of a Credit Interchange report. Unlike some of the agency reports, Credit Interchange reports never present any analysis or interpretation nor do they offer any recommendations or express opinions. They merely present the facts as recited by creditors, arranged in an orderly manner for a quick and intelligent appraisal. Since they do not present anything but an uncolored and impersonal statement of experience of contributing creditors, it becomes essential for the individual credit executive to analyze and interpret the contents as a basis for action. In the paragraphs that follow an attempt will be made to point out the valuable information that is contained in each column of the report. Additional facts can be gained when each column is read vertically as well as horizontally in conjunction with one or more of the other columns.

Business classification. From the data in this column, the wide-awake credit manager may visualize the kind of business in which the risk is engaged and the proportionate composition of his stock of goods. An opportunity is also afforded to study the distribution of purchases between various markets and the reasons therefor. Under each market heading is a code date which establishes the date on which members in that market were canvassed for information. For example, in the specimen report shown in Fig. 17-4, Alabama is shown as the first market. The first section of the number appearing under its name, *viz.*, 1206, indicates that members in that market were canvassed for information

F-6

NATIONAL ASSOCIATION of CREDIT MANAGEMENT
Credit Interchange Report

OFFICES IN PRINCIPAL CITIES

BROWN & JONES   •TABOR, ALABAMA   DECEMBER 22, 1967
                                        MERCER COUNTY

The accuracy of this Report is not guaranteed. Its contents are gathered in good faith from members and sent to you by this Bureau without liability for negligence in procuring, collecting, communicating or failing to communicate the information so gathered.

BUSINESS CLASSIFICATION	HOW LONG SOLD	DATE OF LAST SALE	HIGHEST RECENT CREDIT	NOW OWING INCLUDING NOTES	PAST DUE	TERMS OF SALE	PAYING RECORD DIS-COUNTS	PAYS WHEN DUE	DAYS SLOW	COMMENTS
ALABAMA 1206-136										
D G	yrs	12-67	1520	830		60	x			
Clo	yrs	12-67	2610	1590		8-10EOM	x		30	
D G	yrs	12-67	1978	1462	1069	2-30		x	45	
W App	11-65	12-67	432	120		15		x	30	
Paper	8-65	12-67	370	370	260	2-10-30	x	x	30	
Clo	yrs	10-67	1070			1-10-30	x			
Hdwe	yrs	12-67	92	35		30		x		
ST. LOUIS 1207-307										
D G	yrs	12-67	2876	2876	1150	30			120	Placed for collection
Clo	yrs	12-67	3540	1879	498	60		x	15	
CHATTANOOGA 1208-14										
Gen M	yrs	12-67	214	214	161	30			30	
Knit	yrs	12-67	182	73		30		x		
GEORGIA 1208-412										
W app	yrs	11-67	380	94	94	7-10EOM			30	
Shoe	yrs	12-67	422	263		2-10-30		x		
KNOXVILLE 1207-51										
Shoe	yrs	12-67	1283	124	124	30			30-60	
CHICAGO 1208-3042										
Shoe	yrs	12-67	591	591		2-20-60	x			
Clo	yrs	11-67	2531			30	x			
CENTRAL & S W OHIO 1207-523										
Clo	yrs	12-67	1465	320		8-10EOM	x			
					10841	3356				

Bu 72 JG

CONFIDENTIAL

FOR CREDIT DEPARTMENT PERSONNEL USE ONLY • ANY MEMBER VIOLATING THE CONFIDENTIAL NATURE OF THIS REPORT IS SUBJECT TO SUSPENSION

figure 17-4. *Specimen Credit Interchange report issued by a Credit Interchange Bureau of the National Association of Credit Management. While the data are based on an actual case, the name and address of the subject are fictitious.*

on Dec. 6, and that contributors supplied their information on or after that date.

Market identification of information permits an appraisal of the subject's business ability as evidenced by his buying. Buying in too many markets or in markets which are not normal sources of supply may indicate a badly broken stock of nominal sale value. Intelligent, orderly buying indicates a well-kept, salable stock.

How long sold. The length of time sold to a customer has a significant bearing on the relative merit of a contributor's experience. Other things being equal, the value of the comments, as well as that of the statement concerning manner of payment, varies in direct proportion with the length of time over which dealings have extended. It may also show the degree of confidence creditors have in the subject when the information in the other columns is favorable. If an established business concern has been making first purchases from many creditors within a recent period, it may indicate refusal of credit by former suppliers or preparation to defraud creditors.

Date of last sale. Date of last sale or last shipment tends to disclose the customer's current buying activities. Unusual buying activity serves as a danger signal, calling for an immediate inquiry into its causes and purposes, especially when it is shown in the How Long Sold column that the risk has recently bought from many new sources. The date of a last sale also denotes the recency of the information contributed by the house, thereby aiding in the exact determination of its relative value. This column sheds light on the manner-of-payment columns by indicating the trend of the account.

Highest recent credit. The highest credit extended reflects the opinions and confidence of other creditors respecting the subject, and serves as a valuable guide, particularly when the experiences appear extensive from the standpoint of both time and sales volume. This figure, however, is capable of being easily misunderstood, for the high credit given may be more a matter of necessity than an exact measure of confidence. It does not always suggest that a credit limit of that amount was originally extended the customer, but that sometimes the creditor was willing to continue to carry him for a larger and larger sum as his payments became slower. Under these circumstances, a high credit may be an unfavorable rather than a favorable factor. The highest credit, therefore, should always be checked against terms and paying record. This may indicate whether slow payments are involved, also something of the length of time that particular credit has been outstanding. Comparison of the amount currently owing with the maximum credit extended will indicate whether the buyer is pushing against his ceiling or whether he has reduced the indebtedness at one time allowed him. The appraisal should consider seasonal activities, general trends in business, and similar factors.

Amount owing. Obviously, one of the most important columns is that displaying the amount owing. Without a knowledge of a concern's aggregate indebtedness as revealed roughly under this heading, credit managers may be led to extend credit unwisely, because of the influence exerted by the action of the other creditors in extending large lines to the firm in question. Checking the amount owing against the accounts payable item of the firm's balance sheet, if submitted by the subject, will tend to uncover fraudulent intents and designs, if any, prior to making shipment. Since the Credit Interchange report seldom covers the total indebtedness of the risk, the amount owing, as shown on it, should be much below the figure given on the balance sheet for approximately the same date.

Amount past due. If the ratio of past dues to amounts owing is high, the risk should be regarded with suspicion, and vice versa. Once an account lapses into slowness, the firm is in all probability weakening financially, particularly with regard to its working capital. Then there is the possibility of a past-due account becoming a partial or total loss.

A single amount past due may indicate that the amount is in dispute, but when many suppliers report the account to be slow the information should then serve as a danger signal. Of special value is the ratio of the amount past due to the amount owing, for it indicates the probability of collecting an account on time. Thus, if the amount past due is $50,000 and the amount owing is $200,000, when the past-due amount is deducted from the amount owing we arrive at the amount currently collectible, or $150,000. By dividing this last figure by the total amount owing we obtain an index showing a 75 per cent collectibility. Consequently, a creditor selling to such a customer on 30-day terms may not expect payment until about 10 days after due date, and a creditor selling on 90-day terms will find the bill past due about 25 days after maturity. The data presented under manner of payment will corroborate the conclusion reached by this method.

Sometimes a relatively small amount owing may be shown, and yet the account may be in bad condition. This may be due to the fact that the majority of the bureau members reporting have collected their accounts and ceased to sell to the risk. For this reason, it is important to view this column in the light of the data in the column on date of last sale. If the above is substantiated and the manner of payment is unfavorable, it may then be concluded that the risk's major indebtedness is to nonmembers who have not been privileged to secure the information that led members to stop selling to the subject.

Terms of sale. From the terms of sale, the credit manager, knowing the customary terms prevailing in the various trades, shown in the first column of the report, should be able to ascertain the extent to which confidence is reposed in the subject by other creditors.   An inferior or doubtful risk seldom receives goods on regular terms.   He is usually required to purchase on a C.O.D. or C.I.A. (cash in advance) basis.   On the other hand, exceptionally good risks may be favored with better terms, involving a longer credit period or a larger cash discount, or both.

Paying record. The manner in which a merchant takes care of his bills is an excellent indication of his financial responsibility.   The significance which the manner of payment has on a concern's credit standing and on the successful management of the seller's house has already been discussed fully in another connection.   Suffice it to state that slow pay risks accustomed to take overtime are extremely troublesome.   Some of these accounts may be perfectly safe, but because of carelessness they are chronically and habitually slow; others are apt to become in time poor pay customers, requiring suits or other drastic measures to enforce payment.   While a slow-paying record may indicate a highly unfavorable account, it may also indicate one which is in temporary difficulty but in which creditors have confidence.   The distinction will be shown in reference to other facts in the Amount Past Due and under Comments.

The number of slow pay customers is quite large.   They vary from those just noticeably slow to those very slow, the former meeting their obligations with fair promptness, whereas the latter delay payment until actually threatened with drastic measures.   Hence, the importance of knowing the degree of slowness.

Another thing that needs watching under this heading is the *size* of accounts which are discounted or paid when due.   Some unscrupulous merchants make it a practice to meet their obligations on a few small accounts with great promptness in order to use them as references and otherwise to make a favorable showing.   Again, prompt payment of small accounts at the expense of the larger debts frequently represents a situation where the debtor is at least temporarily confining his buying to amounts considered essential to the operation of his business, for which prompt settlement must be made.

Comments. This column provides space for facts not made clear in the remainder of the report. Among the types of information reported herein are changes in the risk which are noticeable to creditors, credit refusals, collections by attorneys, default on notes, return of checks for insufficient funds, and unfilled first orders.

The amount and number of first orders is especially significant. They show the extent to which new credit is sought by the customer. If unusually large, except where the subject is just beginning in business or where justified expansion is known to take place, a thorough investigation into the causes should be conducted prior to accepting the order. In the course of such an investigation it is essential to ascertain whether the subject is shifting his purchases to a new set of creditors in order to elude settlement of his accounts, or whether he is stocking up with merchandise preparatory to making an assignment or voluntarily going into bankruptcy. The report itself may unmistakably reveal these intentions, when properly interpreted. Thus, when many new accounts are opened at the time that the past dues to old accounts run high, it is perfectly obvious that the subject is attempting to elude payment of his bills.

If any large number of first orders is revealed while at the same time large amounts of past dues are shown, it becomes evident that the customer is allowing his old accounts to lapse into slowness and is endeavoring to obtain additional credit in new markets.

Advantages of Credit Interchange Bureaus. The Credit Interchange Bureaus furnish ledger information the reputation of which for freshness and reliability is well established and recognized by many experienced credit managers. Files on subjects of inquiry are revised at frequent intervals, usually about every 120 days—a feature peculiar to the system. Moreover, reports are furnished within a short time after receipt of an inquiry. This, of course, depends upon the availability or lack of clearance reports on file; also upon the extensiveness of the investigation to be conducted. In any event, preliminary reports can be rendered within a surprisingly short period of time. Even a clearance on a national scale seldom requires more than 10 days to 2 weeks.

One of the paramount advantages of the system lies in the scope of its activities, with respect to both territory and lines of trade. The service is national in scope, making it possible for a credit grantor located, say, in Cleveland to learn through its reports how a customer residing in Nashville is paying his creditors in New York, Philadelphia, St. Louis, Chicago, and elsewhere. The service not only knows no restrictions as to area, but the same is true with respect to lines of trade. All kinds of business are covered in their investigations, so that complete data respecting merchants handling more than one line can be accurately communicated.

Of some significance is the reciprocal feature of the service of some of the bureaus, usually rendered on a limited basis. A contributor of information may thus secure a copy of the completed report or at least of the *local* clearance, if such wish is expressed on the returned filled-in form. This reduces the cost of the service to the member and enables him to maintain up-to-date records on many of his accounts. Because of the costliness of this feature to the bureau, some bureaus have eliminated it altogether and others have curtailed its use.

Ever since the inauguration of the Credit Interchange System steady improvement has been made in its operating procedure. It is now marked by much greater accuracy than during its earlier stages, reports are more complete, and less time is required to complete a clearance and otherwise to serve subscribers. Furthermore, the territory of its operation has been materially enlarged, for even though the total number of bureaus is but 61, attention should be called to the fact that some of the smaller bureaus have been absorbed by and amalgamated with the larger neighboring bureaus.

Objections to Credit Interchange Bureaus. Notwithstanding its numerous advantages, the bureau system has often been criticized; most of this criticism is probably unjustifiable. Some critics claim that the bureau tends to substitute impersonal contact for direct interchange among members. This is, it must be asserted, only partially true. The effectiveness of the system causes it, no doubt, to take the place of the other and cruder methods, as far as regular exchange of ledger experiences is concerned. Direct interchange, however, can still be profitably utilized for the sake of acquiring information which normally does not appear in print and which may decide conclusively the turning point in a given case.

A second group of critics claims that the bureau membership will never attain such dimensions as to become of real importance. In support of their view they point to a large number of credit managers who refuse to subscribe to the service because they feel that it will be necessary for them to give more information concerning their dealings with customers than that received. Again, some credit managers are loath to divulge information respecting a customer who is temporarily embarrassed, for fear of causing undue injury to him. Refusal or neglect to furnish all facts necessarily limits the scope of the report and fails to disclose the exact standing of the subject.

In reply to these critics it may be observed that their arguments run against the current of actual conditions. The probable growth and development of these bureaus are not matters of library philosophy but lie in the realm of actuality. Great and consistent progress is to be noted from the very inception of the enterprise. To be sure, it is still far from having attained completeness and perfection, but if the future growth is to be judged by the progress made heretofore, the prospects are bright.

When to secure a Credit Interchange report. Leading credit executives who have studied the problem seem to feel that a Credit Interchange report should be obtained every time a new account is investigated, when an unusually large order is received, or when a number of direct inquiries on a customer are made; likewise, when a change in a customer's method of payment is first observed, especially if it is derogatory. When receivables are analyzed at the end of the month, a report may be useful on slow accounts prior to determining on any special collection measures. Some credit managers prefer the automatic revision service offered by the system, especially on the principal outlets or on doubtful accounts. Under this plan, a list of such customers is submitted to the bureau with the request that reports on them be furnished every 3, 4, or 6 months as requested. This enables the credit executive to keep a close watch on the affairs of the customer concerning whom there is some doubt and to make sure that he is securing a fair portion of the business from the good accounts.

Credit Interchange also is used by many members as an "early warning system." At the time the bureau is editing the report, if it is obvious to the editor that sufficient change in the total condition of the subject has taken place since the previous report, a copy of the new report is sent to all suppliers listed on the report. Those suppliers whose own ledgers show the subject is discounting with them, for example, are automatically alerted that the subject is not doing the same with others. On the other hand, suppliers who are receiving delayed payments are alerted to improve their collection procedures. In reverse, if a supplier has had to put the customer on C.O.D. terms, the automatic report may show that the latter has improved and the supplier should review his position so that his company's sales will not be unnecessarily restricted.

A series of these Credit Interchange reports can be employed to reveal the "trend" the customer's business is taking. Thus a creative credit manager looking for changes in customers' conditions is automatically notified of such changes. The National Credit Interchange Committee of the National Association of Credit Management is now examining other ways of automating procedures in order to speed the time for completing reports and improving the quality. As most credit executives of business firms need both favorable and unfavorable information on which to base their decisions, the volume of ledger information to be gathered every 90 to 120 days will have a great bearing on the ultimate decisions of procedural changes deemed necessary.

TRADE
CREDIT
BUREAUS

It is estimated that over one-fourth of all national and regional trade associations have found it necessary, as a means of furthering the principal purpose or purposes of the association, to provide some credit information service to its members or to the industry membership generally. Furthermore, in almost one-half of such cases this service represents a major degree of activity of the association.

Nature of credit service. The kind of credit service furnished by a trade association depends upon the special needs of the industry membership and availability of the information to serve those needs from normal commercial sources. Quite often this service is confined to the periodic compilation and distribution of lists covering delinquent and slow accounts. Reference to this type of credit information service on an industry-wide basis is made in more than two dozen sets of Trade Practice Rules promulgated by the Federal Trade Commission. In other cases the service consists of the systematic, periodic collection and dissemination among the members of fairly comprehensive ledger experience on all active accounts. In still other cases the credit information service is rendered to individual members subscribing for it and consists of reports on individual accounts, which may be in the nature of trade opinion information only or may involve complete reports even more comprehensive in scope and content than those furnished by mercantile agencies. When the service is rendered to individual members on individual accounts, it is generally organized into what may be termed a credit bureau or credit department of the association.

Distinctive features of trade credit bureaus or departments. Such an organization may differ radically from the cooperative credit interchange bureaus of the National Association of Credit Management or from similar types of organizations operating for profit. Their operations are under the control of the association. Operating success depends largely upon the voluntary cooperation of the members in supplying credit information in a constant flow and in otherwise contributing time and effort without compensation. Direct exchange of information is fostered, by mail and through credit group meetings.   The service is usually limited from the standpoint of both subscribers and account classes on which it is rendered; no such limitations are ever imposed by the other types of credit service organizations.   Very often the service is unmetered or unlimited in quantity instead of requiring payment on the basis of the number of reports furnished to a subscriber or member.   Sometimes this service may be made available even to nonsubscribing members of the industry when properly referred to the association for it.   Much emphasis is usually placed on activities that tend to prevent financial difficulty of accounts or that help to rehabilitate accounts which have become involved in such difficulty.

Advantages and limitations. One of the advantages lies in the special type of credit information service furnished that may be of peculiar significance in a given line of trade.   Obviously, such service can be tailor-made to suit the needs of the membership.   The other advantage lies in the control that the membership can exert over the quality and kind of information to be supplied.   At the same time the service is disadvantageous to the extent that it is restricted to a single class of persons on which reports will be rendered or to a limited territory.   Any substantial restriction of this nature is apt to make reports incomplete and thus fail to reflect accurately the credit standing of the subjects covered by them.   Furthermore, such service is at best confined to a single line of business or even to a segment of it, so that it may supply but part of the need for credit information by its members.   To be sure, in all such instances this service can be and is supplemented by information available from a variety of other sources.   Despite these limitations, when properly conceived in line with the industry's needs and efficiently executed, this type of credit information service may fill an important gap and tend in no small degree to promote the commercial health and welfare of the industry.

QUESTIONS AND PROBLEMS

1 What is "ledger experience"? Why should a credit manager be especially interested in such information?

2 List all the methods available for the interchange of credit information among creditors without the intervention of any outside agency.

3 Each of customers A, B, and C buys approximately the same amount of merchandise from your house. Your terms are 3/10, net 60 days. A discounts his bill, B pays at maturity, and C is 30 to 60 days slow.

   a Which of these customers is the least profitable to your house? Can you prove your conclusion by the use of figures?

b Which of the customers is entitled to preferential treatment from your firm? Why?

4 You are in receipt of a first order from the Blank Company, located about 125 miles from your city. You are desirous of obtaining the experiences of other creditors who have had dealings with the prospective customer. How can you obtain the names of such creditors?

5 Should direct interchange among creditors be encouraged or restricted? Explain.

6 Compare and contrast interchange bureaus, as a source of credit information, with the direct method of interchange used by creditors.

7 The Association of Credit Management of Bigtown resolved to organize and establish a credit interchange bureau which is to be affiliated with and form a part of the bureaus operated under the supervision of the National Association of Credit Management. You are chosen bureau manager. Outline the various steps that you would take in organizing such a bureau on a working basis. How would you determine your "zone of operation"?

8 What records and files would you deem essential in the operation of your bureau?

9 One of your members, a manufacturer of shoes, sends a member's inquiry ticket, requesting a report on X, who is located approximately 50 miles from your city. What would be the first step in the procedure of furnishing such information to the subscriber?

10 Assuming that a new credit interchange clearance must be made concerning X, what steps should be taken in securing such a clearance?

11 Show by diagram how the data for the above credit interchange report will be gathered.

12 Just how many reports would an inquiring member receive about a subject:
a Under the regular service
b Under the automatic revision service

13 Under what circumstances should a creditor ask for a credit interchange report?

14 In the interpretation of credit interchange reports, can you point out specifically the interdependence existing between the various columns of the report and the necessity of reading any one column in the light of information contained in other columns?

15 Distinguish between credit bureaus maintained by trade associations and those operated by associations of credit managers.

16 Assume that your company is the smallest of a given number in the same line of business who are members of the credit interchange system. Inasmuch as you represent the smallest organization, the larger competitors will receive more orders and thus make more inquiries for reports to which your company will have to contribute. From a practical business viewpoint, should you remain a member of the bureau? Discuss.

17 Analyze the report shown in the text and decide whether the risk is acceptable, indicating the approximate credit limit you would place on the account and any other precaution you would take.

CHAPTER EIGHTEEN

salesmen, attorneys,
and banks as sources
of credit information

Of increasing importance in modern business is the ever-growing tendency toward large-scale operation and equally large-scale management. The twentieth century to date has witnessed numerous and tremendously significant combinations and consolidations, both vertical and horizontal. Individual plants and mercantile houses have also gradually and consistently expanded until they have embraced the entire national market. Because of these developments, purchasers have become further removed geographically from the selling houses, necessitating the substitution of a most indirect contact with the trade for that of personal acquaintance. To say that such a substitution is unsatisfactory is putting it mildly. Although practically all the departments of a selling house are handicapped because of the distance separating them from the customers, none suffers quite so much inconvenience as the credit department.   A personal interview with the *prospective* buyer is no longer generally feasible, and an examination, by the credit manager, of an applicant's place of business, stock of goods, store policy, and the like, prior to rendering a decision, is seldom practical.   For these reasons alert credit managers, recognizing these limitations, usually consult those representatives who have the opportunity of meeting the customer personally.   The more important of these representatives are salesmen, attorneys, and banks.

SALESMEN AS
CREDIT REPORTERS

Probably the oldest source of credit information was the report submitted by the salesman who visited the customer in his place of business.   Even yet the salesman's report is given first consideration, for it logically comes first in chronological order as a source of information, because it accompanies, as a rule, all first orders from new trade.   The salesman is in many instances the only representative of his firm who may ever have the opportunity of establishing relations through personal contact with the customer.   He is the man on the ground and is, therefore, in a superior position to render particularly valuable services to his credit department.

Reluctance of salesmen to furnish credit reports about customers.   That the salesman is in an exceptional position to render valuable assistance by reporting facts based on personal observation remains undisputed.   Whether or not he is willing to supply such information and the extent to which the credit department is justified, as a matter of good business policy, in requiring him to serve as its agent, are entirely different matters.   Both salesmen and sales managers are divided on this question, although much progress has been noted in recent years toward closer cooperation between salesmen and credit managers.

As a rule, salesmen are reluctant to make credit reports about their customers.   They feel that their chief mission is to sell goods, and to this end they ought to devote all their time.   To compel them to spend part of their time on credit work tends to detract materially from selling efficiency.   Furthermore, a salesman's time is valuable.   He spends but a limited number of hours each day face to face with customers and prospects.   Thus his selling time must not be diverted to other channels.   Credit reports can be obtained at much less cost.   Moreover, credit work differs greatly from selling.   The salesman is a constitutional optimist, hence he is a poor judge of the qualities that make a good credit risk.   In this latter work he is often awkward and apologetic, owing to his friendly relationships with customers. Any additional function that in any way conflicts with his main purpose, no matter how remotely, is extremely distasteful to him and he is more than likely to resent it or else assume an attitude of indifference regarding the thoroughness with which it is performed. This is especially true when the method of compensation is based on the volume of sales, as when employed on a commission basis alone or possibly a combination of commission and salary. Under such circumstances, salesmen do not wish to be hampered by anything which apparently has no immediate favorable effect on the amount of sales, and are naturally loath to offend or embarrass a prospective customer by asking numerous questions regarding his financial responsibility for fear of driving away trade to a competitor.

Again, prompted by selfish motives, salesmen are prone even to assume an antagonistic attitude toward the credit department, which, in their opinion, requires their assistance in handling accounts without reciprocating by helping to sell goods. Such an attitude undoubtedly discloses one of the inefficiencies of modern business organization, where, because of the specialization in functions on the part of different departments, the main purpose of the entire machinery is frequently lost sight of and each employee, consequently, considers himself as a department instead of company representative.

Why salesmen should cooperate with the credit department.[1] The credit department is fully justified in insisting upon the salesman's cooperation, and the progressive salesman can be readily convinced of the wisdom of such an attitude. It is full cooperation and mutual understanding of both sales and credit problems that result in maximum earnings of the company and the salesman. No sale is complete until the money is collected, hence credit is in this sense really a part of selling. A lost sale results only in a loss of potential profit, but a credit loss includes not only lost potential profit on the transaction, but also the cost of the merchandise and the expenses incurred on the transaction. There is no denying that the salesman's chief task is to sell, but he must do so in accordance with certain policies and in line with the wishes of his superiors. That is why his nonselling duties are sometimes larger in number than those directly concerned with his selling work. The salesman must be disabused of the idea that he is working solely for the sales department; he must be shown that he is employed by the firm so that his interests should extend beyond his immediate bailiwick.

The fallacies of the salesman's opposition can be pointed out in still another way. If the credit manager in his dealings with customers

---

[1] Numerous articles on this general subject appear frequently in current periodical literature.

bears in mind, as he should, the idea of business promotion, and thus treats them considerately, he thereby aids the salesman in retaining the good will of his trade. Nothing can be of greater value from the standpoint of the salesman than the securing of a quick decision on an order in hand. But to render a credit decision quickly, information respecting the risk's financial responsibility must be readily available. It, therefore, behooves the salesman, in his own interest, to remove all obstacles which may cause undue delay in reaching a credit decision.

It is a relatively simple matter to secure an order from a dealer with a poor credit standing. When such an order is later turned down by the house, all sorts of explanations must be made which inevitably result in ill will. Moreover, the higher the credit standing of an account, the better the sales potentials. Thus, it is to the salesman's benefit to delve into the customer's credit responsibility and to make every effort to improve his standing. In helping his customer with the manifold problems, as he should, the modern salesman is forced to deal with credit matters. For this reason alone, a salesman should be trained to do some credit work. Many salesmen are awkward and incompetent in this regard because of the improper attitude of sales executives and deficient training of the sales force. Again, a salesman is usually required to make only one report on a customer, *viz.*, when a first order is secured. Thereafter, he is seldom called upon to make another investigation unless the customer's account becomes decidedly unsatisfactory and thorough revision of the files is made necessary. It does not seem, therefore, unreasonable to require his assistance in this regard.

As a matter of fact, it is sound policy to require that the salesman keep in constant touch with the credit aspects of his customers. He should be especially watchful for signs that signal warning and call for caution both in selling and in credit handling of the customer. Among these signs are changes in personal habits that are deemed derogatory, indications of heavy buying from a single source, claims against the customer placed in the hands of attorneys, signs of stock deterioration and general business letdown, indications that the customer is planning to sell out his business, or such external factors as pending strikes that might affect the customer's business and creditworthiness. All such matters should be reported by the salesman to his credit department without delay.

Salesmen's credit reports. In view of the foregoing, it is apparent that good judgment calls for a limited amount of information from the salesman. In justice to him, only those facts should be called for which cannot be obtained through the aforementioned channels. He should not be asked to furnish the sort of information which requires an exhaustive investigation and is, therefore, likely to cut heavily into his time and also arouse the customer's suspicion.   Any deviation from this principle invariably results in purchasing data at a price beyond its value, because of the antagonism toward the credit department arising from the embarrassment of customers and consequent loss of sales.

The salesman sees the merchant in his setting and is probably familiar with local conditions.   Because of these facts he is in a position to furnish the following information:

Kind of business.   To a wholesale grocer, for example, it is important to know whether or not the buying merchant handles fresh meats and fresh fruits and vegetables, for these commodities profoundly affect the rate of stock turns and the cost of doing business.   A disclosure of the exact nature of the business is readily procurable from this source, since it calls for a minimum of observation and no direct questioning whatever.

Condition of store.   This involves a consideration of stock arrangement, window and store display, efficiency of the organization, and the manner in which customers are served.   All of these are easily within the range of a salesman's observation, yet they are important.   Gross neglect of any of these factors on the part of a store may eventually precipitate failure.

Condition and value of stock.   The salesman can at a glance ascertain the extent to which the merchandise inventory is out of date, which, in turn, determines the probable rate of stock turnover.   He also knows the customer's buying habits, and if reckless in his buying habits, he is likely to prove equally careless in his manner of payment.   Again, casual observation of the prices at which merchandise is marked will reveal through the apparent gross margin the profitableness of the business.   Whether or not the stock is well kept is also significant as an indication of merchandising ability.   Many houses also require their salesmen to estimate the value of the stock.   However, unless such estimates are made with considerable care, they constitute mere guesses and as such are practically worthless.   To be sure, the proprietor may be consulted regarding this figure, which, when properly discounted, may serve as a better, though still extremely rough, indication of the value of merchandise inventory.

Location.   With greater knowledge of scientific management, the conditions affecting the location of a business are becoming increasingly important. As a result, the progressive merchant, in selecting the site for his business, studies and analyzes all the factors which make for a good location. Among others are its relation to the business center in case of shopping goods; available transportation and parking facilities; the number of passers-by; the character of passers-by; the side of the street, whether shady of sunny in the afternoons; the location with reference to a suburban or other planned business district; and other similar factors. The grouping of businesses is also significant and has a direct bearing on the probable success or failure of the concern in question. On visiting his trade, the salesman ought to be in a position, after proper coaching, to observe the aforementioned factors and on that basis arrive at a correct conclusion respecting location.

Local conditions. The salesman is in a position to keep the credit department informed of these conditions, which have a material effect upon a customer's business. Industries may be removed or shut down, crops may fail, the character of the local industries may be such as to offer only temporary employment, streets in the vicinity may be temporarily torn up, employees of transportation facilities may strike, traffic may be diverted to other streets, and the like.

Habits and reputation. Next to attorneys, probably no one is better fitted than the salesman to gather information concerning the customer's reputation. By direct questioning, assuming confidence on the part of the merchant, and through incidental inquiries in other directions, he will learn whether the customer uses intoxicating liquors excessively, or gambles, and the kind of reputation he enjoys locally as a merchant and as a citizen.

Capital resources. Most houses require their salesmen to furnish figures regarding a risk's capital investment in and outside the business in which he is engaged. Since, however, this information is readily procurable from other sources, it is questionable whether a salesman should be burdened with the task of acquiring it.

References. Since a salesman's report usually accompanies every first order, it is essential to secure some reference to both banks and mercantile establishments with which the risk has dealings. These references may be obtained directly from the merchant or indirectly through inquiries directed at salesmen of other houses and other local merchants with whom connections are well established. Other sources with which the merchant is trading may be determined from the types or brands

NEW ACCOUNT ---- INFORMATION SHEET

Date _____   Salesman_____

Official Name of Store _____

Street Address:_____City _____

Name of Owner (Please Print):_____

Is account registered?_____Federal Narcotic Number _____

Name of Pharmacists (Please Print): _____

_____

How many employed in Store?_____Does Owner work in Store?_____

Is this a new store?_____. If not, from whom was store purchased?_____

_____

Will Owner allow back orders?_____

Does he want a statement every : 15 Days _____Or Monthly _____

Will he pay salesman?_____Or mail direct to Company _____

Is this store affiliated with any other Stores?   Yes _____ NO _____

If Yes, please give particulars:_____

What are shipping instructions?_____

_____

On what days will you call on this Account ?_____

What are Store's approximate sales per month?_____

What is condition of building _____

What is condition of merchandise _____

Would customer be interested in any of the following: Remodeling _____

Pharmaceutical Services_____. Mailing List_____Other _____

Is there any other information you can think of that will help us in being of service to this

account _____

Information sheet prepared by _____

figure 18-1. *Salesman's new-account report used by a drug wholesaler.*

of articles carried in stock.   In smaller communities, attendants at freight depots may supply salesmen with information as to sources of shipments to the merchant.   By obtaining adequate references, the salesman can do the utmost to expedite the credit investigation preceding the filling of a first order, and thus best serve his own interests as well as those of others concerned.

Form of salesman's credit report. Although many forms of salesmen's credit reports have been suggested on various occasions, few appear to conform to the principle enunciated in a previous paragraph, primarily because of the excessive mass of information they purport the salesman to furnish. A reasonable form of report should be confined to the following (see Fig. 18-1):

1 Date.
2 Name and address of firm.
3 How long in business.
4 Kind of business.
5 Condition of store.
6 Estimate of value of stock.
7 Is stock well kept?
8 Buying habits.
9 Location.
10 Competition.
11 Local conditions affecting the business.
12 Capital resources.
13 Firms bought from.
14 Banks dealt with.
15 Remarks concerning experience, habits, and reputation.

In addition to the report to be filled out by a salesman upon the occasion of a first order, a report on a similar form serves a useful purpose for the revision of the credit file. Some of the information initially required of the salesman need not be repeated on similar forms, but the questions upon which revision is to be based can be pointed directly to the facts likely to reveal changes in credit qualification. A questionnaire providing for such information is preferable to questions asked the salesman in letter form, for it prevents his generalizing, covers the entire ground, and supplies him with a convenient means of reply (see Figs. 18-2A and 18-2B).

Value of salesman's credit report. The extent to which the credit data submitted by a salesman should be relied upon depends, in large measure, upon his ability, assuming willingness on his part to do so, to size up a situation and arrive at correct and reliable conclusions. If he is a keen observer and, in addition, possesses knowledge of what constitute good business methods and policies, greater reliance can be placed on his reports than when his opinions are merely a result of sheer guesswork. Another factor determining the strength of his reports is the extent to which he permits himself to become biased by his desire to roll up volume. In the very nature of things, salesmen are prone to be somewhat overoptimistic and may thus allow their judgment to become clouded by their enthusiasm.

A third factor consists in the willingness of the salesman to cooperate with the credit department, which, in turn, depends upon the

QUESTIONNAIRE TO BE FILLED OUT BY
SALESMAN AND RETURNED PROMPTLY TO CREDIT DEPARTMENT

Name of Customer

Address

1. Give your conservative estimate of value of customer's
   stock of merchandise $

2. How is the stock divided —

         Hardware $ _____
         Paint $ _____
         Other lines $ _____

3. How much, and what lines, if any, of slow moving stock does customer carry? Is inventory out of balance?

4. Give your estimate of value of fixtures. Are they suitable under
   present day competitive conditions?

5. What is the appearance of the store? Check your reply —

         Very good   Good   Only fair
         Poor   Very Poor

6. Give names of hardware and other competitors.

7. How does location of store rank — check your reply —

         Best   Good   Poor

(over)

figure 18-2A. *Form of questionnaire used by a hardware wholesaler, which the salesman is required to fill out for purposes of credit file revision.*

treatment accorded customers and salesmen by the latter. Lastly, it is comparatively safe to assume that, when answers are required to a limited number of points, the results will be more satisfactory. Irrespective of all the factors mentioned, it should be borne in mind that, after all, a substantial part of the salesman's report is essentially in the nature of opinions which are, therefore, of no higher quality than that of the person giving them.

8. What is your judgment as to business ability of this customer?
Check your reply —

      Very good   Mediocre   Very poor
      Average   Poor

9. Does customer devote any time to other matters? Explain. If he is
out of the store part of the time, who is in charge during his absence.

10. What records and books does he keep, if any? What franchises (radio,
etc.) does customer control?

11. How many people are employed in the store? How many are relatives?

12. What explanation can you offer as to customer's failure to pay bills
at maturity?

13. Is family extravagent? Does customer have unusual expense at home?
Explain —

14. Does he have any bad habits? Please check or give particulars.

      Drinks   Inclined to be sporty
      Gambles   Spends too freely
      Speculates   Not attentive to business.

      Other remarks —

15. From whom are purchases made of principal lines?

Date _____   _____
                                     Salesman

figure 18-2B. *Page 2 of Fig. 18–2A.*

In addition to reports, salesmen in many houses are required to review, with the credit manager, the customers' list periodically, usually twice a year. This contact affords an opportunity to secure additional pertinent data pertaining to the accounts under discussion and to make the salesmen realize the necessity for cooperation if larger sales are to be made. These contacts should always be encouraged, for they result in the establishment of close and more helpful relations between the two departments thus represented.

ATTORNEYS AS
CREDIT REPORTERS

Not unlike a salesman, an attorney residing in the town of the debtor or prospective customer is favorably situated as a collector and distributor of credit information.   His profession tends to bring him in close contact with the business and businessmen in his community.   Like the salesman, too, he sees the subject in his setting, knows him personally, perhaps, and sees his place of business.   Besides, an attorney invariably has a large circle of business and social acquaintances; this gives him an added advantage in the collection of credit data and opinions.   Again, his daily routine in matters of litigation affords him an extensive field of information valuable from the standpoint of the credit grantor.   Moreover, his special training often qualifies him to judge business conditions accurately.

Many concerns confine their practice of asking for attorney reports to towns of fewer than 15,000 on the theory that in the smaller communities an attorney's profession is more apt to bring him in personal contact with the businessmen in his locality—a feature that is considered essential to the making of reliable reports.   In the large cities, however, many law firms have found this source of revenue sufficiently lucrative to warrant the installation of a special commercial department for the purpose of gathering, filing, and disseminating credit data relative to local firms.   These attorneys chiefly assist in collecting claims for out-of-town creditors against local debtors.   This phase of their work will be discussed in a subsequent chapter.

Attorney directories. To aid in the selection of responsible attorneys, lists bearing the names and addresses of attorneys who have expressed a willingness to serve as collectors of overdue accounts, and, incidentally, as credit reporters, are available for business houses, banks, and collection agencies.   These lists are prepared by various publishing houses, which usually charge each attorney a small annual fee for representation.   These lists are then placed in the hands of houses and agencies likely to be interested.   In many cases no charge is made for the lists thus furnished, in which instances the publishing company relies entirely on the listing fees received from attorneys.   In other instances, substantial charges are made for the directories or lists and credit report forms which may accompany them.

In compiling attorney directories, the aim of the publishers is to secure in each community the name of one or more reputable attorneys from among those seeking commercial business.   Because of the laxity respecting requirements for admission to the bar in some states, the

```
                              City ..................................................... 19 .....
To ............................................................. at ...................................................................
    Dear Sir:-Kindly mail to us in enclosed stamped envelope full information, based on
your knowledge and investigation, as to the age, character, habits, capital, responsi-
bility and promptness in meeting obligations of
Full Name ................................................................ City .....................................
Street and No. ................................... Business ...........................................
Your prompt reply will be greatly appreciated, as Delayed Reports are of no Value.
ANSWER HERE:
Supposed net worth? $ ..........................................................................................
Individual Names (if a firm)?..................................................................................
Married or Single?.............................................. Age approximately?.......................
Reputation for Ability?.................. Honesty?.......................Moral Character? ................
Ever failed?................................................. Been sued?.......................................
How long in business?................................... Business seem prosperous? ....................
Value of stock on hand (estimated)? $................................... Insurance? $.................
Value of real estate above homestead and encumbrance?......................................................
Do you know of any unsatisfied obligations, chattel mortgages, judgments or claims in
hands of attorneys?.....................................................................................................
                            FURTHER REMARKS
..............................................................................................................................
..............................................................................................................................
..............................................................................................................................
All the facts tending in anywise to a just estimate of party's credit-worth are highly de-
sirable. Do not under any circumstances divulge the name of the party desiring this report.
```

figure 18-3. *A typical attorney credit report form.*

selection of reputable attorneys is not always an easy task. If names of undesirable and inefficient attorneys appear on the list, however, they are apt to be weeded out in time, inasmuch as the practice followed in selecting attorneys for listings is to make little investigation at first but to eliminate all those names about which complaints are registered by business concerns. In this manner, comparatively good lists are made available by publishing houses whose experience in compiling attorney directories extends over a period of years.

Attorney credit reports. For the most part, the information secured from attorneys parallels that obtained from salesmen, with the exception of two items (see Fig. 18-3). These are claims and lawsuits.

It is a rather simple matter for an attorney to obtain knowledge of lawsuits instituted against a subject and, once obtained, to follow the progress and outcome of such action. Court records are available to this end, and in most communities all proceedings are published daily and distributed among those concerned with legal matters. Then, too, the attorney is often called upon to represent other selling houses in the collection of claims against the subject of the inquiry.

Status of subject's real property. Many attorneys are thoroughly acquainted with property values in their respective communities. Some of them are experts in this respect.   Hence the valuation submitted in this manner can be used by the credit grantor in checking the figures presented by mercantile agencies or the merchant himself.   Furthermore, attorneys can easily and accurately ascertain from the usual records the encumbrances placed on the real property of the subject.

In regard to the other items, the local attorney's information is apt to be inferior in some respects and superior in others.   Few attorneys, indeed, possess the knowledge of the various factors that determine a good location for a given kind of business or type of store.   Lacking special training in merchandising, they may be no more competent to pass judgment on the condition of the store, buying habits of customers, and value of stock on hand than a casual observer.   The average salesman is far better fitted to supply such information.

On the other hand, the average attorney, because of his associations with various merchants in his community, is able to secure opinions regarding the business ability of the subject and is particularly valuable in giving information on habits and local reputation.   The attorney frequently knows the personal and family history of local merchants either through personal contact or through his wide circle of acquaintances and his information on these points is more valuable, particularly in smaller towns and cities, than that obtained through salesmen.

Value of attorney credit reports. Opinions differ among the larger concerns concerning the value of attorneys' reports.   Some firms have used them successfully for a period of years and are, consequently, staunch supporters of the system; others use them sparingly.   It is obvious, nevertheless, that, not unlike the value of a salesman's credit report, the attorney's credit data depend upon his ability to size up a situation properly, inasmuch as a large part of the report consists of mere opinions.   Another factor is the willingness or diligence with which the investigation is conducted.

On the whole, a report submitted by an average attorney is far less dependable than that of an average salesman.   Several reasons are advanced in explanation of this statement.   To begin with, the attorney may be a friend of the subject under investigation, which is perfectly plausible in smaller towns and cities, and thus renders no unfavorable report, especially in a matter of mere opinion or hearsay.   A second reason accounting for the difference in the quality of reports of salesmen and attorneys, respectively, is the prejudice on the part of the latter against outside creditors.   Reports may be colored in favor of local merchants without at the same time completely disregarding the truth.   This criticism appears to be well grounded in isolated cases in small communities.   Outside of extremely provincial districts, the broadmindedness of attorneys seldom permits of such unfair discrimination. A third cause for the inferiority of attorneys' reports is the difference in credit standards of the house requesting a report and of the attorney rendering it, and hence, possibilities for misinterpreting opinions; whereas a salesman supposedly measures risks by the standards of his house, with which he should become intimately acquainted.

In the fourth place, many attorneys do not give the matter adequate attention because of the subordinate nature of the work. Unless he specializes in commercial work, the attorney is apt to consider the work of collecting claims and reporting on risks as incidental to his main practice. Another and in many instances the most important reason lies in the inadequacy of the compensation for the service rendered. The immediate remuneration is seldom commensurate with the amount of work involved in compiling a report and is, therefore, not conducive to thorough investigations and substantiation of opinion.

In opposition to these criticisms, many houses contend that, notwithstanding his local friendly relationships, the attorney specializing in commercial business can be relied upon for accuracy and completeness of statements, for, prompted by selfish motives, he is anxious to furnish reliable information in order to gain the good will of the house making the inquiry and thereby gain its collection business. The commission earned from collection work is more than sufficient to compensate the attorney for the effort expended in making a thorough investigation. Hence, many of the larger firms employ attorneys as trained credit investigators who have developed a highly efficient system for recording the data assembled. Reports rendered by these firms are necessarily very reliable.

Methods of compensation. Attorneys furnishing credit reports are paid either directly and immediately a small fee for each report or indirectly by the promise of, in return, whatever collection business the house may have in a given locality. As long as the inquiring house has some collections in the locality where the attorney is situated, the latter method of compensation is probably the most satisfactory, provided the claims are actually handed over in accordance with the promise made. When few collections are sent at long intervals, however, attorneys will be found loath to answer many inquiries. Still worse, the free report system is subject to much abuse, and many houses have taken advantage of the opportunity of securing gratis numerous reports from several attorneys in a given town, in return promising each whatever collection business it will have in the town. Obviously, the collections in any given community for one house can hardly be handled by more than one lawyer. Attorneys in some instances, by comparing notes, have discovered these flagrant abuses on the part of some unscrupulous credit men and have, therefore, refused to reply to inquiries or else have given offhand opinions without attempting to substantiate them.   Consequently, the reports were worth no more than the price paid for them.   These abuses also led to the adoption by some bar associations of a schedule of fixed rates for reporting services rendered.

Unless the attorney is actually engaged in making collections for the inquiring firm, it is by far more effectual to compensate him directly and in advance by enclosing a fee, when requesting an investigation, commensurate with the effort used in the process.

BANKS AS
CREDIT REPORTERS

Unlike a mercantile creditor, a commercial bank normally deals with manufacturers, wholesalers, retailers, and other businessmen engaged in various lines of trade and types of operation.   Consequently, it has credit information that is of value to many mercantile creditors.   That fact is fully appreciated by the latter, and hence they attempt to secure it through trade group meetings at which bank credit managers are present or directly on an individual basis in reply to a specific inquiry.

Nature and adequacy of bank credit reports. Many mercantile creditors tend to be critical of the credit information furnished by banks in reply to an inquiry, regarding it as inadequate and generally unsatisfactory.   One alleged reason for this condition is that credit inquiries are handled by banks, purely as an accommodation, by untrained and subordinate personnel.   Another is based on the belief that the bank would make a flattering report regardless of the actual circumstances in order to protect its own position.   A third reason is that the bank withholds much of the information it has because it deems it strictly confidential; peculiar to its operation as in securing guarantees, endorsements, or collateral as security, which, if divulged to mercantile creditors, might be misunderstood to the debtor's detriment; or because it feels that mercantile creditors, having less at stake and operating on a wider margin, do not need so much detail.   Notwithstanding the questionable validity of all points mentioned above, it appears reasonable to expect banks to furnish more complete information than a mere conventional expression, if the reciprocal advantages arising from interchange of credit information are to be fully enjoyed by all parties concerned.   To improve this condition, much can be done by both the inquiring party and the responding bank.

In requesting credit information from a bank, the inquirer should be careful to obtain the correct name of the bank and the particular branch, if any, with which the subject of inquiry does business, together with the exact name under which the bank account is kept and the subject's full address. Furthermore, each request for information should be specific as to the object and scope of the inquiry, the approximate amount of credit under consideration, and should include the references given. At the same time it must be realized that the bank is best suited to give certain kinds of information not available elsewhere and that even such information can be given only in an approximate manner. Such information is best restricted to the following:

1 Age of the account or length of experience with it.

2 Average balances, at least whether in the low, medium, or high figures of a specified number of digits. Thus an average deposit balance in the low five figures would probably refer to an amount of $12,000 or $13,000.

3 Maximum credit accommodations extended recently, as in the past year or two, also stated as in the low, medium, or high of so-many figures.

4 Condition of present loans, whether secured, unsecured, endorsed, etc., and in approximately what amounts.

5 Whether loan experience has been satisfactory.

6 A definite or general expression of opinion regarding the risk.

Interpretation of bank credit reports. Even the limited information supplied by a commercial bank in reply to an inquiry may be of inestimable value when correctly interpreted. This is often facilitated by knowledge of the responding bank's size, operation, and attitude and by familiarity with the terminology in which a bank is wont to express itself. For example, when a bank replies that an account is small, fair, large, medium, or liberal, the inquiring party, in order to interpret the characterization properly, must know something of the size of the bank and the character of the account as already indicated in another connection. The word "liberal" is rather vague but, when used, is considered complimentary to the depositor; when a bank says of its borrower "good for moderate credit," it means that limited credit is permissible. "Good for reasonable credit" indicates some confidence in the account, but bears watching. The expression "good for his requirements" usually indicates that the customer is willing and able to take care of whatever he asks and that he is not likely to ask for credit beyond a reasonable amount.

Sometimes a bank may include in its report fairly exact information as to cash balances maintained by the account as of a certain date and notes payable to it at the time of the report. Both these items are useful, first, in gauging the subject under consideration, and second, for verifying similar items appearing on the financial statement that may have been obtained concerning the subject of the report. In any event, it should be borne in mind that much valuable information can be gained by cultivating a knack for reading between the lines of a bank credit report.

Cost of bank report. The matter of charging for bank credit reports is one of variable policy among banks. In the past, a nominal charge was occasionally made by commercial banks, mainly to forestall abuse of the privilege and to cover so-called "out-of-pocket" expense. This was especially true of banks in smaller communities, which more often were plied with inquiries than they sought such information for their own lending purposes. Increasingly, however, it is recognized by banks that the supplying of credit information is a practice of reciprocity and as a result no charge is made by them. Reports are made as conscientiously to inquirers who do not send a fee as to those who do.

QUESTIONS AND PROBLEMS

1 How do you explain the fact that wholesalers and manufacturers normally require that their salesmen submit credit reports concerning their customers?

2 If you were a salesman employed primarily on a commission basis, what would be your attitude toward the preparation of credit reports on your customers? Why?

3 Assuming that the attitude of the company's salesmen is unfavorable toward the matter of furnishing credit reports, what could the credit manager do to overcome the objections against the practice?

4 What factors tend to determine the value of a salesman's credit report?

5 If you were to prepare a report form to be used by salesmen in credit reporting, what factors would you consider in its construction?

6 In the event that a salesman's report on a given credit risk disagrees with a report secured on the same subject from an attorney, which of the two reports should be regarded as more authentic and of greater value? Give reasons for your answer.

7 Under what circumstances is it advisable to obtain an attorney report on a credit risk?

8 "The salesman's worth to his house is based not upon the volume of orders he secures, but upon the net profit he produces for his firm." Show how a credit manager can use this statement in making a friend and ally of a salesman.

9 In what respects do attorney reports differ from reports generally submitted by salesmen? In what ways are they similar?

10 Account for the fact that banks normally require more detailed information about credit risks than do mercantile organizations.

11 Assuming that banks do have detailed information about the various subjects investigated, why are bank reports often regarded as unsatisfactory?

12 The Blank company manufactured a novelty item that required wide distribution.

In the early period of its growth it confined its operations to the larger cities of the New England and Middle Atlantic states. Here it has developed good banking connections. In addition to Dun & Bradstreet, the company also used attorneys specializing in commercial work as well as banks for credit information.

With the upswing of the business cycle, increased competition, and a growing style consciousness, the company began to expand its market into the smaller towns and into the West. As the business in the new sections increased, the credit manager felt that the sources of credit information previously used were inadequate and proposed that the salesmen of the company be required to submit reports on new accounts as well as on delinquent customers. The sales manager objected, stating that the type of salesman required to sell a line of novelties was not the type that would be able and willing to prepare useful credit reports. Besides, all their time was needed for selling work.

a Explain the basis, if any, for the sales manager's position.

b Would you advise the use of salesmen in this instance? Why or why not?

c If the salesmen were utilized as proposed by the credit manager, would it be necessary to give them any special training? Give reasons.

d What method of compensation would you use if salesmen were required to furnish credit reports?

e Assume that the sales manager's position is tenable in this case; what other sources of credit information can still be tapped by the credit department?

CHAPTER NINETEEN

the personal interview
and miscellaneous sources
of credit information

Much knowledge is needed to draw the line sharply between calculated risks that are acceptable and those that should be rejected or accepted with reservations. Such knowledge is also needed from time to time after an account has been placed on the books. A great deal of this knowledge can be gained from the sources already treated up to this point. Notwithstanding that, it is frequently desirable to establish and maintain a certain degree of personal contact with customers and prospects and to supplement such material with information readily obtainable from a variety of sources bearing on the specific risk or on the underlying conditions—general or particular.

THE PERSONAL
INTERVIEW

Obviously, personal contact is effected through a personal interview, which may be conducted in the office of the selling firm or at the bank where a loan is to be made or at the customer's (borrower's), or prospect's, place of business.

Interviewing customer or borrower in office of selling firm or at the bank. Frequently, when a merchant or other prospective business buyer is seeking a line of credit, he or his representative will visit the credit manager of the supply house or manufacturer with a view toward establishing satisfactory arrangements.   In the case of commercial banks, borrowers usually follow this practice.   Here is an invaluable opportunity of which no credit manager can afford not to avail himself fully.   By displaying a friendly attitude rather than that of a cross-examiner, he may lead the prospective customer to express himself on market conditions, general trend of prices, styles, and other factors directly affecting his particular line of trade.   It should be the aim of the credit manager so to steer the conversation during such an interview as to reveal readily the degree of prudence, judgment, and system exercised in anticipating the demand of his clientele and in the general operation of his business. He will thus discover whether the applicant is a shrewd buyer and so selects his goods as to insure their salability, or whether he is uninformed and buys injudiciously and indiscriminately, in which case he is apt to overstock with a poorly selected line of goods.   Once taken into the credit manager's confidence by an attitude of friendliness and candor, the applicant will talk frankly and freely, thereby revealing facts in regard to his capital responsibility, organization, location, present circumstances, and prospects of his business enterprise.

To avoid any possible resentment against having their credit questioned, it is the practice of many houses to ask out-of-town customers calling on the firm to meet "our Mr. Smith," instead of proposing to meet "our credit man."   The credit manager not being mentioned, the customer will often converse frankly and freely, and thus give all the information that may be required.   It should be borne in mind at all times that entering into details should be avoided during the first or any personal interview at the seller's office, for that sort of information can be secured through the usual channels.   The chief object of an interview is to permit the credit manager to size up the risk, to form a personal impression of his character and business competency, to serve as a basis for future correspondence, and to enable him to interpret more skillfully the information contained in the reports of mercantile agencies and credit bureaus.

Interview at customer's, or prospect's, place of business. In the case of large accounts which present difficult decisions, it is well worthwhile for the credit manager to visit the customer, or prospect, at his place of business. Although it is more or less difficult and, particularly in large establishments, well-nigh impossible to meet all the customers personally, it is nevertheless essential that the credit manager arrange periodically to make credit trips around his trade area, calling on those risks concerning whose credit responsibility he is seriously in doubt.

In visiting the customer's place of business, whether it be a retail establishment, a wholesale house, or a manufacturing plant, the credit man can acquire certain data which are not obtainable through any other channel. He can thus form a personal impression of the customer's methods of doing business, general proficiency, location, arrangement of stock, and many other factors. In addition to this, the credit manager has the invaluable opportunity of sizing up the risk as to his character and business ability, probably to better advantage than when meeting him at the credit man's office, for here the risk is seen in his setting, as he naturally appears from day to day, and is, therefore, likely to be devoid of all artificial and assumed characteristics.

Traveling credit representatives. Some of the larger houses find it advantageous to employ credit department representatives. These are allotted specific territories, the same as salesmen, which they are required to cover periodically with a view to inquiring into the credit standing of applicants and of such old customers as directed by the credit department. Most of the points covered by them in their investigations parallel those secured by traveling salesmen, save for the thoroughness with which the more qualified and better equipped credit specialist conducts his inquiries. In addition, these investigators inquire into the financial condition and other relevant factors determining the customer's debt-paying power.

It is needless to say that the scope of a given investigation and the degree of thoroughness to be exercised in its conduct vary considerably with the relative seriousness of the situation involved. If serious weaknesses are disclosed, the credit department representative may feel warranted even in examining the books of account. In other instances it may suffice to obtain the latest available statement of financial condition or merely to discuss conditions in general. No set rule can be profitably laid down as a guide to a determination of the scope of such an investigation, since the extent of any inquiry will necessarily have to be governed by the circumstances of the particular case.

Many houses follow the policy of sending representatives to visit large accounts which involve some serious doubt or difficulties, even though no special traveling credit investigators are employed. The effect of such a visit may be to lead to a closer and friendlier relationship based on a better mutual understanding between buyer and seller and thus result in increased volume of business, or else it may lead to a decision involving the necessity of closing the account either immediately or gradually and thereby avoiding an otherwise inevitable loss.

MISCELLANEOUS SOURCES OF INFORMATION

Among the miscellaneous sources of credit information are those, like insurance companies, corporation manuals, and the *Credit Manual of Commercial Laws,* that have a bearing on individual risks, and the numerous publications which contain information that has a bearing on general credit conditions.   The more important of these are briefly treated in the pages that follow.

Insurance companies. In accepting any credit risk there is a contingent and uncalculable hazard in the occurrence of circumstances against which one usually protects himself with insurance.   Insurance companies are increasingly cooperating with mercantile creditors in furnishing them information as to the nature and amount of insurance which given risks carry.   A brief résumé on this point is furnished also in some financial statements, wherein the amount of insurance on inventory is listed.   A relevant point is touched also in the Dun & Bradstreet, Inc., report on fire experiences and fire hazards of the risk.   None of these, however, furnishes the degree of detail that is obtainable directly from some insurance companies and their agents.

Insurance statement form. The information which these organizations are prepared to supply is included in what is known as an insurance statement form.   This is usually prepared by the agent of the insurance company for each of his clients, and it consists of an analysis of the insurance program of the individual or his business.   The types and amounts of insurance carried, deficiencies noted, and recommendations made for proper coverage are the subjects usually discussed.   The pertinence of these items to credit evaluation is clearly evident.   If a risk carries insufficient fire, liability, or income insurance, his debt-paying capacity may be cut short without notice or prediction.   In some industries and trades this is of more importance than in others.   Moreover, the insurance program is also a function of other factors, such as the nature of the physical plant, the number of employees, the admission of the public to the premises, and the like.   It is improbable that the decision to grant or to withhold credit would often be based solely upon the insurance carried, any more than upon any other single factor, but it is a significant aspect of the business which is inadequately presented by other sources previously referred to.

Insurance statement forms may be obtained directly from company offices or from agents representing them.   Such analyses are prepared and already available in most cases.   In other instances, insurance companies encourage cooperation between credit managers and insurance agents and brokers, and the opinions of the latter group are sought regarding the adequacy of a risk's insurance program.   In still other instances, credit managers establish their contact with insurance representatives through reference names requested of the credit applicant.   He is asked to give the name of the insurance company or agent who handles the greater part of his business and then that individual is requested to furnish the information desired.

Corporation manuals and services. Concerns which deal with railroads, public utilities, industrial corporations, financial companies, real estate corporations, and municipalities large enough to enjoy a fairly general distribution of their securities will find a substantial amount of valuable information in the various investment and statistical manuals. While these manuals are intended primarily to facilitate the work of the investor, they can be very useful as sources of credit information.   These manuals are practically unabridged encyclopedias of financial and statistical information covering a wide list of individual corporations and political units.   The data in the annual volumes are brought up to date from time to time by supplementary sheets.

The publishers of the financial manuals are Standard & Poor's Corporation, Moody's Investors Service, and the Value Line Investment Survey.

Standard & Poor's Corporation, a subsidiary of McGraw-Hill Book Company, prepares detailed descriptions of the financial condition of the most important corporations.   This information is issued in many different publications including its six-volume reference manuals, *Standard Corporation Records,* which are kept up to date by daily supplements.   Among the other publications of Standard & Poor's Corporation are *The Outlook,* a weekly magazine which reviews market conditions and gives investment recommendations for specific companies, the monthly *Stock Guide,* a pocket-size handbook containing stock ratings and facts on many companies, and *Trade and Security Statistics,* which presents information on past trends and indexes for general business and for the various industries.

Moody's Investors Service, a subsidiary of Dun & Bradstreet,

Inc., also publishes weekly and monthly summaries about industries and individual companies. It probably is best known for its manuals issued annually for companies in the following classifications: industrials, public utilities, transportation companies, financial institutions, and governments. These reference manuals are kept up to date by the issuance of biweekly reports.

The Value Line Investment Survey publishes information on approximately 1,125 companies in 60 industries. This information, including a rating for each company, is published quarterly. In addition, interim reports are issued on any news developments between the time of the regular quarterly reports.

These financial manuals, with their supplements, cover nearly all the available information pertaining to the more important corporations. The information contained for practically each corporation listed other than governments is as follows:

1 A history of the company, its growth and development
2 Territory or market served
3 A description of the property, physical plant, and capacity
4 A description of the company's products
5 Operating statistics
6 Income account data, so far as they are available
7 Balance sheet data
8 Financial policies
9 A description of all security issues
10 Range of market prices of the company's securities
11 Exchanges listed on, if any
12 A list of officers and directors

In addition to the manuals published, these organizations supply many other types of services dealing with market and investment information. Most of them, however, are of little utility for credit work.

Every credit man dealing with railroads, public utilities, or industrial corporations of some size should have at his command at least one of the services referred to, for important information can thus be obtained in convenient form. Nothing more fully reflects a corporation's status than its growth in earning capacity, dividend record and policy, and its comparative financial statement. All these facts and many others are made readily available for the command of the alert and sophisticated credit grantor.

Credit Manual of Commercial Laws. No credit manager's office is complete without this valuable annual publication of the National Association of Credit Management. The *Credit Manual of Commercial Laws* is a condensed and up-to-date reference work, containing the gist of state and Federal legal enactments pertaining to credit matters and some controlling court decisions bearing on them, specimens of various credit instruments, a discussion of terms of payment in commercial transactions, and some feature articles on subjects of general significance to credit managers. It is one of the greatest credit department facilities. Questions frequently arise in analyzing and checking credits which are quickly and explicitly answered by this publication; in a word, it is a handbook which no credit manager can afford to be without.

General credit conditions. A knowledge of the character, capacity, and capital of a credit risk, which might be obtained from the sources discussed elsewhere in this book, is an insufficient basis for the intelligent management of credit in modern business. A fourth credit C, namely, conditions of the economy pertinent to credit, must be taken into account as much as the individual qualifications of the subject risk. The notion that an applicant's creditworthiness may be judged solely upon his own merits is an outmoded concept and one which has never really coincided with the nature of business experience. Beyond the administrative reach or control of any businessman lie influences of the community which have a direct bearing upon his ability to operate his business successfully and which, therefore, must enter into a credit manager's appraisal of his accounts. Every credit risk must be seen in the setting of not merely his particular business venture but also in terms of the general economy and the specific external factors bearing on it. Scientific credit management thus requires a knowledge of the conditions of the general economy and those special phases of it that more directly affect a given business or industry.

It is not easy, however, to appraise general business and economic conditions that affect credit in general and certain types in particular. Such conditions are a matter of relationships, motives, and human endeavors; they must be discerned in the factors that comprise them, which, in turn, have many and different facets. For example, price trends and the degree of competition in an industry determine somewhat the rate of business failures and, consequently, the precariousness of credit risks. The volume of business activity, shown in indexes of production, sales, and consumption expenditures, indicates something of the demands which both industrial and household buyers make for credit. Corporate profits, taxes, and dividends are a reflection of the general business capacity to meet these demands. Credit extended and outstanding during a given period, as well as its rate of turnover, bespeak the character of collective business judgment and the condition of the general economy from that standpoint.   Governmental policies, both foreign and domestic, the pressures of labor and other organized groups, population shifts, savings, optimism, business ingenuity, and the like are other typical factors underlying general credit or business conditions.   These, therefore, are some of the points about which credit management must seek information to support its judgment of individual risks.

The sources of information about credit and business conditions are to be found in numerous general and special publications.   Some of these, published both by governmental agencies and by private publishers, are briefly discussed below, with emphasis upon those characteristics that are of particular importance for credit purposes.

Survey of Current Business.   Published monthly by the U.S. Department of Commerce, the *Survey of Current Business* is one of the more useful and timely compilations of indicators of current business and economic conditions.   Its content is both statistical and interpretive and its data are drawn from the files of information gathered by the U.S. Departments of Commerce and Labor, as well as from other governmental collectors of primary statistics.

Characteristic of its interpretive features is a leading article in each issue reviewing the business situation.   This is based upon the statistics that follow the section of articles and is subdivided with headings corresponding to the principal types of statistical information presented. Among the topics usually included in the survey of the business situation are analysis of general economic conditions, prices, sales, wages, incomes, inventories, capital outlays, employment, construction, production trends, new orders, and consumer credit.   Other timely articles of an economic nature are also published.

Another feature of this publication consists of articles useful to management.   In them are analyzed in detail various important economic developments, and the relations of these developments to business and government operations are shown.   Also included in these issues are articles dealing with such subjects as business financing, distribution of income payments, business turnover and causes of failures, regional department store sales patterns, and international transactions of the United States.

The section devoted to monthly business statistics includes data of interest to all businessmen; most of it has either a direct or indirect bearing upon credit.   Each month current data are published along with those for each of the preceding twelve months.

For a period of years to date, a Supplement to the *Survey of Current Business* has been published biennially.   In this Supplement are included among others all the statistical series covered by the monthly publication, annual averages being given for each year to the beginning of the series, which for most of them is 1909, 1913, 1919, 1929, or 1939, and monthly averages for each of the most recent 4 years. It is thus possible through the various Supplements to trace the business indicators contained therein on a monthly basis for many years past. Finally, a weekly Supplement, presenting tables and charts of weekly data of the same type for the more important series, provides a medium for advancing the information beyond the last monthly issue and considerably in advance of their publication in the next such monthly issue.

Among the other special features of this publication are the so-called "Annual Review" number comprising the February issue and the National Income number making up the July issue. In addition to the national income data contained in the July issue of the *Survey of Current Business,* where the data on Gross National Product and its components as well as data on expenditures and other items are given for some four years, special publications on national income with much more detail are issued as supplements from time to time.

Of the data published in the *Survey of Current Business* and Supplements thereto, the ones that are perhaps of most use in credit management are those that are in the nature of general business indicators or that pertain to the business population, commodity prices, prices received and paid by farmers, retail prices, wholesale prices, consumers' price index, construction and real estate, domestic trade, employment conditions and wages, finance, and industrial statistics. Of growing importance are some of the data on Gross National Product and income, especially those dealing with expenditures by consumers (by type of product), business, government, etc., in forecasting general business conditions and the business of the individual enterprise.

The Federal Reserve Bulletin. Another organ, which is semigovernmental in nature and which contains information of value to credit managers, is the *Federal Reserve Bulletin,* a monthly publication issued by the Board of Governors of the Federal Reserve System. Although designed primarily to depict money and banking conditions of the nation, because of the diversity of the data included in it and the accessibility of certain types of information to Federal Reserve Banks, this publication has a unique place among the economic and business periodicals. Some of its statistical content is compiled originally by other governmental agencies, and in a few instances by private agencies, but for the most part it represents the work of the research facilities of the Federal Reserve System. The *Bulletin* is unlike the *Survey of Current Business,* although both carry some identical indexes and tabulations, in that the *Bulletin's* data are furnished for a number of years whereas those of the *Survey* are characteristically descriptive of current business. Historical figures together with descriptive text for many of the series presented in the monthly bulletin are included in the base book, *Banking and Monetary Statistics*, also issued by the Board of Governors. These publications are supplemented by a *Chart Book*, by the *Annual Report of the Board of Governors of the Federal Reserve System*, and by numerous releases.

Federal Reserve Chart Book. Based upon data assembled by the Board of Governors of the Federal Reserve System, which are published monthly in the *Federal Reserve Bulletin*, and upon other statistics compiled by the U.S. Departments of Commerce, Labor, and Treasury, the Comptroller of Currency, and the Federal Deposit Insurance Corporation, the *Chart Book* is usually an 80-page compendium of charts depicting various phases of current business conditions. They are intended to be used along with, and to be supplemented periodically by, current additions. Charts of particular interest to businessmen and credit managers are those on the following items:

1 Industrial production
2 Manufacturers' orders, shipments, and inventories
3 Employment in nonagricultural establishments
4 Corporate profits, taxes, and dividends
5 Loans and investments of all commercial banks
6 Money rates
7 Gross national product
8 Wholesale prices
9 Consumers' prices
10 Prices paid and received by farmers
11 Personal income, consumption, and savings
12 Consumer instalment credit outstanding
13 Liquid assets ownership by individuals and businesses
14 Stock prices and trading
15 Labor force, employment, and unemployment
16 Department store sales and stocks
17 Weekly series on business activity, by industries

United States Census. Typical of the information of value in credit management coming from the U.S. Bureau of the Census is that found in Volumes I and II of the *Sixteenth Census of the United States: 1939*, pertaining to retail and wholesale trade, and the similar types of information for the year 1948 and later census years. In the volume which relates to retail business is shown the number of stores reporting all cash business, as contrasted with those making both cash and credit sales. Stores are classified by kinds of business and by geographic location, and the ratio of cash to credit business is reported. Accounts and notes receivable outstanding at the end of the census year are also stated. For wholesalers, sales made on cash and credit bases are analyzed for service and limited function wholesalers and for manufacturers' sales branches. Distinctions are made also between cash sales and the credit transactions on various terms of sale. Receivables carried on the books are reported and receivables to sales ratios are furnished.

Credit periodicals. In this category may be included a substantial number of monthly magazines published by associations in the field of credit or by others serving the interests of credit management. In the former should be mentioned *Credit and Financial Management,* a monthly publication of the National Association of Credit Management, and *The Credit World,* the official monthly periodical of the International Consumer Credit Association. Noteworthy of the latter type is *Dun's Review,* the monthly publication by Dun & Bradstreet, Inc., which, among other things, places emphasis on the trend of business and business failures.

QUESTIONS AND PROBLEMS

1 What can be added to information obtained from other possible sources by holding an interview with a mercantile credit applicant? Is it better to hold such a personal interview at the seller's place of business or at the applicant's location and why?

2 Are personal interviews limited in value in connection with an appraisal of a first order or are they even of greater value in connection with an established account? Explain.

3 What additional benefits are to be gained other than gaining information about a risk from a personal interview?

4 What is the significance of a risk's insurance program to a prospective credit grantor?

5 What interest has an insurance company or agent in supplying credit managers with insurance statement forms?

6 Why is the Federal government such a large contributor of data disclosing the nature of current and historical economic conditions?

7 What are the unique and distinguishing features of each of the following: *Survey of Current Business, Federal Reserve Bulletin, Credit and Financial Management?*

8 To what sources would you go to obtain current information regarding each of the following conditions: employment, department store credit sales, interest rates, price changes, current practices in the use of credit and collection letters, consumer loans, physical production in leading industries?

9 Outline the points of major importance in the discharge of credit and collection duties on which reliable data can be obtained from the *Credit Manual of Commercial Laws,* published annually by the National Association of Credit Management.

10 Consult one of the corporation manuals at the library. From it secure the names of three mercantile establishments, giving the information which the manual has about each of the three that would be of value to a credit manager.

CHAPTER TWENTY

financial statements
as a source of
credit information

Accounting data in the form of "financial statements" are probably the most useful source of information about a business firm seeking to buy on credit or to borrow money for the enterprise. These statements have become progressively more significant since the 1920's as the techniques for their analysis and interpretation have become more sophisticated and of more widespread use.

General nature of financial statements. Two of the most common financial statements are the balance sheet, or statement of financial position, and the income statement. Technically and as generally treated by accountants, the former is but a photograph of the financial condition or *position* of the particular business at a given moment, setting forth in some classified manner its assets, liabilities, and owners' equity or net worth.   It is a cross section of the concern's financial standing at a given time, when the business is at a temporary standstill, and thus depicts a *static* condition.   The information contained therein may be presented in a general or highly detailed manner, and the statement may be condensed, consolidated, single, or comparative.

In using financial statements for judging the nature and quality of a risk, the credit manager is also interested in knowing something of the *dynamic* phase of the enterprise.   This is reflected by a form commonly known as the income or profit and loss statement, also frequently referred to as the operating statement or the statement of earnings.   In a sense, this statement presents a moving picture of the business, showing in detail or summary form the sales or income, cost of goods sold, gross profit, operating expenses, net profit or loss, and certain other items relating to surplus and to changes to be made in the net worth.   By showing what has transpired during the period covered, it gives the better view of the earning and debt-paying potentialities of the business, which can be but inferred in part from a comparative statement of assets, liabilities, and net worth for the beginning and end of such period.

The profit and loss statement, or at least the major items included therein, helps to vitalize the information contained in the balance sheet proper.   By means of this information it becomes possible not only to ascertain the value of certain items in the balance sheet more accurately but to judge as well the efficiency with which such items are being managed.   It is thus possible to discover, even from a single statement, i.e., from one covering but a single period such as a year, not only the capital position of the risk but its capacity as well.   In fact, the two statements may be regarded as twin financial reports, one showing the *action* that has taken place during the period covered by it and the other the *result* of such action when added to the position as of the beginning of such period.   Consequently, proper use of the two statements together so enhances their value that the total result is substantially greater than when each is analyzed and interpreted separately.

When a credit manager requests a financial statement from a risk, he expects much more than a skeletal picture of its capital structure. All carefully designed financial statement forms indicate that fact by providing for certain breakdowns of financial statement information, by requiring answers to questions that throw additional light on the items, and, above all, by providing spaces for either a complete profit and loss statement or for some of the major items normally included in it.   In this discussion, therefore, the term financial statement is used in the broader, nontechnical, and practical manner in which it is employed by credit managers. In a word, what credit managers want from a financial statement are answers to two basic questions: (1) How does the risk stand? What is its financial condition? and (2) What happened during the last accounting period and perhaps even in preceding ones to bring it to its present condition?

Reasons for requiring financial statements from credit risks. From the standpoint of the user, one of the most valuable contributions of the statement is in showing with considerable clarity the probable ability of the prospective debtor to discharge his obligations at maturity. Because of the keen competition and attending close margins in most fields of business, successful businessmen do not extend credit without information that tends to disclose an applicant's financial responsibility with almost mathematical precision. Accordingly, from the standpoint of the credit grantor, a signed financial statement is extremely beneficial. It helps him to determine whether the risk has sufficient realizable assets in his business to warrant the belief in his ability to meet his obligations at maturity, if willing to do so.

Also of assistance to the user is the evidence which the financial statement gives of the management efficiency and the character of the maker. While a financial statement indicates primarily the financial condition of the maker, it throws light at the same time on three of the C's of credit, character, capacity, and capital, but in reverse order of emphasis. Its principal bearing is on capital, or the financial condition of the risk as evidenced by the value of each item analyzed. Next, the financial statement contributes to the credit analyst's knowledge of the capacity, or management ability, of the maker. Third, it invariably reflects on the character, or business integrity, of the risk by the presence or absence of any attempt to manipulate the data.

Finally, by requiring signed financial statements, creditors may protect themselves against possible fraud by the makers. Laws have been enacted in many states making it a crime for a person or firm to submit a false statement in writing for the purpose of obtaining credit. Hence, the debtor who contemplates perpetrating a fraud will hesitate to issue a statement for fear of prosecution under these laws.

Consequently, knowing the exact financial condition of the customer or applicant, the credit grantor can exercise better judgment in fixing a credit limit and in the granting of requests for renewals and extensions. Furthermore, the incompetent risks are gradually weeded out, since they are generally unable to furnish satisfactory financial statements. Laxity on the part of credit grantors in requiring statements of such risks obviously leads to the perpetuation of such enterprises in business to the detriment of the sellers.

Reasons for submitting financial statements. Actual or prospective creditors are not the only ones to benefit from the use of financial statements submitted by credit risks, for many benefits are also to be derived by their makers. Reputation or character, although an extremely important factor in credit extensions, is nevertheless not the only factor. The creditor is a contributor of capital and becomes, in a sense, a partner of the debtor and, as such, has a perfect right to demand complete information on the debtor's business resources at all times. Hence a businessman who desires to serve his own interests should recognize that, under prevailing business conditions, the most effective way of proving his basis for credit is through his willingness to submit financial statements of his firm.

One of the beneficial effects which the practice of requiring financial statements has on the debtor is derived from his realization of the necessity for making a good showing. Because of the material influence of the statement upon his credit standing, the debtor is forced to maintain his business in good condition, and prior to entering any hazardous undertaking he is apt to reflect on the probable effect of the outcome of such venture on the appearance of his balance sheet.

A second advantage to the debtor lies in the necessity for keeping books of record. Incompetence is due in large measure not to lack of ability but to lack of information. Lack of information in the retail trade can hardly be due to anything but inferior bookkeeping methods. What they need most is accounts which actually account. Asking for financial statements will encourage and stimulate better methods of accounting and tend to make the conduct of business more scientific. It may also reduce the temptation of a debtor to overexpand.

Moreover, as already pointed out, the probable effect of the practice in requiring statements will be ultimately to weed out the incompetent traders to the benefit of the honest and capable merchants, thereby putting competition on a sound basis. The incompetent merchant frequently offers the meanest sort of competition. When in need of funds, he is apt to undersell the honest and capable dealer, even when required to sell below cost. The inability of these traders to submit satisfactory statements will, through the consequent refusal of credit accommodations, tend toward their complete elimination from the field of business.

Finally, an exact knowledge of a debtor's circumstances, as afforded by the statement of his financial condition, results in the fixing of definite lines of credit which the creditor may prudently give and the debtor may prudently receive. The disaster to the buyer through accepting too much credit may be even greater than the disaster to the seller through giving too much credit.   Statements are, therefore, protective to debtor and creditor alike.   In addition they tend to establish confidence in the buyer, whose trade is on that account solicited by the best houses.

Methods of obtaining statements. Financial statements may be obtained directly from the risk or indirectly through mercantile agencies, some interchange bureaus, and trade credit offices.   Probably most creditors rely on statements obtained through the indirect method.   These are valuable, indeed, and the various agencies are exerting their efforts to secure and incorporate in their reports more complete and more meaningful financial data.   Nevertheless, there are some shortcomings, as financial data thus obtained are often inadequate for careful and intelligent analysis.   At times they are in the form of estimates, perhaps unsigned when given by the makers or too old to be really useful.   To be sure, much improvement is to be noted in all these respects.

All in all, however, it is best to secure a financial statement directly from the risk to be used solely or in connection with those obtained indirectly.   To begin with, it is likely to be fresher, more up to date than when procured otherwise.   It may be more complete, for the maker is generally more conscientious than a somewhat disinterested collector of such information, especially when he is conscious of the specific purpose for which it is being prepared and the immediate use that is to be made of it.   It is likely to be more accurate because such a statement is generally signed and the maker, in consideration of his legal obligations and fear of consequences, endeavors to avoid misrepresentation.   It will probably be in the form in which the information is wanted, for in most instances of direct solicitation of statements a form is supplied by the creditor.   Forms may differ but slightly, but by supplying one's own it is possible to obtain the facts which most nearly answer the questions an analyst requires in studying and analyzing the statement. Furthermore, it may contain information of a special character, disclosing more fully than is done by a statement applicable to all industries the condition of the firm in question.   A profit and loss statement is also more often submitted when the forms used are supplied by the creditor.

In spite of the disadvantages incident to the indirect mode of obtaining statements, relatively few creditors resort to the direct method, except when in doubt as to the debtor's standing and when the statements secured from indirect sources prove unsatisfactory and inadequate. Some houses, including banks, generally follow the practice of requiring statements from all new credit seekers.   Other concerns require statements from all or most of their debtors at regular intervals, usually every year.   This practice serves to impress the debtor with the vigilance of his creditors, thereby inducing him to measure up to their higher credit standards.

Forms of statements. In the light of the analysis which creditors increasingly make of financial statements, it is natural that the information desired from them should tend to become somewhat standardized. Experience has shown that in nearly all instances certain aspects of a concern's financial condition are more important than others; yet the same form of statement is not applicable to all firms and industries. Small organizations lack much of the detail essential to the analysis of larger corporate structures. Trades in which inventories are significant present a different financial picture from the service industries in which there may be no inventories. Similarly, the importance of real estate, accounts assigned, liabilities, insurance, and the like varies from case to case. Consequently, although certain types of information are essential to all analyses, the forms on which they are reported are different and varied.

Some statement forms are developed at the initiative of the creditor providing them for his customers and prospects. Other forms, suited to different lines of business, have been adopted and recommended by agencies which are instrumental in facilitating the exchange of financial information, such as Dun & Bradstreet, Inc. (see Fig. 15-1), the National Association of Credit Management (see Fig. 20-1), and the Federal Reserve Banks. Those of the National Association of Credit Management especially, are widely used, particularly by the smaller concerns. Forms used by larger organizations are also often adaptations of these forms.

An examination of a large number of forms used by houses operating on a substantial scale reflects a special effort on their part to simplify the form so as to contain only the most important items. Experience has shown that many merchants are discouraged at the outset and either refuse entirely to submit a statement or else omit many points if the form they are required to fill out is too intricate and burdened with all sorts of details. Many houses have, therefore, concluded that it is possible to ask for too much information and have simplified their forms accordingly, so as not to make them too comprehensive but to cover merely the essential and vital points.

Composition of a balance sheet. All statements of financial position consist of assets, liabilities, and owners' equity. The fact that the assets of the business, on the one hand, are always balanced by the liabilities and net worth, on the other, and that the arrangement is often such that the asset figures are on the left side of the sheet on which the report is made and the others are on the right, gives point to the designation of such a report as a *balance sheet*. The assets are the proper-

Form 6W

Date_____19_____

FINANCIAL STATEMENT OF_____

Kind of Business_____   Address_____

At Close of Business on_____19___ City_____   State_____

ISSUED TO_____ ←◀ { Name of firm asking for statement

(THIS FORM APPROVED AND PUBLISHED BY NATIONAL ASSOCIATION OF CREDIT MANAGEMENT)

For the purpose of obtaining merchandise from you on credit, or for the extension of credit, we make the following statement in writing, intending that you should rely thereon respecting our exact financial condition.
(PLEASE ANSWER ALL QUESTIONS. WHEN NO FIGURES ARE INSERTED, WRITE WORD "NONE")

ASSETS	Dollars	Cents	LIABILITIES	Dollars	Cents
Cash In Bank			Accounts Payable (for Merchandise)		
On Hand			Notes & Acceptances Payable for Merchandise		
Accounts Receivable			Owe to _____ Bank		
(Amt. 60 Days Past Due $_____)			(When Due_____Secured) (Unsecured)		
(Amt. Sold or Pledged $_____)			Income Taxes. Accrued		
Notes and Trade Acceptances Receivable			Other Taxes, Including Sales Taxes. Accrued		
(Amt. Sold or Pledged $_____)			Interest. Accrued		
Merchandise Inventory. Not on Consignment or			Rental. Payrolls, etc.. Accrued		
Conditional Sale, at Cost or Market whichever is lower			Payables to Partners, Relatives		
(Amount Pledged $_____)			Other Current Liabilities (Describe)		
Other Current Assets (Describe)					
			TOTAL CURRENT LIABILITIES		
			Mortgage on Land and Buildings		
TOTAL CURRENT ASSETS			Chattel Mortgage on Mdse. or Equipment		
Land and Buildings (Depreciated Value)			Liens on Mdse. or Equipment		
Machinery, Fixtures and Equipment (Depreciated Value)			Other Liabilities. No Current (Describe)		
Due from Officers or Non-Customers					
Other Assets (Describe)			TOTAL LIABILITIES		
			Net Worth or { Capital $ / Surplus $ }		
TOTAL ASSETS			TOTAL NET WORTH AND LIABILITIES		

BE SURE TO ANSWER ALL THESE QUESTIONS

ANNUAL NET SALES	COST OF GOODS SOLD	GROSS PROFIT	OPERATING EXPENSE	NET PROFIT FOR YEAR (Before Federal Taxes)
$	$	$	$	$

		INSURANCE CARRIED	
Amount you are liable for as endorser, guarantor, surety $	What books of Account do you keep?	Fire	
Amount of delinquent taxes: Sales tax $____Income tax $	Date of latest inventory	Merchandise $	
		Furn. & Fixt. $	
Property tax $____Other taxes $	Date of latest audit	Building $	
Amount of merchandise held on consignment $	Title to business premises is in name of	Extended Coverage $	
		U & O $	
Amount of machinery or equipment held under lease $	If premises leased state annual rental	Liability	
		General $	
Amount of machinery or equipment under conditional sale $	Name of your bank(s)	Auto & Truck $	
		Burglary $	
Amount you pay per month on lease or conditional sale contract $		Life for Benefit of Business $	

SCHEDULE OF REAL ESTATE	TITLE IN WHOSE NAME	APPRAISED VALUE

BUY PRINCIPALLY FROM THE FOLLOWING FIRMS:		
NAMES	ADDRESSES	AMOUNT OWING

The statement above and on the back of this form has been carefully read by the undersigned (both the printed and written matter), and is, to my knowledge, in all respects complete, accurate and truthful. It discloses to you the true state of my (our) financial condition on the_____day of_____19____. Since that time there has been no material unfavorable change in my (our) financial condition, and if any such change takes place I (we) will give you notice. Until such notice is given, you are to regard this as a continuing statement. **The figures submitted are not estimated.** They have been taken from my (our) books and physical inventory taken as on date shown.

Name of Individual or Firm_____

If Partnership, Name Partners }
If Corporation, Name Officers } _____

How long established_____Previous business experience_____
_____Where_____

Date of Signing Statement_____Street_____City_____State_____

Witness_____   Signed by_____
Residence Address
of Witness_____   Title_____
50M-8-58

50M-2-60

figure 20-1. *One form of financial statement approved and published by the National Association of Credit Management.*

ties used in the operation of the business, while the liabilities are the claims against such assets held by outsiders known as creditors, and the equity, proprietorship, or net worth consists of the residual claims against the enterprise on the part of its owners or stockholders.

Assets. There are three general groups of assets, depending upon the manner in which they function within the business enterprise, as follows:

1. *Current assets* comprise those properties which are in the form of cash or are readily convertible into cash and which are to be used up in the course of normal business conduct within a relatively short period. In this category are included the following: cash, accounts receivable, notes and acceptances receivable, merchandise inventories, investments being held for temporary purposes, loan value of insurance carried on officers, and the like. The importance of these assets lies in the fact that because they are in the form of cash or readily and normally converted into cash in the current operation of the business they are available for the purpose of discharging liabilities incurred in current operations. On the other hand, some current assets are not expected to evolve into cash but represent prepayments, i.e., payments made in advance for values not yet fully used. Prepaid interest, taxes, insurance premiums, and stamps (postage and sales tax) are of this character. Such items are not intended ultimately to increase the cash item of the statement; nevertheless, the fact that these prepayments have been made lessens the withdrawals from cash on hand in the near future. In this fact, therefore, lies the relevance of such items to credit analysis, particularly when comparison is made between the statements of two firms, one making such prepayments and another showing a larger cash balance because it did not make similar prepayments. It is long-standing practice for such items not to be included in current assets, but the increasing tendency is for them to be so classified.

Current assets are sometimes divided by the credit analyst into "quick" assets, comprising cash, marketable government securities and receivables, and "all other" current assets. Even the "quick" assets are sometimes further divided into "quick current" and "slow current," such a division being made when the matter is carried to extremes or when the credit analyst "rides a hobby." Another division of current assets sometimes made, and one that has some validity, is into "working" assets that include cash, receivables, and merchandise inventory, as distinguished from such current assets as marketable government securities or other highly liquid investments of a temporary character. Potentially, however, all of these items are in the nature of "working" assets.

2. Fixed assets are permanent in nature, not subject to radical changes within short periods of time.   Land, buildings, equipment, machinery, fixtures, good will, patents, and trade-marks exemplify this class of properties.

3. A third group consists of *deferred charges,* sometimes called deferred assets.   These resemble prepayments in that they are an advance payment as, for example, bond discounts.   They are segregated, however, in that they do not usually constitute items that would otherwise be paid out of cash in the *near future.*   On the contrary, they more typically represent prepayments which mature over a long period and sometimes are an accounting device for delaying the entry of past expenditures into the operating statement until a future time, as is at times done with organization expense and some repair or modernization expenditures.

Liabilities. These consist of debts and obligations to others and are distinguished in analogous fashion to assets:

1. Current liabilities are those which mature within a year from date of the statement and must be paid promptly, usually out of current assets.   They ordinarily include accounts payable, notes payable, dividends declared but unpaid, taxes, and *accrued* expenses.   The last represent expenses that have been incurred during the period covered by the statement but the payment of which has been postponed to a later accounting period.   Among these accrued items are wages due and unpaid, rent, and interest.   While taxes are of the same essence, they should be shown separately because they are important.   It may be advisable to show separately employees' taxes withheld, Federal and state taxes on income, and other taxes.

2. Fixed liabilities, or long-term debts, consist of obligations which do not mature for a considerable time, usually not less than a year from date of statement.   This class includes all real estate and chattel mortgages, promissory notes falling due at a relatively distant future, and all kinds of bonded indebtedness exclusive of amounts payable within one year.

3. Reserves which are intended to indicate expected shrinkage in specified assets are properly shown in connection with the appropriate assets.   That is true of a reserve for doubtful accounts as a deduction from accounts receivable and of the various reserves for depreciation of fixed assets.   There are, however, some reserves like those for income taxes or for employee benefit plans which cannot be attributed to any particular asset item.   Such reserves are properly shown either in connection with other liabilities or in connection with surplus which is directly affected by them.

Net worth. This section consists of the various components of the owners' equity in the business. In the balance sheet of a firm operated as a partnership, the original investments of the partners may be shown separately from later investments accumulated through retained earnings. The balance sheet of a corporation should show the amount of the various types or classes of capital stock, retained earnings, and other ownership elements.

FALSE STATEMENT LEGISLATION

The significant role of financial statements in the granting of credit is indicated somewhat by the legal precautions which have been taken to make them a reliable source of credit information. This source has become so widely used that great numbers of credit managers employ it as highly indicative evidence of the condition of a credit customer, revealing aspects of his status which no other form of investigation properly discloses. Moreover, because the financial statement is susceptible of thorough analysis and meaningful interpretation, creditors are disposed to place credence upon its contents and the condition indicated by them.

Nevertheless, it is well recognized that statements may depict a business not as a tangible, concrete situation but rather as its managers conceive it. Even in sound accounting theory and practice there are various constructions which may be placed upon certain facts, and a statement may represent what its maker wishes it to do in the light of the *purpose for which it is intended.*

Beyond the realm of legitimate difference of opinion, which may be expressed in statements, lies a further area in which facts are sometimes intentionally distorted to convey erroneous impressions. The temptation so to misuse statements for gaining credit seems especially prevalent. It is for this reason, and simultaneously to safeguard the important uses of statements, that Federal and state laws alike hold certain abuses of statements to be a misdemeanor subject to criminal prosecution.

State laws. Practically every state has a statute, under which a person obtaining or attempting to obtain property by means of a false financial statement may be prosecuted. Such laws are commonly known as "False Pretense Statutes," which are part of the criminal, corporate, and penal codes of the various states. Under them, punishment is provided in the form of fines and/or imprisonment for a specified maximum period of time. In addition, of course, an injured creditor has recourse under the civil codes for damages caused by a false financial statement on the basis of which property was actually obtained.

The New York statute (Penal Law, Sec. 1293-b) is more or less typical of the false statement laws enacted in a majority of the populous commercial states.   It provides that any person

1 Who shall knowingly make or cause to be made, either directly or indirectly, or through any agency whatsoever, any false statement in writing, with intent that it shall be relied upon, respecting the financial condition, or means or ability to pay, of himself, or any other person, firm or corporation, in whom he is interested, or for whom he is acting, for the purpose of procuring in any form whatsoever, either the delivery of personal property, the payment of cash, the making of a loan or credit, the extension of a credit, the discount of an account receivable, the execution, making or delivery by any person, firm, or corporation of any bond or undertaking or the making, acceptance, discount, sale or endorsement of a bill of exchange or promissory note, for the benefit of either himself or of such person, firm or corporation; or,

2 Who, knowing that a false statement in writing has been made, respecting the financial condition, or means, or ability to pay, of himself, or such person, firm or corporation in which he is interested, or for whom he is acting, procures, upon the faith thereof, for the benefit either of himself or of such person, firm or corporation, either or any of the things of benefit mentioned in subdivision one of this section; or,

3 Who, knowing that a statement in writing has been made, respecting the financial condition, or means, or ability to pay himself or such person, firm or corporation, in which he is interested, or for whom he is acting, represents on a later day, either orally or in writing that such statement therefore made if then again made on said day, would be then true, when in fact, said statement if then made would be false, and procures upon the faith thereof, for the benefit either of himself or of such person, firm or corporation, either or any of the things of benefit mentioned in subdivision one of this section,

Shall be guilty of a misdemeanor and punishable by imprisonment for not more than one year or by a fine of not more than one thousand dollars, or both fine and imprisonment.

The Federal law. Of similar nature, although with significant variations, is the Commercial Code of the United States (Title 18 U.S.C.A. Sec. 1341), dealing with Offenses against Postal Service, which provides that:

Whoever, having devised or intending to devise any scheme or artifice to defraud, or for obtaining money or property by means of false or fraudulent pretenses, representations, or promises . . . shall for the purpose of executing such scheme or artifice or attempting so to do, place, or cause to be placed, any letter, postal card, package, writing, circular, pamphlet, or advertisement, whether addressed to any person residing within or outside the United States, in any post office or station thereof, or street or other letterbox of the United States, or authorized depository for mail matter . . . shall be fined not more than $1,000, or imprisoned not more than five years, or both.

In 1952, Sec. 1343 was added which extends the same provisions to the use of wire, radio, or television to defraud "by means of false or fraudulent pretenses, representations, or promises . . ."

Requirements for prosecution. The significance and enforcement of statutes such as those cited in the foregoing paragraphs depend in large measure upon court interpretation of the provisions of such laws. Consequently, the meaning of such terms as "false," "materially false," "fraudulent," "knowingly," and "with intent to be relied upon" has been left to definition by the courts in the many cases involving these subjects. Under the best circumstances, it is admittedly difficult to prove the existence of fraud and the problem is not simplified when the condition pertains to financial statements. Consequently, to give to these statutes the influence intended by the legislators, the construction of the terminology has generally been practical in nature. Nevertheless, even with careful definition and interpretation, some facets of the concepts need yet to be clarified. In the following paragraphs the light which some decisions have shed upon the subject is summarized.

Statement in writing. Both Federal and state laws pertain to statements made in writing—specifically, signed statements. Statements submitted without signature or presented orally, either to a creditor or to a mercantile or other credit agency, are not actionable under the false financial statement laws. That does not mean that such statements may not be accurate nor that they are valueless in credit analysis. On the contrary, a great many statements must be taken at their face value and without the benefit of recourse linked with the signature. Nevertheless, the effort of creditors to obtain signed statements, both for psychological and legal reasons, is readily understandable.

Made with knowledge. The usual requirement of the *state* codes is that the false financial statement be made "knowingly" by the maker thereof. The Federal law does not employ this term, for the reason that it deals specifically with "any scheme or artifice to defraud," the motive of which would be inseparable from a knowledge of the device. The state law requirement, however, has been construed to mean not necessarily *positive knowledge* by the maker of a statement concerning falsities therein. It is enough if in the exercise of reasonable care and responsibility he *should have known* that it was false. An officer of a corporation, for instance, is not absolved from responsibility on the ground that he had no knowledge of the methods his accountants had employed in compiling the statements. Neither is one absolved from responsibility for unintentional errors which constitute a material falsity in the statement, when reasonable care in the course of business would have caused him to know of them. Knowledge of a false statement made in writing, therefore, includes positive knowledge thereof, as well as the responsibility for knowing the character of such a statement.[1]

Intended to be relied upon. There are cases in jurisprudence wherein an accused is absolved from responsibility for a statement which another relied upon, because there was no intention on the part of the maker that it would or should be relied upon. Jesting and facetious remarks are often of this type, as are also statements made to one person which have been taken up and relied upon by another. Financial statements made for credit purposes, however, are obviously intended to be relied upon. The nature and routine of credit investigation are known to suppliers of statements. The suppliers are aware of the credence which credit managers give these statements. Therefore, it is at least implied that the statement is given to be relied upon when it is furnished in connection with a specific request for credit or to an agent whose business it is to deal in and to furnish credit information. Courts have held that statements given with an application for credit are intended to be relied upon. A similar view is held regarding those furnished to mercantile and similar agencies. Nevertheless, it will be noted in the financial statement form illustrated in this chapter that clauses such as the following are usually included in order to remove all possible doubt on this score: "We make the following statement in writing, intending that you should rely thereon respecting our exact financial condition on. . . ."

Made for credit purposes. Financial statements are made for many different purposes and they are, therefore, not only presented in a reasonable variety of forms but some of the data therein may be derived by a legitimate variety of methods and procedures. Statements compiled for credit purposes, for example, may not be the same as those drawn

---

[1] Courts have held that a statement recklessly made, without knowledge of its truth, but which is really false, is a false statement knowingly made, within a settled rule. *Trimble* v. *Reid*, 31 S. W. 861, 863, 97 Ky. 713, 720 (1895), citing *Cooper* v. *Schlesinger*, 4 Sup. Cit. 360, 111 U.S. 148 (1844). "Shepherd's Citations" shows no subsequent change in the decision of either this case or any other cited in this chapter.

up for tax purposes or to be included in a prospectus announcing an issue of securities for sale to the public. One form may not convey an accurate picture of the business when read from the viewpoint of another user. Consequently, the stipulation of the law that the statement should be given for the purpose of securing property, cash, loans, credit, and the like is somewhat of a safeguard for the maker but at the same time a definite commitment as to its intended use.

False statements and fraudulent uses. Although the aforementioned provisions are important, they are secondary in relation to the question of whether a statement is a "false statement" in the eyes of the law or whether its use involves fraud. It is upon these points that prosecution usually turns.

A statement is held to be false when one or more of its constituent items so misrepresent conditions that an ordinarily cautious man, had he known the true facts, would not have extended credit on the basis of such facts or would have acted differently with regard to terms, credit limits, and so on. Such falsity is regarded as "material falsity." In regular court proceedings, the extent or significance of misrepresentation is generally based on testimony of witnesses who are credit experts or by those who are sufficiently skilled in statement analysis and interpretation to be responsive to the degrees of difference which may exist between fact and statement.[2] Even then it is a question as to whether a fair-minded jury or court will be reasonably convinced by such testimony and other evidence that the alleged particular falsity affected the credit situation and would have resulted in an importantly different decision had such falsity been absent. In any event, to be recognized legally as false, a financial statement must be *materially* or *significantly* false.

The distinction between the issuance of a materially false statement and the fraudulent use of such a statement is a legal nicety to which, for practical purposes, not too great significance need be attached; makers of false financial statements may be successfully prosecuted regardless of what the circumstances be called. The distinction may be

---

[2] Not all the items listed on a financial statement are equally susceptible of objective, indisputable determination. Some are definitely matters of fact; others are largely a matter of opinion, or at least subject to variations attributable to the application of dissimilar theories and concepts of valuation. Among the asset items which are statements of ascertainable facts are the following: cash on hand and in the bank, accounts receivable, and notes and acceptances receivable. On the liability side the accuracy of the following items is ascertainable: amount owing for merchandise; amount owing on open account, notes, and acceptances past due; amount owing for borrowed money; liens or chattel mortgages on merchandise and equipment; and mortgages on real estate. Among the items which are more or less subject to fluctuation or variation, depending upon market conditions, basis of computation, or valuations estimated by the management or appraisers, are the following; merchandise at market value and at cost, machinery, fixtures and equipment, and real estate. In general, liabilities are far more definite and real than are assets and are therefore easier to prove.

useful, however, in choosing the most successful procedure for prosecution. If property has been obtained on the basis of a false financial statement, there is in the eyes of some courts a presumption of fraud.[3] Moreover, fraud has been identified in the minds of some authorities with an *intention not to pay*, when credit has been secured on the basis of a false statement.[4] If such be the conditions of a case, the requirements of the laws governing fraud may be met and the plan of prosecution may be determined accordingly. On the other hand, most state false statement laws do not require proof that property was actually *obtained* on the basis of the false statement, misrepresentation alone being a sufficient basis for prosecution. Thus, in the majority of instances, prosecution may be brought under state laws on the basis of the falsity of the statement alone; for prosecution under the Federal code, false representation or fraud must be involved.

Despite the uncertain distinction between a false statement and one that is also fraudulent, it would seem that a distinction must be made so long as it is necessary to prove fraud or fraudulent intent under the Federal law and not under the state laws. So far, intention to pay or not to pay and thus deprive a creditor of his property by means of the false statement seems to be the only real criterion for such a distinction. *It is thus clear that every fraudulent statement is necessarily also false but not every false statement is fraudulent.*

Again, while technically the maker of a false statement can be prosecuted by the state under the state laws regardless of whether or not property has actually been obtained by its means and a loss was suffered by the creditor, in most cases no action would be taken by a *creditor* unless he suffered a loss as a result of a false statement. If the statement was merely an abortive attempt to secure credit, prosecution, except under unusual conditions, would probably not be undertaken.

Decisions as to means of prosecution, however, are contingent not only upon the charges of fraud or misrepresentation but also upon one additional important factor, namely, the use of the mails in submitting the statement.

Use of the mails. When the financial statement as a device for obtaining money or property by means of false or fraudulent representations is sent through the United States mails, the maker thereof may

---

[3] *Record* v. *Rochester Trust Co.*, 192 A. 177, 89 N.H. 1 (1937).

[4] On the other hand, it has been held in a case under the Federal statute that "where there is an intent to obtain money or property by false representation an intent not to pay is immaterial, a purchase of goods without intent to pay being a fraudulent scheme in itself." *Postal Decisions of U.S. and Other Courts, Affecting Post Office Department and the Postal Service.* P.O. Dept., 1939, U.S. Government Printing Office, 1939, p. 244.

be subjected to prosecution under either state law or the Federal laws. That section of the Commercial Code of the United States pertaining to offenses against the Postal Service is designed both to maintain the integrity of the mails and to afford a certain means by which makers of false statements may be justly prosecuted. It is, in fact, sometimes easier to prove the use of the mails to defraud than to prosecute in a state court and under a state statute. Consequently, evidence that a statement has been mailed is carefully preserved, and it is for this reason that the self-mailing or envelope-type form of financial statement blank is widely used. Federal prosecution, therefore, is dependent upon proof of use of the mails, as well as upon evidence that the statement was materially false, intended to be relied upon, and used or intended to be used for credit purposes, much the same as in cases brought under state laws.

Jurisdiction for prosecution. The jurisdiction of cases involving false financial statements is dependent primarily upon the locale of the offense. Under state laws, prosecution must be sought in the county in which the statement was made; under the Federal law, it may be brought either where it was made or where it was received. Usually, however, the offender is prosecuted in the jurisdiction where the statement was made.

The chief purposes of civil and criminal prosecution being different, the former to redress an injured party for damages or loss suffered and the latter to impose penalties for unlawful actions against society, the manner of prosecution differs also under the two types of codes. In civil action, suit is brought by private parties; in criminal cases, prosecution is initiated by the government, through its agent attorneys, against the offender. Action under either Federal or state statutes is usually taken at the instigation of the recipient of the allegedly false statement, but the prosecution is not a private matter, since the offense is against the state or Federal government, as the case may be.

Summary of requirements for prosecution. In general, the requirements of state and Federal statutes for the prosecution of makers of false financial statements are much the same. The terminology employed by each may differ slightly, but for most intents and purposes the significance of the requirements is uniform. The requirements of the two types of codes, therefore, may be summarized in the form indicated below. The points upon which they differ materially are (1) the requirement of fraud; (2) use of mails; and (3) the jurisdiction in which legal action may be taken.

Requirements for Prosecution of Makers of False Financial Statements

Requirements	Federal law	Special state laws
Statement made in writing (signed)	Required	Required
False statement made knowingly	Required	Required
Made for credit purposes	Required	Required
Intended to be relied upon	Required	Required
Statement false (materially false)	Required	Required
Statement fraudulent	Required	Not required
Use of mails	Required	Not required
Place of prosecution	Where statement was either made or received	In county where statement was made

Special legal aspects of financial statements. To make for greater accuracy and to facilitate prosecution, a creditor should require that the statement be completely filled out and signed by the maker. An oral statement is of no value in a criminal action or in barring a discharge in bankruptcy, as can be done when a false financial statement was made in writing. It can be used merely for civil action, as additional evidence in support of the creditor's claims. Unfilled spaces should not be permitted. It should contain a statement that it was given for the purpose of obtaining credit and that it completely represents the maker's financial condition. It should also contain the provision that all debts owed to the creditor in question become due immediately upon the debtor's insolvency or upon transfer of the maker's merchandise in violation of the bulk sales law and under similar conditions.

It is further advisable to have a provision to the effect that not only is the statement true as of the date stated thereon but that it is to be regarded as a continuous statement until the creditor has been notified of any changes of a derogatory character. Even with such a provision on the statement, the courts have held that when the statement is given to establish a general line of credit the representations are continuing for a reasonable period of time, usually 18 months. In the absence of such a provision the apparent intent when the statement was made is a determining factor. If the statement was made for a particular transaction, whether it could be regarded as continuing would depend upon the nature of the transaction. A statement made by a retail grocer as a basis for opening an account at the wholesale house is presumed to be continuing. On the other hand, one made by the grocer, for the purpose of obtaining a loan from a building and loan association or from an insurance company, on his residence and secured by a mortgage, would not generally have such continuing implications. If, however, the statement is given as a continuing one, the debtor is bound to notify his creditors of any unfavorable material changes in his financial condition and such a statement may be relied upon for the reasonable period of about eighteen months. Usually, such a statement is withdrawn either by submission of a new statement or by refusal, when requested, to issue a new statement.

QUESTIONS AND PROBLEMS

1 Explain why a credit manager would want both an income statement and a balance sheet in his evaluation of the nature and quality of a credit risk.

2 Your company is in receipt of an application for credit from the Fit-Well Shoe Company. In order to have a better basis for a credit decision, you requested a financial statement which the Fit-Well Shoe Company refused to furnish. Show how you would proceed to convince the prospective customer of the desirability of supplying your firm with a financial statement.

3 Assuming that the Fit-Well Shoe Company, despite your sound plea, refuses to submit to you a statement of its financial condition, what other means would be available for securing such a statement?

4 Show that the growing practice on the part of debtors in submitting financial statements to their creditors has a beneficial effect upon competition.

5 In what ways is the direct method of obtaining a financial statement superior to the indirect method?

6 Define accrued liabilities and deferred assets. Of what significance are they to the credit man? Classify the following into the two categories:

a Interest due on notes from the preceding accounting period

b Rent received 2 months in advance

c Insurance on buildings paid in advance for 1 year

d Wages due but unpaid

e Dividends declared but not paid

f Employee withholdings for taxes

7 Explain why each of the following reserves is handled in the manner indicated:

a Reserve for bad debts or allowance for doubtful accounts is normally shown on the assets side of the balance sheet as a deduction from the accounts and notes receivable. Furthermore, it is shown only for the periods covered by the balance sheet.

b Reserve for bad debts is sometimes shown on the liability side of the balance sheet.

c Depreciation for plant and equipment is shown on the asset side of the balance sheet as a deduction but in accumulated form rather than for the periods covered.

d If a reserve is set up for certain types of taxes, it is generally shown on the liability side of the balance sheet.

8 Can a financial statement be false and not fraudulent, or vice versa? Explain.

9 Suppose that the Fit-Well Shoe Company was finally persuaded to submit a financial statement to your company. The statement was dated Dec. 31, and showed accounts payable of $56,789. In checking up this item on a Credit Interchange Bureau report cleared at about the same date, you found that the Fit-Well Shoe Company owed creditors approximately $53,265. Assuming willingness on your part to prosecute the maker of the statement, could you secure conviction on the ground that the statement was false and that the accounts payable item was misrepresented?

10 What points must be proved in order to secure conviction under the Federal law for the making and issuing of a false financial statement?

11 In what respects do the state laws specifically governing the making and issuing of false financial statements differ from the Federal law?

12 Which of the two types of law is preferable, from the standpoint of the creditors who rely upon financial statements in the granting of credit?

13 Why does a statement often contain the following words: "We (I) make the following statement in writing intending that you should rely thereon respecting our (my) financial condition as of .... (date)"? Is there any value in adding that "you are to regard this as a continuing statement"? Explain.

14 Why would a statement made for taxation purposes not necessarily be a good one for credit purposes? Does this argue against an all-purpose financial statement for a given enterprise as of a given date? If so, what is the explanation?

CHAPTER TWENTY-ONE

simple analysis and
interpretation of
financial statements

The preceding chapter was devoted mainly to a consideration of the general nature of financial statements as a basis for credit decisions, reasons for using them, methods of obtaining them and in what form, and their overall composition in so far as the static aspects pertaining to assets, liabilities, and net worth are concerned. Special emphasis was placed on the legal phases of the subject, which reflect mainly on the character of the maker and the extent to which reliance upon the statement would be justified.

Need for analysis and interpretation. To be meaningful in credit decision making, a financial statement must be analyzed and interpreted. In judging a credit risk, the value of a financial statement depends in large measure upon the meaning and reliability of the individual items contained therein. A question of truth of falsity may not be involved; the credibility or usefulness of the items may be a function rather of the accounting principles employed in the compilation of the statement and of the ability and time which its maker brought to bear upon its preparation. Consequently, one form of statement analysis is that of ascertaining exactly what is included in each item, in order that its worth may be properly appraised. When statement forms are supplied by the creditor, it is possible to specify thereon the details of the information desired. When choice is left to the maker of the statement, however, it is often necessary to request additional information before a satisfactory study of the statement can be made. Whatever the degree of refinement required, it is recognized by the competent credit analyst that it is worth questioning the seemingly self-evident facts reported in a statement.

Types of financial statement analysis. Much of the value of a financial statement issues from the way in which it is analyzed and interpreted. While the financial analyst may use several different types of financial statement analysis for his purposes, there are in actual practice at least two distinct methods, or types, of analysis in common use for credit purposes. The older and by far the simpler, though less satisfactory, method is sometimes referred to as the valuation method of analysis. It consists of a simple evaluation of the different items appearing on the balance sheet, without reference to proportions or relationships except in the most casual manner. It is a means by which the asset items on the balance sheet are "trimmed" down to figures that are regarded as reasonable and conservative, and the credit decision is based on the financial status of the subject thus revealed by the corrected amounts.

When, however, such an analysis is properly made it reveals much. First, it indicates the debt-paying power of each important asset item. By placing emphasis on the current assets, the current position for billpaying ability is revealed. Second, it makes possible a determination of the subject's net worth and the extent to which it provides a cushion between total assets and total obligations. While it may show how much assets may shrink and still provide safety for creditors, it does not furnish any yardsticks as to the depth of the cushion normally required other than the logic that the deeper such cushion, the better for creditors. Third, through an analysis and interpretation of the figures on sales, gross profit, operating expense, and net profit, it is possible to gauge the subject's earning power.

The other method of analysis, which is the more advanced technique, involves the ratio analysis process. Experience has shown that there are in business certain fundamental relationships. When these relationships are favorable, profitable conditions usually prevail, and vice versa.   These relationships are expressed in ratios, a detailed discussion of which is presented in the following chapter.

Some authorities feel that both analyses should be used at the same time for a given statement, the simpler method being used as a preliminary to the ratio analysis.   This would invariably result, however, in much duplication of effort, since one of the purposes of the ratio analysis is to test the value of each important item in the statement just as in the other type of analysis.

Preliminary procedure and verification. Regardless of the type of analysis to which a financial statement is subjected, certain steps should be taken before proceeding with the analysis proper.   First, it should be ascertained who submitted the statement in order to gauge the responsibility and integrity of its maker.   Second, it should be determined whether the statement was audited and, if so, by whom.   If audited by a responsible firm of chartered or certified public accountants, creditors can feel more certain that the figures presented are accurate and that they reflect the true state of affairs.

An audited report is of little significance unless a certificate by the accountants responsible for the audit is appended, because audits vary in their scope and for that reason certifications vary.   Hence, it is essential that a creditor read the certificate carefully so as to ascertain the character of the audit and the conditions underlying it.   Although accountants find it necessary to conform to the wishes of their clients, nevertheless, no responsible firm will deviate from sound and well-recognized accounting principles in behalf of unscrupulous clients.   Sometimes creditors request and secure verifications on their own forms from the accounting firm that audited the subject's statement.

Third, the date of the statement and that of the inventory should be carefully noted, because both of them have a bearing on currency, accuracy, and importance of the figures.   For example, midseason figures on merchandise inventory or on receivables differ radically in many lines of trade from the corresponding end-of-season figures.   Again, the statement may be too old to be of real value.   Moreover, if any of the figures are to be confirmed, when seeking to verify their accuracy or conservatism, they must be secured from each source as of the same date or approximate time.

Fourth, it is usually a good thing to confirm at least some items. It is relatively simple to confirm a bank balance or to compare certain selected items with those appearing in a mercantile agency report.   Accounts payable may well be compared with the amount owing shown on a credit interchange bureau report as of approximately the same time.

Finally, it is necessary to reclassify the items in the statement

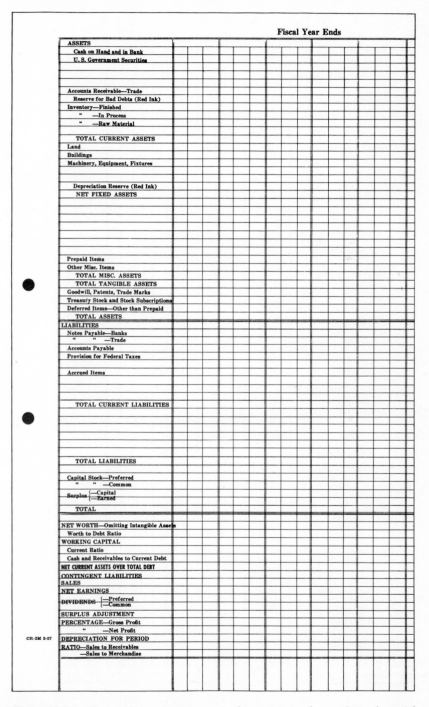

figure 21-1*A. Comparison of statements form commonly used in financial statement analysis.*

NET WORTH TREND—Year End														
Net Worth—Beginning														
Net Worth—Ending														
INCREASE—DECREASE—Net Worth														
Additions:														
Net Profit														
Increase Stock														
Decrease Intangibles														
Surplus Adjustments:														
TOTAL ADDITIONS														
Deductions:														
Operating Loss														
Decrease Stock														
Dividends—Preferred														
Dividends—Common														
Increase Intangibles														
Surplus Adjustments:														
TOTAL DEDUCTIONS														
WORKING CAPITAL TREND														
Working Capital—Beginning														
Working Capital—Ending														
INCREASE-DECREASE-Working Capital														
Additions:														
Increase in Net Worth														
Depreciation														
Decrease Fixed Assets														
Decrease Misc. Assets														
Increase Slow Debt														
TOTAL ADDITIONS														
Deductions:														
Decrease in Net Worth														
Increase Fixed Assets														
Increase Misc. Assets														
Decrease Slow Debt														
TOTAL DEDUCTIONS														
FUNDS REALIZED FROM:														
Increased Working Capital														
Decreased Cash Position														
" Receivables														
" Inventory														
Increased Bank Loans														
" Trade Debt														
" Other Debt														
" Income Tax														
TOTAL														
FUNDS ABSORBED BY:														
Decreased Working Capital														
Increased Cash Position														
" Receivables														
" Inventory														
Decreased Bank Loans														
" Trade Debt														
" Other Debt														
" Income Tax														
TOTAL														

figure **21-1***B*. *Continuation of Fig. 21-1A.*

on a "comparison of statements" form, since the data submitted differ widely in arrangement unless presented on a form furnished by the creditor. This form (Figs. 21-1A and 21-1B) also makes possible the recording of a number of successive statements so that trends over a period of years may be ascertained. Where only a superficial analysis is to be made, this step may be eliminated, as is often the case in acutal practice.

ANALYSIS AND
INTERPRETATION
OF ASSETS

In evaluating the assets of a risk for credit purposes, certain intangibles like good will, patents, or trade-marks are usually deemed worthless for debt-paying purposes and are, therefore, entirely disregarded. As to the other assets, credit analysts deem it necessary not only to ascertain their correctness but also consider it prudent to follow a policy of "shading" them or of writing off a certain percentage. This policy is based on the assumption that the maker of a statement for the purpose of procuring credit, by endeavoring to make a favorable showing, will be prone to list his assets at their highest possible value, which may not at all represent the actual sum which will in all probability be realized ultimately. In this connection it is important to bear in mind that a statement prepared for a going business presupposes voluntary selling and continuity of operations. Consequently, balance sheet items should be valued on a "going concern" basis and not at forced liquidation prices.

The amount by which assets should be "shaded" or "shaved down" is contingent upon a number of factors. Among these factors are the kind of business represented by the statement, the nature of the constituent items, the relationship a given item bears to certain others, whether the statement has been audited by a reputable public accountant, and whether the amounts are stated in round figures and, hence, are mere estimates. Above all, there is the individual judgment of the credit manager as determined by the degree of his knowledge and experience, for statement analysis by the simple method has not been reduced to an exact science.

Cash. This item should comprise the total of cash on hand, in banks, and in other financial institutions such as savings and loan associations and mutual savings banks. In addition, from the viewpoint of the credit manager, short-term government securities are so readily marketable that they may be considered as cash equivalents. In the determination of how much is available in cash for debt-paying purposes as a whole, it is generally essential to separate the amount of cash on hand and cash in the bank. To be regarded as "cash" on hand for accounting purposes, an item should be acceptable for deposit at face value. It would not, therefore, include I.O.U.'s, since their collectibility is frequently doubtful, nor postdated or past-due checks; neither should it include unexpended balances in the hands of salesmen, which are not to be returned as cash to the business; nor should cash include funds subject to liens, or those which are otherwise tied up so as not to be available immediately for payment of debts. If the maker is indebted to the bank in which his funds are deposited, the bank may have a lien on the deposits to the extent of the sum loaned, hence it is advisable to have the cash on hand and that on deposit in the bank listed separately. This does not, however, lessen either the amount of cash in the bank or its debt-paying power, but simply means that to the extent of the indebtedness to the bank it may not be available for payment of obligations to other creditors.

A much more important purpose served in separating the two items is the facility which it offers in arriving at conclusions concerning the probable contents of cash item. Thus, if the cash on hand seems unusually large in amount, it may be reasonably inferred that it contains I.O.U.'s and other items the inclusion of which is forbidden by sound theory and practice, or it may be indicative of poor business judgment. No set rule can be laid down regarding the amount of cash a statement should show, since it is an item which materially varies in size with different types of business and at different seasons. If correctly stated and free from encumbrances, and if the relationship between cash on hand and cash in bank appears reasonable, this item should be accepted at its face value in determining its debt-paying power.

Accounts receivable. Next to cash and "near-cash" items such as short-term government securities, the accounts receivable item represents the most liquid asset. They are merely book accounts, or "open" accounts, with customers. This item should include all unpaid claims against solvent debtors arising from the sale of goods or services. Obviously, only those accounts should be covered by the item under consideration which can be reasonably relied upon for the payment of creditors' claims, as determined by past experience and from information on hand concerning the debtors. They should be shown on the balance sheet at face value, less a valuation reserve for bad debts.

This item should not include amounts reasonably known not to be collectible; advances to salesmen and other employees; loans to officers; overdrafts of partners, which really partake of the nature of withdrawals from the capital investment; balances covering merchandise shipped on consignment; amounts in dispute or placed for collection;

claims against carriers and others; and loans to subsidiaries, which are not to be collected in the normal course of business activity but constitute a rather permanent investment.

In order to bolster up the accounts receivable item, makers of statements not infrequently include mere bookkeeping balances, which are not to be collected in the normal course of business activity and which cannot, therefore, be relied upon for the payment of debts. To provide for such contingencies, allowances should be made in arriving at the net worth of this item. In any event, a normal allowance must be made for bad debts, for even though only solvent debtors be included, it still remains uncertain whether all of them will be willing and able to meet their obligations at maturity. The percentage of such normal allowance or deduction varies with different houses and different lines of trade from less than 0.2 per cent to as high as several per cent. Should no distinction be made between the good and collectible accounts and those which are distinctly inferior, a much larger percentage than normal will necessarily have to be written off.

Treatment of factored and assigned receivables. It stands to reason that if the accounts receivable are financed through factoring,[1] in which case the factor purchases them outright and assumes all credit risks, they do not belong to the subject and should not appear on its financial statement. Under such circumstances, accounts receivable appearing on the balance sheet are either a falsity or consist of the relatively inferior risks which the factor refused to accept. The size of the figure in relation to sales will no doubt help to determine which is the case. If the former is true, all of them should be excluded, and if the latter obtains, the amount should be shaved down by a considerable percentage.

If the financing of the receivables is done through sale with recourse or via assignment as collateral, care must be taken to see that accounts receivable so sold, hypothecated, or pledged are not included in the accounts receivable asset on the balance sheet in the determination of the debt-paying power of such item, but should be included for the development of any ratios that would test the soundness of the subject's credit granting and collection operations. Furthermore, for debt-paying purposes, a much larger reserve for bad debts should be provided for the remaining receivables, inasmuch as the accounts from the better risks are no doubt among those sold with recourse or assigned.

The fundamental significance of assignment. From the standpoint of credit analysis, the crux of the confusion surrounding assignment lies

---

[1] For a fairly comprehensive discussion of factoring and other financing of accounts receivable, see Chap. 14.

in these questions: Does assignment indicate strength or weakness on the part of the firm pledging its accounts?   Is a creditor of the assignor disadvantaged by the assignment?   Is there an obligation to notify creditors and debtors of the assignor concerning the sale of accounts?   Is the assignee placed in a preferred position among creditors of the assignor by reason of the pledge?

Whether assignment indicates strength or desperation depends upon the circumstances of the individual assignor.   It may be a customary practice, resulting in the selling concern's stability of credits and liquidity of assets.   Assignors may similarly be strengthened by their ability to dispose of accounts accumulated through heavy seasonal sales and through aggressive sales promotion, or to purchase in anticipation of price rises.   Moreover, vendors do at times sell their accounts in order to take advantage of cash discounts on their own purchases.   In all these instances, assignment of accounts may work to the advantage of a seller and to the improvement of his financial position.   On the other hand, when working capital is at a low ebb and assignment is resorted to for the liquidation of overdue and doubtful accounts, knowledge of this fact would warn a credit analyst of weakness in the assignor's position.

Whether a creditor of an assignor is disadvantaged by the transaction depends upon the use which is made of the funds secured through hypothecation of his accounts.   If merchandise credit obligations are met with the proceeds, a good purpose is served from the creditor's standpoint, for the assignor's debt status is thereby improved.   On the other hand, if the money is used to meet mere operating expenses which constitute neither a reduction of debt nor an increase in earning capacity, the assets of the organization may be quickly dissipated as a result of inefficient management.   Creditors of the assignor may be further disadvantaged by fraudulent use of the funds so obtained, as when the assignor uses the money to his own advantage, leaving general creditors with the remaining depleted assets.

As a matter of fact, however, such cases have been negligible among the convictions of business debtors under the state or Federal fraud laws obtained by the National Association of Credit Management's Fraud Prevention Department since its inception in 1925.   An honest debtor will not misuse assignments, and a dishonest one is likely to defraud his creditors regardless of whether or not he assigns his accounts.

To be sure, the assignor is morally obligated to reveal to his creditors the situation as to any factoring or assignment of his receivables.   As to the legal obligation to do so, state legislation requires in most instances that such disclosure be made to creditors—actual and prospective—by filing of public notice to that effect. In its treatment of secured transactions that include assignments of receivables, the Uniform Commercial Code (adopted in 49 states and the District of Columbia) requires that a financing statement signed by the debtor and the secured party must be filed with the appropriate filing officer to protect all security interests.

Notes and bills receivable. This item should include only negotiable promissory notes received from solvent purchasers in temporary settlement for goods sold and delivered. If trade acceptances are customarily taken by the firm in payment for goods sold, these trade acceptances should be listed separately in order to facilitate a distinction between the two items for purposes of analysis. The notes receivable account should not include notes given in settlement of loans to individuals, nor should it contain notes covering overdrafts and similar obligations of partners, officers, directors, employees, subsidiary companies, or any other similar obligations. From this account should also be excluded all notes which have been discounted, assigned, or transferred. In a word, only those notes should be listed under this heading which are the outgrowth of normal commercial transactions.

To determine the approximate value of notes receivable, the analyst should know the kind of business and terms of sale granted by the firm under consideration. In most lines of trade, debts for goods sold are usually evidenced by open book accounts. Under these conditions, notes are not taken in the regular course of business. Where this system prevails notes receivable may represent extensions on accounts already past due, put into note settlements. Hence, a substantial amount of notes receivable, unless it is customary in the trade to operate on the basis, frequently indicates a large past-due indebtedness and reflects laxity in the performance of the credit-granting and collection functions. Irrespective of the terms of sale, a certain percentage should be deducted in estimating the value of notes receivable, to provide for bad debts. This percentage is to be based on the average percentage of losses in the given trade and upon the debtor's credit policy, methods, and experience.

Merchandise inventories. Merchandise constitutes one of the most important parts of the current assets, but is appraised with difficulty. This item covers all sorts of goods which are to be sold in the normal course of business. It includes raw materials, goods in process, and finished products to which ownership is claimed by the firm submitting the statement. All merchandise stocks which have been pledged as security or which are subject to liens must necessarily be omitted from this item for the purpose of determining its debt-paying power available to unsecured creditors.   Since, however, such merchandise stocks are part of the inventory, they should be included for purposes of evaluating the size of the entire inventory in relation to sales and otherwise to judge its adequacy.   Again, if the loan for which the merchandise is pledged is shown among the liabilities, the pledged merchandise must be shown on the asset side of the balance sheet but properly footnoted to indicate its position and unavailability for payment of bills to unsecured creditors.

Another item which calls for some consideration in this connection is that of merchandise consigned for sale.   This should be excluded from the merchandise item of the consignee but included instead in the inventory of the consignor.   It constitutes the property of the one who has consigned it and does not, therefore, belong to the consignee.   The latter acts merely as agent charged with the duties specified in the contract governing the relationship between the two parties.   He has no direct financial liability to the consignor, for he is required only to exercise "ordinary care and diligence" in seeing that the merchandise is disposed of in accordance with the provisions of the contract.

In connection with an appraisal of the value of merchandise inventories, several important questions arise, relating to the kind and condition of the stock of goods, mode of ascertaining the quantitative measure of the merchandise on hand, and method employed in pricing the inventory in order to secure a money value of the merchandise in stock.

If the statement is submitted by a manufacturing concern, it is essential to know the proportion of the stock of goods that is in the state of raw materials, goods in process, or finished goods, for merchandise in the shape of raw materials is of much greater value proportionally in case of a forced sale than are goods in process.   Raw materials are not subject to radical style changes and are, therefore, more marketable, i.e., readily convertible into cash, while goods in process require additional material, labor, and time before they are rendered salable.   For the same reason, finished goods can be more readily disposed of than merchandise in process.

In all cases, adequate allowance must be made for old stock and depreciation.   Although merchandise is normally sold at a profit, nevertheless circumstances may arise which greatly diminish its value, since all goods are subject, in varying degrees, to changes in style, declines in value which accompany the downward movement of the business cycle, errors in demand anticipation, and physical deterioration.   Obviously, no uniform basis or scale for writing off the merchandise account, which would apply to all lines of trade, can be profitably established.

A consideration of somewhat less importance is the method employed in arriving at a quantitative measure of the stock of merchandise on hand. It is of some importance to know, in order to gauge the accuracy of the figure, whether the item represents an actual or physical inventory or has been arrived at by means of a perpetual inventory system. In some instances, it may represent simply an estimate. As a rule, when the figures given in the statement are in round numbers, omitting cents and the last digits in the dollars column, the conclusion may reasonably be drawn that the inventory has in all probability been estimated. In this connection, it is also well to note the date of the inventory. If taken at the close of the season, the quantity of goods should be at the low-water mark.

With the adoption of different practices in regard to pricing inventories, it is essential to know what method has been employed. Some houses inventory their merchandise at cost; others at selling price; whereas a third group values its merchandise stocks at cost or prevailing market prices, whichever is the lower. Conservative practice requires that the last of the three methods be used on the assumption that the debt-paying power of a commodity is determined not so much by original cost as by the amount at which it can sell, which is, in turn, reflected in the prevailing market price at which it could be purchased for resale. When inventories are valued at selling prices, appropriations are made of anticipated profits the realization of which is highly problematical. Even though profits are made as a result of a sale, they properly belong to the subsequent accounting period. Moreover, in following this practice, it is easy to overlook the expenses chargeable against a sale of the goods under consideration.

Investments. This includes short-term notes, stocks, bonds, and other securities of subsidiaries or other companies, held by the maker of the statement. These securities may be readily marketable and invested in only temporarily, or may be held for relatively long periods for purposes of control. The value of securities of the first type only should be included among the current assets. Their value for debt-paying purposes is readily ascertainable, if listed on an important stock exchange. Otherwise, they are greatly discounted or entirely disregarded by the credit grantor.

Deferred assets. Having no direct debt-paying power, the significance of these items lies in the fact that they reflect the system of accounting employed by the maker of the statement, which is no unimportant criterion of management ability.

Plant, machinery, and tools. These constitute an important part of the fixed assets and, not unlike the other items of the same class, are not to be sold in the normal course of business activity. They, therefore, do not contribute directly to the ability of the owner to meet obligations currently maturing. Nevertheless, they add to the stability of the business and in event of a forced liquidation the proceeds from their sale will be applied in payment of creditors' claims, according to priority. To be sure, under such circumstances, the sum realized would probably amount to a small percentage of the listed or book value. However, these, as well as some of the other fixed assets, are extremely important in analyzing financial statements, as their ratios to other items disclose methods and policies employed the effect of which is either to increase or diminish the firm's earning capacity and credit responsibility.

In estimating the worth of these properties, an adequate allowance must be made to cover depreciation in value due to wear and tear and obsolescence, if they are listed at cost and no sufficient reserve has been provided.

Many financial statements list each parcel of real estate separately at cost price. By comparing these figures with the assessed valuation, some check is afforded against any overstatement of assets. Such comparison, assuming correct cost price to have been given, also affords an opportunity to study fluctuations in real estate values in the neighborhood in which the debtor's business is located.

Furniture and fixtures. Adequate allowance should be made for depreciation, and since the worth of this item in case of a forced sale is very low, a substantial percentage is sometimes written off by credit grantors. In this connection it should be ascertained, if possible, whether the size of the investment in this item is consistent with the requirements of the business.

Intangible assets. In this group are included good will, trademarks, patents, copyrights, certain contracts, franchises, and other assets of like nature. Most of these are practically disregarded by credit managers in analyzing financial statements, for, it is argued, they can be realized on only when the business is sold and only when they yield satisfactory returns. Although they are not available for debt-paying purposes, if representing real value they should always be included among the assets, inasmuch as intangibles may sometimes constitute the chief and most valuable asset of a concern, as in the case of the patents of the United Shoe Machinery Company.

ANALYSIS AND
INTERPRETATION OF
LIABILITIES AND
NET WORTH

Accounts payable. This item should represent the total sum owing to creditors on open account, and it is advisable, from the standpoint of creditors, to have it segregated into amounts not due and amounts past due. The amount owing for merchandise, if listed as a separate item, should be excluded from accounts payable. The reason for showing the amount owing for merchandise separately is because it prevents understatements, for this figure is readily verified. Such a requirement acts as a deterrent from falsification and aids in detecting tendencies to overstocking.

Notes payable. Under this heading three divisions are to be found:

1 Notes payable to banks, which represent money borrowed by discounting debtor's own notes. If the amount is large, it may represent loans obtained for the purpose of discounting bills of purchase. Good banking accommodations, as represented by this item, are, as a rule, a semblance of strength.

2 Notes payable to merchandise creditors for goods purchased. If the amount is large, it generally represents trade acceptances given and outstanding. Should this be the case, a correspondingly low figure should appear opposite the "owing for merchandise" item. Again, if notes are not regularly employed in the trade in settlement for purchases, these notes probably represent settlements of past-due purchase accounts and are drawing interest, which ordinarily indicates that the debtor's credit is strained.

3 Notes payable to others include notes given when obligations are incurred from sources other than those mentioned, such as officers, directors, relatives, and friends. Their presence in large amounts calls for caution on the part of the credit manager, because these means of securing the necessary funds are resorted to when all banking has probably been exhausted. Moreover, in case of insolvency, it is natural for the debtor to protect his friends and relatives to the detriment of his other creditors.

Mortgages. Liabilities secured in this form may have been assumed as part payment for the property during the acquisition of title or may have been executed at a later date. Ordinary mortgages represent indebtedness secured by a pledge of real estate, whereas chattel mortgages represent indebtedness secured by personal and other movable property, such as a stock of goods, automobiles, refrigerator boxes, cash registers, and the like.   In determining the residual value of the various assets, a knowledge of these encumbrances is absolutely indispensable.

Bonds. In the event of forced liquidation, bondholders' claims, if the bonds are secured by specific property, take precedence over those of bank and merchandise creditors.   Hence, if the bonded indebtedness is large, little or nothing may be expected by others than bondholders upon involuntary dissolution.   This is a consideration requiring particular attention when bank or merchandise creditors are contemplating throwing the debtor into bankruptcy.

Contingent liabilities. These liabilities are potential and do not become real until and unless certain contingencies occur.   Because they do not constitute real liabilities for the present, they are not chargeable, and should not be included among the regular liabilities.   Their existence should be disclosed in supplementary remarks, however.

Contingent liabilities arise through the following transactions:

1 When the debtor guarantees payment of another's account. In case of default on the part of the person whose account is guaranteed the guarantor becomes liable for the sum involved. Thus, his liability is contingent upon the default of the real debtor to pay his obligations. The liability as guarantor also arises out of agreements, leases, and the like.

2 When a merchant indorses his notes receivable or trade acceptances for the purpose of discounting them at the bank. Should the maker or drawer refuse payment at maturity, the indorser becomes directly liable to the bank.

3 By indorsing a note for the accommodation or benefit of another.

4 When commitments for future delivery of merchandise purchases are made. In this case the buyer becomes contingently liable.

Net worth. Net worth represents the equity of owners, partners, or stockholders in the business and is determined by subtracting total liabilities from total assets.   The amount shown on the balance sheet as the excess of assets over liabilities seldom represents the true net worth as viewed by the credit analyst.   A new figure must be developed after the "shading" process has been completed.

Capital stock. If stock has a par value, the aggregate of the par value of the corporation's outstanding shares is ordinarily the figure at which the capital stock is shown on the balance sheet.   If it possesses no par value, the amount of this item usually represents the sum actually received from the sale of the security.   Only that stock which is actually issued and outstanding should thus appear in the balance sheet.

Surplus. This is the difference between the net worth of the business and the value of the capital stock issued and outstanding. It is the excess of book values over the amount which the liabilities and value of the capital stock issued and outstanding represent. A surplus may arise through several types of transactions including the following:

1 Sale of stock for more than par value, forming the so-called "paid-in" surplus

2 Capital stock premiums and purchase by the company of its own securities below par

3 Stock assessments and conversion payments

4 Stock donations, gifts, and contributions from outsiders

5 Sale of capital assets for an amount in excess of their book value

6 Reappraising and writing up the book value of certain assets

7 Normal accumulations of profits as determined by the profit and loss account balances

Under normal conditions only the earned surplus, or that arising from the normal accumulations of profits resulting from the ordinary operations of the business, is available for the payment of dividends. The surplus item, if any, plus the capital stock, constitute the owners' equity in the enterprise. If a deficit is incurred, to determine the owner's equity, the amount of the deficit should be deducted from capital stock instead of placing it on the assets side of the balance sheet, as is sometimes done.

A reasonably substantial surplus is usually looked upon with favor, for it indicates a safe equity. When compared over a period of years, earned surpluses will indicate whether the business is fundamentally sound and is operated on a paying basis, or whether it is retrograding or standing still. However, when the earned surplus becomes so large as to be entirely out of proportion to the capital invested, there is danger of the business being suddenly handicapped by the payment of large dividends out of working capital. Moreover, when surplus represents funds which have been invested in the expansion of the business and are therefore unavailable for payment as dividends, the presence of the surplus item may lead uninformed stockholders to desire or to expect a dividend. It is, therefore, advisable, from the standpoint of credit policy, to capitalize the surplus as soon as it becomes so large as to be out of proportion to the amount of capital invested.

ANALYSIS AND INTERPRETATION OF OPERATING ITEMS

Even by means of a simple and so-called "common-sense" analysis and interpretation of a few of the most important operating items, it is possible to approximate the subject's earning power and ability to meet current obligations. This can best be shown by use of specific information for a hypothetical retail store normally obtainable for such a business as shown below.

THE HYPOTHETICAL RETAIL STORE

Cash	$2,400	Accounts payable	$13,180
Accounts receivable	14,000	Chattel mortgage (current)*	12,960
Merchandise inventory	53,400	Accrued taxes, etc.	3,000
Prepaid sales taxes	800	Chattel mortgage (over 1 year)*	8,640
Supplies, etc.	1,000	Total liabilities	$37,780
Fixtures and equipment	36,000	Net worth	69,820
Total assets	$107,600	Total liabilities and net worth	$107,600

* Mortgage on new fixtures and equipment payable in 24 monthly instalments of $1,080 each; 20 instalments remain to be paid, 12 in current year and 8 in the year following.

Sales average $14,000 monthly at a gross profit margin of 31 per cent; 45 per cent of sales are made on regular 30-day charge account basis; owner's salary in form of drawing account, $1,000 a month; rent, $850 monthly; other expenses, including depreciation of $200 a month, are estimated at $1,300 a month.

Sales and profits. One of the first questions is whether the sales are adequate. Are they high enough to support the expenses? What is the break-even point on this score? From the above data it is seen that the monthly expenses amount to $3,150 ($1,000 + $850 + $1,300). It is assumed that the $1,080 instalment payment is in the nature of a capital investment and not an expense. It follows that in order to break even on the expenses the sales must produce a gross profit equal to $3,150 a month. To do that on a gross margin of 31 per cent of sales, the monthly sales must be at least $10,161 ($150 ÷ 31 per cent × 100). As the actual monthly sales average $14,000, the sales are more than adequate to cover expenses and are substantially above the break-even point.

Whether or not the gross profit margin is adequate depends upon what the average is for the same type of retail store operation on which the credit analyst is no doubt informed. The monthly *net* earnings, however, can be figured from the data, as follows: gross profit equals $4,340 (31 per cent of $14,000), less expenses of $3,150, leaves a net profit for the month of $1,190. Since the chattel mortgage instalment is $1,080, it appears that it will be possible to meet the instalment out of current earnings.

Ability to pay current debts. Assuming that the creditor in question, like the others in the same line of business, sells to the customer on terms of 2/10, net 30 days, it is necessary to ascertain whether the customer will be able to pay his bills on time or possibly also discount some of them. One way of determining it is by an In and Out balance shown below:

	In	*Out*	
Cash on hand	$2,400	$13,180	Accounts payable
Cash sales during month	7,700	2,950	Expenses less depreciation
Collection of prior month's		1,080	Chattel mortgage instalment
credit sales	6,300		
Cash available in 1 month	$16,400	$17,210	Total payable in 1 month

From the above In and Out totals it is evident that even if *all* available cash were to be paid out during the month, it would still be inadequate; hence the customer cannot be expected to pay his bills on time let alone discount them. To be sure, conditions are likely to improve if additional purchases of merchandise will be brought in line with sales, so that the monthly bills on such purchases will amount to only $9,660 (69 per cent of $14,000), and will improve considerably after payments on the chattel mortgage cease and other things remain the same. The latter improvement is not to be expected, however, for some time.

This reasoning assumes, of course, that all currently outstanding accounts payable are to be paid during the month in question and are not to be replaced by newly incurred accounts payable, an assumption that is not warranted. If such an assumption is made, however, then the immediate problem is to determine what can possibly be done in order to enable the subject to meet his current obligations on time. To that end it is advisable to ascertain whether there is not too much inventory for the sales volume done, but that cannot be done by the simple analysis method, for it involves the use of the ratio method discussed in the following chapter.

The above In and Out balance also makes the unwarranted assumption that credit sales will be collected within 30 days. According to available information, 45 per cent of the sales are made on credit; hence the credit sales amount to $6,300 per month (45 per cent of $14,000), or $210 per day ($6,300 ÷ 30 days). Since the accounts receivable amount to $14,000, it means that about 67 days of credit sales are carried on the books ($14,000 ÷ $210). Obviously, an average collection period of 67 days on regular sales terms of approximately 30 days not only indicates that the customer's cash inflow will be slower than shown above but also suggests an extremely lenient if not dangerous credit or collection operation. An attempt might well be made to improve the condition of the receivables, which would automatically improve the subject's immediate debt-paying power. The alternatives are either to refuse to sell to the subject or to grant terms longer than 30 days.

QUESTIONS AND PROBLEMS

1 Why does a financial statement have to be analyzed? Is it necessary to know what is *behind* the figures or can the figures "speak for themselves"?

2 Once the value of the various figures on assets, liabilities, net worth, etc., is determined, is it still necessary that the data be interpreted? Why?

3 Arrange the following assets in the order of their liquidity, placing the most liquid item first, and so on: land, marketable securities, buildings, investments in subsidiaries, cash in the bank, cash value of life insurance, prepaid and deferred charges, cash on hand, sales tax stamps, inventories of merchandise, accounts receivable, leaseholds, notes receivable, trade acceptances, miscellaneous assets.

4 In analyzing a financial statement by the valuation, or simple, method, what specific points would you desire to know about each of the following items appearing thereon?

a Cash

b Accounts receivable

c Merchandise inventory

d Fixed assets

5 Which items would you include in the current assets of The Hypothetical Retail Store for which figures are given in this chapter? Which items would you include among the current liabilities?

6 Why is it desirable that accounts payable for merchandise be separated from other amounts owed by the maker of the statement?

7 Under what circumstances may intangible assets be regarded as valuable from the standpoint of debt-paying power?

8 What is meant by the term "surplus"? What facts concerning it should be of value to the analyst of financial statements? What would be the effect of declaring a dividend out of paid-in surplus?

9 Comparative statements over a period of several years showed that the X company followed a policy of "ploughing in" most of its earnings. Would you as a creditor regard such a policy favorably? Discuss. What effect would an undivided surplus tax have upon such a policy and the credit of such a company?

10 From the information given below about the X Hardware Store, make an analysis similar to that shown in this chapter for The Hypothetical Retail Store, specifically answering the following questions:

a Are the sales adequate and above the break-even point?

b Is the gross margin adequate?

c What is the net profit per month?

d Assuming purchase on 2/10th proximo, net 30 days, which average about 45 days for net payment, can current bills on purchases thus made be paid on time?

e Can the average collection period be sufficiently improved to provide the additional funds needed to meet current obligations promptly?

f What can be done to improve the situation, and what is the real answer to the probable difficulty disclosed by the data?

THE X HARDWARE STORE

Cash	$3,852	Accounts payable	$29,493
Accounts receivable	10,407	Accrued taxes and	
Merchandise inventory	53,978	expense	2,790
Prepaid expenses	1,912	Mortgage (due in	
Fixtures and equipment	8,685	1 year and paid	
Real estate (store and		quarterly)	3,600
residence)	72,000	Mortgage (due after	
Total assets	$150,834	1 year)	33,357
		Total liabilities	$69,240
		Net Worth	81,594
		Total liabilities	
		and net worth	$150,834

Sales average $19,200 a month, or $230,400 annually.   Gross profit margin, 29 per cent.   Monthly expenses: drawing account, $1,125; wages, $1,440; all other expenses, $1,575; estimates for rent of owned building other than what occupancy expenses are already included in "all other expenses." at 2 per cent of sales, or $384 a month.   About 35 per cent of the sales are made on 30-day credit.

CHAPTER TWENTY-TWO

ratio analysis of
financial statements

An analysis of financial statements by a mere valuation of the different items contained therein or by any other simple method as discussed in the preceding chapter is altogether too inadequate. In fact, a mere comparison of amounts may even lead the analyst astray. An examination of bulk figures fails to stress sufficiently the quality and relationship of assets and equities and, consequently, leaves much to be desired in scientific statement analysis. Moreover, such an analysis affords little opportunity for comparison with other concerns operating in similar lines and under substantially similar conditions. It even makes difficult a comparison with the accomplishments of the same enterprise over a period of time.

Most important, the valuation or any other simple type of analysis fails to provide the required answers to the basic questions of the credit analyst.   On the basis of its financial position and operating results, will the subject be able to discount his bills or at least to meet his current obligations on time?   If not, will he be able to pay ultimately or can such payment be successfully enforced?   Can a satisfactory business relationship through credit extensions be established, maintained, and perhaps developed to a higher degree?

To remedy the situation, attempts have been made since the 1920's to formulate a system of financial statement analysis by the ratio method and to develop sets of proportions or ratios which would serve as guides in a systematic and orderly procedure for this work.   So much progress has been made in that area that the ratio method of analysis of financial statements is now commonly accepted by students of the subject and is widely used by governmental agencies like the Securities and Exchange Commission and by most of the progressive credit managers in their daily work in mercantile organizations and in commercial banking and other financial institutions.

The ratio theory. The theory underlying the ratio method of analyzing financial statements for credit purposes is, first, that the true financial position and extent of operating efficiency of a business can be revealed through ratios.   A ratio is the quotient showing the relationship existing between two pertinent and relevant items on the balance sheet, on the operating statement, or one on each, and may be expressed as a percentage or in times that the numerator is of the denominator. Second, it is assumed that there are standard relationships or ratios for each type or kind of business at a given time and general geographic area that indicate sound, or at least normal, financial condition and operations.   Third, it is assumed that no ratio is necessarily meaningful unless it is compared with the standard that has been developed or with some other yardstick that is generally recognized as serving the purpose satisfactorily.

Financial statement ratios are expressed variously.   As used in this treatment, however, an attempt has been made to construct the ratios in such a way that any substantial *upward* deviation from a standard ratio similarly computed would reflect a favorable condition and any substantial *downward* deviation would indicate the opposite.   The same conclusions would be reached when such ratios are compared with similar ones for previous periods for the same subject or risk.

Sources of standard ratios. A number of organizations, governmental and private, have made careful and extensive studies and have developed ratios for a representative number of concerns in a number of lines of business.   Attempts have thus been made to evolve sets of normal or standard ratios representing averages or medians derived from an examination of a number of statements.   One such organization is the Robert Morris Associates, an association of managers of commercial bank credit departments.   Dun & Bradstreet, Inc., is another organization that has been publishing annually certain ratios for 72 lines of business activity.   Trade associations often compile such data.   Among the governmental and semigovernmental agencies from which either developed-standard ratios or basic data from which to compute them may be obtained are the U.S. Department of Commerce, Securities and Exchange Commission, Federal Reserve Board and Banks, and the Federal Trade Commission.

In the absence of prepared standard ratios are of equal soundness or value.   Some may not be based upon a representative number of statements, others may include only the larger enterprises in a given line of business, and still others may develop few *pertinent* ratios for credit purposes.   Very important, also, is the method used in the development of the standard ratios.   In general, two methods are in use.   Unfortunately, a rather common method is to combine the individual statements for a given industry or line of business into a single giant statement from which the ratios are computed.   The only thing to recommend it is the savings in time, effort, and expense.   A suit of clothes made from average measurements of Mutt and Jeff will fit neither one nor the other.   Averages consisting of some of the poorest and the most successful concerns in a given line of business are more than meaningless, for they may even be misleading.   A better method by far seems to be that of determining, through an analysis of a representative number of statements individually handled, the "common" ratios, or those which are characteristic of most of the concerns represented in the study.   Modifications of this are to be found in the use of medians, interquartile ranges (whereby an average is given for each ratio for the upper quartile, one for the lower quartile, and a median), or other results from a frequency distribution.   Once such a norm is established, it can be used as a yardstick for the comparison of the ratios obtained in the analysis of any specific statement of a risk.

In the absence of prepared standard ratios in which a credit manager may be interested or when such ratios are not available to him, standard ratios may be prepared by him for his own use.   This may be done on the basis of statements for a given business and year selected, either at random or for known sound enterprises, from the credit department's own files.   Failing to do that, the credit manager can resort to his experience as a yardstick.   He has no doubt examined many statements from customers of his firm and thus has a fair idea as to what some of the standards should be.   In other words, one way in which ratios for a specific subject can be measured, as they actually are in many cases, though not to be generally recommended, is by comparing them with what the credit manager *remembers to be normal* for such concerns, or with the ratios of the more successful customers of the same type as the one whose statement is being analyzed.

Variables affecting ratios. Financial statement ratios vary with the line of business, location, size, method of operation, method of financing, business fluctuations, and perhaps some other factors. That is why, for example, standard ratios are prepared by kind of business and size of operation and annually. Some of the more important variables are discussed below.

As it is evident that the ratios of the statements for one individual firm will differ from those of another business concern, so is it true that the statements of fundamentally different business groups or lines of trade will be in *significant* contrast to those of other business groups or lines of trade. Consequently, the credit analyst of financial statements must keep in mind the fundamental factors which would modify his interpretations. Three factors to which heed must be given are the following: the line of trade in which the maker of the statement operates, the location of his business, and the date on the statement.

What constitutes a satisfactory relationship or status of affairs in one line of trade may be thoroughly unsatisfactory in another. The greater the style element involved in the merchandise handled, for example, the less certain and stable is the value of the inventory, and vice versa. Moreover, whereas high current ratios would be required for women's ready-to-wear establishments, much lower ones will prove adequate for grocers dealing in staple goods the value of which is not likely to shrink substantially. Hence, it is essential to recognize the difference between lines of trade and to establish a set of normal ratios for each line of business.

Similarly, concerns in the same line of trade will produce different normals in different sections of the country, although the variations by geographic divisions are not very pronounced. Different parts of the country may be affected unequally, however, by transportation, labor, and general business conditions. For these reasons, it is advisable to establish normal ratios not only on a national scale but on a sectional basis as well.

The time of the year in which the statement is prepared will also make a substantial difference in its proportional relationships. Because of seasonal variations in the demand, the stock of goods may be abnormally large during certain parts of the year and exceedingly low during others. A comparison of statements taken at either of these dates with the normal established for the industry will, therefore, prove misleading, unless such differentiation is recognized by the analyst and allowance for deviations made correspondingly.

Among other factors affecting ratios are the size of the enterprise and its method of operation. A large concern with a substantial net worth, for example, may have more of its working capital tied up in merchandise than a small enterprise with less net worth. Similarly, a concern selling principally for cash need not have so high a current ratio as one which operates altogether on a credit basis or one whose credit terms are unusually liberal.

The financial statement in a changing business world. Still another factor causing financial statement ratios to vary considerably is the business cycle. What may be regarded as a satisfactory ratio in a period of prosperity may be entirely inadequate in time of economic stress, and vice versa. For example, in a study of 35 lines of trade made by the senior author, it was found that in 24 lines of trade and manufacturing the current ratio was higher during recession years than in so-called "normal times," in nine lines of business the current position was weaker, and in two it remained the same. Similarly, the sales to receivables ratio in time of recession was higher in but eight lines of trade and manufacturing, 12 lines recorded no change, but in 15 out of the 35 lines of business the ratio was below normal. Thus the tendency during a recession is for the receivables ratio to become weaker, despite a stricter collection policy practiced during such times. This in itself makes necessary a higher current ratio, since the receivables are not in so liquid and so sound a condition. Similar variations are to be found in other ratios during periods of depression. Operating expenses, for instance, increase in time of stress despite all attempts to pare expenditures and to economize, because much of the overhead cannot be eliminated or drastically reduced. The volume of sales in dollars is greatly diminished, but the quantity of goods handled may still be very large. Thus the operating ratio is less favorable. It is therefore erroneous to compare the ratios of a statement made during a year of business stress with standard ratios developed during a year of good business conditions.

What ratios reveal. Contrary to a common conception, financial statements show more than the financial or capital strength of the business which they depict. When properly interpreted and skillfully analyzed, financial statements are equally helpful in measuring *capacity* to manage the different departments or functions of the business and may even reflect the *character* of the makers by the extent to which they have been "dressed up" for the purpose of making a favorable showing. It is important, therefore, that credit managers thoroughly understand the theory underlying statement analysis by means of ratios and possess the training and experience requisite to its effective application.

Practically every ratio aims to test the value of a given item and at the same time serves to indicate the efficiency with which that item has been managed or the judgment used in bringing about the condition of affairs as discovered in the analysis. For this reason the distinction that is sometimes made between static and dynamic ratios may be subject to serious question.[1] All ratios are static in that they indicate a condition at a given moment of time. Similarly, all ratios are dynamic because they reflect the efficiency of operation responsible for the condition shown by them at any given time. In the sense that all ratios have been evolved as a result of some activity they are dynamic. In the sense that they all denote conditions as they existed at the time the statement was prepared they are static. The distinction is indeed a flimsy one and hence will be disregarded in this discussion.

In general, it may be said that in an analysis of financial statements for credit purposes an attempt is made to accomplish the following ends:

1 To ascertain the true ability to pay current debts, by determining the actual liquidating value of the various current assets to a going concern and discovering possible understatments in current liabilities, instead of accepting these items as stated in the balance sheet

2 To discover the extent of reliance of the subject upon borrowed funds

3 To uncover false and misleading financial statements

4 To find out the capacity risk of the subject through ratios that show the relative efficiency of the enterprise and sagacity of the management

5 To determine the direction of the subject's business, whether it is moving forward, standing still, or retrograding

Valuable and pertinent ratios for credit analysis purposes. Authorities on financial statement analysis differ widely with respect to the number of ratios to be used in analyzing a financial statement and even more with regard to the ratios that are deemed pertinent or most important. It is believed that while in some instances exhaustive and detailed analyses of statements may prove helpful and even essential, in the vast majority of instances, especially in the mercantile field, a few ratios will

---

[1] Wherever the distinction is made, static ratios refer to the relationships existing between assets or liabilities, while dynamic ratios involve relationships between various items in the balance sheet with sales. The latter are sometimes called "velocity relationships." Static ratios are supposed to represent the business when at a standstill. Dynamic ratios, on the other hand, presumably suggest a moving picture of the business in the process of actual operation.

suffice to indicate the desirability of credit risk. It would, indeed, be foolhardy for any credit manager in the wholesale grocery business to attempt to analyze each statement submitted by his customers so as to obtain 12 or more ratios, in accordance with recommendations sometimes made by academically inclined statement-analysis zealots. Probably three or four ratios would prove adequate. In other instances, five or six ratios may be all that is necessary for a decision.

As to what ratios are deemed pertinent or most important depends upon, first, whether the analysis is made for credit purposes or for some other ends. From the type of ratios used in some cases, the professed intent to use them for credit intelligence must be seriously questioned. Second, it depends upon what answers are sought through the ratios. Instead of attempting to determine whether payment can be expected on current obligations on time or at least ultimately, the emphasis is sometimes placed on whether the subject has overinvested in receivables, in merchandise, or in fixed assets, on whether the subject has sufficient capital, and on whether he makes sufficient profits. That no doubt accounts for the undue emphasis in some instances on ratios involving working capital, net worth, and net profits. After all, for most businesses, which are generally small, net profits are a relatively minor item and are so nebulous (depending upon use of drawing accounts, use of payless help of members of the family, charge of rent on owned store, and charge of interest on owned capital) that they are easily overemphasized.

While it is recognized that different industries or kinds of business and different forms of business enterprise may require the use of different ratios, the total number with which a credit manager need be familiar is relatively small. From the standpoint of the credit analyst, it appears that the Current ratio is of utmost importance in that it gives a bird's-eye view of the total current financial position of the subject, which is of primary concern to those extending credit on short terms. Next in importance is the ratio of Net Worth to Total Debt, which shows at a glance the long-time financial position of the risk. Third in importance is the Operating Expense ratio, which shows in a general way the approximate efficiency of the operation of the subject's business. Aside from these three overall, or "mountain-view," ratios, those of greatest significance are: Sales to Receivables, Sales to Merchandise, Sales to Fixed Assets, Net Worth to Fixed Assets, Gross Profit to Sales, and Net Profit to Sales. In addition there are some few ratios that are deemed important by some, which have a secondary value in checking on the other ratios, or which are supplementary and throw additional light. These are: the Quick ratios; Fire Insurance to Merchandise; Sales to Net Worth; and Net Profit to Net Worth or to Total Assets.

The more important relationships or ratios will be discussed in some detail in this chapter in the order indicated above, while the others listed will be dealt with rather briefly. It is certainly not intended to convey the impression that all the ratios so listed or discussed are to be used in connection with every statement that is analyzed. They are presented rather as a means of conveying a clear and comprehensive picture of the whole subject and to indicate their relative importance, depending on the judgment of the credit manager in determining which of them are essential for his purposes.

Current ratio. This ratio is derived by dividing the current assets by the current liabilities. It indicates the margin between the amount currently due and that currently owing.

The current ratio has long been regarded by analysts as one of the most useful in interpreting the business subject's liquidity position, or its ability to meet current obligations as they come due. So great was the reliance placed upon it, in fact, that during the second decade of this century, when ratio analysis of balance sheets was first undertaken, this ratio alone was used. It is still significant, but today it is more properly used in conjunction with a number of other ratios, for the immediate debt-paying ability of a business is not the entirety of its financial picture. It is not enough merely to answer the question of whether a debtor is in a position to pay at the present or in the immediate future. Besides, the current ratio fails to reveal the quality of the current assets that are used in its computation and to that extent does not even answer adequately the question as to ability to pay bills currently.

In the development of the current ratio, one of the early and persisting notions regarding it was that it should always be a "2 to 1" ratio or perhaps a bit higher. By that is meant that in order to establish a favorable credit proportion, the statement should show $2 of current assets for every dollar of current liabilities. This 2 to 1 rule was based on the theory that a shrinkage might easily occur in assets but seldom in liabilities. Some accounts receivable may become slow and bad, and merchandise go out of style, become antiquated, or otherwise unsalable, whereas the indebtedness is rarely subject to shrinkage. Hence the necessity of a margin. The 2 to 1, or 200 per cent, ratio allows a 100 per cent margin of safety, which was generally acknowledged as ample and this has been accepted as a standard ratio after considerable experimentation, although it has later, through data revealed by many studies, been invalidated.

In the days immediately following the adoption of the 2 to 1 ratio it was the policy of many banking institutions, it is said, to refuse credit to a businessman who could not produce such a proportion between current assets and current liabilities. In present-day practice, however, the rule is seldom adhered to, because of the recognition of differences in types of business, location, date of issue of the statement, and other similar factors, the effect of which is to vary the proportions that are involved. Whereas for some lines of trade or manufacturing a current ratio of 2 to 1 may be fairly adequate, for others a proportion of as high as 3 to 1 or 4 to 1 may be essential.

From the ratio data published by such organizations as Dun & Bradstreet, Inc., and the Robert Morris Associates it is evident that standard ratios of Current Assets to Current Liabilities of 2 to 1 or less are noted for their absence or rarity and that such ratios vary not only with the line of business but also with the plane or level of economic activity in the same line of business. Furthermore, it may be advantageous for the current ratio of a risk to be higher than the average for the industry. However, to extend credit accommodations to a concern whose current liabilities exceed the current assets, representing a "floating debt," is equivalent to purchasing a lawsuit, since there is no likelihood that the current obligations will be met at maturity or at all.

Need for other ratios. The current ratio alone, as already suggested, gives insufficient evidence of the liquidity of a subject's condition; being based, as it is, upon the total current assets, it may include securities for which there is no market, inventory which is not readily salable, or receivables that are long past due or uncollectible. The current ratio is in itself merely a *quantitative* standard, measuring current assets in bulk against current liabilities in their entirety. It is of equal or possibly greater importance that a *qualitative* analysis of current assets be made to ascertain their character and liquidity, for a smaller than standard current ratio may be more than offset by fresh and rapidly collectible accounts or by merchandise which is readily disposable. For this reason, also because too much stress upon the current ratio often leads to "window dressing" or the employment of methods whereby this ratio can be temporarily improved for purposes of securing credit, other ratios are used to throw further light upon conditions which the current ratio portrays in a general way.

Net worth to debt. Inasmuch as creditworthiness is based upon long-run as well as short-run factors in the risk's financial condition, the current and quick ratios can reveal but one side of the situation. Debt is sometimes not paid out of current assets. Under conditions of insolvency it may be paid out of fixed assets. Consequently, creditors are concerned with the total value or worth of a risk's enterprise, particularly in relation to the debt it has outstanding.

Net worth constitutes the owners' equity in the business. In the case of a corporation it is the difference between the sum of all assets on the one hand and total liabilities on the other. In partnerships and single proprietorships it is designated as capital or net worth. Liabilities represent the financial contributions of others than the owners. They may be in the form of open accounts and short-term notes or in the form of long-term bonds and notes. The ratio of Net Worth to Liabilities, therefore, indicates the proportional relationship which exists between money or goods secured on credit from outsiders and the sum invested by owners of the business; it shows whether the business is operated on a "shoe string," when it depends largely upon creditors' financing, or whether it is "well heeled," as when owners' equity constitutes a large proportion of the total investment in the enterprise. Normally, owners should have about $1\frac{1}{2}$ to 2 times as much in the business as the creditors.[2]

In analyzing this ratio, it is often necessary to make a distinction between current and total liabilities. In different types of enterprises, the credit significance of the ratio varies with the relationship of each to the net worth. Current liabilities generally include accounts and notes payable, acceptances, accruals, and reserves for taxes. Such debts must be met within a relatively short period of time, certainly within a year. In accord with sound principles of financing, it is expected that the owner will have made some provision for meeting at least a part of the current liabilities through his initial investment. Other than current, liabilities include obligations such as bonds, which mature over a longer period, or long-term promissory notes secured by chattel and other mortgages. In all cases it is significant to distinguish between current and fixed liabilities.

As the proportion between funds invested by the owners increases over sums borrowed, the concern becomes less dependent upon the decisions and good will of its creditors for working capital. Another way of putting it is the higher the ratio, the less extended becomes the reliance of creditors upon intangible factors involving character and moral risk. On the other hand, an abnormally low ratio of Worth to Debt calls for considerable care and investigation on the part of the conservative credit grantor. Because of the effective significance of a proper balance between creditors' claims and owners' equities, a low ratio should cause the management immediately to revamp its affairs so as to enable it to maintain the integrity of its credit standing.

In case a considerable portion of the debt is funded, it is recommended that a Net Worth to *Current* Debt ratio be established in order

[2] For the determination of stock market values, a low net worth ratio for a successful concern may indicate high leverage and an advantage to the stockholders, but seldom would it be considered advantageous in ascertaining debt-paying power.

to determine whether or not this ratio is sufficiently high, for, as the proportion of funded debt increases, the necessity for current obligations should be reduced correspondingly.   Yet, on the other hand, when funded debt is involved, a relatively low ratio of Worth to Total Debt may not be as detrimental as where all liabilities are of a current nature, for the necessity of paying them in the immediate future need not be considered.   As a general rule, it is believed that in concerns with a tangible net worth between $50,000 and $250,000 the net worth ratio should be at least 1.5 to 1, i.e., the net worth should approximate $1\frac{1}{2}$ times the liabilities.   For concerns with a large tangible net worth, this ratio may be lower.   Rarely, however, should total liabilities of a commercial or industrial concern exceed the total net worth.[3]

Operating expense ratio. To develop this ratio, divide net sales or gross income by total operating expenses.   Thus, if the sales are $2 million and the operating expense $400,000, the operating ratio may be expressed as 5 to 1.   It means that it costs on an average of $1 to sell $5 worth of goods, or the cost of doing business is 20 per cent of sales.   This ratio serves as an index to relative general business efficiency by comparing it with those of other companies engaged in the same line of trade or by comparing it with a normal established for the line in question.

A rise in the operating ratio normally indicates improvement in the management of the business.   However, such an increase may have been caused, not by an increased rate of turnover, but by some temporary and doubtful economies that may be practiced, such as failure to provide adequate reserves for depreciation, bad debts, and the like.   The economies, although immediately resulting in an improved operating ratio, are obviously detrimental in the long run of events.

This ratio may also be expressed as a percentage of net sales, by dividing operating expenses by net sales.   For standards along this line, the results of the various censuses of business, of the studies made by the Robert Morris Associates, and of the surveys conducted by trade associations are very helpful.

Sales to receivables. Of the current assets, that which ranks in liquidity second to cash is accounts receivable.   The true value of total current assets, however, normally depends in substantial measure upon the degree of liquidity which actually exists in the receivables.   Something of their status can be determined from the Sales to Receivables ratio.

---

[3] Somewhat similar results can be accomplished by a so-called "Proprietary ratio," derived by dividing net worth by total assets, showing the percentage of the total capital or assets in the business that is financed by the owners.

This ratio is found by dividing the total net sales for the year by the total of accounts and notes or bills receivable. To secure a true measure of both the value of the receivables item and the efficiency of the credit department which manages it, credit sales and not total sales should be divided by the outstandings. This ratio indicates the proportion of the annual credit sales which is carried on the books as receivables, and denotes the economy and efficiency observed in handling capital tied up in receivables. The older an account becomes, the heavier the carrying expenses are, the greater the possibility of losses from bad debts, and the poorer the return on the investment. Unfortunately, the yardsticks that are now available are based on total sales, rather than credit sales, divided by the receivables.

A high ratio of Sales to Receivables, within certain limits, more than offsets the disadvantage from a current ratio somewhat below the normal. On the other hand, a low character of collectibility and stale receivables, as reflected by a low ratio of Sales to Receivables, necessitates a much higher current ratio than would have been otherwise required, in order to secure a wider margin of safety against shrinkage caused by bad debts.

To determine the normal ratio of Sales to Receivables, a knowledge of the concern's terms of sale is essential. To illustrate, let us assume that the credit sales for the year amounted to $2,222,063, and that the receivables were $206,896. By dividing the sales by the receivables we obtain a figure showing the number of times these receivables are turned over during the year, which is 10.74 in this case (2,222,063 ÷ 206,896). To determine the number of days of sales carried on the books, divide 10.74 into 365, the days of the year (365 ÷ 10.74), the result being approximately 34. If the firm sells on 30-day terms, the ratio approaches a normal condition. As a matter of fact, under ordinary circumstances, a comfortable condition of affairs is indicated as long as no more than 25 per cent of the previous month's receivables are outstanding at the end of the current month. Thus, 35 to 40 days' receivables outstanding on a statement of a concern selling on 30-day terms would undoubtedly make a favorable showing.

To measure the liquidity of the receivables over a period of time. it is, of course, necessary to make a study of comparative statements. Should such successive statements disclose an increase in the bulk of the receivables, there is no cause for anxiety, provided the sales have increased either in the same proportion or at a greater rate of speed, which fact will be shown by a constant or increasing ratio, respectively. If, however, an increasing volume of sales is accompanied by a decreasing ratio between sales and receivables, it may be presumed that the liquidity of the receivables is diminishing and that a greater proportion of past-due accounts is carried on the books.

It is conceivable that, by adopting too strict a credit policy, this ratio may be raised considerably. Since this would be done at the expense of sales volume, it is seldom, if ever, justifiable; hence it is true that the higher the ratio, *within certain bounds*, the greater the liquidity of the receivables, and consequently, the higher the credit capacity of the risk.

Sales to merchandise. The quality of the current assets, and in turn the current ratio, depends also upon the condition of merchandise in the reported inventory and the rate at which it is moving. Inferences concerning these factors can be drawn from a study of the Sales to Merchandise ratio.

To secure this ratio, divide the net sales by the total merchandise inventory. It shows the number of times a merchant is able to convert his stock of goods into cash or receivables. Thus, if the merchandise on hand amounts to $60,000 and the sales for the year are $240,000, the appropriate number of times a merchant is turning his stock is determined by dividing the inventory into the annual sales ($240,000 ÷ $60,000), which in this instance is 4 times. Although this is the method commonly employed by credit managers in ascertaining the approximate rate of stock turnover, it is nevertheless inaccurate and not in keeping with sound practice, because sales under such circumstances are figured at selling prices, which necessarily include gross profits, whereas the inventory is usually priced at cost, or at cost or buying market, whichever is lower.

Much confusion is current everywhere in the methods of determining stock turnover. The true turnover can be found only (1) by dividing total sales by the average selling value of the merchandise on hand or (2) by dividing the approximate cost of all goods sold by the cost of the average stock kept on hand. Should the inventory not represent the average stock of goods on hand, that fact must be taken into consideration. In order to indicate clearly the two respective correct methods of determining stock turnover, two illustrations are submitted. It is assumed that the merchant under consideration has realized a gross profit of 30 per cent.

1. Sales Price Basis

$$\frac{\text{Total sales at selling price (\$240,000)}}{\text{Inventory at sales price (\$85,713.60)}} = \text{turnover (2.8 times)}$$

2. Cost Basis

$$\frac{\text{Total sales at cost (\$168,000)}}{\text{Inventory priced at cost (\$60,000)}} = \text{turnover (2.8 times)}$$

Another common method of determining the stock turnover on a cost basis is to take the merchandise inventory on hand at the beginning of the fiscal period and add to it the purchases during the year, or the cost of manufactured goods in the case of a manufacturing concern. From this total deduct the merchandise on hand at the end of the year. The resulting figure is the amount of merchandise at cost price that has been sold during the year, which, when divided by the average inventory at cost, gives the stock turnover for the year. For example:

Merchandise on hand at beginning of year	$ 56,000
Purchases during year	172,000
Total	$228,000
Less merchandise on hand at end of year	60,000
Cost of goods sold during year	$168,000

Stock turnover: $168,000 ÷ $60,000 = 2.8 times

Knowing either from normals established in the trade or from experience what the rate of turnover should be, the credit analyst has no difficulty in discovering the degree of business ability possessed by the risk and the freshness and salability of the stock of merchandise. Rapid stock turns indicate good merchandise management, fresh stock, and liquid assets. A slow turnover, on the other hand, reflects possible overvaluation of inventory, too large an investment in merchandise, careless buying, and possibly dead and unmovable stocks.

Sales to fixed assets. This ratio is secured by dividing the net sales by the total fixed assets and serves to indicate the dollars of sales for every dollar invested in plant, machinery, equipment, and other noncurrent assets.

When a low ratio of Sales to Fixed Assets is shown, it means that the degree of plant utilization is relatively low, which amounts to the same thing as saying that the concern is too large for the volume of business transacted. It is to be noted that the amount invested in fixed assets varies considerably with different types of business. Many department stores, for example, show sales of $10 or more to every dollar of fixed assets, whereas large steel companies, where the investment in plant and equipment is exceedingly heavy, often show a ratio of less than 2 to 1; hence the necessity for a norm for every line of trade.

This ratio can be used to advantage in conjunction with that of Worth to Fixed Assets. If both of these ratios are below normal or falling, a condition obtains where plant is enlarging proportionally at a greater rate than worth, and where sales are not keeping pace with the increase in size, which is indicative of a dangerous and pernicious policy of overexpansion. When such a situation is discovered, it behooves both the credit grantor and the credit risk to revamp conditions so that the plant is either decreased gradually or else production and selling efficiency enhanced so as economically to justify the size of the enterprise.

Net worth to fixed assets. This ratio is derived by dividing the net worth by the total fixed or noncurrent assets. It indicates the proportion of net worth or owners' equity tied up in plant, machinery, equipment, and other fixed properties. The margin over and above 100 per cent indicates the proportion of the net worth provided for working capital.

Unless permanent working capital has been provided through the issue of bonds or long-time notes, it is essential that owner-controlled funds be secured for the purpose. Good business judgment argues against relying upon mercantile or bank creditors to supply funds needed for that part of the working capital which is permanently required in the business.

If an increase in net worth is accompanied by a decrease in the ratio of Net Worth to Fixed Assets, the inference that may reasonably be drawn is that the owners have expanded the plant more rapidly than warranted by the normal growth of the business. Such a development, where liquid assets are converted into fixed assets, is likely to occur in a period of rising prices, when optimism prevails and the hope of future large profits stimulates expansion to a point of embarrassment. A declining ratio under such circumstances should be a danger signal to creditors, calling for extreme precautions in their dealings with the subject thus affected.

Gross profit to sales. This ratio is obtained by dividing the amount of gross profit, which is the difference between the net sales and cost of goods sold, by the net sales and is expressed as a percentage of the latter. It is the margin on which the business has to operate. Its adequacy can be readily determined, since this type of information is widely used and is normally available. While the operating expense ratio measures the overall operating efficiency of the enterprise, the Gross Profit to Sales ratio measures the overall, or gross, profitableness of the business. When this ratio is higher than the Operating Expense to Sales ratio, a net operating profit is indicated. It may thus be advisable to develop a subsidiary ratio of Gross Profit to Operating Expense.

Net profit to sales. This ratio is computed by dividing the net profit or net income by the net sales and is expressed as a percentage of the latter. As such data are readily available, the subject's ratio can be compared with a standard even when standards are not available for most of the other ratios. Furthermore, profitableness of an enterprise is normally measured by this type of index.

Quick ratios. A ratio indicating the possibility of current liabilities being met relatively quickly is derived by dividing only cash and receivables by current liabilities. By thus eliminating inventories and any securities held as permanent investment,[4] one may determine the fund likely to be available for paying debts in the *near* future. It may be necessary, however, further to scrutinize the receivables, for they, too, may not be as liquid as might be assumed or hoped. This ratio is often referred to as the "acid test" ratio and is deemed satisfactory in many types of business when the relationship is 1 to 1 or better.

Another quick ratio often employed is that which relates only Cash to Current Liabilities, the amount of cash on hand and in the bank being divided by such liabilities. Many credit grantors desire to see at least 10 to 20 cents in cash for every dollar of current indebtedness. A ratio which reflects less than 10 cents cash for every dollar of current liabilities might indicate lack of ready working capital and failure to maintain the 20 per cent balance in proportion to loans, on which some commercial banks insist. The subject's ability to borrow at a bank would thus be impaired. On the other hand, if the cash item is larger than 20 per cent of total current debt, it might indicate ultraconservatism and failure to put the funds to work for the profit of the enterprise. To find just what the proportion shall be, as in all other ratios, it is necessary to know the common ratio for the business under consideration, either from special studies made along this line or from experience. So far few attempts have been made to develop a standard ratio of this type, although it is of importance in testing both the value of the cash item and the efficiency of the treasurer who manages it. Current emphasis on cash flow analyses should stimulate interest in this ratio.

Fire insurance to merchandise. That the question of fire insurance is very important in considering a credit risk is evidenced by the untiring activity of the Insurance and Fire Prevention Committee of the National Association of Credit Management. Among other functions, this committee has as its important duty to devise methods whereby debtors may be induced to carry adequate insurance against fire losses. A concern selling goods on credit to a merchant who is not protected against fire is assuming a double risk; the ordinary risk incident to credit granting and the risk of loss from fire. Furthermore, neglect to protect himself against fire losses frequently indicates to the creditor that the merchant's business methods in general are more or less loose. If the stock is properly insured in case of fire, the merchant will not only have enough for the payment of his obligations, but will also be able to start anew.

---

[4] Securities which are to be held temporarily for seasonal investment of cash may be regarded as cash for purposes of this ratio.

To produce this ratio, divide the value of the policy by the average merchandise kept on hand, or by the inventory shown in the statement. In the event that the proportion of insurance to merchandise is low, the inference is that the merchant is too careless and is not sufficiently protected or that the merchandise inventory has been overstated. The nearer this ratio is to 100 per cent, or 1 to 1, the more favorable it is, and vice versa.

In this connection, creditors should bear in mind the 80 per cent coinsurance clause. The purpose of this clause is to induce policyholders to carry insurance to nearly full value of the property insured.

Sales to net worth. To produce this ratio, divide the net sales by the net worth. By this means the dollars of sales for every dollar of owners' equity is determined.

The theory underlying the development of this ratio is based on the assumption that there is an optimum point in the activity of owners' invested capital. Assuming a given margin of profit, the greater the volume of sales, the greater the profits on fixed capital and net worth. Hence, a rising ratio indicates greater activity of the funds invested, and, consequently, larger earnings. If such ratio be too high, however, it may reveal a condition where the concern is overextending its operations and transacting too much business for its owners' investment. Such a concern needs either to retrench its activities or else increase its equity investment. It is, therefore, advisable to analyze and appraise this ratio in connection with the proportion of Worth to Debt, for a high Sales to Worth ratio is apt to be accompanied by a low ratio of Worth to Debt, an extreme approaching the danger point of credit.

More frequently, business lacking progressive management does not keep the funds actively employed. If this rate of activity is below normal or falling, it indicates a condition of "dry rot," where the investment is moving too slowly and sluggishly and the funds are not sufficiently productive. It is a symptom either of overcapitalization or of the approach of a natural death of stagnation.

Net profit to net worth or to total assets. The earnings to owners' investment (Net Profit to Net Worth) ratio is found by dividing the annual net profit by the owners' equity. It indicates the general profitableness of the enterprise. A high ratio may mean one of two things, namely, that profits are high, or that the business is financed primarily through the issue of bonds and so-called "short-time" notes. When the ratio is falling, the company is obviously retrograding.

Probably a better measure of the earning power of a business enterprise is the ratio of net earnings to *total capital* investment. This ratio shows the net results realized from the various operations of the concern and the full amount of capital employed. To establish this ratio, the total capital as represented by the sum of the firm's assets should be divided into the net profits for the year under consideration (see Fig. 4-1).

Financial statement analysis of small businesses. The financial statements of many small business concerns do not lend themselves to very detailed analysis. Moreover, credit analysis in such cases is further handicapped by the fact that no financial statements are prepared or available when needed. Lack of proper accounting methods and facilities, as well as indifference of proprietors to requests for what they regard as confidential information, are the major causes. Consequently, it is often necessary for a credit manager to distill his information from a minimum of financial statement data.

The object of all financial statement investigation being to determine the prospect of securing future payment for merchandise sold on credit or money loaned and to ascertain the length of time entailed in obtaining such payment, it is possible to arrive at some conclusions from a knowledge only of a few financial items including sales, markup, accounts payable, and cash on hand and in bank. The logic of this type of analysis is based upon the fact that small businesses, not resorting often to the use of borrowed funds nor being encumbered with obligations for other than merchandise and the usual operating expenses, discharge old and new obligations alike only if and when operating income permits.

Credit used by small businesses usually must be paid directly and entirely out of income. Not all of the income derived from sales, however, is available for use in meeting obligations for merchandise bought on credit. A portion of it must be used for operating expenses and that portion is usually expended before payments are made to merchandise creditors. It is safe, therefore, to conclude that there is available for merchandise payments whatever remains after the operating margin is deducted from net sales. For example, an organization with sales of $100,000 a year, operating on a 30 per cent markup or margin on sales, has available $5,833.33 monthly for merchandise payments

$$(\$100,000 \div 12 \times 70\% = \$5,833.33)$$

In addition to each month's receipts, there is also available for paying creditors cash that was on hand and in the bank at the beginning of the year. It must be remembered, however, that a minimum of cash must be maintained at all times to meet contingencies and for normal current needs so long as the business remains a going concern. If it is assumed that sales are evenly dispersed throughout the year, there is no change in the collection of accounts receivable, and the accounts payable amount to $17,500, it will require about 3 months' income from sales which can be allocated to the payment of accounts payable before such current debt can thus be liquidated ($17,500 ÷ $5,833.33). In this manner it is possible to ascertain in advance the approximate length of time that an account will be outstanding and the terms that may have to be granted in selling to such a customer if at all acceptable. As a matter of fact, such a determination can be made more readily from the subject's paying habits, although not as precisely.

Weighting the ratios. To reduce statement analysis for credit purposes to mathematical precision, it would be desirable to assign a weight to each of the ratios used, provided, of course, one could agree first on what ratios are the most useful. One such system of weighting was developed by the Robert Morris Associates, using but seven ratios. By applying the same technique to the seven ratios which the authors of this book regard as most important and assigning to them the approximate weights indicated below, an index can be developed that will show mathematically how the concern whose statement is being analyzed compares with the standard ratios for the same kind of business. For the sake of the following illustration, an actual statement for a certain type of store was used for the same year for which the standard ratios were available. Obviously, the ratios can be expressed either as so many to one or in percentages. Likewise, the operating ratio may be expressed either as so many dollars of sales per dollar of expense or as a percentage that the expenses are of net sales. It is doubtful whether we have as yet reached the point where ratios can be properly weighted and the

Ratio	Weight, per cent	Standard ratios	Subject firm's ratios	Relation, per cent	Value, per cent
Current	25	3.0 to 1	4.8 to 1	160	40.0
Net Worth to Debt	20	2.4 to 1	1.5 to 1	62	12.4
Operating ratio	15	3.1 to 1	2.8 to 1	90	13.5
Sales to Receivables	10	6.9 to 1	5.3 to 1	77	7.7
Sales to Merchandise	15	6.0 to 1	7.6 to 1	127	19.1
Sales to Fixed Assets	10	3.8 to 1	3.1 to 1	82	8.1
Worth to Fixed Assets	5	1.5 to 1	1.3 to 1	87	4.4
Index	..	....	....	...	105.2

results mathematically computed. Much experimentation remains to be done by credit men before this can be accomplished.

Value of comparative statement analysis. The analysis of a concern's financial responsibility from one statement gives the credit manager an insight into the condition of the business at a given moment—at the time the statement was prepared. The business is inspected and scrutinized, as it were, when at a standstill, especially with respect to ratios that deal only with asset, liability, or net worth items. To be sure, it is possible to ascertain something of the dynamics of the enterprise when the ratios involve one or more of the items from the operating or income part of the total statement.

Much more about the dynamics of the business that will throw light on "what has happened" over a period of time and "how it got there" can be learned, however, when statements can be compared for at least 3 years. Much valuable information can thus be disclosed by comparing the essential items at different dates and by noting changes in ratios at these intervals. From such comparisons the credit manager can thus accurately determine whether the subject's business is improving, standing still, or going down. This, however, need not detract from the great value that can be derived from an analysis of a single statement, which is often all that a credit manager can secure.

Miscellaneous types of ratio analysis. There is no limit to the ingenuity of thinking credit managers in devising methods of dealing with credit and collection problems. The analysis of financial statements by the ratio method is no exception. That may account for some of the unusual ratios, though mostly of doubtful value or significance, encountered especially in the current literature on the subject.

It may be worthwhile, nevertheless, to call attention at this juncture to at least one type of analysis that is used to supplement the more commonly accepted ratios in which emphasis is placed on age—Age of Receivables, Age of Inventories, Age of Conversion, and Age of Current Liabilities. To illustrate the computation of these four ratios, the data for The Hypothetical Retail Store in the preceding chapter are used, with the following results:

$$\frac{\text{Receivables of \$14,000}}{\text{Annual credit sales of \$75,600 (45\% of \$168,000)}}$$
$$\times \ 360 = 67 \text{ days as Age of Receivables}$$

$$\frac{\text{Merchandise inventory of \$53,400}}{\text{Cost of goods sold in year of \$115,920 (69\% of \$168,000)}}$$
$$\times \ 360 = 166 \text{ days as Age of Inventories}$$

Age of Conversion, which indicates the time in days that is required to turn cash into merchandise inventory, then to receivables, and back into cash, is 233 days (67 + 166) for the 45 per cent of the business done on credit and 166 days for the remaining 55 per cent of the volume.

$$\frac{\left\{\begin{array}{c}\text{Current liabilities of \$29,140 (including only}\\\text{monthly instalments on mortgage)}\end{array}\right\}}{\text{Annual sales of \$168,000}} \times 360 = 37 \text{ days}$$

as Age of Current Liabilities, indicating that purchases on 30-day terms are currently being paid about 7 days late but are likely to be paid in a much slower manner unless the store can either increase its rate of conversion or acquire additional long-term funds.

It will be noted that in the above computations only 360 days were used for the number of days in the year, as that is equivalent to 30 days per month in event that the computations are also to be made on a monthly basis. It should also be noted that the Age of Receivables is the same as the average collection period computed in connection with the discussion in the preceding chapter. Finally, the Age of Inventories can also be arrived at by dividing the Merchandise to Sales (at cost) ratio into 360 days. All this corroborates the idea that there are many roads leading to heaven and that, objectively considered, there is probably no one best road.

QUESTIONS AND PROBLEMS

1 Why is an analysis of financial statements by mere examination of bulk figures considered inadequate?

2 What is the ratio theory of financial statement analysis?

3 What two points of special importance does each ratio generally reveal?

4 Show that the financial statement not only gives the analyst a conception of the maker's financial condition but also throws light on his character and capacity.

5 Indicate the three principal classes or types of sources of standard ratio yardsticks:

   a In order of common usage

   b In order of validity

6 Ratios are affected by the date of the statement, time with reference to the business cycle, line of trade or kind of business, geographic location of the business, size of the operation, and method of operation. List these in order of importance in influencing the ratios generally and indicate how a specific ratio may be most seriously affected by one of these factors and not necessarily by others.

7 What is meant by an overall, or "mountain-view," ratio? Which ratios are of this type and why?

8 What is the "2 to 1" ratio?   Show that it is a myth.

9 In analyzing a given statement, how do you know whether the ratios obtained show a healthy condition of affairs or are indicative of unfavorable circumstances?

10 Would a ratio of sales to merchandise for a manufacturing concern bear any different significance than for a trading establishment?   Explain.   What further information would be needed in the former instance?

11 In a year of prosperity and just prior to a predicted recession in an industry where the model ratio of sales to merchandise was 4.8, company A had a ratio of 3.5, while company B had a ratio of 6.2.   Other things being equal, which of these two companies was the better credit risk at the time and why?   Under more normal conditions, which of them would be preferred and why?

12 In what way, if any, would an improper collection policy or undue liberality in credit granting be reflected in a ratio analysis of a financial statement?

13 The Sunnyside Corporation, manufacturers of paints, had property valued at $320,000, consisting of a building, equipment, and materials.   The building alone, which was insured for $150,000, was valued at approximately $230,000. What would be the liability of the insurer if the loss on the building as a result of a fire were $200,000?   Only $160,000?

14 The Smith Clothing Store, selling men's wear exclusively, became interested in adding to its line the furnishings items manufactured by the High Fashion Men's Wear Company.   This would require a line of credit from the latter of $5,000 to $10,000, depending upon the season of the year.   Upon request, the following statements of financial condition and profit and loss were submitted by the Smith Clothing Store:

BALANCE SHEET AS OF JAN. 31, 19XX

Cash on hand and in bank including sales tax	$ 16,339.30
Receivables	53,272.16
Inventory	117,619.30
Fixed Assets	38,402.60
Total assets	$225,633.36
Accounts payable, current	$ 19,423.51
Note payable, bank	25,000.00
Due to officers	9,995.41
Accrued and deferred	6,440.25
Reserve for accounts receivable	8,574.11
Reserve for depreciation	16,864.66
Capital stock	56,250.00
Surplus	83,085.42
Total liabilities and capital	$225,633.36

PROFIT AND LOSS FOR FISCAL
YEAR ENDED JAN. 31, 19XX

Net sales	$662,905.23	
Less cost of merchandise sold	417,959.99	
Gross profit	$244,945.24	
Discount earned	9,356.38	
Bad accounts recovery	3,181.17	
Income from shoe department	5,423.40	
Other income	402.05	$263,308.64
Salaries and wages	$145,066.38	
Fixed expense	34,853.85	
Departmental expense	5,255.88	
Advertising	35,093.98	
General Expense	27,560.30	247,830.39
Net profit before income tax		$ 15,478.25

The credit manager of the High Fashion Men's Wear Company subjected the above statements to an analysis by means of ratios as a basis for his conclusions. In doing so, he was guided by the limited information he had on hand concerning some of the typical ratios obtaining at that time for men's clothing stores in about the same sales volume class. These stores had a turnover of inventory on cost of sales of 2.4 times, a turnover of current assets on net sales of 2.5, a ratio of Tangible Net Worth to Total Debt of 1.2, a ratio of Tangible Net Worth to Fixed Assets of 5.5, Cash and Receivables to Current Debt of 76 per cent, Current Assets to Current Liabilities of 2.3, gross profit of 37 per cent of sales, and expenses of about 33.5 per cent of sales.

On the basis of the ratio analysis, what conclusions seem to be warranted with regard to whether or not the application shall be accepted, the terms of sale to be granted, and the amount of the credit limit? Prepare a report on this matter.

15 In line with its usual practice, the General Wholesale Grocery Corporation submitted the following statements of its financial and operating conditions to all its major sources of supply. By means of ratios, analyze these statements, indicating their significance for credit purposes. Ratios made available by a trading association for wholesale grocers of about the same asset size that might be useful in this analysis are as follows: Current ratio, 1.8; Net Worth to Debt, 0.8; Total Sales to Receivables, 27.0; Total Sales at cost to Year-end Merchandise Inventory, 13.7; Net Worth to Fixed Assets, 2.7; Net Sales to Fixed Assets, 38.2; Gross Profit to Net Sales, 7.9; Net Profit to Net Sales, 0.6; Net Profit to Net Worth, 9.0; Net Profit to Total Assets, 4.0.

YEAR-END BALANCE SHEET, 19XX

Cash	$ 11,448	
Accounts receivable—customers	127,089	
Accounts receivable—other	3,112	
Inventory	548,034	$ 689,683
Land	$ 81,474	
Buildings	200,902	
Refrigerator equipment	69,031	
Furniture and fixtures	30,755	
Trucks and automobiles	40,013	
Total	$422,175	
Less reserve for depreciation	118,502	310,673
Prepaid		3,959
Total assets		$1,004,315
Due banks	$ 75,000	
Current mortgage payments	23,981	
Accounts payable	105,556	
Due affiliated companies	13,963	
Accruals	13,857	$ 232,357
Mortgage loan	$189,905	
Due individuals	34,710	224,615
Total liabilities		$ 456,972
Capital stock		496,600
Surplus		50,743
Total liabilities and capital		$1,004,315

OPERATING STATEMENT, 12-MONTH PERIOD, 19XX

Sales		$4,709,424
Less: Returns	27,738	
Discounts	61,538	
Net sales		$4,620,148
Beginning inventory	$ 698,186	
Purchases	4,126,245	
Freight	29,176	$4,853,607
Ending inventory		548,035
Gross cost of goods sold		$4,305,572
Discounts earned		55,862
Net cost of goods sold		$4,249,710

Gross profit		370,438
Warehouse expense	119,066	
Selling expense	90,111	
Delivery expense	57,234	
General and administrative expense	109,078	$ 375,489
Operating loss		5,184
Other income and deductions		
Income taxes—current year	$ (2,297)*	
Income taxes—prior year	(2,490)*	
Life insurance expense	(1,026)*	
Profit on sale of equipment	33	
Miscellaneous income	429	
Rent and service charges	10,462	
Refund of interest on taxes paid	4,641	$ 9,752
Income transferred to surplus		$ 4,568

16 Hypothetical Department Store X is desirous of establishing a line of credit at your bank. Upon request, it submitted the latest financial statement, and as credit manager of the bank you were asked to analyze it and make your recommendation to the loan and discount committee for its action. The statement presented the following condensed information:

STATEMENT OF FINANCIAL POSITION FOR YEAR ENDED JAN. 31, 19XX

Cash	$ 523,660
Accounts and notes receivable—customers†	1,351,428
Accounts receivable—suppliers, etc.	132,339
Merchandise inventories	1,811,376
Prepaid rent, insurance, and other expenses	117,319
Current assets	$3,936,122
Investments and miscellaneous assets	$ 511,400
Land and buildings (less accumulated depreciation)‡	366,250
Store fixtures and equipment (less accumulated depreciation)	858,358
Fixed and other assets	$1,736,008
Total Assets	$5,672,130

* Amounts in parentheses denote red figures.
† Regular accounts, $1,046,625; instalment accounts and notes, $90,303; revolving credit accounts, $193,403; equity in instalment and revolving accounts sold for the year (in the amount of $1,016,487), $21,097.
‡ Buildings and improvements are on leased property.

Accounts payable	$ 544,457
Accrued accounts	197,108
Taxes (other than Federal income)	151,420
Federal income taxes	263,437
Current liabilities	$1,156,422
Long-term debt*	$ 908,000
Common stock	1,489,170
Retained earnings	2,118,538
Stockholders' equity	$3,607,708
Total Liabilities and Net Worth	$5,672,130

CONDENSED STATEMENT OF EARNINGS FOR YEAR ENDED JAN. 31, 19XX

Net sales (including leased departments)	$12,875,565
Cost of goods sold	8,521,513
Gross margin	$ 4,354,052
Operating expenses	3,848,083
Operating earnings	$ 505,968
Net deductions from earnings	21,897
Net income (earnings before Federal income taxes)	$ 484,071

During the year sales of departments operated by outsiders on a lease or license basis amounted to 6 per cent of total. Of all net sales, 42 per cent were on a cash basis, 39 per cent were on regular 30-day charge accounts, 11 per cent were made up of revolving credit accounts, and 8 per cent consisted of regular instalment or deferred payment accounts.

On the basis of all pertinent standard ratios for department stores of the appropriate size class, analyze the data contained in the above statements, interpret their meaning, and submit the recommendations requested by your superiors.

* Promissory notes maturing in from 3 to 5 years.

CHAPTER TWENTY-THREE

sources of foreign
credit information

With but few exceptions, the task of administering credit involved in foreign trade is essentially the same as that in domestic commerce. The
same factors which make for an acceptable credit risk domestically characterize also the good risk of foreign buyers. All such buyers must present
evidence of possessing character, capacity, and capital, and conditions
must be propitious to the extension of credit. To these four C's of
credit, however, is frequently added a fifth, namely, Country,[1] for in
foreign trade special consideration of the laws, customs, practices, and so
forth of the country of the buyer is imperative. Of particular importance
are special conditions and the currency situation appertaining to a given

---

[1] Although the factors which may be classified as "country" are also fundamentally "conditions," the
pecularities of foreign trade justify the emphasis on the foreign conditions.

country.   In general, virtually the same types of information and sources thereof are available concerning foreign buyers as for those within the United States.

All sources of credit information concerning foreign buyers may be divided into two main classes.   One consists of sources located abroad, particularly in the locality of the customer; the other comprises the various sources available in this country.   The former includes the buyer himself, his banking connections, exporters' representatives abroad, and foreign agencies.   The latter consists of banks, American exporters, trade credit organizations, mercantile agencies, the Foreign Credit Interchange Bureau of the National Association of Credit Management, the American Foreign Credit Underwriters Corporation, publishing companies, and the Federal government through its consular services and the U.S. Department of Commerce.

SOURCES
LOCATED
ABROAD

The most important sources outside the United States are traveling salesmen and the customer himself.   Some information may also be secured from mercantile agencies in the locality of the buyer but the data are often biased and unreliable except in the major countries.   Inquiries may also be sent to banks in the city of the applicant.   Many foreign banks will reply, provided an international money order covering return postage and the small fee which is charged for the service is included.   Other banks refuse to reply unless inquiries are addressed to them through their American correspondents.

Several objections, however, are raised against the use of foreign sources of credit information.   Cabling is expensive, and much time is consumed in the process of communicating by mail, so that when the report is finally received, the need for it might have long since passed.   In the second place, it is difficult to determine the reliability of foreign agencies which sell credit information.   Although many of them are entirely dependable, many others are unworthy.   Then, too, lack of personal contact and close relations with the sources employed result in superficial, biased, and incomplete reports.

Direct information. Relatively little credit information can be obtained from prospective customers.   Financial statements are rarely furnished, and in many countries they should not be asked for, lest the applicants take offense.   This is particularly true of Latin and Oriental countries.   Although in some countries the practice of submitting financial statements has already come into vogue, such places are few and far between.   There is still a general aversion to divulging details regarding their businesses or personal affairs, probably because of the fear that strictly confidential information may fall into the hands of competitors. Another explanation for the general reluctance to supply financial statements is the method of taxation which prevails in some countries.   Taxes are frequently based on the registered capital of the concern.   Where this is true, companies usually register a nominal sum and intentionally refrain from keeping books of account.   Because of this practice, it is frequently impossible to construct an accurate statement, and even if it were possible to do so, the fear that such statement might find its way into the hands of tax authorities serves as a deterrent.   Finally, many foreigners are too sensitive and take offense at any action on the part of sellers which in any way reflects upon their personal qualities of honesty, ability, and integrity.   This general reluctance to furnish a financial statement, however, can sometimes be overcome by the vendor sending the foreign buyer a copy of his own statement as a gesture of mutual confidence.

It should be observed that, even where financial statements are obtainable, they are useful only as a general guide and not as the sole reliance for a credit decision, partly because of inaccuracies, intentional or otherwise, and partly because of the difficulty in interpreting their contents.   Methods of accounting in many foreign countries are loose and unsystematic.   Hence many figures presented are often the result of mere guesswork, and since it is the natural desire of every customer to make as favorable a showing as possible, he may give himself all the benefit of the doubt in estimating the worth of his assets.   Furthermore, credit managers, because of their unfamiliarity with values of real properties and other items appearing on the balance sheet in the country in which the customer resides, find it next to impossible to determine accurately from the figures submitted the actual net worth of the business, as it is done in an analysis of statements in the domestic trade.

Buyer's bank.   When it is preferred not to solicit information directly from the prospective buyer, it is possible at times to obtain it from his bank or from other banks in his locality.   Here, again, the information has a wide range of value, varying from very good to worthless.   It usually consists of a perfunctory report to the effect that the foreign buyer is a highly respected member of the community and is beloved by all.   If such information is not prejudiced, usually it is incomplete and inconclusive, late, and sometimes misleading.   Many exporters feel that little reliance can be placed upon such information.

Traveling salesmen and agents. Many American exporters have traveling salesmen abroad or employ resident agents. Although their chief interest is in securing orders, it is possible, nevertheless, to educate them by proper cooperation to the necessity of giving an unprejudiced opinion concerning the credit responsibility of their customers. Good salesmen generally appreciate the importance of carrying no bad accounts on their books and can be trusted, therefore, to give an unbiased statement of a customer's standing in the community and his management efficiency. They are on the ground, see the customer in his setting, and can learn many important details regarding his habits and the conduct of the enterprise. It should, therefore, be insisted that they furnish at least one report about each customer at the time when it is of most value, namely, when an application for credit accommodations is made for the first time.

DOMESTIC SOURCES

Because of the factors of time, space, language differences, and dissimilarities of credit standards and customs, the most useful information concerning foreign buyers is obtained from sources located within the United States. These are, for the most part, similar to those providing credit information concerning domestic risks.

Banks as a source of credit information. Reliable information about foreign houses sending in orders for the first time may be secured with little delay from the larger American banks. Banking houses which specialize in foreign trade are constantly revising their credit files and securing data on all buyers abroad. This information is obtained from the numerous branches which some of these banks have established in foreign countries, and is supplied free of charge as a part of the regular service to customers. If the exporter's bank lacks the information sought, it is usually secured for him from another bank, since all banks have adopted the practice of freely exchanging credit information. Of the banking institutions performing this service, probably the First National City Bank of New York, the First National Bank of Boston, Morgan Guaranty Trust Company of New York, and the Bank of America are the more prominent.

The information supplied by banks may include a financial statement of the new customer. Where statements of assets and liabilities are not furnished, at least an estimate of worth is given, in addition, of course, to the experience other creditors have had with the risk. Banks are, as a rule, conservative and guarded in their reports. Whatever information they do give is considered reliable. It is often possible to secure information verbally when a close acquaintance has been cultivated by the exporter with his bank's foreign department.   In any event, the data secured from banks, even though deficient in many respects, serve to orient the credit manager with regard to the risk, for they indicate roughly whether the risk is good, bad, or indifferent.   This knowledge is essential before undertaking any exhaustive investigation.

Credit service organizations.   In this group may be included a growing number of cooperative bureaus and services maintained by associations.   Among the more important of these are the National Association of Manufacturers, the American Manufacturers Export Association, and the American Foreign Credit Underwriters Corporation.   The first-named organization has correspondents in leading trade centers of practically every country, through whom it secures data about foreign concerns in addition to the financial statements obtained directly from the risk and trade experiences from American manufacturers.   Although the service is maintained primarily for members, nonmembers can obtain reports at slightly higher rates.   Besides several different types of reports compiled from data obtained in this country and through correspondents abroad, the American Manufacturers Export Association has special facilities for obtaining credit information by cable.

The American Foreign Credit Underwriters Corporation reports the background of foreign buyers, antecedents, and financial credit conditions.   It also assigns to each subject a rating classifying creditworthiness as high, good, fair, borderline, or unacceptable.   In addition to this, it provides a continuing service of notification of rating changes and assists in collection of foreign accounts.

American exporters. Frequently, prospective customers give as references the names of other concerns in the United States with which they have had dealings.   All such references should be investigated before shipment is made.   It is important, however, to bear in mind that concerns given as references are selected with a view of obtaining the most satisfactory recommendations.   It follows that only those exporters are referred to with whom the new customer has had favorable and businesslike dealings.   For this reason it becomes necessary to widen the scope of the investigation beyond the exporters to whom specific reference is made.   Other concerns may be then reached through the various organizations through which such information is commonly cleared.

Mercantile agencies. Dun & Bradstreet, Inc., maintains offices in foreign countries in order to serve exporters as it does merchants and bankers whose operations are within this country.

The company maintains offices outside the United States in Canada, Newfoundland, Mexico, Puerto Rico, South America, Great Britain, Ireland, Holland, Belgium, France, Spain, Portugal, Switzerland, Italy, South Africa, Australia, and New Zealand. Places where no branch offices are located are covered by traveling reporters or correspondents. In some countries the agency has an agreement with similar domestic agencies through which all information concerning risks located therein may be secured.

Over the years, the company has accumulated a vast mass of foreign credit information. Reports on customers located in foreign countries are of the same general type as those prepared for credit risks in the domestic trade, with perhaps a little more emphasis on antecedents and less on financial condition, although in recent years a large number of the reports have contained financial statements. The information gathered in the customer's home market by nationals with a knowledge of local trading customs is translated in the New York office of the agency by credit men with wide experience in export business. In this manner, the Foreign Department of Dun & Bradstreet, Inc., assists American exporters in their sales promotion work, in the selection of foreign outlets, and by supplying general trade information. A "continuous service" is rendered automatically on foreign inquiries, thereby making available for the exporter additional reports, without charge, for a period of 1 year following the original request for information on the risk in question. In addition, the department conducts special surveys on foreign markets and compiles trade lists upon request.

While the general mercantile agency is in an excellent position to render valuable services to export credit managers, it is difficult to match its service in the domestic field. Distance from the foreign customer, sharp competition with local agencies abroad, difficulty in securing reliable data from foreign suppliers, and expense and delay incident to frequent revisions of reports have been factors in the situation.

The Credit & Audit Co. of America, located in New York City, operates a Foreign Department which specializes in furnishing confidential reports on firms all over the world. It has particular facilities for countries in Asia and South America. Special investigations are made in the field and emphasis is placed on trade experiences. The rates charged vary according to the type of report.

For a number of years the National Credit Office, a special mercantile agency, operated a Foreign Department of considerable size, serving especially concerns in the textile, leather, and automotive trades. This work is now conducted at the headquarters of Dun & Bradstreet, Inc., although under certain conditions subscribers of the National Credit Office can be provided with the service without having to subscribe for that of Dun & Bradstreet.

The Foreign Trade Bureau of the Commercial Museum of Philadelphia furnishes credit reports as part of the service it renders to American manufacturers and exporters.   Upon payment of a moderate charge, nonmembers may also obtain such information.   Much of the data for the reports is collected through resident correspondents maintained in practically all countries.

Then there is the Retail Credit Company of Atlanta, Ga., with offices in all principal markets in the United States and branches in Puerto Rico, Guatemala City, and Honolulu, in addition to correspondents covering practically all points of the civilized world.   This company specializes in character reports that are essential in the selection of credit risks and the choice of marketing agency connections.

Finally, there are special mercantile agencies in certain lines of trade which cover, in their rating books and report service, foreign buyers and shippers, especially those located in Central and South America.   There are also some special mercantile agencies, like the Produce Reporter Company, which include in their service reports on firms located in Canada and Cuba, as well as those in this country.   The usefulness of the services of such organizations is limited, however, by their narrow field of operation territorially and by kind of business.

Foreign Credit Interchange Bureau. This bureau was organized in 1919 by a group of foreign trade and credit executives, is operated by the National Association of Credit Management, and is supervised by a committe of its members representing leaders in American export trade.   It is conducted on the same general principles, though adapted more especially to foreign trade needs, on which all domestic bureaus of the Credit Interchange System of the National Association of Credit Management are based.   This bureau is a nonprofit organization whose aim is to serve all its members for a charge sufficient to cover the cost of operation.   For some little time the charge has been $240, covering a year's subscription and entitling the member to 100 interchange reports.   The Bureau is a clearinghouse through which all members may freely and unreservedly interchange the data contained in their ledgers, without the necessity of direct reference each to the other and without divulging the information under their own names.

The members of the Foreign Credit Interchange Bureau constitute the outstanding American and European manufacturing exporters and banking institutions of the United States and Europe.   They represent international traders in almost every line of business and in all world markets.   The products of the members of the Bureau cover all types of American goods sold abroad, such as drugs, chemicals, pharmaceuticals, cosmetics, confections, glassware, hardware, machinery and industrial equipment, steel products, electrical equipment, food products, textiles, men's and women's furnishings, stationery, office equipment, auto-motive products, radios, paper, paints, shoes, rubber products, and specialties.

Members supply to the Bureau promptly and completely their experiences with any concern under inquiry and treat all information fur-nished by the bureau as confidential. The Bureau in turn agrees to supply interchange reports upon request of the member, and supplemen-tary information whenever obtainable, free reciprocal reports to which the member contributes experiences, weekly bulletins, minutes of the monthly round-table conferences, and an exchange of general information of value in the performance of the credit and collection functions. In addition, the Bureau provides a collection service on foreign accounts at specified rates, a consultation service on foreign trade problems, and arranges for industry group meetings.

Securing information directly from the risk. Much information can obviously be obtained directly from the risk, which in this case is the foreign account. To encourage that, the Bureau provides specially de-signed forms of financial statements (see Figs. 23-1A and 23-1B) to be submitted directly to the American seller. In addition, the Bureau itself solicits information from the risk upon request of an interested member, as shown in Figs. 23-2A and 23-2B. In a covering letter, the Bureau assures the foreign customer from whom the information on the questionnaire is requested that its main purpose in doing so is "to assist reputable merchants in the markets outside the continental United States to maintain satisfactory business relations with its members," who "are leading manufacturers, banking and export firms."

Regular Interchange reports. When a member wishes a report on an account or an applicant for credit, he merely sends to the Bureau an inquiry on a form provided him. The request is immediately acknowl-edged with a report or, if no recent information about the subject is on file, with a statement of assurance of a prompt reply upon receipt of information from either the subject himself or from other creditors of his, as the case may require. Information is solicited directly from the subject on the form illustrated in Fig. 23-2, and from other creditors on a "Daily List" form. This latter form is comparable to that used in domestic credit interchange.

All replies are consolidated in tabulated form on a master copy of the report from which an original report is made for the inquiring member. A number of reciprocal copies are prepared for those who have contributed and for the files (see Fig. 23-3). These reports, which are in part keyed, contain information on the length of time sold, terms

Date_____, 19____

The following figures set forth are present financial standing and business operation upon which you may rely for the purpose of establishing our credit:

CURRENT ASSETS:

Cash on hand and in banks . . . . $.............................
Due from customers . . . .
Cost value of merchandise on hand . . ..
Other current assets . . . .
TOTAL $.............................

CURRENT LIABILITIES:

Bank loans payable within a year . . ..
Tax obligations due . . . .
Due to merchandise creditors . . ..
Other debts due within a year . . . .
TOTAL $.............................

FIXED ASSETS:

Business Equipment . . . .
Land used in business . . . .
Buildings used in business . . . .
Other assets . . . .
TOTAL $.............................

INDEBTEDNESS NOT DUE WITHIN A YEAR:

Chattel Mortgages due on merchandise . ...
Chattel Mortgages due on other assets . ...
Real Estate Mortgages . . . .
Other long term debt . . . .
TOTAL $.............................

NET WORTH: . . . . $.............................

Monthly Sales Volume . . . .
% of Sales made on credit . . . .
% of Sales at retail . . . .
% of Sales at wholesale . . . .
% of Sales on time-payment plan . . ..
Peak season of year . . . .
Date of last physical inventory . . . .
Profit shown latest U.S. Income Tax Return ....

Our firm is financially able to meet any commitments we have made and we expect to pay your invoices according to your terms.

Name of Firm or Corporation_____

Street_____City_____Zone_____State_____

Date_____   Signed by_____

Title_____

PLEASE REFER TO THE OTHER SIDE OF THIS FORM WHICH IS A PART THEREOF.

figure 23-1A. *Form for securing financial and other information directly from the foreign risk, approved and published by the National Association of Credit Management.*

of sale, highest credit extended within the past year, the amount now owing (including outstanding drafts), amount past due, length of time past due, manner of payment, rating, and remarks. In addition to this ledger information, the Bureau includes in the report, if obtainable and readily available, supplementary information concerning the subject's vol-

ACCOUNT REVIEW

To: _____   ◄── { NAME OF FIRM
                                                                   { Requesting Statement

The following information is submitted for your consideration as a basis for the extension of Credit to us:

The name of our business is_____

We operate_____business.   We have been established   years.
                (State type and nature of business)

Ours is a: Corporation ☐   Co-Partnership ☐   Limited Partnership ☐   Individual Business ☐

We are incorporated under the state laws of_____

The principal owners or stockholders and officers are, etc., etc.

NAME	ADDRESS	CITY

We bank at_____

Account carried under_____

Our tax returns have been cleared with the taxing authorities through 19_____.

We expect our monthly credit requirements from you to be about $_____.

DESCRIPTION OF INSURANCE PROTECTION CARRIED

Kind	Amount	Kind	Amount
Fire Insurance on:		Employee Fidelity Bonds_____	
Merchandise_____		Burglary Insurance_____	
Buildings_____		Forgery_____	
Furniture & Fixtures_____		Life Insurance for benefit	
Business Interruption_____		of business_____	
Liability Insurance on:_____		Accounts receivable_____	
Premises_____		Miscellaneous:	
Autos_____			
Products_____			
Contractual_____			

YOU MAY REFER TO OUR PRINCIPAL SOURCES OF SUPPLY LISTED BELOW

Name	Address	City	State

Form No. 3C   (This Form Approved and Published by THE NATIONAL ASSOCIATION OF CREDIT MANAGEMENT)   (OVER)

figure 23-1*B. Reverse side of Fig. 23-1A.*

ume of business, capital, kind of goods handled, character of the business he is conducting—whether it happens to be wholesale, retail, etc.—financial data, and antecedents.

Particularly significant in the interpretation of the Credit Interchange reports are those columns which reveal the amounts owed by the importer at the time of the investigation to all contributing subscribers;

FCIB-NACM
44 E. 23rd St.
N.Y., N.Y. 10010
Cable Address: PORCIB
Date of this report_____

Firm name_____Cable address_____

Trade style_____ Affiliated firms_____

Address_____City and country_____

Branches_____

Date established_____Successors to_____Date_____

PRINCIPALS

Name	Title	Age	Stock percentage

Number of employees_____Salesmen_____Years at present address_____

What portion of your real estate is owned outright_____Mortgaged_____

Loans outstanding: Amount   Terms   Interest

Amount	Terms	Interest

Please check: Importer for own account ☐   Distributor ☐   Representative ☐

Corporation ☐   Partnership ☐   Individual firm ☐

What lines do you handle_____Is your merchandise insured_____

Please indicate insurance coverage on merchandise and type_____

Please list firms in which principals have capital invested, or firms in which principals are associated _____

FINANCIAL INFORMATION: (Please indicate type of currency)

Authorized capital		Paid in capital	
Quick assets		Quick liabilities	
Net worth		Annual sales	

After sending us this questionnaire, you may use the name of our Bureau as a reference in the United States.

Please indicate on the reverse side of this sheet references, or remarks   (Over)

figure 23-2*A. Form used by the Foreign Credit Interchange Bureau for soliciting information from foreign importers.*

manner of payment; and terms under which other exporters are selling the applicant.   If it is discovered that the prospective customer is accustomed to purchasing under a letter of credit, the credit manager would naturally feel more at ease in refusing a request for a 60 days' sight draft and in insisting upon terms to which he is accustomed.   Again,

Bank References (local and foreign)

United States firms represented, (name and address), or from whom you are buying

Are you looking for new representations? If so, in what non-competitive fields?

REMARKS

figure 23-2B. *Reverse side of Fig. 23-2A.*

if the "manner of payment" column indicates promptness on the part of the importer in accepting and paying the drafts or in paying his obligations represented by open accounts, the prospective customer is entitled to fair treatment and to liberal credit accommodations. The aggregate indebtedness to the reporting exporters finally shows whether or not a further extension of credit is advisable. In view of the fact that the

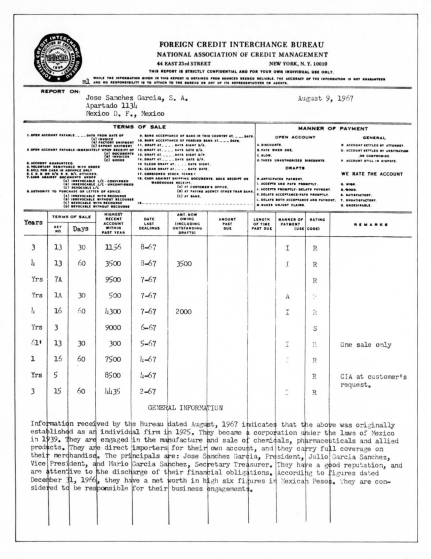

FOREIGN CREDIT INTERCHANGE BUREAU
NATIONAL ASSOCIATION OF CREDIT MANAGEMENT
44 EAST 23rd STREET   NEW YORK, N. Y. 10010
THIS REPORT IS STRICTLY CONFIDENTIAL AND FOR YOUR OWN INDIVIDUAL USE ONLY.

REPORT ON:

Jose Sanchez Garcia, S. A.   August 9, 1967
Apartado 1134
Mexico D. F., Mexico

Years	TERMS OF SALE		HIGHEST RECENT ACCOUNT WITHIN PAST YEAR	DATE LAST DEALINGS	AMT. NOW OWING (INCLUDING OUTSTANDING DRAFTS)	AMOUNT PAST DUE	LENGTH OF TIME PAST DUE	MANNER OF PAYMENT	RATING (USE CODE)	REMARKS
	KEY NO.	Days								
3	13	30	1156	8-67				I	R	
4	13	60	3500	8-67	3500			I	R	
Yrs	7A		9500	7-67					R	
Yrs	1A	30	500	7-67				A	:	
4	16	60	4300	7-67	2000			I	R	
Yrs	3		9000	6-67					S	
61'	13	30	300	5-67				I	R	One sale only
1	16	60	7500	4-67				:	R	
Yrs	5		8500	4-67					R	CIA at customer's request.
3	15	60	4435	2-67				:	R	

GENERAL INFORMATION

Information received by the Bureau dated August, 1967 indicates that the above was originally established as an individual firm in 1925. They became a corporation under the laws of Mexico in 1939. They are engaged in the manufacture and sale of chemicals, pharmaceuticals and allied products. They are direct importers for their own account, and they carry full coverage on their merchandise. The principals are: Jose Sanchez Garcia, President, Julio Garcia Sanchez, Vice President, and Mario Garcia Sanchez, Secretary Treasurer. They have a good reputation, and are attentive to the discharge of their financial obligations. According to figures dated December 31, 1966, they have a net worth in high six figures in Mexican Pesos. They are considered to be responsible for their business engagements.

figure 23-3. *Typical but hypothetical report on a foreign buyer prepared by the Foreign Credit Interchange Bureau of the National Association of Credit Management.*

field of the Interchange Bureau is limited to exporters who are members, the value of the information relating to a customer's total indebtedness or merchandise purchased becomes somewhat uncertain.

One of the things which strongly recommends this source of information is the recency of the data furnished. Moreover, the actual experiences of different exporters in dealing with the subject are usually of far greater significance than the information supplied by other sources, in determining the extent and nature of the credit accommodation that should be extended.

Special reports. When the Bureau is unable to supply adequate ledger information on a particular subject, the special report service may be substituted for the regular interchange report. A special charge is made for this type of report sufficient to reimburse the Bureau for the out-of-pocket expense actually incurred in securing the information. This type of report may also be requested as a supplement to the regular report. Such reports are usually obtained by mail unless cable service is specifically designated. The charge is in proportion to the work required to gather the information. Ordinarily, this type of report gives a detailed running account of the age and size of the firm subject, its management, nature of the business, value of its stocks of merchandise, total assets, real property, reputation of the firm and its officers, bank's opinion, and manner of meeting credit engagements.

Weekly bulletin. Distributed to all members, the weekly bulletin carries information of all current changes in foreign credit, collection, and exchange conditions throughout the world. This helps the exporter interpret not only his own markets but also those in which his customers may be selling, thus giving him a sound basis upon which to formulate his financial policy.

Round-table conferences. Monthly discussion sessions are held by the Foreign Credit Interchange Bureau to cover current export problems and to provide a clearinghouse for information which is valuable to the foreign trader. In the general discussions, the controls and regulations, both at home and abroad, which the trader faces are usually subjects of interest. Minutes of these sessions are prepared and distributed to the members all over the world.

Under the Bureau's auspices also are conducted trade-group meetings of creditors for the discussion of past-due accounts and other pertinent credit matters. Four such groups are now in operation covering the drug field, foods, hardware and allied trades, and textiles.

Consultation service. The Bureau also offers service to members on any unusual problems that they encounter in the administration of foreign financial operations.   The Consultation Service includes the findings reported in surveys made by the Bureau each year covering credit and collection conditions, credit and exchange losses, and other significant phases of foreign credit.   It facilitates the prompt exchange of information between members with common interests and problems, and affords members specialized, individual research and investigation facilities.

Publishing companies. Some foreign trade publications supply their advertisers with credit information free of charge.   Prominent among them are *La Hacienda,* the *Importers Guide,* the *Business Publishers International Corporation,* and *The American Exporter.*   For a moderate fee, others than advertisers may secure similar advantages.   The nature of the information furnished is very much like that supplied by banks and general mercantile agencies, although it is not intended as a substitute for regular credit information.

Governmental agencies. In the United States valuable facts in the form of sales information reports concerning foreign firms can be obtained from the Commercial Intelligence Division of the Department of Commerce.   This division also maintains a "World Trade Directory," compiled from data obtained from several different sources.   Abroad there are United States consuls, trade commissioners, and commercial attachés, all of them officers in the service of our government, who are in a position to secure for the American exporter much valuable information.   Though not in the nature of credit reports, this information bears directly on the making of credit decisions.

QUESTIONS AND PROBLEMS

1 To what extent do the C's of credit analysis apply to the appraisal of risks incurred in foreign credit transactions?

2 Upon what evidences would you judge the creditworthiness of a foreign customer?

3 Contrast the credit information sources located abroad with those located within this country, with respect to their character, variety, services, affiliations, and reliability.

4 Is the analysis of a foreign creditor's financial statement as essential as in the case of a domestic creditor?   Why?

5 Through what sources might a foreign buyer's financial statement be obtained? What reservations might be made concerning its value?

6 Compare and contrast the role played by domestic and foreign salesmen in the supplying of credit information on their respective customers.

7 Show how a regular Foreign Credit Interchange Bureau report differs from one issued by similar bureaus in domestic trade. In what ways is it superior? Inferior?

8 X, an American manufacturer, receives an order for $10,000 from Y, in Buenos Aires. Shipment of the goods is to be made in two equal parts 3 months apart. According to information obtained from an American banker, one of the mercantile agencies, and the Foreign Credit Interchange Bureaus of the National Association of Credit Management, Y pays his bills promptly, is in good standing, the business is capably managed, and the financial statement shows a net worth of around $300,000. Y desires to buy the goods on terms of 90 days S/D under revocable letter of credit. He refuses to furnish a confirmed letter of credit, partly because of the additional expense and partly on account of other reasons. Should X accept or decline the order? Explain.

9 Evaluate the credit interchange report in Fig. 23-3 and reach a decision on whether you would wish to sell to this customer. Give reasons for your conclusions.

10 How valuable are banks as a source of foreign credit information? Give reasons for your answer.

11 List all sources of information concerning foreign accounts and arrange them:
   a In the order in which they are normally used
   b According to the frequency with which they are called into use
   c On the basis of relative value to the creditor

12 Assuming that additional information is needed concerning foreign accounts and all ordinary sources have failed to supply it, what step should be taken?

13 Are sources of foreign credit information likely to grow in number or importance in this country? Why or why not?

management of the collection function

Obviously, collections arise only because credit has been used. It follows, therefore, that collections are an inevitable concomitant of credit granting. Even then, but a small measure of collection effort is an aftermath of *faulty* credit granting. Most of it issues from *sound* performance of the credit-granting function, which calls for the acceptance of predetermined calculated risks.

One of the assumptions underlying credit operation is that credit business is a means of increasing sales and profits. Creditors calculate the risk inherent in this type of business and accept the degree of risk which best serves their promotional purpose, knowing full well that some individual risks may be misjudged, although on the whole and with appropriate collection effort bad debt losses will be kept within a certain range. It must be further assumed that, however well chosen credit risks are originally, some will change for better or worse during the course of the business association. Business conditions change, and debtors become financially handicapped. Capacity may change as a result of unforeseen personal circumstances. Even character may be altered under strain. It must be taken for granted, therefore, that some of the inherent risk in credit will materialize in collection problems. Management of the collection function is further complicated by the fact that, as in credit granting, the objective is to build and retain customer satisfaction and good will. This may have to be accomplished at the expense of obtaining the payment due or the mere collection of a past-due debt.

Thus the credit and collection functions are not only interdependent but are also inextricably interwoven. The weaker the credit-granting function is, the greater the task on the collection end of the business. Similarly, the more lenient the deliberate policy of risk selection, the more formidable is the collection task, and the stricter the granting of credit, the less the burden on the collection function. Some companies follow a policy of sales building through liberal credit extensions and rely heavily on a comprehensive and effective collection system to keep losses within desired limits. Others exercise unusual care in the selection of risks and in the amounts of credit allowed and thus minimize the task of the collection phase of the business.　Most enterprises follow a course somewhere in between these two extremes.

To manage the collection function effectively, there is need for the adoption of sound collection policies and the development of methods and practices for both internal use and in connection with the employment of such outside assistance as collection agencies and attorneys.　To this end it is essential, among other things, to be familiar with all the rights and legal remedies available to creditors and with the best ways of using them.　Much of this knowledge is needed for the proper exercise of normal collection efforts and in effecting adjustments.　For the *enforcement* of payment there is need for further knowledge of usual litigation procedure and consequences, of various special legal means like receiverships and assignments, and of bankruptcy and its administration.　Much of this material is highly technical and of professional substance, but it represents a substantial part of the collection manager's stock in trade.

It is the burden of this part of the book to provide all the basic content essential to the effective management of the collection function as briefly outlined.　Not only that, but an effort has been made to present even the more technical aspects of the subject, such as exemptions, limitations for civil actions, and bankruptcy, in their broader social and economic perspectives.　Such treatment is believed to contribute to a better understanding and appreciation of the reasons for their being and the implications flowing therefrom.　In addition to such cultural values, it should also result in more responsible managerial decision making.

CHAPTER TWENTY-FOUR
collection policies
and practices

It has already been stated that, for the most part, collections are an inevitable concomitant of sound credit granting. This means that normal collection efforts and even some of the special collection problems likely to be encountered are an expected effect of a predetermined credit policy and should therefore be anticipated with clear procedural plans and practices. It means, further, that the work of collecting should be pre-planned. Policies should be established and routines developed that would be followed according to need. Collecting is an orderly and not a sporadic business process. It is universal in the field of credit, and under some circumstances it becomes a highly skilled and specialized operation.

FACTORS AFFECTING
COLLECTION POLICIES

In the formulation of a collection system, the policies of the creditor concern are basic. Policies, in turn, are governed by certain considerations or factors, foremost of which are the classes of debtors, nature of the business, margin of profit, and character and degree of competition faced.

Classification of debtors. Obviously, not all delinquents can be treated alike, because of differences in their temperaments and other personal characteristics, in the quality of the risk which they represent, and in their value to the creditor. Accounts, therefore, are classified into several groups so that each group can be treated in the manner that is likely to be most fruitful of beneficial results.

In order that collections may be expedited, credit customers are generally divided into three classes: good risks, fair risks, and poor risks. Some credit managers divide delinquent accounts into those who can and intend to pay, those who can but won't pay, and those who can't pay. For credit-granting purposes a more elaborate classification of risks is usually made comprising discounting customers, anticipating customers, prompt-pay accounts, slow but good customers, slow and unsatisfactory, and just plain "deadbeats."

The good risk is a customer who is highly rated in regard to his financial ability to pay and is so eager to keep his credit intact that he will make satisfactory arrangements the moment he finds himself unable to meet his bills. He is a good-pay customer, has a high credit limit, and is entirely reliable. Such a customer must be treated with the utmost courtesy in case of delinquency. A little pressure and a proper appeal may be all that is necessary in order to bring about payment of the bill. The delinquency is in all probability due to negligence and not so much to lack of financial resources. Customers in this class are highly sensitive; the treatment must be mild, lenient, and courteous, lest they become offended and withdraw their patronage. No drastic measures whatever need be resorted to and the time between the various steps in the collection series is the longest allowed for the various classes of delinquents.

The fair risk is a customer who is probably good but slow. He has a medium rating in regard to his ability to pay and is entirely willing to meet his bills, but through carelessness or through the happening of unforeseen contingencies beyond his control he postpones payment of his obligations. Such customers have a medium credit limit and, in spite of their occasional delinquency, do not belong to the category of dishonest debtors. They constitute the largest percentage of a retail store's accounts and form the large body of small merchants over whom the credit manager must keep close watch. Many of these delinquents may be finally converted into the first class of debtors. Because of their honesty and good intentions, these cases require careful and special consideration, necessitating a study of conditions responsible for the delinquency before pushing the claim and thereby adding to the confusion and embarrassment of the debtor and further delaying payment. The collection system must allow a longer period of time to elapse between the various letters of the collection series and the other methods forming a part of the anticipated plan.

The poor risk is a customer who apparently has just enough ability to pay and just enough reputation of meeting his obligations with fair promptness to deserve the privilege of an open account involving a small credit limit. In this class are included those customers who can pay but do not intend to do so until forced, as well as customers without conscience or financial responsibility, commonly known as professional "deadbeats." So long as these risks are kept within the credit limit placed on their accounts, they may pay with fair promptness. No credit manager can be certain that he has not extended to some of them more than is warranted by actual conditions, partly because of failure to investigate a customer's reliability thoroughly and partly because even the most careful investigation sometimes fails to disclose the weakness of an applicant for credit. Among these delinquents are persons who are absolutely indifferent to unfavorable credit opinions and upon whom "duns" all the way from pleading persuasiveness to threats to take drastic action have no effect. In dealing with these accounts, the collection system must operate rapidly. Little time should elapse between the first notification and the letter threatening suit. No sympathy should be shown to persons who have earned a reputation as chronic bad-pay customers, because such risks are habituated to strict treatment and will take no offense at the promptness with which they are followed up. Drastic treatment should be reserved, however, until the credit manager has overwhelming proof of the unworthiness of the delinquent. Otherwise, persons in this class should be treated as if they belonged to the class which is composed of the fair risks.

In view of the foregoing, it is apparent that each of the three classes of delinquent debtors requires somewhat different treatment. It is, therefore, essential to ascertain the reason for the delinquency as early as possible in the collection proceedings, so that each account may be properly classified and accorded the treatment which that class deserves.

Nature of the business. Collection methods and practices tend to differ with the line of trade and with the method of operation of the selling concern. Creditors selling on open account, for example, are usually less prompt in pushing collections than are those selling on the instalment plan. The latter group is faced with the possibility of cumulative delinquencies as successive payments fall due and are not met. Service organizations, such as those providing utilities in the form of electricity, gas, heat, or telephone communication, generally follow a prompt collection policy, because indebtedness continues to increase through customers' unchecked use of service during the collection process. Merchants often differ among themselves in collecting, moreover, as when one caters to low income clientele and another to buyers in high income brackets. The latter is usually the more lenient in his collection effort because it is presumed that neglect and oversight, rather than unwillingness and incapacity to pay, are the reasons for the delinquency. On the other hand, still other differences in collection practice stem from the fact that while one vendor emphasizes quality of product and minimizes credit service, a competitor, usually less well established in the trade, seeks patronage through credit liberality.

It is of some significance, too, whether the collections are undertaken by a manufacturer, a wholesaler, or a retailer. The time allowed slow-pay customers by manufacturers or wholesalers is generally short. Terms of sale have been definitely stated and customers have a fairly clear appreciation of the importance of a good credit standing. Retailers, on the other hand, often fail to explain clearly their terms of sale to customers. In collecting, moreover, they resort quite generally to appeals to pride, justice, and sympathy. Finally, efforts to collect on wholesale transactions sometimes necessitate rehabilitative action in order to restore the debtor's capacity.

Margin of profit. The profitableness of the line of business in which a creditor is engaged is another consideration in planning a collection system. In general, the wider the margin of profit on which a vendor operates, the more lenient may be his collection policy and the less urgent his collection efforts. A vendor operating on narrow margins cannot allow delinquencies to continue for very long or engage in prolonged and costly collection activities. Both the risk and cost involved in diverse collection systems must be related to the profit margin on which the creditor operates, and care must be taken that amounts collected are not exceeded by the cost of collection.

A creditor must consider also the profitableness of a *particular* debtor's business to him, as well as his *general* margin of profit, in planning a collection system. Some portions of a vendor's business are more profitable than others.   Some lines, for example, are handled on lower than average margins; some customers order small quantities frequently whereas others place large orders at longer intervals; some sales are made only with high selling cost; some deliveries are more costly than others because of distances involved; some customers are also more bothersome than others, increasing a vendor's costs through numerous returns, complaints, and service demands.   A collection system, therefore, in being well adapted to the situation in which it must operate, is based upon adequate consideration of these factors.

Nature of competition. The collection system depends in some measure also upon the nature and severity of the competition faced by creditors.   Leniency in collections, no less than in credit granting, is a form of service competition.   If faced with strong price competition, a vendor is usually compelled to adopt whatever policies minimize costs, including one of comparatively prompt collections.   If, on the other hand, he seeks to meet price competition on the basis of service rather than price, or if, on the contrary, he is faced generally with strong service competition, under such conditions a creditor may apply less pressure in his collections.   Under either circumstance, his entire collection system tends to reflect both the practices of the trade and his position in the trade.

COLLECTION
POLICIES

Depending upon the factors just discussed, the collection policies adopted by various firms will necessarily differ, especially with respect to leniency or strictness underlying the collection system.   Some of the policies are, however, of such widespread acceptance that they may be regarded as general, while others are of a special character.

General collection policies. In this category are included the collection policies that refer to promptness, regularity, and systematization of effort.

Promptness in collections. The importance of promptness in collection work cannot be overemphasized.   Business success depends upon it for maintaining the turnover of working capital for providing funds with which cash discounts on purchases may be taken, for keeping collection costs and losses low, and for preserving a reasonable standard of efficiency.

Promptness, however, is a relative matter, varying with both creditors and debtors. Collection efforts begun in 30 or 60 days may be prompt for very good customers, whereas 5 or 15 days may be the maximum time allowed a defaulting poor risk. Instalment collections are begun more promptly than those on charge accounts. Again, mercantile creditors act more promptly generally than retailers.

The significance of promptness lies not only in the fact that it brings payment sooner; it also has a psychological effect upon customers, showing them the attitude of the creditor toward the debt and leaving no doubt as to how he expects the debtor to regard his obligation. Moreover, by promptly clearing up past obligations, the creditor opens the way for his customer to buy more, whereas continuing debt often induces a customer to place his subsequent purchases elsewhere.

Regularity in collections. Promptness should be combined with regularity in the collection effort. If considerable time elapses between efforts, the obligation tends to fade from the customer's mind. Few customers object to being reminded of their obligations when the reminder is prompt, regular, and courteous. A house which pays businesslike attention to the collection of its accounts gains the respect of customers. Furthermore, regularity keeps debtors in sound and healthy financial condition.

Systematization of collections. Successful collection depends in large measure upon the development of a collection system. Such a system is a methodical, preplanned program, adapted to differing collection needs, yet providing uniform treatment for all comparable cases. Ideally, each account might be given individual treatment. In practice, however, that is impossible where thousands of accounts have to be handled. Consequently, a routine, or system, is established for accomplishing the desired results.

The collection system must be a regular method of procedure whereby pressure on delinquents is increased gradually but surely until payment is received or until a climax is reached in the use of some drastic means or the account is written off. The impression made upon the debtor by any one step of the system should be deepened by the next. The system should nevertheless be sufficiently flexible that allowance be made for differences in customers' personality, past record, financial conditions, and the value of future patronage. It should not be so rigid as to cause the work to become a mere mechanical process. It should also provide for the individual handling of an account when there is reason that it should not be handled in a routine fashion or where a response to a given collection effort indicates the wisdom of special handling.

Special collection policy problems. In the course of credit granting and collecting, special consideration is often given as a matter of policy to the taking of unearned cash discounts, the charging of interest on unpaid accounts, and the suspension of delinquent customers.

Unearned discounts are those taken after the expiration of the cash discount period. Some buyers may be guilty of this act unintentionally; others may be unable to make payment within the specified time, yet wish strongly to save the discount. When payment unjustifiably omitting the discount is received, the creditor may return the check and request a correct one, hold the check and request an additional one, or deposit the check and bill the customer for the difference. Which action is taken depends upon the amount involved—small sums may not be worth the collection cost; upon the length of time involved—lateness of a few days may be granted as a matter of policy; and upon the character of the debtor—intent to gain personal advantage would not be countenanced in a poor risk and would not be found in a good one.

The charging of interest on overdue accounts depends largely upon the sum involved and the length of time the payment may be delayed. Usually no attempt is made to collect interest on an open account that is past due a short time. When, however, such an account is exchanged for a note, an interest charge is usually added. When it is the intent of the vendor to charge interest on slow accounts, notice to this effect may be given in words printed on all statements, by stickers attached to bills, or by an understanding when originally opening the account.

A third policy problem involves the suspension of delinquent accounts. To speed collections, further credit may be refused an account until payment is made. Often a period of grace may be given. This period may be for 30 to 90 days, depending upon the rate of consumption or sale of the goods for which payments are in arrears and the strictness of the creditor's policy. This policy is especially effectual in lines of business where purchases are made continuously and goods are of the so-called "necessity" type.

COLLECTION
FOLLOW-UP
SYSTEM

One of the first considerations in collection management is the means by which a collection problem is recognized and is pursued to a conclusion. Not every debt presents a collection problem, for receipt of payment during the credit period is not "collection" in the sense that the term is here used. Collection refers specifically to the efforts to gain payment *after* a debt has become *past due.* Keeping track of debts in order that special attention may be given them at the critical time is for the most part a problem of record keeping. Several practices are followed in recording debt so as to aid in the detection and handling of the collection problem. The policies, files, and records pertaining to this work are commonly referred to as the collection follow-up system.

The ledger plan. The ledger plan of follow-up system is based upon the creditor's ledger records. Thus the bookkeeping files are used for collection purposes. The credit manager merely inspects the ledger at frequent intervals to determine which accounts are past due. Notations are made on the ledger opposite each overdue account of steps currently taken to gain payment.

The chief advantage of this system lies in the opportunity it affords the credit manager to keep posted on the development of each account. Furthermore, no separate records need be kept. Such a system, however, is workable only where the number of accounts is relatively small and where the credit and bookkeeping departments are located side by side.

The principal disadvantage of the ledger plan is that it tends to make collection efforts haphazard and irregular. The chore of sorting a multitude of accounts to find the few requiring collection effort tempts one to delay doing it. Thus the work of following up accounts may become secondary to other functions of the department, with the result that collections may be neglected. Moreover, while it is desirable that a credit manager become acquainted with the development of all accounts carried, an inspection at frequent intervals imposes on him a heavy burden. Time thus consumed could be spent to better advantage in other work. Then, too, inspection of the ledger at frequent intervals may interrupt the work of the bookkeeping department.

Card tickler system. The card tickler system is made up of a card for each delinquent account, filed according to dates. Each card contains the amount, terms, due date of the past-due amount in question, and the collection actions so far taken together with the dates thereof. The file is divided into 31 compartments, one for each day of the month. The cards are then placed in the section corresponding with the date on which the next collection step should be taken on those accounts.

A clerk each day inspects the cards filed for attention on that date, checks them against the ledger, posts on the cards remittances received since filing, and refers them to the credit manager or his assistant. If payment has not been received, the card is given to the correspondence unit, and an appropriate communication as dictated by the collection system is then sent to the debtor. Notation of the action taken is made on the card, which is returned to the file in a date compartment when it should again be examined. When all cards scheduled for a given day have been handled, the sections are rotated so that the current date is always in front.

By this plan nothing is left to chance. All matters turn up automatically at the desired time, and overdue accounts are handled systematically and regularly. The plan requires little labor and saves time and energy of the manager. It does necessitate, however, more or less a duplication of records and somewhat additional clerical labor, but only to the extent that the overdue accounts relate to all accounts.

The duplicate invoice system. This method is operated essentially the same as the card tickler system, but in this instance a duplicate copy of each original invoice is used, even though but few of them may become overdue and require collection effort. The tickler card, on the other hand, is made out only for the overdue accounts to which collection effort is to be applied. The duplicate copies of all invoices are filed in a tickler according to maturities, so as to appear on the due date or a few days prior thereto. When the invoice copy appears, if checking it against the ledger reveals that it has been paid, it is destroyed or filed permanently in the general office files. Otherwise, the collection campaign is started and every action taken is recorded on the invoice, which is returned to the file, to come again to attention at a predetermined future date.

The duplicate invoice is to be recommended mainly when the creditor finds that a large percentage of his accounts regularly becomes past due and requires collection effort; otherwise the cost of making the extra copy of each invoice, filing it, and keeping track of payments by that device may become burdensome and in the vast majority of cases is totally unwarranted.

Under the ledgerless accounts receivable system discussed briefly in Chap. 13, a copy of each invoice mailed to a customer is filed in a pocket bearing that customer's name. When payment of an invoice is received, the appropriate copy in the pocket is stamped paid and filed alphabetically in a paid invoice file. By a bright-colored movable signal at the right top edge of the customer's pocket, adjusted to cover the month of the customer's oldest invoice in the pocket, it is possible to determine at a glance how far past due the account is, so that appropriate action may be taken and recorded on the invoice in question. Even this most modern device lacks the tickler feature of the card system and requires handling overdue accounts on an invoice basis rather than in terms of the total amount that may be past due.

THE COLLECTION
SYSTEM

Planning of the collection system is fundamentally the choice of means by which collections can best be effected within a given period of time and under prevailing circumstances. While the same types of specific systems may not be equally adapted to retail and mercantile credit or to instalment and charge account customers, the several factors or elements underlying them are basic and identical and must be taken into account in each case.

Factors or elements in a collection system. The first factor in planning and formulating a collection system has to do with the *length of time* for the entire collection process. This, in turn, depends upon whether a lenient policy is to be pursued and hence considerable time allowed until all reasonable collection effort has been exhausted or whether a strict policy is to prevail and the collection process is to be completed within but 3 or 4 months.

The second factor deals with the selection of appropriate *types or kinds of* collection *efforts.* This choice must be governed by a knowledge both of the various steps that may be taken and of their suitability to the collection system contemplated. The several types or kinds of collection methods, efforts, or steps that may form part of a collection system consist of:

1 Statements
2 Collection notices and reminders
3 Collection letters
4 Personal calls
5 Telephone calls
6 Collection by draft
7 Dunning by wire
8 Use of registered letters
9 Settlement by note
10 Use of collection "services"
11 Use of attorneys and collection agencies
12 Suing the debtor

Third is the decision concerning the *number* of steps to be taken. This is in part dependent upon the policy of the house with regard to leniency or strictness in the handling of delinquent accounts. The more lenient the policy of the house in this respect, the larger the number of measures used in completing the collection process. What the policy is depends, as has been pointed out above, upon the keenness of competition in the particular field in which the vendor is operating, his desire and need for greater volume of business, and the margin of profit obtained.

Once the kinds of effort have been decided upon, as well as their number, the next problem is one of *sequence*. Just how should these various steps be arranged, or in what order should they be called into service? The principle to bear in mind in this connection is that, to be successful, a collection system should be so worked out that the milder measures will be used first so as not to offend the more sensitive delinquents in any given group, followed by the more stringent methods arranged in the order of their severity. It is useless to take a strong step first and then apologize for it by the use of more lenient measures. The probability is that the customer has been so offended that it would be difficult to retain his good will or that he is so calloused to "duns" that more lenient means will be utterly wasted if the stringent measure has been disregarded.

Finally, it is also necessary to determine the frequency with which the various collection efforts should be used or the *interval* elapsing between successive steps. If a relatively lenient policy is followed in the collection of accounts, not only is the number of collection steps relatively large, but the interval between the different measures is likewise lengthened. In all cases, the interval is shortened as the stage of delinquency advances. Whereas as much as a month or 15 days may be allowed between any two steps in the early stages of the collection process, the interval is shortened usually to about 5 days, just to allow for an immediate reply, before the process is brought to completion.

Statements. Regardless of the collection system employed, the first step in most cases consists in sending a bill or statement. Assuming that an original invoice or month-end bill had been sent, one may choose to mail another statement, sometimes flagged with a "reminder" sticker, as his first collection effort. This mild form is based upon a presumption that most debtors are aroused from neglect and forgetfulness by a simple reiteration that payment is overdue.

In a great number of instances, monthly statements as a billing procedure have been discontinued for both economy and efficiency reasons. In these instances it is unlikely that a statement would follow as a collection effort. The first step in collection, rather, would probably be some other form of reminder or letter.

Collection notices and reminders. Such notices or reminders usually take the form of printed forms or "stickers" which are made available in a large variety of forms by publishers and by credit associations (see the next chapter for more detailed discussion). Stickers vary in color and in content, partly to attract attention in different parts of the early stages of delinquency and partly to enable the creditor to use this type of notice more than once for a given account. Such stickers are often placed on the statement or on a blank form of company stationery. Some of the messages on the stickers are simple and straightforward; others are argumentative or make appeals that should be reserved to a more advanced stage in the collection process. It is important that reminders be chosen with care, keeping in mind the purpose for their use and the timing.

Collection letters. The most common method used in collecting is the letter. It makes possible a variety of appeals and varying degrees of directness and forcefulness. It is both a mass means and a highly personalized medium for conveying the collection message. Because of the tremendous importance of letters in collection work, the whole following chapter is devoted to the subject.

Collecting by personal call. Next to the collection letter, the personal call is perhaps the most common method of collecting. Wholesalers' and manufacturers' salesmen are often charged with this function, although many such creditors scrupulously avoid combining selling and collecting. Retail instalment accounts are often collected by personal calls, for time is thus saved in making a collection or in finding out why payment has been delayed. Retail charge accounts are generally not collected by personal call, mainly because of the expense involved but partly to avoid personalizing a delicate relationship between store and customer.

At more advanced stages of delinquency, personal calls in collecting are usually made by collectors or solicitors employed by the creditor. There are times, however, when the credit manager himself goes into the field to investigate a delinquency. Those occasions are of more than common importance, and his purpose may be as much to determine what advice or service he may render the debtor as to effect a full or partial collection. The approach taken depends upon whether the default is occasioned by reasons of capacity or of character. If capacity be lacking or if adverse conditions have impaired the paying power of the debtor, expert counsel may be needed; if unwillingness to pay has caused the default, strong reasoning and persuasion may be the more needed.

A variation of the personal contact for collection purposes is in the debtor's calling upon the creditor, at the latter's request. Such a visit is virtually an acknowledgment of the obligation. It is generally assumed, moreover, that the debtor has come to pay in full or in part, and the interview is approached from that standpoint. At times this meeting brings to light a complaint which the debtor has been harboring and provides an opportunity for discussing and settling it.

Collecting by telephone. Increasing use is being made of the telephone in collecting, both in early and late stages of the collection process, for this method, because of its directness, often succeeds where other methods fail. One of the chief advantages of this method is that it is somewhat surprising to the debtor and may, therefore, catch him unguarded with small alibis and grievances with which to excuse his delinquency. It furnishes the collector a good opportunity to impress him emphatically with the urgency of payment, varying the appeals as the need arises. Frequently, when the reason for nonpayment is understandable, although the failure of the debtor to communicate it is not, a plan of payment may be worked out, usually with a partial payment to be made immediately. Thus, by telephone nearly all can be accomplished that could be gained by a personal solicitation. Telephoning, however, is often the speedier method, the more flexible, particularly in tracing skips, the less costly, even in the use of long-distance service, as long as it is used with efficiency and discretion.

Collecting by drafts. The draft is quite commonly used by wholesalers and manufacturers as a means of enforcing payment. It is one of the more urgent steps in the collection series. In some lines of business the first or second letter may be followed by a draft; in other lines of trade the terms of credit stipulate that if the account remains unpaid after a certain time, a draft will be drawn upon the customer without further notice. It is the common practice, however, to resort to the use of drafts for collection only after most of the collection letters have failed to bring the desired response. Since the draft is one of the more forcible methods, except in trades where payment is commonly made by draft, it is generally advisable to call the customer's attention by letter or special form, in advance, of the intention to draw upon him. Such letter usually contains a simple statement reviewing the steps already taken and stating that unless a response is made by a certain date a draft will be forwarded to the delinquent's bank. This will frequently have the desired effect and bring the remittance. This letter also affords the debtor sufficient time in which to prepare to meet the draft when it is presented by the bank for collection.

The chief purpose of drawing a draft upon a delinquent debtor is to make the bank the creditor's collecting agency, with an implied notice to the debtor's bank and locality that the drawee's credit standing is somewhat impaired. For this reason a draft should be almost as effective as a letter from an attorney or collection agency, except that some of the larger banks refuse to accept the responsibility for presenting this instrument to debtors.

Although there is no way of compelling a bank to present a draft or requiring a drawee to honor it, such a step is nevertheless valuable even when the draft is presented but is dishonored, in that it makes an urgent suggestion to pay.   Furthermore, when a draft is dishonored it is usually returned to the creditor with an indorsement or notation stating briefly the reason for the drawee's failure to pay.   This gives the draft a strategic value, for the way it is treated by the debtor gives the creditor information concerning the following step that should be taken.   From these notations the creditor occasionally learns of the debtor's intentions, thus furnishing a better basis for further treatment. If the debtor gives the bank a reason or excuse for nonpayment, such reason or excuse can be met logically in the next creditor's letter, thereby putting him in such a position that he cannot defend himself, but must either settle the claim or brand himself a bad-paying customer.   If the notation on the slip attached to the draft indicates that the debtor was unprepared at the time to make payment, a second draft may be sent immediately, preceded by a letter stating that fact, calling attention to the first draft, and suggesting forcibly that the debtor be prepared to meet his obligation when the draft is presented by the bank for payment.

When used, the draft is either deposited in the creditor's own bank; which, in turn, forwards it to a bank in the customer's locality, or is sent directly to the bank in the debtor's vicinity.   Many credit managers prefer to send the draft to the debtor's bank, if it is known, while others prefer to send it to another bank in the debtor's town on the assumption that the stranger bank will more promptly present the draft for payment.   On the other hand, a delinquent is more likely to be induced to make payment if the draft is presented through his own bank.   The name and locality of the bank with which the debtor in all probability has dealings may be ascertained from checks sent by him, from mercantile agency rating books, or from law lists, which generally include a list of banks.

Dunning by wire. As long as proper precaution is taken in the wording of the telegram, dunning by wire is permitted by law.   The wire should be largely in the form of an inquiry as to when payment will be made.   Payment may be demanded and even suit threatened, but nothing is permissible which would tend to convey the impression that the debtor is a cheat, or a fraud, or that he unnecessarily or without cause delays the payment of the bill.   Any such inferences, as well as threats of bankruptcy or criminal prosecution, might subject the sender to an action for libel, and in some states are construed as attempted extortion.   A telegram or night letter requesting immediate remittance or an explanation for the delay is usually effective in gaining immediate consideration.[1]

One of the purposes of a telegram is speed, another is emphasis, and a third is its public nature.   Few debtors will tolerate the irritation caused by the publicity of successive telegrams asking for a settlement of an account.   Sometimes the wire may be used in an indirect manner, as when it is sent to the local bank of the debtor requesting the name of a reputable attorney who can take possession of the article, if sold on the instalment plan and subject to repossession, or otherwise handle the case satisfactorily.   The creditor may further inquire whether the bank thinks that a judgment against the debtor can be collected.   A reply by wire is usually called for to add emphasis.   Ordinarily, the bank telephones the debtor to come in and discuss the matter, calling to his attention the seriousness of it and, if his credit is good, the bank may even advance the necessary amount to liquidate the indebtedness.

Registered letters.   A registered letter sent with the express direction to deliver it to the addressee only, and requiring a return receipt, forcibly calls to the attention of the delinquent debtor the condition of the account and gives evidence that great importance is attached thereto and that the creditor insists upon payment.   Upon receipt of such a letter, the debtor will conclude in most instances that his neglect to meet the bill is becoming more serious than it previously appeared to be.   Usually such letters are in the form of an ultimatum.

Settlement by note.   When it is impossible to secure cash, settlement may frequently be made by notes, provided the debtor really intends

---

[1] The Western Union Telegraph Company has prepared the following telegrams that might be used for ordinary collection purposes:

1 Please advise if check covering your account now due has been mailed.

2 You have apparently overlooked your .... (monthly) payment. May we have your check promptly please.

3 Today last day you can take advantage of cash discount.

4 Only immediate compliance my letter .... (date) will save your credit.

5 Urge you wire your intentions on your account immediately to protect your future credit rating.

6 Must withhold shipment of order received today until past account settled. Wire remittance immediately to insure prompt delivery.

7 Urgent we receive payment this week. We value your friendship too much to be compelled to resort to legal action.

8 Imperative remittance on your account sent immediately to avoid action by our lawyers.

9 Wire full payment by .... (date) and we will instruct attorney to withhold action. Failure to send will leave us no choice but to proceed immediately.

10 Payment tomorrow imperative to prevent repossession of items charged your account of .... (date).

to pay at some future time. In taking notes in settlement, a creditor must carefully consider, in addition to the advantages, the disadvantages incident thereto. A note serves practically as conclusive evidence of the indebtedness and facilitates proof if suit is subsequently brought against the debtor. Furthermore, debtors have more respect for their obligations when evidenced by a written instrument. They are more likely to meet their notes at maturity than pay the debt represented by open book accounts. Notes may also be discounted at the bank and the proceeds employed in the business.

On the other hand, many creditors contend that it is not true that notes are usually paid at maturity, that it is not uncommon for debtors to offer only part payment on the due date and to request an extension of time on the balance, for which another note is tendered. It is argued also that the acceptance of notes in settlement of an open account establishes a bad precedent. It later becomes difficult to take objection to this method of payment, once the customer has been permitted to develop the habit. A third argument against the plan is that once a note is accepted, a creditor waives all right to demand payment until the instrument becomes due. He cannot resort to any means of enforcing payment, even though such action were desirable, until the due date.

Attorneys and collection agencies. After all means have been exhausted, and assuming that the creditor stands ready to sever his business relations with the delinquent, a letter is sent to the debtor threatening to place his account in the hands of an attorney or collection agency unless remittance is received within a specified time. If the delinquent debtor fails to respond to the letter threatening such action, the account is handed over to an attorney or collection agency.

This step should not be taken until and unless all reasonable methods have failed and the debtor is no longer deemed a desirable customer. Once an account is handed over to an attorney or collection agency, friendly relations with the debtor may necessarily be ruptured beyond repair and additional costs are incurred in the form of commissions and fees.

Methods employed. The methods of collection agencies and attorneys consist simply in a more forcible application of the procedures used by creditors themselves. They usually write one or more letters to the debtor, urging him to make payment and pointing out the unpleasant consequences of his neglect to do so. If the debtor lives or conducts his business in the same vicinity as the attorney or agency, a collector is usually sent to make a personal demand.

Collection agencies. Many credit managers prefer to utilize collection agencies in place of attorneys. The former are, as a rule, more systematic in following up accounts and usually write a whole series of letters before forwarding the account to a correspondent attorney for possible court action. A distinction should be made, of course, between established, reputable collection agencies and irresponsible concerns, some of which approach the racket category. The former endeavor to preserve the debtor's good will for their clients when collecting because their income from collection fees will naturally suffer if the clients become dissatisfied with the methods used.

All too often the irresponsible collection agencies resort to practices and procedures that have been found to be in violation of Section 5 of the Federal Trade Commission Act. Many of them have been found guilty of misrepresentation of their services and of their status through the use of such words in their name as "Federal," "National," "U.S.," "Bureau of Records," "Department of Claims," and the like.

Illustrative are a few of the numerous agencies that have been found guilty and have been ordered to cease and desist. In one case the agency was prohibited from obtaining information from delinquent debtors by subterfuge by designating its business as the "Bureau of Settlements and Collections."[2] In another case the company was ordered to cease and desist from obtaining creditor-clients through misrepresentation and using subterfuge to get information.[3] Similarly, a respondent was prohibited from making representations or implying that skip-tracing forms, envelopes, or cards were inquiries from government agencies through the use of such words as "Treasurer's Office" or "Disbursement Office" or pictures of an eagle or a seal showing a structure suggesting a government building.[4]

Again, a respondent was prohibited from making false claims to get creditor past-due accounts and getting information through deceptive "skiptracing" forms.[5] Similarly, in one instance, not unlike many others, the Commission forbade an agency's obtaining information concerning delinquent debtors by representing itself as a "United States Government" agency, by calling itself "Office of Labor Statistics."[6] Lastly, a final order to cease and desist, issued Sept. 13, 1967 (Docket 8700), also prohibited the Federal Bureau of Installment Credit, Inc. (FBIC), from misrepresenting its status as a federated organization when in fact it operated but a single office as an unaffiliated collection agency, and

[2] Docket 7679. Consent order, 1960.
[3] Docket 7498. National Board of Trade et al. Order to cease and desist, 1960.
[4] Docket 6648. National Clearance Bureau. Order to cease and desist, 1957. Affirmed CA-3, 1958.
[5] Docket 7043. *U.S. Assn. of Credit Bureaus, Inc.* v. *F.T.C.* (CA-7, 1962). Modified cease and desist order, 1962.
[6] Docket 7506. Consent cease and desist order, 1959.

from using legal-looking documents in its collection work, as if such documents were authorized, issued, or approved by a court or other legal or official authority.

Since there are irresponsible collection agencies, they should be investigated before placing an account in their hands.   For this reason, trade credit bureaus have been formed, one of the functions of which is to collect accounts for their members.   Dun & Bradstreet, Inc., credit insurance companies, and the adjustment bureaus affiliated with the National Association of Credit Management are also equipped to render a collection service for members and subscribers as well as for others. Failure to pay an account placed in the hands of the large agencies or bureaus works to the detriment of the debtors, for the entire business community soon learns that fact through the credit reports which they render, on request to be sure.   Debtors know that and are likely to make payment before suit is brought against them.

House Collection Agencies. Many business firms are so eager to retain control of their bad accounts and to save the commission charged by collection agencies that they have attempted to imitate bona fide collection agencies by the establishment of what is known as "house" collection agencies, which are in reality bogus concerns.   An appropriate name suggestive of its activities is chosen, suitable stationery is printed, and a collection agency blossoms forth.   Every attempt is made to convey the impression that this so-called "agency" is independent and entirely apart from the creditor firm.

While the use of house collection agencies is presumed to have been successful from a strictly financial standpoint, it must be condemned on both ethical and legal grounds.   Ethically, this view is shared widely by businessmen engaged in the collection of past-due accounts as revealed by their respective codes of ethics, as well as by most creditors.   By far more important is the fact that such a device is definitely in violation of law, particularly of Section 5 of the Federal Trade Commission Act. Illustrative is the prohibition applying to two companies engaged in the mail order business from, among other things, implying that the fictitious collection agency used by them is an independent organization engaged in the business of collecting past-due accounts.[7]   Many similar prohibitions have been handed down by the Federal Trade Commission in the form of cease and desist orders, some by consent, in order to make sure that representations to collection agencies or attorneys are to bona fide independent organizations engaged in the business of collecting overdue accounts.

[7] Docket 6288. *Wm. H. Wise Co., Inc.* v. *F.T.C.* (CA–DC, 1957).

Agency substitutes. Some collection agencies, trade organizations, law-list publishers, and collection-letter houses have devised a series of form collection letters for the use of subscribers. These "collection agency" devices are used considerably as a last resort prior to bringing suit against the debtor or before turning the account over for collection. They are sold or given to creditors subscribing for the services of the company, who fill in the blanks and forward them to the delinquent debtors. The purpose is to impress the debtor with the idea that these letters are sent by the agency through which his delinquency may become known, with the result that he is sometimes scared into paying the bill, and this obviates the necessity for more drastic measures.

Most of such forms should not be used until after all other reasonable measures have failed to bring a satisfactory response or unless the account is thought undesirable and the creditor stands ready to sever business relations with the delinquent. They are recommended as a means preceding that of actually bringing suit or prior to handing the account over to an agency or attorney, primarily because of their inexpensiveness. The probable legal justification for the use of this device is threefold: first, the service of a bona fide independent agency is employed; second, the independent agency is being compensated for its assistance and has full knowledge of it; and third, failure to secure payment by such device usually results in a turnover of the account to the agency in question.

Attorneys. In the case of an out-of-town claim, probably the most commonly used method is for a creditor to place the claim in the hands of a local attorney. This attorney usually makes a few collection efforts by correspondence, and if they bring no satisfactory response, the claim is forwarded to a correspondent attorney in the home town of the debtor. Under such circumstances the fee is divided, the forwarding lawyer retaining one-third and the receiving attorney getting two-thirds of the total fee charged for making the collection.

Another method of placing the claim in the hands of an attorney is by forwarding it directly to a lawyer located in the debtor's town. The name of a competent and responsible attorney may be secured for this purpose through the assistance of "bonded attorney lists," "guaranteed attorney lists," or "law lists." Some of these lists even rate each attorney on the basis of integrity, financial responsibility, ability, and promptness in remitting claims collected. Notwithstanding all these guarantees by publishing houses, many credit managers still follow the practice of compiling their own lists of attorneys on the basis of their investigations and experiences.

Partial attorney substitutes. The same reasons that motivate the creation of house collection agencies also prompt some concerns to establish fictitious legal departments on whose stationery one or more letters are written to the delinquents, urging them to make remittance within a specified time, if legal action in court is to be avoided. Both the legality and the ethics of this device are seriously questioned. Another device is to send such letters on stationery bearing the letterhead of some law firm whose permission has been secured for the purpose. In addition to some remuneration for this privilege the law firm whose letterhead is used by the creditor is generally given all the collection business which requires some legal action.

Compensation of agencies and attorneys. The fees or rates that are generally charged by attorneys and collection agencies for complete collection service on mercantile accounts are governed, except where local bar rates apply, by the schedule recommended by the Commercial Law League of America, as follows:

15 per cent on the first $750 or less collected
10 per cent on the excess of $750
Minimum charge of $15
On items of $45 or less, 33⅓ per cent.

Where partial services are rendered by collection agencies, the rates are modified accordingly. Thus, some agencies, in addition to the regular collection service, also render what is known as direct demand service, for which a charge of only 1 per cent may be made, and a special service that does not require personal calls or litigation, for which a charge equivalent to one-half the regular schedule is made. Again, when a claim is forwarded by the collection agency to an attorney, the agency may charge additional amounts to those in the regular schedule, such as 6 per cent on the first $750, 5 per cent on the next $750, and 3 per cent on the excess.

In the retail field, fees charged by collection agencies and attorneys usually range from 25 per cent for all accounts that can be settled without personal calls or litigation and for accounts that are in the same locality, to as high as 33 and 50 per cent for all other accounts. In both the retail and mercantile fields, when accounts are forwarded by the agency or attorney, the practice is for the forwarder to retain one-third of the fee and to give two-thirds to the receiving agency or attorney.

Suing the debtor. Should an attorney or collection agency fail to effect a settlement by amicable means, the creditor will in all probability be asked for authority to summon the debtor into court. The procedure for suit action is fully discussed in Chap. 26, and any creditor forced into this means of collecting should familiarize himself generally with the privileges and limitations of this legal remedy. It is sufficient for present purposes, however, to point out that before granting authority to an attorney or collection agency to initiate suit, the credit manager should satisfy himself that the debtor possesses unencumbered property on which to levy in case a judgment is secured or is earning enough to make garnishment proceedings feasible. The value of the property should be at least the amount of the claim plus expenses incident to the suit. Oftentimes, the attorney or the agency may be able to furnish the requisite information and, if bona fide, such recommendation concerning the advisability of suit should be followed.

COLLECTING
FOREIGN
ACCOUNTS

Foreign and domestic collections. Practically the same principles and considerations apply to the collection of foreign accounts as in making domestic collections. A prompt and systematic follow-up of each account is even more essential here, for the tendency of many foreign customers is to delay payment until greatly pressed. Similarly, sellers who employ prompt and efficient collection methods command the respect of many foreign buyers, while those who allow their accounts to drift along are apt to be taken advantage of by their customers.

Some difference in foreign collections arises from the fact that drafts are in common use as credit instruments when credit transactions are consummated. Letters of credit are also often used to give additional assurance that the drafts will be honored. Collection procedures must be modified, therefore, by these credit practices.

Statements and notifications. Notwithstanding their advantages as reminders, monthly statements are not as a rule desirable in foreign trade. They are at best cold and formal, and, besides, many foreign customers, being less efficient and systematic in their business dealings, feel insulted at the idea of being reminded in such a formal manner before the bill is due.

To eliminate friction and to call the debtor's attention to the fact that the draft will soon be presented to him for payment, it is advisable to send a personal or form letter requesting a verification of the figures, so as to avoid all complaints at maturity of the draft and to call the customer's attention to the approaching due date. When tactfully written in the proper tone, a letter serves to convert what might have been an overdue account into a prompt payment. The letter must be dispatched to reach the recipient two or three weeks before maturity of the draft. This will enable him to make the necessary preparations to honor it.

Collection cables and letters. If the draft is dishonored when presented for payment, immediate action should be taken, lest the customer be led to believe the creditor afraid to protest for various reasons. If the amount is considerable, the customer may be addressed by a cable, in which surprise is expressed at his refusal to pay and an explanation is requested. It is not uncommon to express confidence in the customer's willingness to rectify the mistake immediately. If the account is small, a letter of similar contents is substituted for the cable. As a result of the use of such letters or cables, immediate settlement is secured on many accounts.

At the same time that an explanation for refusing to honor the draft is demanded from the customer, the collecting bank should be instructed as to the action it should take in regard to the draft. The bank may be of invaluable assistance in ascertaining the reason for non-payment. It may also suggest means of enforcing payment.

If payment is not forthcoming and a reply to the cable or first letter is not received within a reasonable time, a second letter should be dispatched to the debtor. In this letter a suggestion of the credit grantor's willingness to grant an extension, if the debtor is temporarily out of funds, may be made. At any rate, he is asked to explain the reasons for his refusal to meet his obligations, with the assurance that reasonable cooperation will be extended him in order to bring about a settlement which is mutually satisfactory.

Enforcing payment. Reliable collection agencies in foreign countries are scarce. Much help can be obtained through the world-wide collection service of the Foreign Credit Interchange Bureau of the National Association of Credit Management. It represents United States companies in every line of business and collects commercial claims of every variety, whether complicated, disputed, contested, or backlogged. The rates charged for such service are contingent upon collection, as in the collection of domestic accounts, but are necessarily higher than on domestic collections, being 20 per cent on the first $750 or less, 15 per cent on the next $750 or fraction thereof, 13 per cent on amounts in excess of $1,500, and 5 per cent additional on "Attorney Accounts." The American chamber of commerce in the foreign community may also be of some assistance in collecting overdue accounts.

It is extremely difficult to force payment of foreign accounts by legal means. In the first place, exporters know much less about collection laws of foreign countries than the customers themselves. Hence, in order to display force effectively and make threats, the exporter must be sure that the threat can be fulfilled. Furthermore, collection by legal means is almost impossible in some countries on account of the inadequacy of the laws. Then, too, suits are very expensive.

Nevertheless it would be wise for every export credit manager to familiarize himself with at least two types of laws of the countries in which he is interested: those relating to the collection of accounts, and those dealing with the form of business organization. In practically every country there is to be found at least one form of business organization which is peculiar to that country, just as the corporate type of business organization has come to prevail in the United States. Thus the prevailing form of business organization in France is the *société anonyme;* in Mexico, the *sociedad anónima,* abbreviated S.A.; etc.

Knowledge of the particular form of organization of a customer is essential in order to determine a creditor's rights and limitations in enforcing payment. In many countries there is a definite limit placed on the liability on the various members of the firm.

Foreign commercial laws are so numerous, bulky, inadequate from the standpoint of protection to the creditor, and are changing so frequently that it becomes rather difficult to keep well informed of the proper steps to be taken in enforcing payment by legal pressure and causes one to doubt the wisdom of attempts to collect accounts in this manner.

In view of the foregoing, it is advisable to secure a settlement through amicable means by compromising with the debtor, not necessarily as to the amount of the bill but also in regard to terms or the time of payment. Once a willingness on the part of the seller to compromise is evidenced, it is said that in most cases it will result in the payment of the bill and in the retention of the customer's good will and patronage.

Whenever legal action does become necessary as the only means of settling an account, it is advisable to consult the Division of Commercial Laws of the Bureau of Foreign and Domestic Commerce. This division has prepared articles on the subject of collecting overdue accounts in foreign countries. It also has compiled lists of names of reputable attorneys in foreign countries who specialize in serving American creditors and is otherwise prepared to assist creditors in adjusting cases involving errors or misunderstandings.

QUESTIONS AND PROBLEMS

1 "The function of the collection department is to collect *all* overdue accounts." Do you agree? Why or why not?

2 Why do authorities on credit advocate promptness in collecting accounts?

3 Is promptness in collections synonymous with strictness? If not, what is the difference?

4 Assume that you have been called in, in the capacity of consultant, to work out a collection system for a mercantile institution. What factors would you have to consider in accomplishing your purpose?

5 How would these factors differ in the preparation of a collection system for a retail establishment in contrast to one for a wholesale establishment?

6 Point out the logic in arranging the appeals to be used by the collection department in a certain sequence?

7 What relationship, if any, is there between the leniency of a firm's *credit* policy and the leniency of its *collection* policy? Should they be related and, if so, in what manner?

8 At what stages throughout the granting of credit and the making of collections would a credit manager have a good opportunity to classify an account as a good, fair, or poor risk?

9 List all possible methods that can be used in the collection of overdue accounts by:

a Wholesalers and manufacturers

b Retailers selling on regular charge account; on the instalment plan

c Exporters

10 Arrange these collection methods in the order in which they are likely to be applied.

11 When does the use of collection letters begin and when does it end in the collection process?

12 Why is the draft regarded as a fairly effective collection device? How do you explain the failure of some drafts to result in payment?

13 Indicate the reasons for advance notices of drafts. Which of these reasons, in your opinion, is the most important?

14 A draft may be returned because the bank has neglected to present it. Can you suggest any reasons for the bank's action?

15 Is the personal call equally adaptable to the retail and mercantile fields? At what stage in the collection process should a personal call be made and by whom? Would the answer to this question be the same for all cases, regardless of whether collection is to be made from a consumer or from a business establishment?

16 At what stage in the collection process would you recommend the employment of a collection agency or an attorney? Why?

17 What may be done by a creditor who desires to hold on to an account as long as possible before turning it over to an outside agency for collection?

18 In selecting a collection agency or an attorney, what precautions must be exercised and why? What facilities are available for the purpose?

19 When an account has reached the stage when the employment of an outside agency is demanded, what would govern your choice between an attorney or a collection agency?

20 What makes the forceful collection of accounts especially difficult in the foreign field? What is the alternative? To what agencies in this country and abroad may a creditor turn for assistance in securing payment?

21 Is it correct to say that the credit-granting function and the collection function are interdependent? Explain.

22 What is the impact of the credit-granting function upon the collection task? Does the same explanation apply to the impact of the collection task upon credit-granting policy? Explain.

23 Give examples of the types of practices employed by irresponsible collection agencies which have been found to be in violation of Section 5 of the Federal Trade Commission Act.

CHAPTER TWENTY-FIVE

collection letters

Of the various methods of collection employed, the letter is in several respects the most important. It is at least the method used sooner or later by virtually all creditors, and it is the sole method used by many of them. Undoubtedly one reason for its universal adoption is the fact that everyone is prepared and equipped in some measure to write letters; moreover, the naturalness with which letters are received by the public also lends an advantage to their use. Over and above these merits, the letter possesses other qualities essential to a collection medium: namely, flexibility, timeliness, economy, and personality. It may be used individually or in series, with serious or humorous appeal, regularly or intermittently, and with adaptations to individuals or to groups. The preparation of the collection letter or the collection series is, however, a problem demanding both business acumen and writing craftsmanship.

THE SINGLE
COLLECTION
LETTER

Collections can often be made by a single letter. At least this should be the expectation of the writer, for there is no point in sending a letter which does not state the case for collection clearly and convincingly. To send anything less, or to doubt the efficacy of what is sent, is to waste time and effort. The expectation, of course, is not always realized, and more letters, or means stronger than letters, may be required. Each letter that is sent, however, should be regarded as the last one necessary, so far as the writer is concerned. Otherwise an absolute standard for the collection letter would be difficult to establish.

Form and content. Exactly what the collection letter should contain and how it is stated varies, depending upon circumstances of the writer and of the debtor. The delinquency may be the first default of the customer after a long period of patronage; it may be the first default of a new customer; it may be one of a number of failures to pay by a customer of little value to the creditor. On the other hand, the creditor may be handling an account in the usual routine of collecting; he may be pressing his claims in an urgent effort to turn over his working capital; or he may be acting in anticipation of unfavorable changes in the economic climate. The account in default may be small or it may be large. All such factors bear directly upon the character of the collection letter. In general, however, every collection letter should have certain characteristics relating to the beginning, the body, the ending, tone, and personality.

Ordinarily, the *beginning,* being the most emphatic position in the letter, should be used for making a definite, positive statement of its purpose. This often consists merely of a statement that a debt of a certain amount is due. Oversimplified beginnings, however, tend to become repetitious, impersonal, and consequently trite and ineffectual. A remedy is to combine with the fact about the debt some statement relating to an item of mutual or reader interest. To avoid the overworked beginning, the point of contact must be one of some real interest, sincerely made, and not a glib or effusive remark made merely for the sake of *creating* a beginning.

The *body* of the letter may include a number of things relevant to the situation. It may explain the urgency of the writer's need; it may review the original understanding of the credit terms; it may inform the debtor of consequences of his failure to act; it may offer advice subsequent to a former discussion of the conditions upon which credit was granted.

The *ending* almost invariably states or restates the request for payment. All that need be said after giving the facts of the case is what is expected of the debtor. He may be requested to make immediate payment, to communicate with the credit manager, to make at least partial payment, or to indicate the arrangements he has made for payment. The more specific the request, generally the more action-impelling it is.

Characteristics. The *tone* of the letter is that intangible quality which reflects the writer's attitude. Apart from the strictly intellectual content, it is the aspect of the letter which expresses the emotions of the writer and arouses those of the reader. The tone of sincerity, above all, is essential in collection letters; closely second to it is that of just firmness in a businesslike dealing. Doubt, fear, unwarranted suspicion, unprincipled leniency, and uncertainty on the part of the writer imbue the letter with a tone that antagonizes the reader and makes him incompliant to the writer's requests. Most damaging to tone is the use of such terms as "our demand," "we insist," "require," "you failed to," "be compelled to," "delinquent," etc. The negative connotations of these words betray the self-centered and constrained attitudes of writers.

Contributing alike to tone and content of the letter is the writer's *attitude* toward debt. Only an immature and unqualified credit manager would offer excuses for requesting payment. No apology need be made for seeking settlement. There is no reason to beg; money due should be paid without further delay. Credit obligations are assumed with mutual agreement, and there need be no reluctance in requesting a debtor to live up to his part of the bargain.

Finally, the collection letter should have *personality* and naturalness. If the writer expresses himself naturally, and not with the restraints so commonly found in letters in general and in collection letters in particular, the result will be in accord with the criteria here established. If this is achieved, the letter will also have a personality, or distinctiveness of its own, and exceed the ordinary letter in effectiveness. The requirements of the single collection letter are embodied in some measure in the following example:

> Dear Mr. . . . . :
>
> Haven't you at some time tried to keep from looking at the clock when a welcome friend overextended a visit?
>
> We have been reluctant in the same way to notice by the calendar that payment for our last shipment has considerably overrun the credit period. Your account for $. . . . . is past due.
>
> We know from experience, however, that it is not only good manners but good business to call this to your attenion. Both of us will be more at ease if a prompt settlement is made.

Won't you send us your check today? Let us open the way for another "visit," instead of prolonging this one.

Sincerely yours,

PLANNING THE COLLECTION LETTER SERIES

While collection may result from a single letter, collection correspondence is generally based upon assumptions which place even the single letter in the perspective of a planned series. It is true that some collection tasks cannot reasonably be stretched out over a long series. This is the case when small sums are involved, when subsequent instalment payments will be falling due, and when nonpayment justifies cessation of a continuing service in order to prevent accumulating indebtedness and greater loss. On the other hand, collection often results only from repetition and variation of appeals, with the consequence that the planning of letters in a series is an essential activity in the collection process.

Factors underlying the collection series. Underlying the collection correspondence and determining the character of the series are essentially the same considerations discussed in the preceding chapter as fundamental to the entire collection system. Among them, particularly, are the following: the importance of promptness, regularity and system in collection, classification of debtors, the competitive situation, and consideration of profits and costs involved in the performance of the task.

To acquaint himself with the facts of a case, the collection correspondent should review the history of an account, the circumstances of the current debt, and the efforts made thus far to collect. Personal recollections of the customer and information in the credit file will help him orient the case for writing purposes. When the debtor is not individually known by the collection correspondent, it is necessary to make certain assumptions concerning him and his reasons for not paying. When payment is not immediately forthcoming, it may be assumed that the debt has escaped his attention. Reminders are in order. Continued nonpayment suggests that the customer may be experiencing some financial difficulties. Letters discussing the situation from the creditor's viewpoint or inviting the debtor to explain his reason for not paying are appropriate. If no explanation or payment is forthcoming, it is eventually assumed that the customer is unreasonable and unwilling to meet his obligations. At this point, friendly relations may be ruptured and the customer made to feel that his obligations must be met, otherwise he should be prepared to suffer the consequences of his failure to act.

STAGES IN
COLLECTION
CORRESPONDENCE

In general, there are four stages through which the collection process runs its course: notification, reminder, discussion, and compulsion. Not every account in the collection process necessarily passes through all these. Some accounts are collected after the first effort; others, following a second or a third attempt. Again, the particular circumstances of a given account may justify a prompt transition from the first to the last stage without reminding the customer of his delinquency or without any discussion concerning his reason for the delay in making settlement. Nevertheless, most accounts do pass through the successive stages, until payment is made or the account is abandoned as worthless and is written off as a bad debt.

The stages of a mercantile credit system are usually more condensed than those of retail stores. Because accounts are fewer and larger, relations more direct and businesslike, and reasons for default more serious, manufacturers and wholesalers soon get to the point of finding out why an overdue debt is not paid. They do not rely upon the customer's responding to letters alone; they resort to other more direct means of reaching an understanding about the debt. Retailers and service establishments, however, dealing with many charge customers and often being preoccupied with selling rather than with record keeping and collecting, are more inclined to use a system of letters involving the traditional stages.

Stage of notification. The customer may receive two types of notification. The first is a statement sent with the invoice at time of shipment. It serves to verify the amount as to correctness and forestalls possibility of mistakes, misunderstanding, or excuse. The second is another statement timed to arrive the day the account becomes due. This emphasizes the fact that payment is expected.

Stage of reminder. This stage begins at the time that the account matures, when the matter is brought to the debtor's attention by one of several different means. Additional statements are sometimes sent, to which specially prepared reminder stickers are attached. Brief, mimeographed, printed, or typewritten notices, as well as short impersonal letters, are also used to remind the customer of his overdue account.

The assumption underlying this stage is that nonpayment is the result of oversight or neglect. This will be a true assumption in most cases; consequently, the honest debtor possessing means of payment will generally make a settlement upon being reminded. On the other hand, debtors whose delinquency is not accurately explained by the assumption will probably not be moved to action by a mere reminder. If, therefore, they are either unable or unwilling to pay, they will be screened through this stage and left for stronger treatment.

Types of reminders. Formal reminders generally take one of four forms. Some consist of a mere phrase of varying length, such as "reminder," "past due; please remit," or "The above account is past due, this has no doubt escaped your attention. A prompt remittance will be appreciated." A reminder containing such words may be stamped on the statement which it accompanies by means of a rubber stamp, attached to it in printed form, or printed on the body of the statement.

The second type is a more elaborate printed form which accompanies the statement. It is frequently printed on a card which is then clipped to the statement. It may read somewhat as follows:

> We call your attention to the accompanying statement, which, no doubt, has escaped your attention.

The third type consists of a printed or lithographed form with no introductory address or complimentary close, containing blank spaces for the insertion of the name and address of the customer, the amount owed, and the period in which the purchases were made. It is an obvious form reminder and is intended to make an impersonal impression. The blank spaces are filled in with ink or on the typewriter. This form may also be printed on a card. Its probable contents are as follows:

> We call your attention to your account of .... amounting to $.............. Your prompt attention will be appreciated.

Or

> We call attention to your account for .... (month, etc.), amounting to $.............. We hope it will have your immediate attention.

The fourth style of impersonal reminders consists of a series of typewritten or multigraphed forms of letters with blank spaces in which all necessary information may be inserted. These letters are, as a rule, carefully watched and personally signed, and contain a salutation and complimentary close. Where this style of letter is employed, the first reminder is very courteous and mild, excluding all sharp phrases. It is based on the assumption that the debtor has overlooked the account, and all blame for possible mistakes is taken by the creditor. Following are illustrations of the first formal reminder of this type:

> Dear Sir:
>> We are sending you a copy of your invoice of .... amounting to $............, in order that you may check its correctness. Our books show the amount as unpaid.
>> If there is any error please let us know. We will gladly correct it.
>>> Respectfully yours,

> Dear Customer:
>> We call your attention to your account which is now due. Has it been overlooked?
>> A check in settlement will be greatly appreciated.
>>> Very truly yours,

Should this secure no response, one or more formal reminders, the exact number of which will depend upon considerations mentioned in the earlier part of the present chapter, are sent to the delinquent debtor at intervals determined by the timing and dating plan of the collection system of the house. Although courteous assumptions are still proper, these reminders are made somewhat stronger in tone by the inclusion of a sharp phrase, making the request for payment more definite and insistent. Following are illustrations of such reminders:

> Dear Sir:
>> Your invoice of .... for $............ has been past due for two months and is still unpaid. We wrote you regarding this matter on .... but have received no reply. We call your attention again to the need for settlement.
>> If there is any error or misunderstanding, will you let us know immediately?
>>> Respectfully yours,

> Dear Sir:
>> We again call your attention to your past-due account of .... for $................, a detailed statement of which we have previously mailed to you. We shall appreciate a remittance in settlement of this amount by return mail.
>>> Very truly yours,

Stage of discussion. In this stage, personal collection letters are employed, in which the appeals are graded in strength and in the tone of insistency. The creditor here assumes that the debtor has good reason for the delay in settlement, or is in difficulties. Accordingly, attempts are made at this point to secure a response explaining the reasons for the delay. The customer's confidence is invited, and the house may either offer to allow additional time or else become more insistent and proceed to the next and last stage of the collection process.

Personal collection letters. The personal letters, which constitute this discussion stage, are undoubtedly the most important part of the collection process. They are written only after reminders have been used unsuccessfully. To secure the best results, the letters must lead to a climax. Accordingly, it is necessary that their tone and the appeals they make be graded in strength and insistency.

In order to make the first of the personal letters mild, sales material is sometimes included, which may suggest the value of continuing business relations with the creditor by maintaining a good credit standing. It may consist of a sentence calling attention to a special sale or offer, or expressing the hope for both payment and further orders. Such material as this, when it is used, is placed most advantageously at the end of the letter.

Since at this stage accounts usually call for individual attention, the correspondent, before starting to write, should familiarize himself with the actual condition of the account, the personal characteristics of the debtor, and the like. Only then is he in a position to select the appeal and the tone which he wishes to express in the letter. Because these are personal letters, they should be personal in style, and the somewhat mild or ordinary language appropriate in the preceding stage should not be used.

Collection-letter appeals. The heart of the collection letter is the appeal around which it is built; this constitutes the body of the letter. The appeal is chosen with an eye toward motivating the debtor with the ideas which seem most likely to move him to make payment. The five most commonly used appeals are sympathy, pride, justice, self-interest, and fear.

Appeal to Sympathy: The appeal to sympathy makes the customer feel that the concern which has favored him with credit is now inconvenienced, perhaps suffering, as a result of his failure to pay. This is a weak and sometimes misused appeal. If the organization using it is large, the average debtor believes that the reason given is untrue and implausible. On the other hand, where it is sincerely made, it may be very effective. One believable use is that of pointing out that although this particular customer's account is small, the sum owed by several thousand such customers is considerable and significant. The following letter illustrates some of these points:

> Dear Sir:
>
> Your check for $. . . . . to cover the invoice of . . . .
> (date) has not yet arrived. You wouldn't want to be the straw that breaks the
> camel's back, would you?
>
> Although in itself this amount is small, when multiplied by the several
> thousand accounts that we have which are similar to yours, even the little
> ones become very significant to us.
>
> Won't you do your small part in helping us to reduce a big load? Let
> us have your check covering this amount.
>
> Very truly yours,

Appeal to Self—respect: Men are motivated by their respect
for themselves and by the respect which others have for them. This,
then, constitutes an effectual appeal for the collector, as is illustrated
in the following letter:

> Dear Sir:
>
> We could not help holding in high esteem the standards which you had
> for prompt payment of your account in the past, and we want you to know
> that we have appreciated this.
>
> At present, however, your account is past due in the amount of $. . . . . . ,
> and we are reminding you of it, knowing that you would not generally permit
> it to remain this long in arrears.
>
> May we have your check covering the amount stated? We are counting
> on your cooperation.
>
> Sincerely yours,

Appeal to Justice: The purpose of this appeal is to make
the customer feel that he is not dealing fairly with the creditor. It points
out that the bill is due for value received, that the creditor has carried
the account long after it became due, and that it is not fair and just
to compel him to wait any longer for payment.

> Dear Sir:
>
> We confidently expected a remittance on your account of . . . .
> (date) for $. . . . . , as a response to our last letter.
>
> Frankly, we were disappointed, for we cannot believe that you would in-
> tentionally impose upon us. And that is really what it amounts to, for by not
> remitting promptly you do impose upon the difficulties incident to carrying the
> account longer than we had agreed to do.
>
> Without our elaborating, you know the importance of prompt collections.
> We are still confident that we can count on you to be fair and just with us in this
> instance.
>
> Very truly yours,

Appeal to Self–interest: A letter containing this appeal is stronger and may be more insistent in tone than those previously discussed. Logic and argument become more effective. The customer can be shown that it is to his own interest to pay his overdue bills immediately, that prompt payment improves his credit standing and enables the supplier to sell at reduced prices.

Dear Sir:

We have several times called to your attention the unpaid balance of $................ on your account for our invoice of .... (date). Why have we heard nothing from you?

In simple language, we are disappointed. When you asked for credit, we felt warranted in placing confidence in you. You have not done your share to uphold our confidence.

It is unnecessary to point out to an astute businessman like you that only by meeting obligations justly can a firm maintain its credit standing in the community. You cannot afford to lose the good will of your suppliers by allowing knowledge of your nonpayment to circulate among the trade.

We hope, therefore, that you will restore our original confidence with a prompt payment. Put your check in the mail today. Let's close this past chapter and start anew with a fresh slate.

Very truly yours,

Another way an appeal to self-interest may be made effectively is that employed by retailers who are members of some retail merchants' association. They write the slow-pay customer that the stores are required periodically to report all unpaid accounts and that this opportunity is given the customer to make his account current and avoid embarrassment. Any suggestion of threat should be carefully avoided, inasmuch as some states prosecute collectors using threatening appeals. Even where permitted by law, the plan has the disadvantage of implying a process of blacklisting, which is, on the whole, a bad practice, although it may under these circumstances be fully justifiable. A more detailed discussion of the legal aspects pertaining to collection letters is presented later in this chapter.

Dear Customer:

May we make a suggestion for your benefit?

At the next meeting of the .... Credit Association, it will be necessary to report your name among those who have been owing merchants for a considerable length of time.

This is only in line with rules of the Association and we have no choice in the matter.

We thought you would like an opportunity to prevent our having to submit your name by paying the $............ which you now owe us.   Unless satisfactory arrangements are made by .... (date), your name will be reported.

We hope you will act promptly to clear up your account with us.   That will be the much better thing for you in all ways.

Very truly yours,

Part payment. At times it is advisable to send what is generally regarded as a letter of courtesy, in which the customer is given one more opportunity to explain his neglect or to make payment.   An attempt may be made to secure at least part payment and arrange for additional payments at definite intervals.   A proposition to this effect rarely fails to bring a reply, since it is plausible and appeals to the debtor.   This method is usually resorted to by wholesalers and manufacturers where the accounts carried involve relatively large sums.   In such instances a real service is rendered the debtor who is unable to accumulate an amount large enough to pay his bills in their entirety.

Stage of urgency and compulsion. Ultimately the creditor must forcefully point out the customer's obligation and the consequence that might result from continued nonpayment.   In mercantile credit, it is at this late stage that a draft may be employed as means of enforcing payment.   Then is sent a letter announcing that if amicable efforts for settlement fail, the account will be placed in the hands of an attorney or collection agency.

Use of drafts. One of the more urgent steps, taken particularly by wholesalers and manufacturers, is the sending of a draft.   Its use has already been discussed in the preceding chapter.   The letter announcing the intention to send a draft, if a letter is used in place of a printed "Advance Notice of Draft," consists of a simple statement reviewing the action already taken and stating that unless a response is made within a certain time, a draft will be dispatched to the debtor's or some other designated bank.

Dear Sir:

Your account amounting to $............is now 95 days overdue, as we have pointed out in several letters.

This is as long as we feel we can carry the account, and unless we hear from you by ...., we assume that we have your permission to draw a draft on you for this amount.   It will be drawn through the First National Bank at ....

We hope that you will avoid this inconvenient and roundabout method of paying, and at the same time prevent the unfavorable reflection on your credit standing at the bank, by remitting to us directly before the date indicated. Let us hear from you by return mail.

Yours truly,

Appeal to fear. If the draft is dishonored and all the personal appeal letters have failed to secure a response or payment of the obligation, the creditor may send a personal collector, or the credit manager himself may call upon the debtor under certain circumstances. If none of these actions is feasible, threat letters are resorted to. They appeal to fear and are the harshest of collection letters. The debtor is usually threatened that he will be sued unless payment is forthcoming on or before a specified date, or that the account will be placed in the hands of an attorney or a collection agency. Its purpose is to point out that disagreeable consequences will result from further delay and that the debtor cannot escape payment of his just obligations. It is sometimes desirable to write a rather lengthy letter in which the seriousness of the matter is dwelt upon. It is often advisable to use language with a veiled threat to take drastic measures. If this fails to bring a response, the threat is made openly and at length as pointed out above.

Dear Sir:

Despite the fact that we have sent you numerous notices and letters regarding your past due bill of $............ for ...., we have heard nothing from you and we are at a loss to understand the situation. We feel that we have waited long and patiently and now urgently request your immediate attention.

We have no desire to embarrass or trouble you, but it is necessary that this account be settled at once and that you make satisfactory arrangements to do so without delay.

Very truly yours,

Where permitted by law, retailers who are members of some merchants' association are furnished with one or two form letters (or printed forms) that are supposed to have been sent by the bureau which the association maintains and which read as though coming from the bureau. These letters have been found very effective. They read somewhat as follows:

Dear Mr. ....:

In preparing the files of this bureau, organized for the mutual interchange of credit infomation, we find that .... (name of store) reports an account against you which is past due.

We would suggest that you make settlement with your creditor at once so that your record may be clear in our files.

Members of the bureau will, under our rules, report to us within five days as to whether or not settlement has been made.

Very truly yours,

Dear Mr. ....:

We wrote you on .... (date), stating that .... (name of store) had reported an account against you which is past due.

Our letter was sent in order to give you an opportunity to make settlement with your creditor and to avoid an unfavorable credit report with us.

Operated, as our bureau is, by the leading retail merchants of ......, our aim is to conduct negotiations with you in confidence and with utmost fairness. It is our business to give accurate and truthful information as to the paying habit of customers when inquiry is received from members of the bureau. We feel sure you will appreciate the value of a good credit standing with these merchants.

We shall expect you to make settlement with your creditor at once. Under the rules of our bureau, unless this is done within 5 days, the matter will be turned over to our attorneys for whatever action they deem necessary.

Very truly yours,

Collecting by unusual appeals. Occasionally the traditional routine of collecting is varied by the introduction of uncommon appeals, not the least useful of which has been that made to the debtor's sense of humor. So successful have fresh, novel approaches been in many instances that their returns have exceeded the results of more usual pleas. That this might occur need not seem strange; neither should it seem accidental or irregular. To the contrary, the humorous appeal is based accurately upon the well-discerned assumption that most individuals— including debtors—are capable of seeing the light side of situations. Thus they may be made to appreciate the creditor's demand and, consequently, to accede to his request.

To be successful, however, the humorous appeal must be genuine. It is best when it bears a close relationship to the immediate credit situation. It is least effective when forced, sarcastic, or offensive, under which circumstances, although it may amuse, it will seldom yield expected collection results. The principal element of good humor is its incongruity and its surprising turn of thought. Originality is also essential, for, while stock humor has been profitably adapted to new situations, the effectiveness of an unusual appeal is rapidly dissipated through repetition and familiarity. Consequently, the humorous collection letter may not only be the more difficult for the average writer to compose, but it may also be the least effective when used without skill and good judgment. In rare instances it may constitute the sole collection effort, but under most circumstances it serves best as a variation from the more businesslike collection approach.

Legal phases of collection letters. In writing collection letters, especially during the advanced stages of delinquency when strong appeals are likely to be made, it is prudent to be cautious about their contents in order to avoid possible liability. If the contents are intended to harass, or have the effect of harassing, the debtor as a means of coercing payment, the sender may be subject to possible liability for extortion. This may be true, for example, if the letter contains a threat of criminal prosecution, of bankruptcy, or even of an unfavorable report to members of a credit association. This would not be the case if the letter contains a threat to sue for the money due or a statement to the effect that as a member of a certain credit association the past-due indebtedness of the debtor will have to be reported after a certain date. The line of demarcation is thus at times rather thin. Again, in many states it may be deemed legally offensive to send a letter or form that simulates a legal process and is thus calculated to scare the debtor into paying even when no direct threat is made.

Liability for libel is no doubt the greatest risk involved in the use of questionable collection letters. If the contents, which would be considered published when a third party sees them (like the stenographer to whom it was dictated or the secretary of the recipient who would open such mail in the normal course of business), tend to degrade the debtor or hold him up to public ridicule and this causes him injury, the sender of the letter would be actionable for libel. Some of the statements in the letter may be libelous per se, such as a charge of fraud, deception, or dishonesty, without the necessity of proving actual injury.

Finally, there is the possibility of liability for invasion of the right of privacy, as in the mailing of postal cards or letters with contents on the outside cover which would tend to reflect unfavorably upon the character of the addressee. As a matter of fact, such matter is nonmailable and, if mailed, may subject the sender to a heavy fine or imprisonment. This should be a warning, for example, against sending postal cards indicating that the addressee is being dunned for a past-due account.

None of the above types of letters fall in the privileged communication category as does the interchange of credit information among interested creditors even when such information proves damaging to the subject involved. To be sure, also, there are legal defenses to all three types of possible liability briefly discussed above, especially to those of extortion and libel, but it would seem far safer not to have to resort to them by avoiding the use of language in the letters that might give cause for such action.

QUESTIONS AND PROBLEMS

1 Collection letters possess several qualities that are essential to a collection medium. What are these qualities?

2 What should be accomplished in the beginning, body, and ending of the single collection letter?

3 Prepare a list of negative terms and expressions that should not be used in collection correspondence.

4 Why is it usually necessary to use a collection series instead of a single letter?

5 Upon what assumptions are the stages in collection correspondence based?

6 Contrast the stages of notification and reminder.

7 Comment on the impersonal nature of reminders.

8 How do discussion letters differ from reminders?

9 What are the most common discussion appeals?

10 Write a letter using one of the common appeals?

11 In what ways may one recognize that the series has shifted from discussion to the stage of urgency?

12 What place has humor in collection letters?

13 Under what circumstances is collection possible by a single letter?

14 In bringing an obstinate debtor into line, a creditor may use improper language in his letters that would subject him to one of three possible liabilities. What are these liabilities? Are there any defenses against such action by a debtor?

special rights and
remedies of creditors

The business policies, methods, and practices of making collections discussed in the two preceding chapters are, except when abused in certain
respects, all legal or lawful.   There is nothing extralegal about them.
They deal with rights on the part of creditors and obligations on the
part of debtors arising out of credit transactions.   These are founded
on common law and Federal and state statutory law and are supported
by ethical considerations and social mores affecting business conduct.
They involve human behavior, interactions of creditor and debtor, and
actions by creditors from the mildest form to the use of strong moral
suasion and threat of enforcement.

There are times and conditions, however, in which regular procedure in effecting payment of a debt arising out of a commercial transaction
is inadequate, inappropriate, or ineffective.   Under such circumstances

it may be necessary for creditors to resort to specified rights and remedies available to them under appropriate laws. In this chapter consideration is given only to the *state* laws that are pertinent to the subject matter treated. In the order of treatment, they relate to sales, attachment, litigation, garnishment, bulk transfers, and special types of liens. The limitations placed upon creditors' rights and remedies are pointed out *specifically* in connection with each of the various laws or parts thereof involved and *generally* in the discussion of the statutes of limitations and those bearing on exemptions. Furthermore, while most of the discussion in this chapter is with reference to debts arising out of commercial transactions, much of it also applies to personal debts incurred in connection with the consumption of goods and services by individuals.

RIGHTS AND REMEDIES
OF AN UNPAID SELLER

Being a form of contract, a sale is governed by general rules pertaining to all contracts. As a *particular* form of contract, however, a sale has been subject to certain special rules of law that have been in existence in all states as common law or in statutory form under the Uniform Sales Act adopted by many states. All of these special rules of law have been superseded by the Uniform Commercial Code, which has been adopted by 49 states and the District of Columbia. In this brief discussion attention is given only to those aspects of the Uniform Commercial Code which deal with the rights and remedies of an upaid seller.

Some general rules and statements. Under the Uniform Commercial Code it is obviously the obligation of the seller to transfer and deliver and that of the buyer to accept and pay as required by the contract. Unless otherwise provided in the contract:

1 All goods called for must be tendered by the seller in a single delivery, and payment is due only on such tender.

2 Place for delivery is the seller's place of business unless the identified goods are known by both parties at time of contracting to be in another place, which then becomes the place of delivery.

3 Payment is due at time and place at which buyer is to receive the goods, which place may be the same as place of shipment, or upon receipt of documents of title.

4 If the seller is required or authorized to ship the goods on credit, the credit period runs from time of shipment except when the invoice is postdated.

Again, under the Uniform Commercial Code, until otherwise interpreted and ruled by the courts, the importance of *title* to the goods in determining questions of risk of loss or certain rights of a seller is deemphasized and is replaced by *possession* of the goods as the controlling factor, except in cases of breach of contract where the loss falls on the breaching party. Of course, it may well be that courts will still tend to follow the precedence long established under title theory and thus in a way defeat or modify the intended emphasis on possession theory. As this entire area is likely to remain legally far from clear, only future court decisions or specific amendments to the Code will throw needed light on the matter.

Subject to subsequent clarification by court decisions, title to the goods usually passes from seller to buyer in any manner and on any conditions explicitly agreed on, at time and place the seller completes his performance with respect to physical delivery of the goods. Moreover, a purchaser acquires all title which the seller had or had the power to transfer, and when the goods are delivered, the buyer has such power even though (1) the seller was deceived as to the identity of the buyer, (2) the delivery was in exchange for a check which was later dishonored, (3) it was agreed that the transaction was to be a "cash sale," or (4) the delivery was procured through fraud punishable under criminal law. Not only that, but a merchant-buyer, regularly dealing in such goods, to whom possession was entrusted has the power to transfer all rights of the entruster or seller to other buyers in the ordinary course of business. Furthermore, where the goods are to be shipped by seller to buyer, except on destination contracts, possession, and thus risk of loss, passes to the buyer when the goods are delivered to the carrier. Finally, rejection or other refusal by the buyer to receive or retain the goods, whether justified or not, revests title to the goods in the seller.

Seller's remedies in case of buyer's insolvency. When the seller discovers that the buyer is insolvent, he may refuse delivery except for cash and require payment for all goods previously delivered under the contract and stop delivery of goods in possession of a carrier. If the buyer has received goods on credit while insolvent, upon such discovery the seller may reclaim the goods on demand made within 10 days after their receipt. Usually, however, as already pointed out in the preceding paragraph, a seller may not base a right to reclaim goods on the basis of the buyer's fraudulent or innocent misrepresentation of solvency or of intent to pay. If the reclamation is successful, all other remedies with respect to the goods are excluded.

Seller's remedies in general. If a buyer wrongfully rejects or revokes acceptance of the goods contracted for, fails to make a payment due on or before delivery, or repudiates part or the whole of a contract, the seller can exercise certain remedies with respect to any of the goods directly affected or with respect to the whole undelivered balance, as the case may be.   For one thing, the seller may withhold delivery of such goods as are identified to the contract that are still in his possession or control and treat them as subject of resale to others.

Second, upon discovery of the buyer's insolvency or for any other reason that would give him a right to withhold or reclaim the goods, the seller may exercise his right of stoppage in transit.   This is done by serving notice to the carrier or other bailee in possession of the goods to stop delivery.   The carrier or other bailee must then hold the goods and deliver them as directed by the seller, who remains liable to bailee for any ensuing charges and damage claims.

Third, the seller may resell the goods concerned or the undelivered balance thereof and recover damages, measured by the difference between the unpaid contract price and the market price at the time and place for tender, plus incidental damages to an aggrieved seller such as commercially reasonable charges and expenses incurred in stopping delivery, in the transportation, care, and custody of the goods after the buyer's breach, in connection with the return and resale of the goods, etc.   Any expenses saved as a result of the buyer's breach must be deducted.   If such measure of damages as just outlined is inadequate to put the seller in as good a position as performance of the contract would have accomplished, then the measure of damages would be the profit, including reasonable overhead, which the seller would have made from full performance by the buyer plus incidental damages as indicated above.

Fourth, if the buyer fails to pay the price as it becomes due, the seller may take action for the price, together with any incidental damages, of goods accepted or of conforming goods lost or damaged within a commercially reasonable time after risk of loss (possession) has passed to the buyer, as well as of goods subject to the contract that the seller was unable after reasonable efforts to resell at a reasonable price or that the circumstances reasonably indicate such efforts to resell are unavailing.   When suing for the price, the seller must hold for the buyer any goods covered by the contract still in his control except where a resale becomes possible prior to collection of the judgment.   A seller who is not entitled to the price may nevertheless be awarded damages incident to the buyer's breach of contract.

Buyer's rights and remedies.   Under the Uniform Commercial Code buyers, too, have extensive rights and remedies against nonperforming sellers.   For example, if the seller fails to make delivery, repudiates the contract, or the buyer rightfully rejects or justifiably revokes acceptance of the goods, the buyer may cancel part or all of the contract, recover as much of the price as has been paid, and recover damages for nondelivery. He may under certain conditions recover incidental damages resulting from the seller's breach, such as expenses reasonably incurred in inspection, receipt, transportation, and care and custody of the goods rightfully rejected, any commercially reasonable charges, and expenses incident to the delay or other breach. Consequential damages may result in the nature of loss resulting from requirements and needs of which the seller was cognizant at time of contract or of injury to person or property resulting from any breach of warranty.

In the treatment of this subject, however, principal interest is in the rights and remedies available to sellers in the collection of amounts owing by debtors. As part of the collection process, consequently, such interest is emphasized to the apparent neglect of the substantially equal protection afforded to buyers against nonperforming sellers.

ATTACHMENT

Attachment is a provisional legal remedy whereby the defendant's property is seized and taken out of his control and held for the payment of a debt on which suit has been or is about to be brought by a creditor. If an attachment has been made prior to bringing suit, such action must be taken within a certain time, usually 30 days, after service of the writ of attachment; otherwise, jurisdiction over the property attached ceases.

The purpose of this provisional remedy is to prevent a debtor, during the pendency of a suit against him, from disposing of his property or from placing it beyond the reach of his creditor. It is a precautionary measure to prevent debtors with ample assets from causing them to disappear and thus making themselves execution-proof after a judgment has been obtained.

Grounds for attachment. The right of attachment is purely statutory, the statutes usually specifying in great detail the classes of action in which the writ may be issued and the peculiar circumstances and relationships which must exist in these areas before the writ may be issued.[1] Attachment proceedings are highly technical in most states, and if these technical requirements are not strictly complied with, the defendant may cause the attachment to be vacated.

Although the statutes differ widely in certain particulars, the principal grounds for resorting to this remedy are substantially the same

[1] In some jurisdictions, as in the New England states, practically all legal actions are commenced by attachment.

in practically all states. These grounds for attachment are as follows:

1 That the debtor is a nonresident of the state where the writ of attachment is sought against the debtor's property located within the state. This is one of the most usual grounds for granting an attachment. Thus, for example, in most jurisdictions it is sufficient if the defendant is a foreign corporation.

2 That the debtor has absconded from the state with intent to defraud creditors or to avoid service of legal process.

3 That the debtor keeps himself concealed with intent to defraud creditors or to avoid service of legal process.

4 That the debtor has removed property or is about to dispose of property for the purpose of defrauding his creditors.

In the state of New York there is the additional ground that the debtor has secured property from the creditor by fraudulent representations, such as the making of a false statement in writing regarding his financial condition.

Thus it will be seen that in general, aside from nonresidence, an element of fraud or concealment or removal from the jurisdiction must usually be proved to sustain the issuance of a writ of attachment.

Attachment procedure. Prior to the issuance of a writ of attachment, the plaintiff or creditor is required in most states to make an affidavit stating the amount of the indebtedness; that the claim is just; that no part of the debt claimed has been paid; the manner in which the debt accrued; that he is not indebted to the defendant; that the sum demanded is actually due; and the ground or grounds for attachment. The affidavit may be made by the creditor himself, his agent, or his attorney. Another condition precedent to the issue of the writ of attachment in practically all states is the requirement that the plainiff give a bond, or undertaking, with sufficient sureties, to protect the debtor against any injury which would result from a wrongful attachment, as where the debtor recovers judgment, or causes the attachment to be vacated. The attachment is not to be construed as wrongful, if the plaintiff had good cause to believe the grounds for attachment true, although cases to the contrary may be found in some states.

As soon as the writ of attachment is issued, the sheriff to whom it is directed immediately proceeds to execute it, by attaching enough property, which is not exempt from levy, to satisfy the creditor's claim, together with costs and expenses. If the original levy is insufficient, additional levies may be made from time to time until a sufficient amount of property has been attached. On the day specified in the writ, the sheriff returns a report of the procedure together with an exact and specific description of the property attached. The attachment then constitutes a lien on the debtor's property dating from the date of the actual execution of the writ. This lien is afterwards made absolute by judgment. In this connection it should be observed that in most states an attachment may be dissolved and the attached property released by the defendant tendering a bond for the payment of whatever judgment may be rendered against him, usually in the same amount as the creditor's bond.

COLLECTION
BY SUIT

Collection by suit is undertaken usually only when other rights of the unpaid creditor are inapplicable, when all other methods employed in commercial practice have been exhausted, and when there are assets of value in the hands of the debtor against which a judgment, if obtained, may be executed, or, in the case of consumer debt, when action in garnishment proceedings is to be contemplated. Suit action, whether brought before a judge or jury, serves two primary purposes: first, to establish the fact of the debt and agreement as to the amount and, second, to provide the creditor with a legal remedy and aid in collecting the proven debt. In justice to both parties to a debt, however, the law provides safeguards for the debtor as well as for the creditor; it also establishes standards of settlement which are in the interest of society in general.

Procedure for suit action.[2] Suit generally consists of three separate stages of action: namely, *pleadings, trial,* and *execution of judgment.* The pleading of the case is that stage in which the contentions of the litigants are expressed and in which the matters to be decided by trial are determined. In most instances in which suit is brought to enforce payment, the creditor engages the services of an attorney to represent him as plaintiff. The attorney, with appropriate and sufficient copies of the original orders for merchandise and invoices establishing the fact and terms of shipment, files a *petition* in the court having jurisdiction of the case (see Fig. 26-1). He also files with the court a *precipe* (see Fig. 26-2), asking for the service of a *summons* upon the debtor or defendant. After service of the process (see Figs. 26-3*A* and 26-3*B*), the debtor is allowed, within a specified time, to file an *answer* denying the allegations of the complaint or setting up such defenses as he may think he has. Anything introducing new matter, other than a general denial, necessitates, in turn, a *reply* by the plaintiff. This reply may then be followed by a *rejoinder* by the defendant, after which the issues of the

---

[2] This discussion and the several forms presented in connection therewith are merely illustrative of the procedure followed and forms used in most jurisdictions in exactly the same or in a modified manner.

In the Municipal Court of the City of Toledo, Lucas County, Ohio

Plaintiff

No._____

PETITION

Defendant

Plaintiff says there is due_____ from the within named defendant __the sum

of_____ ($_____) Dollars on an account

for _____to defendant by plaintiff at defendant's special instance

and request, that; said sum is justly due and owing and demand has been made for

the payment thereof, but that defendant ____ ha ___ neglected and refused and still

neglects and refuses to pay the same.

WHEREFORE plaintiff pray_____ judgment against said defendant _____ in the

sum of _____ ($_____) Dollars with interest

thereon at the rate of 6% per annum from the _____ day of _____19___,

until paid, and the costs of this action.

_____
Attorney for Plaintiff

STATE OF OHIO

    SS.

LUCAS COUNTY

_____ being first duly sworn, according to

law, deposes and says that he is _____ the plaintiff herein, and

duly authorized in the premises; that he has read the foregoing petition, and that

the facts stated, and allegations contained therein are true, as he verily believes.

_____

Sworn to before me and subscribed in my presence this_____ day

of _____, 19___.

_____
Notary Public, Lucas County, Ohio

figure 26-1. *Typical form of petition by a creditor in initiating suit for the collection of money, replevin, attachment, or garnishment.*

allegations are sufficiently clarified for presentation to the court. If no answer is made by the debtor, a default judgment usually results.

Following the pleadings, the action is placed on the calendar of the court for trial, which may be heard by a judge alone or by a judge and jury. Where the case is heard by both, the judge passes

The State of Ohio, FRANKLIN COUNTY, CITY OF COLUMBUS, } ss.

PRECIPE

IN THE COLUMBUS MUNICIPAL COURT OF COLUMBUS, OHIO.

.... } Plaintiff

VS.

.... } Defendant

Doc...................................

Case No. ....

To the Clerk:

Please issue ....

.... in the above entitled case

....

Filed .... Attorney for..............................

P.P.Co.

figure 26-2. *Precipe, used by attorneys when requesting the court to take a desired action.*

Summons in Action for Money Only

CASE No. ....

THE STATE OF OHIO, FRANKLIN COUNTY, CITY OF COLUMBUS, }

To the Bailiff of the Columbus Municipal Court of Columbus, Ohio
You are commanded to notify

....

....

that .... ha...... been sued by ....

.... in the Columbus Municipal Court of Columbus, Ohio, and

that unless .... file .... answer in writing on or before ....

the petition of said plaintiff...... against .... filed in the Clerk's office of said Court, will be taken as true and judgment rendered accordingly.

Witness, TED HYSELL, Clerk of said Court
and the Seal thereof, at the City of Columbus,

(SEAL)

....

TED HYSELL, Clerk

By .... DEPUTY CLERK

Amount claimed, $ .... and interest as follows at .... per cent

on $ .... from ....

on $ .... from ....

and the costs of suit. Judgment will be taken if you fail to answer or appear.

Returnable by Bailiff ....

Plaintiff's Attorney ....

ANSWER MUST BE MADE UNDER OATH

figure 26-3A. *Summons ordering the debtor or defendant to appear before the court.*

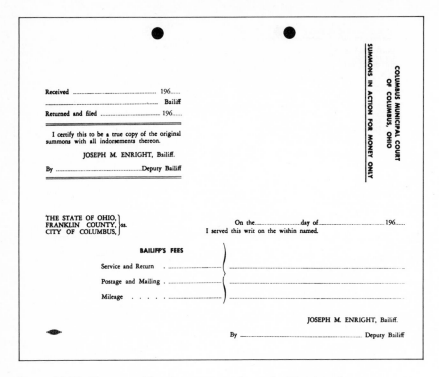

figure 26-3*B. Reverse side of summons shown in Fig. 26-3A.*

upon all questions of law, while the jury determines the facts of the case.   In most jurisdictions, trial by jury may be waived, although the defendant has a right to such a hearing if he wishes it.   After the rendition of a decision by the judge, or a verdict by the jury, *judgment* is entered either for the plaintiff or for the defendant.   The judgment is, if in favor of plaintiff, a court decree determining the amount due from a defendant.   The judgment becomes part of the permanent court records and, depending upon the laws of the jurisdiction, may become a lien upon the defendant's real estate and personal property.   In some jurisdictions, however, a lien may not be established until the issuance of an execution on the judgment.

Execution must follow the entering of a judgment in order to make the judgment effectual.   An execution is an order of the court directing the sheriff, bailiff, marshal, constable, or other executive officer of the court to collect the amount of the judgment from the property of the judgment debtor (see Figs. 26-4*A* and 26-4*B*).   Information may be given the bailiff by the judgment creditor's attorney, instructing him

EXECUTION IN CIVIL CASES
THE COLUMBUS MUNICIPAL COURT, COLUMBUS, OHIO Docket No._____ Case No._____

THE STATE OF OHIO
FRANKLIN COUNTY } ss   TO ANY BAILIFF OF SAID COURT:
CITY OF COLUMBUS

WHEREAS, on ....

.... obtained a judgment

against ....

Before THE COLUMBUS MUNICIPAL COURT, City Hall, Columbus, Ohio for the sum of

.... dollars .... cents,

.... dollars .... cents costs:

YOU ARE THEREFORE COMMANDED to collect the amount of said judgment, with costs indorsed and

increase, out of the personal property of the said ....

....

and pay the same to the Clerk of this Court, and make return of this execution and a certificate thereon, showing

the manner in which you have executed the same, in thirty days from the time of your receipt hereof.

Amount of Judgment Debt - $................

Judgment Creditor's Costs - - ....   *Given under my hand* ....

Judgment Debtor's Costs - - ....

Interest - - - - - - - - - - - ....   *TED HYSELL, Clerk of The Columbus Municipal Court*

This Execution and Filing - - ....   *By* .... *Deputy Clerk*

Bailiff's Fees on This Writ

Service and Return - - - - - - ....

Mileage....................miles - ....

Advertising - - - - - - - - - ....

Storage - - - - - - - - - - - - ....

Sum'g and Swear'g Ap. ....

Custodian's fee - - - - - - - - ....

Poundage - - - - - - - - - - - ....

Levy - - - - - - - - - - - - - - ....

....

....   *Returnable* ....

Total - - - - - - - - - - $................

JOSEPH M. ENRIGHT, Bailiff, ...

By........................Deputy Bailiff   *Plaintiff's Attorney*

figure 26-4A. *Execution form issued by the court instructing the bailiff to collect the amount of the judgment.*

upon what to levy execution, particularly in replevin cases. The officer then levies by seizing the property of the debtor and in making demand upon him for payment. If property is seized, it is advertised for sale and sold at public auction. The proceeds are turned over to the court, and after deduction of charges and expenses of the officer, the remainder

EXECUTION IN CIVIL CASES

The Columbus Municipal Court
City Hall, Columbus, Ohio

RETURN

Received this writ ....19........ By virtue of this writ ....

JOSEPH M. ENRIGHT, Bailiff,

By .... Deputy Bailiff

figure 26-4*B. Reverse side of execution form shown in Fig. 26-4A.*

is paid to the judgment creditor, who, upon receipt of payment in full, executes and delivers to the judgment debtor an instrument known as a *satisfaction piece*. If no property is available for seizure, however, the officer *returns* the execution to the court unsatisfied, and the judgment is *docketed* for future use if and when the debtor acquires property against which an execution may be levied.

Statutes of limitations. A claim or a judgment cannot be held forever against a debtor. On the contrary, in every state there are statutory limitations to the length of time that a debt may be pursued and specifications concerning the renewal of the limitation period.

Such relief for debtors is based upon several principles of social theory. The law, for one thing, looks with suspicion upon very old claims. They are difficult to prove, because evidence becomes lost, memories become dimmed, and witnesses are removed by death or otherwise from the jurisdiction. They would encourage, moreover, inefficiencies in business and collection practice. Furthermore, statutes of limitations are consciously or instinctively predicated upon a philosophy that every debtor should ultimately be relieved of his debt. Precedent for this action is found even in the Mosaic writings recorded in Deuteronomy, whereby every seventh year creditors released their debtors, giving either full remission or at least suspension of the debt for the period of a year.[3] Modern bankruptcy affords a similar release for those who choose to and can avail themselves of it.

The limitations imposed by the various states differ widely, however, and creditors must familiarize themselves with the statutes of the particular jurisdiction. The limitations also vary with respect to the several types of claims, different lengths of time being provided for bringing action on promissory notes, open accounts, instruments and contracts under seal, ordinary contracts, judgments in courts of record, and judgments in courts not of record. In the state of Ohio, for example, a creditor has a legal right to bring action on an unpaid promissory note for a period of 15 years. Open accounts which are not evidenced by a written contract are outlawed after 6 years, as are other ordinary contracts made orally. Domestic judgments entered in a court of record continue in effect for a period of 21 years, provided that at the end of the sixth year and every 5 years thereafter the judgment is kept alive by execution. Other civil actions have a limit of 15 years. The provisions of other state codes are similar to these in general respects although widely varying in detail. For example, open accounts are outlawed in Texas in 2 years, in fourteen states in 3 years, in seven states in 4 years, in six states in 5 years, in 22 states in 6 years, and in the state of Wyoming in 8 years. Again, in three states (Kansas, Nebraska, and Oklahoma) domestic judgments may be kept alive indefinitely by execution every 5 years.

These statutory time limitations, on the other hand, are not without

---

[3] Chapter 15 provides that "At the end of *every* seven years thou shalt make a release." "Every creditor that lendeth *ought* unto his neighbour shall release it," etc. It also provides for a similar release of slaves, saying that if a Hebrew person "be sold unto thee, he shall serve thee six years; and in the seventh year thou shalt let him go free from thee."

some elements of flexibility which work advantages to creditors as well as to debtors. In the first place, a debtor seeking defense on the ground that the statutory number of years had elapsed must plead this claim affirmatively, otherwise the statute is deemed waived and a recovery may be had in spite of the age of the debt. Furthermore, the period of limitation may be started to run anew as a result of certain actions of the debtor, thus prolonging the period within which action may be brought to enforce payment. Three actions of the debtor may produce this effect: namely, the making of partial payment of the debt; acknowledgment of the validity of the debt; or by a new promise to pay the same.

Exemptions. The effectiveness of collection by suit is tempered also by exemptions which are commonly allowed the debtor under the statutes of the various states. Exemptions are allowed on the theory that an injustice is done both to the debtor and to society by depriving him of all his assets or property. Completely stripped of possessions, debtors may become public charges, particularly if also their entire earnings are subject to seizure through judgment and garnishment. Consequently, every state stipulates what property and what per cent of earnings cannot be taken by suit.[4] Most states exempt some homestead holdings, expressed either on an acreage or value basis. All states exempt certain items of personal property, usually valued up to a specified amount and consisting of objects of apparel, household goods, and materials and stock necessary for carrying on the trade or business of the debtor. Most states provide an exemption also for a portion of the debtor's earnings, placing beyond reach of creditors either an absolute minimum dollar earnings or a percentage of the debtor's current (monthly) income. Holdings and earnings in excess of the stated exemptions may be levied upon for the satisfaction of a judgment on a debt.

Supplementary proceedings. Frequently, when a judgment has been docketed as unsatisfied, execution thereon having been unsuccessful, it is desired further to investigate the judgment debtor with respect to his property and ability to pay. This examination of the debtor is made possible through proceedings supplementary to the execution. Acting under the governing statutory provisions, the judgment creditor may, by order or subpoena direct the judgment debtor to appear before the court or referee and answer questions concerning the whereabouts of his property, suspected transfer thereof to a third party, indebtedness of others to him, earnings, employment, and the like. Any or all persons indebted to the judgment debtor may also be examined in supplementary proceed-

---

[4] For a classified list of exemptions, as well as statutes of limitations, by states, see *Credit Manual of Commercial Laws*, published annually by the National Association of Credit Management.

ings. All assets so discovered may then be applied to the satisfaction of the judgment, subject to exemptions specified in the statute under consideration. Thus are fraudulent transfers and concealment of assets ferreted out. Such proceedings may be resorted to at any time within the period permitted by the statute of limitations.

GARNISHMENT

Garnishment, sometimes termed "trustee process," or "third-party proceedings," is a process resembling that of attachment; it is a species of seizure by notice. Under these proceedings the creditor acquires a lien or right to hold the garnishee, in whose possession the goods, money, or credits of the debtor are found, liable for his debt to the defendant.

A garnishee is supposedly an innocent third party owing money to the defendant or in whose possession property of the defendant is found without his fault or blame. When such property or debt is attached, the garnishee is regarded in the eyes of the law as a trustee or custodian of the property or debt and is restrained from paying the debt or returning the property to the defendant. Instead, he is notified or warned to the effect that he is not to settle with the defendant but to answer to the suit of the creditor. The purpose obviously is to apply a debt due to a defendant from a third party to the satisfaction of a judgment against such defendant.

In practically every state the right of garnishment exists in one form or another, although in some few states it exists under a different name.[5] In all instances the remedy is statutory; hence there are wide differences in its application. In many states it is limited to actions on contract but not permitted in actions in tort. In some states it is permitted only after an execution against the debtor has been returned unsatisfied, while in other states it is used in connection with a writ of attachment. The statutes differ also in other respects.

Procedure. Despite these differences in the various states, it is believed that a brief explanation of the procedure followed in the state of Ohio, which is typical in many respects, will serve to elucidate the matter somewhat.

A person bringing an action must first make a demand in writing for the excess over and above 80 per cent of the first $300, and over and above 60 per cent of the balance, earned within 30 days preceding

---

[5] In some of the New England states garnishment goes under the name of "trustee process," in Pennsylvania it is known as "judgment execution," and in South Carolina it is completely unknown. Furthermore, in Montana it is executed by means of an attachment and in New York by the statutory proceedings supplementary to execution.

issue of process, assuming that the third party is the debtor's employer, 5 days and not more than 30 days before such action is actually commenced. The minimum exempted from garnishment is $150 per month. If the defendant debtor tenders payment for the amount demanded, no additional charges are made, otherwise there is a charge of $2.50 to cover costs of the action. The law prohibits the making of such demand by the same creditor at closer periods than 30 days.[6]

Failing to secure payment as demanded, the creditor files an affidavit for attachment and garnishment setting forth the facts and conditions of the case and praying for an order on the garnishee. Such an order is then issued by the court requiring the garnishee to appear and answer to the liability to the defendant debtor. This document, sometimes referred to as a "Notice of Garnishment," or an "Aid in Execution," serves as a notice to withhold all property, moneys, or credits in his possession until further orders from the court.

Failure of the garnishee to appear or to answer to the notice entitles the plaintiff to proceed against him in his own name. If the debt is admitted on the "Answer of Garnishee" form, an order is issued for its payment into court. It should be borne in mind that garnishment proceedings as well as all other rights given to creditors in enforcing payment are subject to the exemption provisions of the various states.

Wage garnishment under Federal law. For the first time in our history, effective July 1, 1970, the garnishment of wages or other compensation for personal services is to be regulated by Federal legislation, which supersedes all state laws on the subject except where the latter are more restrictive. Under provisions of the Consumer Credit Protection Act, the maximum part of a workweek's compensation subject to garnishment may not exceed the lesser of (1) 25 per cent of the debtor's aggregate disposable earnings for the week (the so-called take-home pay) or (2) the amount by which such weekly earnings exceed 30 times the Federal

---

[6] The laws differ greatly in this matter. For example, in South Dakota there is no provision for a wage exemption, which means that all wages can be garnished. In Rhode Island the wage exemption does not exceed $50, and in many other states such exemption is altogether too low. At the other extreme, as in Florida, the entire wages of the head of the family due for personal labor or services are exempt. In still other states the wage exemption provisions are antiquated and anachronistic, as, for example, in Georgia, where wages are exempt from garnishment up to $3 per day and 50 per cent of excess thereof. This is still lower in Kentucky, where $67.50 of monthly earnings are exempt from garnishment. On the whole, however, the tendency has been to adjust the wage exemptions upward and provide more liberal protection from garnishment. This trend is justified by the rising costs and higher standards of living, as well as by the reduced purchasing power of the dollar caused by various inflationary factors. Such protection, if adequate in amount, should also minimize the need of wage earners for bankruptcy proceedings, although, despite notable pronouncements to the contrary, there is no consistent relationship between harshness or mildness in garnishment laws and the number of personal bankruptcies. See, for example, Table 6 in Harry Lee Mathews, *"Causes of Personal Bankruptcies in Ohio"* doctoral dissertation at The Ohio State University, Columbus, Ohio.

minimum hourly wage. For any other pay period than a week the Secretary of Labor is to prescribe the applicable multiple to be used in this formula. The law also forbids the discharge of an employee on the ground that his wages were subjected to garnishment for any *one* indebtedness, under penalty of a fine of up to $1,000, imprisonment of up to one year, or both.

This part of the Act is predicated upon questionable findings and assumptions. One is the allegedly disruptive effect of garnishment upon interstate commerce. The other is that disparities in the state garnishment laws destroy the uniformity of the Bankruptcy Law, on the unproven assumption that harsh garnishment laws lead to the bankruptcy courts. As far as is known, no scientific study has revealed any substantial support for such a position or any assertions to this effect.

BULK SALES
AND TRANSFERS

Purpose of law. From time immemorial dishonest debtors have attempted to defraud creditors by one means or another. A not uncommon device has been to sell their entire stock of goods in bulk quickly and at ridiculously low valuations and, by concealment of the proceeds, render themselves execution- or judgment-proof. A practice somewhat similar to selling out to a third and bona fide purchaser would be one where the goods in bulk are transferred by a single proprietor or partnership to an organization into which the business was previously incorporated, in exchange for capital stock.

To prevent such sales and transfers being consummated to the detriment of creditors, bulk sales statutes have been enacted in substantially similar form in every state and the District of Columbia. These have all been replaced by the adoption of the Uniform Commercial Code, again in substantially similar form, by all states but one and by the District of Columbia. Some 21 states have also adopted the Uniform Fraudulent Conveyance Act, which declares that every conveyance made or obligation incurred by a person who is or will thereby be made insolvent is fraudulent as to creditors regardless of actual intent unless justified by a fair consideration. The discussion herein is confined, however, to the provisions of the Uniform Commercial Code with regard to bulk sales and transfers.

Coverage or scope. This part of the Uniform Commercial Code applies to concerns whose principal business is the sale of merchandise from stock or manufacture and covers transactions involving the sale or transfer of all or a major part of a stock of merchandise or other inventory, not only in bulk but *also* out of the ordinary course of business of the seller or transferror. To be sure, some bulk sales or transfers are excepted from the law, as, for example, general assignments for the benefit of creditors; sales by executors, receivers, or any other public officer under judicial process; transfers of property which is exempt from execution; and other types of transfers specified by the law in question. Furthermore, there are certain transactions in bulk that may or may not be subject to the bulk transfer provisions of the Uniform Commercial Code, which may be at variance with certain state statutes, such as goods covered by a chattel mortgage, sales at public auction, or transfers to a corporation or partnership organized to take over the business of the transferror. On all such matters the specific state law that governs needs to be considered.

Principal provisions. The transferror must furnish a list of his existing creditors and a schedule of the property involved to the transferee, which must be preserved by the latter for a period of 6 months to permit inspection by any creditor of the transferror. Such lists may be filed with the county clerk in the county in which the property was located at time of transfer; in California this filing is mandatory. Notice must then be given by the transferee or purchaser to all listed creditors and to all other persons known by him to hold or assert claims against the transferror or seller, usually at least 10 days before he takes possession of the goods or pays for them. Failure to give such notice makes the transfer or sale, depending upon the specific statute, void, ineffective, or presumptively fraudulent and void. In addition to giving notice, in many states and under the provisions of the Uniform Commercial Code, the transferee or purchaser is required to apply, or to see to the application of, the purchase price to the payment in full or pro rata among the creditors of their claims against the transferror or seller. Ordinarily, creditors may bring proceedings to set the transfer aside within 6 months from the date of possession by the transferee or, if concealed, within such period after discovery. But, except in cases of collusion between the transferee and subsequent purchasers, creditors may not pursue the property into the hands of the latter.

If a bulk transfer subject to the law is made through an auctioneer, a list of creditors together with a schedule of property to be sold must be furnished to him and retained for a period of 6 months for possible inspection by creditors. The auctioneer must give notice of the auction personally or by registered mail at least 10 days before it takes place and assure that the net proceeds are applied to the payment of the creditors in full or pro rata. Failure to do these things does not affect the validity of the sale or title of the purchasers, but, if the auctioneer knows it to be a bulk sale, such failure renders him liable to the creditors as a class for the sums owing to them by the transferror up to the amount of the net proceeds of the auction.

SPECIAL TYPES OF LIENS

In addition to unpaid sellers' liens already discussed, there are two types of liens which are of special interest to creditors and in which possession of the goods may not be essential. They are factors' liens and mechanics' liens.

Factors' liens. Originally the factor sold merchandise for his clients and made loans to them on it prior to sale. As the merchandise under such circumstances was often in the factor's possession, he could exercise a common law lien on it as security for his loans and commissions and fees. Later the factor specialized in financing operations, checking credits, cashing sales, and making loans on merchandise not in his possession. To give the factor a lien on goods *not* in his possession, special factors' lien laws were enacted by most of the states, making such a lien possible if a public notice is filed in the county recording office to that effect and his name is placed on the premises holding the goods so pledged. These statutory enactments have been replaced by the Uniform Commercial Code in its provisions concerning secured transactions.

Mechanics' liens. Under special statutes enacted by all states and the District of Columbia, a mechanics' or materialman's lien may be obtained for services rendered or materials furnished on credit in connection with the construction, repair, or alteration of a building or other improvements upon realty. To obtain such a lien and thus protect the credit involved, the services rendered or materials furnished must have been based upon the credit of the building or other realty and not merely upon the general credit of the owner or contractor. Such liens are not only important to contractors who supply both services and materials, but are also of great significance to wholesalers and others who sell to contractors materials for installation and other uses on construction projects or when such concerns sell directly to home owners fixtures and similar articles that become an integral part of the realty.

Illustrative is the California law, which provides that such a lien becomes effective if filed in a county recorder's office generally within 60 days after completion of the work, but the lien does not bind the property for more than 90 days after filing, unless proceedings are commenced to enforce it, and even then such action must be brought to trial within 2 years after it is commenced.   Such a lien takes priority over any lien, mortgage, or other encumbrance which was unrecorded at time work commenced under the lien in question or which attached subsequent to such commencement.   Public improvements are not subject to this type of lien, but improvements on gas and oil wells are.

QUESTIONS AND PROBLEMS

1 Why and when is it necessary for a seller to resort to so-called "legal means" of collecting an account rather than merely commercial methods?   What is the real distinction between the two?

2 With a change of emphasis from transfer of title to transfer of possession as effected by the Uniform Commercial Code as compared with previously existing common law or the Uniform Sales Act, what basic changes have been made in the rights and remedies of a creditor:

a Against a buyer who misrepresented his solvency?

b Against a buyer who deceived a seller as to his identity?

3 Under what conditions can goods be reclaimed, and what are the consequences of a successful reclamation?

4 List the general rights and remedies which an unpaid seller can exercise:

a When the seller discovers the buyer to be insolvent.

b When the buyer breaches the contract.

5 From the relatively detailed discussion of a *seller's* rights and remedies, should it be assumed that similar protective devices are not available to buyers?   Why or why not?

6 What are the nature and purpose of attachments, and under what circumstances may they be used?   What is the relationship of attachments to the legal actions involved in suing a debtor and to garnishment proceedings, respectively?

7 Explain the steps involved in collection by suit yielding a judgment.   What variation of the procedure would there be in a suit to collect a debt evidenced by a cognovit note?

8 Assuming that a judgment has been obtained against the delinquent debtor, what is the procedure in enforcing it?   Suppose no property is available at the time, what can be done with the judgment and for how long a period can the judgment be kept alive?

9 What are statutes of limitation?   Why are there such laws?

10 How may an account, barred by the statute of limitations, be revived?

11 Consult a copy of the *Credit Manual of Commercial Laws* and report on the character of exemptions which are allowed debtors located in your state.

12 What are the purpose and nature of supplementary proceedings?

13 Explain the use of garnishment proceedings and discuss the relationship between them, exemptions, and the number of personal bankruptcies.

14 What is the principal purpose of the provisions of the Uniform Commercial Code with respect to bulk sales and transfers, and how is it to be achieved? If the bulk sale is made by auction, are creditors equally protected?

15 A retail grocer in Indianapolis, Ind., purchased a large bill of goods from a local wholesale house. Being in some difficulties with his bank and other creditors, the retailer left the state for parts unknown. Can the wholesaler in question obtain possession of the goods? If yes, by what proceedings can this be done and under what conditions?

16 Mr. X, who is engaged in the capacity of salesman for a clothing store in Santa Fe, N.M., bought a diamond ring for his wife from a local store. He promised to pay the purchase price at the end of 90 days, but he defaulted. How much can the seller recover by means of garnishment proceedings? Would your answer be the same if the bill were owed to a grocery store for the purchase of various items of food? Give reasons for your answer.

17 A sells his business to B, including the entire stock in trade. C is one of the creditors of A and was unaware of the transaction until shortly after it was completed. What can C do to protect his interest in the matter?

18 A hardware merchant, seeing financial difficulties ahead, stocks up with large quantities of goods purchased on credit terms. He then sells his store and stock and conceals the cash received from the sale. Is such a sale legal? What makes it legal or illegal?

19 Why is it necessary to have special laws providing for factors' liens instead of using those pertaining to unpaid sellers' liens? Does the same reasoning apply to mechanics' liens?

20 List the various classes of retailers, wholesalers, and manufacturers who are affected by the laws governing mechanics' liens. Is this effect direct or indirect? Explain.

CHAPTER TWENTY-SEVEN

extensions and
friendly adjustments

In the preceding three chapters the collection problem has been handled from the standpoint of the individual creditor. It was also assumed that the debtor could pay or could be made to pay the *full* amount of the indebtedness. It is the purpose of this chapter to deal with the collection problem mainly from the point of view of a group of creditors interested in the same account and especially under conditions, other than those involving extensions, which make full payment well-nigh impossible. Furthermore, the discussion will center on the various methods of *adjusting* the debt in a friendly manner, i.e., out of court. The legal treatment of insolvent debtors through arrangements or by the bankruptcy road has been reserved for the chapter immediately following.

Types of insolvency. The term insolvency is used with at least three different meanings. First, there is what may be called commercial insolvency.   In that sense, a debtor is deemed to be insolvent if he "either has ceased to pay his debts in the ordinary course of business or cannot pay his debts as they become due," even though his assets may exceed his liabilities and he may ultimately be able to pay all of his obligations. A second type of insolvency exists when a debtor becomes financially embarrassed, notwithstanding the fact that his assets at a fair valuation exceed his liabilities.   Such a state of financial embarrassment may exist when the debtor lacks working capital and when his assets cannot be easily converted into cash, without substantial loss in their value.   If this is a temporary condition, the debtor may ultimately be able to pay the full amount of his indebtedness; if it is of a serious character, only a portion of the obligations may ultimately be paid.   A debtor who is insolvent in this sense may continue in business in this condition for some time, and yet remain immune from bankruptcy proceedings.   The third form of insolvency is the permanent insolvency contemplated under the bankruptcy law, whereby the liabilities of the debtor exceed the assets at a fair valuation.   In addition, for some specific purposes as for credit insurance policies, the term insolvency may be used in a very broad and special sense to cover anything from the nonpayment of a single bill in a stated period of time to assignments, receiverships, and bankruptcy.

General causes of insolvency. Among the causes of business insolvency most frequently cited are incompetence; lack of experience in certain lines of merchandise, in management, or in some of the business functions; lack of working capital; personal neglect of the business because of poor health, marital difficulties, or bad habits; fraud on the part of the principals as reflected by premeditated overbuying or the irregular disposal of assets; and disaster such as fire, flood, burglary, strikes, or fraud on the part of employees.

In general, all failures may be classified, according to the causes which produced them, into two major divisions, the first comprising failures the causes of which lie within the business itself, and the second containing insolvencies which are considered not to be due to the faults of those failing.   Insolvency of the latter type may be caused by specific conditions beyond the control of the failing concerns, such as wars, floods, and disasters, or by failures of others.   Insolvencies falling in the first classification either arise out of incompetence, such as overbuying or careless selection of a stock of goods, unwise credit granting, carelessness in following up collections of outstanding accounts, inaccurate accounting system, poor business location, or any one of numerous other causes generally lumped under "bad management"; or they may result from a lack of adequate working capital, which is ordinarily caused by more fundamental or real factors, such as failure to keep a sufficient amount in liquid form, an injudicious disbursement of capital in interest and dividend payments, or unwarranted withdrawals by principals to cover their living beyond means.

Almost as involved are the causes of individual or consumer insolvency. Some of them, to be sure, are causes for which the individual must assume personal responsibility, such as living beyond his means, injudicious use of credit, and imprudent financial management. Some may be beyond the individual's control, such as loss of employment caused by external factors, rising costs of living, or acts of God in the form of natural disasters like floods and windstorms. Others may be incident to the involuntary assumption of considerable indebtedness, resulting from major medical expenses, marital difficulties, or personal liability suits.

Treatment of insolvent debtors. Once a debtor becomes insolvent, there are several possibilities whereby either he may be extricated from his financial embarrassment and a readjustment worked out, or his property may be seized, liquidated, and distributed among his creditors. Thus the insolvent debtor may make but part payment and arrange to pay the balance in instalments; he may ask for an extension; he may request a composition settlement; he may make an assignment of all his property for the benefit of his creditors; or a receiver may be applied for by the debtor or his creditors. Finally, if insolvency occurs in the sense that his assets at a fair valuation fall short of satisfying his liabilities, there is a possibility of his going into bankruptcy voluntarily, or of waiting until forced into bankruptcy by his creditors. Whatever the treatment, it should be humane and constructive, aimed at the debtor's financial rehabilitation without unduly sacrificing the long-run interests of the creditors. Furthermore, some of the adjustments, such as those of extensions and compositions discussed in this chapter, can also be effected under the nonbankruptcy provisions of the Bankruptcy Act, discussed in the chapter immediately following, under the several arrangement and reorganization proceedings therein covered.

EXTENSIONS

For some cases of insolvency an extension of time for the payment of the already past-due indebtedness may suffice. In essence, an extension is an agreement of a creditor or among creditors of the insolvent debtor, granting him the extended period of credit deemed necessary for an adequate rehabilitation of the impaired financial condition.

When to grant an extension. If a debtor's financial responsibility is not seriously impaired and causes of the insolvency are but temporary and remediable, an extension may be all that is needed. While an extension may be agreed to by a single creditor in a given situation, the discussion here is concerned mainly with such action by creditors collectively.

Prior to granting an extension to a business debtor, creditors should satisfy themselves that the conditions warranting it are prevalent. In the first place, it should be evident that the debtor is fundamentally honest. A dishonest debtor is not entitled to any consideration on the part of creditors. If he lacks the all-important qualities of honesty and integrity, an extension of time will simply afford him an excellent opportunity to perpetrate a fraud upon the creditors.

Another consideration for creditors to ponder before granting an extension is the seriousness of the debtor's embarrassment and the causes therefor. If the weakness is but temporary, and if there is reason to believe him sufficiently capable of continuing in business and extricating himself from his difficulties, there is no reason why creditors should not lend their assistance and cooperation in order to effect a quick recovery. Where the causes are temporary and curable, the prospects for improvement are bright. Thus it frequently happens that a merchant has too much capital tied up in salable merchandise inventories, or in accounts receivable which are good and collectible but slow-paying. In either of the cases cited a lapse of time will usually remedy the situation.

Furthermore, if the debtor is likely to require large quantities of additional merchandise in order to continue in business and meet the demands of his trade, it behooves the present creditors, if an extension is granted, not only to pledge their moral support but also to supply the debtor with fresh merchandise to replenish his stock. When a debtor exposes his financial condition by requesting an extension, his credit standing in all markets is at once weakened, thereby automatically shutting off his credit in new markets. To the extent to which he finds it impossible to secure new credits, to that extent he must rely upon his old creditors, whose failure to supply the necessary stocks precludes any possibility of paying the original indebtedness involved in the extension. If, however, the additional amount of credit required is large in proportion to the existing claim, it would be bad policy to agree to an extension; it amounts to sending too many good dollars after those already impaired.

Similar considerations underlie extensions granted by a creditor or creditors acting jointly on behalf of consumer debtors. Honesty of the debtor, temporary nature of his financial embarrassment, and additional requirements for credit during the extension period are all important factors, but the last one is probably less significant than in the case of business debtors requesting an extension.

Method of granting extensions. The usual method of arranging an extension where a number of creditors are involved is to execute and enter into a trust agreement between the debtor and an adjuster representing the creditors. The adjuster acts as agent for all of the creditors who are willing to assign their claims to him, thus indicating their willingness to cooperate in the extension agreement. The debtor is then enabled to deal with one individual instead of with a large number of creditors, some of whom may be located at considerable distances from him. Such an assignment of claims operates to the advantage of creditors, as well as to the debtor. It obviates the possibility of creditors having to contend with parties among themselves who might otherwise retard settlement by insisting upon more prompt settlement or by threatening to take more drastic action. Moreover, the pressure which such joint action brings to bear upon the debtor is also an advantage to creditors who are represented by an adjuster. The debtor is thereby made to feel that all creditors are cemented by a common interest, acting in unison as an individual through the medium of the adjuster, and should he compel them to legal action by his refusal to submit to terms, such action is greatly simplified and expedited.

The trust agreement usually provides for a continuation of the business by the debtor himself under the supervision of the adjuster, who is often a representative or the manager of an adjustment bureau, or it places the business under the direct control of the latter until the original indebtedness is fully paid.

It is not uncommon, however, for the debtor to seek to arrange informally with one or two creditors, usually the largest, for an extension of time. In such a case, he may give a single promissory note or a series of instalment notes payable at stated intervals. The terms of his account are thus made definite and the maturity of the debt is postponed.

Legal aspects of extensions. To the debtor, the significance of an extension lies in the restraint it places upon creditors, preventing them from exercising more drastic means of collection during the extension period. An agreement by one creditor to give a debtor an extension of time, however, without consideration therefor, is not binding on the creditor. Every contract or agreement must be supported by sufficient consideration to be binding.

This matter of consideration poses two questions. First, what is consideration? Second, when is it to be regarded as sufficient or adequate? In essence, consideration is the surrender of a legal right, as in doing or promising to do something, in return for something he is to receive from another under a contract. This at once implies that

a promise based upon a past consideration or upon a moral obligation would be unenforceable, for it does not involve mutuality of consideration as of the time of the agreement. Generally, to be sufficient or adequate the consideration given must be equivalent to what is received for it, especially where money is involved. This means that an agreement by a creditor to accept a lesser sum than is actually due, except in those states that permit it when such an agreement is in writing, is invalid unless some additional consideration like paying in advance of due date or changing the place of payment, etc., is included in the contract.

Obviously, if the debtor gives the creditor a note or other security, including guarantees, in consideration for an extension of time granted, the agreement is binding and the creditor would have to wait until the expiration of the extended period before he would have the legal right to bring action against the debtor. The principle underlying this is that the giving and the acceptance of the note or other security in place of the old account constitute a substitution of a new contract for an old one and are, therefore, equally binding on both parties.

On the other hand, where two or more creditors agree among themselves and with the debtor, that in consideration of each creditor's forbearance each of the other creditors will agree to an extension, there is deemed to be adequate consideration to support the promise of each creditor. Once such an agreement is entered into, no one creditor, at least without the consent of all others, would have the right to demand payment before the expiration of the extended time. The agreement is binding only on the creditors who sign it, and no creditor can be compelled to sign it. For this reason, small creditors who do not assent to the trust agreement are sometimes paid in full to prevent them from filing bankruptcy proceedings on some sufficient cause.

COMPOSITIONS

A composition is a contract entered into by an insolvent debtor and two or more of his creditors (not necessarily all) whereby, in consideration of the mutual promises of the creditors to release the debtor from the balance of his indebtedness and thus to forego their legal rights for the enforcement of their claims, the debtor settles the claims against him at an agreed percentage of their face value. This type of agreement is binding only upon those who accept it by signing. Such a *common law composition* constitutes in effect a discharge or release from further obligation to all agreeing creditors, not by the operation of law, but through the mutual consent and valuable consideration.

A composition, or compromise, settlement is usually the result of the debtor's initiative. He submits the terms of compromise, offering to pay a certain percentage of the claims held against him.   The proposal may be submitted to the creditors individually or at a creditors' meeting called for the purpose.   The latter is preferable, particularly when the creditors are numerous and widely scattered.

When to agree to a composition. A composition settlement is worthy of consideration only when the debtor's financial embarrassment is serious and when it seems probable that, relieved of the excessive burden of his debt, he could continue to operate the business profitably.   It is never intended as a bribe or inducement to a financially sound but "chiseling" customer in order to effect payment of a past-due account.   Much of the discussion of this subject in current literature seems to be based upon this misunderstanding.   Even when the debtor is really insolvent, such settlement should never be considered when any suspicion of fraud attaches to the insolvency.   On the contrary, creditors should relentlessly prosecute fraudulent debtors to the fullest extent, for creditors owe it not only to themselves but to their fellow businessmen, competitors and customers alike, to prevent the perpetration of fraud on the part of debtors.   It is, indeed, also a protection in future transactions for a creditor to distinguish nicely between conditions warranting composition settlement and those demanding more stringent treatment, for unscrupulous debtors stay shy of those who are willing to sacrifice large dividends in order to prosecute frauds.

The advantages of a composition settlement to creditors arise from the fact that the continuation of an honest and capable, though currently insolvent, customer is generally preferable to the dissolution of such a debtor's business.   Assets of a defunct organization are seldom worth to others what they are worth to the owner if he can employ them properly.   An insolvent debtor's balance sheet may show, for example, a deficit of 20 per cent, i.e., the liabilities exceeding the assets 20 cents on the dollar.   If the valuation is conservative, the business is worth 80 per cent of the liabilities so long as it remains a going concern.   A forced liquidation, however, would result in the realization of much less than the book value of the properties, seldom more than one-half that amount.   Furthermore, if the business went through bankruptcy proceedings, much of the proceeds from a forced sale would be dissipated by expenses incident to such proceedings, until a payment of 10 per cent to unsecured creditors would begin to look generous.   Obviously, therefore, it is much more businesslike for creditors to accept a settlement of 45 or 50 per cent and leave the debtor the remaining 30 or 35 per cent with which to continue and rehabilitate his business.   Creditors, however, may thus be benefited not only in the realization of a greater amount on past debt than by another method, but also in the prospects of future business. Even the losses actually sustained may be ultimately recouped in profits arising from continued business relations with the debtor. Such possibility is completely precluded when the debtor is forced into bankruptcy. Furthermore, by making a composition settlement, the creditor dispenses with the time, trouble, and worry attending all bankruptcy cases.

Humanitarian as well as selfish motives should prompt creditors in considering a composition settlement. Honest debtors are entitled to such consideration. In modern times, as a result of the spirit and widespread recognition of commercial interdependence, the idea prevails that the credit grantor is in a measure a partner in the debtor's business. Because of the risk in any business enterprise, losses must be expected, and the creditor should stand ready to bear his proportionate share. For these reasons, offers made by honest merchants should be accepted and even encouraged, so that they may retain their business and save themselves and their dependents from disaster and the stigma of bankruptcy.

Forcing composition settlements. It is evident that under some circumstances the effort to reach agreement for the acceptance of a composition settlement may be impeded by recalcitrant creditors. It may then seem advisable to *force* a proposed composition settlement upon such creditors. This may be accomplished by filing a petition under Chapter XI of the Bankruptcy Act, for an arrangement covering the debtor's unsecured debts. Such a petition may be filed in a pending bankruptcy proceeding either before or after adjudication, or it may be filed in the absence of any bankruptcy proceeding. In the former instance, bankruptcy proceedings are stayed pending the outcome of whatever arrangement is presented by the debtor at a meeting of creditors called under court auspices.

At the meeting of the creditors, the debtor is examined as to the state of his affairs, after which he submits the terms. Assuming that the terms call for a compromise settlement, it is necessary that a majority of the creditors *in number and in amount of claims* agree to it before further action is taken with respect to it. An application is then made to the court for the confirmation of the adjustment. If the composition is confirmed by the court, it becomes binding upon all unsecured creditors, and the debtor obtains the desired relief, if timely, without being adjudged a bankrupt.

FRIENDLY LIQUIDATION THROUGH ASSIGNMENTS

When the debtor's affairs are so badly involved that the granting of an extension is not warranted and no terms of composition can be agreed upon, there is still another course to follow, namely, to wind up the estate and distribute the proceeds among the creditors pro rata. This may be accomplished in either of two ways: through an assignment executed by the debtor of through bankruptcy proceedings. The former is regarded as a friendly liquidation, not because the debtor voluntarily and without pressure relinquishes control of his property, but because the liquidation takes place out of court and is not subject to strict legal supervision. Such liquidation is accomplished, rather, through the work of a creditors' committee or by an adjuster representing creditors.

Nature and kinds of assignments. An assignment for the benefit of creditors is a voluntary action taken by a debtor, who generally is insolvent, whereby he transfers in trust some or all of his property to an assignee, for the purpose of applying such assets or the proceeds thereof to the payment of his debts.

Such an assignment may be made either at common law or under state law, for many states have some form of law whereby property may be turned over by a debtor to an assignee for the purpose of sale and division among the assignor's creditors pro rata. Common law assignments are used throughout the country as the legal basis for friendly adjustments. They differ from statutory assignments principally in the following respects: (1) they are usually not filed, and (2) the administration of the estate is under the supervision of a committee of creditors or other representatives rather than under control of a court. Both types of assignments, however, have certain things in common. In both instances the conveyance is presumed to be voluntary; both are recognized and regulated by law in most jurisdictions; and both types, because they constitute an act of bankruptcy, may be set aside and invalidated by the filing of a petition in bankruptcy within 4 months after the execution of the assignment.

Advantages and disadvantages of assignments. The principal advantages of a friendly liquidation through an assignment over liquidation of an insolvent estate in court are: speed with which the task can be completed, securing of a larger fund for distribution among creditors through superior opportunity for marketing the assets, elimination or reduction of court costs and fees of a multitude of officials provided for in the Bankruptcy Act, elimination or reduction of attorneys' fees, freedom from restraint by the court, and the privacy with which the work can be done. Obviously, if the assignment is statutory, these advantages are not realized in full.

There are, however, a number of limitations to liquidation through assignment. In the first place, such an assignment constitutes an act of bankruptcy. Consequently, nonassenting creditors, by initiating bankruptcy proceedings, may take the administration of the estate out of the jurisdiction of creditors or the state insolvency court, since bankruptcy supersedes all other forms of liquidation of insolvents. Second, there is no power under friendly assignments to subject the debtor to an examination under oath. Third, there is no machinery for the recovery of preferential payments. Fourth, from the debtor's point of view, the chief objection is that he cannot secure a discharge from his obligations except by the consent of all creditors. Fifth, there is the territorial limitation, since assignments are governed by different laws under varying jurisdictions. Especially is this true of statutory assignments. Sixth, there is lack of uniformity in the laws and requirements of the various states. Finally, there is no direct effective supervision over the assignee in the administration of the estate. Debtors have the power to appoint their own assignees and in some states they are not compelled even to consult the creditors or to obtain their consent to the appointment. This objection, however, is largely theoretical, since the assignment, while presumably voluntary, is made under the pressure of creditors who are in a position to dictate terms.

Assignment procedure. In handling common law assignments the procedure is much simpler and less formal than in the case of statutory assignments, but it is believed that a brief description of the latter procedure, which is definitely codified, may be helpful to an understanding of the subject. The first requirement is to make the assignment in writing, to serve as protection against fraud and collusion and to give effect to the instrument itself, which lists and describes on one schedule the property transferred and the disposition to be made of it as per another schedule on which are listed all of the debtor's creditors for whose benefit the assets are appropriated.

The second step in the proceeding is to execute the assignment by the assignor and in some states also by the assignee. Next, the instrument must be recorded in a specific public office in order to make it valid. Fourth, the assignment must be delivered to the assignee. Failure to do so may render the act void and fraudulent against judgment creditors. Fifth, possession of property must be delivered next and should follow immediately the deed making the transfer. To give the assignment validity, the assent of creditors must be secured, unless it is made to a trustee for the benefit of creditors who are not parties to the agreement. In most jurisdictions the consent of creditors is not essential to the validity of an assignment.

The specific steps taken in the assignment procedure are not unlike those involved in a bankruptcy or other dissolution of a debtor's estate for the benefit of creditors.   Briefly stated, they consist of the following:

1 Notice of the assignment given by assignee to creditors, who are requested to file their claims.

2 Liquidation of the estate through the conversion of all assets into cash by sale as expeditiously as possible.

3 Deductions of all expenses incurred, including specified or reasonable compensation of the assignee, as the case may be.

4 Distribution of dividends to creditors, according to priority, from remaining proceeds without unreasonable delay.

5 Final accounting by the assignee of all transactions, receipts, and disbursements to creditors.

6 Close of trust and discharge of the assignor upon his petition and common consent of usually two-thirds of all creditors residing in the United States.

EQUITY
RECEIVERSHIPS

From the standpoint of the purpose for which a receiver may be appointed, all receiverships may be divided into those of equity and bankruptcy.   The former are used mostly in connection with friendly adjustments and the latter are used in bankruptcy proceedings as discussed in the next chapter.

A receiver in equity may be appointed by a Federal court in an action brought by one or more creditors as plaintiffs against the debtor as defendant, provided that at least one of the petitioning creditors is a resident of another state from that of the debtor and the amount of the petitioners' claims is in excess of $10,000.   A state court may appoint an equity receiver either for a solvent or insolvent debtor in proceedings of various kinds, including dissolution, and for temporary purposes pending the outcome of litigation.   Such a receivership may be requested either by the debtor or by creditors, but when a state court appoints him, the receiver can take possession of only the property in the jurisdiction of the court.

Purpose of equity receiverships. An equity receivership is usually sought when the debtor is *solvent in the bankruptcy sense* but is unable to meet his obligations as they mature.   The object of a receivership is to preserve the estate during the readjustment, reorganization, or litigation which is to decide the rights of the litigants, and to establish a so-called "moratorium" on behalf of the debtor.   To warrant the appointment of such a receiver, the court must be shown by the plaintiff that such action is necessary to prevent loss or injury to those financially interested.   A mere default in payment of an obligation is not sufficient ground, for under such circumstances the ordinary processes of the law can be resorted to as a remedy.

Powers and compensation. An equity receiver is an officer of the appointing court. It is his duty to take possession of the property of the debtor and to operate the business, often with the cooperation of creditors, for the benefit of all persons interested, until it is liquidated or the receivership is terminated and the property returned to the debtor. Sometimes the business is thoroughly reorganized under the receivership, which is terminated upon completion of the reorganization process, and which is really one form of liquidation. Pending receivership, all persons are enjoined from interfering with the assets in the hands of the receiver, who is not even amenable to suit except by express permission of the court.

On all matters of policy and on questions outside of ordinary management and operation, the receiver must apply to the court for authority and instructions. He is held responsible for all debts incurred with third parties and for any fraud or negligence resulting in injury to the property under his management. For this reason, the receiver is usually required to execute a bond, the amount of which is fixed by the court.

In the matter of compensation of equity receivers, some states regulate the amount to be paid, but in most of them it is left to the discretion of the court and is determined by the circumstances of the particular case. The amount allowed is usually in excess of the corresponding fees allowed in bankruptcy proceedings, partly because of lack of regulations and partly on account of the difference in scope of activity.

Termination. An equity receivership is terminated by the appointing court when the necessity for the office ceases to exist and a formal order is issued to that effect, either upon the receiver's own application or upon petition of other interested parties. The court itself, of course, has authority to terminate that which it has created. Before the receiver is discharged from his trust, he must render a final accounting, at which time creditors and others interested may appear and raise objections. In no case can a debtor, however, receive a discharge from his unpaid debts under an equity receivership.

DEALING WITH INSOLVENT DEBTORS THROUGH ADJUSTMENT BUREAUS—MERCANTILE AND RETAIL

To secure more effective cooperation of creditors in dealing with embarrassed merchants, members of many of the various lines of trade have organized themselves within their respective industries and have established local representatives or secretaries in the larger market centers for this purpose. The National Association of Credit Management, in particular, has been instrumental in the development and widespread use of such mediums by establishing local Adjustment Bureaus within their organization.

All activities of the Adjustment Bureaus of the National Association of Credit Management may be divided into four parts. The first function consists in personal investigations made by representatives of the bureau upon request of a member of the association. These representatives investigate the debtor's condition and adjust the account. A second function is that of effecting friendly adjustments, including service in a fiduciary capacity in any action of any character except bankruptcies. These adjustments are made in behalf of two or more creditors and for the common good of all. Bureaus are also equipped to serve in a fiduciary capacity during bankruptcy proceedings. Bureau representatives attend hearings and otherwise investigate bankruptcy cases, irrespective of whether or not a representative of the bureau is elected receiver or trustee. Finally, most of the bureaus are equipped to handle collections in their respective zones or to forward them for collection to other bureaus and attorneys.

The main purpose of all bureaus, and the sole activity in some of them, is to handle in behalf of all creditors the affairs of insolvent and embarrassed debtors, whether in friendly adjustment or in bankruptcy.

Mercantile adjustment bureaus are not alone in this type of activity. Many retail credit bureaus, as part of their collection service or incidental thereto, provide arrangements for refinancing the debt owed to a number of its members, for pooling the indebtedness with the consent of its creditor members and distributing payments received on a pro rata basis, or even for a scaling down of the debt by means of a friendly composition settlement. In this way, many bankruptcies have no doubt been avoided and a number of consumers have been rehabilitated financially, with their credit standing remaining relatively unimpaired, especially through counseling service inaugurated in recent years by the bureaus and other agencies concerned with consumer credit.

QUESTIONS AND PROBLEMS

1 You have been asked to address a group of credit managers representing wholesalers and manufacturers on the subject of "Friendly Adjustments." Some of the members of the group to be addressed believe in the use of harsh methods in making settlement of overdue accounts, while others do not quite appreciate the value of friendly settlements. It is your task to enlighten them all on the subject assigned. What special reasons would you advance in your address in favor of friendly adjustments, wherever possible, in preference to forcible methods?

2 What is an extension? Under what circumstances would you, as a creditor, agree to it? Is it really an adjustment?

3 Why is it essential that a debtor be honest in all cases of friendly adjustments?

4 Mr. Blank, who is operating a drug store, owes the X Wholesale Drug Company $1,200 on open account. The account is now 40 days past due, but Mr. Blank is still unable to meet his obligation. He requests that the X Company grant him an extension of 90 days, believing that at the end of that time the larger seasonal sales will enable him to pay his bills. The X Company, believing its customer to be honest and deserving, agreed to the extension. Ten days later it obtained information through a mercantile agency showing an impaired condition in Mr. Blank's character, and other facts contained in the report pointed to the advisability of enforcing payment at once. Can the X Wholesale Drug Company enforce payment immediately, despite its previous agreement to extend the time 90 days, or must the creditor wait until the expiration of the 90 days covered by the extension?

5 Would your answer be different if the agreement to grant Mr. Blank an extension were reached jointly with two additional creditors at a meeting held for the purpose?

6 Suppose the X company had accepted a 90-day promissory note before it agreed to extend the time of payment for Mr. Blank; could the X Company set the extension aside and enforce payment before the expiration of the 90-day period?

7 If a debtor is seriously embarrassed but is honest and deserving of fair treatment by the creditors, which of the methods of amicable adjustment would you recommend?

8 What is a composition settlement? How does a common law composition differ from a composition in bankruptcy?

9 Under what circumstances should creditors agree to a common law composition settlement?

10 Suppose 15 out of 20 creditors agree to a common law composition; what is the status of the remaining five creditors? Must they accept the terms agreed to by the majority of creditors or can they proceed to enforce full payment of their claims?

11 Why should a debtor ever agree to a friendly liquidation?

12 What is an assignment? When can it be set aside?

13 What advantages can be claimed for assignments, from the standpoint of both debtor and creditor, over bankruptcy proceedings?

14 Suppose an assignment has been made in favor of creditors, but a few recalcitrant creditors fail to approve of it; what action can they take in the case?

15 An assignment has been made to a trustee for the benefit of creditors. In the meantime one of the creditors obtained a judgment. Can such judgment be executed or is the assignment valid even though this creditor did not agree to it?

16 What are the two types of receivership and how do they differ?

17 If you were appointed an equity receiver for a business establishment, what would be your duties? As receiver in bankruptcy?

18 When do equity receiverships terminate and how? Does the same answer apply to receiverships in bankruptcy discussed in the next chapter?

19 How do creditors benefit from the use of Adjustment Bureaus in the handling of overdue accounts and various types of adjustments?

20 John Doe operated a very popular and well-patronized cafeteria in the center of the retail district of Wichita, Kans. Domestic trouble, followed by a separation of debtor from his wife, together with some other unwise activities on his part, caused the debtor to lose heavily in his business. When a creditors' meeting was finally called, it was ascertained that the debtor owed approximately $20,000, and that the only assets of the debtor and his wife consisted of the cafeteria fixtures, which debtor later sold for $1,000, the half interest in a restaurant which the debtor's wife later sold for $3,000, and the lease on the cafeteria (in the wife's name) which had 5 years to run, together with various items of personal assets which were exempt.

At the creditors' meeting, the manager of the local association of credit managers proposed to let the debtor keep his cafeteria fixtures, and that the wife be given the undivided half interest in the restaurant hereinbefore referred to. This was to be done on condition that the debtor would execute a note for his indebtedness, payable 3 years after date, to the said manager of the association, with interest at the rate of 8 per cent from date until paid, and providing further that the said note be secured by an assignment of the lease on the premises where the cafeteria was located. This was agreed to by all parties concerned, the upstairs of the lease was subleased for $292.50 per month, and the downstairs was subleased for $650 per month, which made a gross profit of $507.50 per month on said lease, for a period of 5 years.

Was this case properly handled? What were the alternatives?

21 The X Company is a hardware and mill supply wholesaler, selling to hardware stores, furniture stores, and to manufacturers. It has about 1,500 active accounts and some others that buy only seasonally. One of its customers, Y, is a proprietor of a hardware store located in a small town 10 miles from the wholesaler's city. He became slow in his payments. In an effort to continue operations, Y placed his son in charge of the store and secured a position for himself elsewhere.

When the account became 3 months past due, the credit company demanded and received a cognovit note to cover the total indebtedness. The note was to be paid in instalments. After making two small payments on it the debtor stopped making further remittances. A suggestion that he go into receivership did not meet with the debtor's approval. Instead he attempted to borrow the money, and failing to do that he wanted to sell out to a prospective buyer, who suddenly became aware of the Bulk Sales Law and, as a result, stopped negotiations.

The X Company then came to the conclusion that Mr. Y's store should be liquidated for the benefit of the creditors through an assignment but leaving his real estate as an exemption. To this the debtor agreed, and all 38 creditors, some of whom were very small, finally got out of the liquidation about 41 cents of the dollar of claims. As in this case bankruptcy was probably the only alternative, was it wise for the creditors to go with the proposal made by the X Company and to which the debtor agreed? Assuming that the value of the real estate equity of the debtor exceeded the exemption provided by state law, was it wise for the creditors to let the debtor retain all the real estate? Why?

22 Which of the several types of friendly adjustments are appropriate and practically essential under conditions of a debtor's permanent financial embarrassment as distinguished from a temporary impairment?

CHAPTER TWENTY-EIGHT

bankruptcy

Bankruptcy occupies a position of extreme resort for creditors in their collection procedures and for honest debtors in securing relief from over-burdening indebtedness. For creditors it may be the final expedient for retrieving some values on their claims when sole reliance must be placed on the capital position of the debtor. For honest debtors it is a way of securing permanent relief from a financial embarrassment, which may have resulted from injudicious actions on the part of debtor or creditors or from external and emergency conditions beyond their control.

Bankruptcy is a legal rather than a commercial remedy for insolvency, and it is one for which either the debtor or creditors may petition. Being essentially legal in nature, the process thereof is largely the province of attorneys. The discussion in this chapter, however, is not intended so much for attorneys as it is for those interested primarily in the commercial and business aspects, as well as social phases, of the subject.

NATURE AND
DEVELOPMENT
OF BANKRUPTCY

Although the term bankruptcy is often used promiscuously to signify various conditions of insolvency, it has through many years acquired a technical and legal meaning of considerable exactitude.

Conception of the term. The etymology of the word "bankruptcy" is somewhat in dispute. Among the various explanations offered is the following, which seems both plausible and authoritative. During the existence of the temple in Jerusalem, Hebraic custom required the deposit in the temple on certain occasions of sums of money. This money had to be in Hebraic currency, but, since Roman coins were generally used at the time, money-changers established places of business consisting of tables or benches (banks) on which they displayed their supply of Hebraic coins which were to be exchanged for Roman money. Money *lending* was another function which was later added to the practice of money *changing*. Some of these ventures proved unsuccessful and creditors, therefore, drove the failing moneylender from his table or bench. Thus he found himself "bench-broken" (*bancus ruptus* in Latin) or "banch-rupted," bankrupted.[1]

Bankruptcy today, not unlike in the days described in the preceding paragraph, consists of a condition coupled with an outward act. The condition is admission in writing of inability to pay debts and willingness to be adjudged a bankrupt in case of voluntary bankruptcies or insolvency of the debtor in the case of involuntary bankruptcies. The outward action indicating the existence of such a condition is a decree of bankruptcy handed down by a Federal court instead of a physical act of destroying the bench. Thus bankruptcy may be defined as *a legal process whereby an insolvent debtor,* presumed or actual depending upon whether it is voluntary or involuntary, *is declared a bankrupt, his assets* (if available) *are seized and liquidated, and the proceeds are equitably distributed among his creditors, after which he is discharged from certain further liabilities.*

Early bankruptcy legislation. As far as recorded history is concerned, the earliest concepts with regard to bankruptcy are to be found in Mosaic law (about 1500 B.C.), first in connection with the release from indebtedness at the end of every 7 years, including the release of certain servants (Deuteronomy 15) and, second, in connection with each fiftieth, or jubilee, year in which liberty was to be "proclaimed throughout *all* the land," and the inhabitants were ordered to "return every man unto his possession" and "every man unto his family" (Leviti-

---

[1] R. P. Ettinger and D. E. Golieb, *Credits and Collections*, Prentice-Hall, Inc., Englewood Cliffs, N.J., 1917, pp. 331–332. See also pp. 328–330.

cus 25). It was emphasized at that point that "The land shall not be sold for ever" but shall, if not redeemed sooner, be returned to the original owner during the year of jubilee, which is probably the forerunner of the modern types of 50-year and 99-year leases.

In the light of this liberal attitude toward debtors, it is most difficult to understand the harsh treatment of debtors under later laws. For example, under the ancient laws of the Twelve Tables, enacted in Rome in 459 B.C., creditors could have a delinquent debtor put to death or could certainly sell him and his family into slavery. A law enacted in Rome in 239 B.C. finally prohibited corporal punishment for indebtedness but still permitted imprisonment. As part of the Lex Julia, enacted by Julius Caesar, the first bankruptcy statute of the more modern type was put into effect.[2]

Until comparatively recent times, the English laws permitted the imprisonment of those who could not or would not pay their debts. The earliest English bankruptcy law dates back only to 1542 and was designed primarily for the protection of *creditors* against fraudulent debtors.

During the early days of the American republic no crime brought so many to the jails and prisons as the crime of debt. Persons likely to get into debt were for the most part defenseless and dependent, and consisted of the great body of artisans, laborers, and servants. As one historian is said to have put it, obviously referring to the early part of the nineteenth century, "one hundred years ago the laborer who fell from a scaffold or lay sick of a fever was sure to be seized by the sheriff the moment he recovered and be carried to jail for the bill of a few dollars, which had been running up, during his illness, at the huckster's or the tavern."

The early state insolvency laws were of a drastic nature, designed primarily for the protection of creditors. Because of the dependency of most debtors on their daily wages for their subsistence, a creditor's right of action against a debtor's property bore little significance. Hence, the surrender of the person of the debtor for his imprisonment was considered necessary to protect the interests of creditors. Many of the early laws were extremely drastic in the punishment provided for debtors. No debtor had the right to petition himself into bankruptcy and be discharged from his obligations. The laws provided merely that creditors could under certain circumstances throw the debtor into bankruptcy, seize his property, and divide it among themselves. The balance had to be paid thereafter in the best way possible, else the debtor went to jail or prison.

Nineteenth-century Federal legislation. Beginning with the nineteenth century, the views respecting the relationship between debtors

---

[2] M. Marks, *How to Correct Credit Abuses,* Harper & Brothers, New York, 1930, pp. 61–64; see also pp. 69–73 for historical bankruptcy procedure in France and Germany.

and creditors underwent a decided change. The spirit of commercial interdependence had given rise to the idea that the creditor is in a sense a partner of the debtor. In accordance with this development and with the improvement in business ethics, a more humanitarian feeling toward insolvent debtors was implanted in the hearts of the public at large, and new laws were consequently passed, abolishing imprisonment for debt or any other corporal punishment for such offenses. These laws held the debtor responsible merely to the extent of the amount of the property he possessed at time of failure.

Today, the commercial world has progressed even much farther than the law. Creditors have established organizations, called "adjustment bureaus" and described elsewhere, for the assistance of failing but honest debtors, as well as creditors. These quasi-public organizations not only secure the best results expeditiously but also aid the debtor, in that they obviate the necessity of placing upon him the stigma of bankruptcy.

Article 1, Section 8, of the United States Constitution, provides that "Congress shall have power to establish . . . uniform laws on the subject of bankruptcy throughout the United States." This has been interpreted to mean that a Federal Bankruptcy Act supersedes any act of the states, although the right to make a general assignment for the benefit of creditors is not precluded by the passage of the Federal Bankruptcy Act.

Under the power granted by the aforementioned clause of the United States Constitution, Congress passed the first bankruptcy law in 1800, which was repealed in 1803. The next bankruptcy act was passed in 1841, but this, too, was repealed two years later. In 1867 another law was passed, which was amended in 1874 and repealed in 1878. It was not until 1898 that the national Bankruptcy Act was passed, which has, though with a number of amendments, remained in force to date.

The current bankruptcy law. As already indicated, the organic bankruptcy law under which we essentially operate at present was passed by the Congress in 1898. This law was amended a number of times, but it was not until 1938 that it was so thoroughly revised in many respects that it is often referred to as the Bankruptcy Act of 1938, or as the Chandler Act. Even this revised version has been amended in some respects a number of times since. The two most recent amendments were enacted in 1966 after "almost ten years of extensive work by the National Bankruptcy Conference and consistent pressure upon Congress by the National Association of Credit Management."[3]

In so far as what is now generally regarded as "straight bank-

---

[3] *Credit Manual of Commercial Laws, 1967*, National Association of Credit Management, New York, p. xxvi.

ruptcy" is concerned, whereby the estate (if any is available beyond the exemptions) of the bankrupt debtor is seized and liquidated and thus ceases to exist, the law now in effect has retained the essentials of the 1898 Act in modified form. Even today, however, a debtor can still be imprisoned in this country for nonpayment of alimony, because such a debt is not affected by a discharge in bankruptcy and presumably because such debtor is in contempt of court.

Since the 1930's some more modern concepts in the treatment of financially embarrassed debtors, in a manner short of bankruptcy, have been added through the inclusion of relief provisions in certain chapters of the Bankruptcy Act. These new items deal generally with the matter of arrangements or reorganization and will be discussed briefly after the treatment of bankruptcy proper. While included in the Bankruptcy Act, it is felt that the subject matter covered by the special appendages to the bankruptcy law, as well as the statistics pertaining thereto, should be treated separately and not as an integral phase of what is *commonly* known as bankruptcy and now referred to as "straight bankruptcy" in the government statistics.

Purposes of bankruptcy legislation. Obviously, the necessity for bankruptcy legislation arises from the nature of present-day trade and is based on the principle that much of our commerce is built on credit and that credit implies risk. The most honorable merchant may be ruined without actually committing any crime. It is partly to relieve such an honest debtor from the load of his debt and to save him from going to an almshouse, as well as to distinguish between fraudulent bankruptcies and honest misfortunes, that bankruptcy legislation has been enacted. The second, and probably in many respects the more important purpose of bankruptcy legislation, is to provide a just treatment of creditors. It aims to prevent preferences, and to secure a fair and equitable division of the estate among all creditors, regardless of how far or near they are to the debtor's location or whether they are large or small, strict or lenient in their collection follow-up. More specifically, the purposes of present-day bankruptcy proceedings may be summarized as follows:

1   To establish judicially the bankruptcy of debtors
2   To provide facilities for locating and collecting the debtor's assets
3   To provide for the uniform administration of insolvent estates by taking such administration out of the hands of state courts
4   To provide remedies and punishments to insure the orderly administration of the properties in accordance with the intention of the law
5   To provide means whereby the debtor may, upon agreement of his creditors, retain his assets on payment of a certain agreed percentage of his indebtedness and otherwise to rehabilitate a distressed business enterprise

6 To effect a distribution of the bankrupt's assets equitably among the creditors

7 To discharge debtors, if not guilty of fraud, from further legal obligations to their creditors, and thereby relieve them from the unbearable pressure of creditors

Kinds of bankruptcy. Bankruptcy is divided into two main types: voluntary and involuntary. The fundamental distinction is that in the former instance the debtor himself requests the court to adjudge him a bankrupt, whereas in the latter case he is forced into bankruptcy by his creditors, presumably against his will.

In voluntary bankruptcy the debtor himself files a petition admitting his inability to meet his obligations and expressing his willingness to be adjudged a bankrupt on that ground. The purposes of voluntarily going into bankruptcy are, first, to secure relief from burdensome obligations so as to be able to begin anew and unencumbered, and, second, to have the assets equitably distributed among all creditors. During the 1960's the number of voluntary straight bankruptcy cases filed for every involuntary bankruptcy has risen from 73 to 140 during fiscal 1967.

REQUIREMENTS
FOR BANKRUPTCY

As already indicated, and for added emphasis, it should be pointed out that not every action taken under the Bankruptcy Act involves bankruptcy proceedings, in the sense that the debtor is declared a bankrupt, his estate (if any) is seized and liquidated, the proceeds are divided among the creditors pro rata, the business ceases to exist, and the debtor secures a discharge from specified obligations. As a matter of fact, there are a number of chapters included in the present law which have nothing to do with what may be termed *regular* bankruptcy as indicated above. This is certainly true of Chapter X, which deals with corporate reorganizations; of Chapters XI and XII, which deal with arrangements for unsecured debts and for real property indebtedness, respectively; and of Chapter XIII, which deals with wage earners' arrangements. These are discussed briefly late in this chapter as nonbankruptcy provisions of the law. While these are optional measures provided by the law, it does not mean that everyone can take advantage of bankruptcy proper.

Who may become bankrupts? Although the principal requirements for the initiation of bankruptcy proceedings are insolvency of the debtor or declared inability to pay debts and the commission by him of an act of bankruptcy, not everyone who may have so qualified is eligible to petition for, or to be forced into, bankruptcy. Five types or classes of debtors may not voluntarily petition themselves into bankruptcy:

namely, municipalities, railroads, insurance companies, banking corporations, and building and loan associations. Similarly, neither may these five types of debtors be *forced* into bankruptcy. This exemption from bankruptcy proceedings, which in the normal sense involve dissolution and liquidation of the enterprise, has no doubt been prompted by two reasons. One is that these institutions are strongly tinged with public interest and their continued operation may be essential, as in the case of the fire and police protection services of municipalities or the transportation services of the railroads. A second reason is that these institutions, other than the municipalities, are under the supervision of special governmental agencies—Federal and state. This is illustrated by the supervision of railroads by the Interstate Commerce Commission and, in the case of intrastate systems, by state commissions. Another illustration is afforded by the banks, which are supervised by such agencies as the Comptroller of the Currency, the Federal Reserve System, and the Federal Deposit Insurance Corporation in the case of national banks; and by state banking divisions, and frequently also by the last two Federal agencies, in the case of state banks.

Two other types of classes of debtors may not be forced into bankruptcy. They are wage earners (individuals who work "for wages, salary, or hire, at a rate of compensation not exceeding $1,500 per year") and farmers (individuals "personally engaged in farming or tillage of the soil" including dairy farming or the production of poultry and livestock). Organized political influence of each of these two groups has no doubt been responsible for this exemption. However, while wage earners and farmers may not be thrown into bankruptcy, they are entitled to the benefits of this law as voluntary bankrupts.

Conditions required for bankruptcy proceedings. In order to qualify for voluntary bankruptcy, a debtor must admit in writing his inability to pay his debts and his willingness to be adjudged a bankrupt. In involuntary proceedings, a debtor must be *insolvent* in the sense that his liabilities exceed his assets at a fair valuation. Furthermore, a petition must be filed by three or more creditors with provable claims amounting in the aggregate, in excess of collateral or securities held by them, to at least $500. If the creditors are less than 12 in number, 1 creditor with a net provable claim of $500 or over may file the petition. In determining the number of creditors for this purpose, all creditors are excluded who were employed by the bankrupt at time the petition was filed, relatives, stockholders and officers of the bankrupt corporation, and creditors whose claims are fully secured, who have received voidable preferences, or who have participated in the act of bankruptcy charged in the petition. Furthermore, the debtor must owe $1,000 or more at time of filing of petition and must also be insolvent in the sense that the entire mass of his resources at a fair valuation falls short of satisfying his existing indebtedness.   Finally, the debtor must have committed one or more of the six acts of bankruptcy within 4 months before filing of petition.

In cases of voluntary bankruptcy no restrictions are placed on the amount that must be owed by the person who petitions himself into bankruptcy.   The practice should be confined nevertheless to debtors who wish to secure a discharge from *substantial* obligations because of the expense of the proceedings and the stigma it places on the bankrupt, but such is often not the case.[4]

Acts of bankruptcy. The second requisite for involuntary bankruptcy proceedings is that the debtor should have, within 4 months of the filing of the petition, committed an act of bankruptcy.   In voluntary proceedings the very admission of insolvency and petitioning for bankruptcy constitutes an act of bankruptcy.   The six acts of bankruptcy set forth in Chapter II, Section 3, of the law consist of his having done one or more of the following:

1 Concealed, removed, or permitted to be concealed or removed any part of his property, with intent to hinder, delay, or defraud his creditors or any of them, or made or suffered a transfer of any of his property, fraudulent under the provision of section 67 or 70 of this Act [which deal with Liens and Fraudulent Transfers and Title to Property, respectively. Under this Act the burden of proving solvency rests upon the alleged bankrupt.].

2 Made or suffered a preferential transfer, as defined in subdivision a of section 60 of this Act [which deals with Preferred Creditors.   Such preferences obtain when a debtor, while insolvent, transfers any of his property to one or more of his creditors within 4 months before bankruptcy. As the matter of solvency or insolvency while such a transfer has been made is crucial, the burden of establishing the condition rests upon the debtor.].

3 Suffered or permitted, while insolvent, any creditor to obtain a lien upon any of his property through legal proceedings or distraint and not having vacated or discharged such lien within 30 days from the date thereof or at least 5 days before the date set for any sale or other disposition of such property.

4 Made a general assignment for the benefit of his creditors.

5 While insolvent or unable to pay his debts as they mature, procured, permitted, or suffered voluntarily or involuntarily the appointment of a receiver or trustee to take charge of his property.

[4] During the 6-year period 1956–1961, the average total indebtedness of 2,097 or 5.4 per cent of all the discharged personal bankrupts in Ohio was but $775. This means that for many of these it was considerably under $500. George Allen Brunner, *Personal Bankruptcies: Trends and Characteristics*, The Ohio State University, Bureau of Business Resarch, Monograph 124, Columbus, Ohio, 1965, Table 14, pp. 56–57.

6 Admitted in writing his inability to pay his debts and his willingness to be adjudged a bankrupt. [Under this Act it is immaterial whether the debtor is solvent or insolvent.]

Payment, while insolvent, of a preexisting or antecedent debt constitutes sufficient evidence of the commission of the second act of bankruptcy. But payment of a debt which arises simultaneously with or after the payment does not constitute a preference. Thus, payment made for the purchase of merchandise on C.O.D. or "cash" terms does not result in a preference, since the effect of such transaction is not to diminish the insolvent's estate, but merely to substitute one asset for another, namely, merchandise for cash.

Not until the debtor commits one of these acts may the court adjudicate him bankrupt. It is possible, however, to create one of these acts of bankruptcy or to cause the insolvent debtor to commit it. Thus, one creditor, with the approval of others who are desirous of placing the debtor in bankruptcy, brings suit for a claim, obtains a judgment, and levies execution against the debtor's property. In this manner, the third act of bankruptcy is committed, thereby allowing other creditors to file their petition, for the result of suit and execution of judgment is to secure a preference the effect of which is to deplete the insolvent's estate for the benefit of one creditor and to the detriment of all others.

ORDINARY, REGULAR, OR STRAIGHT BANKRUPTCY PROCEDURE

From the fulfillment of the requirements for bankruptcy to the final granting of a discharge from debt in bankruptcy, the successive steps in the procedure are fully detailed in the Bankruptcy Act. Appropriate forms to be used are specified, and the time interval required or allowed for each step is stated. The following, in general, are the steps taken in ordinary, regular, or "straight" bankruptcy cases:

1 Filing of petition in the Federal district court

2 Appointment of a receiver, on application, to preserve the insolvent estate

3 Jury trial, if proceedings are contested, and examination of debtor on petition of involuntary bankruptcy; adjudication of bankruptcy by the court; reference of the case to a referee in bankruptcy for administration

4 Notification of creditors, by the referee, of the adjudication

5 Filing proof of claims by creditors

6 First meeting of creditors; allowance of claims; examination of bankrupt; election of trustee

7 Liquidation of estate; payment of dividends to creditors from the proceeds; filing of final accounting of trustee with referee

8 Final meeting of creditors; submission of final report to the court; granting of discharge

Important modifications. The procedure outlined above and discussed in some detail in the pages that follow has always been modified on the basis of whether asset, nominal-asset, or no-asset cases were involved. By amendment in 1959, however, some modifications were provided by the law itself. Since then, for example, the filing of a voluntary petition in an ordinary bankruptcy case (by a person or by a partnership when all partners do so jointly) automatically operates as an adjudication. While in some districts adjudication may have been made for some time more or less automatically on reference by the court clerk, in others this change in law may have encouraged voluntary bankruptcies. Moreover, the adjudication of any person, except a corporation, operates automatically as an application for a discharge in bankruptcy unless the bankrupt waives in writing his right to a discharge before the hearing on the matter.

Filing the petition. Irrespective of the kind of bankruptcy, proceedings are always begun by filing a petition in the Federal Judicial District in which the bankrupt has his or its principal place of business, resided or had the domicile for the 6 months preceding filing of the petition or for a longer portion of the preceding 6 months than in any other state.

The petition is a written document, alleging the essential facts necessary to warrant the court in adjudicating the insolvent debtor a bankrupt. For involuntary proceedings, the petition may be prepared in any given case by the creditors' attorney, or a form such as that shown in Fig. 28-1 may be used for the purpose. For voluntary cases, the petition is prepared on a prescribed legal form (see Fig. 28-2), uniform throughout the United States, to which are annexed five schedules showing (see Fig. 28-3):

1 A statement of all creditors who are to be paid in full, or to whom priority is secured by law

2 Creditors holding securities

3 Creditors whose claims are unsecured

4 Liabilities on notes or bills discounted which ought to be paid by drawers, makers, acceptors, or endorsers

5 Accommodation paper

U. S. S. OFFICIAL FORM No. 5

UNIFORM BANKRUPTCY BLANKS
COL. BLANK BOOK CO.
Form No. 4818

CREDITORS' PETITION

In the District Court of the United States for the

....District of...

In the matter of

....,
Bankrupt.

In Bankruptcy

No..........................

PETITION

To the Honorable...,

Judge of the District Court of the United States

For the...District of..

The Petition of..., of.., and

...., of..., and

...., of..., respectfully represents:

1. ...., of............................, has had his principal place
of business (or has resided or has had his domicile) at...,
within the above judicial district, for a longer portion of the six months immediately preceding the filing of
this petition than in any other judicial district.

2. Said ....owes debts to the amount of $1,000, and is
not a wage-earner or a farmer.

3. Your petitioners are creditors of said..., having
provable claims against him, fixed as to liability and liquidated in amount, amounting in the aggregate, in
excess of the value of securities held by them, to $500. The nature and,amount of your petitioners' claims are
as follows:

....

....

4. Within four months next preceding the filing of this petition, the said.................................
....committed an act of bankruptcy, in that he did
heretofore, to-wit, on the..................day of..., 19.......,..............................

Wherefore Your Petitioners Pray, that service of this petition, with a subpoena, may be made upon said
...., as provided in the Act of Congress relating to bankruptcy, and that he may be adjudged by the court to be a bankrupt within the purview of said Act.

....,

....,

....,

Petitioners.

Attorney.

State of..
County of.. } *ss.*

...., ..., and
...., the petitioners above named, do hereby make solemn oath that the
statements contained in the foregoing petition, subscribed by them, are true.

....,

....,

Petitioners.

Subscribed and sworn to before me this..................day of........................, 19.........,

....,

[Official Character.]

figure 28-1. *Petition in involuntary bankruptcy filed by creditors.*

U. S. S. C. OFFICIAL FORM No. 1

UNIFORM BANKRUPTCY BLANKS
COLUMBUS BLANK BOOK CO.
Columbus, Ohio   4500

DEBTOR'S PETITION

In the United States District Court for the

....District of..

In the matter of

....
Bankrupt. $\Big\}$

In Bankruptcy

No.................................

PETITION

To the Honorable..,

Judge of the United States District Court

For the...District of..:

The Petition of..,

residing at No..Street, in..,

County of..., State of..., by occupation a

...., and employed by ....

....

(or engaged in the business of..), **Respectfully Represents:**

1. Your petitioner has had his principal place of business (or has resided, or has had his domicile) at

....,

within the above judicial district, for a longer portion of the six months immediately preceding the filing of this petition than in any other judicial district.

2. Your petitioner owes debts and is willing to surrender all his property for the benefit of his creditors, except such as is exempt by law, and desires to obtain the benefit of the Act of Congress relating to bankruptcy.

3. The schedule hereto annexed, marked Schedule A, and verified by your petitioner's oath, contains a full and true statement of all his debts, and, so far as it is possible to ascertain, the names and places of residence or business of his creditors, and such further statements concerning said debts as are required by the provisions of said Act.

4. The schedule hereto annexed, marked Schedule B, and verified by your petitioner's oath, contains an accurate inventory of all his property, real and personal, and such further statements concerning said property as are required by the provisions of said Act.

Wherefore Your Petitioner Prays that he may be adjudged by the court to be a bankrupt within the purview of said Act.

....
Petitioner.

....
Attorney

State of................................... $\Big\}$ ss.

County of...................................

I,..,

the petitioner named in the foregoing petition, do hereby make solemn oath that the statements contained therein are true according to the best of my knowledge, information, and belief.

....
Petitioner.

Subscribed and sworn to before me this...................day of...................................., 19..........

....
[Official character]

figure 28-2. *Petition in voluntary bankruptcy filed by debtor.*

U. S. S. C. OFFICIAL FORM

UNIFORM BANKRUPTCY BLANKS
Columbus Blank Book Co.
Columbus, Ohio 4801

SCHEDULE A—STATEMENT OF ALL DEBTS OF BANKRUPT

SCHEDULE A—1

STATEMENT OF ALL CREDITORS TO WHOM PRIORITY IS SECURED BY THE ACT

Claims which have priority	Reference to Ledger or Voucher	NAMES OF CREDITORS	RESIDENCES (If unknown, that fact must be stated).	When and where incurred or contracted	Whether Claim is Contingent, Unliquidated or Disputed	Nature and consideration of the debt, and whether incurred or contracted as partner or joint contractor and, if so, with whom	AMOUNT DUE OR CLAIMED
							$

a—Wages due workmen, servants, clerks or traveling or city salesmen on salary or commission basis, whole or part time, whether or not selling exclusively for the bankrupt, to an amount not exceeding $600 each, earned within three months before filing the petition.

b—Taxes due and owing to

(1) The United States.

(2) The State of ....

(3) The County, district or municipality of ....

State of ....

(c)—(1) Debts owing to any person, including the United States, who by the laws of the United States is entitled to priority.

(2) Rent owing to a landlord who is entitled to priority by the laws of the State of ....

accrued within three months before filing the petition, for actual use and occupancy.

U. S. S. C. OFFICIAL FORM—SCHEDULE A—
STATEMENT OF ALL DEBTS OF BANKRUPT

UNIFORM BANKRUPTCY BLANKS
Columbus Blank Book Co.
Columbus, Ohio 4802

SCHEDULE A—2

CREDITORS HOLDING SECURITIES

[N. B.—Particulars óf securities held, with dates of same, and when they were given, to be stated under the names of the several creditors, and also particulars concerning each debt, as required by the Act of Congress relating to bankruptcy, and whether contracted as partner or joint contractor with any other person, and, if so, with whom.]

Reference to Ledger or Voucher	NAMES OF CREDITORS	RESIDENCE OR PLACE OF BUSINESS (If unknown, that fact must be stated.)	Description of Securities	When and where debts were contracted, and nature and consideration thereof	Whether Claim is Contingent, Unliquidated or Disputed	VALUE OF SECURITIES		AMOUNT DUE OR CLAIMED	
						Dollars	Cts.	Dollars	Cts.

U. S. S. C. OFFICIAL FORM—SCHEDULE A.
STATEMENT OF ALL DEBTS OF BANKRUPT

UNIFORM BANKRUPTCY BLANKS
Columbus Blank Book Co.
Columbus, Ohio 4803

SCHEDULE A—3

CREDITORS WHOSE CLAIMS ARE UNSECURED

[N. B.—When the name and residence (or either) of any drawer, maker, indorser, or holder of any bill or note, etc., are unknown, the fact must be stated, and also the name and residence of the last holder known to the debtor. The debt due to each creditor must be stated in full, and any claim by way of set-off stated in the schedule of property.]

Reference to Ledger or Voucher	NAMES OF CREDITORS	RESIDENCE OR PLACE OF BUSINESS (If unknown, that fact must be stated).	WHEN AND WHERE CONTRACTED	Whether Claim is Contingent, Unliquidated or Disputed	Nature and consideration of the debt, and whether any judgment, bond, bill of exchange, promissory note, etc., and whether contracted as partner or joint contracter with any other person; and if so, with whom.	Amount Due or Claimed	
						Dollars	Cts.

U. S. S. C. OFFICIAL FORM—SCHEDULE A—
STATEMENT OF ALL DEBTS OF BANKRUPT

UNIFORM BANKRUPTCY BLANKS
Columbus Blank Book Co.
Columbus, Ohio 4804

SCHEDULE A—4

LIABILITIES ON NOTES OR BILLS DISCOUNTED WHICH OUGHT TO BE PAID BY THE DRAWERS, MAKERS, ACCEPTORS, OR INDORSERS

[N. B.—The dates of the notes or bills, and when due, with the names, residences, and the business or occupation of the drawers, makers, acceptors, or indorsers thereof, are to be set forth under the names of the holders. If the names of the holders are not known, the name of the last holder known to the debtor shall be stated, and his business and place of residence. The same particulars shall be stated as to notes or bills on which the debtor is liable as indorser.]

Reference to Ledger or Voucher	NAMES OF HOLDERS AS FAR AS KNOWN	RESIDENCE OR PLACE OF BUSINESS (If unknown, that fact must be stated).	Place Where Contracted.	WHETHER CLAIM IS DISPUTED	Nature and consideration of liability, whether same was contracted as partner or joint contractor, or with any other person, and if so, with whom.	Amount Due or Claimed	
						Dollars	Cts.

U. S. S. C.—OFFICIAL FORM—SCHEDULE A.—
STATEMENT OF ALL DEBTS OF BANKRUPT

UNIFORM BANKRUPTCY BLANKS
Columbus Blank Book Co.
Columbus, Ohio 4805

SCHEDULE A—5

ACCOMODATION PAPER

[N. B.—The dates of the notes or bills, and when due, with the names and residences of the drawers, makers, acceptors, and indorsers thereof, are to be set forth under the names of the holders; if the debtor be liable as drawer, maker, acceptor, or indorser thereof, it is to be stated accordingly. If the names of the holders are not known, the name of the last holder known to the debtor should be stated, with his residence. Give same particulars as to other commercial paper.]

Reference to Ledger or Voucher	NAMES OF HOLDERS	RESIDENCE OR PLACE OF BUSINESS (If unknown, that fact must be stated).	Names and Residences of Persons Accommodated	PLACE WHERE CONTRACTED	Whether Claim is Disputed	Whether Liability was contracted as partner or joint contractor, or with any other person; and, if so, with whom.	AMOUNT DUE OR CLAIMED	
							Dollars	Cts.

OATH TO SCHEDULE A.

State of ....
County of .... } *ss.*

I, ..., *the person who subscribed to the following schedule, do hereby make solemn oath that the said schedule is a statement of all my debts, in accordance with the Act of Congress relating to bankruptcy, according to the best of my knowledge, information, and belief.*

.........., *Petitioner.*

Subscribed and sworn to before me this .... *day of* ...., *19*....

..........,

....
(Official Character)

figure 28-3. *Schedule A in bankruptcy, listing the bankrupt's creditors and debts owed to each of them.*

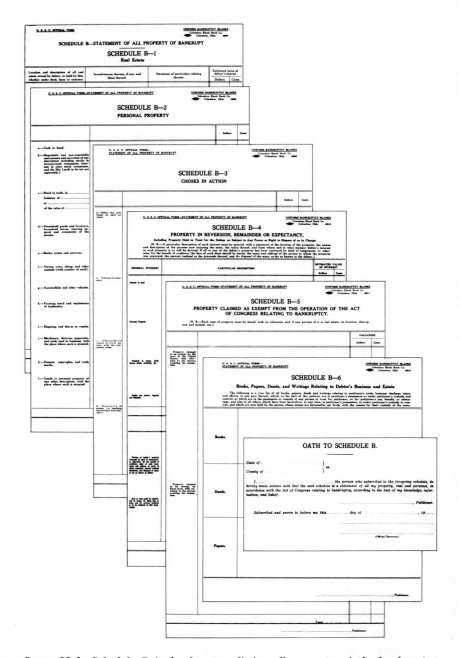

figure 28-4. *Schedule B in bankruptcy, listing all property of the bankrupt.*

Another list of six schedules (see Fig. 28-4) is made out and annexed to the petition showing a statement of all property of bankrupt, including real estate, personal property, choses in action, property held in trust for the debtor, property claimed as exempted from the operation of bankruptcy laws, and books, papers, deeds, and writings relating to bankrupt's business and estate. All schedules must be filed with the petition in voluntary cases and within 5 days after adjudication in involuntary bankruptcies.

The truthfulness of the statements contained in all these schedules is verified by oath. A summary of debts and assets is then drawn up (see Fig. 28-5), the petition is filed with the clerk of the district court, and a fee of $40 is paid, except when a fee is not required from a voluntary bankrupt who takes the pauper oath. The petition is prepared in quadruplicate, three copies being filed with the clerk of the court, one copy for the clerk, one for the referee, and one for service on the bankrupt.

Finally, at least 5 days before the first meeting of creditors, the bankrupt must file a statement of affairs in such form as the district court may prescribe. In this statement the bankrupt supplies the court with information concerning himself which otherwise would have to be solicited in oral examination. The form shown in Figs 28-6A and 28-6B is typical of the statements required of a debtor engaged in business. A similar, although slightly different form, is required also of bankrupts not engaged in business.

Appointment of receiver in bankruptcy. The function of the receiver in bankruptcy is to preserve the estate, if that should seem necessary, until the trustee can be elected. His appointment may be made at the request of any interested party or parties, at any time after the filing of the bankruptcy petition and in either voluntary or involuntary proceedings. A receiver may be appointed by the Federal court under Chapter II, Section 2 of the Bankruptcy Act in different capacities: as a custodian, which is his usual position; with full powers; with authority to conduct the business; or in an ancillary capacity.

A petition for such a receiver is filed in those cases where there are substantial assets and where it is found necessary in order to preserve or prevent loss to such assets. His principal duty is that of custodian of the insolvent estate, unless the court allows him to continue the business for a limited period of time. Thus it is his duty to take an immediate inventory of the estate of the alleged bankrupt, seize all his books and records, close the place of business, and take all necessary steps to collect and appropriate the property and effects belonging to the debtor, for the benefit of creditors. He remains in control until the petition

U. S. S. C. OFFICIAL FORM

UNIFORM BANKRUPTCY BLANKS
Columbus Blank Book Co.
Columbus, Ohio 4514

SUMMARY OF DEBTS AND ASSETS

[From the statements of the debtor in Schedules A and B.]

Schedule A	1-a	Wages		
Schedule A	1-b (1)	Taxes due United States		
Schedule A	1-b (2)	Taxes due States		
Schedule A	1-b (3)	Taxes due counties, districts and municipalities		
Schedule A	1-c (1)	Debts due any person, including the United States having priority by laws of the United States		
Schedule A	1-c (2)	Rent having priority		
Schedule A	2	Secured claims		
Schedule A	3	Unsecured claims		
Schedule A	4	Notes and bills which ought to be paid by other parties thereto		
Schedule A	5	Accommodation paper		
		Schedule A, total		
Schedule B	1	Real Estate		
Schedule B	2-a	Cash on hand		
Schedule B	2-b	Negotiable and non-negotiable instruments and securities		
Schedule B	2-c	Stock in trade		
Schedule B	2-d	Household Goods		
Schedule B	2-e	Books, prints, and pictures		
Schedule B	2-f	Horses, cows, and other animals		
Schedule B	2-g	Automobiles and other vehicles		
Schedule B	2-h	Farming stock and implements		
Schedule B	2-i	Shipping and shares in vessels		
Schedule B	2-j	Machinery, fixtures, and tools		
Schedule B	2-k	Patents, copyrights, and trade-marks		
Schedule B	2-l	Other personal property		
Schedule B	3-a	Debts due on open accounts		
Schedule B	3-b	Policies of insurance		
Schedule B	3-c	Unliquidated claims		
Schedule B	3-d	Deposits of money in banks and elsewhere		
Schedule B	4	Property in reversion, remainder, expectancy or trust		
Schedule B	5	Property claimed as exempt		
Schedule B	6	Books, deeds, and papers		
		Schedule B, total		

figure **28-5.** *Summary of debts and assets filed by the bankrupt.*

U. S. S. C. OFFICIAL FORM No. 3

UNIFORM BANKRUPTCY BLANKS
Columbus Blank Book Co.
Columbus, Ohio   4500-B

In the United States District Court for the..District of..

In the Matter of

}

In Bankruptcy

....
Bankrupt

No................................

STATEMENT OF AFFAIRS.
(For Bankrupt or Debtor Engaged in Business.)

(Note.—Each question should be answered or the failure to answer explained. If the answer is "none," this should be stated. If additional space is needed for the answer to any question, a separate sheet properly identified and made a part hereof, should be used and attached.

If the bankrupt or debtor is a partnership or a corporation, the questions shall be deemed to be addressed to, and shall be answered on behalf of, the partnership or corporation; and the statement shall be verified by a member of the partnership or by a duly authorized officer of the corporation.

The term, "original petition," as used in the following questions, shall mean the petition filed under section 3b or 4a of chapter III, section 322 of chapter XI, section 422, of chapter XII, or section 622 of chapter XIII.)

1. *Nature, location and name of business.*
  a. What business are you engaged in?..
      (If business operations have been terminated, give the date of such termination.)
  b. Where, and under what name, do you carry on such business?..

  c. When did you commence such business?..
  d. Where else, and under what other names, have you carried on business within the six years immediately preceding the filing of the original petition herein?..

      (Give street addresses, the names of any partners, joint adventurers, or other associates, the nature of the business, and the periods for which it was carried on.)
2. *Books and records.*
  a. By whom, or under whose supervision, have your books of account and records been kept during the two years immediately preceding the filing of the original petition herein?..

      (Give names, addresses, and periods of time.)
  b. By whom have your books of account and records been audited during the two years immediately preceding the filing of the original petition herein?..

      (Give names, addresses, and dates of audits.)
  c. In whose possession are your books of account and records?..

      (Give names and addresses.)
3. *Financial statements.*
  a. Have you issued any financial statements within the two years immediately preceding the filing of the original petition herein?..
      (Give dates, and the names and addresses of the persons to whom issued, including mercantile and trade agencies.)
4. *Inventories.*
  a. When was the last inventory of your property taken?..
  b. By whom, or under whose supervision, was this inventory taken?..
  c. What was the amount, in dollars, of the inventory?..
      (State whether the inventory was taken at cost, market, or otherwise.)
  d. When was the next prior inventory of your property taken?..
  e. By whom, or under whose supervision, was this inventory taken?..

  f. What was the amount, in dollars, of the inventory?..
      (State whether the inventory was taken at cost, market, or otherwise.)
  g. In whose possession are the records of the two inventories above referred to?..

      (Give names and addresses.)
5. *Income other than from operation of business.*
  a. What amount of income, other than from the operation of your business, have you received during each of the two years immediately preceding the filing of the original petition herein?..

      (Give particulars, including each source, and the amount received therefrom.)
6. *Income tax returns.*
  a. Where did you file your last federal and state income tax returns, and for what years?..

7. *Bank accounts and safe deposit boxes.*
  a. What bank accounts have you maintained, alone or together with any other person, and in your own or any other name, within the two years immediately preceding the filing of the original petition herein?..

      (Give the name and address of each bank, the name in which the deposit was maintained, and the name of every person authorized to make withdrawals from such account.)
  b. What safe deposit box or boxes or other depository or depositories have you kept or used for your securities, cash or other valuables, within the two years immediately preceding the filing of the original petition herein?..

      (Give the name and address of the bank or other depository, the name in which each box or other depository was kept, the name of every person who had the right of access thereto, a brief description of the contents thereof, and, if surrendered, when surrendered, or, if transferred, when transferred and the name and address of the transferee.)

figure 28-6*A. Statement of Affairs filed by a bankrupt engaged in business.*

8. Property held in trust.
    a. What property do you hold in trust for any other person? ....

          (Give name and address of each person, and a description of the property and the amount or value thereof.)
9. Prior bankruptcy or other proceedings; assignments for benefit of creditors.
    a. What proceedings under the Bankruptcy Act have been brought by or against you during the six years immediately preceding the filing of the original petition herein? ....

          (Give the location of the bankruptcy court, the nature of the proceeding, and whether a discharge was granted or refused, or a composition, arrangement or plan was or was not confirmed.)
    b. Was any of your property, at the time of filing of the original petition herein, in the hands of a receiver or trustee?

          (If so, give the name and location of the court, the nature of the proceeding, a brief description of the property, and the name of the receiver or trustee.)
    c. Have you made any assignment of your property for the benefit of your creditors, or any general settlement with your creditors, within the two years immediately preceding the filing of the original petition herein?..................

          (If so, give dates, the name of the assignee, and a brief statement of the terms of assignment or settlement.)
10. Loans repaid.
    a. What repayments of loans have you made during the year immediately preceding the filing of the original petition herein? ....

          (Give the name and address of the lender, the amount of the loan and when received, the amount and date when repaid, and, if the lender is a relative, the relationship. If the bankrupt or debtor is a partnership, state whether the lender is or was a partner or a relative of a partner, and if so, the relationship. If the bankrupt or debtor is a corporation, state whether the lender is or was an officer, director or stockholder, or a relative of an officer, director or stockholder, and, if so, the relationship.)
11. Transfer of property.
    a. What property have you transferred or disposed of, other than in the ordinary course of business, during the year immediately preceding the filing of the original petition herein? ....

          (Give a description of the property, the date of transfer or disposition, to whom transferred or how disposed of, and, if the transferee is a relative, the relationship, the consideration, if any, received therefor, and the disposition of such consideration.)
12. Accounts receivable.
    a. Have you assigned any of your accounts receivable during the year immediately preceding the filing of the original petition herein? ....

          (If so, give names and addresses of assignees.)
13. Losses.
    a. Have you suffered any losses from fire, theft or gambling during the year immediately preceding the filing of the petition herein? ....

          (If so, give particulars, including dates, and the amounts of money or value and general description of property lost.)
          (If the bankrupt or debtor is a partnership or corporation the following additional questions should be answered.)
14. Withdrawals.
    a. What personal withdrawals, including loans, have been made by each member of the partnership, or by each officer, director or managing executive of the corporation, during the year immediately preceding the filing of the original petition herein? ....

          (Give the name of each person, whether a partner, officer, director or manager, the dates and amounts of withdrawals, and the nature or purpose thereof.)
15. Members of partnership; officers, directors, managers, and principal stockholders of corporation.
    a. What are the names and addresses of each member of the partnership, or the names, titles and addresses of each officer, director and managing executive, and of each stockholder holding 25 per cent or more of the issued and outstanding stock, of the corporation?..

                                                         Bankrupt [or Debtor].

State of..⎫
                           ⎬ ss.
County of...⎭

    I, ... the **person who subscribed to the foregoing statement of affairs,** do hereby make solemn oath that the answers therein contained are true and complete to the best of my knowledge, information, and belief.

                                          Bankrupt [or Debtor].

Subscribed and sworn to before me this................day of......................................, 19........

                                    [Official character].

figure 28-6B. *Reverse side of Fig. 28-6A.*

in bankruptcy is dismissed or, in event of adjudication, until the first meeting of creditors, which must be called by the referee within 30 days but not less than 10 days after the debtor is declared a bankrupt. At this meeting a trustee is elected to whom all assets belonging to the insolvent estate are transferred immediately by the receiver and the receivership is terminated automatically. Before the receivership is terminated, a special meeting of creditors is called for the purpose of approving the receiver's final report and the application for allowances to him and his attorney.

Compensation of the receiver varies with the functions he performs and with his responsibilities. It is in the form of a percentage of moneys disbursed or turned over by him to any persons, including the trustee. The schedule of his commissions is as follows:

As custodian	Up to 2% of first $1,000 or less
	0.5% on all amounts above $1,000
With full powers	Up to 6% on first $500 or less
	4% on from $500 to $1,500
	2% on from $1,500 to $10,000
	1% on all amounts over $10,000
As operator of the business	Not more than twice the maximum allowance permitted when operating with full powers

Trial and examination of bankrupt. Immediately prior to the adjudication of bankruptcy, usually soon after the filing of the petition in a case of involuntary bankruptcy, the debtor is entitled to a jury trial at which he may be examined by the court or enter a protest to the proceedings. At such a time, he may contest the allegation that he is insolvent or that he has committed an act of bankruptcy. He may also be required by the court to supply certain information concerning his status, assets, and obligations, essential to the bankruptcy action. He may even successfully challenge and contest the jurisdiction of the court over the case. Obviously, this step in the procedure of bankruptcy pertains only to involuntary petitions, for when a debtor voluntarily petitions the court he automatically admits the conditions requisite to bankruptcy and furnishes the evidence otherwise sought by the trial process.

If the bankrupt elects to contest the proceedings, a jury trial is necessary (unless waived by failure to apply for such a trial) before the court can sign the decree adjudicating him bankrupt. Such suits are not commonly contested; hence at the expiration of about 15 days the debtor is assumed to have waived the trial and the case is either dismissed or a decree is entered, depending upon the proof and circumstances.

Actions of the referee. The referee in bankruptcy is an officer of the Federal court, appointed and reappointed by the district judge for a term of 6 years each time.   The jurisdiction which he has as representative of the public in the administration of the Federal Bankruptcy Act is clearly set forth in Chapter V, Section 38 of that Act.   Subject always to a review by the judge, it is the duty of the referee to consider all petitions referred to him by the clerk of the Federal district court, to hold trials, to make adjudication, or to dismiss petitions.   He administers oaths and examines witnesses, requiring the production of documents in proceedings before the bankruptcy court.   He may, under certain conditions, exercise the power of the judge to take possession or to release the property of the bankrupt.   It is he who grants, denies, or revokes discharges and who confirms or refuses to confirm arrangements or wage earner plans.   He also must perform the duties conferred by the Act on courts of bankruptcy and, during the proceedings, upon application of the trustee, authorizes the employment of stenographic help, at the expense of the estate, for reporting and transcribing the proceedings.

Following adjudication, the referee's principal duties, as prescribed in Chapter V, Section 39, are to give notice to creditors and other parties in interest of the adjudication and of meetings; to prepare and file schedules of property and lists of creditors, in cases of involuntary petitions, when the bankrupt neglects them; to examine all schedules of property and lists of creditors filed by bankrupts; and to declare dividends and to prepare and deliver to trustees dividend sheets showing the amounts declared and to whom payable.   The other duties deal with the preservation and handling of all records of the proceedings and the furnishing of information to all interested parties.

Compensation of referees is fixed by the judicial conference of the United States not to exceed $22,500 per annum for full-time referees, and not to be more than $11,000 for those engaged part time, the specific sums paid any referee being based upon the average number and types of cases handled, average amount of gross receipts realized, cases closed and pending, and other similar factors.   Payment of such salaries, as well as referees' expenses, is made up in part from the $32 allocated from the bankruptcy filing fee for each estate to the referee's salary and expense fund, but mostly from funds charged against each estate based on the net proceeds realized, against each arrangement confirmed, and against each wage earner plan confirmed.   All such receipts, as well as those received when acting as conciliation commissioners and as special masters under the Act, are placed in the Treasury of the United States for the account of the referee salary and expense fund.

The number of referees and the territory covered by each depend upon the amount of business under the Bankruptcy Act.   At the end of fiscal 1967 there were 174 authorized full-time referees and 41 part-time such functionaries, a total of 215.[5]

Filing proof of claims. A first duty of the referee following adjudication is to notify creditors of the bankruptcy. This notification constitutes an invitation to creditors to submit proof of their claims and to attend the first meeting of creditors at a time announced. Prompt filing of such claims is essential, for only those creditors whose claims have been filed and subsequently allowed may participate in the election of a trustee; however, claims may be filed with the referee at or before the first meeting or thereafter within 6 months from adjudication.

Claims are filed on certain forms which were adopted and prescribed by the Supreme Court of the United States (see Fig. 28-7). On these forms, a creditor sets forth his claim and the consideration therefor, payments made on the claim, and the amount justly owing from the bankrupt. If any securities are held for the claim under consideration, that fact must be stated on the "proof of debt" form. It is advisable to attach itemized bills setting forth the nature of the claim. If a claim is based on a written instrument, such instrument or a copy thereof must be filed with the claim. In event the instrument is lost or destroyed, a statement to that effect must be filed under oath with the claim.

All debts owing at the time the petition is filed, though not payable until a later date, may be proved. Other provable debts consist in claims for torts reduced to judgment before the adjudication; claims of persons contingently liable for the bankrupt; and all liquidated claims of a contractual nature, such as breach of contract.

First meeting of creditors. Following adjudication, notification, and proving of claims, a creditors' meeting must be held not less than 10 nor more than 30 days after the decree of bankruptcy has been signed. According to Chapter VI, Section 58, creditors or a committee appointed by them are entitled to 10 days' notice by mail, unless they waive notice in writing. Such notice must be published at least once, not later than 1 week prior to the meeting. Not only must notice be sent of all meetings of creditors, but the same applies to all examinations of the bankrupt, all hearings for the confirmation of a composition, all proposed sales of property or compromises of any controversy, declaration and time of payment of dividends, the filing and examining of the final accounts of the trustee, and the proposed dismissal of the proceedings; creditors are also entitled to 30 days' notice of applications for the discharge of bankrupts.

[5] *Tables of Bankruptcy Statistics Fiscal Year Ending June 30, 1967,* Administrative Office of the United States Courts, 1968.

BK-28a (Rev. August '61)

UNITED STATES DISTRICT COURT
FOR THE

....

In the matter of

In Bankruptcy

No. ....

(Important—Insert name of bankrupt or debtor above).

PROOF OF CLAIM IN BANKRUPTCY

...., of No. .... Street,

in ...., County of ...., State of ...., says:
(City)

IF CLAIMANT IS AN INDIVIDUAL:
   1. *(a)* That he is the claimant herein.

IF CLAIMANT IS A PARTNERSHIP:
   1. *(b)* That he is a member of ...., a copartnership, composed
of the undersigned and ...., of ...., in the County
of ...., State of ...., and carrying on business
at No. .... Street, in ...., County of ....
                               (City)
State of ...., ...

IF CLAIMANT IS A CORPORATION:
   1. *(c)* That the undersigned is the .... of..., a corporation organized
                                   (Official title)   (Creditor)
under the laws of the State of ...., and carrying on business at No. .... Street
in ...., County of ...., State of ...., and is duly
   (City)
authorized to make this proof of claim on its behalf.

IF MADE BY AGENT OR ATTORNEY:
   1. *(d)* That the undersigned is the agent or attorney of ....,
                                            (Creditor)
of No. .... Street, in ...., County of ....
                              (City)
State of ....; that he is duly authorized by said ....
to make this proof of claim in his behalf; that said proof cannot be made by said ....
                                            (Creditor)
in person because ....

   2. That the above-named bankrupt (or debtor) was at and before the filing by (or against) him of the petition herein (for adjudication of bankruptcy), and still is, justly and truly indebted (or liable) to the claimant (or copartnership or corporation), in the sum of .... dollars ($....................).

   3. That the consideration of this debt (or liability) is as follows:

   4. That no part of the debt (or liability) has been paid except ....

   5. That there are no set-offs or counterclaims to the debt (or liability), except ....

   6. That claimant (or said copartnership or said corporation) does not hold, and has not, nor has any person by his or (its) order, or to the knowledge or belief of the undersigned, for his (or its) use, had or received, any security, or securities for the debt (or liability), except ....

   7. [If the debt or liability is founded upon an instrument of writing.] That the instrument upon which the debt (or liability) is founded is attached hereto (or lost or destroyed, as set forth in the affidavit attached hereto.)

   8. [If the debt is founded upon an open account.] That the said debt was (or will become) due on .... (or that the average date thereof is ....; that no note, or other negotiable instrument, has been received for such account, or any part thereof (or that the said debt is evidenced by a note, or other negotiable instrument, which is attached hereto; and that no judgment has been rendered thereon, except ....

   9. This claim is filed as an { UNSECURED / SECURED / PRIORITY } CLAIM

Dated at ...., this .... day of .... 19.........

               Signed ....
                              (Name of individual, agent, officer, or partner signing this claim)

PENALTY FOR PRESENTING FRAUDULENT CLAIM.— Fine of not more than $5,000 or imprisonment for not more than five years or both — Title 18, U. S. C., §152.

   (When signed mail this proof of claim to Referee in Bankruptcy)

figure 28-7. *Proof of claim filed by creditors.*

The purpose of the first meeting of creditors, at which the judge or referee presides, is to allow or disallow the claims of creditors, to elect a trustee, to place the debtor on the witness stand for an examination by creditors or their representatives, and to appoint a committee of three or more creditors to consult and advise with the trustee.

Allowance of claims. Ordinarily, before the first meeting of creditors, many claims will have been filed; others are filed at this meeting. If filed in proper form and in the class of probable claims, the next thing is to determine whether they shall be allowed. Generally, all provable claims are allowable. To this there are two important exceptions. Secured claims, for example, are allowable only to the extent of the difference between the amount of the claim and the value of the property securing the claim. Again, claims with voidable preferences will not be allowed till such preferences are surrendered.

A preference is voidable if (1) it was given for a preexisting debt, (2) within 4 months before the filing of the petition, or after filing the petition and before the adjudication, and (3) the person receiving it or benefiting thereby had reasonable cause to believe that the debtor was insolvent at the time and therefore apparently intended to give the recipient a preference. The purpose in making such preferences voidable is to enable the trustee to recover every payment made to creditors within 4 months prior to filing of petition or before adjudication, in order to provide for an equitable distribution of the insolvent estate.

Examination of the bankrupt. One of the most important phases of the proceedings is to place the bankrupt on the witness stand, where he may be questioned personally by any bona fide creditor or through an attorney or other representative of creditors, with a view to ascertaining and establishing the fraud or preference of which the creditors may be suspicious. To make such an examination possible, Chapter III, Section 7 of the Bankruptcy Act, provides that the bankrupt shall submit to an examination concerning the conduct of his business and all matters directly relating to the cause of his bankruptcy, his dealings with his creditors and other persons, the whereabouts of his property, as well as all matters which may affect the administration and settlement of his estate. This testimony, however, may not be used against him in any criminal proceeding.

Other well-defined duties which devolve upon the bankrupt are the following: to attend the first meeting of his creditors, the hearing upon his petition for a discharge, if objections are filed, and such other meetings as the court may direct; to comply with all lawful orders of the court; to examine the correctness of proofs of claims against his estate; to cooperate with the trustee in collecting and protecting the assets; to prepare and file schedules of assets and liabilities; and to file at least 5 days before the first meeting of creditors a statement of his affairs.

Should the bankrupt, upon examination, prove hostile or otherwise unsatisfactory, because of his evasive replies; or should he refuse to answer questions or to produce records; or should he otherwise manifest a desire to withhold necessary and helpful information, the court may confine him for contempt of court. He is also subject to arrest if he refuses to appear for examination when so ordered or when satisfactory proof by affidavits is given that the bankrupt intends to leave the district in order to avoid examination or otherwise defeat the proceedings in bankruptcy. Under such circumstances the judge is given power to issue a warrant to the marshal directing him to bring the bankrupt before the court for examination. When so confined, the bankrupt may be kept in custody not exceeding 10 days.

Subsequent meetings may be called from time to time whenever the referee deems it necessary, or within 30 days whenever one-fourth or more in number of creditors who have proved their claims file a written request to that effect. When the affairs of the estate are ready to be closed, except in no-asset cases, a final meeting must be ordered.

The trustee—election and office. One of the chief objects of the creditors' first meeting is to elect a trustee, who represents the creditors in bankruptcy proceedings, as the referee represents the court. The trusteeship may consist of one or three persons, and the election is made by those creditors whose claims have been proved and allowed. A majority vote, in both number and amount of claims, is necessary to effect such election.[6] The election of the trustee, however, is subject to the approval of the referee, and in event the creditors cannot agree on a trustee, as where the vote on the per dollar claim basis conflicts with the per capita basis, the referee appoints one. Where there is conflict in the results of the two votes, the choice of the majority of creditors is usually appointed by the referee. In no-asset cases, on the other hand, no trustee may be necessary and none will be appointed.

At the first meeting, in addition to electing a trustee, creditors are permitted to elect a committee the purpose of which is to consult

---

[6] Claims of $50 or less are counted only in computing the amount but not the number of voting creditors, thereby minimizing the influence of collection agencies and others who corral many small claims for control purposes. Relatives of the bankrupt or stockholders and officers of the bankrupt corporations are precluded from voting for the election of a trustee or for a creditors' committee. Creditors with claims that are secured or with priority can vote only to the extent of the excess of such claims over the values of the securities or priorities.

with and to advise the trustee in the administration of the estate. A majority vote, computed as in the election of a trustee, is necessary to elect. Such a committee, however, has no responsibility for controlling the estate or engaging in its administration. It does have a right, nevertheless, to be heard by the court on any question affecting the administration.

A creditor who is unable to attend the creditors' meeting personally may be represented by an attorney if he fills out the blank power of attorney. No special advantage, save that of convenience, can ordinarily be gained from such representation. On the other hand, there is a possibility of placing such claims in the hands of unscrupulous attorneys who are overanxious to secure a large number of claims in order to obtain contol of the estate through the appointment of a trustee who is to represent *them* rather than the creditors. If not in a position to control the insolvent's estate, such attorneys may hold out in a composition settlement in order secretly to secure additional compensation for themselves from the debtor. For these reasons, some attorneys make it a practice to solicit claims against insolvent estates and offer to represent creditors without any fee. It is against such attorneys as these that creditors must be cautioned in the exercise of their power to authorize an attorney to represent them at creditors' meetings. It is unjust, however, for credit men to maintain a contemptuous attitude toward the commercial attorneys, as such, for relatively few of them are in the class of dishonest bankruptcy practitioners.

A much better practice in vogue at the present time is to file the claim with the referee and to give a representative committee of creditors or an adjustment bureau, where one is available, a proxy to vote at the meetings, or else assign the claim to the bureau, which will itself file it and take whatever action it deems advisable. In either case, the creditor may be certain that a more competent trustee will be elected.

A trustee, in order to qualify for the position, before entering upon his official duties must file a bond, the amount of which is determined by the court and may be increased or decreased at any time if there is ample cause for such a change. This in a measure indicates the importance of his position, for creditors may administer the insolvent estate only through the medium of their trustee. Hence, to insure the largest possible dividends it is essential that a competent trustee be elected in order that the estate may be handled in an honest and businesslike manner. It is urged, therefore, that all creditors be present or else properly represented at the first meeting, when such election takes place.

Following his appointment and qualification, the trustee takes title to all the bankrupt's property as of date the debtor was adjudged a bankrupt, except in so far as exemption to the property is claimed and allowed. He is vested with the title of all documents relating to the bankrupt's assets; interests in all sorts of intangible assets, including patents, patent rights, copyrights, and trade-marks; property fraudulently transferred by the bankrupt to his creditors; and rights of action arising from contracts, etc. In a word, the trustee practically stands "in the shoes" of the bankrupt as far as title to the property is concerned. He holds the property and may convey title to the purchaser thereof subject to all legal and equitable liens. Naturally, he acquires no better title to the property than the bankrupt had.

The duties of a trustee are outlined in Chapter V, Section 47, paragraph (a) of the Bankruptcy Act. He is required to examine proofs of claim and object to their allowance if deemed improper; to examine the bankrupt; to reduce all property to possession, liquidate it under the direction of the court as expeditiously as compatible with the best interests of all parties concerned, place the proceeds received in one of the designated depositories, and distribute the moneys among the creditors as required by law; and, at the expense of the estate, to oppose the discharge of the bankrupt if deemed advisable. Real and personal property belonging to the bankrupt estate, after being properly appraised by three disinterested appraisers appointed by the court, is usually sold subject to the approval of the court, and the sale must receive approval if the property realizes less than 75 per cent of its appraisal value. He must account for all receipts and disbursements; furnish information concerning the estate to all parties in interest; lay before the final meeting of the creditors detailed statements of the administration of the estate; make final reports and file final accounts with the court 15 days before the day fixed for the final meeting of the creditors; and pay dividends within 10 days after declared by the referee. If three trustees are placed in charge of an estate, at least two must concur to make their acts valid.

Compensation of trustees. Except when a fee is not required from a voluntary bankrupt, a trustee in bankruptcy receives a fee of $10 for each estate deposited with the clerk at time of filing of petition and such other compensation as the court may allow. For normal administration, when the trustee does not conduct the business of the bankrupt, the trustee is allowed a maximum of 10 per cent of the first $500 or less, 6 per cent on all in excess of $500 but less than $1,500, 3 per cent on all above $1,500 and less than $10,000, 2 per cent on moneys in excess of $10,000 but not more than $25,000, and 1 per cent on moneys disbursed or turned over by them to any persons in excess of $25,000. When the trustee also conducts the business for limited periods as authorized, if deemed necessary in the interest of the estate, a higher compensation is allowed by the court, which must never be in excess of twice the maximum allowance permitted for normal administration.

Declaration and payment of dividends. Before any dividends may be declared and paid on the allowed claims of general creditors, certain debts having priority must be paid in full out of the bankrupt estate. The following debts are given priority by Chapter VII, Section 64 of the Bankruptcy Act, in the order in which they are listed herewith:

1 Costs and expenses of administration, including actual and necessary costs and expenses of preserving the estate subsequent to filing of petition, fees for referee's salary and expense fund, filing fees paid to creditors, reasonable costs and expenses for recovery of property for the benefit of the estate, trustee's expenses in opposing bankrupt's discharge and criminal prosecution of offenses connected with the estate, and for all other administrative purposes.

2 Wages, not to exceed $600 to each claimant, which have been earned within 3 months prior to the commencement of the proceeding.

3 Reasonable costs and expenses of creditors in obtaining a refusal, revocation, or setting aside of a discharge by the bankrupt or a confirmation of an arrangement or a wage earner's plan, or in adducing evidence for such purpose.

4 All taxes to the United States or any state or subdivision thereof that became legally due and owing *within 3 years* preceding bankruptcy. Unpaid tax claims entitled to such priority are not dischargeable, but unpaid tax claims not entitled to priority rank as general unsecured claims and are equally subject to discharge.

5 Debts other than for taxes owing to any person, including the United States, who by the laws of the United States or some state law is entitled to priority.

After the above claims have been paid in full, the remainder is distributed pro rata among all other creditors. In this connection it should be observed that a judgment creditor has no priority over other unsecured creditors unless an execution has been levied on specific property at least 4 months prior to filing of the petition.

As already indicated in a previous connection, the referee must declare dividends and prepare dividend sheets showing dividends declared and to whom payable. It then devolves upon the trustee to pay the dividends thus declared within 10 days after the declaration by the referee. Chapter VII, Section 65 of the Act provides that the first dividend must be declared within 30 days after the first date set for the first meeting of creditors, if the money of the estate in excess of the amount necessary to pay in full all priority claims amounts to 5 per cent or more of the allowable claims. Not more than 50 per cent of the funds on hand in excess of the amount needed to satisfy prior and lien claims may be paid out on the first dividend. Subsequent dividends must be declared whenever the amount to be distributed equals 10 per cent or more, as well as upon closing of the estate. Dividends may be declared oftener and in smaller proportions upon the order of the judge. The final dividend, however, is not to be declared within 3 months after the first dividend has been declared. All dividends which remain unclaimed for 60 days after the declaration of the final dividend are to be paid by the trustee into the court. If unclaimed for a period of 1 year, the judge may direct that such dividends be distributed among creditors whose claims have been allowed but not paid in full, the balance, if any, going to the bankrupt. Unclaimed dividends belonging to minors must remain intact until 1 year after such minors arrive at majority.

Discharge of bankrupt. One of the main purposes of the Bankruptcy Law is to enable creditors to take possession of an insolvent debtor's assets and equitably to distribute the proceeds among themselves. The second chief object of the law is to release the bankrupt debtor, through a discharge, from his unpaid liabilities, thereby allowing him to start anew and unencumbered. In accordance with this object, Chapter III, Section 14 of the Act provides that the adjudication of a bankrupt other than a corporation automatically acts as a discharge application unless waived by writing to the court to that effect. If the bankrupt is a corporation, it must file an application for a discharge within 6 months following adjudication.

After the bankrupt has been examined, the court fixes a time for the filing of objections to the discharge. Notice must be sent to creditors, trustees, and the U.S. District Attorney at least 30 days in advance, also at least 30 days' notice is given to the bankrupt, his attorney, and objecting parties of a hearing to be held on the objections filed.

Conditions preventing discharge. After hearing the application for a discharge and proofs and pleas in opposition thereto, the court will grant the discharge unless the bankrupt has committed one of the acts expressly prohibited by Chapter III, Section 14 of the Bankruptcy Act. According to this section a discharge shall not be granted if the bankrupt has:

1 Committed an offense punishable by imprisonment, as provided by the Act, such as concealing property from the trustee, making a false oath or account in bankruptcy proceedings, or presenting under oath a false claim against his estate

2 Destroyed, mutilated, falsified, concealed, or failed to keep books of account or records from which his financial condition might be ascertained, except where the court feels that such acts might have been justified by all the conditions in the case

3 Obtained a new credit or an extension or renewal thereof through a false statement issued in writing concerning his financial condition

4 Transferred, removed, destroyed, or concealed any of his property, or permitted others to do so, with intention to hinder, delay, or defraud his creditors, within 12 months immediately preceding the filing of the petition

5 Has been granted a discharge in bankruptcy within 6 years, or had a composition or a wage earner's plan confirmed within 6 years

6 Refused to obey any lawful order of, or to answer any material question approved by, the court in the course of the proceedings

7 Failed to explain satisfactorily any losses or deficiency of assets to meet his obligations

If there has been any fraud in bringing about the proceedings, or in concealing property which should have been surrendered for the benefit of creditors, any of the defrauded creditors may apply to the court within a year after the discharge has been granted and have it revoked. It must be proved that knowledge of the fraud has been acquired by the petitioners since the granting of the discharge, and had such facts been known in time, the discharge would not have been granted. It, therefore, behooves insolvent debtors to be honest in their dealings with creditors, particularly in bankruptcy proceedings.

Debts not affected by discharge. Chapter III, Section 17 of the Bankruptcy Act provides that a discharge in bankruptcy releases the bankrupt from all his provable debts, whether allowable in full or in part, incurred before the petition was filed, except the following debts, which remain a claim against him even after a discharge in bankruptcy has been granted:

1 Unpaid taxes which became legally due and owing by the bankrupt to the United States or any state or subdivision thereof within 3 years preceding bankruptcy, including taxes that were not assessed because the bankrupt failed to make a return as required by law, failed to report on his return basis for the assessment, or made a false or fraudulent return in an attempt to evade the assessment

2 Liabilities for obtaining money or property by false pretenses or false representations, or malicious injuries to the person or property of another, or alimony due or to become due, for maintenance or support of wife or child, or for the seduction of an unmarried female, or for breach of promise of marriage accompanied by seduction, or for criminal conversation

3 Unscheduled claims unless creditors had notice or actual knowledge of the proceedings in bankruptcy

4 Debts created by the bankrupt's fraud, embezzlement. misappropriation, or defalcation while acting as an officer or in any fiduciary capacity

5 Wages earned by employees within 3 months prior to date of commencement of proceedings in bankruptcy

6 Moneys received from an employee to secure the faithful performance of such employee in accordance with the terms of the contract

To the above may be added all debts incurred *after* the petition has been filed. All creditors whose claims fall in any of the above groups may proceed with the enforcement of collection as if no bankruptcy proceedings had taken place.

NONBANKRUPTCY RELIEF PROVISIONS OF THE BANKRUPTCY ACT

Adjudication of bankruptcy and the discharge of a debtor's obligations resulting from these proceedings are obviously not the best solution, from the standpoint of the debtor or his creditors, for many problems of insolvency. Friendly adjustment is frequently an alternative, but while this means avoiding some of the expense and stigma involved in bankruptcy, it lacks some of the force and finality of settlement made under court jurisdiction. Consequently, there have been provided in the Bankruptcy Act several legal remedies which are short of bankruptcy yet which provide some of the advantages desired. Among them are three discussed briefly below: namely, settlement by arrangement, corporate reorganization, and wage earners' plans.

Settlement by arrangements. It has already been brought out in Chap. 27 that a composition at common law is a contract entered into by an insolvent debtor and his creditors, whereby the debtor settles the claims against him at an agreed percentage of their face value, provided the creditors mutually promise to release him from the balance of his indebtedness. Such a settlement is binding, however, only upon those creditors who consent to it. To effect similar adjustments and make them binding upon all creditors is the purpose of Chapter XI, having to do with compositions and extensions of unsecured debts, and Chapter XII, covering real property arrangements by persons other than corporations. An "arrangement" is defined therein as "any plan of a debtor for the settlement, satisfaction, or extension of the time of payment of his unsecured debts, upon any terms."

Composition arrangement for unsecured debts. Under Chapter XI a debtor may file a petition, stating that he is insolvent or unable to pay his debts as they mature and setting forth the terms of his proposed arrangement. The petition must be accompanied by a statement of the debtor's executory contracts, his schedules, a statement of his affairs, and the filing fee. If proceedings in bankruptcy are already pending, no new filing fee need be paid nor is it necessary to file new schedules or a new statement of affairs. Furthermore, such proceedings may be stayed by the court pending action on the petition for an arrangement.

The judge may refer the proceeding to a referee and upon application of interested parties appoints a receiver unless the estate is already in the hands of a trustee in bankruptcy. Appraisers may then be appointed to prepare an inventory and appraisal of the debtor's property. Upon 10 days' notice, a meeting of creditors is called, the notice being accompanied by a copy of the proposed arrangement and a summary of assets and liabilities as shown by the schedules. In this notice may also be named the time for filing of the application to confirm the arrangement as well as the time for the hearing on the application and objections thereto. Either the judge or the referee may preside at this meeting, where proofs of claim are received and allowed or disallowed, the debtor is examined, and written acceptances of creditors on the proposition are received and passed upon. At this meeting or thereafter a receiver or trustee is appointed whose task it is to receive and distribute the consideration to be deposited by the debtor. Creditors may also appoint a committee and nominate a trustee who is later appointed by the court if it should become necessary to administer the estate in bankruptcy.

If at the meeting of creditors an arrangement has been accepted in writing by all creditors affected thereby, the court confirms it. Otherwise, it must be accepted by a majority in number of all creditors and amount of all claims allowed before an application for confirmation of the arrangement may be filed with the court. If creditors are divided into classes, such as small versus large creditors, or borrowed money versus merchandise creditors, it is necessary to obtain a majority both in number of creditors and in amount of claims in each class. The judge thereupon confirms the arrangement, if he is satisfied that: (1) it is for the best interests of the creditors; (2) it is fair, equitable, and feasible; (3) the debtor has not been guilty of any act or failed to perform any duty which would prevent the discharge of a bankrupt; and (4) the proposal has been offered and accepted in good faith.

Upon confirmation, the terms of the arrangement are binding upon the debtor and *all* creditors. The court retains jurisdiction of the case until all claims subject to the arrangement have been allowed or disallowed. But the debtor is discharged from all his unsecured debts immediately after the confirmation and the fulfillment of his obligations thereunder, except for debts that are not dischargeable in bankruptcy. When the proceeding is consummated, the court enters a final decree discharging the receiver or trustee and closing the estate.

If an arrangement is withdrawn or abandoned prior to its acceptance, or is not accepted, or its terms are violated by the debtor, the court either dismisses the proceeding or, upon hearing after due notice to all interested parties, enters an order adjudging the debtor a bankrupt. If the case is already in bankruptcy, proceedings, if stayed, are resumed upon failure of the arrangement to materialize. But even here no adjudication can be entered against a wage earner (in the archaic sense used for bankruptcy purposes) or farmer without his consent in writing.

An evaluation of the efficacy of arrangements under Chapter XI is most difficult to make. From one point of view it has fallen far short of reasonable expectations. For example, during fiscal year 1966 only 1,060 such relief cases were concluded, and of these, about 10 per cent were dismissed, 52 per cent were adjudicated bankrupt, and only 406, or 38 per cent, were concluded as confirmed arrangements in the form of compositions and extensions. From another point of view, this relief provision may be considered successful even in the limited sense. First, the 406 arrangements concluded represented big cases with average liabilities about fifteen times those of the 18,532 asset cases concluded under straight bankruptcy during the same year. Moreover, the 406 cases under arrangements involved in total debts affected as much as 32 per cent of total claims allowed in the 18,532 bankruptcies with assets. But even more important, the amounts paid to creditors under the arrangements ($22,883,529 under composition and $31,259,694 under extension) were 38.6 per cent of the liabilities as compared with 6.9 per cent paid to unsecured creditors in the straight bankruptcy asset cases concluded.

Corporate reorganizations. Chapter X, which provides for corporate reorganizations (except banks, insurance companies, municipalities, railroads, and building and loan associations), is an adjunct to the Bankruptcy Act intended for true reorganizations involving a readjustment of the rights of secured creditors or holders of securities and not for the purpose of effecting ordinary compositions with unsecured creditors. It places under the jurisdiction of the bankruptcy courts proceedings formerly handled under Federal equity receiverships, combining for the most part the procedure used in equity cases with that used in bankruptcy. A petition for reorganization may be filed voluntarily by the corporation itself, by three or more creditors with total claims of $5,000 or more, or by an indenture trustee of outstanding securities.

In order to qualify for relief under this chapter of the Act, the corporation must be insolvent in the bankruptcy sense or unable to meet current obligations as they mature and to have committed an act of bankruptcy within 4 months prior to filing of petition.   It must also state that one of the conditions specified in Chapter X, Section 131, exists. Approval of the petition is usually based on the allegations contained therein, although the debtor and the creditors are given a chance to file a controverting answer and to be heard.   If the petition is approved, no order of adjudication is entered.   Creditors, stockholders, indenture trustees, and the Securities and Exchange Commission are then notified of a hearing to be held not less than 30 and not more than 60 days after approval of petition, to determine whether the debtor shall remain in possession of the property or a trustee shall be appointed.   In the meantime, the judge may appoint a temporary trustee to take over the business, and if the debt involved is $250,000 or over, the appointment of a trustee becomes mandatory.   A reorganization plan is worked out and filed with the court, on which a hearing is held, upon due notice to creditors, for the consideration of and, perhaps, definite action on the plan.   No definite time limit for the filing of reorganization plans is fixed by law.   Plans may be proposed by creditors, stockholders, the debtor, the trustee, or the examiner.

Prior to confirming a reorganization plan, the judge must be sure that the plan approved by him has been accepted in writing, filed in court, in the case of insolvency of the corporation, by at least two-thirds of each class of creditors affected by the plan, *in amount,* and if solvent, by a majority of each class of stock.   The number of creditors, unlike ordinary bankruptcy proceedings and compositions, is irrelevant, the amount of claims consenting to the plan being the main consideration. Moreover, creditors have no voice in the choice of a trustee and can only vote upon acceptance or rejection of a reorganization plan, although they may be heard on other questions.   When the plan is confirmed, its provisions are binding upon the debtor and all creditors and stockholders, including a dissenting minority which in an equity court is able to block all plans of reorganization.   The judge then enters a decree discharging the debtor and the trustee and closing the estate.   Failure to consummate a plan may result in a dismissal of the proceeding or in an adjudication in bankruptcy.

Wage earners' plans. Prior to the enactment of the substantially revised bankruptcy law in 1938, an insolvent wage earner was faced with two alternatives: either to go through regular bankruptcy or to leave his wages subject to attachment and garnishment under the various state laws.   The latter, of course, often resulted in loss of employment, for an employer does not wish to be harassed by court orders at frequent intervals. Consequently, although a wage earner cannot be forced into bankruptcy by his creditors, little real protection is afforded by this limitation even to honest debtors, partly because the archaic definition of a wage earner for bankruptcy purposes as a worker earning less than $1,500 a year probably applies in modern times to less than a sixth of the employees going into bankruptcy but largely because of the pressure by creditors referred to above. Chapter XIII of the Bankruptcy Act was intended to correct this condition, first, by broadening the scope of the term "wage earner" for purposes of these plans, and second, by providing the machinery for nonbankruptcy relief discussed below.

Under Chapter XIII, a wage earner is an individual "whose principal income is derived from wages, salary or commissions," rather than one earning a maximum of $1,500 from wages, salary, or hire, as defined for purposes of straight bankruptcy. A petition filed under this chapter must state that the debtor is insolvent or unable to pay his debts as they mature. It is filed with the Federal court in his jurisdiction stating his desire to effect a composition settlement or an extension, or both, out of his future earnings or wages. With this petition he submits his schedules of assets and liabilities and a statement of affairs and pays a fee of $15, of which $10 goes to the Treasury of the United States for deposit in the referees' salary and expense fund and $5 to the clerk.

The proceeding may be referred by the judge to the referee, who promptly calls a meeting of creditors, giving them 10 days' notice thereof. At that meeting, proofs of claims are received and allowed, the debtor is examined, witnesses may be heard, and the debtor submits his plan and deposits with the referee not more than $15 to cover expenses of the proceeding. If any other costs are involved, they are to be paid out of the fund as it accumulates from future earnings of the debtor. From this point on, the proceeding is no different from that followed in effecting an arrangement.

Under this plan the wage earner subjects his future earnings to the supervision and control of the court, thereby removing the possibility of garnishment by creditors. The portion agreed upon is paid over to the court at regular intervals, and out of this fund an equitable distribution is made among the creditors. Usually, a wage earner's plan includes only unsecured creditors, although it may contain provisions dealing with secured creditors provided all of the latter affected by the plan agree to it.

Altogether, 26,206 cases were concluded in fiscal 1966 under this chapter. Of these, nearly 49 per cent were dismissed, 11 per cent were adjudicated in bankruptcy, and about 40 per cent were in the nature of confirmed arrangements. Most interesting is the fact that of the 10,529 arrangements under these plans, involving a total of over $20 million in debts, or about $2,000 per case, creditors were paid as much as 92 per cent, which means that relatively few of the arrangements were in the nature of composition settlements. It is also significant that over 10,000 persons with considerable debt were spared the stigma of bankruptcy and that presumably satisfactory arrangements could be effected between reasonable debtors on the one hand and reasonable creditors on the other. Perhaps this offers much encouragement for greater use of such plans in the future.

APPRAISAL
OF REGULAR
BANKRUPTCY
PROCEDURE

Despite the many good features and laudable purposes of the Bankruptcy Act, there are some important weaknesses in it. Some of the defects are inherent in the legislation, some may be laid at the doors of creditors, and most of them relate more specifically to the administration of the law.

Major weaknesses of the Bankruptcy Act and its administration. The weaknesses pointed out below refer only to regular or ordinary bankruptcy procedure and do not relate to the application of the several non-bankruptcy provisions included in the Bankruptcy Act, some evaluation of which has already been made at appropriate places.

First, the procedure is too cumbersome. It is highly legalistic and thereby impedes expeditious disposition of cases. This is evident from the very enumeration of all the parties involved in an ordinary bankruptcy case, including bankrupts and their attorneys, creditors and their attorneys, receivers and their attorneys, trustees and their attorneys, referees, appraisers, auctioneers, and others (see, for illustrative purposes, Table 28-1).

Second, and probably because the procedure is so complicated and cumbersome, an inordinately high expense is incurred in the administration of bankruptcy cases, absorbing about one-fourth of all proceeds realized in asset cases, about 40 per cent of such costs being for attorneys' fees. Each bankruptcy case is administered separately and must carry the expense of a separate and independent management by receivers, trustees, appraisers, auctioneers, and attorneys.

Third, and probably one of the greatest weaknesses, is the apparent gross inefficiency with which bankrupt estates are generally administered. Even in the very prosperous years covered by the data in Table 28-1, when merchandise and other property could be readily disposed of at good prices, the proceeds realized in asset cases averaged below 30 per cent of the liabilities involved. In poorer years this is likely to fall considerably below 20 per cent. It would seem that many trustees elected to take over the bankrupt estate and liquidate it for the benefit of creditors either know next to nothing about the business or do not care, taking too much time to perform their duties or selling out the entire stock of goods to a single buyer for a small fraction of its true value, thus ridding themselves of the job.

A fourth and perhaps an even more important explanation for the small amounts realized from the liquidation of bankrupt estates is to be found in the dishonesty which has pervaded the administration of our bankruptcy laws; not dishonesty in the courts or on the part of referees, but dishonesty on the part of many of the attorneys, trustees, and others involved in such cases. There has hardly been a city of real size in the United States which has not had one or more bankruptcy rings. The common method of operating a bankruptcy ring is for an attorney, or a group of attorneys, to solicit claims against a bankrupt from the different creditors. With these claims in their possession they are then in a position to elect as a trustee one of their colleagues who, in turn, sells the property of the bankrupt at ridiculously low figures to another member of the ring, and, when the case is finally closed, the property is disposed of at its real value and the difference is split among all the parties in the ring. Many attempts have been made by associations of credit men, bar associations, and the Federal judges to break up these rings. These attempts have not always been successful.

Fifth, many dishonest debtors have frequently escaped by the door of bankruptcy. In many instances all the assets are not collected, and discharges are not fought by creditors, except in extraordinary cases. Bankruptcy has thus become a means of enrichment to persons with fraudulent designs and so far has failed to accomplish fully the fundamental purposes for which it was designed. This is attested to by the number of bankrupts who have been denied a discharge and even more by the much larger number that waived a discharge or did not apply for it, probably because they could not have gotten it.

Sixth, even in the prosperous years covered by the data in Table 28-1, the dividends received by unsecured creditors from the proceeds in asset cases approximated only 8 cents on the dollar of their allowed claims. Such dividends seldom exceed 10 cents on the dollar, and quite often they approach but one-half that amount on the average. This is usually enough to discourage unsecured creditors from participating actively and interestedly in bankruptcy cases, yet the effectiveness of the law's administration is predicated on creditors' active interest and participation. To make the law effective, creditors must exercise their preroga-

table 28-1 *Statistical Summary of Bankruptcy* Cases Handled in the United States District Courts during Recent Specified Years*
(Amounts expressed in thousands of dollars)

	Year ending June 30			
Item	*1950*	*1955*	*1960*	*1966*
Cases pending and concluded:				
Pending at close of previous year	30,566	48,428	84,273	162,372
Commenced during the year	33,392	59,404	110,034	192,354
Terminated during the year	25,582	52,240	99,317	186,219
Pending at close of the year	38,376	55,592	94,990	168,507
Cases referred or commenced during the year:				
Voluntary	32,008	58,147	108,729	191,181
Farmers	290	386	453	551
Employees	22,933	46,163	89,639	160,299
Businesses	6,561	7,343	10,041	14,093
All others	2,224	4,255	8,596	16,238
Involuntary	1,384	1,257	1,305	1,173
Businesses	1,375	1,239	1,295	n.a.
All others	9	18	10	n.a.
Cases concluded during the year:				
Without declaration of bankruptcy	5,083	10,249	15,372	31,020
Dismissed	2,923	4,710	9,050	20,028
Under nonbankruptcy sections or chapters	2,160	5,539	6,322	10,992
After declaration of bankruptcy:				
Asset cases	3,792	6,320	10,485	18,532
Nominal- and no-asset cases	18,755	35,671	73,460	136,667
Discharges:				
Asset cases:				
Granted	2,898	4,848	8,490	15,920
Denied	126	123	167	140
Waived or not applied for	978	1,349	1,828	2,472
Nominal- and no-asset cases:				
Granted	15,913	34,603	71,983	135,006
Denied	211	319	932	666
Waived or not applied for	583	749	545	995
Amount of liabilities:				
Asset cases	$97,748	$156,601	$235,449	$440,395
Nominal-asset cases	23,595	45,520	117,191	349,926
No-asset cases	93,956	201,463	469,866	n.a.

table 28-1 *Statistical Summary of Bankruptcy* Cases Handled in the United States District Courts during Recent Specified Years (Continued) (Amounts expressed in thousands of dollars)*

Item	Year ending June 30			
	1950	1955	1960	1966
Proceeds realized from asset cases:				
Gross amount	$29,174	$38,381	$63,282	$99,385
Per cent of total liabilities	29.8%	24.5%	26.9%	22.6%
Distribution of proceeds realized in asset cases:				
Administrative fees and expenses	$6,827	$10,211	$16,130	$24,617
To creditors	21,408	26,772	44,150	71,410
All other payments	939	1,398	3,002	3,358
Proceeds realized in asset cases paid to creditors, as per cent of claims allowed;				
Priority creditors	30.6%	24.4%	37.7%	36.2%
Secured creditors	72.1%	60.4%	66.8%	62.6%
Unsecured creditors	9.7%	7.8%	8.4%	6.9%
Distribution of administrative fees and expenses, as per cent of gross proceeds realized in asset cases:				
Receivers; commissions and expenses	1.5%	1.5%	1.3%	1.2%
Referees; salary fund, expense fund, etc.	3.1%	4.4%	3.6%	3.5%
Trustees; commissions, expenses, etc	6.6%	6.1%	6.0%	6.4%
Auctioneers' fees and expenses	1.6%	1.7%	1.6%	1.7%
Appraisers' fees and expenses	0.5%	0.5%	0.5%	0.4%
Rental expense	1.0%	1.4%	1.5%	1.3%
Attorneys for:				
Creditors	0.6%	0.6%	0.5%	0.4%
Bankrupts	1.5%	1.8%	1.6%	1.4%
Receivers	1.0%	1.4%	1.1%	1.0%
Trustees	6.0%	7.2%	7.8%	7.1%
Others	......	......	......	0.4%
Total expense	23.4%	26.6%	25.5%	24.8%

* Including in some of the data cases coming under the relief or nonbankruptcy provisions of the Act. n.a. not available.

SOURCE: Adapted and computed from the *Tables of Bankruptcy Statistics*, published annually by the Administrative Office of the United States Courts, Washington, D.C., for submittal to the Congress in accordance with the provisions of Section 53 of the Bankruptcy Act.

tives, attend creditors' meetings, insist upon a thorough examination of the bankrupt before accepting an offer for an arrangement, and, above all, must cooperate with other creditors instead of acting alone or through the medium of dishonest bankruptcy practitioners. Creditors must realize that the bankrupt estates are their property and that larger dividends will be forthcoming if they would protect that property as if it were in their own possession. If bankruptcy abuses continue, no longer is it possible for creditors to blame faulty legislation to the same extent as in the past. A larger share of such responsibility must be assumed directly by the creditors themselves and it is now mainly in their hands that the remedy lies.

Finally, the cumbersome and expensive procedure that is used in asset cases has been applied to what is known as nominal-asset cases and even to no-asset cases. The latter two types of cases make up over 80 per cent of all bankruptcy cases and account at times for over 70 per cent of the liabilities involved. As there is nothing for creditors in these cases, whatever becomes available in nominal-asset cases being eaten up by expense, it is sheer folly to apply to them the same techniques and complicated procedures as those used for asset cases, yet that is just what is being done. Obviously, there is need for a simplified business procedure for the handling of such cases. That would clear the legal and other machinery for more effective performance in asset cases for the legitimate benefit of all concerned.

Criticism of bankruptcy from a social point of view. The relatively large increase in the number of bankruptcy cases filed in recent years, as shown in Table 28-2, has given rise to much criticism of the Bankruptcy Act and, more specifically, of the possible causes. What the exact nature of the criticism is depends upon the position of the critic. For example, creditors feel that the number of bankruptcies should be discouraged by allowing the Federal judge or the referee in bankruptcy leeway in determining whether straight bankruptcy adjudication should be replaced by action under the relief provisions of such chapters (especially XI and XIII) as might require repayment of the full amount. They also feel that if the minimum indebtedness required in filing an involuntary petition were raised by law from the present requirement of $1,000 to $2,000 and a similar requirement were applied to voluntary cases, the temptation for bankruptcy adjudication would be substantially diminished. Two studies indicate that such a requirement would reduce the number of personal bankruptcies by as much as 20 to 25 per cent.[7]

Critics concerned with social legislation take a different view of

---

[7] Brunner, *op. cit.*, p. 56; and Harry Lee Mathews, "Causes of Personal Bankruptcies in Ohio," unpublished doctoral dissertation, The Ohio State University, 1966, Table 16.

the situation. To them the figures shown in Table 28-2 are alarming because they are supposed to reflect much suffering of the underprivileged, and to that end they cite the proportion of total bankruptcy filings that is made by persons not in business or the professions. Furthermore, they attribute this plight to a probable overextension of credit, for which all blame is placed upon creditors rather than its users, and to harsh state laws on garnishments and wage assignments for which there seems to be little evidence of any causal relationship.[8] To some critics the

---

[8] *Mathews, op. cit.,* **pp. 34–41, including Table 6.**

table 28-2 *Bankruptcy Cases Commenced during the Fiscal Year Ending June 30, 1950-1967*

	Total		*Straight bankruptcy*		*Nonbusiness cases**	
Year	*Number (col. 1)*	*Rate of increase (col. 2)*	*Number (col. 3)*	*Per cent of col. 1 (col. 4)*	*Number (col. 5)*	*Per cent of col. 1 (col. 6)*
1950	33,392	28.3	26,632	79.8	25,040	75.0
1951	35,193	5.4	27,693	78.7	27,806	79.0
1952	34,873	(0.9)	26,949	77.3	28,331	81.2
1953	40,087	15.0	30,879	77.0	33,315	83.1
1954	53,136	32.6	42,733	80.4	44,248	83.3
1955	59,404	11.8	48,899	82.3	50,219	84.5
1956	62,086	4.5	51,899	83.6	52,608	84.7
1957	73,761	18.8	61,524	83.4	63,617	86.2
1958	91,668	24.3	77,461	84.5	80,265	87.6
1959	100,672	9.8	86,790	86.2	88,943	88.3
1960	110,034	9.3	95,710	87.0	97,750	88.8
1961	146,643	33.3	125,830	85.8	131,402	89.6
1962	147,780	0.8	123,881	83.8	132,125	89.5
1963	155,493	5.2	129,814	83.5	139,191	89.5
1964	171,719	10.4	143,167	83.4	155,209	90.4
1965	180,323	5.0	151,137	83.8	163,413	90.6
1966	192,354	6.7	163,013	84.7	175,924	9.15
1967	208,329	8.3	173,884	83.5	191,729	92.0

* Practically all voluntary cases. Includes so-called "personal" bankruptcies.
SOURCE: *Tables of Bankruptcy Statistics* published annually by the Administrative Office of the United States Courts, Supreme Court Building, Washington, D.C.

personal bankruptcy figures reflect a moral deterioration of our people, lack of prudent financial management of personal affairs, or the results of living hazards involving illness, accidents, liability judgments, etc.

The truth of the matter is that there is little, if any, justification for some of the criticisms in the last two categories, mainly because of absence of reliable factual data as a base, as well as because of failure to distinguish between *apparent* and *true* causes of bankruptcy. To begin with, the so-called "factual data" used from the *Tables of Bankruptcy Statistics* are not what they are interpreted by their users to be.   In the first place, the filings data generally used include filings under the nonbankruptcy provisions of the Act, which in the 6-year period of 1961–1966 represented 15.8 per cent of all filings, of which but a small proportion (from 10 to 15 per cent) wound up as adjudicated bankruptcies.   Second, many of the filings, especially of the personal bankruptcy type, are duplications, for in many cases the wife who may have signed a note on the husband's borrowings or purchases simultaneously files a *companion* petition in bankruptcy when her husband files a petition. Third, filings are not synonymous with bankruptcies.   During 1961–1966, the same 6-year period referred to above, 4.5 per cent of all straight bankruptcy cases concluded were dismissed without adjudication, which means that they did not turn out to be bankruptcy cases at all.   Finally, the data on so-called "nonbusiness" or "personal" cases are inflated by the fact that quite a number of the cases filed by employees at the time had really incurred the indebtedness from which relief was sought when they were in business; this can be seen from the information given in the "Statement of Affairs" for the preceding 6 years as well as from the nature and amount of the indebtedness.   Apparently, as interpreted, the number of personal bankruptcies is grossly exaggerated, perhaps by as much as 25 per cent or more.

It would seem that until accurate information is obtained on the number of straight bankruptcies and the exact status of those filing petitions in that way it would be preposterous to attempt to find causes or to place major responsibility for the increase, if any, in the number of bankruptcies or in the liabilities involved.   For many years sociologists and social workers have been dealing with this problem and have developed a number of *theories,* but there is need for facts and verification of the theories.   With this in view, two elaborate studies, but still on a limited scale, were undertaken under the senior author's supervision, the results of which have shed some needed light on the subject.[9]   Much more remains to be done.   Until that void is filled, there will remain an open field for crackpots, social welfare "do gooders," and many well-

---

[9] See Brunner, *op. cit.,* also Mathews, *op. cit.*

meaning and otherwise sophisticated thinkers concerned with the problems of efficient business management and social well-being for all sorts of speculation and for many questionable diagnoses, prognoses, and remedies.

QUESTIONS AND PROBLEMS

1 What was the public attitude toward debtors and their possibility of going through bankruptcy under:

  a Mosaic law

  b Roman law

  c Old English law

  d Our state insolvency laws prior to the adoption of the Federal Bankruptcy Act

2 Does your answer to the above question and the history of bankruptcy legislation from 1800 to 1898 suggest a narrow or enlightened position along economic lines? How is that to be explained?

3 A called B a bankrupt because B could not or would not pay his bills to A. Could B have any legal recourse against A?

4 What are the two *major* purposes of bankruptcy legislation? Which, in your opinion, is the more important of the two?

5 Under what circumstances would resort be made to bankruptcy rather than to some form of friendly adjustment? What provisions for settlement are made by the Bankruptcy Act other than outright, or straight, bankruptcy?

6 What condition or conditions must exist before bankruptcy proceedings can be successfully initiated: voluntarily? involuntarily?

7 Does a debtor have the opportunity to defend himself against being forced into bankruptcy? In what way?

8 Outline the steps in bankruptcy procedure, showing specifically the duties and responsibilities of the following: the debtor; a creditor; the receiver, if any; the judge or clerk of the district court; the referee; the trustee. Whom does each of these represent?

9 What is the purpose and business of the first meeting of creditors?

10 What debts can never be discharged in bankruptcy? Are there any reasons for such provision in the law? Are all such reasons equally valid?

11 Under what circumstances is a debtor denied a discharge in bankruptcy:

  a In voluntary proceedings

  b In involuntary cases

12 Contrast settlement by arrangement under the Bankruptcy Act with a composition settlement as a friendly means of adjustment.

13 Is the provision of the Bankruptcy Act governing corporate reorganizations an alternative to bankruptcy proceedings? For whose benefit is this intended?

14 If you were a wage earner considerably in debt, under what circumstances might you resort to each of the following to meet or otherwise discharge your obligations:

    a Borrow from a personal finance company

    b File a petition in bankruptcy

    c Seek a settlement under a wage earners' plan

    d Merely allow the debt to continue unpaid

15 Mr. X, a wage earner, has had considerable sickness in his family. As a result, his indebtedness ran up to about $5,000. Would you recommend that he secure a discharge from his obligations through bankruptcy proceedings? Why or why not? How else can the situation be handled under the present bankruptcy law? Would your answer be different if the indebtedness were only $1,700?

16 Mr. A, an operator of a drugstore, is in financial difficulties and finds it impossible to meet his obligations with promptness. In fact, there are a number of creditors with claims against him which are 6 months ovedue. Assuming that the creditors wish to throw A into bankruptcy, what kind of proceedings would have to be instituted? In order to have the debtor declared a bankrupt, what conditions must be fulfilled?

17 What are the possibilities of establishing the following as prior claims in bankruptcy?

    a A check given by a customer in payment of an account just before the customer goes into the hands of a receiver in bankruptcy

    b Wages owed to the employees of a bankrupt corporation

18 X was discharged in bankruptcy. Some time later he promised one of his creditors that he would pay him the unpaid balance on a bankrupt account within 1 year. At the end of the year, X refused to pay his creditor, claiming immunity because of his previous discharge of that obligation in bankruptcy. Can the creditor enforce payment or has his claim been fully discharged once and for all?

19 On the basis of the data in Table 28-1, make an analysis of the major defects in our bankruptcy law and its administration, and indicate possible remedies.

20 In the absence of any other knowledge or information, what conclusions might you draw from the data presented in Table 28-2? Would such conclusions be of any social significance? Explain.

21 In what ways may responsibility for increased numbers of personal bankruptcies be placed upon creditors, debtors, and society, respectively? List them for each.

22 Do the analysis and correct interpretation of official and published data on bankruptcy justify most of the criticisms often made against bankruptcy from the viewpoint of causes? What light is shed on this phase of the subject by recent academic studies of causes of personal bankruptcies? Explain.

management control of credit and collection operations

From a strictly managerial viewpoint, the ultimate aim in credit and collection management is not, as is often claimed, a mere control of or reduction in risk incident to this phase of a firm's business. That is but one of the major objectives. Others, as previously discussed, are to maximize both sales and business volume as well as the productivity of the capital invested in receivables. In effect, then, the ultimate aim in the long run is to maximize profitability of the enterprise through the effective and efficient performance of the credit and collection functions. Just how this may best be done has been the basic substance presented throughout this book wherever it was treated from the standpoint of the individual enterprise engaged in credit business.

Whether sound credit and collection management has been used by a given firm, in accordance with accepted valid theory and good practice as discussed throughout this volume, is to be judged largely by results achieved. Such results are in the form of prerogatives used in minimizing risk of loss from bad debts through such possible transfer as discussed in the first chapter of this part dealing with credit insurance and the use of credit limits as discussed in the second chapter of this part. To a considerable extent, the results obtained must be evaluated by use of standards of performance and the development of devices for proper measurement as discussed in the last chapter of this book. The extremely dynamic nature of credit management calls for frequent measurement and evaluation as tests of the effect of changes instituted from time to time. It is the task of this part of the book to provide credit and collection management with a perspective as well as with essential guides for an impartial evaluation of accomplishments.

CHAPTER TWENTY-NINE

credit insurance

As shown in Chap. 14, it is possible under certain limited circumstances for a mercantile creditor to shift all credit risks and even the functions of credit and collection management to a factor. It is also possible to shift losses in part to an insurance carrier. This latter type of credit protection or control through risk shifting is known as credit insurance. This does not, however, obviate the necessity for the adoption of measures which make for effective management of the credit and collection functions and the use of such controls as are discussed in the two chapters that follow.

Nature of credit insurance. The basic principle underlying this type of insurance is identical with that upon which all kinds of insurance are founded, namely, the law of averages applicable to the type of risk in question. This field of insurance is probably riskier, however, for the insurance company because it lacks the time dimension in risk diversi-fication characteristic of other types of insurance. While the commercial credit insurance company can diversify its risk within a given period of time, such as a year (the usual term of a policy), its operation is superimposed upon cyclical fluctuations that may affect both quality and quantity of risks it accepts.

Credit insurance does not provide protection against *all* losses which a creditor may experience from bad debts; it is instead the applica-tion of the insurance principle to the probability of *losses in excess of an agreed amount* known as "primary loss," which approximates the nor-mal loss incident to the particular business of the insured. Within the limitations spelled out by the several provisions of the policy, variously styled as the bond of indemnity or the policy of credit guaranty, credit insurance is protection that the merchandise shipped on credit terms will be paid for and that bad debt losses over and above those normally anticipated by the insured will be kept under some degree of control.

Finally, the commercial credit insurance discussed in this chapter should be distinguished from so-called consumer credit insurance, which is really credit *life* insurance that insures borrowers to cover loans in case of death, and retail credit insurance. Properly used, credit insur-ance has nothing to do with life insurance of any form or with any opera-tions on the retail level.

Development and present status. Credit insurance has been available on some scale since the early part of the nineteenth century and today is provided for creditors in a number of the important commer-cial countries of the world. Credit insurance is known to have been offered as early as 1837; however, prior to 1898, when the national Bankruptcy Act was passed, credit insurance business was largely in an experimental stage, the only policies written being of a restricted nature and at relatively low premium rates. After 1898, policies were liberalized from time to time until they have come to include all types of legal insolvency and, in addition, the nonpublic insolvency of compro-mise. With regard to the latter, it is possible for a debtor to compromise his indebtedness with the majority of his creditors without any public record of the adjustment.

Two insurance companies have been foremost in the development and promotion of credit insurance in the United States. The American Credit Indemnity Company of New York, at present the leading credit insurance underwriter, was incorporated in 1893. In 1936, it was ac-quired by the Commercial Credit Company, one of the large finance com-panies, and under this ownership it continues today to write policies for members of a wide variety of lines of business. The second company is the London Guarantee and Accident Company, Ltd., which established a credit insurance department in this country in 1892.

In the United States,[1] credit insurance is designed entirely for use by manufacturers, wholesalers, advertising agencies, and certain other service organizations dealing with business firms as partial protection against excessive or unanticipated bad debt losses within the limits of the policy. The protection is not available to retailers, i.e., concerns that sell to the ultimate consumer. While policies are carried by firms of all sizes and in most lines of business, the average-sized firm with sales between $1 million and $10 million constitutes the largest percentage of policyholders, followed by those with a volume of less than $1 million; the two groups account for more than 90 per cent of the insured concerns. Certain lines of trade are not insured because they are considered too hazardous from the standpoint of the nature of the goods handled, the flexibility of terms of sale, or the types of persons engaged in them. Rules as to what businesses are to be insured naturally change from time to time.

Basis of credit insurance rates. In insuring against a given contingency, the degree of risk must be determined by experience with respect to the average outcome of numerous similar cases handled over an extended period of time. Obviously, the accuracy with which the risk may be determined varies directly with the amount of data available regarding similar contingencies in the past, and the more accurate and scientific the computation of the risk, the less, within certain limits, the cost of insurance. To determine scientifically the degree of risk in a proposed extension of credit, it would be necessary to resort to a compilation of records covering failures of commercial houses, the causes therefor, and the financial condition of such concerns sometime prior to failure. Only from such records carefully kept over a period of years is it possible for credit insurance companies to determine with reasonable accuracy the extent of the risk in a given credit transaction.

No such statistical data were available until early in 1918, when the *Manual of Credit Insurance Rates,* now known as the *Standard Manual,* made its appearance. The Manual was the result of a long succession of mathematical calculations based on the experience of the credit insurance companies as revealed by their records covering a period of years.

As a result of this method of approach, the *Standard Manual* contains four primary loss tables for various businesses to which credit

---

[1] For discussion of the major features of "export credit insurance," which provides coverage on debtors located outside the United States, see Mark R. Greene, "Export Credit Insurance—Its Role in Expanding World Trade," *The Journal of Insurance,* June, 1965, pp. 177–193.

insurance is made available. One table applies where more than 50 per cent of the product is shipped to manufacturers and wholesalers; another, where more than 50 per cent of the product is shipped to dealers; a third, which represents by far the lowest primary loss figures, is used where the debtors covered are restricted to the prime risk; the fourth, the highest of the primary loss tables, is used with the L policy which represents the greatest hazard.

The system developed in the first Manual has been revised and expanded from year to year to keep pace with changing economic conditions, legal requirements, and degree of risk. This may signify that credit insurance is still in the experimental stage or is flexible, depending upon the point of view, or it may mean that the condition and soundness of certain lines of business are undergoing constant changes which call for adjustments in classification, changes in rates, and other modifications.

The American Credit Indemnity Company of New York acts as the statistical agent for both major companies in the business. It accumulates loss experience data based upon actual performance as shown by the historical record, and it applies these data in the calculation of primary loss rates and of premium rates. Thus, mortality tables and a factual basis have been developed for the rate structure. Obviously, because of the peculiar nature of credit insurance and the influence of business fluctuations, credit insurance cannot be as close to an exact science as are life and certain types of casualty insurance. That is why underwriting *judgment* plays an important role in the conduct of commercial credit insurance business.

Types of policies. In the past, individual account policies, as well as general coverage policies, were offered by both companies. The former types were designed to cover only single accounts selected by the insured. They have been discontinued by the American Credit Indemnity Company because for the most part such policies resulted in an adverse selection of risk against the insurance company and prevented adequate diversification of risks. While a few individual account policies were being written by the London Guarantee and Accident Company as late as 1960, practically all policies are now of the general coverage types which provide insurance on all the accounts of the insured subject to the provisions discussed below.

The two major groups into which credit insurance policies may be broken down are back-coverage and forward-coverage policies, respectively. Under the back-coverage policy the insurer agrees to reimburse the policyholder for losses occurring within the term of the policy, which usually covers a period of 1 year, including losses on sales made, shipped, and delivered prior to commencement date of the policy within a period not exceeding the longest terms of sale of the insured.

In the case of a first-year policy, this coverage obtains only on accounts that were not past due at date of policy commencement. For each renewal of that policy, the insurance company goes back for a full 12-month period and picks up all amounts owing whether they are past due or not. About 85 per cent of the premium income is derived from policies of this type.

Under the forward-coverage policy the losses covered must result from sales, shipments, and deliveries of merchandise within the term of the policy, the coverage continuing forward on the shipments made when the policy was in force until the debtor pays the bill or the account is filed with the insurance company as a loss. This type of policy naturally must have a definite termination date during which time the policy-holder must file his claims. Under the forward-coverage policy, the last day of the policy term is the final date by which accounts must be filed to be acceptable as claims against the policy.

Credit insurance policies may also be classified according to whether or not they contain a provision for the proving of past-due accounts as losses under the contract and for the handling of such accounts for collection purposes by the insurance company. As already indicated, most forward-coverage policies contain a compulsory filing provision of accounts for collection when they are 90 days past due. Under the back-coverage policy this is optional, although most of them contain the provision relating to past-due accounts. Only under two forms of policies, which are of relatively little significance premium-wise, is the policyholder required to handle his own accounts for collection purposes; these are generally written for policyholders who have their own established and well-organized collection departments and hence prefer to handle collections themselves.

Even the threefold classification indicated above falls far short of the mark in really characterizing credit insurance policies for the simple reason that all policies are tailor-made to fit the specific needs and, perhaps, desires of the insured. This is accomplished, as a result of both study and negotiation, by the attachment to the basic contract of a number of riders or endorsements which amend the terms of the basic contract.

It is thus possible, by means of endorsement and an additional premium or charge, to provide extraordinary coverage, i.e., coverage on certain accounts in amounts exceeding the maximum set by the insurance company for the various agency rating classifications, provided that co-insurance on all such extra coverage is raised from the normal of 10 per cent to 20 per cent. Again, by means of a limited coverage endorsement and an additional premium or charge, it is possible to cover debtors not otherwise included in the policy; but here, too, the coinsurance is 20 per cent or more.   In addition, a limit is specified as to loss allowable on a single debtor and as an aggregate for all accounts covered by the endorsement.

There is also a conditional exemption coinsurance endorsement, by means of which the coinsurance feature applying to debtors with a first or second credit rating may be waived.   Similarly, there is a conditional exemption of primary loss endorsement, whereby the primary loss applying to certain accounts with first or second credit ratings may also be waived.   Both of these conditional exemption endorsements may be attached to a given policy.

In 1960, both companies began offering a new standard policy, available in either the back-coverage or the forward-coverage form, in addition to their other standard types of policies.   Under this new policy, often referred to as the A or B $Form$, there is no coinsurance, and hence it is possible for the insured to be reimbursed in excess of the primary loss for the full invoiced price of the goods shipped.   The premium is naturally higher than in the case of policies requiring coinsurance.

Insolvency for purposes of policy. Credit insurance policies provide indemnity against losses occurring because of insolvency of debtors. The definition of the twelve conditions under which an account is accepted as being insolvent for the purpose of credit insurance policies is far more liberal (in the sense of being favorable to the insured) than the popular or legal concepts of the term.   As set forth in the policy, these conditions are as follows:

1 A debtor shall have absconded.

2 A sole debtor shall have died.

3 A sole debtor shall have been adjudged insane.

4 A receiver shall have been appointed for a debtor.

5 A debtor shall have transferred or sold his entire stock in trade under the appropriate provisions of the Uniform Commercial Code.

6 A writ of attachment or execution shall have been levied on a debtor's stock in trade and said stock sold thereunder, or the writ returned unsatisfied.

7 A debtor shall have made a general offer of compromise to his creditors for less than his indebtedness.

8 Possession shall have been taken under a chattel mortgage given by a debtor on his stock in trade.

9 A debtor's assets shall have been assigned to or taken over by a committee for the sole purpose of liquidation.

10 Possession shall have been taken of a debtor's assets under an assignment or deed of trust executed by the debtor for the benefit of his creditors.

11 A voluntary or involuntary proceeding shall have been instituted to adjudge a debtor bankrupt.

12 A proceeding for an arrangement of the debts of a debtor shall have been instituted in a court of bankruptcy.

In addition to the foregoing conditions of insolvency, most policies provide that, when the insured elects to file with the insurance company, for collection, an account which is not over 3 months past due under the original terms of sale, that account shall be treated in any adjustments under the policy as though the debtor had become insolvent.

BASIC ELEMENTS
OF A CREDIT
INSURANCE CONTRACT

In most general coverage policies there are four basic features: primary loss, coinsurance, coverage, and premium. All of them are necessarily interdependent, inasmuch as the premium charged depends not only upon the coverage afforded, but also indirectly upon the primary loss agreed upon. It is to some extent dependent also upon the percentage of coinsurance borne by the policyholder.

Primary loss. The primary loss is the bad debt loss which is intended to reflect the experience of the class of business of the insured, modified by the latter's own experience. In general, it is that amount of receivables which is *normally* lost or anticipated as a loss in a given business. Since the primary loss is calculable and anticipated, it must be considered a normal expense item like any manufacturing or selling cost incurred in the operation of the business. To insure against it, the premium would of necessity be equal to such loss and would have to provide in addition for the overhead costs and net profits of the insurance company. That is why credit insurance is intended only for losses which exceed the primary loss and are to that extent unexpected and unknown in advance.

There are separate tables of primary loss in the Manual; depending upon the type of coverage, the more liberal the coverage of the policy is, the greater the amount of primary loss. For general coverage policies, this loss has been averaging in recent years about 0.15 per cent of the estimated total sales of the policyholders. Final computation of the primary loss depends upon not only the loss experience in the particular line of business as shown in the Manual but also upon the insured's own experience. If the insured has had an unusually high loss ratio, his own experience governs. If, on the other hand, he has had an unusually good experience, then the loss ratio in the Manual is "merited" so as partially to reduce it in line with this good experience.

Coinsurance. Deductible in the credit insurance contract is what is known as coinsurance, which means that the insured is usually required to bear a portion of each loss covered by the policy, usually 10 per cent on accounts with first or second credit ratings and 20 per cent on off-rated accounts. This is sometimes compared to the 20 per cent coinsurance that may be deductible on business fire insurance or the $50 or $100 deductible on collision coverage in automobile insurance policies. For various reasons, especially because of the primary loss deduction in credit insurance for which there is nothing comparable in the other cases, the two are not exactly comparable. It should be pointed out, however, that the larger the coinsurance deduction, the smaller the premium charged. The coinsurance is deducted only from the covered portion of the account. If the policyholder should ship in amounts greater than the coverage in the policy, the entire amount of the excess obligation is borne by him and hence no coinsurance is deductible from such excess. To illustrate, on an account with a first or second credit rating, if the obligation were $4,100 but the coverage is only $3,000, the coinsurance would be $300, or 10 per cent of the amount covered.

For an additional premium the coinsurance deduction on first- and second-rated accounts can be eliminated in various policy forms. In the case of the newest standard form made available by the insurance companies, the *A* or *B Form,* no coinsurance is included.

Face amount and coverage. The protection afforded by a credit insurance policy lies in an area of loss determined, on the lower side, by the maximum primary loss the insured is willing to assume and, on the upper side, by the maximum losses which the underwriter will assume. This protection is determined by two principal factors. First, there is the *face amount of the policy,* which is the maximum *aggregate* loss for which the insurance company assumes responsibility. It is normal in any policy in any line of insurance to have a maximum liability defined. This *face amount* can be increased or decreased by the insured from the figure indicated in the original insurance proposal, with a consequent increase or decrease in the premium he pays. Legally, each of the credit insurance companies can go high in the face amount of a single policy, but in actual practice only a few insureds have needed as much as $1.5 million in face amount and have that maximum in their policies. Second, there is the maximum loss stipulated in the policy for individual accounts. Here, again, the amounts may change with a consequent change in the cost of the insurance.

The coverage afforded by a policy on any one account or rating group of accounts is dependent primarily upon two factors: the capital and credit rating of an account and the demand of the insured for specific coverage. Ratings are taken from standard rating books, a choice of which may be allowed the insured, although those of Dun & Bradstreet, Inc., are most often used for the purpose. The mercantile agency[2] whose ratings shall govern, as agreed upon by both parties when the policy is written, is specified in the policy. By an endorsement and an addition to the basic premium, it is possible to provide for the use of more than one mercantile agency, in which case there would be more than one governing rating for some of the customers of the policyholder.

For any rating group, the maximum coverage acceptable to the insurance company is published in a schedule such as shown in Fig. 29-1, wherein it is evident that the maximum coverage allowed varies not only with the pecuniary strength of a risk but also with the credit grade.

When a table like that illustrated in Fig. 29-1 is incorporated in a policy, it means that the insurance company is willing, without knowing who the debtor is, to provide the amount of coverage listed opposite each rating on each and every debtor having that rating at date of shipment. In addition, if desired, the insurance company will provide by special endorsements coverages by names of debtors where special lines are needed and/or an open single limit of coverage for nonrated accounts and for debtors with low ratings. Obviously, the extent and amount of coverage depends upon how much is needed and how much the insured is willing to spend for it.

It may be assumed that generally the insured buys only the coverages he needs. For example, as indicated in the table in Fig. 29-1, he can buy as much as $50,000 coverage for customers having a C + 1 rating, but if none of his customers with such a rating owe him more than $20,000 at one time, he will no doubt stipulate $20,000 as the amount he wants for that rating and pay correspondingly.

In buying increased lines of coverage for various debtors specifically named in the policy, there is no aggregate limit to the amounts

[2] Other mercantile agencies of a specialized type, the use of whose ratings is permitted by credit insurance companies in determining coverage, provided that they are specified in the policy, include:

    1 The Feakes Mercantile Agency, Inc.
    2 Jewelers Board of Trade
    3 Lumberman's Credit Association, Inc.
    4 Lyon Furniture Mercantile Agency
    5 Motor and Equipment Manufacturers Association
    6 Packer Produce Mercantile Agency
    7 Produce Reporter Company
    8 Smith Mercantile Agency

	Column one			Column two	
Rating		Gross amount covered	Rating		Gross amount covered
AA	A1	$150,000	AA	1	$50,000
A +	A1	$ 50,000	A +	1	$50,000
A	A1	$ 50,000	A	1	$50,000
B +	1	$ 50,000	B +	1½	$50,000
B	1	$ 50,000	B	1½	$50,000
C +	1	$ 50,000	C	1½	$25,000
(Blank)	1	$ 50,000	(Blank)	2	$15,000
C	1½	$ 30,000	C	2	$15,000
D +	1½	$ 25,000	D +	2	$12,500
D	1½	$ 20,000	D	2	$10,000
E	2	$ 10,000	E	2½	$ 5,000
F	2½	$ 5,000	F	3	$ 3,000
G	3	$ 2,500	G	3½	$ 1,500
H	3	$ 1,500	H	3½	$ 750
J	3	$ 1,000	J	3½	$ 500
K	3	$ 500			

figure 29-1. *Table of ratings and coverage, based on Dun & Bradstreet ratings.*

of such coverages on first- and second-rated accounts except with reference to the face amount of the policy. In the case of increased lines for accounts with lower ratings and nonrated accounts an aggregate is agreed upon because of the greater hazard represented by such customers.

The mercantile agency rating of the debtor at *date of shipment* governs the coverage in the credit insurance policy. If a debtor has more than one governing rating, the maximum indebtedness covered is limited to the largest amount set opposite either of the ratings. The latest published rating book must be used for determining the customer's rating, except where that rating is changed by a report of the agency or a supplement issued before such changed rating could appear in the regular reference or rating book. If the name of the debtor does not appear in the latest published rating book, the shipment is governed by the rating appearing in the latest agency report if compiled within 4 months prior to date of shipment; otherwise the shipment is governed by the rating appearing in the first report of the agency compiled within 4 months *after* date of shipment.

The insurance premium. There are two principal practices with respect to the determination of the premium paid by the insured for the risk underwritten by the insurance company.   In the majority of cases the entire premium is determined and paid in advance.   On policies with an available coverage endorsement, a portion of the premium is paid in advance and additional amounts are paid each month, calculated at the predetermined rate for first- and second-rated accounts, on the coverage actually used from month to month as shown by the policyholder's monthly reports.   On the average, the credit insurance premium tends to be around 0.089 per cent of the projected sales volume of the insured or that part of it which is covered by the policies.   In any event, for a proper gauge, the premium of around 0.089 per cent of projected sales, plus the primary loss which averages about 0.15 per cent of such sales on all general coverage policies, plus the coinsurance actually borne by the insured, should be compared with total losses from bad debts by all wholesalers, as shown in Chap. 13, of 0.19 per cent of credit sales.

Under all circumstances, the amount of premium varies with the degree of risk assumed by the underwriter and is determined after a careful consideration of the following factors:

1 The type of policy
2 Terms of sale, including dating
3 Projected total sales volume for the year ahead
4 Amount of coverage provided on first- and second-rated accounts
5 Amount and type of coverage provided for off-rated accounts
6 Extent of extraordinary coverage provided
7 Amount or face value of the policy
8 Other special endorsements

POLICY ANALYSIS

A clear understanding of the provisions of any insurance policy is of prime importance to the policyholder or to any collateral beneficiary, for the policy with its endorsements attached is the evidence of a legal contract containing warranties and representations of the insured, as well as duties, rights and privileges of the insurer.

Application. The application, signed by the applicant, is always part of a credit insurance policy.   General coverage forms of policies include 20 or more questions to be answered and filled in by the applicant, stating the total amount of coverage desired; percentage distribution of sales, by product; mercantile agency on which coverage is to be based;

the applicant's line of business; usual and longest terms of sale; approximate number of customers; territory served; previous collection experience; and sales and losses for the past 3 years and fractional year to date. Terms of sale not longer than those listed in the application should appear on all invoices that are to be covered under the policy. Further, a policyholder should be alert to the necessity for including in the policy any new product which he may add to his line of business during the policy term, in order that sales thereof may be covered.

The answers in the application represent warranties or representations upon which the insurer relies when assuming the risk. At common law, if a warranty is not absolutely true or fully performed, the insurance company may refuse to accept liability under the contract. In a few states, however, statutes have been passed which provide, in effect, that warranties are to be considered as representations which will not void a policy if they are *substantially* true or performed.

Insuring clause. The policy declaration contains the name, address, and line of business of the insured, face amount and term of the policy, percentage of coinsurance, and the primary loss stated both as a percentage of sales and as a minimum dollar amount. It should be noted that the face amount of the policy is the maximum amount for which the insurance company may be held liable under any combination of circumstances attaching to the policy, and not necessarily the amount of payment to the policyholder for any commensurate amount of credit losses. Coinsurance usually appears as 10 per cent in the insuring clause, but it normally applies only to first, second, and third grade credits, with endorsements to the policy changing the coinsurance to 20 per cent in the case of fourth grade and other off-rated accounts. Moreover, the minimum dollar amount of primary loss as listed in the insuring clause does not govern if covered sales during a policy term are higher than the estimate on which this amount was based, although the *percentage* of primary loss as stated in the insuring clause would apply to any experienced higher sales volume.

Filing of claims. With one insignificant exception, all policies provide for the privilege of filing accounts which are not more than 3 months past due under the original terms of sale when received by the insurance company, for treatment in any adjustment under the policy as though the debtor had become insolvent. Under back-coverage policies, the policyholder may elect not to file a past-due account with the insurance company, but failure to do so within 3 months after due date would mean that this account would thereafter be covered only to the extent of an actual insolvency as defined occurring during the policy term.

Under forward-coverage policies, the policyholder forgoes coverage entirely if he fails to file past-due accounts on or before the last day of the policy term. However, any past-due accounts which he files within 3 months after their due dates are accepted by the insurance company as claims on the same basis for settlement purposes as insolvent accounts. An account that is once filed and later withdrawn by the insured ceases to have coverage under any policy form.

In order that the loss on an insolvent account be covered, the policyholder must file notification of claim with the insurance company within 10 days after acquiring knowledge of a debtor's insolvency and must place the account in the hands of the insurance company for collection. A report of insolvency issued by a mercantile agency to which the insured subscribes is considered as knowledge of insolvency.

On all accounts placed with the insurance company for collection, the policyholder receives 10 days' free service. The insurance company also gives free service before adjustment on all insolvent accounts to the extent that they are covered by the policy. Commercial law league rates are charged for collection service if an attorney is used; otherwise, reduced rates are charged.

Time and method of adjustment. If any claim for loss is to be made under the policy, it must be made by the policyholder within 30 days after the expiration of the policy term, on a Final Statement of Claim form furnished by the insurance company. Adjustment will then be effected by the insurance company within 60 days of receipt of the final statement. Under the general provisions of the policy, a policyholder collects for a loss only after expiration of the policy, even though the loss may have occurred during the first few months of the policy term. By means of an interim adjustment rider and an additional premium, however, losses may be adjusted within 60 days after the interim claim is filed.

To ascertain the net loss on any adjustment, there is deducted from each gross loss covered, filed, and proved:

1 The net amount realized on any claim in which the insurance company has no interest

2 The net amount realized on any claim in excess of the gross amount covered, and

3 That portion of the net amount realized on any claim, equal to the percentage of coinsurance deducted in claim settlement

A loss must be an undisputed claim, and the burden of proof naturally is upon the policyholder. In determining claims under the policy, only those covered under the ratings and endorsements of the policy are allowed. If the indebtedness is in excess of the gross amount covered by the policy, then the first two deductions are made pro rata, in the ratio that the gross amount covered bears to the whole indebtedness. Then the coinsurance is deducted, after which the primary loss is deducted from the balance. The remainder, if within the policy amount, is payable to the policyholder.

All accounts admitted in adjustment must be assigned to the insurance company. The insured retains an interest in accounts so assigned to the extent of amounts not covered by the policy and coinsurance, which must be remitted to him on a pro rata basis as salvage is derived from the account, but after deduction of all charges and expenses incurred in recovery of salvage. If the insurance company realizes eventually from the account more than the aggregate sum paid the insured, the net excess must be refunded.

Termination and cancellation. No commercial credit insurance policy can be canceled during the term of the policy, mainly for the protection of the policyholder. Otherwise the insurance company might be tempted to cancel the policy on or about the time the primary loss seems to be reached. The insurance company reserves the right, however, to cancel, upon written notice, all coverage on accounts insured by name in riders to the policy. Such cancellation applies only to future shipments, and the unearned premium is refunded on a pro rata basis.

MERITS OF
CREDIT
INSURANCE

Where risks are borne by business establishments, it is customary, wherever possible, to pass them on to specialists, as in the case of fire, storm, theft, and public liability hazards. Such shifting of risk is also practiced in credit extension by some manufacturers, wholesalers, and advertising agencies by the use of commercial credit insurance. This insurance, like other forms of insurance, has its limitations, advantages, and disadvantages depending on the particular situation of the individual firm concerned, on proper or improper uses, and to some degree on the inherent nature of this particular form of protection.

Limitations to the use of credit insurance. While it is often argued that every person should buy life insurance and every business should carry fire insurance, no such sweeping claims can be made in the case of commercial credit insurance. This particular type of protection is simply not available to retailers and others dealing directly with the ultimate consumer, nor may any direct sales to such consumers by manufacturers or wholesalers be covered. Again, credit insurance is not available to various other classes of firms: those making their sales on consignment; those dealing in specified lines of business regarded as too risky; and those with unsatisfactory records indicating a speculative policy in credit extension.

There are also many other classes of firms for which such insurance may be totally unnecessary or of little real advantage. These include businesses which factor their receivables; sell machinery, equipment, or other goods on conditional sales contracts; lease, instead of sell, their products; sell their output on a cash, C.B.D. or C.O.D. basis; sell most or all of their product to Federal, state, or local governments; or have both considerable financial strength and a minimum exposure to risk.

The crux of the matter as to whether a business which can qualify for commercial credit insurance may find it advantageous or not depends in large part upon the relationship between (1) the loss-absorbing capacity and (2) the possibility of excessive credit losses in the case of the particular firm. With regard to the loss-absorbing capacity, firms naturally differ substantially. Some have built up great financial strength and could absorb abnormal losses of very large amounts without crippling their planned programs or without causing possible bankruptcy. Others are not in such a fortunate position. With regard to the possibility of sustaining abnormal credit losses, risk is minimized mainly through effective credit management, particularly in the case of firms whose customers represent a wide diversification from many angles. In other firms the possibility of credit losses may be much greater because a large proportion of their receivables may be owed by a small number of debtors, by accounts in a single line of business which may be especially vulnerable to the effects of unanticipated developments, by customers located in the same geographic area which may be affected by an occurrence confined to such a region, and so on. Hence, commercial credit insurance, like any other business device, may be advantageous to some firms and unnecessary or not worthwhile to others.

Reasons for use of credit insurance and their evaluation. Among the firms making use of commercial credit insurance, the primary reason, of course, is to obtain a guarantee against excessive credit losses. To be sure, many insureds whose actual abnormal losses over a period of years have been small or moderate continue to carry such insurance as a matter of practice in their operation. Whereas the excess losses actually experienced in the past may not have been heavy, it is not certain that the same results will follow in the future. Besides, policyholders obtain additional advantages, of varying importance to different firms, discussed in the paragraphs that follow.

The collection service offered by credit insurance companies to their clients on a free or reduced cost basis, except in the case of accounts requiring the use of outside attorneys, is the additional advantage most mentioned by policyholders. In fact, investigations have revealed that in some cases the collection service is such an important factor as to be the chief reason for carrying credit insurance. The insurance company is necessarily more vitally concerned with the past-due accounts reported to it (since it will have to reimburse the insured, subject to the provisions of the policy, whether it collects the accounts or not) and, hence, makes greater efforts to recover than, say, collection agencies, even though the collection charges made by insurance companies are overall much lower than the costs involved in the use of other outside means for collection purposes.

Third in importance from the standpoint of the insureds is the claim that credit insurance enables them to maintain and increase sales volume by safely elevating credit lines and thus penetrating markets more deeply. A firm may have an established policy that, in view of its resources and total sales volume, it will allow no customer regardless of how high rated he may be a credit limit in excess of $50,000. While it is true that there may be only one chance in a hundred or even less of such a top-rated customer going bad, the seller may feel that he cannot take that one chance and sell the account up to $100,000 or more. With credit insurance, the seller may obtain coverage of $100,000 or $150,000 on each such high-rated account and be able to increase his sales volume and profits with safety. Doing this does not mean that he is taking unjustified chances, becoming unduly lenient, or gambling in credit extension, but merely that he is allowing the law of averages to work for the insurance company. It means that, by extending higher credit lines where the risk is shared between him and the insurance company, he is following a long established business practice of the insurance companies themselves. For example, a life insurance company will not issue a policy for more than a certain amount to any person, regardless of how good a risk he is, except in the case where it turns around and reinsures, i.e., gets other insurance companies to take shares in the large risk it has assumed on the person in question. Also, each of the credit insurance companies, when issuing policies of large face amounts, reinsures these risks with other insurance companies which do not engage in directly writing such policies.

Fourth, some insureds are said to find that credit insurance enables them to obtain larger borrowing lines from their bank or larger lines of credit from a principal supplier as a result. Without charge to either the bank or the insured, a "bank" endorsement may be added to the policy giving the bank greater security in making unsecured loans or advances on accounts receivable to the insured.   Similarly, a "collateral benefit" endorsement may be added to the policy naming a principal supplier of the insured as beneficiary.

Fifth, by carrying credit insurance a business firm is relieved of the necessity of creating a large reserve fund with which to meet abnormal bad debt losses.   Credit insurance, within the limits of the policy provisions, provides the equivalent of such a fund, just as life insurance is said to create an "estate."   In this manner, the insured avoids the accumulation of a taxable reserve fund and at the same time reduces his taxable income by deducting the insurance premium as an allowable expense.   With regard to the usual, normal, or expected losses, the insured, of course, maintains reserves indicated in his records against his primary loss, any amounts which would not be covered in full under the policy, and coinsurance, if such sharing of risk is included in the policy.

Sixth, undoubtedly one of the important reasons why many insureds carry policies is to be found in their desire to be protected against the full effects of the frequent recessions to which business is subject. While recessions cannot be prevented by credit insurance, it can no doubt mitigate their effects on those firms which do have the protection in such measure with respect to face value of the policy and other provisions as it will allow.

Seventh, there are also a number of other reasons why business firms carry credit insurance.[3]   Some of these are merely derived from other major reasons.   For example, credit insurance is presumed to increase working capital turnover and to decrease expenses caused by slow accounts mainly as a result of the collection service and other aids provided for the collection of past-due accounts.   Again, in budgeting and planning ahead and when adequate credit insurance is carried as to policy amount and as to each account sold (which would probably seldom be the case), credit losses and other costs incident thereto can be more closely estimated than otherwise.   Others are of an auxiliary nature as when customers named in a policy for extraordinary coverages are continuously investigated by the insurance company throughout the term of the policy, with the result that it frequently advises the insured of favorable or adverse developments affecting certain customers before such knowledge would be obtained in the ordinary course of the insured's business.

---

[3] For a complete and detailed discussion of the subject, see C. W. Phelps, "Commercial Credit Insurance as a Management Tool," *Studies in Commercial Financing* No. 3, Commercial Credit Company, Baltimore, 1961.

Proper and effective use of credit insurance. Naturally, the firms making use of commercial credit insurance generally favor it; critics and opponents among business firms are probably those that have not used it because it was not advantageous in their particular situations or because of their unawareness of its real nature or they may be among those who have not applied it properly in their credit operations. Hence, a few observations with this general setting in mind may be quite appropriate at this juncture.

It stands to reason that a business firm, in buying credit insurance, should buy only the coverage it needs. Typically, it will find that the coverages available for purchase under the policy are higher than it needs to buy in view of the balances owed by its various customers. At the same time, the coverages bought must be adequate both as to face amount of the policy and as to individual accounts and classes of accounts. If sales to certain accounts should increase beyond the limits originally stipulated, higher coverages should be requested, just as in the case where the value or replacement cost of a building rises because of inflation, fire insurance coverage should be increased.

Selling, with or without credit insurance, to slow-paying submarginal accounts is generally unprofitable because it slows down the turnover of working capital, unless it is done on a calculated risk basis that may spell higher sales volume and a bigger share of the market in the longer run. Whether or not credit insurance is used, blindly following mercantile agency ratings, shirking responsibility for investigating risks thoroughly, or conducting credit management in a mechanical, routine manner by clerks, leads to unsatisfactory results. Neither credit insurance nor rating services, credit bureaus, or other mere tools can replace the need for the human judgment, experience, and skill of a properly educated and competent credit executive. Credit insurance is definitely not a substitute for the credit department; it is simply an additional tool which may be placed at the use of the credit executive for the purpose of achieving enhanced efficiency in the performance of his multifarious tasks essential to sound credit and collection management.

QUESTIONS AND PROBLEMS

1 What is credit insurance and exactly what does it insure?

2 Are there any limitations to the use of credit insurance from the standpoint of type of business or size of operations?

3 What is the exact meaning of each of the following terms used in connection with credit insurance: face amount of policy, coverage, coinsurance, premium, primary loss, *Standard Manual?*

4 Of the threefold classification of credit insurance policies, which is the most important and why?

5 In what ways does the term "insolvency" differ in credit insurance from that used in connection with bankruptcy?

6 How is primary loss determined and what use is made of it for purposes of credit insurance?

7 What two factors make it impossible to know in advance what the coinsurance will be during the term of a policy?

8 Under what circumstances is it possible to have more than one governing rating for a shipment under a credit insurance policy?

9 What is the distinction between a rated and an off-rated account for credit insurance purposes?

10 What factors are considered in arriving at the premium to be paid for any one insurance policy? Is it fair to express this cost as a per cent of net or gross sales (actual or estimated)? Explain.

11 In arriving at the net allowed loss on any one debtor for which a claim has been filed, what deductions must be made from the gross loss filed and proved? What additional deductions must be made in arriving at the *total* net allowed loss under the policy?

12 "Credit insurance is analogous to fire insurance. If you believe in fire insurance, you certainly must believe in credit insurance." Criticize this argument that is so often advanced in favor of credit insurance.

CHAPTER THIRTY

credit limits

The decision to extend credit is but one of three important and virtually inseparable decisions.   On what terms and under what conditions the credit shall be extended is a second decision.   The third and very important decision relates to the setting or determination of a limit to the amount of credit to be extended under the specified terms and conditions. Limits are necessitated by the very nature of credit, which is, in turn, based on factors that are in themselves existing in but limited quantities. Limits are essential also for practical reasons, because moderate credit is an incentive to serviceful and profitable activity for risks to whom unlimited or unwarranted credit may cause overextension of their activities.   On the other hand, in certain instances there seem to be no reasons for limiting credit, so favorable appear some risks.   Nevertheless, even gilt-edge risks warrant "unlimited" credit only so long as other things are equal—only so long as there is no material change in the extremely favorable conditions upon which their willingness and ability to pay are predicated. Consequently, the concept of limits is inherent in the institution of credit itself, and an understanding of the role which limits play in its administration is indispensable to the proper control of credit.

Purposes of credit limits. Although limits are sometimes used, literally, as absolute maxima of credit, their general use is in the nature of danger signals, just like the warnings posted at approaches to railroad crossings. In each case an *area* of danger is indicated, rather than a line which must not be crossed. A credit limit thus represents an *approximate* ceiling that reflects the considered judgment of the creditor as to the amount of credit which might be safely extended to a given customer. It is the amount which analysis of the C's of credit indicates to be in proper proportion to the customer's needs and ability to repay in the usual or other specified credit period. A limit must, therefore, be arrived at from the viewpoint of both customer and creditor.

The principal purpose of credit limits is to serve as *guides* to credit management and control. They serve to improve the granting or establishment of credit, its authorization or approval in specific transactions, credit promotion, and collections. The setting or determination of limits before an account is opened necessitates careful investigation and comprehensive analysis of the elements composing a given risk. This, in itself, is conducive to improved credit granting. Sharing this information with the sales force results in more effective sales work, less wasted sales effort and expense in securing orders in excess of the limits which will have to be rejected, and a higher degree of cooperation between the credit and sales functionaries in the enterprise. After accounts have been opened, limits simplify credit authorization, for orders may be passed upon merely by checking to see that the appropriate limits are not being exceeded. In retail stores, purchases on charge accounts are thus largely authorized by clerks and refer authorizers. In a way, limits mark the point at which authorization requires the manager's approval or consideration.

Limits serve also as guides to the promotion of sound credit business. Notwithstanding the fact that limits are by nature restrictive, they furnish the occasion for repeated consideration of a customer's business as he proves himself worthy of more extensive credit. Particularly in the field of mercantile credit, where customers are commonly informed of the limits on their accounts, justified increases of the limits, whether initiated by the debtor or the creditor, constitute a valuable opportunity for the credit manager to promote and to increase the volume of credit business soundly. Limits should permit no less than that amount of business which could safely be done on credit if no limits had been set; limits, on the other hand, restrain unwarranted sales promotion by allowing only the expansion of sound credit business. Finally, limits serve to improve collections and to provide the numerous advantages attending the maintenance of a proper rate of turnover of accounts receivable. By eliminating or restricting questionable risks, the credit business can be carried on in an orderly, businesslike, and profitable way.

Advantages of credit limits. From the foregoing it is clear that credit limits operate as an overall device for the control of credit extensions, the promotion of sound credit business, and the effective collection of accounts. Set up in advance, they prevent misunderstandings with the sales force and with customers, minimize wasted sales effort, and provide to some degree a more or less automatic control over the accounts receivable. More specifically, credit limits aid in reducing the cost of credit management and in enhancing its efficiency. By routinizing credit authorization or checking, they minimize the functions performed in this operation, the simpler duties being allocated to the clerical staff, thus conserving the manager's time for the more important problems. The reduction of credit department operating costs, bad debt losses, and interest on capital invested in slow-turning accounts results, in turn, in increased profit on credit business. Limits are advantageous also to debtors. For them they generally act as a check against reckless buying and extravagance, and through their use are sometimes brought to the attention of the buyer observations of the creditors which redound to the improvement of the buyer's business condition.

Objections to credit limits. Notwithstanding the advantages incident to the use of credit limits, some objections toward them have been voiced. One of the most common objections to the use of limits arises from the fact that they are difficult and costly to keep up to date. Unless they are current, limits are presumed to be of little value. Facts and figures, it is alleged, must be constantly gathered from a variety of sources and carefully examined and reflected in the limits set. Furthermore, every order that causes an account to approach or to exceed its limit imposes upon the credit manager the necessity to review the circumstances, to revise the limit, or to reply to the request for additional credit. Discussions revolving around credit limits often prove fruitless and embarrassing. Finally, the delegation of authority which the use of credit limits makes possible may cause the credit manager to lose the necessary intimate contact with his accounts.

Although these objections may seem formidable, it should be pointed out that, in reality, they are of no special significance. Limits, after all, are but approximate amounts. For this reason alone it is not necessary to revise them at short intervals, nor is it necessary to reject an order when a limit is slightly exceeded.   Credit limits are not intended to reflect actual conditions so accurately as to require constant adjustment.   Instead, they are regarded as outposts, warnings, or danger signals.   Normally, credit managers allow a leeway of 25 or 30 per cent beyond the limit so long as the customer is discounting his bills or is paying promptly in accordance with the terms of sale.   Moreover, the method used in setting limits may relieve the firm of the embarrassment in revealing its extent to any customer.   Even when no such method is used, tact in revealing the limit does much to prevent any ill feeling.   Finally, no sagacious credit manager fails to keep track of a customer's orders and remittances, no matter how much of his authority is delegated on routine matters.

Extent to which limits are used. Notwithstanding the evident advantages and practical necessity of credit limits in most cases, it should not be inferred that they are universally employed.   Limits may not be used in small concerns in which there is close personal contact with customers; where the vendor's salesmen assume responsibility for collections and credit losses; where the accounts are protected by a mortgage lien or some other form of sound collateral; where the risks are of the highest order and consist of large and excellently rated concerns to which individual attention is constantly being given; or where, as in large retail stores, the costs of administering credit limits on the many thousands of accounts may be deemed to outweigh the advantages gained therefrom.   For some of the reasons just indicated, limits may be used in a given enterprise for some of the accounts but not for others.   By and large, however, and on all levels of the production and distribution systems, as well as by commercial banks, credit limits are in common use and highly regarded as an effective device for the control of both credit granting and collections.

Factors involved. The same factors considered in arriving at a decision to extend credit are the basis also for determining the credit limit.   Due attention must be given to character, capacity, capital, the customer's past performance, and to general prevailing conditions.   All must be studied with reference to the customer's particular line of business and his type of organization, and they must in turn be related to the policy of the house with regard to such matters.

These factors should indicate whether or not the customer will be willing and able to pay.   However, it is not *ultimate* payment that is the point of interest, but rather whether he will be willing and able to pay the amount to be extended within the time specified by the terms of the sale.   Consequently, not only the past and present must be evaluated but also future conditions of the subject, for potential conditions may be more significant than those which actually exist.

Another factor to be considered is the length of the credit period. While it may be hazardous to extend a given amount to a customer on 90-day terms, such amount may be safely granted on a 10- or 30-day basis, because of the shorter duration of the risk and also because under such circumstances the debtor will be more cautious in incurring obligations, knowing full well that they must be met within a short period of time. Above all, the credit manager must give due regard to the customer's requirements and keep all credit extensions within those limits; otherwise, capital so obtained may be used for purposes of paying other creditors or for needs outside the business.

Two fundamental bases for credit limits. Essentially there are but two real bases for the determination of credit limits, all others being purely arbitrary. One of these fundamental bases involves sole or main reliance upon the subject's debt-paying power or ability to pay. This may be termed the financial approach to the problem of setting credit limits. It is primarily a question of whether the subject can meet his current obligations on time and in what amounts. If his financial responsibility is great and his debt-paying power of current obligations is extremely high, there is no need for any credit limit on such an account. In all other cases it would be limited by what the subject can pay currently.

The other fundamental basis deals mainly with the subject's requirements in the seller's line of merchandise and may be called the sales approach to the problem of setting limits. Here it is primarily a question of determining how much the subject will need or require during an *effective* credit period, as distinguished from the stated customary credit period. If the debt-paying power warrants it, the limit will be set at such requirements; if not, the figure will be reduced to bring it in line with ability to pay.

As a matter of fact, in but relatively rare instances can either of the two bases be used alone in any proper determination of credit limits. In actual practice and certainly in theory, it is purely a question of emphasis or perhaps one of a starting point. When debt-paying power is emphasized it is determined first, followed by an ascertainment of the requirements. If the latter are in line with the former, the limit is set at the requirements level; if not, the figure is reduced to what seems justified by the debt-paying power. If the requirements are lower than what is justified by ability to pay, the limit is still set at requirements in order to prevent the subject from using the seller's credit for other than intended purposes. This is a potent argument in favor of using requirements as the principal basis. Another argument in its favor is that if the limit is set below requirements, the subject will be prone to buy more heavily from competitors. The most important reason for using requirements as the principal basis is that requirements can be fairly approximated while debt-paying power can at best be only "guestimated."

From this brief discussion it is clear that both approaches must be used in setting credit limits, even though one of them may prove to be the governing factor in any given case. Which of them will govern in a given situation cannot be determined until each is examined separately. After all, it is the goal of a creditor to sell to a customer on credit all that is required in the line of merchandise in question, so long as payment can be reasonably expected in line with the effective terms of sale. This, of course, suggests the wisdom of ascertaining the requirements first and then probing into the debt-paying power in order to see whether it would support a limit set at requirements and, if not, by how much such a limit is to be modified.

DETERMINATION
OF MERCANTILE
CREDIT LIMITS

Some of the best examples of the use of credit limits are to be found in connection with mercantile credit, where the procedure is usually more businesslike than in retail charge account credit and the amounts involved are much larger. Yet even here there is no unanimity of opinion as to the best methods of setting credit limits. Some of the methods in actual use are almost purely arbitrary, some place sole reliance upon debt-paying power, others are limited to requirements, while still others make use of a combination of methods.

Arbitrary methods. Among what may be termed as arbitrary methods are those that involve following the example of other creditors or those that are of a trial-and-error type. It is altogether too common practice, for example, to allow as much credit as other creditors have been allowing to the same account on similar lines of merchandise. This is often based on the average amount of highest credit extended by other suppliers in the same line of business as shown on credit interchange or mercantile agency reports. It is simply a matter of depending upon the judgment, and perhaps experience, of still others. This may or may not be sound. First, it is not based upon the amounts of credit other like suppliers are *willing* to extend but on the amounts actually extended. Second, and more important, it does not call for the use of independent judgment or for an appraisal of the risk and the facts underlying the judgment of the other creditors.

On new accounts and for a limited period of some 6 months or a year, some trial-and-error method is often used in setting limits. This may take the form of allowing credit on a "bill-to-bill" basis. Another method frequently encountered is to start a new customer with a small amount arbitrarily determined and raise this amount gradually, as the risk proves satisfactory, until a certain limit is reached on the basis of experience. Those using the arbitrary limit technique allow a new account an arbitrary amount of $100, $200, or some other amount based on the size of the customer's business. When this limit is exceeded, the account is reviewed as a basis for any change. After the test period the credit limit is revised in accordance with information then on hand, including the creditor's experience with the risk.

A modification of the plan just outlined is to start a customer with an amount of credit covering his purchases over a certain period of time, say, 1 week. If the terms are complied with promptly several times in succession, the amount is increased to cover purchases over a longer period of time more or less arbitrarily determined, or based on requirements and custom. In a number of mercantile concerns an opposite practice is followed and no limits are set on an account as long as it discounts its bills or pays promptly. This means that new customers have practically unlimited credit for a while, but are rigidly controlled as to the amount and terms if they become slow-pay.

Limits based primarily on debt-paying power. Mercantile credit limits of this character are founded either on the tangible net worth or the net working capital concept, and most of them contain elements of arbitrariness. In terms of net worth, the limit is obtained by dividing tangible net worth by the number of principal sources of supply, which may be taken from the creditor's own experience with similar types of business. In doing so, it is assumed that net worth fairly measures a subject's debt-paying power, especially when the assets consist largely of fixed properties and very little is invested in current assets. It must be remembered, however, that fixed assets included in net worth are not available for payment of current indebtedness in the normal course of business operations and to that extent a limit thus determined is baseless and misleading. Furthermore, such a limit is not related to any period for which credit is to be extended.

A somewhat similar method is the one in which mercantile agency ratings are used as a basis for assigning credit limits, either as absolute amounts based on certain rating brackets or as a per cent of the capital rating. When the latter is used, the rule normally followed is to allow a credit limit amounting to 10 per cent of the higher capital rating figure if the account is rated in the first or second general credit grade ("high" or "good" in Dun & Bradstreet's reference books) and 10 per cent of the lower capital rating figure if the account's general rating is in the third or fourth grade ("fair" or "limited" in Dun & Bradstreet's). Especially is this true of concerns carrying credit insurance. In such instances the common practice is to follow the limits of coverage indicated in the policy opposite each rating of whatever agency has been chosen for the purpose. Despite fairly popular use of this method of credit limit setting, it cannot be recommended. First, it is subject to the same weaknesses as is the method based on tangible net worth. After all, the mercantile agency capital rating is based on tangible net worth and is less accurate than the former because it is in the nature of a range rather than a specific amount that applies to the subject in question. Second, it means that too much reliance is placed on ratings, regardless of the fact that ratings change frequently and that they are merely approximations based to no inconsiderable degree on the judgment of mercantile agency officials, which may not in many instances coincide with the judgment of the individual credit manager.

Of perhaps somewhat greater value are the limits that are based on the working capital concept, if by working capital is meant net working capital (current assets less current liabilities) or net current assets. In using this method, common procedure is to divide the net current assets by the number of the subject's principal suppliers. The assumptions underlying this process are that net current assets measure the debtor's ability to pay within a short period of time and that he buys equally from the number of firms used as a divisor. Should such assumptions be unwarranted, as they probably are, necessary modifications must be made in order to make the calculation more realistic. A modification of this is to allow, say, 10 per cent of the merchandise inventory shown on the customer's financial statement on the assumption that the customer probably buys only from about 10 principal sources of supply. Another modification is to use an arbitrary stated percentage of the net current assets as the credit limit.

Limits based primarily on subject's requirements. On this basis, too, the methods used in actual practice or advocated for use are many and varied, and some of them are of the arbitrary type. In all cases, even when expressed in quantitative terms, the limits are related to a stated period of time and hence are temporal in nature. Furthermore, they are all related to sales at cost or to merchandise inventories.

One of the methods of setting credit limits on the basis of requirements is by having the salesman, in connection with a first order, indicate on his credit report or on the credit application what the customer's probable requirements will be.   A similar method is that of asking the customer, when making a direct application for credit, to state how much he believes he will require from the supplier in question.

A third method is to set credit limits altogether on a temporal basis, without stipulating any amount, such as one week's purchases, which may with experience be changed to some other period of time. This method is especially applicable to perishable goods like dairy or bakery products and particularly when such products are purchased from but a single supplier.   Under such circumstances, the customer is not likely to overstock or to use the credit of one supplier to finance purchases from a competitor.

A fourth method calls, first, for a determination of the subject's total merchandise requirements for the year, which is equivalent to the estimated cost of goods to be sold during the ensuing year.   Dividing this figure into the normal rate of merchandise turnover results in average merchandise requirements.   When this is divided by the number of principal suppliers, a credit limit is obtained.   Such a simple method is fairly satisfactory so long as each supplier carries about the same assortment of merchandise and the purchases are evenly distributed among them.

Suggested methods of setting mercantile credit limits. It is probable that practically all methods now in use can be justified in part one way or another.   At the same time it must be admitted that some of them are arbitrary, rule of thumb, emulatory, and otherwise unscientific in either the approach to the problem or in the results obtained.   On the other hand, it is believed possible to calculate limits mathematically, logically, and with a fair degree of accuracy, without oversimplifying the matter or complicating it unduly.   In this kind of approach it is necessary first to decide which of the two bases should be emphasized.   From the preceding discussion it appears that precedence in this regard must be given to the subject's requirements, and but secondarily attention should be given to his ability to pay or debt-paying power, for as yet no method has been found that would enable a creditor even to approximate such ability.   In all cases, however, it must be assumed that the subject is *willing* to pay his bills and that his character is unimpaired; otherwise credit may be refused altogether or the limit confined to a relatively small and nominal amount.

Suggested methods of computing limits on basis of requirements. In the methodical determination of credit limits, one logically considers first the requirements of the subject.   Presumably his requirements are based upon sound anticipation of sales volume.   Suppliers have the privilege as well as the duty to society to make available the merchandise which is demanded. Consequently, any creditor, in seeking to determine the amount of credit business possible with a particular customer, would reasonably estimate the portion of his requirements which he might hope to fill.

In this connection, however, one should be warned against the common practice of indirectly allowing the debtor himself to fix his limit. Many a credit manager works on the theory that the proportion of goods purchased from any one source would be regulated by the customer himself, and that such a customer will not exceed his requirements. Quite frequently, credit agencies state in their reports that the subject "is good for his requirements," implying that he is entitled to all the credit desired by him. That this assumption is unsound is witnessed by the large amount of overbuying on the part of many merchants and a considerable amount of buying beyond what the purchasers are able to pay for within the credit period. What is suggested here is that the requirements be determined by the credit grantor and not by the purchaser.

The steps in this calculation are as follows:

1. Obtain the *customer's annual volume of business.* This may often be estimated by the salesman and noted in his new-account report or by the credit manager himself. This estimate may be made on the basis of the number employed by the subject or some other factor on which statistical information is available. Experience has shown that the task of estimating a given customer's business is not so difficult as it may appear at first blush. Very often sales are given in the mercantile agency report or in the financial statement submitted by the risk. Let us assume that the subject is in the retail drug business, that his sales are $200,000 a year, and that the creditor is a drug wholesaler.

2. Find out what *proportion* of his business is *in your lines.* This information can be obtained from an analysis of some of the firm's customers' businesses, as has been done in a number of cases or from governmental sources, especially the censuses of business, which show sales by commodities for different wholesale and retail businesses, and from reports issued by the United States Department of Commerce. Let us assume that the retailer's business includes merchandise handled by your firm amounting to 60 per cent of the total. His requirements in your line are, therefore, $120,000 a year.

3. Determine what proportion of this business you can reasonably *expect to obtain.* This amount will vary, of course, with the nature of competition and with the type of customer. We shall assume that since the standing of your firm with your customers is such as to warrant one-half of the business in your lines of merchandise, you may expect to obtain one-half of $120,000 during the year, or $60,000.

4. The next question is: How many *days of sales* will you allow the customer *on credit?* Since your terms are, say, 1/10 E.O.M., net 30 days, with an average of 45 days outstandings carried on the books, we shall assume that as many as 45 days of sales will be allowed. The credit limit, at retail prices, is then determined by dividing 45 days into 360, and dividing the result into the amount to be extended, at retail prices, during the entire year: $360 \div 45 = 8$; $\$60,000 \div 8 = \$7,500$.

5. Reduce the credit limit thus determined by the average gross *margin of profit* on which retail druggists normally handle your line of goods, say, 30 per cent, and you have a credit limit of approximately $5,250.

This method may be expressed by the following formula:

$$\frac{\left\{\begin{array}{l}\text{Annual sales} \times \text{percentage in seller's line} \\ \quad \times \text{percentage in seller's line, seller expects to obtain} \\ \qquad \times \text{cost of goods sold, as percentage of sales}\end{array}\right\}}{\text{Average turnover of seller's accounts receivable}} = \text{credit limit}$$

Substituting the data used in the above illustration, the results are as follows:

$$\frac{\$200,000 \times 60\% \times 50\% \times 70\%}{8} = \$5,250$$

Another way of determining roughly a customer's requirements is, first, to ascertain the cost of goods sold during the year, which can be obtained from the financial statement, and which may be regarded as approximately equivalent to the annual merchandise requirements. This figure must then be divided by the customary credit period to obtain the amount that would be required during such time. Finally, the amount is divided by the number of principal suppliers to arrive at the credit limit to be set by each of such suppliers. Thus, if we assume the cost of goods sold to be $180,000 for the year, and the customary credit period 60 days, then the amount needed for such a period is $30,000 worth of goods. This amount is then divided, say, by 15 principal suppliers, resulting in a credit limit of $2,000. This calculation can be expressed by means of the following formula:

$$\frac{\text{Terms in days} \times \text{cost of goods}}{\text{Days in year (360)} \times \text{number of suppliers}} = \text{credit limit}$$

The best recommendation for this method of ascertaining credit limits is its relative simplicity. The naïveté of the underlying assumptions, however, is more than surprising. It assumes, for instance, that the customer deals in but a single line of merchandise, or else how can one apply the same terms of credit to all of his goods? Even in the same line of merchandise the terms offered by different suppliers vary greatly. It assumes, further, that payments are made exactly within the credit period, which is pure fiction, as the outstandings of any creditor will show. It disregards the relative position of the vendor in the competitive market, and the numerous secondary suppliers. Then it requires information from outside sources which the first method suggested does not.

On old accounts the requirements can be determined by past sales to them, the limit being fixed at a number of days of sales to the customer commensurate with the days of sales outstanding for the business as a whole.

Suggested method of computing limits on basis of debt-paying power. Requirements alone, however, are not a sufficient basis for determining a credit limit, particularly if the creditor assumes the position of a source of supply *additional* to the customer's other normal sources. There is the question also of the subject's *ability to pay* for goods brought from yet another supplier. Assuming that present relations continue uninterrupted, the new supplier necessarily looks to the net working capital of the customer for evidence of his debt-paying power. The estimation of the credit limit on this basis consists of the following five steps:

1. The expected revenue of the subject is ascertained, since from this source all payments must be made. Anticipated sales of the subject for the ensuing period, including those which the new creditor contemplates selling to him, must be estimated. This, obviously, is a task difficult of attainment and in many instances it may be necessary to rely upon sales of a recent past period as the base.

2. From estimated sales are deducted the subject's gross margin, for operating expenses generally have a prior claim on revenue. The remainder, after deduction of the gross margin, represents the cost of goods sold, from which all merchandise creditors, including a new one, are to be paid.

3. The probable claims of all existing merchandise creditors against the funds available for payments on merchandise purchases must be estimated. Their claims at any one time are represented by the accounts and notes payable for merchandise shown on the subject's financial statement. Their claims over the period of a year are determined by multiplying the sum of the accounts and notes payable to merchandise creditors by the rate of turnover of such obligations. Such a rate may be ascertained from reports on the subject's paying habits, such as furnished by interchange bureaus or by mercantile agencies. It is computed by dividing 360 days by the average length of time taken by the subject in paying his bills. The product of the payables and the turnover rate represents the likely claims of existing merchandise creditors upon the annual earnings.

4. The portion of earnings available to pay a new creditor, as-suming that he did not displace old ones, is the difference between the total cost of goods sold (step 2) and the obligations to existing creditors (step 3). The remainder represents the total which a new creditor might expect to sell to the customer in a year's time.

5. The credit limit for any given period depends upon the length of time that the creditor is willing to carry the subject on his books. The total annual sales that he may hope to make to the subject are divided by the turnover rate which he would expect of the particular account. Terms may be for a period of 30 days, but if he is willing to carry the account for 60 days, one-sixth (360 ÷ 60) of a year's sales to the subject may be allowed to remain outstanding on the books at any one time. This, then, constitutes the customer's credit limit, determined on the basis of his ability to pay.

This entire procedure may be summarized in the following formula:

$$\frac{\text{Anticipated} \times \begin{array}{c} \text{per cent of} \\ \text{sales repre-} \\ \text{sented by cost} \\ \text{of goods sold} \end{array} - \left(\begin{array}{c} \text{accounts} \\ \text{and notes} \\ \text{payable} \end{array} \times \begin{array}{c} \text{rate of turnover} \\ \text{of accounts and} \\ \text{notes payable} \end{array} \right)}{\text{Seller's turnover of receivables}} = \begin{array}{c} \text{credit} \\ \text{limit} \end{array}$$

As an illustration of the computation of credit limits by the debt-paying power method, it be assumed that the anticipated sales of the subject are $120,000. His gross margin being 20 per cent of sales, the cost of expected sales amounts to $120,000 × 80 per cent = $96,000. Accounts and notes currently outstanding as payable for merchandise are $6,000, and reports show that the subject generally pays when due on 30-day terms. Thus, he has a turnover rate of twelve times on his payables (360 ÷ 30). Consequently, the total claims of other creditors upon his earnings over and above his operating expenses amount to $6,000 × 12 = $72,000. This amount, deducted from the cost of merchandise expected to be sold, leaves $96,000 — $72,000 = $24,000, which a new creditor might hope to realize in sales to the subject. However, this amount of sales is to be made over a year. Although terms of the new creditor are 30 days net, if he is willing to extend the subject as much as 60 days of credit at a time, the turnover expected of that account is 6 times. Therefore, a credit limit of $4,000 is set on the account. Expressed in terms of the above formula, the statement is as follows:

$$\frac{\$120,000 \times 80\% - (\$6,000 \times 12)}{6} = \$4,000$$

Obviously, the limits predicated upon requirements must necessarily be related to those based upon debt-paying power. From requirements must in some measure come the ability to pay debt, and from anticipated debt-paying ability stem to some extent the requirements for merchandise to provide such paying capacity. Thus both these methods are related, each presenting its own emphasis of certain factors.

SETTING RETAIL
CREDIT LIMITS

The methods employed in setting retail credit limits are generally less detailed and less methodical than in cases of mercantile credit, both because the sums involved warrant less expenditure of time and effort and because consumers do not lend themselves to the types of analyses which are made for industrial and commercial buyers. Nevertheless, the factors upon which the simpler limits are set in retail credit are not unlike those upon which others are based.

Assigning limits on retail charge accounts. A method somewhat favored by retail credit managers is to inquire of the prospective customer at the time the application is filled in as to what amount he would like to have credit with the firm. If the reply is indefinite, it may then be possible for the credit clerk to inquire as to whether a certain amount will cover it. Such an understanding places the credit department in a favorable position later when the limit is exceeded. It is then possible to call the customer's attention to the arrangement and use it as pressure to reduce the indebtedness to the desired figure.

When limits are assigned by the credit manager without any aid from customers, one of several methods may be used. In some houses the amounts assigned are governed largely by the method of checking or authorizing, depending upon whether the system is centralized or decentralized. Thus one prominent concern places its limits in six groups, from $25 to $200, depending upon whether the risks have limited buying power, are fair, need watching, are good, well-to-do, or wealthy. Another house classifies its accounts for rating purposes as follows: employees' accounts; temporary and "accommodation" customers; $25, $50, $100, and $500 accounts; and those which have an unlimited paying capacity.

Some stores base their credit limits on the reports from credit bureaus, by taking the average figure of the customer's other accounts and allowing him the highest amount he has met within a certain number of days, the latter being governed by what the terms of the store under consideration are. Occasionally, limits are based on time. Under such conditions, a store will allow a customer, say, purchases over a 2-month period. Similarly, when an account becomes 60 days past due it is closed until payment has been made. Dairy companies ordinarily set a limit on purchases by consumers from their drivers on the basis of time. One such company, for example, classifies its customers into weekly, biweekly, triweekly, and monthly, expecting each account to be liquidated within the time specified, giving the usual amount of grace.

A fairly common method is to set the limit on a 30-day charge account at a figure that approximates the customer's salary for a period of 2 weeks. Even then the precaution is taken of placing the maximum debt at any one time on such an account as a certain amount in relation to the customer's annual income, as, for example, $150 for those having an annual income of $6,000 to $7,500, $250 for those with incomes of $7,500 to $10,000, and a $400 or $500 credit limit for those with incomes over $10,000.

Setting limits on charge accounts by calculation. As seen from the foregoing, in most cases limits appear to be set arbitrarily. It is because of this fact that limits are frequently nothing but figures above which charges become refers, requiring more than the usual attention given in the normal routine of authorizing purchases. A variety of bases are used in setting limits, including personal appearance, financial standing as obtained from the banks, agency ratings, place of employment, income, and location of residence.

Assuming willingness on the part of the customer to pay his bills, probably the best method of determining limits in a retail store is to calculate the amount that the customer might be expected to purchase from the store within the credit period allowed, plus the usual number of days of grace. A store selling on 30-day terms would then be justified in allowing credit covering the purchases over a period of about 50 days, provided, of course, that such purchases are confined to a single store of the type under consideration. If it is found that patronage is divided among two or more such stores, only part of the requirements in this particular line of merchandise over the period stated should be taken as a basis for setting the limit on the account. The problem of making limits low enough to prevent overbuying and yet high enough to avoid too many refers is one that requires judgment and skill. Fortunately, as a result of studies made by the Bureau of Labor Statistics and the Department of Agriculture, much valuable information is available on budgets of families of various sizes and in different income groups. An increasing number of credit managers also are utilizing data processing equipment to provide more sophisticated and up-to-date statistical studies on the buying and paying habits of various classes of customers. Such data should aid the credit manager in computing a credit limit at least semiscientifically, taking into consideration both the customer's requirements and his ability to pay.

Setting limits on deferred payment accounts. On instalment transactions, the limits set are ordinarily much higher than those used on charge accounts, because high-priced goods are bought on deferred payments, the time for the liquidation of the debt is longer, and much of the merchandise so purchased is durable so that more security is had. Nevertheless, a limit must be set to prevent customers from overbuying and to keep the store's losses down to reasonable proportions. To do this, the capacity of the customer to pay becomes a cardinal factor. In measuring ability to pay, all obligations on the instalment plan must be taken into account and it is suggested that the *total* of such obligations should not exceed 10 or 12 per cent of the customer's monthly income for a period of 1 to 2 years, depending upon the nature of the merchandise bought, the period within which the particular instalment contract is to be liquidated, and the customer's earning stability. This method of determining a credit limit on instalment purchases is sometimes further refined by deducting from the 10 or 12 per cent of income referred to above 1 per cent for each dependent. It is further modified by the usual resale value of the product involved and the rapidity of its depreciation. Thus, on an automobile which retains substantial resale value much more credit can be extended than on a product that depreciates rapidly, has little or no resale value, and may be difficult to repossess. All in all, in actual practice, setting limits on instalment customers is still a matter of rule of thumb.

Finally, in the case of revolving charge accounts, limits vary with the paying capacity of the debtor and the length of time over which the account revolves. As a rule, credit managers establishing such an account seek to determine the amount which the customer can normally pay each month for the types of commodities he would be buying in that store. This sum is then multiplied by the number of months embraced in the plan. Some stores operate on a 6-month revolution of the accounts, others on a 12-month plan. Thus, if the customer could pay $20 a month and the store had a 6-month basis of operation, a credit limit of $120 is established. It is $240 on an anuual revolving program.

LIMITS SET
BY LENDERS
OF CASH

Cash credit limits are based upon essentially the same considerations as those that underlie the limits used on sales credit. In the lending of cash, however, by reason of the character of the lending institutions, as well as by reason of the different substance of the credit, some special factors pertain to the setting of limits. Limits for some lending institutions, like small-loan companies and certain types of credit unions, are regulated by statutes. Within such limits which pertain to maximums that can be loaned to any one borrower, the cash lender must still determine what specific limit shall be placed on any one particular borrower, which in many cases is substantially less than the maximum allowed by law. Typical of credit limit determination by other types of lending organizations are the practices followed by commercial banks; hence the following discussion is intended to be illustrative of such practices in general.

Limits for business borrowers. Commercial banks frequently set a credit limit, known as a line of credit, for their business borrowers. Sometimes no formal arrangement is made to that effect so that it cannot be used for advertising or insurance purposes, but it may take the form of an understanding or gentlemen's agreement. This gives the borrower an idea of how far he can go in relying upon the bank for accommodations during a season or the ensuing year. When conditions are uncertain or bad, as during periods of recession, banks often refuse to commit themselves by setting lines of credit but wish to handle each application for a loan on its merits.

In setting lines of credit, a bank is governed by several considerations. First, there are regulations which limit the amount that can be loaned to any one borrowing interest. It is usually limited to 10 per cent of the bank's paid-up and unimpaired capital and surplus, although there are some exceptions to this provision arising out of the nature of the loans. This provision is intended to prevent a concentration of risk, so that the failure of any one borrower would not cripple the institution, and to bring about a wide distribution of banking funds throughout the community. Second, the bank's policy in dealing with certain kinds of business is a factor. A bank that has specialized knowledge of a given type of business is more apt to advance a larger line of credit to borrowers in that field than one that is unfamiliar with it and hence overcautious. Third, rigidity of the bank's requirements of borrowers in maintaining bank balances and in clearing up the account at least once a year will have a bearing on the line of credit extended.   Ordinarily, a commercial bank, especially in cities, requires from its borrowers a balance of about 20 per cent of the amount actually borrowed, but this percentage in actual practice is said to vary from 10 to 25 per cent. Other requirements may be set up by some banks and not by others. Fourth and most important are the borrower's banking needs.   If a bank is to perform its function properly, within the limits specified above, it behooves it to serve the legitimate needs of its business clientele.

In establishing a line of credit, the banker prefers to have the applicant make the request and state the amount needed, although the former may solicit information on possible *requirements* during a given period of time.   If the borrower deals with more than one bank, account must be taken of his total bank borrowings; otherwise the bank will consider the customer's needs, and, if they can be served in line with the bank's policy and legal requirements, the line of credit requested will be granted.

Limits on personal loans.   Many of the commercial banks maintain personal loan departments, and practically all of them make some personal loans.   When this type of business is departmentized, an upper limit is usually established, within which the credit limit of any one borrower is set on the basis of his *ability* to pay as agreed and *requirements* as judged by the purpose for which the loan is made.

INFORMING CUSTOMERS
OR BORROWERS
OF CREDIT LIMIT

Should customer or borrower know what credit limit has been set for him?   This is a question that has been much debated among credit managers.   To be sure, in certain types of credit, as in revolving credit accounts, such knowledge is inevitable.   It is equally clear that the same would be true when the customer is asked when applying for credit how much he would intend to buy on the account.   This is also true of specific types of transactions, such as buying an automobile, and borrowing from a small-loan company or credit union and of other types when the amount of credit extended is limited by the specific purchase or loan.   In many other cases, however, the question arises to plague the credit manager. Many times commercial banks may refuse to set a line of credit for a borrower but insist on treating each application for a loan on its own merits; but when a line of credit is determined, the prospective borrower is always aware of it and proceeds with his own commitments accordingly. In the mercantile field, the matter is quite debatable.   If the limit set is lower than what the customer can buy from a competing supplier on credit, it works to the disadvantage of the creditor who has notified the customer of the lower limit. Failure to notify the customer of the limit, however, may make later control of the account rather difficult. This area is even more sensitive when dealing with ultimate consumers, especially in charge account credit. On the whole, it would seem best that both parties to credit transactions have as much knowledge as possible of the amounts that can be bought on credit or borrowed. It must be remembered that there is no credit business without risk and one of the risks may be that of losing an occasional customer or borrower because of such knowledge.

QUESTIONS AND PROBLEMS

1 What is the purpose of credit limits? Is there but a single purpose?

2 Explain what is meant by the statement that the concept of limits is inherent in the institution of credit.

3 Distinguish between quantitative and temporal credit limits and show what use is made of each. Is this distinction basic? Explain.

4 To what extent is it true that some firms use "no credit limits"? To what extent are such limits formally determined in practice?

5 Are credit limits of value only to the creditor? Explain.

6 Under what circumstances, if you were a manufacturer, would you be likely to use or not to use credit limits? Would your answer be the same if you were a wholesaler? A retailer?

7 What are the advantages attributed to credit limits? The alleged disadvantages? Evaluate the two and reach a conclusion as to their justification.

8 Suppose the manufacturer were following a policy of selling through a limited number of outlets; would the adoption of credit limits be as necessary and as valuable?

9 Criticize the present-day practices of determining or setting credit limits:

   a In the retail field

   b By mercantile institutions

10 What factors should govern the determination of credit limits?

11 Which of the two suggested basic methods of setting credit limits is superior? Why? Can one be used to the exclusion of the other?

12 Mrs. Jones wishes to open a charge account at your store, one of five department stores in the city. She also has an account at another department store with which she has traded on open credit for some 4 years. Mrs. Jones has a family of three; her husband is a railway engineer, earning approximately $1,000 a month. They live in their own home, the rental of which is equivalent to $175 a month. The family drives a Ford sedan. Mrs. Jones appeared during the personal interview to be very well dressed, the coat she wore costing probably around

$1,200. What credit limit would you place on her account, assuming that your terms require settlement on or before the tenth of the month for all purchases made during the preceding month?

13 You are in the wholesale grocery business selling directly to retail grocers. You received a first order from the ABC retail grocery store, which has an annual volume of business amounting to $400,000. The store is located in your home town, where you occupy a rather strong position in the sale of groceries, so that you normally obtain about one-half of such business in your community. It is estimated that approximately 60 per cent of all sales in a grocery store in your community is in dry groceries. Assuming that the order has been approved, what credit limit would you allow the customer? Show how this limit should be determined.

14 Where the matter is discretionary, should an applicant for credit be notified or otherwise made aware of the limit set on his account? Discuss the arguments for and against such a procedure.

CHAPTER THIRTY-ONE

credit and collection
management effectiveness
and control

At various points throughout this book the subject matter discussed, while treated primarily from a managerial viewpoint, was also considered broadly in its social, economic, and business setting with due attention being given to the effect and implications of credit and collection management problems and decisions upon business generally and upon our economy as a whole. In this chapter, however, the subject matter covered is discussed entirely from the standpoint of management on a micro basis, i.e., as an individual enterprise operating in a competitive business and economic environment.

As indicated in Chap, 4, the three basic objectives of primary importance in credit management are those of maximizing or optimizing sales or business volume, controlling the amount of assets invested in receivables or other outstandings, and controlling the costs of credit and collections. To attain these objectives, the credit department or any other part of the business enterprise charged with the responsibility must develop an appropriate organization, establish sound policies, institute good methods and practices, and generally perform the numerous and multifarious routine and other activities in a most effective manner. Whether all that is done, and to what extent, depends upon the results achieved. It becomes necessary, therefore, to devise ways and means for the measuring of results. Only thus is it possible to gauge the effectiveness of the important phases of credit and collection operation and management. More important, only thus is it possible to exercise proper control over the various aspects of the work, so that the necessary changes and modifications may be made that will enhance efficiency and insure the attainment of the essential goals of an effective credit and collection organization.

Choice of measurements governed by conception of credit and collection objectives. What indexes are to be chosen for the measurement of a credit department's effectiveness depends largely upon the conception of the primary purpose of such a department. For example, it is sometimes argued that a credit department exists mainly for the purpose of dealing with so-called "marginal accounts." When thus conceived, its effectiveness would have to be determined by measurements that bear more or less specifically on such accounts. On the credit side, for example, there would be emphasis on measures of the extent to which potential business was lost by rejecting poorly rated accounts and the degree of risk exposure by accepting such accounts. On the collection side emphasis would necessarily be on losses sustained on marginal accounts and on the aging of receivables.

That this concept is not only unsound but utterly fallacious is clearly evident even from the brief discussion that follows. First, it assumes that it is easily possible to identify marginal accounts, which is far from true. It is even more difficult to draw the line, or even to distinguish between such accounts and those adjacent to them on the upper side on the one hand and the adjacent submarginal accounts on the other. Second, the quality of accounts does not remain static. A "limited" or even a good account may develop into a marginal account, just as the latter may graduate to a higher classification. Third, it is assumed that there are no important credit and collection management functions to be performed in connection with accounts other than marginal. This is the same as saying that 80 or 90 per cent of the credit business does not involve any work for the credit department other than sheer routine. It obviously overlooks the important tasks of extracting more business volume from the accounts above the marginal, of preventing a deterioration of some of those accounts, and of dealing with them when they become involved. Fourth, the highly questionable nature of this concept is indicated by an analogy to the sales function, for it is analogous to saying that the primary purpose of a sales department is to deal with sales that are hard to make. Assuming that it were possible to identify such sales and to distinguish them from others on either side, there would be practically no sales clerks in our department stores, and very few salesmen would be employed by the manufacturers and wholesalers of life's necessities. Salesmen would justifiably be paid commissions only on hard-to-make sales, and about 80 or 90 per cent of all sales work and expense would be considered a total waste.

It is believed that the choice of measurements should be governed by the principal objectives of a credit department and by the main goals it is to attain. Such objectives and goals clearly issue from the major functions of credit and collection management. This calls for indexes that would measure the effectiveness of the credit department, first, in maximizing or optimizing sales, second, in employing funds invested in receivables, third, in controlling the costs of credit and collections, and fourth, in the extent of cooperation given and secured.

To be sure, credit granting and collecting and the several major functions thereof, like most other phases of business activity, are not susceptible of appraisal by any single or simple standard. To the contrary, performance records which may be thought by one authority to be relevant or highly satisfactory, by another may be regarded as immaterial, fair, or faulty. Credit and collection activity in business is, however, so well established that there is widespread agreement concerning many of the criteria by which credit management may be judged. Consequently, there are actually in use a number of means and measures, other than credit limits, by which credit and collection activities may be controlled. Some of these and others deemed proper and valuable are presented in this chapter in the hope of further advancing the science of credit management. Even so, the measures suggested here are by no means exhaustive. Rather they are deemed to be the more important ones and those that may prove useful in almost all kinds of business when properly adapted.

CONTROL MEASURES FOR MAXIMIZING SALES

It is axiomatic that credit sales stimulate total sales, hence the larger the proportion of business done on credit, other things being equal, the larger the total business of the enterprise and, within certain limits, the more successful the performance of the credit operation.   Results along this line may be measured by one or more of the indexes discussed in this section.

Credit sales index. In all business enterprises in manufacturing, wholesaling, and retailing, it is important to know what percentage of the total sales is represented by credit transactions.   This percentage or index is secured by dividing credit sales by total net sales:

$$\frac{\text{Credit sales}}{\text{Total net sales}} = \text{credit sales index}$$

It is sometimes advisable to determine also the percentage of business done on each type of credit, as, for example, instalment credit, charge account business, revolving charge account volume, C.O.D.'s, and so forth.   When comparisons are made from month to month or over a period of years, this measure affords a valuable picture of the firm's credit business and of some of the effects of its conduct regarding its credit policy.   Comparisons with similar figures for other firms operating under substantially similar conditions indicate something of the relative success achieved in obtaining credit business.

To illustrate, a department store operating on a cash, open credit, and instalment credit combination basis may compare its results with those shown in annual surveys.[1]   Although the proportions of business done in these categories change somewhat from year to year and vary according to locality and size of the firm, all such stores in terms of weighted averages have in recent years done about 59 to 60 per cent of their total business on credit, 37 per cent of total business from regular charge accounts, and 23 per cent consisting of instalment and other term-account credit volume.   If a department store making a comparison of its sales by such divisions with these average figures finds that it had a much smaller than average amount of credit business in one or all of these categories, it behooves its officers to seek an explanation of this condition.   It may be the result of a strict credit-granting policy, or it may be due to lethargy in developing such business.   Whether it is the former can be verified by a study of the rejection index discussed below.   If, on the other hand, the store has a higher than average percent-age of credit business, the bad debt index is consulted to see whether such business is being obtained at a higher cost than warranted.   In

[1] See *Credit Management Yearbook*, published annually by the National Retail Merchants Association, Credit Management Division. See also *Financial and Operating Results of Department and Specialty Stores*, National Retail Merchants Association, Controllers' Congress.

any event, the index of credit sales to total volume reveals in a general way the effectiveness of the concern's policy with regard to one of the principal functions of the credit department, namely, that of maintaining sales at a maximum.

Number of new accounts opened. The number of new accounts opened during any given period will indicate the extent to which emphasis is being placed upon credit service and whether or not the business enterprise is alive to its opportunity for attracting new trade to the house. In the retail field, the number of new accounts opened may serve as a means of measuring the effectiveness of store publicity. In all types of concerns, this figure together with the rejection percentage will measure the strictness of the concern's credit policy. It may be of added value to express the number of new accounts opened as a ratio, in relation to the total number of accounts currently active.

It may be useful also to record the number of accounts definitely closed during the period. Perhaps this figure should be limited to those accounts the closing of which has a bearing on management aspects of the credit and collection operation, excluding accounts that have been closed for other obvious reasons like death, cessation of the business, or removal to a different geographic area. Whatever the decision as to what accounts to include among those definitely closed during the period, such number should be deducted from the total number of accounts opened in order to provide additional intelligence that would show the net growth or decline in the number of customers served.

Rejection index. A measure of growing importance is the rejection index or percentage showing the proportion of applications for credit which are rejected, as follows:

$$\frac{\text{Applications rejected}}{\text{Applications received}} = \text{rejection index}$$

In department and women's ready-to-wear specialty stores this percentage varies from 8 to 30, depending upon whether the store is lenient or conservative in its credit-granting policies and the stage of the business cycle. One source reported that the percentage of applications rejected by department stores in a given year on regular charge accounts was 10.28 and on instalment applications it was 6.3. One large mail order house is said to reject about 30 per cent of all applicants for credit despite its most liberal policy.[2] A similar rejection percentage is not

[2] Article about Spiegel, Inc., by Carl Rieser in *Fortune*, June, 1961, p. 203.

uncommon among small-loan companies. It is believed that in commercial banking many applicants for credit are completely rejected or the amounts requested are substantially reduced. In the mercantile field the rejection percentage is no doubt smaller than in the other areas mentioned, although no statistics of a reliable nature are available on this point.

Not only is it valuable to have the percentage of applications for credit declined, but it may also be worthwhile to know how much business is lost by refusing to approve orders from old customers. Only then could an estimate be made of the total amount of business that has been rejected, which can be used as a gauge in determining the relative strictness or leniency of the credit policy followed.

Inactive accounts index. Credit sales and hence total sales volume may be increased by credit sales promotion directed at securing new accounts, making active accounts more active, and arousing and reactivating the dormant and inactive accounts. The extent to which the last step is taken by a seller may be measured by a ratio of dormant and inactive accounts to the total of current or active accounts. The lower this ratio, the more effective the effort exerted in this direction.

**CONTROL MEASURES
FOR EFFECTIVE
UTILIZATION OF
FUNDS INVESTED
IN RECEIVABLES**

A business must over time recover the amount of funds invested in accounts receivable in order to meet its financial obligations or to reinvest in other assets that would increase its profits. It is, therefore, an important duty of credit management to safeguard capital invested in receivables. Many control devices have been developed in this area of a credit department's activity. Prominent among them are the indexes discussed below.

Collection percentage index. The collection percentage, one of the most commonly used of the credit control indexes, is determined by dividing the total amounts collected during the month by the total accounts and notes receivable outstanding at the beginning of that month, as shown below:

$$\frac{\text{Collections made during period}}{\text{Receivables outstanding at beginning of period}} = \text{collection index}$$

By plotting successive collection percentages on a chart, the general trend in collections is indicated by the resulting curve.   When collections are unfavorable, improvements in the handling of accounts may be inaugurated and other steps taken to inquire into external causes that may be responsible for the condition.   By extending such a study over a period of time, a credit manager will be able the more closely to estimate his collections, an item of considerable importance to concerns operating by use of budgets.   Thus, if experience has shown that collections for a given concern amount to 80 per cent in June and 75 per cent in July, figures might be drawn off in the following fashion:

June 1, receivables	$340,000
Estimated collections for June	272,000
Overdue June receivables	$ 68,000
Estimated credit sales for June (furnished by sales department)	310,000
July 1, receivables	$378,000
Estimated collections for July	283,500
Overdue July receivables	$ 94,500

Collection being highly dependent upon not only general but also local conditions, interpretation of differences between one's own collection percentage and a standard must take into consideration not only the month but the size of enterprise and its location.   For this reason the data for retail stores, for example, are usually presented by cities or other geographic areas and by size of store group.   Moreover, they are published monthly.   If, therefore, a store has a collection percentage that is higher than the comparable index or ratio, this may be indicative of a sound collection policy, provided it does not result in too low a credit sales index.   If the collection percentage is much below the average and the credit sales index is also much lower than the average, then the fault must lie with the collection policy and system of the store.

Average collection period. A derivative of the collection index is an estimation of the average length of time that receivables are outstanding.   If, for example, terms in a particular line of business are net 30 days and the collection index is 50 per cent, indicating that only one-half of the outstanding receivables were collected during the month or, in this case, within the credit period, receivables would *on the average* be outstanding 60 days.   This estimate is made by dividing the number of days in the credit period, allowed by the terms of sale, by the collection index, as follows:

$$\frac{\text{Net credit period}}{\text{Collection index}} \times 100 = \text{average collection period}$$

The estimated collection period, which may also be regarded as the *effectual* credit period, is, like all averages, not necessarily indicative of the actual experiences upon which it is based. It is possible that, although only one-half of the receivables were collected during the month, the remainder were paid during the few days immediately following. Nevertheless, as averages go, this is a significant and indicative measure of collection activity and of the quality of accounts receivable.

The collection period may also be obtained by dividing the month's credit sales by the month-end receivables and then dividing the result *into* the exact number of days in the current month.

Delinquency index. This measure of credit management involves a determination of the proportion of all accounts, in amount and in number, that is past due. It is usually derived by dividing the total past-due amount by the total outstandings, as follows:

$$\frac{\text{Total past due}}{\text{Total outstandings}} = \text{delinquency index}$$

When this index is computed for several successive periods it serves as a barometer indicating whether the general trend of delinquency is downward or upward. If this percentage increases faster than it should at any given time, proper steps can usually be taken to curb the trend or, perhaps, to bring it back to the normal position, which can be ascertained after such record has been maintained for some time.

It is of utmost importance in this connection to make allowance for differences in amount of sales. For example, the percentage of past-due accounts may be 16 on Dec. 1, and 12 on Jan. 1, although the amount of past-due indebtedness in dollars and cents remains the same. This is so because the preholiday sales during the month of December effected a considerable increase in the sales figure over the previous month, on which this percentage is based. As soon as some of the accounts receivable are liquidated, the tendency is for the percentage of overdue acounts to increase, unless a material improvement is at the same time effected in collections of the more stubborn accounts.

While the delinquency index is ordinarily expressed as a percentage of amounts, it may be quite useful to express it also as a percentage of the number of delinquent accounts per 1,000 currently active accounts. It may well be that a high amount percentage of delinquency may be accompanied by a low index in terms of the number delinquent, in which case effort can be concentrated for a more effective remedy.

Accounts receivable turnover. Receivables outstanding beyond terms of sale are in a sense somewhat analogous to slow-moving merchandise inventories; both affect the productivity of the investment, and the activity of the investment in each is susceptible of some measurement in the form of a turnover rate or index. The rate of receivables turnover is found by dividing the total credit sales by the average receivables outstanding, as follows:

$$\frac{\text{Total credit sales}}{\text{Average receivables outstanding}} = \text{receivables turnover rate}$$

In practice, because of the absence of more complete information, it is often necessary to rely upon the receivables outstanding at the end of the year, as shown in a financial statement, rather than upon an average figure, for the computation of this rate. However, unless the business is highly seasonal, this does not materially affect the result. If the turnover rate for an organization is higher than the average in its line of business, it indicates that collections were made promptly and effectively or that with a given amount of capital invested in receivables a larger amount of credit business was obtained. Whether an opposite condition of the rate was due to either lax collections or inefficient sales must be determined by analysis also of the collection index and the credit sales index.

The activity of the investment in receivables may be expressed as a rate or in terms of the number of days required for one turn of the accounts. This may be computed by dividing 360 days by the receivables turnover rate, as shown below:

$$\frac{360\ \text{days}}{\text{Receivables turnover rate}} = \begin{array}{c}\text{days for one turn of accounts} \\ \text{(number days of credit sales} \\ \text{outstanding)}\end{array}$$

Another way of computing the number of days of credit sales carried in the accounts receivable is by the following ratio:

$$\frac{\text{Accounts and notes receivable}}{\text{Average daily credit sales}} = \begin{array}{c}\text{number of days of credit sales} \\ \text{outstanding}\end{array}$$

This measure in terms of days, however, should not be confused with the number of days in the average collection period. For example, let it be assumed that a vendor's credit sales for the year amount to $120,000, his average receivables outstanding are $12,000, and his collections in a typical month are $10,000. The rate of receivables turnover is 10 times ($120,000 ÷ $12,000), and the accounts are turned once in 36 days (360 ÷ 10). The collection index is thus approximately 84 per cent ($10,000 ÷ $12,000), and the average collection period is also 36 days, assuming that terms are net 30 days (30 days ÷ 84 per cent and × 100). Although both measures are expressed in the same number of days, they are not synonymous. Each must be compared with its own particular standard. Suppose that in its line of business accounts normally turn every 30 days, and that the average collection period is 40 days. The performance of this particular firm, therefore, indicates, first, that the activity of its capital invested in credit business is subnormal, but, second, that collections are made more promptly than in other firms. Still other indexes reveal whether this was the result of conservative credit granting, lack of promotions, too aggressive collection efforts, or of other or all of these factors.

Receivables as a percentage of total assets. A practice commonly employed by financial analysts and sometimes used by credit management for measuring the effectiveness of funds invested in accounts receivable is to express the amount of receivables as a percentage of total assets. When comparisons are made over a period of years, this percentage reveals in a general way the trends in accounts receivable investment. Comparison with similar figures for other concerns of about the same size in the same industry also can be used as a gauge of efficiency of capital invested in receivables.[3] An unusually low percentage of assets in the form of accounts receivable would suggest unnecessarily tight credit and collection policies. In contrast, an abnormally high percentage would indicate a congestion of slow-moving funds in accounts receivable.

Age analysis of accounts. It is generally recognized that the distribution of accounts receivable, by months of origin or by the length of time they have been outstanding, has a direct and important relationship to the rate of collection and the probable net loss from bad debts. It is advisable therefore to age the accounts at least once or twice a year, and usually even on a monthly basis. When such a practice is followed, the past-due accounts are usually divided in case of a retail store into those that are 30 to 60 days past due, 60 days to 6 months past due, 6 months to 1 year past due, and over 1 year past due. Mercantile establishments age their accounts on a shorter interval basis, namely, accounts 30 days past due, 30 to 60 days past due, 60 to 90 days past due, and 90 days and over past due.

[3] A valuable source of data for this purpose is the *Annual Statement Studies*, published by Robert Morris Associates and which provides a percentage distribution of items on the balance sheet for many different lines of business.

CODE		REPORT OF PAST DUE ACCOUNTS					

O—Skipped Bill. Usually Prompt.
D—In Dispute. Usually Prompt.
T—Tracing Shipment.
X—Customer Wants Sales Assistance.
SU—Slow but Satisfactory.
SU—Slow and Unsatisfactory.
A—Preparing to Place for Collection.
AA—In Hands of Attorney.

Company _____   Date _____

At _____   Sheet No. _____

LIMITS ON PAST DUE ACCOUNTS	NAME, CITY & STATE	LEDGER BALANCE	PAST DUE				CODE and / or REMARKS
			1-30 DAYS PAST DUE	31-60 DAYS PAST DUE	OVER 60 DAYS PAST DUE		
					INV DATE	AMOUNT	

figure 31-1. *Top part of a sheet used by a leading mercantile concern in listing its past-due accounts when making an age analysis.*

Many houses have adopted the wholesome practice of compiling lists periodically, usually monthly or quarterly, giving the names of the customers whose accounts are overdue, the amounts involved, and the extent to which they are past due.   Such lists are often arranged by salesmen, especially when salesmen are used extensively in the collection of accounts.   They may provide spaces in which to list the various amounts becoming due each month over a period of 3 to 6 months, and the total past-due indebtedness at the end of such period (see Fig. 31-1).

In this connection it is interesting to note the relation between the age of past-due accounts and the amount of business that may be expected from them.   An analysis made for a wholesale automotive firm showed that only 11 per cent of all customers who were listed during the month of May as delinquent 90 days and over purchased during the month on regular terms and in usual amounts.   A little less than 8.5 per cent bought on credit but in smaller amounts than usual, while over 82 per cent made no purchases during the month on open account. This last percentage was even higher during the month of June, with the total accounts delinquent 90 days and over increasing about 20 per cent.   Of the total number of such delinquents appearing during the month of June, only approximately 49 per cent also appeared on the slow list for May.   Some of the customers in the last mentioned group purchased a little on a C.O.D. basis, but the bulk of them made no purchases whatever.   This would seem to indicate that the easiest way of losing a customer is to allow him to become delinquent over an ex- tended period of time.   An analysis made for a grocery firm in the South showed similar results.   Moreover, accounts depreciate with age.   Ac- cording to one study, the depreciation in the value of the receivables followed the course indicated in the following chart:

Age of accounts	Depreciation, per cent	Worth per dollar
30 days	5	$0.95
60 days	7	0.93
90 days	10	0.90
4 months	14	0.86
5 months	19	0.81
6 months	37	0.63
1 year	58	0.42
2 years	74	0.26
3 years	83	0.17
5 years	100 (almost)	0.00

A credit executive in one of the largest institutions, after testing hundreds of thousands of accounts, reported the following results, based on the time an account is past due, as in the preceding analysis:

Age	Depreciation, per cent	Worth per dollar
90 days	10	$0.90
4 months	15	0.85
5 months	25	0.75
6 months	50	0.50
1 year	70	0.30
2 years	80	0.20
3 years	90	0.10
5 years	100	0.00

Similar data showing the shrinkage of the delinquent account dollar in the retailing field are presented in a publication by a leading concern as generally experienced.[4] They show that a current account dollar decreases in value to 90 cents when overdue 3 months, to 30 cents when overdue 1 year, to 23 cents when overdue 2 years, to 15 cents when overdue 3 years, and to 1 cent when overdue 5 years.

Slow accounts also call for extra collection effort and expense.

[4] "Credits and Collections," *Better Retailing*, Merchants Service, The National Cash Register Company, 1960, p. 18.

additional bookkeeping, extra interest costs in money tied up, and a higher cost of doing business.   Furthermore, they may cripple the creditor financially, make it impossible for him to discount his bills, necessitate additional borrowing at the bank, and otherwise cause unpleasantnesses and annoyances.   Knowledge of the exact situation on this score is likely to lead to improved collections and to efforts to remedy it in time.

CONTROL MEASURES FOR CONTROLLING COSTS

Traditionally, though erroneously, businessmen have often considered it to be the prime, if not sole, duty of the credit manager to minimize or even eliminate all losses from bad debts.   Probably for that reason, more emphasis has been placed on the use of control devices in this area of credit department activity than any other.   Included among them are the indexes discussed in this section.

Bad debt loss index. Even though losses from bad debts cannot be regarded as the sole or even the major criterion of a successful credit department, they are important nevertheless.   Their importance is expressed by the relationship which they bear to sales—specifically to credit sales—except where practically all the sales of a firm are on credit terms. This relationship is shown by dividing bad debts incurred during the period under consideration by total credit sales, as follows:

$$\frac{\text{Bad debt loss}}{\text{Total credit sales}} = \text{bad debt loss index}$$

The bad debt loss index is usually considered to be the second most important measure of a credit department's efficiency, next to the credit sales index.   It shows mainly how the second of the three primary objectives of a credit department is being attained, that of keeping losses down to a minimum commensurate with a given sales volume.   Percentages of bad debt loss naturally vary with different lines of business, with competitive conditions, with the month or season of the year, and with general business conditions.   They also vary inversely with the collection percentage, as might be expected.   Thus, a creditor with a comparatively high bad debt percentage may have either a lax collection policy or a lax policy of granting credit.   Whether it be the former can be further disclosed by the collection percentage index.   If it is the latter, this would be reflected also by the credit sales index and by the rejection index.

Suspense and profit and loss ledger indexes. It is the practice of some firms to transfer all doubtful accounts of a certain age—say, accounts that are 90 to 120 days past due, depending upon how lenient a policy any given vendor is following—to what is known as a suspense ledger.   Thorough collection treatment is applied to all accounts thus transferred.   If the treatment has been unsuccessful, the account is then transferred to the profit and loss ledger.   In other firms, all accounts of a given age are transferred directly to the profit and loss ledger, dispensing entirely with the suspense ledger routine.   Transfers to either of these ledgers are made periodically, usually once or twice a year. Monthly transfers are much to be preferred, inasmuch as they make available information that is timely and may lead to some unexpected recoveries.

Whichever method is being followed, it is advisable to prepare a chart at certain intervals showing the number of accounts and amounts charged to suspense; the amount recovered; net loss or amount charged to profit and loss as uncollectible; the percentage of bad debts to total sales and to credit sales, respectively; and the balance in suspense.

From this it is apparent that a number of indexes might be profitably developed from the data appearing in these ledgers.   One of them may pertain to the percentage of all amounts first written off that is recovered, to be used as a measure of the credit department's effectiveness in following up such accounts.   Another may deal with the amounts transferred each month to such ledgers as write-offs in relation to total receivables.

Cost of carrying accounts receivable. Much light could be shed on the policy of charging interest on all overdue accounts, on the construction of terms of sale, and on other important credit and collection policies, if more knowledge were available concerning the cost of operating on a credit basis and of carrying receivables on the books.   To be sure, bad debts afford one such measure, but losses from bad debts are but one item in the operation of a credit department.   In addition to bad debts, there are other expenditures the total of which normally exceeds all losses from bad debts by three or more times.   Wages and salaries of persons employed in credit and collection activities are the most important single category of expense, which in addition to interest on outstandings, fees and dues for credit information, and charges for outside assistance in making collections constitute the bulk of the costs incurred in credit operations.[5]

Every credit manager should attempt to learn what the costs of operating a credit department in his line of business should be or

---

[5] For costs of operating credit departments in department stores, see Table 7–2 in Chap. 7. For some items of cost in operating a mercantile credit department, see Chap. 13.

at least what such costs are for other enterprises similarly operating. Such knowledge would provide him a standard by which to judge his own costs and would indicate where control is especially needed. To be sure, credit department expense is affected by many factors, such as average size of accounts, average amount of each transaction, sales per active account, number of accounts serviced, amount of field assistance given, territory covered, collection methods used, type of equipment used, and many others. By the same token, there are many opportunities for enhancing efficiency of operation, once it is known that it is below par and by how much.

Control measures for effective cooperation. As indicated in Chap. 4, in order to attain the three basic objectives of credit management the credit department must cooperate to a high degree with other business organizations as well as with other departments in its own company. Unfortunately, however, so far no indexes or any other means have been devised for the measurement of the effectiveness of a credit department's cooperation with other credit departments and with other departments in its own business concern. There is certainly need for such measures, and some of them will no doubt be developed in time. They may relate to the number of replies received from other creditors in relation to the number of requests made, the number of replies made to other creditors giving requested information, the number of meetings attended— trade group, local association, state or regional convention, and national association types—cooperative efforts of credit managers in collecting accounts and results obtained in number of cases and amounts involved, and extent of cooperation with all types of credit agencies and organizations that contribute to the professionalizing of credit management.

Conclusion. While this final chapter deals with specific measures that might aid in the control of credit and collection operations, it must not be concluded that credit management is essentially a matter of finding the correct indexes, formulas, ratios, or other statistical devices and applying them indiscriminately to all situations. When properly used, they are all helpful, just as are the various reports obtained from the numerous sources of credit information. Paramount, however, are the fundamental knowledge, practical experience, and sound judgment of the credit manager, for which there is no substitute.

QUESTIONS AND PROBLEMS

1 How does the conception of the primary purpose of a credit department determine the devices to be used in measuring its efficiency? Why should there be a difference in such a conception?

2 Is there a single index or standard for measuring credit department efficiency? Is there a single index or standard for measuring the efficiency of a major function of the credit department?   Explain.

3 Is it wise to judge the efficiency of a credit department by the amount or percentage of loss from bad debts?   Why or why not?

4 What are probably the four best indexes of credit department efficiency?

5 Of what significance is a knowledge of the relation of credit business to the total volume of sales?

6 What is the meaning of an abnormally high bad debt loss ratio?

7 Explain the meaning of the collection index and point out the assumptions underlying the computation of the average collection period on the basis of the collection index.

8 If the average collection period and the days for one turn of accounts are identical, is there but one meaning for the figure?   Explain.

9 In what ways is the receivables turnover rate analogous to the rate of merchandise turnover?   In what ways are they dissimilar?

10 What purpose or purposes can be served by an age analysis of accounts re-receivable?   How is it done?

11 Is the rejection percentage alone an adequate indication of a firm's credit policy? How can it be checked up?

12 What is involved in the cost of carrying accounts receivable?   What factors tend to influence such cost?

13 Store A has an annual volume of business about $5,000,000, approximately 60 per cent of which is done on a credit basis.   Its losses from bad debts average $15,000 a year.   What is the percentage of loss from bad debts for the store?

14 The collection percentages for Company B are 70 for the month of September, 85 for October, and 80 for the month of November.   The receivables at the beginning of September were $65,000.   The credit sales during the month of September and October are estimated to be $150,000 and $98,000, respectively. What collections can be expected during the months of October and November as a means of providing for cash disbursements?

15 What specific indexes might be properly developed for the measuring of performance in cooperating:

 a With other departments of the business

 b With credit departments of other businesses

APPENDIX

customary terms of
sale in domestic trade

The following customary terms of sale prevailing in the mercantile field are presented to indicate at once the great variety of such terms employed in different lines of trade and the relative uniformity in credit terms within a single line of business. This information in part has been gathered as a result of original investigation by the senior author and in large measure has been garnered from a number of authoritative sources, including the Board of Governors of the Federal Reserve System, Dun & Bradsteet, Inc., the National Association of Credit Management, the U.S. Department of Commerce, studies made by governmental agencies in connection with various economic programs, and the Federal Trade Commission.

  To be sure, terms of sale have undergone considerable change since the early days of our economy. and even today they may tend to vary some with general conditions of the money market. At any given time any one concern in a given trade or industry may deviate substantially from the terms normally used by that trade or industry. By and large, however, there is general adherence by members of a trade or industry to the common or customary terms, and there is relatively little change in such terms from year to year.

Airplane Parts and Accessories 1/10, net 30, except to large accounts, which are billed on terms of 1 per cent on the 10th and 25th of the month, net 30 days.

Anthracite Coal S.D.-B.L. to 30 or 60 days net. In certain cases terms are ½/10, net 30.

Automobile Parts and Accessories By manufacturers, 2/10th prox., net 30 extra; by wholesalers, 2/10th prox., net 20th prox.

Automobile Tires and Tubes 2/10th prox. and 2/10, net 30.

Automobiles To dealers, S.D.-B.L. attached.

Automotive Supply House 2/10th prox., net 30.

Bakers Most sales are made on a net cash C.O.D. basis; more responsible restaurants are sold on net 7-day terms; larger chain restaurants and hotels are sold on net 30-day terms.

Bale Goods 2/10, net 60.

Bars (Sheet) ½/10, net 30.

Beans ½/10, net 30.

Bearings 5/10, net 30.

Bedding and Pillow Material 2/30, net 60.

Bedsprings and Mattresses 2/10 prox., net 60.

Blankets (Retail) 2/10, 60 extra.

Blanks (for Cut Glass) 1/30, net 60.

Bolts, Rivets, Nuts Less than ½ inch, 1/10, net 30.

Bottles 1/10, net 30.

Boxes 1/10, net 30.

Brass, Copper, Rods, Wire, Sheeting, and Tubing 1/10, net 30.

Breweries Selling terms of breweries are controlled by the state in which sales are made. For example, in New York sales to retailers are on net 10th prox. and to wholesalers on net 30; in Virginia all sales are C.O.D; and in Connecticut all sales are on net 30.

Builders' Supplies 2/10th prox.

Building Wire (Rubber Covered) 2/10 prox., net E.O.M. prox.; to wholesalers, 2/15 prox., net E.O.M. prox.

Butter, Eggs, and Cheese Wholesalers' terms are net 10 days from date of invoice, with invoices usually rendered on Friday for purchases made during that week.

Candy (Bulk) 2/10, net 60.

Canned Goods (General) 1½/10, net 60.

Carpets (Made to Order) 4/10, net 60.

Carpets (Regular Stock) 4/10, 60 extra.

Cement   3/10.

Chemicals (Industrial)   Most frequent terms are net 30. Terms vary widely for different products, some being 1/10, net 30 and 10th prox. Chemicals Pacific Coast, 1/30, net 60.

China   Net 10.

Cigars   Manufacturers' terms most commonly used are 2/10, net 30 to jobbers and large distributors including chain stores; 2/30, net 60 to retailers. Terms used by wholesalers of cigars, cigarettes, and tobacco are usually net 7 days from invoice date.

Clothing (Children's Dresses and Wash Suits)   8/10, E.O.M., 25th counted as end of month.

Clothing (Men's and Boys')   Net 30 and net 60.

Coal and Coke   S.D.-B.L. to 30 or 60 days net; to retailers: no cash discount, net 30.

Coat Leather   2/10, net 30.

Coats and Suits (Women's)   8/10, E.O.M., the end of the month usually being considered the 25th and in some instances the 20th. Wholesalers offer terms of 8/10, E.O.M. and net 10 days, E.O.M., with the 8 per cent discount considered a trade discount and deducted before invoicing.

Coffee   Green, to small jobbers, ½/10, net 30; roasted, 2/10, 30 days extra; roasted, in West, 2/10, net 60; green 2/10, net 90 days; jobbers to retailer, roasted, 1 to 2/10, net 30 days.

Confectionery   Manufacturers' terms, 2/15, net 30; wholesalers' terms, 2/30 or net 30 with 2 per cent deducted before invoicing.

Corduroys (Men's and Women's)   General terms, 10/10 days; also 8/60 days.

Corsets   Local trading, 2/10, net 30; Pacific Coast, 2/10, net 60; terms 5/10 used to moderate extent; retail terms, 5/10, 60 extra, also 7/10 days.

Cotton (Raw)   S.D.-B.L. attached.

Cotton Cloth Mills   Gray goods, net 10 days; duck, 2/10; finished goods, 2/10, 60 extra. Also season's dating, which is October 1 and April 1. Delivery is usually made from May for October dating, and from November for April dating.

Cotton Goods   To "cutters up," 2/10, net 60; 2/10, net 30, or 2/10, net 60, or 3/10 E.O.M. depending upon the merchandise involved and size of buyer.

Curtains, Draperies, and Bedspreads   Manufacturers' terms, to retailers 2/10 or 3/10, E.O.M. or net 70; to jobbers, 2/10, 30 or 60 extra.

Cut Glass   1/30, net 60; also 2/10, net 30 days.

Decorations (Interior)   6/10, net 60 days.

Dresses (Rayon, Silk, and Acetate)   8/10, E.O.M., 25th counted as end of month.

Drugs   Manufacturers' terms, 2/10, net 60, and 1/10, net 30; terms by wholesalers of drugs and drug sundries, 1/10, E.O.M.

Dry Cells   2/10 or 10th prox., net 30 or 60 days.

Dry Goods   Wholesalers' terms, 3/10 E.O.M. and 2/10, net 60.

Electric Arc Welding Apparatus   Net 30.

Electric Fans   2/10, net 30.

Electric Heating Appliances (Domestic)   2/10, net 30 and 2/10, net 90.

Electrical Parts and Supplies   Manufacturers' terms, 2/15th prox., net 60 or 2/10, net 30.   Wholesalers' terms, 2/10, net 30.

Electrical Products   2/10 to 5/10, net 30 to 60.

Envelopes   Wholesale, 3/10.

Fabrics (Worsted)   7/10, 60 extra.

Feathers   To manufacturers, 10 per cent E.O.M.

Fish (Canned)   1½10, net 30.

Flashlights   2/10 or 10th prox., net 30 or 60.

Flour   1½/10, net 60 used extensively; 1/10, net 30 used in rare cases. Terms vary according to grade, size of shipment, keenness of competition, and the like.   S.D.-BL. often employed on carload shipments.

Food Products   Wholesalers and manufacturers selling to retailers, no cash discount, 30 days; 1/10, net 30; 2/10, net 30.

Foundries   Gray iron, net 30; malleable iron, ½/10, net 30 and net 30; brass and bronze foundries, ½/10, net 30, 1/10, net 30, or net 30.

Fruits and Produce (Fresh)   Wholesalers' terms, net 7 to small accounts, terms running from 7 to 45 days for restaurants, institutions, and hotels.

Fruits and Vegetables (Canners)   Slight draft, bill of lading attached, are most commonly used terms; 1½/10, net 30 granted to large, established accounts. Some Florida canners grant an option of 2/10 on sight draft, or 1½/10, net 30.

Fur Garments   Seasonal dating allowed small retailers with usually at 4 months' note given.   Terms to large buyers, net 10, E.O.M., 25th counted as end of month.

Furnishings (Men's)   1 to 3/10, net E.O.M., 25th counted as end of month.

Furniture   2/10, net 30 on metal kitchen furniture; 2/10 net 30 and 2/30, net 60 on upholstered furniture; and 2/30, net 60 on case goods.

Furs   2/10 on cheap grade; 7/10 on best grades.

Gasoline and Lubricating Oil   Wholesalers' terms, gasoline, net 30 to established accounts, C.O.D. or load-to-load on other accounts; lubricating oil, 1/10, net 30 and C.O.D.

Glass   Window plate, 1/10, net 30; flint and lime, 1/15, net 30.

Glove Leather   1/10; also 2/10, net 30; also 2/10, net 60; also 3/10.

Gloves   5/30; also 6/10; 6/30; and 7/10.

Gray Goods (Unfinished)   3/10, net 60.

Groceries   Wholesalers' terms to retailers, net 7, or C.O.D., or 1/10, net 30; to hotels, restaurants, and institutions, 1/10, net 30.   Also net 10 or net 30 often used.

Hams   ½/10; also ½/10, net 30.

Hardware and Tools   Manufacturers' terms, 2/10, net 30; wholesalers' terms, 2/10, net 30 to industrial buyers, 2/10, net 30, E.O.M., to retailers. On "builders' hardware" proximo terms are frequently employed. "Shelf hardware" is often sold on 2/15, net 30 and R.O.G. terms; also 2/10, E.O.M.

Harness Leather   2/30, net 60.

Harvesting Machinery   5/60; 5/30 used as a seasonal variation.

Hats (Panama)   2/10, net 30; also 5/10.

Hides and Skins   S.D.-B.L.

Hosiery   Manufacturers' terms, net 30. Wholesalers' terms, 10 E.O.M. and net 30.

Implements (Agricultural)   2/10, net 60 with season dating.

Ingots   ½/10, net 30.

Iron (Pig)   Net 30.

Iron (Rolled)   ½/10, net 30.

Jewelry   5/30, net 4 months. Plain gold rings sold on 30 net. Loose diamonds sold on 6 to 9 months, settlement being commonly made by note or acceptance. Silverware, of both flatware and hollow ware, is sold on 2/30, net 4 months.

Laces   7/10, 60 extra; small industries, domestic, 8/10.

Lard   2/10, net 60.

Lead (Chemical Sheet)   1/10, net 30; to manufacturers, 2/15, net 60.

Leather   1/10 on glove leather; on fancy goods, russet, collar and coat, 2/10, net 30, and 2/10, net 60; also 3/10; shoes, soles, 3/30; and 4/10; uppers for shoes, 4/30 and 5/10.

Leather Garments   To retailers, 2/10, E.O.M., 15 extra; to wholesalers and larger chains, net 30 or net 60.

Lever and Disc Harrow   1/30, net 60.

Luggage   2/10, net 30, E.O.M., 25th counted as end of month.

Lumber   1/10, and 2/30; wholesale, 2/10, net 30; 2/10th prox., net 30; 2/10, and 2/30, net 90. Also S.D.-B.L. to net 30 or 60 on timber lien notes, freight net cash upon receipt of each car.

Lumber and Building Materials   Wholesalers' terms, 2/10, net 30.

Machine Tools   Net cash or net 30; also 1/10 or 2/10, net 30.

Machinery (Industrial)   For smaller machines, net 30 after completion and delivery; for larger contracts, an agreed down payment and instalments.

Meats and Provisions   Packers usually ship carload lots on terms of sight draft, bill of lading attached; less than carload lots on net weekly terms. Packers' salesmen usually collect on first call after delivery. Wholesalers' terms: net 7 days, to biweekly and 30 days.

Metal Stamping   Net 30; 1/10 to 1/20, net 30 to regular customers. On new accounts, up to ½ down payment with the balance due 10 days following completion and delivery.

Milk (Condensed and Evaporated)   To wholesalers, 2/10, net 30.

Mill Supplies   2/10, net 30.

Millinery   General, 4/60; 5/30; 7/10, 60 extra; and 9/10; millinery and braid; 6/10.

Motors, Electric (Fractional Horse Power)   net 30.

Musical Instruments   2/10, net 30.

Neckwear (Men's)   6/10, 60 extra, or 7/10, E.O.M.

Nightwear   2/10, 30 extra; 2/10, 60 extra; and 3/10.

Office Appliances   2/10, net 30; and 2/10, net 60.

Oils   1/10 net 30; branded, carload or less, 1/10, net 60; linseed oil, 2/10, 30 extra.

Outwear (Knitted)   Manufacturers' terms, net 10 E.O.M., 25th counted as end of month; wholesalers' terms, 8/10 E.O.M.

Overalls and Work Clothing   Net 30.

Paints, Varnishes, and Lacquers   Manufacturers' terms, 2/10, net 30; 2/10, net 60 to wholesalers and retailers; 1/10, net 30 to maintenance accounts. Wholesalers' terms, 2/10, net 60 to retailers; 2/10, net 30 to industrial buyers.

Paper   Manufacturers' terms, 1/10, net 30 and 1/10, net 11 on coarse paper; 2/10, net 21 on fine paper.   Wholesalers' terms, 1/10, net 30 and 2/10, net 30.

Paper Boxes   2/10, E.O.M. for set-up boxes; 1/10, E.O.M. for fiber boxes.

Peanut Butter   1/10, net 30.

Petroleum (Integrated Operators)   For gasoline and lubricating oil, 1/10, net 30; for fuel oil, net 30.

Piece Goods   7/10, net 4 months; woolen, 10/10, net 30.

Pipes, Tubings, and Fittings   2/10, net 30 or 60.

Plumbing and Heating   Wholesalers' terms, 2/10, net 30.

Pottery   1/10, 2/10, net 30.

Preserves   2/10, net 30.

Printers (Job)   Net 30; 2/10, net 30; and net 10th prox.

Rayon, Silk, and Acetate Piece Goods (Converters)   Net 60 or 70 to the cutting-up trade, and 10 days, E.O.M. or 10 days, 60 extra to jobbers and retailers.

Rivets   Half inch and larger, 1/2/10, net 30.

Rods (Wire)   1/2/10, net 30.

Sardines (Maine)   1/2/10, net 60.

Sauces   1/10, net 30; 1-1/2/10, net 30; 2/10, net 30.

Saws   2/10, net 30.

Scarfs (Men's)   3/10 E.O.M. or 2/10, 60 extra.

Seeds, Vegetable and Flower   1-1/2/10, net 60; 2/10, net 60; farm and grass seeds often sold on cash terms.

Shipping Containers (Shooks)   1/10, net 30; 2/10, net 60.

Shirts (Work)   1/10; 2/10; 2/10, 60 extra; others 2/10, net 60.

Shirts, Underwear, and Pajamas (Men's)   To large buyers such as mail order houses, chains, and department stores, 3/10, E.O.M.; to small buyers, 2/10, net 30.

Shoes Manufacturers' terms, net 30, with discounts ranging from 3/10 to 10/10 given to large buyers. Selling prices are generally adjusted when such discounts are given. Wholesalers' terms, net 30.

Soft Drinks (Bottlers) 30 days net to hotels, chains, and other large buyers; cash or bill-to-bill term to all others.

Soups (Canned) 1/10, net 60; 1½/10, net 30.

Spices 1/10, net 30; 2/10, net 60; whole, 1½/10, net 30.

Stationery 2/10, net 60.

Steel (Structural) For materials fabricated, net 10th prox., or net 30; for materials erected by the seller, payment on the 10th of each month of not less than 90 per cent of contract value of materials shipped, stored, or ready for shipment, and the balance payable 30 days net after completion of contract.

Stoves, Ranges, and Ovens 2/10, net 30 and net 10 on domestic gas ranges; 1/10, net 30 on coal stoves and ranges.

Sugar (Refined) To wholesalers and manufacturers, 2/7 R.O.G.

Teas Importer to wholesaler, 3/10, net 4 months; wholesaler to retailer, 2/10, net 120 and 5/10, net 60 to 120.

Textiles Cotton cloth, 2/10, 60 extra. Cotton in the gray, net 10. Woolens (piece goods), 7 to 10 per cent discount with net period varying from 30 days to 4 months. Dress goods, including worsteds, 7/10, 60 days' dating; also season datings; sometimes net 30 E.O.M. Silk goods, 6/10, 60 days' dating; sometimes 7/10 E.O.M. Linens, "regular terms," 6/10, 60 days' dating; "net terms," 2/10, 60 extra; "net net," spot cash, with no discount and no dating; also 3/10 E.O.M. and 3/10 R.O.G. Velvets, including plushes, 6/10, 60 days' dating, with season dating as of April and Oct. 15; to manufacturers in the millinery trade datings are as of Jan. and July 1.

Tiles General, 3/30, net 60; hollow, building, 5/15.

Tin Plate 2/10, net 30.

Tires (Rubber) 5/10th prox. used extensively when discount is given.

Tobacco Smoking, twist, plug, 2/10, net 60. Tobacco products sold to re-tailers: 2/10, net 30 and 2/10th prox., net 30.

Towel Material 3/10, net 60.

Tubes Seamless, 2/10, net 30; welded, 2/10, net 60.

Underwear Knit, wholesale and retail 1/10, net 30; heavy weight, wholesale and retail, 1/10, net 60; light weight, wholesale and retail, 1/10, 60 extra; cloth, wholesale and retail 2/10, 60 extra; general, 2/10, net 90; women's silk, rayon, and acetate, 8/10, E.O.M.; light weight cloth, wholesaler, 2/30; cotton, women's 7/10, 60 extra; muslin and cotton, women's, 8/10.

Upholstery (Auto) 2/10, net 60; 6/10, net 60.

Varnishes 1/10, net 30.

Varnishes and Mixed Paints 2/10, net 60.

Watches Trade-marked, 6/10 to 30 days, net 4 months.

White Goods 2/10, net 60; also 2/10, 60 extra.

Wines and Liquors Net 7, net 30, and 10 days, E.O.M., as specified by state regulations.

Wire Goods 2/10, net 60.

Woolen and Worsted Piece Goods 1/10, net 60, and net 30.

Yarn 1/10; 2/10, net 60; yarn and thread, rare instances, 1½/10, net 60.

Zinc High-grade, usual terms are ½/10; for purchasers of high standing, ½/10, net 30.

NAME INDEX

Names of persons, business firms, institutions, trade associations, publications, and government bureaus and agencies are included in this index.

SUBJECT INDEX

For names of persons, business firms, institutions, trade associations, publications, and government bureaus and agencies see Name Index.